America Toons In

America Toons In

A History of Television Animation

DAVID PERLMUTTER

McFarland & Company, Inc., Publishers
Jefferson, North Carolina

LIBRARY OF CONGRESS CATALOGUING-IN-PUBLICATION DATA

Perlmutter, David, 1980–
America toons in : a history of
television animation / David Perlmutter.
          p.   cm.
Includes bibliographical references and index.

ISBN 978-0-7864-7650-3 softcover : acid free paper ∞
ISBN 978-1-4766-1488-5 (ebook)

1. Animated television programs—United States—
History and criticism.   2. Animated televison programs—
Social aspects—United States.   I. Title.
PN1992.8.A59P47 2014   791.45′3—dc23   2014003864

BRITISH LIBRARY CATALOGUING DATA ARE AVAILABLE

© 2014 David Perlmutter. All rights reserved

*No part of this book may be reproduced or transmitted in any form
or by any means, electronic or mechanical, including photocopying
or recording, or by any information storage and retrieval system,
without permission in writing from the publisher.*

On the cover: (inset) Characters from the
Rocky & His Friends animated program (ABC/Photofest)

Manufactured in the United States of America

*McFarland & Company, Inc., Publishers
Box 611, Jefferson, North Carolina 28640
www.mcfarlandpub.com*

Table of Contents

Preface 1

Introduction 3

1—Pencil Tests (1900–1948) 9

2—Marginalia (1948–1956) 32

3—Silhouette Storytelling (1957–1969) 40

4—House Arrest (1970–1979) 114

5—Sweet and Sour (1980–1990) 170

6—Songs of Innocence and Experience (1990–1999) 230

7—Dreams Deferred (2000–Present) 304

Conclusion: Where Are We Going? 368

Chapter Notes 371

Bibliography 391

Index 403

Acknowledgments

The writing of this book covered an extended period of time, in part because of the amount of time dedicated to background research, the constant addition of new programs to the established television animation canon, and the writing of my M.A. thesis based on a portion of the material in this text. During this time, a number of people provided assistance and encouragement, and I wish to thank them now:

My mother and father, Bill and Kris Perlmutter; my sisters, Sara Perlmutter Thrift and Signy Perlmutter; and my brother-in-law, Charlie Thrift, were entirely supportive and understanding through the process of the project's development. My mother and my aunts—Lorna Jakobson, Irene Marks and Thora Delaquis—read drafts and offered many valuable suggestions. Numerous other relatives have observed from afar and are awaiting their autographed copies.

My thesis advisors, David Churchill and Sarah Elvins at the University of Manitoba, who guided me through the process of writing and presenting the material pertaining to my M.A. thesis. I also want to thank four of my undergraduate instructors at the University of Winnipeg—Cory Lewis, Tamara Myers, Seth Wigderson and especially Garin Burbank—for encouraging me in the serious pursuit not only of history as a whole, but in this particular subject.

My interview subjects, who aided me immensely with first-person accounts—Charlie Adler, Amy Keating Rogers, Rob Renzetti, Lou Scheimer, and Fred Seibert—were all very helpful and generous with their time.

The staff of the libraries of the University of Winnipeg, the University of Manitoba and the Winnipeg Public Library, whose resources I taxed to the limit in pursuing my research.

Various friends and acquaintances who have known about this project from the start, and have endured me talking about it for so many years. I particularly want to thank Gloria Romaniuk, volunteer archivist at the Anglican Diocese of Rupert's Land, for giving me a welcoming weekly refuge from the wider world these past two years.

The published authors whose work has influenced my own, and who are well represented in the bibliography.

And, finally:

All of the people—actors, directors, producers, writers, artists, etc.—involved in the production of American television animation, past and present. You have made this book possible, and you have made my world a brighter and much more optimistic place to live in, just as you have for millions of others.

Preface

This is a scholarly study of the history of television animation in the United States from 1948 to 2012, covering and analyzing the work of the most influential studios and producers. While theatrical animation has received much scholarly attention, television animation has not, and my work redresses this while providing an overview of television animation that can be an accessible basis for future scholarship.

Television animation has been viewed negatively because of biased and erroneous concerns about its content and ideology, and this has severely impacted scholarship of the genre as a whole, as opposed to the occasional in-depth study of popular programs such as *The Simpsons*. There is a considerable body of television animation programs that has not received this scholarly attention, and my intent is to provide the justification for studying them on equal terms to more popular ones. I also provide a historical overview of the entire genre, so that individual programs can be better understood within a historical context.

American television animation has long been one of my great interests, and I was shocked to find that there was little in much-established literature that did not display some bias against it: for being on television, being directed toward children and supposedly "exploiting" them, perpetrating so-called "violence," and so on. I wanted to offer a more balanced view.

My research method combined traditional primary and secondary research, Internet scholarship, and a close "reading" of as many of the programs that were available to me as possible. I also perused materials related to the fields of animation and television, and the larger social and historical contexts related to them.

My work is particularly indebted to the works of Leonard Maltin, whose *Of Mice and Magic* is the definitive history of theatrical animation in America, and Hal Erickson, whose monumental encyclopedia, *Television Cartoon Shows*, provides an insightful overview of the field. I applied Maltin's narrative structure to tell the story of television animation and I expanded on Erickson's highly informative introduction to his work by going into greater depth regarding the historical origins of the methodology of television animation and how it has managed to evolve and endure within both the wider animation industry and the world beyond.

A note on the use of italics and quotation marks: italics are used for programs consisting of a half an hour of content or more; quotation marks are used for programs less than half an hour, aired either independently or as a segment of a longer program.

Introduction

The critical viewer of television animation is faced with two alternating but interconnecting streams of thought. There is, first of all, consideration of the actual narratives and characters involved. They are a complex and diverse lot indeed—human beings, as well as animals, fish and reptiles who act very convincingly *like* humans. In television animation, there are very few things that can be considered "normal"; the opposite is more often the case. Perhaps this is one of the reasons television animation has been marginalized, and why it has often been marketed to groups of consumers, like children, who are likely to view it at face value, rather than judge it based on what it is *not* rather than what it actually is.

Less understood is the reasoning behind the production of these programs in the first place. Producers of television animation have been less successful than other producers of television at managing to divorce their economic concerns from their artistic ones, at least in the eyes of the public. They have been accused of exploiting children for money—to the point that they have been, in the past, publicly accused of being "child molesters"[1] by one overzealous FCC commissioner. This is a heavily biased accusation against the genre, albeit a persistent one. The original generation of television animators clearly understood who their audience was, and tailored their product accordingly. Their successors expanded this bond between creators and audience, even to the point of straining the latter's patience at times.

Television animation is in a unique position among the various components of television. It is one of the relatively few genres to span the entire history of television in America. It has an entirely flexible format, with lengths ranging from a spare few minutes to two hours. It is able to take on, in both comic and dramatic forms, the major issues of the day, and to find unique ways of addressing them. This has helped to make a unique place for animation in television, and to sustain and preserve it within the rapidly changing media landscape in America.

In spite of this, however, there remain obstacles to its full understanding and acceptance by the viewing public. Though the genre has diversified far beyond the traditional "cartoon" stereotypes it began with, these stereotypes persist due to the reluctance on the part of some producers to abandon them. There are also the problems that much of the best work in the genre continues to be shown in daytime and weekend timeslots, which traditionally have been given less critical attention than the more visible "prime time" ones, and that much of this work remains unavailable for closer scrutiny on DVD, with several obvious exceptions.

There are obvious differences in technique and approaches to the genre used by the producers themselves (evident upon comparative viewing), which hinder rather than enhance our ability to understand the genre as a whole. This conundrum began with the genre's origins in theatrical animation, and has only become more complex as the number of producers and studios involved with television animation has increased.

The present work examines television animation with these pluses and minuses in mind, in order to separate the genre's positive qualities from its negative ones. In other words, it aims to help scholars and viewers separate the gold from the dross.

◆ ◆ ◆

Because of stereotypes related to television animation—the "peripheral" nature of television as a whole; marketing aimed at children as the major consumers; the prominence of comedy in the narratives; the backlash from the animation community at large because of its "limited production values"; and the view of it as a purveyor of "violence"—past criticisms of many television animation programs in the media were slanted. Consequently, it has only been in the past decade that a historically minded study of television animation has commenced. In order for this process to continue, and for us to establish criteria for the study of television animation as a genre, it is important to set out what a genre consists of. A definition which works as well for film and television studies as it does for literary ones is provided by literary critic Robert Scholes in his book *Textual Power*:

> The genre is a network of codes that can be inferred from a set of related texts. A genre is as real as a language and exerts similar pressures through its network of codes, meeting similar instances of solid conformity and playful challenge. No one who has ever studied seriously the history of any art can doubt the importance of precedent, schema, presupposition [and] convention ... in the actual production of texts. The more one knows about a given historical situation, the more one realizes the struggle behind even the smallest innovation in any art or craft, a struggle first to master and then to transcend a given generic or stylistic practice.[2]

By Scholes's definition, we can interpret television animation as a genre in a unique position within the study of television. As a form of programming often seen as being primarily or exclusively for children, it has, in the past, been subjected to the scrutiny of censors, parents and sponsors. Yet it has defied categorization through the variety of its narrative structures and strategies. Therefore, the "network of codes" (to use Scholes's term) that are related to television animation must be carefully and thoughtfully interpreted to be fully understood.

Drawing on literary antecedents, scholars of television history and production processes, such as David Marc and Robert Thompson in their book *Prime Time, Prime Movers*,[3] have stressed the importance of viewing individual television programs as "texts," with their producers labeled as the "authors." The very nature of much television programming, which divides programs into individual episodes or segments, each with their own writers, directors and other key staff, fragments the creative process and gives everyone involved in the production of a series a potential share in the "authorship." For these reasons, it is important to establish, on both an overall and an episode-by-episode level, who the key contributors to a work are and what specific contributions they make. As historian and critic John Kenneth Muir has suggested, the analysis of television requires a very specific set of responses, including a consideration of the impact of the visuals on the audience.[4] The use of cameras to film from particular angles with special lenses, as well as editing choices such as slow- or fast-motion photography or freeze frames, provide important clues to the nature of the story and the personalities of the characters in an eye-catching shot-hand manner, which dialogue on its own simply cannot. The truism of a picture being worth a thousand words is a crucial dictum in television production. The definition by Muir of television as a visual medium gives an important form of support to the study of television animation. Because it is a genre whose existence is entirely dependent upon the creation of physical and mental illusions for its success, visual and aural effects and imagery are crucial to the development of a sustained image that separates it from the live-action television environment.

◆ ◆ ◆

As a cultural art form, television animation inherited a number of production processes and cultural interpretation structures from its immediate ancestor, theatrical animation. This is most evident in the first two decades of television animation's existence, where the personnel consisted largely of theatrical animation veterans, and much of the humorous ambience had strong roots in the prior form. This did not, however, prevent television animation from being heavily criticized by certain members of the theatrical animation community as being a bastardized, for-profit-only art form—an exaggerated position that would dog television animation for decades.

The most obvious separation between the two art forms was an emphasis, within television animation, on curtailed production processes, an effort designed to save costs but interpreted as reflecting a lack of respect for the traditional painstaking artistry involved in theatrical animation. In early television animation programs, such as Jay Ward's *Crusader Rabbit* (discussed more fully in Chapter 2), this argument was seemingly borne out, as the action unfolded in limited movements that did not meet the flowing, artistic aspects of theatrical animation. Yet, in other aspects—particularly the average seven-minute length and the narrative content—the connection to theatrical animation was very evident. Even when programming expanded in the 1950s from seven-minute segments to full half-hours—in individualized segments or later, in the 1960s, in full-length half-hour storylines—the production methodology kept close to a bare-bones level, with a close eye on production costs. Whether it was the "limited" animation employed by Hanna-Barbera, or the "runaway" method employed by Jay Ward (both discussed in Chapter 3), the methods used to produce quality work on a budget came with obvious problems.

The gradual decline of the theatrical animation divisions of the Hollywood studios in the 1950s led to an increase in available talent for television animation producers, which in turn led to an increased level of production. The Hollywood-based animation industry had traditionally risen and fallen with the success and failures of the industry as a whole, and it became weakened as a result of the 1948 Supreme Court decision *Paramount v. United States*, which forced the Hollywood studios to relinquish control of the motion picture theater chains they owned to avoid violation of federal anti-trust laws. As a consequence, the studios were forced to curtail their animation production or shut it down entirely, leading their artists to enter television animation production in search of work. It was these artists who pioneered the television animation industry, out of both economic necessity and the enormous potential for artistic advancement television promised them.

Even as the genre ascended commercially and creatively, creating numerous memorable programs and characters along the way, it could never entirely escape its status as a "marginal" genre—a work of art or a group of such that has fallen into "critical disrepute," and therefore ends up chiefly appreciated by "an extraordinarily small audience—almost a cult following."[5]

As a consequence, appreciation of television animation has often been isolated around certain popular individual programs rather than being directed at the genre as a whole—with scholarship inevitably following suit.

Television animation, even with its growing artistic and commercial plurality in the 1990s and 2000s, has remained marginal, even when individual programs manage to achieve a high level of acceptance. Why does this situation continue to exist?

◆ ◆ ◆

There is a gap in the study of television animation in America. While several texts and anthologies have been produced in relation to television animation in the past few years, in keeping with the rising levels of respect for television animation, no single survey texts exist that examine the genre of television animation and its history as a whole. The present work seeks to fill this gap by providing a history of all the major television animation production companies, the roots of the technology, and the types of storytelling used in the genre, and by discussing future directions of the genre. In describing the history of television animation, I cover its roots in prior live- and film-entertainment, the lives of its creators, and the diverse programs it has produced between 1948 and 2012.

America Toons In: A History of Television Animation is divided into seven chapters and a conclusion. Chapter 1, "Pencil Tests (1900–1948)," begins with a discussion of the roots of television animation storytelling within the context of live and film media, particularly vaudeville and silent film comedy, and, finally, the earliest theatrical animation films. The rise and fall of the theatrical animation industry in this period is discussed to provide an understanding of the production processes and social outlook that television animation would inherit, as well as an understanding of the social and political tensions that caused television animation to be seen as less valuable than theatrical animation when it emerged.

Chapter 2, "Marginalia (1948–1956)," discusses the rise of television and its positive and negative consequences, since this initial period was responsible for shaping social and political opinion related to all of its features, including television animation, for several decades. In terms of the actual presence of television animation, the use of the art in advertising and as a feature of local children's programming established the contradictory manner in which it would be seen in the future.

Chapter 3, "Silhouette Storytelling (1957–1969)," highlights the maturity of television animation, symbolized by the rise of Hanna-Barbera to supremacy and the rise and abrupt fall of Jay Ward, among many studios. The rise of Saturday morning television, and the relegation of television animation to it, is examined, as well as the major backlash against the use and potential promotion of violence in its plotlines.

Chapter 4, "House Arrest (1970–1979)," addresses the limitations placed on television animation in the 1970s, which severely curtailed its artistic growth as a result of overzealous internal censorship by the major American television networks. The ongoing conflicts between producers and censors are examined, as are the psychological studies and reportage that stereotyped television animation.

Chapter 5, "Sweet and Sour (1980–1990)," discusses the impact of the new vehicle of syndication in the 1980s. The use of this independent distribution system helped to break network control of television animation but, in certain cases, turned it into exactly the kind of blatant commercial programming its critics feared it would become. At the same time, continued network censorship created further blandness in the programming by forcing the use of overtly moralistic storytelling.

Chapter 6, "Songs of Innocence and of Experience (1990–1999)," depicts the epic changes that gripped television animation and television as a whole in the 1990s. Positive changes were the emergence of a wide range of broadcast outlets, including the new "fourth network," FOX, and the cable channels Nickelodeon and Cartoon Network, which produced a wide variety of programming that reshaped both television animation's artistic aims and its commercial position. New programming was produced in a larger range of styles and approaches and showed a new attitude. This resulted in a remarkable and unexpected artistic diversity. Television animation could no longer be seen as "one" genre under these conditions—it now had to be considered as a pluralistic set of sub-genres which required a more intellectual understanding of media processes in order to be fully comprehended. These major gains allowed the genre to survive the loss of what had been its major forums in the previous decades—the decline of syndication due to new, restrictive federal legislation, and the networks' abandonment of Saturday morning animation formats because of declining profits.

The new diversity of television animation has continued in the present day, as shown in the final chapter, "Dreams Deferred (2000–Present)." Despite perceptions of a backlash against "ironic" humor in the years following the events of September 11, 2001, television animation has largely continued to mine this vein in its humor. This "maturity" was frequently at odds with the genre's traditional child-friendly approach, a reflection of the often unspoken tensions among the producers in the field about what television animation was supposed to "be."

The conclusion, "Where Are We Going?," is a comment on the current state of television animation in America. Particularly noticeable is how, rather than being evasive about addressing social concerns as in the earlier narratives, it is now very much a part and a reflection of our contemporary world. I will argue that it is possible to address television animation in serious critical terms, even as the producers continue to bring us the bizarre humor and escapist adventures that are at the genre's core.

Television animation has been marginalized for much of its existence, and continues to be in some cases, but this in no way demeans its artistic value as a cultural product of the 20th and early 21st centuries. The programs discussed here and the *modus operandi* behind them certainly demonstrates this. A close examination of the genre, and its programs, characters and plots, more than justifies Marshall McLuhan's view of it as "the optimal mode"[6] of television.

Chapter 1
Pencil Tests (1900–1948)

The structure and evolution of television animation in America is inextricably tied to that of its immediate predecessor, theatrical animation.[1] In turn, theatrical animation cannot be fully understood without understanding how it developed from the styles of artistic endeavor that influenced and preceded it. These influences were infused into its practitioners, who then brought them with full force into the development of theatrical and, later, television, animation.

The historical origins of the structure, practices and ideas of television animation were inherited from vaudeville, silent films and other sources via the influence of theatrical animation. Many of the pioneers of television animation had worked in theatrical animation before the inauguration of the newer form. This helps us to understand the how and why of the development of the theatrical animation industry in America prior to the invention of television and illuminates why television animation, when it emerged, was seen as such an "inferior" art form, and why it was shunned by most practitioners of theatrical animation. Television animation has been marked as "inferior" to theatrical animation for much of its existence, a major reason it has been shunned by serious criticism.

The irony of this situation, however, was that television animation, in spite of its many initial technical limitations, continued to practice many of the artistic and technical practices it inherited from theatrical animation, and which had been bestowed upon it from other, previously existing art forms. This makes it all the more important to understand the roots of theatrical animation, for, in spite of all the artistic and commercial differences over the course of the 20th century, it served to be the foundation of television animation in its beginnings—and this legacy continues today.

Pre-Film and Non-Animation Silent Film Influences

VAUDEVILLE

Prior to the development of visual media, the most prominent forms of entertainment in America was a live, theatrical experience, where performers engaged the expectations and fears of audiences even as they entertained them. While such acts were prominent on a local level prior to the Civil War, it was only after this time that they came to be standardized and distributed on a national scale. By far the most popular and longest-lasting of these formats was vaudeville, a diverse form of theatrical exhibition that would have a lasting influence on all performance-based media that would follow in the years to come, including television animation.[2] Vaudeville was influential not only because of the large number of star performers who eventually came to modify the development of film comedy, but also because the essential structure and ideas of comic and dramatic performance that it shaped were to be critical in developing theatrical animation's representation of these ideas, some of which remain prominent in television animation today.

Named after a French term meaning "voice of the city," vaudeville emerged following the Civil War to become the preeminent form of live entertainment of the late 19th and early 20th centuries.[3] As historian Robert Snyder has suggested, the premise behind it was simple: to provide stage entertainment for a wide variety of people rather than the few that the stage shows had originally targeted.[4] What complicated the situation was the need to provide diverse attractions that would engage and entertain both the middle-class and working-class sections of the audiences, whose ideas on what constituted "entertainment" were frequently at odds. A compromise was reached in the final model that emerged: "a synchronized succession of daredevils, comics, tearjerkers and crooners,"[5] along with more novelty-oriented attractions such as animal acts. The speed of presentation set this new format apart from its forerunners. Working within strict time limits, the vaudeville performer had to establish an almost immediate connection with the often-fickle public or else they would end up getting the infamous "hook," which would bring their performance—and sometimes their career—to a definite end. Consequently, performers would go to great lengths to meet exacting standards of perfection, standards that became even more exacting as vaudeville expanded from simply a regional New York phenomenon to a national and international performance mode. As more forums were established, performers were required to be traveling almost constantly between destinations. Yet New York remained the center of the vaudeville universe, where the legendary mecca of the form, the Palace Theatre, stood ever ready to make or break careers.

It was necessary for comedy performers in vaudeville to make a direct connection with their audiences by way of their material, their appearance, their delivery or other factors. As historian Susan Douglas has argued, a new approach to comedy had to emerge in vaudeville under these conditions. And one most certainly did:

> Vaudeville ... popularized a new kind of humor ... more brash, defiant and aggressive, more reliant on jokes and punchlines than on tall tales and monologues. It threw verbal [and, later, actual] pies in the face of Victorian gentility ... and it acknowledged that *disorder, not order*, governed everyday life [my emphasis]. This was the humor of resentment and retaliation ... the humor of the underdog trapped by verbal misunderstandings and barricades. This humor spoke especially to working-class men, to their frustrated ambitions and wounded pride, their respect and need for quick wittedness, and their need to get even, if only verbally, with a system that rewarded some men at the expense of others.[6]

These attributes are fundamental to understanding the evolution of modern media humor in America. Attacks on pretension and gentility, the preference for the unpredictability of disorder over and above the stability of order, the boiling over of resentment based on arbitrary lines and divisions, the badly treated underdog, quick-witted defensive action as a means of equalization, and the desire to "get even" would remain persistent themes within the comic narratives which pervaded the media that would succeed vaudeville in public prominence in the years of the twentieth and twenty first centuries. And nowhere would these narrative and stylistic approaches end up resonating more than in television animation, a narrative form that survives and thrives on disorder in its stories while at the same time repeatedly allowing underdog figures to "get even" in the smoothest and funniest ways possible. Yet vaudeville was also ultimately evident elsewhere in the more dramatic aspects of television animation narrative, as television animation has frequently explored the plight of the social and political outsider hauntingly in both comic and dramatic forms, and occasionally in both at once.

Although it may appear that the performances of vaudeville were unaffected by censorship, this was definitely not the case. E.F. Albee, the reigning impresario of vaudeville for much of its existence, through his ownership of the highly influential Keith-Albee-Orpheum theater circuit (of which the Palace was the centerpiece), was a stickler for making sure that performances under his watch met the refined standards he set for his theaters. Most evident of this was a series of notices posted backstage in all of his theaters:

> You are hereby warned that your act must be free of all vulgarity and suggestiveness in words, action and costume ... such words as liar, slob, son-of-a-gun, devil, sucker, damn, and all other words unfit for the ears of ladies and children ... are prohibited under fear of instant discharge.[7]

Under these conditions, performers were under a double bind: they had to please the audience while at the same time respecting the concerns of those who managed their affairs, or else they would be fired and prevented from working. This internal conflict over which side of the creative equation knew what was "best" for the audience—the performers and producers of the work, or those financing and regulating it—would persist across the media of the 20th century. Television animation, as it evolved creatively, would become drawn into the center of the debate. Yet, in spite of these internal restrictions on performance, the audience members were free to interpret each on its own merits and judge the level of offensiveness as opposed to entertainment it provided them. As historian Henry Jenkins notes, "The program as a whole offered no consistent message; individual acts might offer conflicting or competing messages."[8] As a consequence, performers became adept at structuring their material so that it would balance internal censorship with the need to keep the audience entertained—and occasionally enlightened—by their work. This was a crucial skill needed to keeping them employed in vaudeville, and, as they migrated to other, newer forms of media, in particular film, radio and early television, this system of internal monitoring, albeit in a much more expansive fashion considering the increased size of the audiences, influenced the way these newer art forms told their stories. Animation was no exception to this rule; in truth, because of its eventual stereotyping as an art form expressly for children, it would have to maintain and police these standards with more vigor, on its own terms or those imposed by theatrical and television regulators and sponsors.

Vaudeville declined with changing times after World War I, and was virtually extinct by the mid–1930s. Yet its influence has persistently remained in contemporary media, then and now. The movies, which succeeded vaudeville as the major public art form in America by the early 1900s, essentially picked up where vaudeville left off in a number of ways. The most obvious was the fact that the vaudeville theater chains, in essence, became motion picture theater chains when the media changeover occurred. But, where motion picture comedy was concerned, the essence of the manner in which vaudeville communicated with and engaged its audience remained. The vast majority of the major stars of motion picture comedy, including Charlie Chaplin (the most dominant and influential figure of them all), were veterans of vaudeville, and they saw no reason to change the manner in which they performed their material and engaged their audiences in spite of the change of venue. By preserving their "acts" on film, they secured their place as the founders of a unique comedy heritage that all the makers of film comedy after them—including the makers of television animation—would both directly and indirectly borrow from repeatedly.

Sennett, Chaplin and Other Live-Action Comedy

By the mid–1910s, motion pictures had evolved rapidly from a fleeting novelty into a major industry. With the growing industrialization that came with this rapid economic growth, the fly-by-night nature of the enterprise gradually gave way to the interests and demands of a series of businessmen—or "moguls," as they came to be called—who used their interests and demands to shape the manner in which the fledgling industry told stories and engaged with its audiences. In terms of the initial shaping of American film comedy, the major figure in this regard was Mack Sennett.[9]

Sennett, a Canadian immigrant who had evolved from a failed actor into a modestly successful film director, established Keystone Studios in 1912, the first major American film studio whose primary objective was the production of film comedy.[10] For the next few years, Sennett reigned as Hollywood's unofficial "king of comedy," as he pioneered many of the modern staples of film comedy. Particularly noteworthy, as critics Scott and Barbara Siegel have noted, was the fact that Sennett shared with the vaudeville humor that preceded him "a healthy tradition of irreverence; nothing—certainly not authority—was immune from his good natured jabs."[11] Among his inventions were such soon to be commonplace devices as throwing pies in the faces of unsuspecting victims, extended, frenetic chase sequences, and buildings falling apart, all delivered in a fashion that emphasized speed and impact. Sennett also had a penchant for the bizarre, expressed when he made stars out of such unlikely figures as rotund Roscoe "Fatty" Arbuckle and cross-eyed Ben Turpin, as well as giving Charlie Chaplin his first break as a film performer. His disdain for the conventional was also reflected in one of his most popular creations, the Keystone Cops, one of the first and most effective satires of law enforcement captured on film.

While Sennett burned out creatively and financially after several years, and suffered declining fortunes that drove him out of business by the 1930s, his legacy was far more lasting. For Sennett not only set the template for what live-action silent film comedy was supposed to be, he also inadvertently did so for theatrical animation, and, ultimately, early television animation as well. As the first major comedy film producer, Sennett set templates for what storylines could be told effectively in film comedy and how they could be told. His emphasis on telling these stories rapidly to gain impact would not be lost on the pioneer generation of animators, who almost certainly were exposed to his films and those of the people he influenced, such as Chaplin, at a young age. Particularly important was the fact that his work emphasized a variety of character "types." Angst could be drawn from their conflicting needs and desires, something taken to heart by animators in the sound era in particular.[12] Yet, Sennett's pioneering influence on film comedy has rarely been adequately acknowledged, in part because his perspective on the world did not serve the purpose it was originally intended for during the television era.[13]

In his heyday, however, Sennett was popular enough to be imitated, and also to have his ideas taken in different directions, by other who had worked with, or been influenced, by him. One such direction was chosen by Sennett's closest rival and, ultimately, the successor to the title of "king of comedy," Hal Roach.[14] Roach's work (especially in terms of the films of his most popular performers, Stan Laurel and Oliver Hardy) resembled Sennett's in a number of ways. However, a key difference rested in the approach they chose. Whereas Sennett was fast-paced, frenetic, and openly disrespectful, Roach tended to allow his films to build up to a boiling point, at the same time allowing a feigned gentility in his characters to emerge, allowing them to better earn the audience's respect and sympathy along with their laughter, in a way that was virtually impossible in Sennett's films.[15] The Laurel and Hardy films, in particular, emphasized this model, throwing these unrefined but likeable characters into predictable situations and allowing them to raise good-natured havoc within them. By removing and toning down the more anarchic elements of Sennett's work and substituting elements that would be more palatable to film viewers with more refined taste, Roach created an alternate model for film comedy that allowed it to be accepted in ways and in venues Sennett's could not. The underlying tension between the Sennett and Roach models of film comedy, as being the proper ones for comedy conduct, persist to this day.

It was, however, a Sennett alumnus—Charlie Chaplin—who reigned as the dominant comedy force in America from the mid–1910s to the sound era.[16] After leaving Sennett, Chaplin began to de-emphasize the ensemble patterns his mentor had established in favor of a more individualized focus on a single lead character. His legendary character, "The Little Tramp," was truly the focus of the film rather than simply a part of an indecipherable mass of characters, as had been the case in Sennett's work. In developing this character in a series of ambitious short subjects and, eventually, by becoming the first major director of comedy feature films, Chaplin was responsible for the increasing maturation of film comedy and its growing ability to effectively portray scenes of pathos as well as laughter. As short subjects were gradually phased out in favor of feature films as the dominant mode of production, Chaplin's single-character–driven model of focus soon became the dominant means. This strategy was taken up with equal success by others in the field as well, particularly Buster Keaton and Harold Lloyd, who joined with Chaplin in exploiting the potential for developing screen comedy in the silent era to its fullest potential. It was also to be a dominant force in film animation, as Walt Disney and others soon realized, for a star character à la Chaplin not only led to consistent success and popularity for those playing them, but also made sure that their art form could be considered in some way legitimate. Consequently, like the Sennett and Roach models of film comedy, the Chaplin model remains an important and consistent legacy to both film and television comedy, and, in particular, the animation models.

The lessons that major producers of film comedy such as Sennett, Roach and Chaplin gave to aspirants to their level of success, were not lost. And, as animation sought to find its own place in the artistic world, they were not only borrowed and adapted, they were enhanced in only ways a truly fantastic medium like animation could do.

Early Silent Film Animation

At the same time that screen comedy was beginning to come into its own, the animated cartoon was also beginning to transcend its humble origins as a novelty item to become a popular sensation.[17] By elevating the traditions of Sennett, Roach and Chaplin to an art form where, it seemed, literally "anything" was possible, the pioneers of theatrical animation created the ground rules of the form and set the standards for all future manifestations of animation as a genre. First of all, however, theatrical animation had to prove to its initial audiences that it was indeed worthy of serious attention and not simply a passing fad.

There had been fleeting attempts at creating moving drawings, notably with the popular novelty device called the Zoetrope,[18] prior to the 20th century, but serious attempts to produce actual films consisting of moving drawings did not begin until the 20th century. Though the American J. Stuart Blackton and the Frenchman Emile Cohl had made the first advancements in the creation of the animated film, it was another American, Winsor McCay, who took the first major steps toward actually producing narrative and character in the form rather than simply producing static imagery or unconnected humorous moments.[19] As the creator of the popular comic strips *Little Nemo in Slumberland* and *The Dreams of a Rarebit Fiend*, McCay had a means of public exposure that lent credibility to his efforts. After an early attempt to bring *Little Nemo* to the screen, McCay had a greater level of success with the creation, in 1914, of Gertie the Dinosaur, the first true "cartoon character." Ingeniously, McCay chose to exploit his creation by using her in a unique interactive vaudeville performance, during which he pretended to interact with her while going through the traditional tropes of the vaudeville animal act. The exception to this was the end of the film, when an animated version of McCay entered the screen and rode away in the film on Gertie's back. As Leonard Maltin has noted, McCay's wringing of natural behavior and true, actual emotion from what was essentially a series of static drawings stunned audiences. He had, in essence, invented the animated cartoon as we know it today, as he himself later claimed erroneously.[20]

With the exception of an elaborate film reproduction of the sinking of the *Lusitania* in 1915[21] and some other minor projects, he abandoned animation by the 1920s, increasingly disturbed by the exploitable commerciality of something he had always regarded as purely art. As he noted before a gathering of animators, in his honor, at the end of the 1920s, animation was no longer an art; it had become a trade instead.[22]

This statement suggested a divide that has continued to exist in the debates among those in the production of animation. Was animation simply an "art," to develop simply and only in the aesthetic, not-for-profit manner of fine arts, or was it a "trade" that could be profited from as a commercial medium? The answer was simple: it became both. But whether or not it was an "art" or a "trade" would mostly depend on whether you were working at it on your own, as McCay was, or if, increasingly, you were part of a vast studio machinery that produced product *en masse* for public consumption. For fans and scholars of television animation, this question would loom even larger. Unlike theatrical animation, it was produced in a studio atmosphere from its very beginnings, and did not have the advantage of maverick pioneer figures like McCay to act outside of such a setting. In this manner, its position of being a "trade" was evident from the start, and, unlike those of theatrical animation, the pioneers of television animation did not have the advantage of having their work seen as an "art" form until much later on.

It was John Randolph Bray, another former newspaper cartoonist, who first shaped the commercial potential of what theatrical animation was to be. He inaugurated the first popular theatrical animation series (the first animated cartoon seen on its own merits without being seen as part of a vaudeville act, as McCay's and others' had) with the character of Colonel Heeza Liar, a traveling adventurer. More importantly, however, Bray and another cartoonist, Earl Hurd, developed a major advance in animation production—the creation of background paintings with separate images of the characters drawn onto sheets of celluloid, with the characters thus being able to be moved independently of the background. This was the first major advancement of the form, and until the late 20th century, it remained the major method by which animated images were filmed and photographed.[23] This process greatly improved the speed by which animated films could be produced, since the tedious reproduction of every single detail from frame to frame was no longer necessary; only the characters and not the background needed to move for a sustained illusion of movement. Other animators, particularly the Canadian Raoul Barre, proceeded to invent further developments, such as the "slash" system, that refined this method even further to produce smoothness in the final product.[24]

The emerging popularity of the animated cartoon, by 1916, was such that newspaper tycoon William Randolph Hearst sought to increase the popularity and exposure of his comic-strip characters by producing animated cartoons featuring them—the first of many cross-media collaborations between the two forms. The longest lasting of these collaborations was the adaptation of Bud Fisher's *Mutt and Jeff*, which lasted well into the 1920s. However, Fisher never gave proper credit to the animators, headed by Raoul Barre and Charles Bowers, who adapted the characters for the screen; instead, he perpetuated the myth that the cartoons were entirely his own inventions.[25] As will be shown later on, this lack of acknowledgment of the creative "help" would be a major source of contention within the animation industry as it grew, particularly as it became more unionized in the 1930s and 1940s. Other adaptations, such as George Herriman's *Krazy Kat* (which would be adapted again, less successfully and accurately, in the sound era), struggled to maintain the integrity of the strips which they were based on under extremely primitive production conditions—until 1918, when Hearst closed his studio.[26] Bray continued onward, giving early experience to two future animation producers—Max Fleischer and Paul Terry—until he shut down operations in 1927.[27]

The most successful producer of the theatrical cartoon in the latter half of the silent era was Pat Sullivan, an Australian emigrant who had become a successful newspaper cartoonist; a typical path, as we have seen, toward gaining experience in animation at that time. Sullivan was chiefly a producer; his young associate, Otto Messmer, was the chief animator of most of his product, though Sullivan, like Bud Fisher, took singular credit for the work. Sullivan, in 1919, brought to the screen the most popular animated cartoon character of the silent screen: Felix the Cat.[28] Over the course of the 1920s, through the inventiveness of Messmer and others on the expanding Sullivan staff (which briefly included Raoul Barre), Felix became the first cartoon character to become a recognized celebrity. More importantly, as Leonard Maltin has noted, Felix had not only a penchant for getting himself into difficult situations, but also ingenious ways of getting himself *out* of them as well:

> Felix had a mind, and he used to think his way out of a tough spot. From this foundation came the trademarks of the series: Felix's pensive walk, with head down in a thoughtful position and hands clasped behind his back, and his unique gift for turning his tail into any implement necessary at the moment—an oar, a baseball bat, a fishing hook, a telescope. This talent was complemented by Felix's frequent excursions into unreality: He could jump into a telephone and squeeze himself through the wires; cross over a chasm on a "bridge" of question marks that emanated from his head; disguise himself as a suitcase in order to take a free trip; and so on.[29]

With these cartoons, Messmer and his colleagues were essentially inventing the visual vocabulary that would distinguish much of theatrical animation in its golden age: a blatant disregard for the conventions of "realistic" filmmaking that implied—and even insisted—that, compared to live-action, animation filmmaking was a horse of another color that could never be fully accepted or understood on the terms of "conventional" filmmaking. Much like Charlie Chaplin (to whom he was occasionally compared), Felix the Cat inaugurated a long-lasting tradition that served his chosen medium well right into the advent of television, when it was finally forced to change as a result of differences in the composition of the audience itself.

Yet Sullivan was neither willing nor able to adapt his studio's product to the next major step in the evolution of animation filmmaking—the addition of sound. This cost him heavily in the end. As a result, with the advent of sound, Felix's popularity was in limbo, and by 1933, Sullivan was dead and his business in tatters. Messmer would not see true recognition for his work on the Felix films until much later on.[30]

It was left to the next generation of animators to make further advancements in the field of theatrical animation and to shape, unknowingly, the numerous ways it would later appear on television.

The Major Theatrical Animation Studios of the Sound Era

The addition of sound tracks (and, later, color) provided means for theatrical animation to further shake off its status as a novelty and develop more and more into a legitimate art form. Much of this was the result of an increasingly bold and brash new generation of animators who were willing to expand the limits of the form and then test those limits repeatedly. It was these animators who built on the traditions of their predecessors in the silent era to invent the procedures, the characters, and the ideas—as well as the stereotypes, unfortunately—that the animators of television would re-invent in their new medium many years later. And, in spite of the hostility that would come to exist between the theatrical and television animation camps, the irony was that many of the animators who pioneered theatrical animation did almost the same thing for television animation, using nearly similar but more limited processes of production. Consequently, if we are to understand how television animation was to "invent" its "wheel" in the 1950s, we need also understand how theatrical animation invented its own between the late 1920s and the late 1940s, for that was precisely the model that was being drawn from in this process of creation.

This chapter concludes, as a result, with a brief overview of the major theatrical animation studios of the sound era, the major technical and artistic contributions they made, and how they set increasingly high standards for what animation was supposed to "be"— the exact standards by which television animation would long be judged, and found wanting.

WALT DISNEY

The name "Walt Disney" means many things to many people. To some, it means the greatest animated short films (and, later, feature films) ever produced. For others, it means an important cultural influence through his weekly television programs. To still others, it represents the name of a company that is representative of a repressive corporate oligarchy that unofficially governs contemporary American popular culture. Yet the man behind the name remains something of a mystery to scholars, in spite of repeated attempts to analyze him and his cultural legacy.[31]

However, in animation, the field in which he first made his cultural mark and to which he remained committed until his death, the evidence is indisputable. Walt Disney was a visionary figure who fundamentally reshaped the manner and means by which animation communicated with its audience and the way in which it told stories in both considerable artistic and technological terms. As Leonard Maltin has sagely indicated, "[Disney] did not invent the medium [of theatrical animation], but one could say that he *defined* it [emphasis in original]."[32]

The penultimate child of Elias Disney, a perennially itinerate farmer and businessman (Leonard Maltin goes so far as to call him a "ne'er-do-well"[33]), Disney had from his youth a desire and a striving to succeed where his father had failed. In fact, "he was determined to become the most successful man in his field, and he expended himself mentally and physically to achieve that goal."[34] When he had obtained this position in theatrical animation short films, he continued exerting himself to pioneer and succeed elsewhere: in theatrical animation feature films, live-action feature films, television, theme parks, robotics and many other concerns.

Walt Disney with Mickey Mouse, circa 1930 (United Artists/Photofest).

But while he achieved success in most of these fields, this came at a cost. As a workaholic and a perfectionist, Disney expected others employed by him to give similar efforts—at the expense of giving them individual credit for *his* achievements. Particularly in animation, which was supposed to be, in theory, a collaborative medium, this attitude would eventually cost him.

After service in the military during World War I, Disney returned to his hometown of Kansas City and began producing films for local theatrical exhibition.[35] While he was successful enough to form his own company, Laugh-O-Grams, his increasingly ambitious production desires soon caused the company to go bankrupt. Consequently, in 1923, he relocated to Los Angeles to be closer to the burgeoning film industry. While modestly successful, he suffered from financial and distribution issues for much of this time, which limited what he could achieve in the silent film format. The advent of sound changed this. In 1928, the Disney company produced, after much trial and error, the first major animated film with a synchronized sound track, *Steamboat Willie*. It was nothing less than an overnight sensation, and, immediately, its star character, Mickey Mouse, became an international celebrity, and remains so to this day. Disney quickly began producing more films in the same vein, reaping considerable acclaim for his emerging oeuvre while also profiting immensely from the marketing of Mickey as a commercial entity.

Pioneering media critic Gilbert Seldes observed in 1932 that "the great satisfaction in the first animated films was that they used sound properly—the sound was as unreal as the action; the eye and the ear were not at war with each other, one observing a fantasy, the other an actuality."[36] He was referring, in particular, to Disney's films, which had unexpectedly and inevitably become the gold standard for the changed industry. The films—with his star characters Mickey Mouse, and later Donald Duck, Goofy, Pluto, and others—represented one area of this development. While retaining the traditional emphasis on "gag" comedy inherited from live-action films,[37] Disney and his staff developed these figures as actual *characters*, with defined personality traits, expected reactions to being placed in difficult situations, and distinctive individualized voices. These served to make these characters more multi-dimensional and able to engage the attention and sympathy of the audience. Disney's ability to bring elements of complexity to his characters forever changed the manner in which the stories of animation were told: they could no longer be simply random collections of gags as in the past; they had to include and emphasize character, story and plot instead. Whether simple or complex, it was a model Disney refined and one that his competitors and imitators regularly strived to emulate.

Disney was equally successful in expanding his model beyond star-driven vehicles to embrace one-shot films that showed off the emerging technological virtues of the medium to its greatest potential. His long running *Silly Symphonies* series, inaugurated in the early 1930s, repeatedly showcased his brand of animation at its height, embracing all the advantages that sound (and, later, color) could use to enhance the experience of watching an animated film. Classic films such as 1932's *Flowers and Trees*, 1933's *The Three Little Pigs*, and 1935's *The Tortoise and the Hare* showed off what could be achieved with the application of all the artistic and technological resources at Disney's disposal to his advantage. Not surprisingly, he was repeatedly awarded Academy Awards during this time for his virtual re-invention of the animated cartoon.

Much of this success came because Disney, unlike many of his contemporaries, was willing and able to use advances in film technology to improve his product. He was one of the first producers to openly embrace sound tracks and color film photography, both of which he used to great advantage. But he also advocated other changes that were less noticeable to the eye of the average viewer, though they were certainly understood by those in the industry itself. He was, for example, one of the first producers to use a storyboard for his films, which essentially provides the same functions for an animator that a blueprint does for an architect. While few films before had been made without some prior sense of what was needed to be produced, Disney's studio was the first one to map out the story of a film *as a whole*, with the result that a common goal could be planned for directly by the animation staff and achieved in a much quicker time span.[38] It also provided a clearer and more linear look for the finished film, eliminating the visual and stylistic inconsistencies that had occurred in earlier films. He inaugurated views of animation based on early drawings and ideas, called "pencil tests," which were examined personally by Disney in his personal theater (which came to be known as "the sweatbox" to the often concerned animators) so he could provide commentary and corrections before they went to full animation. Likewise, he was one of the first to embrace multi-dimensional, deep-focus cinematography, as emphasized by his development of the "multiplane" camera, which challenged the animators further into creating material that was truly worthy of being shot in this fashion.[39] Finally, and perhaps most importantly, in the depths of the Depression he provided steady work for numerous talented animators who would develop and refine their skills across the theatrical film era, working for both Disney himself and other animation producers in both film and television.

However, many of these innovations were not developed so much to expand the artistic and technological vocabulary of theatrical animation—even though they certainly did— but to assist Disney in the achievement of a new, ambitious goal: the production of the first major theatrical animation feature film. Begun in 1934, and debuting in 1937, *Snow White and the Seven Dwarfs* essentially created a new and more ambitious vehicle for the art of animation. A major artistic and commercial success, the film set theatrical animation on a new path. Suddenly animation could be seen and viewed in a manner that was equal to that of live-action storytelling. But while this new vehicle helped animation gain a new respectability, and one that Disney would build on and expand with his further films in the format over the next 30 years (and which the studio and others would continue with following his death), it suddenly made the animated short film be seen with less value, Disney's own films included. For the studios that tried and failed to emulate Disney with their own features and short films over the following years, the tenuous and fluctuating state of the animated cartoon in theatrical programs would be of even greater concern.

Adversely affected by World War II, a bitter and protracted 1941 strike that drove many of the younger artists away from the studio permanently, and changing audience tastes, the animated short films of Disney began retreating after this point into more formulaic conventions, though special projects continued embracing the technology of the film medium and being rewarded for it. While Disney remained innovative through his theatrical feature films, he was increasingly overtaken by others in the short films department. With costs escalating, it was no surprise that he finally ceased production of short subjects in 1955.[40] Yet his innovations and ideas remained, particularly with both theatrical and television animators in later years striving to equal his achievements and technological innovations in the field. And, as it turned out, short form animation at Disney was not as "dead"[41] as Leonard Maltin suggests—it merely had to wait another 30 years, and for an entirely new forum, for its services to fully blossom before it reasserted itself with a vengeance.

Max Fleischer

Much like Walt Disney, who followed and initially imitated him, Max Fleischer was a pioneering figure in the development of animation. He shared with Disney a commitment to excellence in his field and a consistent desire to improve and refine the technology with which it was made. Unlike Disney, however, he lacked a significant business model from which to work, a consistent personal drive, and a desire to improve his product artistically as well as technologically. His inability to provide consistent artistic innovations as well as technological ones, coupled with various financial and personal setbacks, was what ultimately caused him to lose control of his studio at the very height of its success.[42]

The Fleischer family were Jewish emigrants who left their native Austria in the late–19th century to settle in the United States, where father William developed a successful tailoring business in New York.[43] From an early age, Max had a deep and abiding interest in mechanics, and this led him, as an adult, to become a commercial artist and publication editor on just this topic. His curiosity was piqued by the early development of animation, and in 1915 he invented what became known as the rotoscope, which allowed animators to manually trace drawings based on live-action film images and thus create animated characters who could move and act in more realistic ways than they had before.[44] Following military service in World War I, Fleischer, assisted by his younger brother Dave as an artistic and financial partner, began producing animated films based around the rotoscope process. The result was *Out of the Inkwell*, one of the most famous and innovative short film series of the silent era, built around the animated character Koko the Clown and his interactions—in real life—with Max Fleischer himself at the drawing board, filmed in live-action. The series superbly blurred the boundaries of fantasy and reality through innovative animation and camera work, and it led to further projects in both non-commercial and theatrical animation for the studio.

Fleischer had formed his own distribution company, Red Seal Pictures, in 1924, but the company soon went bankrupt. In 1927, he signed a distribution deal with Paramount, which would carry his studio's films for the remainder of its existence. The resulting financial security of this relationship allowed Fleischer and his team a relief from the more stressful aspects of film distribution, but it also made them increasingly constrained by what Paramount wanted them to do rather than what they felt they could do. It was a business pact that would ultimately cost the Fleischers dearly, and serve as a key example of how animation and its practitioners were truly valued by the Hollywood studio system.

Once the relationship with Paramount was established, Fleischer eagerly entered the arena of sound cartoon filmmaking with the *Talkartoons* series.[45] In many respects, these cartoons represented the height of the "rubber hose" or "squash and stretch" approach to animation in the 1930s, in which character and even background movement was heavily syncopated, essentially moving in time to the pre-recorded background scores commissioned for the films rather than allowing the reverse to be possible.[46] Fleischer's approach was emulated with less success by most of the second- and third-tier studios of the era, including the Terrytoons studio of Paul Terry, the Van Beuren Studio (both of which, like Fleischer, were based in the New York area and had a deep "urban" ambience like his), the short-lived Ub Iwerks studio (headed by the legendary former Disney animator), and the early cartoons of Columbia Pictures (initially produced by former Disney distributor Charles Mintz before the company established its own in-house operation; these were Hollywood-based concerns).[47] However, Fleischer's studio was the only one that truly used the format with any innovation, given Max Fleischer's desire for technological progress and Dave Fleischer's facility at coming up with gags and encouraging his staff to do the same. Thus, they proved most able, like Disney, to transcend the limitations of their format and provide means for animation to enhance its appeal to audiences.

Much like Disney, the Fleischers found their greatest successes by developing "star" characters that had the capacity for sustaining the studio artistically and financially. This resulted in a troika of powerful series that, just as much as Disney's had, profoundly restructured and reshaped what was possible for theatrical animation to achieve. Each of them was a Pandora's box in its own way: they defined essential and emerging sub-genres in theatrical animation and wrote new rules for what could happen there. Yet, in terms of issues related to gender, conflict and censorship issues, each would also ignite major concerns and critiques about animation that lasted well into the era of television animation and, consequently, deeply affected that medium's artistic growth.

The first and, arguably, the most controversial of the trio was Betty Boop, the first— and, largely, the only—major female cartoon star of the theatrical animation era. Black haired and flirtatious to a fault, she represented, as Leonard Maltin notes, the "perfect flapper, who could flirt and tease but still remain innocent."[48] But, at the same time, she was as much a sexual "predator" as the men who openly lusted after her. Much of this open sexuality, notes historian Paul Buhle, was a reaction to the manner in which the Fleischers tied Betty to the predatory nature of the American city itself:

> [Betty] ... had a teasing manner that more than hinted at her sexuality as evildoers visibly stroked her thighs and breasts.... [S]he radiated musical syncopation, the gravitational force of constantly "animated" creatures ... all of them apparently moved by the liberation of the urban space, while also being threatened by its spooky downside.[49]

Both Maltin and Buhle, along with other historians, have indicated that this series emphasizes the key elements that the Fleischers used to distinguish their work from their competitors. They and their staff were lifelong urbanites and Easterners, and their approach to comedy reflected this influence, rather than that of the more polished, family-friendly producers such as Disney. In addition, they rejected appealing primarily to the younger members of the audience in favor of targeting the adult members' sensibilities, which allowed them to move their product in entirely new directions.[50] Consequently, while the Boop series benefitted from inventive gag writing, it was also heavily criticized for being what was seen as a contradiction in terms—a cartoon series that openly trafficked in "smut." The introduction of the Production Code in 1934 changed this, as it firmly locked Hollywood filmmaking into a period of sexual and social chastity that would last for over 30 years.[51] Betty Boop was adversely affected by this trend, as the efforts of the studio to remake her into a "good" girl largely failed, and she was "retired" in 1938. However, although her time in the spotlight was brief, she was unquestionably a pioneering figure in American animation, and she remains something of an icon for the period in which she thrived.

The second series commenced just as the Boop series was winding down, and introduced one of the most popular and enduring figures in American animation history. Popeye the Sailor had been entertaining newspaper readers since he debuted in E.C. Segar's comic strip *Thimble Theater* in 1929,[52] and his larger-than-life persona, coupled with a colorful supporting cast, made him a natural for adaptation to animation. At least Max Fleischer seemed to think so, which is why he purchased adaptation rights to the character from his owner, King Features Syndicate, in 1933.[53] For the next decade, Popeye, his lady friend Olive Oyl, and friendly nemesis Bluto managed to star in a series of films that accurately reflected the chaotic nature of Segar's storytelling style while also showing the studio's increasing sophistication in both devising innovative gags and plots for the characters and providing sleekly designed black-and-white photography with which to film them, reflecting the particular expertise of Dave and Max Fleischer respectively at the height of their abilities. Both the studio and its distributor benefitted from the prestige the series created, and they capitalized on it by featuring Popeye and company in a trio of 20-minute short color films which were advertised and occasionally treated as if they were full-length features,[54] namely 1936's *Popeye the Sailor Meets Sinbad the Sailor*; 1937's *Popeye Meets Ali Baba and His Forty Thieves*; and 1939's *Popeye Meets Aladdin and His Wonderful Lamp*. Much as Disney's shorts prior to *Snow White* emphasized the increasing sophistication of his studio's production process, this trio of films indicated the amazing advances Fleischer's product was now making to alter the process by which animated films were made. A particularly noticeable innovation was a new "3D" process called the "tabletop" or "turntable" method, in which miniature sets were built on a turntable attached to an animation camera, upon which the character designs were overlaid. The results were a stunning breakthrough in multi-dimensional filmmaking rivaling

Disney's multiplane camera in its effects, though economic feasibility limited the studio's ability to use it on a regular, effective basis as Disney would use his own effects later on.[55]

The Popeye series was a consistently popular attraction, and the Sailor Man managed to survive the upheaval that occurred when Paramount fired the Fleischers in 1942 and re-established their studio under their control as Famous Studios.[56] In both old and new incarnations, he would remain a consistent audience favorite in the era of television, but few of his later incarnations were able to depict him with the kind of zest and feeling provided by his early Fleischer cartoons. These set a standard that was nearly impossible to match by successive generations of animators.

The third member of the Fleischer troika was the last to emerge, and the one whose films cast the largest shadow over the future of the medium. Like Popeye, Superman was a character already well known from another medium—the just-burgeoning comic-book industry—who was well suited for adaptation to animation.[57] It was the powers that be (Paramount) who suggested the idea of the adaptation to the Fleischers, to which they initially objected: it would require, they said, a considerably larger per-cartoon budget than was possible because of the need to produce realistic-looking characters and special effects. Dave Fleischer suggested that it would cost at least $100,000 to produce each film—four times the average per film cost for the studio. Much to the Fleischers' surprise, Paramount agreed to produce the series with exactly that budget in mind.[58]

Much as they had earlier with Popeye, the Fleischers managed to reproduce the comic-book series as originally produced by Jerry Siegel and Joe Shuster with astonishing clarity and fidelity. The studio made great use of the extra resources given to them by Paramount in making the series look and feel far more realistic than anything that had preceded it. The animators proved to be adept not only with mirroring the structure of the comic-book stories but in enhancing the product with finely tuned art deco design and dazzling camera work, both far ahead of their time. As Leonard Maltin notes, the series was likely "the most cinematically sophisticated" series produced by the Fleischers—or perhaps any other studio—in the theatrical era:

> The camera angles are indeed dramatic, and thoughtfully chosen. Each shot flows into the next, with a variety of pans, dissolves and other linking devices. Effective use is made of shadows in practically every scene, and such qualities as speed, weight and depth are vividly realized.... These films are among the best fantasy cartoons ever produced and feature a gallery of spectacular and memorable highlights.[59]

With this series, the Fleischers substantially expanded the storytelling vocabulary of the animated film, and introduced a sub-genre of the form—the animated superhero—that would substantially enrich the medium (particularly in television animation) in its later years. Yet it came at a cost. The substantial budgets of the original *Superman* series dwarfed those of its contemporaries, and especially those of the later television animators, who initially were unable to duplicate its scale on their more modest budgets. But, in the 1990s, the pioneering influence of the Fleischers in developing animated super-heroics would become increasingly evident as television animation finally became able to mirror their mature artistic sophistication. Just as he had in his comic-book incarnation, Superman set the standard for every hero figure to emerge after him, and their artistic worth would be forever judged by how successful they were in escaping his considerable shadow.

Despite these considerable artistic achievements, the Fleischer studio was in constant turmoil from the late 1930s onward that adversely affected it. A bitter 1937 labor dispute led Max to pull up stakes and re-locate the studio to Miami, Florida, on the promise of tax incentives. He began producing new series in color in imitation of Disney, the majority of which were failures. But the studio was much more adversely affected by Paramount's insistence on its commencing feature film production à la Disney, an area it was ill-equipped to handle. Not surprisingly, the two feature films it produced—1939's *Gulliver's Travels* and 1941's *Mr. Bug Goes to Town* (later retitled *Hoppity Goes to Town*)—were far less successful artistically and commercially than Disney's features. An emerging rift between Max and Dave Fleischer did little to stem the problems. Consequently, in 1942, in "what was possibly, and even probably, an illegal maneuver,"[60] Paramount removed the brothers from control of their own studio and re-established it in New York under its own terms.

In spite of what had to be a humiliating end for the Fleischer brothers, the greatest productions of their studio have stood the test of time and remain as joyous and entertaining as when they were first conceived. Their artistic and technical excellence in their prime was rarely equaled elsewhere, and they retained their appeal to subsequent generations of viewers. And, as the years would pass and television animation came into its own, the true influence of the Fleischers on the development of the younger medium's artistic maturity would become increasingly undeniable.

Walter Lantz

Unlike Disney and Fleischer, Walter Lantz's aims and achievements as a theatrical animation producer were more modest, but, in many ways, they were also more subtle. Lantz broke no new ground artistically, as he tended to follow the models set by others that were popular elsewhere. Likewise, he did not exploit the technology available to him, even though he was affiliated throughout his career with a major film studio—Universal—that could have provided him with these opportunities. Where Lantz truly made his mark, however, was in understanding both the skills of his staff and the desires of his audiences and accommodating them both effectively. In turn, he understood the ability of the appeal of the unconventional in animation and cannily exploited it—as in the case, for example, of his longtime star character, Woody Woodpecker. For these reasons, Lantz was virtually the only animation producer who had begun in the silent era who was still producing theatrical animation in the 1960s, when the market for this forum had rapidly decreased. He was unquestionably a survivor where others had failed: as Leonard Maltin suggests, "Anybody who operated an [animation] studio for forty-five years, well past the point of endurance for many of his competitors, has earned this designation."[61] Lantz's ability to survive as a producer—and, indeed, to be the only non–Disney producer to be able to introduce his films to a new generation via a national television show—marks him as an important, if often unnoticed, influence on the growth of animation on television, and makes it equally important to analyze how this influence came about.

Lantz came in on the ground floor in the history of animation, and its influence remained with him throughout his career. While still a teenager, he joined the staff of the Hearst animation studio and quickly advanced to the status of full-fledged animator.[62]

In 1918, he joined the John Bray studio as a director and remained there until Bray closed his doors in 1927. At this point, he joined the growing exodus of animators to Los Angeles, where he worked as a gag writer and animator for Mack Sennett before joining Universal, first as a gag writer and then, after a fateful meeting with studio founder Carl Laemmle, head of a newly incorporated animation division.

Lantz, working chiefly with William Nolan in this early period, inherited the character of Oswald the Lucky Rabbit, whose films, originally produced by Walt Disney, had been distributed by the studio for several years.[63] The product, 26 films per year, was generally undistinguished but competently done by the non–Disney standards of the day. In 1936, Lantz changed his relationship with Universal, becoming an independent producer distributed by the studio rather than working directly for them. With the exception of a brief stint at United Artists during 1948, he remained with Universal in this capacity for the remainder of his career.

In the wake of Disney's success with *Snow White*, Lantz briefly toyed with the idea of making a feature film version of *Aladdin and His Wonderful Lamp*, but he abandoned it on the grounds that the risks and cost of the venture were far too prohibitive for him to continue.[64] But his greatest innovations in the short animated film were yet to come. Lantz, as Leonard Maltin notes, spent much of his career actively looking for ways to differentiate his product from his contemporaries, chiefly by anthropomorphically adapting animals that had never before received this treatment.[65] This resulted in his two most popular and long-lasting series characters: the mild, Mickey Mouse–like Andy Panda at one end, and, on the other, the brash, hyperactive and destructive Woody Woodpecker, who became one of the iconic figures of his kind in a career spanning just over 30 years. Many of these films, especially those directed by Shamus Culhane, carried a depiction of violence "to such an outrageous extreme that the potential pain [exhibited by the characters] is tempered by sheer absurdity."[66] As a result, these films would be heavily censored in the television era, where even the minor presence of violence in animated films would suddenly be raised to the level of a sociopolitical issue to which Lantz and other producers would object. The "sheer absurdity" of the scenarios, as Maltin notes, was a credible defense for this, even if it was one critics patently ignored.

Lantz was forced to close his studio for over a year in 1949–50 due to business troubles before resuming distribution through Universal. Working on a less ambitious scale than before, he concentrated on cartoons starring Woody Woodpecker, and a new character called Chilly Willy, a mute penguin. He also, in 1957, began appearing on television with *The Woody Woodpecker Show*, which combined exhibitions of old cartoons with sequences where Lantz explained to the audience the minutiae of making animated films. He was, however, unable to prevent severe censorship from occurring to his product, which often served to diminish the quality of the TV versions of the films.[67]

Despite the occasional presence of an innovative director in his ranks—Culhane, Don Patterson, Dick Lundy, Tex Avery, Jack Hannah and Sid Marcus among them—Lantz's product descended further into the formulaic during the 1950s and 1960s. The quality of his established series faltered, and newer projects failed to meet their potential. The declining market for theatrical short cartoons did not help matters any. Remarkably, Lantz remained in business until 1972, when he laid off his staff and retired. Universal continued issuing older films for exhibition, while, in semi-retirement, Lantz became something of an elder statesman for the animation business.

Walter Lantz was not an innovator in the same sense Disney and the Fleischers had been, but he made his mark on animation history in a similar, if more modest, manner. In a career that spanned nearly 60 years, he developed an acute understanding of how animation was both an art and a trade, and therefore he was better suited than most to understand how these seemingly incompatible goals could be balanced. His product consequently came to be better suited to television than most of his contemporaries for, while he favored formula storytelling, he worked hard to create variance within the formulas. His most successful work—especially the films with his one true star character, Woody Woodpecker—have remained popular for specifically that reason, because they represent the fact that animation can often achieve its greatest successes when its goals are modest rather than grandiose, much like Lantz's own goals were. Through his methods and his presence on television, Lantz came to represent a second-tier level of production achievement that, in both positive and negative ways, would serve as a major influence on television animation in its formative years.

Warner Bros.

Other than Disney, when the general public normally thinks about "cartoons," it is often the legendary product of this studio that they have in mind. The star characters of the "Looney Tunes" and "Merrie Melodies" produced by Warner Bros. between the mid–1930s and the early 1960s represent what is perhaps the most formidable and memorable stock company in animation history. Certainly, few other cartoon characters are as immediately recognizable through their voices and catchphrases alone, not to mention their very names and physical appearances. Nor, for that matter, have any of them been subjected to the large volume of critical and historical analysis their films have received.[68] Not that this is in any way undeserved. The Warner studio at its peak, during the 1940s and 1950s, was a fountain of creative and technological innovation in theatrical animation, employing many of the greatest names in the field and exploiting their talents to their greatest advantage. Yet, in spite of their individual and creative excellence, the enduring popularity of the characters was developed and reinforced as much through a long-standing series of television compilations, as well as newer materials produced for television and theaters, that have allowed the characters a long residency within the broadcast media of the world, an unprecedented achievement considering their origins. And though this served to heighten the visibility of the characters, and enrich the bottom line of their parent company, the consistent presence of the classic Warner characters in Saturday morning and daytime programming schedules aimed at children in both network and cable schedules has frequently prevented the analysis of television animation on its own, independent virtues. The mere presence of these films *on* television has often reinforced the view among those ignorant of the history of animation that they were somehow *made* for it. Consequently, the Warner house style (anarchic, flippant, irreverent and filled with a large amount of both actual and implied violence) would be allowed, especially in the 1960s and 1970s, to stand in for the entire animation medium— theatrical *and* television—and thus allow it to be easily and erroneously written off by media critics as an unhealthy "waste of time." And, in spite of the growth of television animation artistically in the 1990s and 2000s, there were many programs that reflected the view of the classic Warner studio as the "only" way of producing animation by openly aping its style, with mixed levels of success—including a reactivated television animation production unit from Warner Bros. itself.

The studio began in 1930, when Disney veterans Hugh Harman and Rudolf Ising persuaded Hollywood veteran Leon Schlesinger to financially back production of animated cartoons; Schlesinger, calling on connections at Warner Bros., persuaded them to serve as the films' distributor in turn.[69] Like most non–Disney studios, its work initially (and slavishly) imitated Disney. Harman and Ising's lead character, a caricatured African American named Bosko, launched and initially starred in the *Looney Tunes* series, while a second series,

Merrie Melodies, was designed to illustrate and exploit songs from the studio's back catalog. The studio continued producing competent, if pedestrian, films in this line until Harman and Ising split with Schlesinger in 1933. The animators moved to MGM (see following entry) while Schlesinger reorganized the studio under his direct control, hiring talent away from both Disney and Harman and Ising themselves. From this latter group came Isadore "Friz" Freleng, a veteran animator turned director who was to remain associated with the studio for the bulk of his long and distinguished career.

The addition of several younger animators to the staff (headed by Frederick "Tex" Avery and including future studio stalwarts Bob Clampett and Chuck Jones) led to a radical overhaul in the studio's creative agenda. While still working within established story frameworks, this group and their colleague Frank Tashlin began pushing the boundaries of the execution of comedy in animation. Combining a lightning-fast pace with unprecedented technical virtuosity, they began to help the Warner studio finally come out of Disney's shadow and establish its own independent creative agenda. By the end of the 1930s this had begun to coalesce into the Warner studio style that would become known and loved throughout the world. Two gifted non-animators also served to begin enhancing the Warner product in these years. Musical director Carl Stalling, a Disney veteran, developed a musical style as unique as the studio's emerging visual product, which he maintained until retiring in the 1950s.[70] Actor Mel Blanc, meanwhile, began contributing voices for the characters. In doing so, this amazingly versatile and durable performer virtually invented the art of "voice acting," giving animated characters all the emotions, acting ability and audience sympathy of their live-action counterparts, which would prove to be an indispensable element for the success of television animation.[71] Blanc would remain a major part of the Warner arsenal—and later, in the television era, an important contributor to Hanna-Barbera as well—until his death in 1989.

The establishment of this central team, coupled with the introduction of its first major star characters—Porky Pig in 1935, Daffy Duck in 1938 and Bugs Bunny in 1940—coalesced into the studio's definitive and influential style. Especially in the works of Avery and Clampett, the surreal aspects of the animated cartoon were delved into and mined to their greatest potential. But there were also milder statements, such as Friz Freleng's *You Ought to Be in Pictures* (1940), a unique combination of animation and live-action that highlighted the engaging personalities of the characters, and, if only temporarily, gave off the suggestion that they could easily exist in the "real" world. The jubilant anarchy and extravagant personalities of the characters were well suited to the changing national tenor during World War II, and the studio cannily exploited them in this way, especially after Leon Schlesinger sold his studio outright to them in 1944 upon his retirement.[72]

Despite the departures of Avery in 1942 and Clampett in 1946, the studio's high standards were maintained—and, in some ways, surpassed—during the early postwar era. With production centralized into units headed by Friz Freleng, Chuck Jones and veteran animator Robert McKimson, the remainder of the studio's existence built on what had come before, if in a slightly more restrained fashion, while introducing innovative new characters to the animation screen. While developing unique takes on the studio's established stars, each director was also able to develop his own characters and produce innovative one-shot films as well, which enhanced the studio's reputation and showed its increasing versatility. Freleng concentrated much of his efforts on the feuding cat and bird duo Tweety and Sylvester, while McKimson depicted the adventures of the braggart rooster Foghorn Leghorn with equal success. It was Jones, however, who came to dominate the studio's production and set the house style by the early 1950s. He had been directing since the early 1940s, but now, out of the shadow of his contemporaries Avery and Clampett, he became the theatrical animation director most deserving of the title of *auteur*. Working in close collaboration with writer Michael Maltese, Jones created two of the studio's most durable properties: the long-running (and infamously "violent") Road Runner series, and the incurably romantic skunk Pepe Le Pew. He was also responsible for numerous innovative series films and one-shots, which culminated in 1957 with the satirical mini-opera *What's Opera, Doc?*, which a poll of one thousand animation professionals declared to be the greatest short animated film ever produced.[73]

Inevitably, by the early 1960s, the studio's product began winding down. The loss of personnel to other venues, including television animation, hurt immensely, and the changing economics of Hollywood had made theatrical animation less of a necessity than it had been in the past. Consequently, in 1963, the studio ceased production of animated films, though it briefly resumed it later in the decade. However, these later products, chiefly done by Friz Freleng's new DePatie-Freleng[74] studios, did nothing to enhance the reputation of the studio; instead, it cheapened it. It was left to television, where the characters debuted in *The Bugs Bunny Show* on ABC in 1960,[75] to keep the characters and their antics alive for a new generation.

The enduring presence of the characters in television compilation programs, VHS and DVD issues, and the odd original special or film, has made it hard for subsequent generations of animators to fully escape their shadow. By firmly setting in place the idea of what "cartoons" were supposed to "be" in the eye of the public, the Warner studio set, in many respects, standards that were impossible for the more modestly budgeted world of television animation to recapture or surpass until recently. As a consequence of its regular presence as an attraction on television, this studio inadvertently created a major ideological obstacle to the independent study of television animation apart from its theatrical counterpart. The shadow would loom even larger when Warner Bros. itself began producing television animation in the 1990s, though, in their case, that was somewhat intentional.

METRO-GOLDWYN-MAYER (MGM)

The most financially affluent and artistically extravagant of the major studios of Hollywood's Golden Age, MGM had no interest in animation during the silent era and seemed generally uninterested in it until Disney's revolutionary success in the late 1920s and early 1930s. It failed to lure Disney himself into its fold, but did succeed in providing backing for one of Disney's most distinguished former employees, Ub Iwerks, to set up his own business in 1929.[76] This arrangement produced generally undistinguished product, and the studio ceased the arrangement in 1933. The following year, it established a new arrangement with two other Disney veterans, Hugh Harman and Rudolf Ising, who had recently fallen out with their previous distributors, Leon Schlesinger and Warner Bros. (see previous entry). Offered the chance to work in color, and with larger budgets than before, Harman, Ising and much of their previous Warner staff jumped at the chance.

Working in the pattern set earlier at Warner—Harman and Ising sharing a corporate by-line while each made his own films—the producers "concentrated on one-shot stories concerning cute, cherubic animals (Ising's specialty) and stylized characters personifying a particular character or theme (Harman's forte)."[77] A conscious decision was made to emulate Disney's "personality animation,"[78] and while the studio succeeded in producing levels of realism in character and design that certainly rivaled Disney's in some respects, it failed to distinguish the characters and films as a body of work. The indulgences of the producers resulted at times in work that was overlong by theatrical animation standards and failed to produce stories that matched the ambitious visuals.[79]

Tiring of the cost overruns on Harman and Ising's films, MGM, in 1937, decided instead to establish its own in-house animation unit, headed by Fred Quimby, a veteran studio executive with very little knowledge or understanding of animation. Quimby recruited veterans of the Harman-Ising studio, members of the New York animation community, and even lured Friz Freleng from Warner Bros. briefly. Despite this new aggregation of talent, problems ensued. MGM purchased the rights to the popular comic strip *The Captain and the Kids* in hopes of making it into a short film series, but the series was a spectacular failure. Comic-strip artist Milt Gross brought some of his characters and ideas to the studio, but he and they did not last, and another comics artist, Harry Hershfield, contributed even less during his time as Gross's replacement.

Forced to eat crow, MGM brought Hugh Harman and Rudolf Ising back to head the studio. Ising introduced a new starring character, Barney Bear, while Harman concentrated primarily on one-shot films. The highlight of this latter phase of their stay at the studio was Harman's *Peace on Earth* (1939), an ambitious anti-war cartoon which received an Academy Award nomination.

The following year saw the release of *Puss Gets the Boot*, a film that introduced the cat-and-mouse duo Tom and Jerry, who would be the closest thing the studio would have to sustained "stars" à la Warner Bros.[80] They were the creation of a new and innovative creative team at the studio: William Hanna, a Harman-Ising veteran, and Joseph Barbera, a veteran of the New York animation community. Hanna's skill at timing action felicitously complemented Barbera's innovative gag writing, and the duo managed to convert what could have become a stale and repetitive situation into a series of amazingly versatile and ambitious films. The fact that the series won seven Academy Awards between 1940 and 1957, along with additional nominations, says much for both its initial appeal and its enduring attractions, as well as for the high level of preparation and quality work Hanna, Barbera and their staff put into it. In spite of heavily adverse criticism, this would be no less the case when the duo relocated to television in 1957, with much of the same staff intact.[81]

In 1942, another, even more creative force began working alongside Hanna and Barbera at the studio. Frederick "Tex" Avery had been one of the major architects of the Warner Bros. house style (see previous entry) before coming to a parting of the ways with the Warner management. He built on this approach at MGM, and pushed it so far that it became uniquely his own.[82] Totally and entirely separating themselves from the realism of Disney, Avery's films were a self-contained universe where nothing was sacred and even the most illogical things were taken for granted. His break-neck pacing, disregard for standard animation conventions, and, in particular, the overplayed, forceful and intensely emotional "acting" of his characters mark Avery as a true *auteur* both among his contemporaries and within the modern standards of animation as well. But, as with the Warner studio, the lasting impact of his work has had both positive and negative consequences for the future of animation in America. The enduring popularity of his work served to inculcate into viewers not understanding of the diversity of animation a narrow idea of what the medium's capabilities were. This has been particularly the case with television exhibition of the films, though this has not been as extensive or continuous as the Warner product. Nevertheless, just as the Warner studio served to establish a false understanding of the methodology of the animated cartoon to the general public, Avery's films served to provide a *modus operandi* for how the stereotypical "cartoon character" was supposed to "act." The enduring influence of Avery in television animation's approach to gags and acting—especially in the post–1990 modern era—says much about the degree to which this attitude was accepted and reinforced in the animation community itself, not to mention the general public.

Avery, after exhausting himself through overwork, left MGM in 1955; he worked briefly as a director for Walter Lantz before exiting theatrical animation permanently.

That same year, Fred Quimby retired and Hanna and Barbera took over as the joint heads of the studio. Their reign was short-lived, however. In 1957, MGM chose to close its animation studio for financial reasons, the belief being that they could simply reissue older cartoons to theaters rather than be encumbered by the cost of producing new ones.

Consequently, Hanna, Barbera and their staff chose to enter the new and burgeoning medium of television—with spectacular results, as this book will show later on. MGM would briefly revive its animation production unit with Chuck Jones at the helm during the mid–1960s, producing both television and theatrical animation before finally ceasing animation production in 1967.[83]

UNITED PRODUCTIONS OF AMERICA (UPA)

The last major animation studio of the theatrical animation era was also the one whose shadow ended up looming the largest over television animation, due to chronological, artistic and personnel symmetry. UPA represented the work of a new generation of animators who, tired of the conventions of Hollywood animation, deliberately chose means of artistic expression that defied it in every conceivable way possible. The commitment of this studio to the production of animation as "art" served to elevate theatrical animation in the eyes of the public, making it easier for television animation to be dismissed for a relative lack of production values. The irony was that television animation would not have been able to grow and mature if it were not for the input of veterans of theatrical animation—especially those who had worked at highbrow-minded UPA.

UPA grew from the dissatisfaction of a younger generation of artists, many of whom had been hired by Disney during the period of expansion required for the making of *Snow White and the Seven Dwarfs*. As these younger artists tended to have more progressive views than the elder artists, they became the brunt of anti-art attacks from the elder group, seeing that the elder artists did not have the same fine arts background as they did and resented them for it.[84] In the aftermath of the Disney strike of 1941, these artists demanded the time and resources need to produce "a progressive, intelligent approach to animation ... and [the] realization that it is an expressive and not a mechanical medium."[85] The artists found ideal means of expressing their new approach to animation working at the Columbia-distributed Screen Gems studio and also in the production of war and political-themed animated films, such as the 1944 pro–Roosevelt campaign film *Hell Bent for Election*.

When the war ended, three members of this group of animators—Stephen Bosustow, David Hilberman and Zachary Schwartz—established UPA in order to continue production of films on a regular, commercial basis. Hilberman and Schwartz soon left to form Tempo Productions, a pioneering television animation studio (see Chapter 2), while Bosustow consolidated his control as the head of the new studio. Soon afterward, Bosustow secured a distribution deal with Columbia, and the studio was off and running.

With the exception of a popular series featuring the elderly, nearsighted human being Mr. Magoo (voiced memorably by Jim Backus), UPA eschewed regular series production in favor of well-designed and artistically stylized one-shot films. The most famous of these was *Gerald McBoing Boing*, based on a Dr. Seuss story, about a boy who can only speak in sound effects and is ostracized until he finds a useful place for himself. This 1951 Academy Award winner was hailed as a breakthrough in the artistic use of graphic design in animation. Gilbert Seldes, who had praised the early work of Disney, was equally enthused about the UPA product. "In a sense," he wrote, "the UPA product is not so much new as it is a return to the principles of the animated cartoon, those fundamentals which Disney understood and exploited more fully than anyone before him, and which he has abandoned."[86] He went on to describe the essentials of the UPA style, which he believed formed the core of its appeal, and also indicates what the studio's greatest legacy would be, especially to television animation:

> The UPA cartoons are flat; whatever sense of depth you get comes from perspective.... And because they use one drawing for every two or three frames of the film, instead of Disney's one for each frame, the figures move less smoothly; they have a galvanic animation.
>
> ...The positive virtues of UPA are their impudent and intelligent approach to subject matter and a gay palette, a cascading of light colors, the use of color and line always to suggest, never to render completely, a great deal of warmth, and an unfailing wit. Some of the cartoons recall stock episodes ... but the best of them are as fresh in concept as in execution.[87]

As Seldes suggests, what the UPA was creating was a more streamlined approach to the production and execution of animation storylines—one that was not as labor intensive as those that had come before. It was work that contradicted Winsor McCay's old pronouncement: in the hands of skilled artists, animation could now be both an art and a trade. And it also heralded major changes in how the animation industry viewed its product. Following UPA's success, all of the other major studios—even Disney—began producing films that openly embraced UPA's innovations, including streamlined backgrounds and creative uses of color and design, in particular. But UPA's production methods proved to be most beneficial to the television animation industry, since the traditional time-consuming production methods of theatrical animation could not be used in a medium where product had to be produced on a consistent level on a weekly basis. Consequently, UPA's methods played a major role in preparing the animation industry for this major transition between media.

While the studio also contracted to produce advertisements for television to secure its financial survival,[88] it continued the production of adventurous animated short films by veterans such as John Hubley and Robert "Bobe" Cannon, and by relative newcomers such as Bill Hurtz and Ted Parmelee. This latter pair were responsible, respectively, for literary adaptations of James Thurber's *A Unicorn in the Garden*, and Edgar Allan Poe's *The Tell Tale Heart*—both of which remained astonishingly faithful to their source material while advancing UPA as a source of progressive animation ideas. The studio also advanced into other areas, expanding its advertising division into a separate New York branch, producing a television series, *The Gerald McBoing Boing Show* (see Chapter 3), and producing a feature film, *1001 Arabian Nights*, in 1958. This expansive schedule taxed the studio's resources and drove most of the key talent away. Writer Bill Scott, for example, moved to television in partnership with Jay Ward, and lured UPA veterans Ted Parmelee, Lew Keller, Bill Hurtz and Pete Burness over to direct. The resulting *Rocky and Bullwinkle* series benefitted much from their expertise (see Chapter 3). In 1959, Bosustow sold the company to Henry Saperstein, and the second, lesser phase of the company's history began as a television animation provider (see Chapter 3).

UPA's legacy far outlived its short existence as a commercial entity, however. As Leonard

Maltin notes, the company "expanded the horizons of animation within the commercial context, and paved the way for new ideas that otherwise might have lain dormant."[89] Quite a few of those "new ideas"—from *Rocky and Bullwinkle* to *The Powerpuff Girls* and *My Life as a Teenage Robot*—would come from television animation in the following 50 years, and nearly all of them would bear, either directly or indirectly, the artistic imprint or the commercial blueprint that UPA set for the industry in the late 1940s and early 1950s.

Conclusion

Television animation was not created in a vacuum. There were clear structures and ideas in place, as we have seen, long before television itself existed. There were also increasingly high standards that animators were setting for themselves that needed to be dealt with—as well as the views of outsiders that also needed to be mediated. How animation moved from the theater to the TV screen, how it adapted to both positive and negative changes to its mindset from this shift, and how it has consistently struggled to produce work equaling that of the classic theatrical animation studios who were its models and forebears, forms the basis of the arguments at the heart of the remainder of this book.

Chapter 2
Marginalia (1948–1956)

The period in which television was introduced into American life was a transitional one in the lives of everyone involved in the enterprise. This profound new medium's emergence into the world provided both considerable potential for enriching the scope of its viewers and (as its critics more pessimistically warned) the potential to turn viewers into zombie-like "addicts" whose ability to resist the seductive lure of television would harm themselves and their lives. For this reason, until it had proved its worthiness to millions of still-skeptical Americans, television's first decade was marked by a need to balance the enlightening abilities it possessed alongside fears that it would become solely an addictive instrument.

Although the entire medium of television was viewed skeptically by critics, no art form depicted on it was presented or viewed as being more "marginal" than animation. Yet, the truth was that animation was at one of its lowest ebbs at the time of television's emergence, and it literally needed television to survive. With the major motion picture studios drastically reducing their production of theatrical animation or curtailing it altogether, thousands of artists in the field were suddenly unemployed. Television provided solutions to this problem, but also had problems of its own. Television used animation in its advertising, exhibited old theatrical animation films as part of children's series, and, most significantly, began producing original animation series during this period. But artists who were involved in producing animation for television had to operate cautiously or incognito—especially if they were still employed by the major film studios, who viewed television as competition during the early 1950s, although this attitude would change by the end of the decade. There were also antagonistic attitudes from the remaining theatrical animation community, who viewed television animation as an "inferior" product because of its limited budgets (a necessity of the times, as well as the technical limitations of the new medium) and apparent lack of creativity. As a consequence, the view of television animation as a marginal and inferior product was set early in its history, and it would take decades to fully recover from this bias.

In spite of these restrictions, there was a new generation of artists working in the field who believed in the potential of television animation and helped it to grow artistically across the decade. Eventually, they would help it to walk, but it had to learn how to crawl first.

The Advent of Television, and Its Apparent "Threat"

Until the advent of the Internet several decades later, no form of mass media has been viewed with as much suspicion as television was when commercial television broadcasting was introduced in the United States in 1948. The reactions—both positive and negative—were varied, from its educational potential to the addiction issues already discussed. All of them would provide considerable fodder for study and debate at a later time.[1] The debates about television represented two sides of a coin, and arguments about the pros and cons of the new medium were divisive. However, both positions were supported by hard facts in the form of how the predecessors of television had succeeded—or failed—in managing similar divides.

The evolution of mass media and public entertainment in America was something that had never gone unopposed. Most commonly, opposition came in the form of socially, politically and religiously conservative people who feared that the "corruptive" influence of these entertainment forms, perceived and actual, would cause their consumers to deviate from cultural and social norms. Opponents of the American circus in the 19th century, for example, feared that the spectacle offered by the shows would entice innocent young people to abandon normality and "run away" with the shows, which some actually did.[2] Opposition to the most prominent popular literary form of the day—the dime novel—was based on similar pretexts. To critics of the time, they were "villainous sheets which pander greedily and viciously to the natural taste of young readers for excitement, [whose] irreparable wrong ... is hidden from no one."[3] Variations on these themes would be replayed and revised in the forthcoming years as new and ever more potentially objectionable forms of media and entertainment worked their way into American life.

This is not to say that the practitioners of live and literary entertainment were entirely negligent regarding their obligations to their audience. In vaudeville (the pre-eminent live media form of the time) the opposite was true. The founders of the influential Keith-Orpheum vaudeville circuit, in particular, demanded a strict model of decorum that forbade (among other things) profanity, broad sexuality in dress and speech, and anything perceived to have the ability to offend the audience, "on pain of instant discharge"—though this did not include the racist, sexist and political forms of humor that were commonplace in the era's comedy. And, as vaudeville became the essential training ground for the founding entertainers of film and radio, these sentiments attached themselves to those media as well.[4]

The advent of visual culture, exemplified by the rise of motion pictures and then television, gave force to arguments against the "corruptive" influences of the mass media. As historian Robert Sklar has suggested, the ascension of the motion picture coincided with the rise of the Progressive reform movement, which "drew much of its energy from the middle classes' discovery that they had lost control over—and even knowledge of—the behavior and values of the lower orders; and the movies became prime targets of their efforts to reformulate and reassert their power."[5] Concern over film-industry conduct widened, culminating in the Payne Fund Study and Experiments of the late 1920s, whose results were published in 1932.[6] The first systemic study of a mass media of any kind, the Payne Fund studies examined the scope of what motion picture narratives were capable of instructing people in, particularly the young. In response, the Hollywood studios, with the influence of interested parties in the American Catholic Church, set up the doctrinal system of regulation for filmmaking which became known as the Production Code.[7] Adopted in 1934, and in force until the mid-1960s, the Code locked American filmmaking into a narrow doctrinal system, forbidding the use and display of profanity, overt sexuality and scatology on the screen while at the same time encouraging and supporting an idealized portrait of American life and the Christian faith. In the short term, this served the purpose of limiting the growth of ideologically threatening ideas in filmmaking, including animation. The value system imposed by the Code was carried over into television, since the vast majority of television's pioneers had received their start in the prior medium, and were well aware of its rules and code of behavior. As a consequence, when commercial television broadcasting began in the United States in 1948, reactions to it and attempts to limit its influence already had at least a half century of incubation. The severe backlash from critics toward television, particularly with regard to its impact on children, thus had traceable roots noticeable in debates over earlier media. Still, nothing could have prepared television producers for more than three decades of criticism they would receive, simply for being part of the industry.

A key reason television was seen as a threat was the fact that, by importing outside views and ideas into the home, it was violating the traditionally "feminine" atmosphere of the home through its presentation of "masculine" value systems. As historian Lynn Spigel has noted, social activities within the home were supposed to follow the genteel model, with the "masculine" elements outside of the home designed to be socially and politically isolated and more exposed to outside regulation.[8] This separation of "feminine" and "masculine" entertainments was a key stimulus for the negative views toward many forms of entertainment taking place outside of the home in the late–19th and early–20th centuries, such as the circus, vaudeville, and, ultimately, the movies. Television, however, was different because it existed *within* the home. Thus, while television's backers promoted it as the ideal form of "family" (i.e., "feminine") entertainment, there remained opposition to what was seen as its more coarse and vulgar aspects, particularly from religious and family-minded social groups who would demonize television animation, in particular, in later times. This debate persisted into the early 21st century, until the Internet began to usurp television's position as a "threat" by luring away large portions of its audience, and by providing uncensored access to an almost unlimited range of viewing subjects.

But in the late 1940s and early 1950s, there was no medium more scrutinized, or misunderstood, than television. It would be under the lens of this scrutiny that television animation would begin to undergo the difficult and divisive process of distinguishing itself from its theatrical counterpart, as hard as that might have seemed at the time.

Animation Needed Television

Animation came to embrace television sooner than other aspects of the film industry did for a simple reason: it needed to survive. As noted in Chapter 1, the contraction of the Hollywood film industry during the late 1940s as a result of the *Paramount v. United States* Supreme Court case caused a number of the film industry's products, including animation, to become valued less as part of the Hollywood filmmaking machine. As a consequence, many film studios either reduced the size of their animation production units or closed them altogether. With work scarce and often temporary, the Hollywood animation industry became less secure, as an employer, than it had been in the past. This created the feeling among a newer generation of animators entering the field that they were part of a "lost generation"[9] whose opportunities were fewer than those of their predecessors, and had to be taken when they were available or chances for work would be lost.

Television seemed to offer some partial relief to this situation. The new medium required a large amount of material to fill its broadcast days, much more than had been produced on a yearly basis in the heyday of the film industry. Animation was a major part of this, even if its role was not always directly acknowledged. Commercials were made using animation, and older material was repackaged for broadcast as part of local children's programming and elsewhere. But the most significant breakthrough was the beginnings of production of *original* television animation programs, a significant development that would ensure the presence of animation as an art form in a new medium as its older one began to fade and falter.

However, the use of animation in the new medium was not something that was entirely accepted by those in the profession itself, or in the film industry as a whole, during this period. In the late 1940s and early 1950s television was still regarded as a threat by the film industry, who could only see it as a newer and more attractive entertainment form that was cutting into its bottom line. Therefore, it was not surprising that the film industry did not approve of its employees working for the "competition." The relatively few who did this were forced to work undercover without credit, a common position for animators since credit was rarely given even when due in theatrical films themselves. An additional problem was the contempt that many established theatrical animators felt for what was being undertaken in the name of animation on television. Working with budgets that were mere fractions of what theatrical animators had at their disposal, it was no surprise that the earliest television animation was crude in comparison to the more established and distinguished theatrical animation industry. This supposed "cheapness" was something television animation would have to fight against for much of its first three decades, even when budgets increased and became more comparable with theatrical animation. The simple reason for this was the fact that theatrical animation veterans often erroneously believed television animation was trying to undercut the artistic value of the form—something for which little true evidence existed.

The truth was that a new generation of animators was entering the field through television and they had fewer qualms about working in it because they could foresee the more lasting and enduring value of the medium, as well as the place that animation would be able to hold within it. It was, therefore, this generation of animators that would maintain the faith in animation as an art form during this uncertain time period in the field's existence.

The First Major Television Animation Series: "Crusader Rabbit"

"Crusader Rabbit" was the first major television animation product to be seen as a weekly or daily series, one of the first to feature continuing characters and plotlines, and one of the first to be broadcast as part of a regular broadcasting schedule. But it is also important for another reason. It was the first production of the man who would become one of the most controversial—and influential—figures in the history of television animation production: Jay Ward. Viewed in this light, the significance of this program cannot be overstated.

Unlike so many involved in the film industry at that time, Jay Ward was a native of California, born in San Francisco in 1920.[10] Educated at UC Berkeley and Harvard, his original aim was to operate as a realtor, which he did into the 1980s. However, his enthusiasm for realty dimmed when he was involved in a bizarre automobile accident on his first day on the job. A lumber truck lost braking power and crashed through the front window of Ward's office, injuring him severely in the process.[11] He was forced to undergo a long period of recuperation, during which a good friend approached him with a business proposition that he could not refuse.

Alex Anderson, a childhood friend of Ward's, was an aspiring animator who was interested in the new potential that television seemed to provide for animation. He even had theatrical animation connections: his uncle was Paul Terry, founder of the New York–based Terrytoons studio. However, when Anderson approached his uncle for assistance with the venture, Terry refused for a subtle, but obvious, reason. As noted earlier, the theatrical animation and film industries were closely tied, and the latter did not approve of any in the former being too closely associated with the new, threatening medium of television. As Terry informed his nephew, if he was to become involved in television production, his distributor, 20th Century–Fox, would sever its ties with Terrytoons "just like that."[12] Having nowhere else to turn, Anderson approached Ward, whose enthusiasm for the burgeoning new medium equaled—if not surpassed—his own.

In 1948, Ward and Anderson established Television Arts Productions, one of the first companies specifically established for the production of animated films for television.[13] Assembling a staff and working on a budget of $350 per cartoon,[14] they produced a trio of pilot films for potential sale as syndicated products. They were "Hamhock Jones," a parody of Sherlock Holmes; "Dudley Do-Right of the Mounties," a melodramatic farce that would later re-emerge as part of Ward's oeuvre (see Chapter 3); and "Crusader Rabbit," based on a concept that Anderson had developed while working at his uncle's studio.[15] Presenting the films as a package called *The Comic Strips of Television*, they approached NBC in the fall of 1948. "Crusader Rabbit" proved to be the piece that attracted potential buyers the most and, soon, the producers had signed a deal with pioneer television producer Jerry Fairbanks, who would serve as the program's distributor through his exclusive arrangement to supply NBC with film products.[16]

Working with a thin staff, and out of a makeshift studio behind the house of Anderson's parents in Berkeley, California,[17] the producers set to work. One hundred and fifty episodes, each five minutes long, were produced, making their debut in the fall of 1950. The series documented the adventures of Crusader Rabbit (voiced by Lucille Bliss), a surprisingly pugnacious "good deed" doer,[18] and his sidekick Rags the Tiger (Vern Louden) as they traveled from their home base in Galahad Glen in search of adventure.[19] It had a serialized adventure format combined with a hip sense of humor, which allowed it to attract both children and adults.[20] The success of the format was something that was not lost on Ward, and he would later find success by continuing to mine this then-unique combination in the following decade.

Though few of the episodes survive for examination today,[21] what remains provides evidence of a series that pioneered many standard elements of television animation programs to come, and stood in contradiction to other soon-to-be standard elements. As pioneering television animation historian Hal Erickson has argued, the first story sequence—in which Crusader and Rags travel to Texas to confront the harsh conditions being endured by Crusader's fellow rabbits—is particularly revealing:

> Animation is not the strong suit in the first *Crusader Rabbits*. No more than four poses are seen within any five seconds of screen time (sometimes not even that many); most often, movement is conveyed by rapid cutting from scene to scene, or "simulated" by the energetic narration, the evocative musical score and the two-reel comedy sound effects. It isn't really important how the characters move, however. What gives [the series] exuberance is its impeccable sense of timing. The setups, punchlines and throwaway gags occur at such

"right" movements that the series stands as a model of brilliant comic editing. Adding to the fun is the character of Crusader Rabbit himself. After years of [seeing] relatively mild mannered TV cartoon characters ... it's a real eye opener to see this furry little bunny from half a century ago, who charges unprovoked into a room and threatens to punch out all comers. This guy doesn't have adventures—he's *making* the adventures [emphasis in original].[22]

Erickson's statement that Crusader is "making" his adventures marks him out, even this early in television animation's history, as a truly groundbreaking character. However, it would take some time—as well as changes in the economic structure of television and the attitudes regarding television animation in the eyes of the general public—before the likes of him would truly be seen again.

Flushed with the success of *Crusader Rabbit* as a daily syndicated product, Ward and Anderson began making plans to expand the reach of their company. In addition to doing some contracted advertising work for their program's sponsors, they also began to consider ideas for new programs. The most prominent of these was "The Frostbite Falls Review," featuring a cast of animals who would deliver programming from their station in rural, woodsy northern Minnesota. "For years these amazing creatures have been hiding their dramatic abilities away out yonder in the great North Woods [*sic*]," a promotional flyer for the series claimed. "Now at last, through the wondrous medium of television, they plan to launch their remarkable talents upon our unsuspecting nation."[23] This hyperbolic statement proved to be partially true: the setting, and a revised version of two of the characters, would later emerge as successes in their own right, but this remained some years away.

The bubble burst for the studio soon afterwards, however. NBC withdrew its support for *Crusader Rabbit* in the spring of 1951, and by 1952, Television Arts was out of business.[24] Ward retreated to realty, and Anderson began a new career in advertising. The following year saw Jerry Fairbanks's business collapse and, with it, Ward and Anderson's ownership of the *Crusader Rabbit* property—a loss over which they lodged a lawsuit against Fairbanks.[25] Ward attempted a failed revival of the series in 1956, but a more successful version was launched instead by Shull Bonsall, the Los Angeles businessman who had inherited Fairbanks's properties upon the closure of Fairbanks's business. Bonsall's version did not involve the participation of Ward and Anderson, and therefore this later, color version was less distinguished than its predecessor.[26]

However, Jay Ward would not be out of the television animation business for long; indeed, eventually, he would return to the field with a vengeance.

The First Major Television Network Series: "Tele-Comics"/ "NBC Comics"

While *Crusader Rabbit* was aired through syndication on NBC affiliated stations, this series was actually the first television animation program to air on an actual television network schedule.[27] As Hal Erickson has noted, the program "was essentially what its title described: filmed comic-strip panels, with the camera panning from one panel to the next as the story progressed."[28] Little is known about the series save for what Erickson describes in his seminal book, *Television Cartoon Shows*: the various components of the program were adventure serial formats much in the same fashion as *Crusader Rabbit*. They included "Johnny and Mr. Do-Right," the tale of a boy and his dog; "Danny March," a juvenile delinquent turned detective; "Kid Champion," a boxing serial; and "Space Barton," the tale of a jet pilot. Because the program was filmed in black-and-white, as opposed to color, it did not survive many of the changes that came to the television industry in later years. It has thus remained known chiefly to historians and collectors—a victim of the fact that preservation was not a priority at that time.

Side Shows: Children's Show Packages and Original Advertising

Despite the success of *Crusader Rabbit* and *Tele-Comics* in proving that television animation could be a stand-alone attraction, the industry was not yet able to provide the economic framework to allow it to develop beyond the limitations of the short-film format. As a consequence, it was far more common to see animation on television during this period through two less noticed and understood formats: the distribution of older theatrical animation through local children's programming, and the use of animation as a feature of early television advertising.

Children's television was one of the earliest forms of television production, and many local programs emerged as the medium grew, with many lasting for decades.[29] These programs featured friendly hosts who entertained children both with their own antics and with filmed entertainment from bygone eras (chiefly, old comedy shorts dating back to the silent era) as well as, increasingly, animated films. By the late 1950s, the attitude of Hollywood toward television was starting to change. The studios were beginning to understand that they could no longer beat television, but now had to join it, in order to survive financially. They not only were beginning to produce original material for the medium, but were also starting to release their earlier material for exhibition there. This was chiefly material produced prior to 1948 due to the Screen Actors Guild's insistence on the payment of residuals for the post–1948 "TV era."[30] As a consequence, animated films from the theatrical era began to be exposed to a new and appreciative audience (albeit one that was often unaware of their prior existences and incarnations), and in a way that denied both credit to the original producers and an understanding of how and when they were produced. Still, it is likely that these characters (particularly Bugs Bunny and Popeye, whose films proved to be the most popular) would not have had significant exposure to an audience any other way than this. Their exposure in this forum undoubtedly contributed to at least one generation of children developing a strong fondness for animation that, if television ratings could be believed, would only grow stronger in the following decades.

A similar fate met those involved in the production of television advertising, which was likely the most visible but most unnoticed form of television animation during this period. Involving both veteran studios such as Disney and UPA as well as smaller companies such as Playhouse, Academy, Elektra and Tempo, these companies brought a patch of color into what was still largely a black-and-white medium.[31] The production of animation primarily for commercial use, while profitable during the early part of the decade, was a trend that reversed itself as the advertising industry began using filmed commercials in the early 1960s, in lieu of the animated inserts that these studios had once provided. Tempo, the brainchild of UPA cofounders David Hilberman and Zachary Schwartz, suffered a particularly bad end shortly after its founding in 1953 when it was suspected of having Communist ties due to the politics of its founders.[32] Consequently, the halcyon period of the relationship between television, animation and advertising was short, but, as with exposure through children's programming, the use of animation in advertising was a vital link between the techniques of theatrical animation and the manner in which they would be used in the new medium of television.

Conclusion

The actual, physical evidence of animation produced for television between 1948 and 1956 is limited, given the absence of videotape and other forms of preservation. The first decade of television's existence provided a period in which the new medium was able to experiment and give all of its wares—including animation—a chance to reach as many people as possible, in as many forms as possible. In both old forms and new, animation was making its presence felt, even if it was unknown to, or unrecognized by, the public at large. In establishing itself as a medium of entertainment in this formative period, animators who produced films for television came to understand how the medium could provide them with both a means of strong, personal artistic expression and the means for establishing a firm, solid business model. The period between 1957 and 1969 would further deepen television animation as both a form of artistic expression and as a commercial product—even if, to some, these positions seemed increasingly contradictory.

Chapter 3

Silhouette Storytelling (1957–1969)

The period between 1957 and 1969 saw the emergence of television animation as a genre independent of theatrical animation. As new forums opened for animation on television, and influential figures began to support it, the genre was able to expand beyond its initial orientation toward children and gain a following among adults as well. This increased its social and economic cache in the competitive field of television. However, by the end of the period, a wave of draconian censorship imposed by that same field served to imprison television animation in a series of mechanical, repetitious formats that would limit its artistic growth for over two decades.

The producers who dominated the genre in this time period would become the most prolific and influential of their kind in the field, imposing a lasting influence on its styles and formats. William Hanna and Joseph Barbera brought their expertise as theatrical animation directors and their intelligence as businessmen to a medium and genre lacking in both and, in doing so, they helped to create legitimacy for a field that had little or none prior to their entry. In spite of criticism of their production methods, particularly their use of the controversial practice of "limited animation" (a circumscribed version of the traditional animation process) and the view that their work, like that of other producers, was a for-profit entity bereft of artistic merit, Hanna and Barbera played a major role in establishing animation as a programming format in television, and successfully adapted it to the vast changes that both television and animation would undergo over the course of the 20th century.

Hanna and Barbera's success inspired others to follow in their wake. The dominant creative voice of this group was Jay Ward, now working in collaboration with theatrical animation veteran Bill Scott. Ward and Scott's work was the polar opposite of Hanna and Barbera's, both technologically and philosophically. These producers embraced an irreverent attitude in their work that was unheard of in television at that time and, as a consequence, they were heavily criticized, marginalized and, finally, nearly driven out of the business altogether. However, their classic shows and characters have endured nearly as long as Hanna and Barbera's, and consequently have proven to be nearly as influential on the development of television animation as an artistic forum and challenger of the social and political status quo. Other producers made their mark in this time, but few of their works would endure in the same way as those of Hanna and Barbera or Ward and Scott. Their work was not fully rediscovered until it became available for re-release on VHS and DVD years later.

A major shift occurred in the middle of the 1960s that limited the exposure of television animation and served to limit the public image and artistic value of the productions. The programming of animation on Saturday mornings beginning in 1965 was, in theory, designed to exploit the cultural appeal of animation to children, but the economic underpinnings of the schedule were nevertheless ever visible, and thus never truly free from controversy. This left television animation vulnerable to controversial interpretations—and misinterpretations—from people who did not understand its history, and, ultimately, to censorship that jeopardized its artistic intentions. At the other end of the broadcast day, another, more benign format for exposure developed for television animation in the form of the holiday special. Particularly during the period examined in this chapter, this became a fecund area of creativity for the field, producing several classic programs that have remained holiday staples to this day.

The period between 1957 and 1969 was a seminal period in the artistic and commercial development of television animation and its legitimization in the television landscape. But, as the 1970s began, television animation was still continually under challenge.

Hanna-Barbera

The endurance of the professional partnership between William Hanna and Joseph Barbera between two artistic media and over nearly 50 years is all the more remarkable when one considers the extreme differences in the personal attitudes and personalities of the two men.[1] Hanna possessed a generally laid-back, laconic personality; Barbera, an openly gregarious one. Hanna generally kept himself out of the public eye; Barbera was an entertainer in both public and private. Hanna preferred the company of friends and family to the world of Hollywood; Barbera reveled in rubbing shoulders with powerful, influential people, especially as he became one himself. The bond they shared professionally, however, was an enduring belief in the value of animation as an art form and in its ability to gain large audiences of both children and adults. Using their respective talents in this heavily specialized field, and relying on the many varied talents of the artists who passed through their studio gates over the years, they were able to achieve enormous success making their dreams and aims for the genre a reality. This was in spite of the fact that they, even more than other producers in the field, endured a heavy level of criticism directed at their product, both within and outside of the industry.

The two men came to their partnership through a circuitous series of events. William Hanna was born in Melrose, New Mexico, in July 1910, and was raised in Utah, Oregon and California. His father (also named William Hanna) worked as an engineer, surveyor and construction worker, and instilled a love of nature in his son that would be evident in many of Hanna's later films. An early interest and involvement in the Boy Scouts led to a lifelong involvement with that organization. From an early age, Hanna displayed musical and artistic talents that came to be of use to him as an adult.

Following his graduation from Compton High School, Hanna briefly attended Compton Junior College as a journalism student, but was forced to drop out because of the Great Depression. He then attempted to follow in his father's footsteps as a construction worker, but a fall from a scaffold convinced him that he was not cut out for that job. After other odd jobs, he landed a job at the Harman-Ising animation studio as a janitor, and slowly worked his way up to animator, composer, writer, and, finally, director. When Harman-Ising ended its distribution deal with Warner Bros. in 1933 and signed a new arrangement with

William Hanna (left) and Joseph Barbera with characters from *The Jetsons* (top, from left): Mr. Spacely, George, Jane, Astro (bottom, from left): Elroy, Judy, Rosie the Robot (Columbia Pictures/Photofest).

MGM, Hanna went with them. He remained at the studio when the producers left over financial issues and MGM centralized the operation as an in-house division.

Hanna's first major directing assignment was as a segment director of an adaptation of the comic strip *The Captain and the Kids*, a project that proved so disastrous that MGM was forced to re-hire Harman and Ising to head the department and get it back on track. By this time, Hanna had met, befriended and had begun working with Barbera, with whom he would be professionally associated for the rest of his life.

While Hanna had spent much of his life in and around the great outdoors, Joseph Barbera had been a lifelong resident of New York City until moving to California in the late

1930s. He was born in March 1911, the child of Sicilian immigrants, and grew up in an impoverished neighborhood in Brooklyn. His father, Vincent, was a successful barber, but a gambling addiction minimized both his finances and his involvement with his family's life. This may have contributed to Barbera's later displays of strong resilience, self-confidence and self-reliance as a businessman in particular.

From an early age, he displayed prodigious talents as an artist, so much so that the nuns who taught him assigned him to draw scenes from the Bible on a chalkboard.[2] In high school, he edited the school paper and developed a passionate interest in the theater, which ultimately would lead to his writing plays of his own. He had hoped to attend college, but this was not financially possible. Instead, he took a job as a tax auditor at the Irving Trust Company, occasionally managing to sell editorial cartoons on the side.

Exposure to the early work of Walt Disney was inspiring to him, and he began taking art classes at night to improve his draftsmanship. He moonlighted briefly at the Max Fleischer studio, but did not pursue animation as a full-time career until he was laid off from his day job. He gained a position as an animator at the New York–based Van Beuren Studio, and began making his mark as an animator and writer, but this did not last. The Van Beuren Studio was forced out of business in 1936 when it was dropped by RKO, its distributor, who began distributing the arguably superior work of Walt Disney instead. Unmoved by this setback, Barbera relocated to California, hoping to earn a position at the Disney studio. Failing in this, he ended up instead at MGM, where he first teamed up with Hanna. Initially, Barbera was simply an animator in Hanna's unit, but they soon discovered that their respective strengths as animators—Hanna's ability to create precision timing in the action, and Barbera's to write and stage jokes and gags—were much better suited to dividing the directorial chores between them.

Their initial projects were undistinguished, but, in 1940, they began to achieve a high level of critical and commercial success. A film called *Puss Gets the Boot*, featuring the cat and mouse duo Tom and Jerry, was a huge hit with audiences, and the young directors were instructed to create more films in the same vein. What resulted was a long-running series that lasted 17 years, won seven Academy Awards, and is generally considered one of the highlights of the golden age of theatrical animation.[3] During the production of these films, Hanna and Barbera established strong working relationships with their colleagues—particularly animators Gene Barge, Irv Spence and Ken Muse and layout artist Richard "Bick" Bickenbach—that would later become crucial to their later artistic and commercial survival.

By 1957, however, the fortunes of the theatrical animation industry were at a low ebb. By this time, Hanna and Barbera had succeeded their longtime producer Fred Quimby as the joint heads of the MGM animation department, but even this success did not save them or their colleagues from being dismissed. The reasoning was simple: animation cost money to produce, and MGM's executives reasoned that they could make more money reissuing existing, already produced animation than shelling out money for new animation. Thus, the MGM animation department was closed, and Hanna, Barbera and their colleagues were out of work.

As both men later recalled, the decision came as a shock to them, and, at least initially, they were unsure about what to do next. "A whole career had disappeared," Barbera told Ted Sennett in 1989:

> We had built this supposedly impregnable monument to success, and suddenly we are *out* [emphasis in original].... We had the dreadful feeling that we had to start over again in another business.... We weren't kids, you know. We'd been through a career.[4]

Fortunately, however, as Hanna added later in his autobiography, they soon realized where their future and the future of animation itself lay: in television.

> Television could either be our doom or our possible deliverance. While we cleaned out our desks we also pondered. We were damned good at what we did. If we couldn't make cartoons for the big screen anymore, then why not try to sell them for the small screen? ... There was one thing we would not have to give up if we chose, and that was our partnership. It had worked for nearly eighteen years and somehow, some way, we'd continue to make it work.[5]

Indeed, it was not very long before their new business, Hanna-Barbera Productions, began to "make it work," both for themselves and for the still nascent medium of television animation.

Initially, they were greeted with responses ranging from skepticism to hostility when they presented their radical new ideas for producing animation for television. The criticisms were that either animation was too expensive an art form to be effectively marketed on television, or, within the animation community itself, that Hanna and Barbera were simply using "cheap" shortcuts in production to stay involved in the industry and were thus tarnishing it. Fortunately, the producers soon found an ally in John Mitchell, the head of sales at Screen Gems, the television production division of Columbia Pictures. Mitchell was enthusiastic in his support of the producers' ideas and encouraged them to keep developing them. Although Columbia founder Harry Cohn was not interested in backing Hanna and Barbera, Mitchell managed to persuade him to fund their venture. In July of 1957, with their own limited financing and Columbia's investment, Hanna and Barbera were able to set up their company's first studio, in a historic location on Highland Avenue once used by Charlie Chaplin.[6]

Hanna and Barbera's success was established through their use of a novel but relatively underused practice in the field known as "limited animation," which simplified some of the more complicated aspects of the animation production process in order to meet the shorter deadlines of television. As historian Ted Sennett has noted, the appeal of limited animation was that it managed to preserve the artistic integrity of animation in spite of the short cuts taken to achieve the final result:

> As opposed to the intricate details of classical animation, a few moving parts of the principal characters were animated and then photocopied on to the cells to simulate talking or simple action. The character walks and other standard movements were codified and reused in cycles, while a single background could serve for entire sequences. With this system, a complete cartoon could be made and timed to its exact length in a much shorter period than before. Although a loss of life-like and richly varied detail was inevitable, the savings in time and money were incalculable. Television animation on a massive scale became possible for the first time with these stripped bare procedures.[7]

It was exactly this "loss of life-like and richly varied detail" that would earn Hanna and Barbera the enmity of many animation purists, who felt that limited animation compromised the artistic integrity of the genre, and thus they did not completely acknowledge the merit of the studio's work. Yet Hanna and Barbera understood that the timing and economics of television required an animation process that was not the same as that used in theatrical animation, and tailored the product of their studio accordingly.

Hanna and Barbera also benefitted from the contraction of the theatrical animation industry that had caused them to lose their positions at MGM. That studio was not the only one to see the writing on the wall in this regard. Most of the major studios, and even Walt Disney himself, either curtailed their production of short theatrical animation or ended it altogether as the 1950s progressed. Consequently, Hanna and Barbera, in setting up their studio, had a bumper crop of available talent from which to choose, and many talented artists, writers, and actors jumped at the chance to work with them in the new medium of television.

As seasoned veterans of the animation industry themselves, Hanna and Barbera understood that their employees would be more productive if they knew that they would be respected and valued, a rarity in the hierarchical structure of the film studios. Thus, as Barbera recalled, the company, at least initially, was built around attempting to produce quality product while achieving and maintaining this respect for the staff:

> We ran our shop in the kind of loose, anti-corporate, no-bullshit way we knew animators respected and under which they did their best, most imaginative work. We had no time clocks to punch or sign-in sheets to initial. Our artists and animators came and went as they wished. We paid them by the foot. For each foot of film an animator produced, he [sic] received so much. In those days, a good animator—if he were lucky enough to find work—made between $175 and $225 a week. Paying by the foot gave our animators an incentive to work at a blazing pace, using all the effective shortcuts their expertise commanded, and they made as much as fourteen hundred dollars a week.[8]

Given the gap between the standard animator's salary and the potential for what they could earn at Hanna-Barbera, it was not surprising that the studio soon acquired the services of many of the best in their fields of expertise in the business. It was equally unsurprising that many of these figures remained at the studio for years, even decades, to come.

Hanna and Barbera were thus able to establish a familiar "house style" whose approach would become standard in the field. In addition to the aforementioned Barge, Spence, Muse and Bickenbach, who quickly adapted to the time demands of the new medium, two other MGM veterans—layout artist and character designer Ed Benedict and animator Lewis Marshall—formed the core of the original animation staff. The in-house writing department, headed by Barbera, came to include such notables as Warren Foster, Michael Maltese, Charles Shows, Tony Benedict, Joe Ruby and Ken Spears. As the studio grew during the 1960s and the size of the staff increased, other creative voices began making their mark as well. Animator/production designer Iwao Takamoto and layout artist/character designer Jerry Eisenberg made critical contributions to updating and refining the studio's approach to layout and design in the mid to late 1960s. Veteran animators Charles "Nick" Nichols and Ray Patterson supplemented and ultimately succeeded Hanna as the principal line directors during this period.[9]

Hoyt Curtin, a veteran of the advertising industry, served as the studio's musical director, writing original background music (or compiling it from "needle-drop" stock music themes) and authoring the theme songs for the programs in collaboration with Hanna and Barbera, who wrote the lyrics. As Curtin later recalled, the producers approached him over the telephone. They had the lyrics for the first theme already written, and they needed music for it. Curtin responded by writing what he thought was an appropriate melody and then called them back. Initially hearing silence when he had finished his presentation, Curtin feared he had failed. However, the producers were impressed, enough so to offer him a job. Curtin remained at the studio into the early 1980s, and his reliable musical gifts made him an enduring asset to his employers.[10]

Two other versatile and reliable voice actors became the backbone of the studio's cast in this period: Daws Butler, who portrayed most of the lead, "star" characters, and Don Messick, who specialized in supporting character roles and narration.[11] Butler, born in Toledo, Ohio, in 1916, began performing professionally while still a young man, honing his skills as a mimic and impersonator in particular. Following service in the Navy during World War II, he traveled to Hollywood to work as a radio actor. In the early 1950s, he and Stan Freberg served as the puppeteers/stars of Bob Clampett's popular, Emmy Award–winning live-action fantasy series *Time for Beany* (itself adapted for television animation, as *Beany and Cecil*, in the early 1960s[12]). Butler also appeared on many of Freberg's popular comedy recordings, and was a regular on Freberg's short-lived CBS radio show. Due to his experience in television and his versatility as an actor, with a knowledge and understanding of a wide variety of accents and dialects that often surprised his employers,[13] Butler became a valuable contributor, helping to develop the characters through his portrayals in ways the scripts and animation could not have done on their own. Messick, a native of Buffalo, New York, ten years Butler's junior, also began performing as a young man, initially as a ventriloquist. Like Butler, he traveled to Hollywood following military service to seek work. Butler and Messick became friends and began performing together, and their joint professional respect is often evident in their collaborative vocal performances. However, while Butler was chiefly a comic actor, Messick proved to be equally skilled as a dramatic actor, and, as the studio's product diversified into more "straight" non-comic animated series during the mid–1960s, his expertise in this area became more evident, and his workload increased. Much as Mel Blanc had done in his Warner Bros. voices for theatrical animation, Butler and Messick made it perfectly clear in their voice performances that this work was being done by legitimate *actors*, not by people simply reading lines. They provided a clear-cut example for the many other actors who would follow in their field, and many of these people have openly acknowledged their influence. In helping to create classic characters, Butler and Messick played as vital a role as did the writers and animators, and helped to establish the idea that animation voice acting was a field worthy of dignity and respect.

With this talented staff in place, Hanna and Barbera were prepared to make their mark in television history as prolific and influential producers within a small and often misjudged genre.

◆ ◆ ◆

The first series to bear the Hanna-Barbera imprimatur was *Ruff and Reddy*, which debuted in the fall of 1957. A serialized adventure program after the fashion of Jay Ward's *Crusader Rabbit* (see Chapter 2), it aired on NBC as part of a nationally broadcast children's program. The protagonists were Ruff (Butler), a stocky, dimwitted dog, and Reddy (Messick), a diminutive cat. Foreshadowing future television animation programs, in particular Ward's *Rocky and Bullwinkle,* this mismatched but friendly pair frequently found themselves at odds with the forces of evil. The antagonists included such figures as the Mastermind of the planet Mini-Mula, the Chicken Hearted Chickasaurus, Scary Harry Safari, Killer and Diller (the terrible twins from Texas), and the Goon of Glocca Morra. On the heroes' side were Professor Gizmo, an eccentric scientist with a head shaped like a light bulb, and Ubble-Ubble, a young boy who (much like Mordecai Richler's later literary creation, Jacob Two Two) could speak only in double talk. The series was a success and helped to launch the Hanna-Barbera organization. Time, however, has not been kind to this dog-and-cat duo. The short, serialized format of the program was a disadvantage for rebroadcasting, as the focus of the animation industry moved toward half-hour self-contained narratives in the 1960s. In addition, while much of the studio's output has been issued for viewing on VHS and DVD in the past 30 years, *Ruff and Reddy* has been curiously absent. This lack of exposure has left it as a footnote in television animation history rather than being viewed as the pioneering series it was.

Having established the credibility of their studio and production methods, Hanna and Barbera, through much supportive goading by John Mitchell, now began to aspire to a new goal: producing a television series that consisted *entirely* of television animation, not simply featuring it as a mere component, as *Ruff and Reddy* did. First, however, they needed to acquire a sponsor, one of the "modern potentates"[14] who then controlled the off-camera aspects of the industry. Since television animation was seen as a genre whose principal audience was children, it made sense for the producers to attract the attention of an advertiser whose business focused on them. With this in mind, Barbera set up a meeting with executives of the Kellogg's cereal company and their advertising agency, Leo Burnett, in the hopes that both would bankroll the projected half-hour project. Flying to Chicago for the meeting with pilot films for the three proposed segments in hand, Barbera hoped for the best but feared for the worst. In spite of some technical problems that marred the presentation,[15] Kellogg's agreed to support Hanna-Barbera's venture. Much like the alliance between Hanna-Barbera and Screen Gems, it was a mutually beneficial arrangement: Hanna-Barbera gained a level of trust and support in the eyes of the public through being associated with an influential sponsor, while, over the years, Kellogg's gained exposure and a wide variety of colorful spokescharacters for its products.

The first star character, cheekily referred to as the studio's "Barrymore" in a 1961 *Saturday Evening Post* article,[16] was Huckleberry Hound (voiced by Daws Butler), whose eponymous program debuted in the fall of 1958. "Huck," as he was affectionately known, was a blue-furred, humanized dog who possessed a "laid back, sow-belly and greens" Southern accent and an unflappable, idealistic personality which immediately endeared him to both children and adults.[17] Written chiefly by Barbera and Warren Foster, the series cast Huck after the fashion of Chaplin, Keaton, Harold Lloyd et al. in the silent era, putting him into situations he was ill-equipped to handle and letting chaos ensue. In spite of the often dangerous situations he was put in, Huck tended to respond in a low-key fashion, which added to the humor of the narratives immensely. In his first episode, for example, Huck is cast as a policeman assigned to arrest a large gorilla with the ironic name of Wee Willie, who has escaped from a local zoo. In the course of the adventure, Huck ends up captured by the gorilla, who consumes his gun and handcuffs, and drags him into a dangerous construction site.[18] His reaction—"I guess I hurt his feelings"—is a hilarious lesson in verbal understatement.

Further episodes deepened this formula and managed to avoid repetition by finding a wide variety of inappropriate roles in which Huck could be cast. He played the roles of lion hunter, Mountie, knight, swashbuckling hero, Western lawman, detective, teacher, etc., with predictably disastrous results. Always, however, he managed to emerge remarkably unscathed from the experience, with his idealistic personality and laconic dialogue delivery completely intact. As Ted Sennett notes, the series "displayed not only a keen appreciation of the venerable art of slapstick but also a brash, impudent irreverence toward the standard genres of movies and television."[19] It retains this flavor today, even after years of reruns and the overt familiarity of some of the comic material. In its own time, it was received well by its target audience, which was willing to accept anything that was original in television animation. Huck was also popular among adults: there were rumors that some taverns on the West

Coast requested complete silence from their patrons during broadcasts of the show.[20] The television industry was equally supportive: following its first season, the series received an Emmy Award, making it the first television animation program to earn this honor.[21]

The second segment of the program would also become an enduring favorite among viewers, although it returned Hanna and Barbera to more familiar terrain. Pixie and Dixie (Messick and Butler, respectively) were a pair of gray-furred mice (Pixie wore a blue bow tie, Dixie a red vest) who continually fell afoul of the jaunty cat Mr. Jinx (Butler, speaking in "a loose, New York type of attitude"[22] reminiscent of the young Marlon Brando). It was an exercise in "genial, basic slapstick"[23] that did no harm to the audience—though one could not say the same for Mr. Jinx, who, like others before him, ended up as the victim of his scheming instead of the beneficiary he imagined himself to be. His regular exclamation of how he hated "those meeces to pieces!" became a popular catchphrase among viewers.

The third feature of the program was the one that endured the longest, with its lead character becoming an unofficial social and corporate mascot for the studio. Yogi Bear proved to be so popular, in fact, that he was able to "graduate" to his own series in 1961 (discussed later on in this chapter). As voiced by Daws Butler, Yogi, a brown, upright-walking bear wearing a green hat and necktie, proved to be one of the best examples of the traditional use of anthropomorphism for satirical purposes in animation.[24] In his case, it was used to spoof the then-popular figure of the con artist, as defined in the live-action sitcom by Phil Silvers's popular character, Sergeant Bilko. For his part, Yogi was a genial inhabitant of the fictional Jellystone Park, where he was continually "on the make" for the food of the picnicking tourists in particular. He was aided and abetted by his little bow-tie–wearing associate Boo Boo (Don Messick), who served alternately as Yogi's biggest fan or his devil's advocate. Yogi was fond of noting how he was "smarter than the average bear," but this mental aptitude was frequently tested by his friendly nemesis, Park Ranger John Smith (Messick), whose attempts to outwit and/or punish him were a major component of many episodes.

These early episodes cast Yogi in a variety of settings: as a Goofy-like demonstrator of the "right" way to do things, a Good Samaritan of the forest, even as a would-be mascot for the Chicago Bears football team. Eventually, however, the series settled down into the familiar con artist pattern that would serve as its hallmark. In this setting, Yogi represents several aspects of the archetypal male con artist. He has, to begin with, an inordinate faith in his own abilities and an unyielding belief that his approach to the situation at hand will work. He is prepared to do anything to maintain his standard of living. As historian Hal Erickson has noted, he displays many of the expected emotional traits of the con artist: "grovelling in the face of Authority, sniggering behind Authority's back, gleefully scamming everyone in sight to further his own comfort, and never losing rapport with an audience who'd give anything to get away with what Yogi got away with."[25] By managing to accomplish his goals while remaining in the audience's good graces, Yogi is able to succeed on a double level.

In spite of Yogi's success, however, the character was unable to avoid the status of "outsider" that con artistry inevitably creates for its practitioners. While he tries to get something he feels he deserves, he is frequently perceived by the tourists as a force of menace trying to harm them—regardless of his real intentions. An early episode, "Bear on a Picnic," is instructive in this light, as Yogi's interest in stealing food from a middle-aged couple is compromised by his sympathetic interest in their infant son. As the child wanders into dangerous situations in the forest, Yogi protects the boy without interest in recompense, even when he gets into a fight with a mountain lion as a consequence of some of the child's actions. However, it is Yogi himself who is considered the threat to the child by the parents, who drive him away through this misguided interpretation. The metaphor is made clear at this point: Yogi is being judged based on his outward, "threatening" appearance rather than his inner heart, and becomes a victim of prejudice for precisely this reason.

As Erickson suggests,[26] the character of Ranger Smith represents Authority, and the need to repair the rifts in the social order which Yogi has created. Smith's relationship with Yogi can be interpreted in two significant ways. There is clearly a sense that one is the "master" of the other, but our preconceptions about who fills what role are often challenged by Hanna and Barbera. While Smith is theoretically Yogi's "master," he is also manipulated into having to "correct" the damage which Yogi's cons inflict and is, therefore, made a "slave" to Yogi in this sense. Yogi, in turn, is willing to play the "slave" role in discussions with Smith, even though his actions clearly demonstrate that this role is merely assumed. Also evident are traces of a coded father/son relationship between the pair, with Smith frequently issuing warnings and punishments designed to correct Yogi's behavior, which Yogi ignores and manipulates to make his "father" look like a fool for trying to control him. This undoubtedly enhanced his appeal to child viewers having to deal with their own "controlling" parents.

A deeper edge exists to this relationship, however, which reveals the subversive nature of television animation in the light of the exclusionary politics of American television in the 1950s, where racial minorities were seen only rarely, and then only in heavily stereotypical roles. Especially in light of the then-ongoing civil rights movement, it is possible to look at the Yogi/Smith relationship as a coded white/black relationship, with Yogi as the "black" figure and Smith the "white" authority figure trying to control him. In this light, as well, Yogi's often antagonistic relationship with the Park tourists, always drawn as caricatured "white" people, can take on a notably racial edge, as in the "Bear on a Picnic" episode noted earlier.

Even at this early stage in its development, it is possible to see how the *Yogi Bear* series would become one of the most seminal in television animation history, with many later series echoing, in both direct and indirect ways, its con artistry theme and its satire of exclusionary politics toward "outsiders." When Yogi got his own program in 1961, Hanna and Barbera would further develop this format beyond its obvious limitations in surprising and often unexpected ways.

◆ ◆ ◆

The success of the *Huckleberry Hound* program led to Hanna-Barbera and Kellogg tightening their alliance through the production of two similarly formatted programs: *Quick Draw McGraw*, which debuted in the fall of 1959, and *The Yogi Bear Show*, debuting in the fall of 1961. The segments featured on these programs, while derivative of the earlier series in some ways, were equally as entertaining and memorable. They showcased the Hanna-Barbera studio at the height of its powers, creating clever, facetious characters whose humorous antics satirized the culture and society of the America of their time in spite of their limitations.

Nowhere was this more evident than in the adventures of Quick Draw McGraw (Daws Butler), an equine Old West lawman with an inflated reputation as a sharp-shooter. As expected, these films satirized the Western, a staple element of Hollywood movies which had become the most dominant genre on television during this period.[27] Quick Draw was a typical Western hero, laconic in speech, but, mostly, quick to action. Unlike his live-action role models, however, he was completely and utterly incompetent, a trait reinforced by his ignorance toward the usually sensible advice provided by his sidekick, the Latino-accented burro Baba Looey (Butler). This was typified by one of Quick Draw's regular exclamations: "I'll do ... the thin'in around here ... [a]nd do-o-n't you forget it!," a statement whose validity was soon contradicted by his actions. An occasional ally was a dog named Snuffles (also voiced by Butler), who had a deep passion for dog biscuits, shown by an extended, almost orgasmic response to their consumption which the producers milked for all the comic value it was worth. The series gained much of its humor from the overt familiarity of the audience toward the Western scenarios being presented and the decidedly *un*familiar approaches the writers chose to resolve them. Similarly, the stupidity of Quick Draw was further reinforced by statements about him made by Baba Looey directly to the audience. A further level of satire was added by a subseries within the program, where Quick Draw masqueraded (incompetently, of course) as the Zorro-like, black-clad "masked avenger" El Kabong, so called because he preferred to use an acoustic guitar (or "Kabonger," as he called it) to the traditional sword as a weapon, both through his horrible singing while accompanying himself on it, and, more effectively, by hitting his opponents over the head with it while shouting "Kabong!" Absurdities like these inserted into traditional storylines added immeasurably to their comic impact, and pointed the way for others to satirize other television genres in a similarly absurd fashion in later years.

The two other segments of the program were equally effective satires of two other dominant TV genres: the detective drama and the family sitcom, respectively. "Super Snooper and Blabber Mouse" focused on a pair of trench-coat–clad detectives: the former a cat wearing a Sherlock Holmes–like deerstalker, the latter a fedora-wearing mouse who functioned as a hero-worshipping Dr. Watson (Daws Butler played both characters). Naturally, "Snoop" proved to be not nearly as competent in the job as he believed himself to be, while "Blab" provided little in the way of assistance. In a similar vein was the third feature, "Augie Doggie and Doggie Daddy," featuring a green-shirted puppy (Butler) and his dimwitted father (Doug Young, impersonating Jimmy Durante). This series focused on the troubles Augie got both of them in, though things were usually fixed by Augie showering his father with effusive, unnecessary praise. Both of these series added to the appeal of the lead feature and clearly indicated, as had earlier projects, that Hanna-Barbera was becoming a comic force to be reckoned with in terms of spoofing the culture of its times.

This approach was also typical of *The Yogi Bear Show*, whose lead feature continued the adventures of the title character.[28] These episodes concentrated particularly on the underlying tension that existed in the relationship between Yogi and Ranger Smith. In "Booby Trapped Bear," for example, Yogi disguises himself as the park's "health inspector" in order to more easily divest the unsuspecting tourists of their food. Smith promptly "busts" Yogi and initially imprisons him in a cave lined with metal bars (making it not unlike a prison cell), but he relents when Yogi loudly protests that his "rights" as an animal living under the protection of the American government are being compromised by this action. Nevertheless, unknown to Yogi, the release has a string attached. Smith has strategically placed booby-trapped picnic baskets throughout the park, which are designed to inflict physical punishment on Yogi if he attempts to take food from them. The scheme succeeds with the intended results, and Yogi is soon on the point of permanently swearing off picnic baskets. However, Smith's triumph is short-lived. Just as he reveals the insidious nature of his scheme to Yogi, his superior makes a surprise appearance—and is promptly injured by one of the booby-trapped baskets. In the final scene, we see Smith imprisoned in exactly the same cave he had earlier used to hold Yogi. When Smith accepts a stolen sandwich Yogi offers him, Yogi observes that being confined seems to have helped Smith to think more like the animals he watches over.

This episode is notable not only for the comments it makes about the relationships between the characters, but also because it closely reveals the connection between television animation and the thesis of sociologist Erving Goffman's book *The Presentation of Self in Everyday Life*, published only two years prior to the production of this episode.[29] Goffman's thesis was that human life roles, such as jobs, family relationships, and friendships, were essentially "roles," and that humans were the "actors" portraying them; they are "assumed" and executed in the same way actors "assume" their characters. Goffman's work thus provides an important insight into understanding television animation—that the characters are essentially "acting" on the stages of their creators the same way humans "act" in real life, and that they need to be looked at and examined as such to be fully understood.

As the *Yogi Bear* series evolved, it became clear that, while the series framework necessarily made Yogi and Smith antagonists, a systematic symbiotic relationship existed between them; it was as if each needed the other to truly survive and thrive.[30] Two episodes in particular highlight this often contradictory relationship. In "Iron Hand Jones," Smith temporarily leaves his position and is replaced by the title character, a stereotypical U.S. Army sergeant figure who behaves in the fashion of a martinet, frequently ordering those around him to march in military fashion to reinforce his need to command. Understandably, this clashes with Yogi's free-wheeling approach to life, and he pulls strings to get Smith back and restore the status quo. Similarly, in "Home, Sweet Jellystone," Smith leaves the park after inheriting the estate of a rich relative. However, the change does neither he nor Yogi any good. Yogi misses his "worthy opponent," while Smith finds his new life boring and returns to the park, saying to the audience that, while Yogi was much on his mind, he would have done the same thing "for any dumb animal." These episodes suggest that, in spite of their differences of opinion, these characters had developed a need for a close relationship with each other. Even this, however, could not prevent them from being on opposite sides of regular conflicts. This was particularly the case in "Bear Foot Soldiers," one of the last and most satirical episodes of the series, when Yogi and Boo Boo's unintentional meddling in U.S. Army training maneuvers leads to the army, with assistance from the Park Rangers, declaring full-out war on the bears of Jellystone!

The humor in the other two segments of the program was no less absurd or biting. "Snagglepuss" focused on a genial, pink-furred lion with overtly theatrical mannerisms who had earlier appeared as an antagonistic character in two episodes of "Quick Draw McGraw." His voice (delivered by Daws Butler) was clearly based on comedian/actor Bert Lahr's portrayal of the Cowardly Lion in the 1939 film version of *The Wizard of Oz* (enough for Lahr to consider legal action against Hanna-Barbera[31]), though Butler's biographers contend that the Lahr-derived elements had been reduced substantially by the time "Snag" became a star in his own right.[32] Regardless of the voice's origin, the character became popular, and his regular exclamations, such as "Heavens to Murgatroyd!" and "Exit, stage left!" soon became viewer favorites. The third feature was arguably the studio's most Disney-esque in terms of its tone. Yakky Doodle (voiced by Jimmy Weldon, after the fashion of Clarence Nash's portrayal of Donald Duck) was an innocent young duckling protected by the kind-hearted bulldog Chopper (Vance Colvig, à la Wallace Beery) from the advances of Fibber Fox (Daws Butler). Neither of these segments upstaged Yogi, but, as Hal Erickson has observed, that was probably the point.[33]

Clearly, by this time, Hanna-Barbera had become the dominant force in television animation through the success of these popular series, but their greatest gambles in the field—and perhaps their biggest payoffs as well—still lay ahead.

◆ ◆ ◆

Once again, it was John Mitchell who convinced Hanna and Barbera to take on a risky venture in terms of television animation production. He noted that, while children were the primary audience for the studio's product, given their scheduling in late afternoon timeslots in most areas, the programs were also attracting a number of adult viewers, who clearly appreciated the studio's wry approach to comedy in a way children did not or could not. Why, Mitchell asked, couldn't the studio produce a series aimed *directly* at an adult audience, to be aired in prime-time on a major TV network?

The producers were interested in the idea, particularly in the concept of attracting a more lucrative section of the TV audience and improving their bottom line. There was only one problem: it had never been done before, and, especially at that time, the three networks who controlled the majority of prime-time real estate tended to be risk-aversive when it came to new ideas. Looking at this issue from a time in which television animation—both old and new—is now broadcast every night on some cable TV providers with no objections or even notice, it seems absurd that Hanna and Barbera would have a problem selling a prime-time television animation program to a network or cable TV program provider. But, in the far more conservative world of television of the late 1950s and the early 1960s, they faced exactly this problem.

First, they needed an idea for a series—and not just any idea, if it was going to be successful.

Following a period of intense deliberation, Hanna, Barbera and their staff decided to use a familiar television format, the situation comedy, as the framework for their project. But they soon realized that they needed to inject an element of novelty into a format that, even then, was somewhat cliché ridden, if the program was to succeed. "Rather than dishing up roast beef," Hanna later observed, "we might barbecue the meat a little."[34] To this end, they decided to develop a sitcom whose uniqueness could be derived chiefly by placing a modern American family in a historical setting far removed from modern America. But what kind of family and, more importantly, what kind of historical setting could they use? That, as Barbera noted later, came to be something of an obstacle for the studio:

> We thought of an ordinary American family, like any other on television at the time. We thought about a family with kids, without kids, with a tall husband, a short wife, a nagging mother-in-law, a dog, a cat, no pets. Then we thought about a farmer and his family, which led to a hillbilly family. And, soon, we were slipping backward in history. We came up with a Pilgrim family, with wide collars and high hats, [and] then a Roman family, with togas and helmets.
>
> Nothing worked. Nothing clicked. And the weeks and months glided by. The project seemed pretty much [like] a lost cause.[35]

It was at this point that inspiration struck, and neither television nor television animation would ever be the same again. It is not known who first came up with the idea; in fact, who truly "created" the series remains heavily contested among animation historians. But the truth remains that the studio's exploration of the potential historical settings eventually led them as far back as they could go—to the Stone Age. The idea of the characters dressed like cavemen—in loincloths made of animal pelts—plus the humorous potential the writers and artists found in reconceptualizing the world around them in a fantastic Stone Age far removed from historical reality, soon got everyone's creative wheels rolling, and, before long, the series that would come to be known and loved as *The Flintstones* began to take shape.[36]

There remained, however, the task of earning the backing of a sponsor, and, in this case, the support of one of the three networks as well. Once again, Joseph Barbera was pressed into performing a role he disliked, but was quite effective at: the company's traveling salesman. He disliked it, as he recalled, because it required much time and effort on his part, doing literal performances of the pilot storyboards for interested clients at least once a day or more:

> It was a performance.... By the time you give a preamble about what it's all about, go through two storyboards, and then watch their eyes and their reactions, to see if they're smiling or they're falling asleep, you're worn out....
>
> We would meet in the Screen Gems office.... There would be anywhere from one to forty people waiting to see the presentation. The word had gotten out that this was *not* the usual presentation [emphasis in original]. I had to act out all the parts, jumping around and making all kinds of noises. That's what it took. Sometimes I had to do five presentations in one day.... The pitch went on for eight long weeks.[37]

While everyone who witnessed Barbera's performances was impressed with the project, considering it a boldly original idea, there was less interest in actively backing it precisely for that reason. That was the reasoning, at least, behind both CBS and NBC refusing to air it. ABC, the perennial "third network," however, was more accepting; they had less to lose and more to gain given their current status in the ratings. Thus, in March 1960, Hanna-Barbera began another relationship with a corporate supporter that, over the years, would work to both parties' advantage.

Next came the drive to acquire sponsorship. With this in mind, Barbera and company headed to Winston-Salem, North Carolina, where they made their pitch to a potential sponsor, the Reynolds Tobacco Company:

> We convened on their beautiful conference room, with walls paneled in a rich wood. We couldn't put tacks into these walls, so we taped every drawing to the walls. We came back after a coffee break to find that all the drawings were on the floor, and we had to do it all over again in only two hours. We managed to make the presentation ... but it seemed like a disaster. The chairman of the board wasn't smiling—he wasn't even chuckling. We learned later that he was [simply] in pain from ... gout.[38]

Reynolds was willing to commit to sponsorship of the show, on behalf of their chief cigarette brand, Winston. However, they were only willing to back half of the show, requiring another sponsor to be found for the remainder. To get this, Barbera, with John Mitchell and ABC executive Oliver Treyz in tow, converged on Chicago to approach Miles Laboratories, a medical supply company:

> We had all these boxes with the artwork. And we boarded an Electra—a two-propeller plane that flew to Chicago. These were the planes that turned out to have a fault—they began to disintegrate in the air. A few weeks later, there were two crashes [of similar planes]. We arrived at midnight, after the wildest, bumpiest ride I have ever had. We got to their offices and pinned up all the drawings until my thumbs were bleeding. We finished at three in the morning and then came back again at eight to make the presentation. And lo and behold, they bought the other half. Now we were fully sponsored.[39]

The relationship between Hanna-Barbera and Miles would ultimately result in an important economic side project: the creation of Flintstones-brand vitamins for children, which continue to be sold today.

With the economic issue of sponsorship now resolved, Hanna and Barbera were prepared to commence production of the series. They had to be, if they were to meet the deadline for the series' premiere in September of 1960.

◆ ◆ ◆

While it was generally perceived in the 1950s and 1960s that men had control in the public world, such was not the case in more domestic settings. Traditionally, home life in American entertainment narratives had been portrayed as a battlefield, where women either had the edge or were capable of manipulating men to see their point of view. The "tyrannical" wife had long been a stereotype used for comic effect in narratives, either to humble men or to excuse the abuse they doled out to keep women "in their place." The situation comedies, or "sitcoms," of radio and early television only served to confirm, internalize and institutionalize these viewpoints in their viewers, bringing these common conflicts into the slightly more enlightened sphere of the modern world. Until the early 1970s, as a result, these narratives were predicated upon seeing women as junior partners, while suggesting that women used more negative routes in order to "have their way." *The Flintstones*, which ultimately ran for six seasons on ABC, and other, later narratives with a similar format, were, at least in their original incarnations, demonstrations of these roles. The series satirized the real positions and concerns of men in the postwar era vis-a-vis the idealistic images of masculinity served up by the mass media at this time.

The sitcom format's adaptability to changes in American society was most evident in the 1960s, when a large number of such programs began using fantasy elements as a means of distancing audiences from contemporary concerns while, at the same time, using that distance to ridicule them.[40] In planning to expand their studio's reach into prime time, Hanna and Barbera were essentially riding the crest of a wave, even if they were unaware of it at the time.

The territorial template within which Hanna-Barbera set its Stone Age follies—American suburbia circa 1960—was still a contested ground both of obvious affluence and obvious exclusions. As historian Lynn Spigel has argued, the suburb emerged after World War II as a "promised land" that provided hope for a better life for those who participated in it. Yet this "promised land" was exclusively for the middle class; "undesirables," such as racial minorities, were kept out through such discriminatory measures as restrictive covenants and "redlining" zoning practices.[41] Consequently, the live-action sitcoms of the 1950s which depicted white suburbia were essentially depicting a world that was seen by outsiders as a lie even in their time. Later periods of nostalgia would remove the truth from the picture and distort this world view even more. It was this bias toward a normative "white middle class" standard of living in the suburbs, and its depiction within the environment of television, that would give *The Flintstones* much of its satiric thrust. In using *The Honeymooners* (CBS, 1955–56), a sitcom with an unvarnished "blue-collar" setting, as its template, Hanna-Barbera was reflecting on and spoofing the tension between an established middle class and "arrivistes" from the working class, such as Fred Flintstone, who attempted to negotiate and establish a harmonious environment in which to live together in spite of differences in class and politics in particular.

Debuting in the fall of 1960 on ABC, *The Flintstones* initially met with mixed and even hostile reviews. Typical of the reaction was *New York Times* television reviewer Jack Gould, who referred to the show as "an inked disaster" while despairing the fact that "the humor was of the boff-and-sock genre, nothing light or subtle."[42] Gould's harsh assessment is certainly applicable to the earliest episodes, when it was truly structured toward an "adult" mindset, but it does not account for the staying power of the series as a whole. The manner in which the producers manipulated the characters and the underlying socio-political attitudes of the time are a subject for further close historical analysis.

It should be noted at the outset that the setting itself is perhaps the most enjoyable aspect of the program. The town of Bedrock is devised as a modern American community in Stone Age disguise, with characters wearing modified animal skins, commuting by means of foot-powered transportation, and using dinosaurs in place of heavy equipment. In addition, sports and activities such as bowling are given a heavy and humorous Stone Age twist. Much of the show's humor, in fact, comes from the disjunction between modern life and the pseudo-prehistoric world presented by the series and the attempts made by the producers to reconcile these differences. These attributes provided some of the program's most memorable moments. It is in discussion of the issues and politics of the show's lead characters and their relationships with their wives that the show's true age is actually revealed. The two distinct eras of the program—the "adult" period (1960–63) and the "kid" period (1963–66)—mark the main changes to the program during its run. The show, initially defined as an adult-oriented situation comedy, was forced into a new existence as a kid-friendly family show by changes in the target audience.[43]

The tone of any fictional television program, animated or otherwise, is usually set by its lead characters, since the producers use them as a fulcrum to keep it going on a weekly basis. Therefore, it is essential that the characters be "likeable," at the very least, if the series is to thrive. Examining Fred Flintstone (voiced by Alan Reed[44]) in this light is significant, for his "likability," as well as his masculinity, is frequently limited. Fred is loudmouthed, overweight and domineering, embodying many of the stereotypical traits of the "blue-collar" working-class male, especially in the early episodes. He hopes to dominate others simply with his presence and voice, though this is not often the case. Like many real-life men who lived in the 1960s, he suffers from a psychological inability to live up to his own, inordinately high life expectations[45] and reacts by resorting to both real and threatened violence (verbal and physical) to get others to react to and support him in his aims. In contemporary language, he has an "anger management" problem, which is frequently aggravated when he does not get his way. Fred misguidedly (and mistakenly) believes that his status as a man allows him privileges, and that he, therefore, should have all the luck in the world. Thus, when his schemes for improving his lot in life backfire, he is reduced to throwing childish temper tantrums. He opposes the efforts of his wife, Wilma (Jean Vander Pyl), to earn money for herself because of his backward social views (which were, nevertheless, consistent with societal attitudes during the original broadcast period), ignoring how this possibly might benefit them as a family. Most significantly, and perhaps most regrettably, he is willing to risk his friendships and happiness over minor issues based on his stubborn refusal to admit that he is wrong about anything, a particularly stereotypical "male" trait that endures in many later male television animation characters. This attitude frequently tests his relationship with Wilma, although they display affection toward each other as well.

Providing a foil to Fred is his best friend and neighbor, Barney Rubble (Mel Blanc), who embodies a more even-tempered and good-natured form of masculinity than Fred, much as his wife, Betty (Bea Benaderet, 1960–64; Gerry Johnson, 1964–66), is generally kinder and gentler in nature than Wilma. Barney is able to engage the sympathy of the audience much more than Fred because of his constant humorous commentary on their joint predicaments, his happy-go-lucky personal nature, and the fact that he is occasionally victimized by Fred in the name of achieving a goal (e.g., his pretending to be Fred's infant son in "Baby Barney" (1962) so that Fred can lay claim to an inheritance[46]). Barney is, however, as much of a man as Fred is, since his ability to become petty and irritable can rival Fred's, especially when they are on opposite sides of a dispute. The ability of these two "friends" to fall out over relatively minor issues, especially in the first season's episodes, was remarkable, though Wilma and Betty, watching from the sidelines, knew implicitly that these childish displays of temper on both sides were simply the men working off inner frustrations in the only way they knew.

The first three seasons of *The Flintstones*, in this sense, are quite certainly an "adult"-oriented sitcom, since the disputes between Fred and Wilma and Fred and Barney over various trifles are what drive the plots. Children of the time might not have understood what was going on with this, but adults did. The series, like any other in its time period, was constrained by the normative expectations of its target audience—specifically, that it would portray life "as it was" humorously in spite of its fantastic setting. Certainly, while the series was capable of felicitously exploiting the Stone Age setting at times, the true comic potential of the series was often squandered by the producers' need to conform to the normative sitcom standards of the era—feuding husbands and wives, feuding friends, money, work issues, etc. Hanna and Barbera could have chosen a different approach and taken greater advantage of available technology, but they and the network and sponsors knew that they had to work within a set pattern of narratives in order to present what their audience wanted. For an adult audience of the period, what mattered most was seeing the concerns of their time presented.

Among the more gratuitous sins of the program in the eyes of contemporary viewers is the sexism displayed by the male characters. As literary and media critic M. Keith Booker has noted, while this may have been typical for the show's original broadcast period, it is rankling to viewers accustomed to more modern, "enlightened" attitudes toward gender relations.[47] Referring to women as "girls" and using condescending diminutives for their wives, as Fred and Barney do, is not exactly an enlightened viewpoint by feminist standards, but, given the time period of the original broadcasts and the majority attitude toward women within it, it is not surprising that this language was used, and that the wives simply accepted it. This does not mean that the women were defenseless; indeed, turnabout was often fair play. In many of the early episodes, for example, Wilma was capable of streaks of violence, resulting "in blows to the head for Fred or anyone else who got in her way!"[48] Other male characters were portrayed in a light that reflected their lack of ability in the home sphere, resulting in a shift in the balance of power toward women.[49] Fred's employer, Mr. Slate (John Stephenson), for example, was clearly in charge on the job, but viewers saw him as being dominated by a controlling and bossy wife at home.

The *ne plus ultra* of this particular divide between the sexes was Fred and Barney's fraternal lodge, the Loyal Order of Water Buffaloes, which figures prominently in a number of episodes in the series.[50] Clearly modeled on similar real-life men's groups (Elks, Masons, etc.), but shorn of those groups' desire to promote and conduct acts of charity for their communities, the Buffaloes exist primarily as a means of escape for harried members from the prototypical, tyrannical "little woman" at home. This allows the members to cavort in bacchanalian (albeit sanitized for TV) exploits that they would not care to let their wives know about, especially cavorting with attractive dancing girls. The point of this organization, both implicitly and explicitly, is to provide a place in the overly controlled and regulated society of Bedrock for men to free themselves from inhibitions and actually be *men* without being fearful of their wives' controlling concerns. Wilma and Betty can only enter this domain by disguising themselves as men, which they actually do in one episode. Yet, even within this sanctified area, the "real" world can enter and irrevocably shatter the façade of illusion. The Buffaloes' supreme leader, the exalted Grand Poobah,[51] projects a mystic and powerful image as someone in complete control of his surroundings, and the members honor and respect him for that reason. Yet he, too, is merely a man like them, with a wife who dominates him.

Midway through the series' run, in 1963, a sea change occurred in the issues and concerns addressed by the program. Specifically, Fred and Barney, like many members of their adult audience, became fathers for the first time,[52] and the show's format abruptly switched from an adult's view of the world to one much more suitable for children in consequence. The arrival of Pebbles Flintstone and Bamm Bamm Rubble, while part of a calculated ploy to improve series viewership,[53] also served to "domesticate" the rougher edges of the series. Gone were the conflicts about the men staying out late, the "extravagances" of the wives, and much of the more detailed social satire. In their place came a more fantastical element, seen particular in a changed emphasis toward such ideas in the plots, which was much more in tune with a series whose primary audience was now seen to be young people rather than adults. This philosophical regression was made complete by additions to the series of new elements that highlighted the program's fantastical setting. In particular, Fred became much more of "a rugged individualist with a feeble brainbone"[54] and, consequently, a slightly gentler figure than he had been in the past.

In relation to this change, there was a greater emphasis on Fred's efforts to transcend his "blue-collar" existence to provide a better environment for his new family. As historian Paul Wells has noted, while the series nominally remained in a "blue-collar" setting, the characters increasingly began aspiring to more refined, "middle class" norms. They thus aped the mannerisms and activities of the middle class, often failing in the process but creating escapist liberation for themselves and their audience.[55] In this context, the series was able to explore wider social and political terrain than would have been allowed in a more traditionally formatted live-action sitcom. Fred's various experiences—as a popular singer, a songwriter, a Hollywood (or, rather, Hollyrock) actor, a race-car driver, a college athlete, etc.—helped to develop and enrich the series beyond the limitations of its original format. It also pointed the way for future programs, most notably *The Simpsons*, to re-explore these contexts in a changed social atmosphere, where the gently mocking approach of *The Flintstones* gave way to a more barbed, pointed and critical form of humor.

The new status of the Flintstones and Rubbles as parents forced the producers to rethink their characterizations, specifically by adding Fred and Barney to an ever-growing list of well-meaning but inept father figures of the television era. In earlier episodes, children had been caricatured largely as intruding nuisances, and served to indicate the differences in the personalities of the two men. In "The Baby Sitters," a first-season episode, Fred's "expertise" at handling a crying child consists largely in yelling at it to be quiet.[56] Barney, in contrast, takes an active interest, playing with the child in a memorably constructed sequence. Judging by this, one would think that Fred lacked the skill and patience needed to deal with children and thus be a "good" father, so the fact that he eventually became one for his own daughter was an abrupt about-face, although not one without mishaps. In particular, Fred learns a hard lesson about parental responsibility in the 1964 episode "Daddies Anonymous" when he joins a group of henpecked husbands who play poker under the guise of "looking after" their children, and is given grief from Wilma when he accidentally returns home with the wrong child.[57] By the final episodes, the children began to play major roles in the episodes, and their fathers became considerably less aggressive than they had once been in their presence. The implied message of this phase of the show's evolution was that it was perfectly fine for a man to show a healthy interest in children—so long as they were his own.

A final major element of contentious masculinity is seen in the addition to the show's cast in the last season of The Great Gazoo (Harvey Korman). A supernaturally gifted alien being, Gazoo has been sent from his home planet to study the Earthlings. While he befriends Fred and Barney, and often uses his abilities to help them, he still assumes a condescending attitude toward them, frequently referring to them as "dum-dums." In contrasting Gazoo with Fred and Barney, the producers cast him as an arbiter of taste and sophistication, areas in which Fred in particular is seen to be lacking. This provides a heavier level of contrast in the streams of masculinity represented by the program. The fact that Gazoo causes much more trouble than he solves, however, negates any notions of superiority his presence might imply, which may have been the producers' intent.

As the first major prime-time television animation program, *The Flintstones'* legacy is significant on both aesthetic and political levels. As much as it broke ground as an animated television series, it was mostly unable to transcend the expectations of its viewers because it relied so heavily on the accepted notions of its time and place. By placing the series in prime-time television, Hanna-Barbera was forced to negotiate a difficult and choppy divide between the juvenile-oriented humor at the heart of the studio's work and the need to reflect, at the series' core, the bare realities of American life, circa 1960–66, in a prehistoric setting. The writers had to make the lead characters "mature" in a way few other animated characters had been before, but in ways that did not disrupt the essential fantasy at the heart of the program's setting. The enduring conflict between plots involving accepted notions in the outside world and the essentially fantastic nature of television animation as an art form would become a problematic issue for the genre in the future, not just for Hanna-Barbera, but for their contemporaries and successors in the field as well.

◆ ◆ ◆

The success of *The Flintstones* prompted ABC to ask Hanna-Barbera for more of the same, and they responded in kind. Their next project for the network was a colorful variation on the "Yogi Bear" format that Barbera reputedly sold on the basis of a single drawing of the title character.[58] The result was *Top Cat*, which aired on ABC during the 1961-62 television season.[59] *Top Cat* is interesting because it took an existing narrative structure and reshaped it to the new ideals and demands of television animation, as Hanna-Barbera had previously demonstrated with *The Flintstones*. Borrowing on the popularity of a previously existing network series, *The Phil Silvers Show* (CBS 1955–59),[60] the program's characters aped the adventures of Sergeant Bilko and his platoon in feline form. However, in contrast to criticism leveled against them, Hanna-Barbera was not simply copying an existing idea but rather adapting one to serve its own devices.

The imprint of the *Silvers* program was, nevertheless, still visible at times. Top Cat (voiced by Arnold Stang) was developed as the lead Bilko figure, with the supporting cast following the "Runyonesque"[61] character "types" set by the prior program. As with Bilko, the lead character was surrounded with a loyal group of followers who were memorable both individually and as a group. The group, always loyal and deferential toward "T.C.," consisted of Benny the Ball (Maurice Gosfield), Top Cat's general factotum and devil's advocate; Choo Choo (Marvin Kaplan), the New York–accented, over-eager leg man; Spook (Leo De Lyon), a genial hipster; the ironically named Brain (De Lyon); and Fancy Fancy (John Stephenson), a self-infatuated ladies' man whose voice actor cheekily referred to him, aptly, as "the Cary Grant of Brooklyn."[62]

Providing nominal opposition to the group's activities was the local cop on the beat, Officer Charlie Dibble (Allen Jenkins). Dibble, like Ranger Smith before him, is drawn as a flawed but respectable caricature of traditional white male authority, in his case the often deceptively bucolic, beat-walking neighborhood policeman so common in urban centers of the period. However, he lacks the Ranger's intelligence and guile, and is therefore much more easily swayed by friendly words or a perceived need for his involvement. Dibble appears, at first glance, to be simply a cipher of outside controlling forces but, in fact, he has an implicit sense that his feline antagonists need him around more than even they suspect at times.

As with other Hanna-Barbera series at this time, a between-the-lines reading deepens what would otherwise be interpreted as a simple situation. As M. Keith Booker has noted, there are undertones of both class division and racial antagonism in the relationship between Dibble and the cats, but the producers, bowing to the pressures of prime-time narrative expectations, frequently soft-pedaled the latter element.[63] However, traces of defiance remain within the structure. Booker discusses the character of Spook, for example, as being reminiscent of the so-called "White Negroes" that Norman Mailer had identified in a 1957 essay— white men who openly embraced African American culture, norms and mannerisms at a time when this was socially unacceptable.[64] The urban setting of the program also grounded it within one of the most potent battlefields in the civil rights movement, and significantly predates the concerns resulting in the urban race riots of the following decade.[65] As with Yogi Bear's earlier encounters with "white" humanity, it is possible to look at the relationship between the Top Cat gang and "white" human characters, including Dibble, in a racial light. The gang members are portrayed as outsiders, but, like other outsider figures, they have constructed a small, independent universe within the larger community through which they can exist with minimal persecution. It is only when they move out of this universe, and into the light of the larger community, that they truly become vulnerable to the threat of "racism" from the "white" human characters. However, thanks to Top Cat's manipulation of the system for his and their benefit, this rarely occurs. More controlled elements of rebellion also exist. The cats' independent and active operation and Dibble's inability to control them in particular mocks the conformist attitudes of the era, in particular their stress on group unity over individual effort and input.[66] These elements, however, were communicated strictly in a subtle fashion—the only way they could have been in network television during this time.

The majority of the series' installments tended to focus on Top Cat's elaborate plans to become wealthy overnight. As with Bilko, this involved considerable scam artistry, over-the-top impersonations, cunning ploys, and as little actual "work" as possible. Yet, as noted earlier, Hanna-Barbera was not in the business of overtly imitating other media forms; they gave as much as they took away in developing ideas. In this regard, *Top Cat* was no exception. For this reason, the program is indebted both in narrative and psychology as much to *Yogi Bear* as to Bilko. Like the earlier program, the disruption and restoration of the status quo forms the basis of several installments.[67] In "Naked Town," both Top Cat and company and Dibble are conned by a pair of robbers who stage a robbery with their unwitting aid. As in the "Iron Hand Jones" episode of *Yogi Bear*, Dibble is temporarily relieved from office and replaced with a less sympathetic figure, making Dibble's restoration a major priority for the gang. Similarly, in "Farewell, Mr. Dibble," a rival policeman named Prowler engages in Machiavellian manipulation to get Dibble discharged so he can take his place. Top Cat and his associates retaliate by fingering Prowler's citation book and littering the city with tickets. Dibble is reinstated when Prowler overzealously arrests both his superior officer and the mayor, and is sent home to rest.

Other episodes indicated that, while Dibble was the cats' "friend," he was also the key "mark" for their cons. In "The Long Hot Winter," the cats con Dibble into letting them spend the night in his apartment, but they place the policeman outside on the fire escape when his snoring bothers them. He responds by ejecting them when he wakes. As a counterattack, Top Cat calls "Strife" magazine and pitches a story to them about Dibble performing the Good Samaritan deed of rescuing "unfortunate" cats from the cold outside. To save face, Dibble is forced to readmit the cats to his domicile when a "Strife" reporter arrives to cover the story. An arrangement is made so that the cats can stay until spring.

Top Cat, unlike *The Flintstones*, was not a success in prime time for a number of reasons. As Hal Erickson has suggested, it was not simply because it garnered poor ratings, but that it was simply too much of an "adult" fantasy to be translated effectively into a "children's" format, which television animation was largely perceived to be at this time.[68] The series certainly had the potential for attracting an audience of children, which it later did in Saturday morning reruns. But children were considered a minority group among prime-time television viewers, and, if Hanna-Barbera were to continue to succeed in prime time, they would have to develop ideas that had more relevance to the adult viewers who comprised the majority of the audience.

◆ ◆ ◆

In some respects, this inability to connect with an adult audience was countered by the studio's next project, *The Jetsons* (ABC 1962–63; Syndicated, 1985–87),[69] which served to adapt the sitcom to the stereotypical worldview of the future the same way *The Flintstones* did to the stereotypical view of the past. Here again, however, the studio was forced to make compromises in order to achieve popular acceptability.

As with the earlier series, the setting of *The Jetsons* is its biggest asset. Set in the near future (or, more accurately, what the future was thought to be like in 1962), the community of Orbit City is, like Bedrock, a "modern" American community retrofitted to suit a new setting and standard of living. Cars float on the air via rocket power, and most of the citizenry is equipped with electronic communication or transportation devices that eerily anticipate many technological revolutions of the late–20th and early–21st centuries. Most ingeniously, a large percentage of functions once performed or produced through manual labor—eating, dressing, bathing, walking, etc.—are now done through automation or robots. Despite the apparent advantages of the setting, a considerable number of conflicts and concerns arise.

The Jetsons is particularly reminiscent of a sub-genre of literary science fiction which historian Lisa Yaszek has recently dubbed "Galactic Suburbia": that is, a series of stories "set in high-tech, far futures where gender relations [especially] still look suspiciously like those of 'present day, white middle-class suburbia.'"[70] This is not surprising, considering both the stories and *The Jetsons*, as commercial products, were geared toward exactly that white middle-class audience. Just as the female science fiction writers discussed by Yaszek had to tailor their work to accepted normative standards in order to be published, Hanna and Barbera had to make their series acceptable to a diverse prime-time television audience. Once again, the producers tailored their fantastic structure to accepted social and sitcom stereotypes, although they also attempted to deepen them, with mixed success.

The focus of the series was the titular family, in particular family patriarch George Jetson (voiced by George O'Hanlon), who frequently conveyed a world-weary cynicism that clashed felicitously with the program's futuristic setting. A digital index operator (i.e., button pusher) at Spacely Space Sprockets, George is the futuristic equivalent of the 1960s "wage slave" in the same way that Fred Flintstone was its Stone Age prototype. Yet George is a different kind of man from Fred, both physically (he is taller and less muscular) and emotionally (his displays of violence are only the verbal kind). Though he complains regularly about his supposedly taxing job (three hours a week and an annual income of $100,000) and the fact that he is often taken for granted by his family, these seem empty complaints simply because he is modestly well off for his time, unlike Fred.

This is a significant difference, and points specifically to the fact that *The Jetsons* is concerned with social status in a different way than *The Flintstones*. George Jetson is seen and portrayed as a solid member of a respected middle class, the kind of status to which Fred Flintstone could only aspire. Unlike Fred, George does not have to be concerned about "making it" in society because, at least in his own mind, he already *has* made it. What George secretly fears, however, is that, somehow, he or his family will do or say something that will unravel this secure situation. For this reason, he polices himself and his family, through various patriarchal pronouncements and pontifications, to try to ensure that such a situation never occurs.

George keeps his home life more ordered than Fred's, though it also escapes his control to become chaotic at times. His wife, Jane (Penny Singleton), is a stay-at-home wife and mother who has no intention, nor desire, to compete with him economically. In addition, George is a father to two growing children, pre-teen Elroy (Daws Butler) and teenaged Judy (Janet Waldo), who, though providing him with problems on a regular basis, still respect him in the normative patriarchal fashion of the 1960s. The family setting is completed by Rosie, the robot maid (Jean Vander Pyl), and Astro, the overly emotional family dog (Don Messick), who provide their own complications at times. Still, the majority of episodes focus on George and his ability (or inability) to adjust to a changing social order.

Because there is less conflict in George's home than in Fred Flintstone's, a different arena is used to show the audience why George feels discontented with his life. Much more than in *The Flintstones*, George's job and the various "roles" he must play within the context of it form a major component of the series. This is also the source of his most complex and contentious personal relationship: that with his employer, Cosmo Spacely (Mel Blanc).[71]

The "boss-as-tyrant" was a familiar figure to listeners and viewers of radio and television sitcoms of the 1940s and 1950s. Considerable humorous mileage was gained out of this figure and his (never her) use of economic leverage over his employees. Cosmo Spacely is perhaps representative of this character type at its most rapacious. A Napoleonic tyrant figure at worst, and only mildly likeable at best, the diminutive, balding Spacely is the show's most formidable character, and one of the most formidable characters in the entire Hanna-Barbera arsenal. He represents a negative version of masculinity that mirrors the more positive one represented by George. Power has gone to this man's head, and, other than the expected mollifying attitude toward his wife, he answers to nobody, and will do anything and everything to stay in business. George, as would be expected, is the primary target of Spacely's aggressive bullying tactics, which seem humorous, if only briefly, due to the extreme size difference between the two men. At times, Spacely takes almost sadistic glee in tormenting George, assigning him large amounts of work that will guarantee that he will be working overtime instead of being at home with his family. George's occasional, accidental bursts of incompetence, as well, occasionally motivate Spacely to threaten to fire him or to actually do this ("You're fired!" was practically his catchphrase). At other times, however, when he sees something of value he can get out of George, he treats him with over-the-top, obsequious kindness, making both George and the audience suspicious of his true motivation until the plot collapses like weak floorboards beneath them both.

Some of the program's most incisive episodes concern the relationship between George and Spacely as it plays out against the complex economic and technological conditions shown to exist in this period, particularly as they relate to Spacely's Machiavellian power struggles with his chief business rival, Cogswell of Cogswell Cogs (Daws Butler). Two episodes in particular stand out here. In "Test Pilot"[72] George is drafted to be the subject for a series of tests of an "indestructible" jacket developed by Spacely's lab, a role he accepts only because he mistakenly believes that he is terminally ill. A number of successful tests of the jacket are completed, during which George displays a swaggering macho bravado that is firmly punctured with the news that the diagnosis was false. George is offered an executive position with the company as a reward; however, Jane ends up destroying the supposedly "indestructible" jacket in the wash! Even more trenchant and satiric is "Private Property,"[73] with the focus of the episode clearly on the Spacely/Cogswell conflict. When Cogswell erects a new headquarters near Spacely's building, George is assigned the task of devising a ten-foot wall between the properties. However, through George's blundering and the respective greed and opportunism of Spacely and Cogswell, Spacely not only ends up with Cogswell's building (and vice versa), but discovers that his new building has to be demolished for violating building code standards. This episode and similar ones in the series expose big business as a petty, childish game. Like Fred and Barney in the early *Flintstones* episodes, Spacely and Cogswell are unwilling to use diplomacy, negotiations and other more mature tactics to coexist peacefully, instead constantly scheming to drive each other out of business. George, the Everyman, simply becomes a pawn in the ongoing financial tug-of-war between them. These installments were often the closest thing to subversive liberal social satire à la Jay Ward that the markedly conservative Hanna-Barbera studio ever produced.

George is not always this easily manipulated, however. In his own home, he is (or, at least, would like to be) the manipulator. This side of him comes out most prominently in "A Date with Jet Screamer."[74] Judy Jetson, portrayed as a stereotyped teenager whose thoughts seemed to rarely go beyond boys and rock music,[75] always seemed to bring out the protective, conservatively valued side of her father with her antics. This episode was a definitive portrayal of George in this sense. In the episode, Judy becomes entranced by the Elvis Presley–like singer Jet Screamer, and enters a song-writing contest to win a date with him. George, harboring many of the concerns of the white American middle-class "establishment" toward rock and roll (i.e., that it was too "loud," the performers were loutish and uncouth, the music was too suggestive, etc.),[76] is not impressed with Mr. Screamer, and sabotages Judy's efforts by substituting a secret code of Elroy's for her entry. Ironically, the "song," "Eep Opp Ork Aah Aah," ends up winning the contest. George's paternal protective attitude gets the better of him, and he secretly tails the pair on their date to a concert where Screamer is performing. In the process, George's attitude toward Screamer shifts rapidly from fear and jealousy toward admiration. A moral lesson exists here: that supposedly "threatening" musicians such as Jet Screamer are simply normal people, and that, if rock music's critics were able to forgo their initial negative impressions of the music, they might actually enjoy it. However, this attitude was very much a minority viewpoint in the time that this episode was actually produced.

With *The Jetsons*, just as with *The Flintstones*, Hanna-Barbera demonstrated that it was possible for television animation to achieve a prime-time audience—albeit at a cost. The characters and situations had to be structured in a way that made them acceptable, and this often involved the use of social and artistic stereotyping rather than genuine creativity. Nevertheless, with both programs the studio succeeded in putting some puncture wounds in the situation comedy format with broad animated humor, particularly where the inflated expectations of masculinity in the postwar era were concerned. They were less successful, however, when they tried to do the same thing by playing it straight.

◆ ◆ ◆

The final Hanna-Barbera series to air in prime time on ABC in the 1960s was, suffice it to say, a departure from their previous work in a number of ways. Airing on the network during the 1964-65 season, *Jonny Quest*[77] represented a throwback to an old-fashioned, thrill-packed style of adventure storytelling that had flourished prior to World War II in comic strips, pulp fiction, radio and the movies, where escapism and fun were considered the norm. It was a series drawn with realistic characters and backgrounds, ambitious special-effects animation, and straight-faced performances from the characters. Yet, while it managed to re-create some of the thrills of the prewar era, this was compromised by a racist, Orientalist worldview and an idealized take on masculinity that could not as easily be explained away as it could have in an earlier time.

As historian Christopher Lehman has argued recently, it is impossible not to view *Jonny Quest* as an attempt to recreate an older and, arguably more racist world view as envisioned by past media in a time when, in the "real" world, America was preparing to go to war in a particular "backward" country, namely Vietnam. Specifically, by depicting "the travels of white figures across the globe and the dangers they face[d]," as well as "countries inhabited by people of color as simultaneously exotic and threatening," the series served to reinforce, if unintentionally, traditional notions of white male superiority.[78] This idea cannot be ignored on a historical level of study, even if the producers did not intend to make the series political in this or any other way.

External politics aside, the actual narratives of the series were less complicated, even though they certainly voiced this worldview. The blond-haired title character (Tim Matheson) was an idealistic young boy who was the son of Dr. Benton Quest (played first by John Stephenson, and later by Don Messick), a globetrotting scientist doing vaguely defined secret scientific work for the U.S. government. They were accompanied by Jonny's mentor and guardian secret agent Race Bannon (Mike Road), his heavily stereotyped East Indian friend Hadji (Danny Bravo); and his dog Bandit (Don Messick). Though technically sound, the series has aged poorly in terms of its plot and character development. Key to this problem were issues common to many of the programs aired during this time period, especially the animated ones. Although the program was designed to be set in a "near future" time period while reflecting contemporary concerns,[79] it tended to reinforce social and political viewpoints of a time long since past. Race Bannon and Dr. Quest, in particular, were constructed as knights in shining armor, using their physical and mental abilities, respectively, to provide solutions to problems. The idealized and deified status of these characters reinforced their privileged white masculine status as the dominant one of their society, and significantly undermined the position of the racial minority characters, who were portrayed either as outright villains or threats in other ways. The group's major enemy, for example, was a Fu Manchu–styled Chinese scientific genius named Dr. Zin, whose megalomaniacal desire for world domination made it hard to see him as anything other than a racialized threat to the

United States whom the heroes were almost duty-bound to stop. This attitude persisted toward various other minority groups, whose members were uniformly seen as ethnically inferior "savages" and "devils."[80] Our heroes, who represented a highly "white" view of America, were shown to be morally and ethnically "superior" to these "backward" folks. Perhaps this view was acceptable in the early, immediate post–World War II period, in keeping with the demonization of "enemy" ethnicities in the war period and before, but it is insulting from a modern, multicultural viewpoint, which is perhaps one reason this series has been in limited circulation in broadcast television for so many years. Hanna-Barbera was guilty here of kowtowing to the expectations of the "average" viewers of the time period, in this case by using an adventure format to reinforce a centralized and biased "American" viewpoint. What was worse was the fact that, because this program had such a deadly serious tone, the producers could not use the defense, as they could for other aspects of their work, that they were simply creating a "comic" world view. Despite this, *Jonny Quest* established a formula that would be repeatedly employed by the studio for the remainder of the decade and beyond, particularly as they began restructuring their products to new areas of television programming whose audience demanded less artistically and ideologically from them.

◆ ◆ ◆

The end of *The Flintstones* in 1966, caused chiefly by a loss of sponsorship, also marked the end of Hanna-Barbera's adventures in prime time, and, concurrently, led to television animation becoming mostly absent from that venue for over two decades. Yet the studio itself remained productive as ever, continuing to syndicate their programming on daytime schedules as well as being regular contributors to the newest forum for television animation, which eventually would become one of its more restrictive.

Although the studio's work was becoming more repetitive and derivative than it was in the past, it was no less entertaining than before. In 1963, the studio produced what was loosely referred to as *The Hanna-Barbera New Cartoon Series*, a package of three short animation series that could be run together or separately as the individual stations wished.[81] The first project featured yet another animal con artist, Wally Gator (Daws Butler, impersonating Ed Wynn). Described in the theme song as the "swinging alligator from the swamp," Wally was a zoo resident forever trying—and often succeeding—to escape to the outside world, in spite of the efforts of the zookeeper, Mr. Twiddles (Don Messick), to stop him. The two other segments of this program operated in a similar vein. "Lippy The Lion" was another animal con man (Butler, impersonating Joe E. Brown) whose high-energy level was complemented by the lugubrious nature of his sidekick, a hyena ironically named Hardy Har Har (Mel Blanc). "Touche Turtle," in contrast, was somewhat reminiscent of *Crusader Rabbit*, featuring a "heroic," sword-wielding turtle (Bill Thompson), who advertised himself and his services through the motto: "Hero work done cheap, all credit cards accepted." Touche was assisted, or, rather, hindered, by a slow-moving sheepdog aptly named Dum Dum (Alan Reed).

Much more successful and memorable was the lead segment of the studio's next syndicated project, *The Magilla Gorilla Show*, which debuted in syndication in January of 1964. The series had a straightforward yet surprisingly adaptable premise: Magilla (Allan Melvin), a jovial but dimwitted primate, was the major attraction at the pet shop operated by Mr. Peebles (Howard Morris); his only real friend was a girl named Ogee (Jean Vander Pyl), who often tried to purchase him and came up short. Magilla was, however, often purchased or otherwise liberated from the pet shop for various adventures. He often returned to the shop by episode's end, much to the dismay of Peebles, although the latter was secretly fond of him. His adventures took him into the French Foreign Legion, into basic training in the U.S. Army (which leads him to become an unlikely astronaut), attempting to control an out-of-control automobile, and into an airplane which wrecks a movie shoot and a toy shop. "Modest ... affectionate, and forever hopeful,"[82] Magilla remains one of Hanna-Barbera's most endearing creations.

Adding to the fun were the additional segments of the program. "Ricochet Rabbit," much like "Quick Draw McGraw" before it, was a parody of the TV Western, although done in a slightly different style given the characteristics of the leads. Ricochet (Don Messick) was an old–West lawman who was always on the move. Naturally, his associate, Droop-A-Long Coyote (Mel Blanc), was his complete opposite, moving at an incredibly slow pace that hindered their efforts as much as Ricochet's speed aided them.[83] The third segment was initially "Breezly and Sneezly," set at the fictional U.S. Army base Camp Frostbite, appropriately based in Alaska. Yet another animal con-artist scenario, the title characters were, respectively, a foolish polar bear (Howard Morris) and a more intelligent seal (Mel Blanc) attempting to either cadge food or become soldiers, much to the chagrin and fervent opposition of Camp Frostbite's commanding officer, Colonel Fusby (John Stephenson, impersonating character actor Paul Ford, of *Phil Silvers Show* fame). The derivative nature of this segment was apparent even to the studio, which removed it from the series at the commencement of the next round of production. It was replaced by a bizarre variation of "Tom And Jerry" called "Punkin Puss," which featured the title character, a cat (Allan Melvin), and his enemy, Mush Mouse (Howard Morris), as feuding hillbillies in the vein of the legendary Hatfields and McCoys. The studio had employed parodies of these kinds of figures earlier in their work, and handled those one-shot portrayals better than they did the characters in this series.

Airing concurrently with *Magilla Gorilla*, under a similar structure and sponsorship, was *The Peter Potamus Show*. Devised by animator Jerry Eisenberg, the title character was a humanized hippopotamus (Daws Butler, again impersonating Joe E. Brown) who, outfitted in safari gear and pith helmet, went exploring through time and space in a "magic flying balloon" with his sidekick, a monkey named So So (Don Messick). When they were in trouble, Peter would respond with an ear-piercing "Hippo Hurricane Holler" that often got them out of it. The featured segments were "Breezly and Sneezly" (see above) and "The Three Goofy Guards," featuring three zany musketeer-type humanized dogs—Yippee (Doug Young), Yappee (Hal Smith) and Yahooey (Daws Butler, impersonating Jerry Lewis) working in the service of a diminutive king (Smith). "Ricochet Rabbit" (see above) replaced "Breezly and Sneezly" when the latter became a *Magilla Gorilla* component in 1965. While the series was serviceable and entertaining, it also suggested that perhaps Hanna-Barbera's creative well was beginning to run slightly dry. Yet the studio still had some interesting tricks up its sleeve, which a change of broadcast venue served to emphasize.

The next item on the studio's agenda was an important transitional program, both in terms of shifting the studio's output toward the newly emerging field of Saturday morning programming and, gradually, shifting the content of the programs away, albeit temporarily, from broad comedy toward straightforward action-adventure à la *Jonny Quest*. A one-hour series debuting on ABC in the fall of 1965, *The Atom Ant/Secret Squirrel Show* was a clear attempt by the studio to embrace some new popular culture staples while at the same time parodying them, at least in the title sequences. The remainder was mostly business as usual.

"Atom Ant," a humorous superhero saga, was based on a traditional cartoon stereotype which was, in turn, based on biological reality—that the small, helpless-looking ant is capable of carrying large amounts in excess of its own weight. The title character (initially voiced by Howard Morris, and later by Don Messick), outfitted in orange shirt and white helmet was "the tiniest but most relentless defender of law and order on television."[84] Having gained superpowers through a pair of atomized eyeglasses, he frequently left his underground laboratory to battle with villainy, crying out, "Up and at 'em, Atom Ant!" His enemies included a bank robbing monster, the Glob; Mr. Mooto, a karate expert ant; Ferocious Flea, an evil doppelgänger of our hero; and Anastasia Antnik, a seductive pseudo–Russian spy.

"Secret Squirrel," in contrast, took its cue from the popularity of fictional spies, ignited by the James Bond movie franchise and fanned on television by such series as *The Man from U.N.C.L.E.* and *Get Smart*, among other examples. The title character (Mel Blanc) was outfitted in traditional spy gear, a trench coat and a fedora covering his entire face, with holes for his eyes. Working for the International Sneaky Service, he was partnered with the fez-wearing Morocco Mole (Paul Frees, impersonating Peter Lorre). Secret's adventures were highlighted by his employment of a number of Bondian devices whose usefulness was equaled only by their comical attributes. These included the Anti-Blowout Button, the Skeeter-Beater, the Super-Atomic Neutralizer Bazooka, and the Instant Grandma Cottage, whose names alone were clearly designed to create laughs, especially for those familiar with their live-action prototypes.

While these two features were funny and innovative, such could not necessarily be said for the other features of the program. Supporting "Atom Ant" were "Precious Pupp," focusing on a mischievous dog (Don Messick) who engaged in adventures with and away from his mistress, the elderly but feisty Granny Sweet (Janet Waldo); and "The Hillbilly Bears," concerning a stereotyped family of ursine hillbillies: patriarch Paw (Henry Corden), matriarch Maw (Jean Vander Pyl); daughter Floral (Vander Pyl); and son Shag (Don Messick). Airing in support of "Secret Squirrel" were "Squiddly Diddly," whose title character (Paul Frees) was a cephalopodic continuation of the animal con-artist formula, often in conflict with Chief Winchley (John Stephenson); and "Winsome Witch," featuring a good-natured magic practitioner (Jean Vander Pyl) who aided those in distress while defying the stereotypes common to her kind. These projects were entertaining, it was true, but they were not without precedent, and, in that light, they seemed to indicate how Hanna-Barbera was moving on a limited creative treadmill.

It was at this point, however, that the studio gained fresh opportunities to take television animation in new directions, which allowed it to take the form beyond the built-in limitations they had created through formulaic repetition and expand the genre's artistic and commercial growth potential in innovative and surprising ways.

◆ ◆ ◆

The remainder of the 1960s saw Hanna-Barbera become a major player in Saturday morning television, the newest and most visible forum for television animation, and one which would virtually imprison it artistically until the 1990s. The originator of this new format was Fred Silverman, recently installed as the head of daytime programming at CBS; he would later become a more visible and controversial figure as president of ABC in the late 1970s and NBC in the early 1980s.[85] Silverman, the son of a television-set repair man, had been involved with television for much of his life; his master's thesis at Ohio State had discussed ABC's programming strategies of the late 1950s and 1960s, and he had used this as a springboard to executive positions at several independent television stations before arriving at CBS. Here, Silverman became a force to be reckoned with, involving himself in the minutiae of the production and development of series far more than any other executive in the field, before or since. As an animation fan, he was particularly interested in developing television animation and other children's programming as a competitive arena comparable to prime time. Silverman's interest and developmental role in television animation programming at this time was unique. Few other television executives assigned to television animation in the future would display the caring attention that he gave to it during this period.

Silverman was particularly interested in developing superheroes as a more prominent sub-genre than it had been in the past. As he later explained to historian Ted Sennett:

> Everything up to that point [in Saturday morning] was kind of soft. It was either live-action or it was a lot of little animals running around. This was a departure. I guess I projected what I liked into a brand-new schedule, what you might call a "superhero morning."[86]

Fred Silverman, circa mid–1970s (Photofest).

This "superhero morning" format debuted on CBS in the fall of 1966, and it and similar formats would become the dominant ones for the remainder of the 20th century. Hanna-Barbera, as the most dominant name in television animation, in turn dominated this new format, with its fortunes constantly rising and falling with the new format's own peaks and valleys over the years.

This shift in the artistic and production approach of the studio necessarily required the introduction of new figures who understood the need for a more state-of-the-art approach to programming. The writing team of Joe Ruby and Ken Spears, for example, became more prominent since, as Spears later recalled, they understood how to write action-adventure programming in a way the studio's more comedy-oriented writers did not:

> Hanna and Barbera called us in and showed us a few of the series they were working on. They were having problems because until then they had worked on funny cartoons, and the staff writers didn't grasp the action adventure [or] science fiction type of show. So Joe and Bill explained the series [ideas] to us and we went out of there with two or three approved ideas. We wrote the first two scripts on spec and we delivered them under a mat at Joe's house. They were shipped to CBS, who thought they were terrific. From then on we wrote many of the scripts for the superhero series.[87]

Comic book artist Alex Toth was recruited to help develop series and characters in collaboration with Hanna, Barbera and Silverman. In this line, he was following his contemporary Doug Wildey, who had done similar work on *Jonny Quest*. As Toth later explained, these were intense but productive sessions that got fast results:

> We would have long brainstorming sessions. With someone like Fred Silverman, who knew exactly what he wanted, there would be lively, round-the-table discussions, with everyone taking part. Joe Barbera and I would be doodling while Bill Hanna and Silverman were talking, thrashing out what a new character ought to look like. Very often it was that kind of mutual input. After my rough drawings were approved, I would give them a final trimming, running back and forth until they were right. It was hectic, but it was fun.

> Once we locked in the characters, we made as many designs as possible, to move the characters around and show how they would look, how they would interact with other characters, and what devices they would use, whether they required a special plane, a rocket ship, or a clever gadget. The approved model sheets would be distributed to the studio.[88]

The animators, in turn, had to develop a more realistic approach to developing human figures, making them act and move realistically within the confines of animation. But, as Barbera pointed out, there was less need to move the realistic human figures as constantly as the distorted animal figures, and the process became simplified:

> You didn't have to move the human figures as much.... One of the reasons you achieved a feeling of fluidity was that they were zooming through space a lot. If a character puts his arms out and he sails through the air at terrific speed, you get the feeling of smoothness, but you have to realize that there's really no animation there. The character is not sitting or standing or scratching his nose—he's sailing through the air at great speed.[89]

Once again, Hanna-Barbera was developing new and innovative ways of producing television animation to suit its production and economic needs, or, in the eyes of its critics, taking the actual "art" out of the process of animation. But the results spoke for themselves.

The fruits of the alliance between Hanna-Barbera, Silverman and Toth first manifested themselves with *Space Ghost and Dino Boy*, debuting on CBS in 1966.[90] The opening feature was an interplanetary superhero (voiced by Gary Owens) who traveled through space in his "Phantom Cruiser" and battled inter-planetary villains such as Zorak, Brak, Metallis, Iceman, Sorcerer and The Black Widow. He was assisted in his efforts by his masked and caped sidekicks, Jan (Ginny Tyler) and Jayce (Tim Matheson) and their pet monkey, Blip (Don Messick). Supporting this feature was "Dino Boy," featuring a young man (John Carson) who parachuted back in time, to the Stone Age. Working with a caveman named Ugh (Mike Road), he fought a variety of often vaguely defined foes, such as the Worm People, the Ant Warriors, the Rock Pygmies, and the Mighty Snow Creature.

A similar, if more comically oriented series, debuted on the same network during the same broadcast year: *Frankenstein Jr. and The Impossibles*. Despite the name of the former, historian Ted Sennett assures us that "Frankenstein Jr. bore no resemblance to the obsessed scientist of Mary Shelley's novel or to the monster he created in his laboratory."[91] He was, instead, a 50-foot-tall robot superhero wearing a mask and cape (Ted Cassidy). Rather than Dr. Frankenstein, he was the creation of the Tom Swift–like "boy scientist" Buzz Conroy (Dick Beals), son of the eminent Professor Conroy (John Stephenson). The robot was activated by Buzz's "radar ring" and a ringing cry of "Alakazoom!," which sent them into battle with the likes of one-dimensional villains, such as Dr. Spectro and Mr. Menace. Supporting them were The Impossibles, a rock-and-roll band who led a double life as superheroes. They consisted of Coil Man (Hal Smith), able to extend his legs like a spring; Multi Man (Don Messick), able to duplicate himself indefinitely; and Fluid Man (Paul Frees), able to take the form of any type of liquid. As expected, they triumphed easily over the likes of the Fiendish Fiddler and the Terrible Twister.

Jealous of CBS's success, the other two networks began programming animation on Saturday morning in 1966, and Hanna-Barbera soon began producing material for them as well. For NBC in 1966, and particularly aimed at a younger audience than the CBS shows, they produced *Space Kidettes*. Based on the premise of a group of children involved in science fiction adventures, the group consisted of Scooter (Chris Allen), Snoopy (Lucille Bliss), Jenny (Janet Waldo) and Countdown (Don Messick), accompanied by their dog Pupstar

(Messick). Their chief enemy was the Cockney-accented braggart Captain Skyhook (Daws Butler), who frequently complained about his inability to beat his "itty bitty" nemeses.

Back at CBS, the studio debuted three new action-oriented series in the fall of 1967, each continuing the early programs' pattern of emphasizing action-based plots over characterization and in-depth storytelling. *The Herculoids* was by far the most ambitious of these. Set on the distant planet of Quasar, it involved a super-powered trio of animals who effectively acted as the bodyguards for the planet's ruler, King Zandor (Mike Road), his wife, Queen Tara (Virginia Gregg), and their son Prince Dorno (Teddy Eccles). The title trio consisted of Zok (Road), a flying dragon capable of firing laser rays from his eyes and tail; Tundro the Tremendous (Road), a rhinoceros with ten legs and a horn that doubled as a cannon; and Igoo (Road again), an immensely powerful gorilla. Their weekly enemies included the likes of the Purple Menace, the Firebird, the Electrode Men and the Faceless People. The Firebird episode,[92] however, was a departure from the Manichean norm of the series of the time, in that the Firebird was a female protecting her egg inside a volcano; the heroes helped her to retrieve the egg before completing their mission of sealing up the volcano to prevent its eruptions from causing harm. The end moral—"No animal on Earth is completely evil"—was something of a surprise to viewers of the time, though it and others like it, both literally and metaphorically, would become far more commonplace in the series of the years ahead.

More troublesome was the second series debuting that year, *Shazzan*. Here the focus was on the teenage twins Chuck (Jerry Dexter) and Nancy (Janet Waldo), who discover a mysterious chest in a cave off the coast of Maine; the centerpiece of this was a magic ring in two halves, which form the word "Shazzan." When this word was uttered, the twins were transported back to the realm of the Arabian Nights, where they encountered the title character (Barney Phillips), a 60-foot-tall genie who became their protector—on the condition that they return the magic ring to its rightful owner. Assisted by the flying camel Kaboobie (Don Messick), Chuck and Nancy confronted a variety of exotic enemies, from whom Shazzan inevitably rescued them. Although it was far better animated than some of its contemporaries, *Shazzan* suffered from the common problem of the series of this era: a lack of characterization and plot development. As Fred Silverman later noted, the issue was simple: "We had a concept problem. The genie had no weaknesses. Once you summoned him, the story was over."[93]

The third and final CBS series of that year also came via the pen of Alex Toth: *Moby Dick and the Mighty Mightor*. The lead character was a powerful whale who resembled Herman Melville's vicious leviathan in name only. This whale was the protector of two teenage boys named Tom (Bobby Resnick) and Tub (Barry Balkin), who frequently found themselves in a variety of underwater perils. This forced Moby to come to their aid, often with the aid of a seal named Scooby (Don Messick). The secondary feature was much more imaginative in nature. Set in the Stone Age (done in a far more realistic fashion than *The Flintstones*), it focused on the teenage cave-dweller Tor (Bobby Diamond), who lived with his father, Pondo (John Stephenson), his sister Sheera (Patsy Garrett), and his younger brother Lil' Rok (Norma McMillan), along with a winged dinosaur named Tog (Stephenson) and a bird named Ork (Stephenson). After Tor rescued an old hermit from death, the hermit gave him a magical club in gratitude. When Tor raised this club to the heavens, he was instantly transformed into the superhero Mightor, and Tog into a fire-breathing dragon, and they went into battle against the likes of Numo and his Sea Slavers and the Plant People. The theme of the young protagonist with secret superpowers would become more commonplace in later years; other, later producers would treat the theme with more complexity than the producers did here.

The ever-productive studio did not restrict itself to CBS during this season. As Ted Sennett aptly notes, "In the enthusiasm for intrepid comic-book crusaders against crime and evil, other networks decided to offer their own contributions."[94] For NBC, Hanna-Barbera offered another variation on the transformative theme, *Samson and Goliath*. Samson (Tim Matthieson) was a seemingly average teenager; Goliath, his pet dog. However, when trouble loomed, Samson rubbed two gold bracelets together while shouting, "I need Samson power!" Instantly, Samson was transformed into a strongman reminiscent of his Biblical namesake, while Goliath became a powerful lion. Their opponents included the likes of The Colossal Coral Creature, The Thing from the Black Mountains, and The Terrible Dr. Desto.

For the same network, the studio produced a slightly more imaginative series, *Birdman and the Galaxy Trio*. Birdman was the secret identity of Ray Randall (Keith Andes), saved from death by the Egyptian sun god Ra and given the power of flight in return. Reporting to the eye-patched Falcon 7 (Don Messick), he possessed formidable weaponry as well: Solar Ray Beams emerging from his knuckles that could melt everything in their path, and a Solar Shield which served as protection against his enemies' weapons. These included the "evil genius" Morto and the various agents of the criminal agency F.E.A.R. (what the acronym stood for was never explained, and it was spelled out rather than said as a single "word"). The Galaxy Trio was a similarly straightforward series focusing on a trio of space adventurers who traveled across the galaxy to right wrongs. The trio consisted of Vapor Man (Don Messick), capable of assuming the form of gas or mist; Gravity Girl (Virginia Eiler), able to defy gravity by flying through space at will, and Meteor Man (Ted Cassidy), possessing superhuman strength and pointed ears reminiscent of those of *Star Trek*'s Mr. Spock. The trio traveled in their spaceship, the *Condor 1*, to a large number of interplanetary destinations.

A far more groundbreaking group of comic-book characters was adapted for animation by Hanna-Barbera the same year for ABC. *The Fantastic Four*, created by writer/editor Stan Lee and artist Jack Kirby for Marvel Comics in 1961, were among the first superhero characters to display more realistically human behavior, allowing them and the characters that followed to make a deeper connection with their audience. Coincidentally, it also allowed Marvel, long an also-ran company, to seriously begin challenging the industry leader and standard, DC Comics, for the first time.[95] Indeed, in later years, the company's influence over the production and structure of both comic-book heroes and their television animation counterparts would prove to be vast. The television animation adventures of the Four, however, mostly lacked the complexity of character and plot structure of the comic books, for logistical reasons. Yet other aspects of the series, particularly the voice casting (which seemed to be nearly the way the characters would have "talked" in the comics) were remarkably faithful to the source. As in the comics, the Four received superpowers after being irradiated while traveling in space. They consisted of the de facto leader, Reed Richards, a.k.a. Mr. Fantastic (Gerald Mohr), able to stretch his body in remarkably flexible ways; Reed's wife, Sue Storm Richards, a.k.a. Invisible Girl (Jo Ann Pflug), able to become invisible and project force fields to defend herself and others from attack; Sue's brother Johnny Storm, a.k.a. The Human Torch (Jack Flounders), who could burst into flames that covered his body at will (by shouting "Flame On!") and fly in the air while doing so; and Ben Grimm, a.k.a. The Thing (Paul Frees, with a delightful Brooklyn accent), transformed into a large super-powered creature made of orange rock (his battle cry was "It's Clobberin' Time!"). The Four's opponents included nemeses from their comic-book adventures, such as the silver-metal–faced

Dr. Doom and the Mole Man, as well as more original figures, such as the wicked alchemist Diablo, who created mischief after being freed following a century of entombment. This series was one of the best produced of the late 1960s superhero cycle, but it was also, unfortunately, one of the last.

The Fantastic Four was more of a deviation from the norm for Hanna-Barbera's adventure series of the time, as it came via an outside source. For the 1968–69 campaign the studio reverted to running their formula for this cycle into the ground. Three series from this time reflected this increasing decline in quality, as they were based very loosely on literary sources with none of those sources' literary merit. They were *The Adventures of Gulliver* (ABC), based on Jonathan Swift's satiric fantasy *Gulliver's Travels*; *The Arabian Knights* (NBC), from the *Arabian Nights* story cycle of the Far East; and *The Three Musketeers* (NBC), from Alexandre Dumas' legendary adventure story. All of these had been done elsewhere in the history of both television and theatrical animation with mixed results.

It was at this time that the studio began to return to form by backtracking to its older strengths. This was partially the result of creative decline and partially due to outside influence. Increasingly, television animation, because it was one of the major forums for attracting children to television watching, became the target of "watchdog" groups attempting to "clean up" television, mostly consisting of otherwise well-meaning parents trying to act in the name of "protecting" their children. As Ted Sennett notes, "A swell of protest began to rise against *what was perceived* as *the excessive violence* in many of the series, and especially against the proliferation of commercials for expensive toys and sugar-coated cereals [emphasis added]."[96] At the head of the pack was the Massachusetts-based Action For Children's Television, headed by housewife-cum-social activist Peggy Charren, which would play a major role in forcing a major cultural and ideological shift in television animation in the following decade.[97] "The industry met with her," Barbera later recalled, "and listened to her side of the story. She made a loud enough noise so that the producers began to wonder what they were doing."[98] Fred Silverman, however, contended that "the [ratings] influenced [us] more than anything else [in deciding to cancel the programs]. They just weren't good enough."[99]

Producing shows that did not offend the sensibilities of ACT while at the same time drawing ratings that were "good enough" to keep them on the air was a tricky divide, but Hanna-Barbera wisely responded by taking a new spin on the comic narratives that had long been their stock in trade. The first flowering of this was in *Wacky Races*, which debuted on CBS in the fall of 1968. The product of the inventiveness of Iwao Takamoto, Jerry Eisenberg, and the newer, younger members of the animation staff, the show was an extension of a theme featured in a number of popular movies of the time, involving high-speed, rapid-fire, slapstick-based comic races featuring elaborate means of transportation, such as *The Great Race* (Blake Edwards, 1965) and *Those Magnificent Men in Their Flying Machines* (Ken Annakin, 1966). The show was built around an aggressive, cross-country competition for the title of "World's Wackiest Racer." The group, on their marks and getting set to go, was an incredibly diverse and comically exaggerated lot. Among them: the villainous "double-dealing dobadder"[100] Dick Dastardly (Paul Winchell), who used elaborate means of sabotage to attack his opponents, but always got his in the end, with no thanks to his snickering, sibilant canine accomplice Muttley (Don Messick). Others in the group were stereotyped "hero" figure Peter Perfect (Daws Butler) in the "Turbo Terrific"; "Hillbillies" Luke and Blubber Bear (both played by John Stephenson) in the "Arkansas Chugabug"; Professor Pat Pending (Messick), an eccentric inventor, in his "Convert-a-Car"; Lumberjack Rufus Ruffcutt (Butler) and Sawtooth (Messick) in the Buzz Wagon; The General (Stephenson), The Sergeant (Butler) and Private Pinkley (Winchell) in the Army Surplus Special; Cavemen Rock and Gravel Slag (both Butler) in the Bouldermobile; Penelope Pitstop (Janet Waldo) in the Compact Pussycat; Aviator The Red Max (Butler) in the Crimson Hay-Bailer; The Gruesome Twosome (Butler and Messick) in the Creepy Coupe; and the diminutive Ant Hill Mob (all by Mel Blanc) in their Bulletproof Bomb. This show was entirely unique, employing traditional "cartoon" slapstick and innovative background and character designs to create an entirely appealing package, and it was very popular with viewers. As a consequence of this popularity, however, its basic formula would be done to death by Hanna-Barbera and other studios over the course of the following decade, in the process robbing the idea of its freshness.

Before that happened, though, Hanna-Barbera took advantage of an emerging trend in television: taking popular supporting characters from hit series and making them into leads in their own programs. Two *Wacky Races* characters were given this bells-and-whistles treatment for the 1969-70 season. In *Dastardly and Muttley in Their Flying Machines*, Dick Dastardly (again played by Paul Winchell) was only slightly recast as an inept World War I flying ace, hindered rather than helped by Muttley (again played by Don Messick) and two inept airplane mechanics, incoherent Klunk and cowardly Zilly (both Messick). Under orders from the General (heard only as an often angry telephone voice), the villainous quartet attempted—and repeatedly failed—to capture Yankee Doodle Pigeon, a courageous American message courier outfitted, like Jay Ward's Rocky (see below) in goggles and flying helmet. Guess who survived the weekly contests unscathed? The series was also notable for its zesty theme song (written, as always, by Hanna, Barbera and Hoyt Curtin), "Stop That Pigeon!" (the original working title of the series).

The other character to get the star treatment was Penelope Pitstop (again played by Janet Waldo), recast as a Pearl White–type serial heroine forever in peril and in need of rescue from danger. This danger specifically took the form of her supposedly benign benefactor, Sylvester Sneekly (Paul Lynde,[101] making his [uncredited] Hanna-Barbera debut; Lynde and Paul Winchell would both contribute many voices to the studio in the following decade). Sneekly masqueraded à la Snidely Whiplash with green hat and cape as the notorious Hooded Claw. However, he neglected to remove his pince-nez glasses in the process of disguising himself, and thus gave himself away (to the audience, but not the characters, which made the show much funnier than it would have been otherwise). In Penelope's corner were the Ant Hill Mob, still in their bulletproof limousine (now anthropomorphized with the name Chug-a-Boom and portrayed by Mel Blanc with the same broken-down-engine-of-a-car noise voice he had once used on radio to "play" Jack Benny's notoriously decrepit Maxwell). The Mob themselves were now given individualized personalities à la Walt Disney's Seven Dwarfs. By name, they were known as Clyde, the leader (Paul Winchell); Zippy, Pockets, Dum Dum, Snoozy (all Don Messick), Softy (Winchell) and Yak Yak (Blanc). In the Hooded Claw's corner were the inept Bully Brothers (both Blanc), whose name was self-explanatory.

Narrated by Gary Owens,[102] *Penelope Pitstop* was an effective recreation of the thrills of the silent film and early talkie adventure serials, where black and white portrayals of forces of good and evil were not only accepted but commonplace. However, while the earlier serials had emphasized the helplessness of the leads, Hanna-Barbera took a more progressive approach to the material. While Penelope constantly cried for help when in peril, and the Ant Hill Mob often rescued her, she also showed unexpected agency in escaping from peril, and spoke the occasional bit of witty dialogue. As would be expected, as with *Dastardly and Muttley*, the writing of this series (Ruby and Spears did the action; Michael Maltese, the comedy) was above average in comparison to the blandness that, in response to the anti-"violence" campaign of the late 1960s and early 1970s, was becoming the new industry standard.

That blandness was particularly the result of another amazingly popular series which debuted in 1969 on CBS. Though Hanna and Barbera had achieved financial security for themselves and their staff by selling Hanna-Barbera to the Ohio-based Taft Broadcasting group in 1967,[103] they still had to answer to the sponsors and networks, and were more than willing to indulge Fred Silverman for that reason. At this time, he suggested a series that would be a combination of horror and comedy, not unlike the old NBC radio series of the 1930s and 1940s, *I Love a Mystery*, created and written by the legendary Carleton (*One Man's Family*) Morse, and similar Abbott and Costello film comedies, such as *Hold That Ghost* (Arthur Lubin, 1941) and *Abbott and Costello Meet Frankenstein* (Charles Barton, 1948), Silverman having been a fan of both. In a process reminiscent of the modern idea of "mashing up" seemingly incompatible cultural products, he suggested to the producers that they make the lead characters teenagers to appeal to the Saturday morning audience, along the lines of an early TV series he admired, *The Many Loves of Dobie Gillis*, whose main characters ended up serving as the models for the human lead characters.[104] In what was then standard studio practice, a goofy dog was created to be their sidekick, possibly to create ancillary merchandising revenue. Initially known as *Mysteries Five* and then *Who's Scared?*, the series was structured in the middle of the schedule by Silverman, who then presented the schedule to network president Frank Stanton and the board of directors for their approval. Here, trouble reared its head. Silverman takes up the story:

> I went to present the whole schedule, and we finally got to this show. It turned out that the artwork was [unintentionally] very frightening. Stanton looked at it and said, "[w]e can't put that on the air." [Then we knew] [w]e were in trouble. We had placed this show at 10:30 [Eastern Standard Time], right in the middle of the schedule, and without this show we wouldn't *have* a schedule [emphasis in original]. "Well," I said, "let me see what I can do." Flying back to Los Angeles that night, I happened to have the [in-flight] earphones on and was listening to Frank Sinatra ['s recording of] "Strangers in the Night." I was struck by the phrase "Scooby-dooby-doo" [which Sinatra improvises during the closing moments of the recording]. [Immediately] I went back and said, "We'll call the show 'Scooby Doo, Where Are You?' and we'll make the dog the star of the show. [The show as it was animated and aired] ... was the same basic show, except that we brought the dog up front, and all the other characters supported him.[105]

Thus began a programming phenomenon which became one of Hanna-Barbera's hallmarks, running continuously in various formats on CBS and ABC between 1969 and 1986, and in various new incarnations in the 1990s and 2000s on Cartoon Network, as well as being the subject of two live-action feature films during this latter period.

Initially, at least, except for the shift in focus toward the dog, the show did fulfill Silverman's desire to "mash up" *I Love a Mystery* with *Dobie Gillis*. Besides Scooby (Don Messick), the goofy, ungainly and ravenously hungry Great Dane, the group consisted of Fred (Frank Welker), tall, blond, white-shirted and ascoted, the de facto leader; red haired, trouble-prone Daphne (Heather North); bespectacled, orange-sweatered Velma (Nicole Jaffe); and particularly Shaggy (future star DJ Casey Kasem), an unkempt hippy/beatnik type whose appetite rivaled that of Scooby. (Shaggy alone among the characters most resembled his role model—*Dobie Gillis*'s Maynard G. Krebs [Bob Denver]—especially the latter's slacker, cowardly attitude to life). Traveling in a customized van dubbed "The Mystery

Machine," painted in psychedelically inspired orange, blue and green, the "gang" (as Fred frequently referred to them) investigated what appeared to be supernaturally devised "mysteries" (revealed chiefly as mundane, non-supernatural perpetrations at the climax), which followed a disappointingly repetitious format at times. Fred, Daphne and Velma were the "straight" characters responsible for solving the crimes at hand, while Shaggy and Scooby handled the comedy, particularly in their inspired, over-the-top reactions to the "monster" of the week. Inevitably, in the fashion of pre–World War II mystery fiction in particular, the "monster" was usually revealed to be a person the gang had somehow encountered during the course of the episode. This individual would inevitably say something to the effect that they "would have gotten away with it if it weren't for you meddling kids" as he/she was led away by the stony-faced local authorities.[106] *Columbo* it was not.

The producers spiced up the mundane aspects through creative use of the animated monsters, which became less "fake" and more "real" as the series progressed until it could be accurately considered a predecessor of *Ghostbusters* by the end of the original cycle. There were also other minor and more eccentric touches that enhanced the show's appeal. The dog-treat Scooby Snacks, for example, were frequently used as a carrot to goad Scooby (and often Shaggy as well) to forgo his cowardly attitude and leap into action. However, the show suffered from what would become the major flaws of television animation in the 1970s and 1980s—wooden characters, simplistic plotting, and the mere suggestion of "comedy" and "action" that were neither funny nor exciting but simply purported to be. Still, as Timothy and Kevin Burke have noted, these absences in the narrative just provided an unexpected form of food for thought for the viewers, who could simply use their imagination to speculate about the things related to the story that Hanna, Barbera and the studio had no desire, nor time, to go into.[107]

While *Scooby Doo* was a success, it was also a bad omen. Rather than bringing prestige to Hanna-Barbera as its other work of the 1950s and 1960s would, it would increasingly bring shame to the studio for both its method of production and its limitations as drama and comedy. And, as other studios openly began to imitate *Scooby Doo*'s production and narrative approach, it tainted television animation for much of the following decade. If Hanna and Barbera noticed this, they only rarely commented on it. They were too busy laughing all the way to the bank.

Jay Ward

After his experiences producing *Crusader Rabbit* (see Chapter 1), one might think that Jay Ward would have become bitter and resentful and would simply abandon the television animation business altogether. Not so. By the late 1950s, he had begun production again, working and producing under his own name this time. It was in this period that he truly made his mark on the still nascent genre. If William Hanna and Joseph Barbera were clearly the "fathers" of animation's success in the new medium, Ward was its godfather, its hip, eccentric uncle, and—to his detractors—its skeleton in the closet.

This was chiefly because Ward set high standards for himself and his staff, which in turn led to conflicts with network management over content and promotion and ultimately led to his being ostracized from network television. More's the pity, for despite his eccentricities, Ward was one of the few television animation producers prior to the 1990s who was able to give his work a unique, individualized sensibility that allowed him to stand both

Rocky and His Friends ran on ABC from 1959 to 1961. From left: Bullwinkle J. Moose, series creator Jay Ward and Rocket "Rocky" J. Squirrel (ABC/Photofest).

away from and above his peers. The fact that his work remains accessible to viewers, and influential to active and potential animators today, is a sign of how far ahead of the times he truly was. Unfortunately, as a path-breaker and a maverick, he paid a heavy price for maintaining his independence.

Working with a talented staff, in particular actor/writer/producer Bill Scott, Ward fashioned a series of narratives that included remarkably frank sentiments for their time, although to contemporary viewers most of these are safely disguised under the mask of comedy. Unlike Hanna-Barbera, which was adaptable to the marketplace and the demands of advertisers and network executives, the Ward studio refused to make any commercial or artistic concessions toward its product. While this may have prevented Ward from developing a secure business, it also ensured the high quality of its work and its endurance in later years, regardless of the limited reception it had in its original broadcast period.[108]

Ward's work was (and remains) shockingly ahead of its time in many respects, particularly when compared to that of Hanna-Barbera. There were, of course, obvious similarities in characters and subject matter: both used animals as their star characters, and both regularly satirized television and popular culture in their work. The difference lay in the approach. Hanna-Barbera, in spite of their use of symbolism for satire, far too often diffused the satiric potential of their ideas to retain the respect of audiences, advertisers and network executives. Ward, on the other hand, did no such thing. The raw, satiric humor in his programs was a revelation to viewers, and continues to remain influential today. In particular, he felicitously succeeded in debunking the "heroic" image of masculinity his generation had been presented with in their youth, in a style far more corrosive than that of the competition.

What follows is a brief overview of the career of this singular television animation producer.

♦ ♦ ♦

Following his failure to revive *Crusader Rabbit*, Ward struck out, as the narrators of his programs might say, for further adventures. Establishing Jay Ward Productions in 1957, he first attempted to collaborate with veteran theatrical animator Shamus Culhane on a new series called *Phineas T. Phox, Adventurer*, but Ward's role in the project was reduced and ultimately shelved after a falling out with Culhane.[109] The aborted project, however, did lead to a lasting partnership with another animator who would play a vital role in future studio productions: Bill Scott.

Scott was born in Philadelphia in 1920, and raised in Trenton, New Jersey, and Denver, Colorado, moving to the latter place with his family after contracting tuberculosis. An animation fan from his childhood, he hoped to pursue a career in it after gaining university degrees in drama and English, as well as beginning a performing career on radio and doing amateur animation work. He briefly worked as a high school teacher, but then enlisted in the air force during World War II. Trained as a photographer and cameraman, he was assigned to the Hollywood-based First Motion Picture Unit, where he was able to indulge in his love of filmmaking and animation.[110]

Following his discharge, Scott decided to remain in Hollywood to pursue a career as a professional animator and actor. At Warner Bros., he worked with Lloyd Turner, later a member of the Ward writing staff. However, Scott's stint was short-lived, as he became a victim of internal politics at the studio; yet he was forever grateful for the on-the-job-training experience the studio gave him. After an aborted attempt to establish an acting career in Hollywood, he spent the next few years working as a writer on Bob Clampett's *Time for Beany* series (see above and below) before striking out on his own again. (Turner and another future Ward employee, Chris Hayward, also worked on the show.[111])

After being fired by Clampett for fronting the demands of the writers for more money, Scott joined the staff of UPA (see Chapter 1 and below) in 1950. UPA had already hired director Bill Hurtz (later a charter member of the Ward studio) and background artist Phil Monroe, both of whom had worked with Scott in the First Motion Picture Unit. Coming to work for UPA was thus a natural for Scott. He worked producing scripts for the Mr. Magoo series under director John Hubley (another FMPU colleague) as well as co-authoring the scripts for their elaborate adaptations of *Gerald McBoing Boing* and *The Tell Tale Heart* (see Chapter 1). Fired for his progressive politics during the McCarthy era in 1952, Scott concentrated on freelancing, including returning briefly to UPA in 1956 to oversee the studio's first attempt at television production, *The Gerald McBoing Boing Show*. Though this lasted only one season, the expertise Scott gained as a television producer would become invaluable to his later work. It was after this period that Scott and Ward first met and joined forces.[112]

Recommended for *Phineas T. Phox* by an already-hired friend and colleague, Charles Shows (also, later, a Hanna-Barbera writer), Scott had already begun scripting the series when the Ward-Culhane partnership imploded and the series aborted. But Ward wanted to continue producing series based on his own ideas, and he asked Scott, whose work impressed him, to help him develop these into a new series:

> Jay was enthused [Scott later recalled]. He'd gotten his feet wet with Hollywood animation again, and this time he wanted to do it properly. Anyway, a few days later Jay wrote to me and asked if I'd be interested in working with him on another series. So I met with him, and he pulled out some ideas that he and Alex Anderson hadn't been able to sell—particularly one called *The Frostbite Falls Review*, which concerned a TV show, sort of like *Hee Haw* combined with *The Today Show*. All the characters were animals, in a "rube" setting; kind of a small-town comedy.
>
> Jay was very entranced with the kind of characters he'd had in *Crusader Rabbit* ... the little guy teamed with the big guy. In this ... show, there was a flying squirrel named Rocky, and a moose named Bullwinkle. Jay asked if we could do an adventure strip with these two characters.... I said, "Well, sure. Why not? Anything for money." So we wrote a script together which became the pilot film.[113]

It was during this period that Ward discovered Scott's acting talents, particularly his facility at making funny "cartoon" voices, and offered him additional duties besides writing on the new project:

> Scott would read the dialogue aloud in various voices, "and Jay was just delighted. He'd fall about laughing. Then[,] when we discussed hiring people for the pilot, I asked him, Who do we get to play Bullwinkle? And he said, well, you do it. So I said, 'Sure, why not. Sensational!' So I read the role of Bullwinkle."[114]

Inadvertently, Scott the writer had allowed Scott the actor to achieve the role that would make him famous and beloved throughout the world to at least two generations of fans. Bullwinkle would, however, be just one of the many Ward characters Scott would play during his career, a testament to his versatility and skill as both a writer and an actor.

There were still several problems that needed to be addressed. The first was hiring an animation concern to produce the series' nuts-and-bolts animation. "Above the line" work such as scriptwriting, voice acting and storyboarding would remain in Hollywood. In this, Ward pioneered an industry tactic that would become as widespread—and controversial—as limited animation. "Runaway" animation—the use by American animation producers of foreign animation houses to produce material faster and take advantage of the absence of American wage and labor laws—would become more commonplace in the following years as the costs of animation production skyrocketed. Yet, at the time Ward was producing animation, it was still considered something of a novelty. As Keith Scott notes, Ward and his financial manager, Len Key, were eager to embrace this tactic because, unlike Hanna-Barbera's U.S.–based approach, it involved no budgetary or artistic sacrifices of any kind.[115] Initially contracting with a Japanese studio, they ultimately made connections with the Mexican studio Val-Mar (later Gamma), who would animate the earliest of the Ward studio products before a dissatisfied Ward made the switch back to Hollywood production. Mexico was also the home base for another important Ward staffer: composer Fred Steiner.

Another major need was to assemble a cast of voice actors. Ward found that Hollywood had a bumper crop of talented radio actors from which to choose. Ultimately, the Ward audio staff proved to be one of the most talented and versatile in animation history. In addition to Bill Scott himself, the major members of this legendary group were:

- *Paul Frees* (1920–86): Born in Chicago, Frees began performing while still a youth on stage and radio, performing initially under the stage name "Buddy Green." He became an established radio actor after World War II, with this work initially helping him to support his beloved, frail, first wife, Annelle, and then to help him move on following her sudden death at the age of twenty-one. An exceptionally versatile actor and a gifted mimic (particularly of Hollywood figures such as Peter Lorre) whose repertoire included a wide range of dialects and accents (including the Russian one he would use for Boris Badenov), Frees was also a good-humored man who contributed much in the way of lively fun to the recording sessions.[116]

- *June Foray* (1917–present): This Springfield, Massachusetts, native remains one of the best-known and most beloved female voice actors. She began acting as a child, and when her family moved to California during the 1930s she began to pursue this vocation in earnest, working both in radio and as a regular contributor to theatrical animation. She also recorded extensively for Capitol Records, doing many children's albums and appearing alongside Daws Butler on a number of Stan Freberg comedy records. This work led her to be recruited by Ward. A 1960 ABC publicity piece indicated that she kept a library of new voices recorded for future use,[117] which has, no doubt, helped her sustain her career over an astonishing 50-plus-year period.

- *William "Bill" Conrad (né John William Cann, Jr.)* (1920–94): Perhaps best known for his role as the corpulent, mustachioed private investigator, Cannon, in the 1970s television series of the same name, Conrad's career extended nearly 50 years, and included acting, narration, writing, production and direction in radio, film and television. Born in Louisville, Kentucky, Conrad moved to California with his family as a teenager, where he began work as a radio announcer. After military service during World War II, he began to accumulate a long list of radio, film and television credits, including originating the role of Matt Dillon in the radio version of *Gunsmoke.* Later credits included narrating the original TV version of *The Fugitive* and starring in *Jake and the Fatman.* Conrad's jaunty narration of the "Rocky and Bullwinkle" episodes, which added considerably to their comic impact, was his chief contribution to the Ward oeuvre, although later he would also voice characters in Ward-produced commercials. He had a long association with Paul Frees through radio that affected their joint work; as Keith Scott notes, the two "knew each other's styles the way twins know each other's moods."[118] Consequently, Conrad was the principal target of Frees's jokes and horseplay, which frequently reduced the often gruff-appearing Conrad to unrestrained laughter.[119]

- *Edward Everett Horton* (1888–1971): The narrator of the "Fractured Fairy Tales" segments, Horton was in his seventies at the time of their recording. As Scott noted, the veteran character actor was recruited "to lend a certain air of reverence to otherwise irreverent stories."[120] In a career dating back to the silent era, Horton, a closeted homosexual, was frequently cast as an effeminate character with a sly giggle and knowing facial movements that communicated much more than mere words could suggest alone. He cleverly invoked this image in his work for Ward, in particular through his often pained reactions to the bad jokes and horrific puns he was forced to deliver.[121]

- *Charles Ruggles* (1892–70): Another veteran Hollywood character actor, Ruggles's career spanned both films and television. He was employed by Ward as the voice of Aesop in the revisionist "Aesop and Son" segments of the program. He did this uncredited, however, so his contributions to the program have never been fully acknowledged.[122] Ruggles's extensive experience playing dimwitted authority figures contributed greatly to his successful portraying of Aesop, done in the manner of an "unctuous school principal raining platitudes down from his Olympian heights on a captive assemblage of students."[123] He was also, however, capable of infusing some genuine warmth in the character, particularly in his interactions with his son, Junior (Daws Butler), a rare feat in and of itself for any animation voice actor.

- *Hansel "Hans" Conreid* (1917–1982): Yet another veteran Hollywood character actor, Conreid was, like Horton and Ruggles, known for portraying eccentric comedy roles, though he was also capable of more sinister portrayals, such as the title role in 1953's *The 5,000 Fingers of Dr. T.* He proved to be a natural for Ward's style of comedy, as demonstrated by his excellent portrayal of the overacting Snidely Whiplash in the "Dudley Do-Right" segments. Like many of the other actors, he remained in the Ward fold when *Rocky and Bullwinkle* ended, voicing "Uncle Waldo" in the *Hoppity Hooper* series and serving as the unctuous host of *Fractured Flickers* (see both below).[124]

- *Walter Tetley* (1921–1975): Tetley, a midget, sounded perennially young because a hormonal condition prevented his voice from breaking. As an actor, this limited him to child parts, but he proved to be one of the best essayers of such roles on radio between the 1930s and the 1950s. It was this skill that led Ward to recruit him to play Sherman, the "pet boy" of the intelligent canine Mr. Peabody. This became a highlight of the later part of his career, which ended as a result of injuries sustained in an automobile accident.[125]

- *Daws Butler.* See Hanna-Barbera section above. Butler's extensive work for Ward, chiefly in irregular character roles, was not credited onscreen because of the conflict between Hanna-Barbera's sponsor (Kellogg's) and Ward's (General Mills).[126]

◆ ◆ ◆

As mentioned earlier, the Mexico City animation studio Val-Mar/Gamma became the studio's animation producer when an attempted bid to produce through a Japanese company fell through. Operated by wealthy speculator Gustavo Valdez, with Jesus Martinez as head of production, the company, funded by General Mills and Ward's company, P.A.T., set up and hastily began production in order to meet the fall 1959 production deadline set by ABC.[127] Communication issues and conflict between the producers and the animation studio resulted in heavily uneven animation material (such as having Boris Badenov's moustache appear in one scene and disappear in another[128]), but both parties managed to stay on course. Much of this was due to the refinements of the material done by the veteran and talented series directors (Bill Hurtz, Ted Parmelee, Lew Keller, Pete Burness) and writers (Scott, Chris Hayward, Lloyd Turner, Chris Jenkyns, George Atkins and future *Mary Tyler Moore*

Show co-creator Allan Burns) based in Los Angeles, whose work transcended the limitations caused by the animation's weaknesses. The contrast between the excellent writing and the uneven animation was jarring at times, but it made clear to the viewer that this series was not of the average, Hanna-Barbera variety—which was likely Ward and Scott's point, after all.

That being said, the written content was of the highest quality possible, given Ward and Scott's commitment at this end to high standards, and though, especially in the earliest episodes, the animation sometimes marred it, this remained a hallmark of Ward's work for the duration of his career. It becomes especially notable through a close reading of the individual segments of *Rocky and His Friends*, as the series was known during its 1959–61 daily run on ABC, and *The Bullwinkle Show*, as it was renamed when it became a weekly series on NBC from 1962 to 1964.

◆ ◆ ◆

Most discussions of Ward's work have to begin with his most famous characters, Rocket J. "Rocky" Squirrel (Foray) and Bullwinkle J. Moose (Scott). This mismatched, but firmly loyal, pair of characters were structured in such a way that they could be admired by children for their openly "heroic" behavior while being laughed at by adults because of their all-too-obvious Achilles heels. Rocky, the "brains" of the duo, is a thoughtful, agile and courageous figure who displays surprising levels of resourcefulness when faced with danger. Nevertheless, he is limited by both his youthful idealism, which blinds him to the idea that anything bad could be done to him or his friend, and his naïveté, which occasionally causes him to fall into fairly obvious traps set by the villains. Bullwinkle, the "brawn," is a study in emotional contrast to his friend. Constantly spewing a variety of insouciant wisecracks, he never takes anything too seriously, even when his life depends on it. In spite of his wit, however, he is innately stupid, and is victimized by the villains on this basis in the same way that they manipulate Rocky's idealism. The stories repeatedly reinforce the fact that Rocky and Bullwinkle are limited in ways that prevent them from being the truly heroic "men" that their adventure-based narratives demand them to be. They are, in a sense, "boys" (as the narrator often calls them) doing a "man's" job. But this is something no one bothers to tell them, so they go along on their idealistic way, and their efforts to be "TV-type heroes" become far more comical than they would otherwise be. Despite this, the residents of their home town, Frostbite Falls, Minnesota, admire and respect them for their "heroic" achievements in a way that borders on adulation.

The villains in these narratives, like many animation "bad guys" before them, had villainy written into their very names. Boris Badenov (Frees) and Natasha Fatale (Foray) were spies from Pottsylvania, clearly a satire of Soviet Russia.[129] While Rocky and Bullwinkle were overtly structured as parodies of traditional media notions of heroism, Boris and Natasha represent a similar caricature of such notions of villainy. This is represented by their ghoulish physical appearance, their pseudo–Slavic accents, and their constant application of "fiendish plans" meant to destroy their enemies. Boris, unlike Rocky and Bullwinkle, appears unhappy, however, with his limited role in the narrative, and subverts the expectations of the audience by often inserting his ideas and opinions into the narrative when they are unwanted. On these occasions, he seeks to take control of the show itself by challenging the narrator's version of the story arc, by putting himself in the narrator's place, and other similar tactics. In one episode of the "Topsy Turvy World" sequence,[130] for example, he orders everyone in the story to "hold it!" while he outlines his latest "fiendish plan." All of the other characters promptly stop *exactly in place*, suggesting the breadth of Boris's influence over the "offstage" aspects of the narrative. Similarly, in an installment of "The Treasure of Monte Zoom,"[131] Boris believes he overheard the narrator giving away a crucial piece of information regarding the show's plot. When the narrator denies this, Boris makes the producers *rewind* the episode tape so he can make sure he heard it properly. Actions like this add a sinister edge to Boris's otherwise comic and non-threatening "villainy," suggesting that, because he can resort to these means to take control of the narrative construction, he can control the outcome of events to help him succeed in his aims. Thus, there is irony when Rocky and Bullwinkle ultimately defeat him, since, even when Boris has been constantly scamming and tricking them, they are frequently oblivious to the fact that he is doing anything wrong.

Even with his ability to manipulate the outside narrative, Boris is still made to answer to a higher power: Fearless Leader (Scott), the menacing and ruthless dictator of Pottsylvania. This character stands out among his cartoon contemporaries due to the fact that he is genuinely frightening and intimidating, a figure of totalitarian power and influence. It is perhaps no wonder that he resembles a caricatured Nazi officer. What makes him so fearful is that his power is so concentrated. Unlike many of the Hanna-Barbera authority figures, he has no one to answer to, no wife or employer to limit his activities, abilities or desires. Consequently, he represents masculine power at its most extreme and cruel. This adds a level of tension to his relationship with Boris that is similar to, but more extreme than, that between George Jetson and Mr. Spacely. Fearless Leader can not only fire Boris if he is displeased with him, he can have him *killed*. Boris knows this, and constantly plays up to him to remain in his good graces, though this does him little good when he cannot succeed in his efforts due to Rocky and Bullwinkle's often unwitting interventions.

A final element of caricature existed with the narrator himself (Conrad). Narrators in the past served as links between the audience and the story; the narrator was supposed to speak from a distance, with this distance giving him the authority and objectivity to tell the story "properly." This hardly occurred here. This narrator was not an empowered omniscient figure; rather, he was simply another character, subjected to the same travails of the narrative as were the other characters. Pointing to his physical as well as his metaphysical presence limited the amount of "authority" he could project as the story's "teller" and, along with other factors, limited the ability of the audiences to view the ongoing story in any "realistic" way. It also made him vulnerable to being captured along with Rocky and Bullwinkle. In one episode, this is done in order to "halt" the "official" version of the story so the villains could tell it their way instead. By challenging the narrator's ability to do his job properly, the producers made it clear to the audience that this whole thing was simply an extended joke, and the only reasonable thing they could do was treat it as such.

These elements helped to make the "Rocky and Bullwinkle" segments funny and memorable, as well as highlighting the essential point made by the writers: that Hollywood and fiction narratives were essentially limited and repeated sets of characters, plots and ideas manipulated by outside hands, and, if the writers did not challenge the tide of endlessly repeated machinations, their characters would be reduced to caricatures. This was particularly true of the male characters who played the leading roles in this series; they either accepted their position and went along with it, as Rocky and Bullwinkle did, or demanded to be something other and more, as Boris did. The limitations of these type of fictions were found to be equally constricting in the other segments of the program as well.

◆ ◆ ◆

One segment that proved to have a similar irreverent attitude toward its subject was "Fractured Fairy Tales."[132] Rejecting the lavish approach Walt Disney had long advocated in his feature-film adaptations of fairy tales, Ward, Scott and their staff, much like some of the theatrical animators who had preceded them, used them instead as a source of parody and satire, as much of the contemporary world around them as the world of the tales themselves. This clever series was highlighted by the effervescent narration of Edward Everett Horton, in particular highlighting his bad reactions to the puns that were used to end the narratives.

Two episodes in particular highlight the program's unique and enduring approach. "Snow White" is redone in one installment in a modern fashion by having the Seven Dwarfs act as a group of con artists à la *The Phil Silvers Show*. The Wicked Queen comes in succession looking for Snow White, and instead ends up finding the Seven Dwarfs' "Health Club," "Dance Studio," "Charm School," etc., in her place. In succession, the Queen is taken to the cleaners each time by the dwarfs through the elaborate scam. We are led to believe that Snow White is simply nonexistent until an ugly woman bearing the name arrives, causing the lead dwarf to exclaim, "There really *is* a Snow White?"

Another take on an established fairy tale, in this case "Sleeping Beauty," is much less disguised in terms of intent and tone. Walt Disney had released a lavish feature-film version of this story in 1959, prompting Ward to release a version that was much more mass market in nature. In Ward's version, Disney, complete with moustache, is drawn as the prince, with Daws Butler intoning his lines in the archetypal Phil Silvers/Sergeant Bilko manner he often used with Ward. The connection was obvious: Disney was being portrayed as a con man who used fairy tales to enrich himself. This was made clear when, rather than choosing to free the princess from her slumbering enchantment, he builds a successful amusement park, "Sleeping Beauty Land." This catches the eye of the greedy Wicked Fairy, who wants to gain a cut of the park's profits. The prince attempts to get rid of her, but with little success. Ultimately, the prince, the fairy and Sleeping Beauty herself are all exposed as pretenders: the fairy is not really a fairy, the prince is not a prince but a "hog flogger" (a subtle reference to masturbation[133]) and Sleeping Beauty merely one of many people trying to "make it" in show business. That latter theme became a prominent sub-theme of the series, allowing for many humorous satires of Hollywood and/or the mechanics of fairy tales to be produced in this memorable series of programs.

A similar attitude was expressed in the fairy tales' companion/successor series, "Aesop and Son," which ran concurrently for much of the show's run. Though not as consistently funny as the fairy tales, they utilized many of the same storytelling devices to create similar effects in narrative and storytelling. Much of the humor here came from the casting of veteran character actor Charles Ruggles as Aesop and Daws Butler as his son Junior, who managed to create a very convincing relationship in spite of the limitations of the format.

Butler and Bill Scott, in the stories proper, played an amazingly diverse number of anthropomorphic characters. In addition to modernized variations on the standard fables, such as "The Tortoise and the Hare," the series also presented bizarre original stories in the format, such as "The Sick Lion," involving a lion with delusions of becoming an opera star, and "The Fox and the Hound," set in Hollywood and based on a down-on-his-luck Hollywood agent.

Bullwinkle, meanwhile, befitting the star status he had assumed, also became the host in a number of supporting features, all with humorous results. The first of these was "Bullwinkle's Corner," a poetry reading whose initial set aim was to provide the series with "a bit of culture," but which inevitably descended into comic chaos. Initially, the readings were relatively straightforward comic illustrations, but they soon became more elaborate. The reading of "Little Miss Muffet," for example, was highlighted by the comic banter between Rocky (as the spider) and Bullwinkle (in drag as the title character), and the latter's humorous asides within the proceedings, which generally set the tone for what was to come. Boris Badenov was also involved in many of the later segments. Particularly noteworthy in this regard was Boris and Bullwinkle turning "Simple Simon" into an extended vaudeville wordplay routine ("Not your what—your ware"). Much like the other segments of the program, the writers seemed to take delight in updating and transmogrifying early works and converting them into modernized travesties. Thus, "Wee Willie Winkie" is arrested as a potential flasher, Poe's "Raven" turns out to be an aggressive woodpecker, and Longfellow's "Excelsior" became an advertising campaign for a lumber company. This collision of low comedy and high culture made for one of the program's more entertaining segments.

Something that proved to be even more effective was casting Bullwinkle in the unlikely role of "Mr. Know It All," which effectively took over the "Bullwinkle's Corner" segments later in the program's run. In a similar fashion to the poetry segments, these segments demolished their intended "how to" intentions by making it comically impossible for Bullwinkle to demonstrate his supposed "expertise" on the subject at hand. These included a variety of direct burlesques of professional roles in society ("How to Be a Star Reporter" was a highlight here), as well as more absurd, exaggerated subjects ("How to Escape from Devil's Island"), and even social satire ("How to Be a Beatnik," "How to Be a Successful Member of the Peace Corps," etc.). Boris again was the principal foil, perennially stymieing Bullwinkle's efforts. A third, minor series supplemented these segments toward the end of the program's run: "The Bullwinkle and Rocky Fan Club," which consisted *only* of members of the show's cast, and most often involved futile efforts to increase the membership.

◆ ◆ ◆

Two other long-lived segments completed the program's content, and, like the main "Rocky and Bullwinkle" feature, deserve to be discussed in detail because of their enduring cultural influence.

"Peabody's Improbable History" made its debut as part of the original *Rocky and His Friends* series in 1959 and remained a major component of the *Rocky and Bullwinkle* series for the entirety of its run. Like the other Ward products, it exists as a satiric and subversive work, but the target of its satire was not Hollywood culture directly but historical education and the narrative construction of history (although Hollywood did play a secondary role in this with its film versions of historical events). In particular, it attacks and undermines the hypothetical "Great Man" theory dominating historical study in the 19th and early–20th centuries.

To begin with, the form, characters and function of the series are unorthodox for television at any part of its history and in any genre. Devised by *Saturday Evening Post* illustrator Ted Key,[134] the series focused on Mr. Peabody (Bill Scott), a dog with well-cultivated intelligence, his "pet boy" Sherman (Walter Tetley), and their adventures in time, courtesy of Peabody's "Waybac" time machine. The "pilot" episode of the series set the tone for much of what was to follow, and showed the audience exactly what kind of "man" Peabody was to be. After a shot of Peabody's penthouse apartment, we see Peabody standing on his head. "Please excuse the position," he says in his cultured, somewhat arrogant voice. "Just practicing my yoga." He introduces himself ("My name is Peabody.... I presume you *know* yours") and fills us in on his background. A "puppy prodigy" and university graduate, he has extensive experience in business (they called him "The Woof of Wall Street") and as a foreign diplomat (he can speak several languages, including English, occasionally all at once). He "adopted" Sherman out of feelings of loneliness and despite the fact that the authorities questioned his ability to be a proper guardian, which he proved that he was. (There are limits to his sympathy, however. When Sherman addresses him as "Daddy," he sternly rejects the appellation, telling—rather than asking—Sherman to call him "Mr." Peabody, "or, informally, Peabody.") The "Waybac" was developed by Peabody as a means of amusing Sherman, and was refined to the point where the duo could interact with people from the past. This was a good thing, considering that, in Ward's words, the historical characters that they met were all portrayed as "complete boobs."[135] Peabody was, however, *always* up to the task, as he never failed to remind both Sherman and the audience, since he was also the program's narrator, and therefore completely in charge of the story.

Historical accuracy was not apparent in these segments; indeed, the facts were more often distorted and ignored by the producers in favor of a few good laughs. We are repeatedly led to believe that history might have had to be rewritten without Peabody's interventions. The narratives gave their subject matter a beating with irreverent, anachronistic and modern topical humor, superimposing social and ethnic stereotypes over unlikely settings, and significantly devolving both the intelligence and resourcefulness of the human characters in relation to Peabody, the *ubermensch* figure who carefully and easily solved all of their problems every time. Throughout these installments, Sherman played the perfect "son" to his "father," asking questions and raising concerns for which Peabody always provided solutions. This was *Father Knows Best* played to its most absurd extreme, and the humor was heightened by the fact that "Father" was actually a dog. In the process, just as other segments of the *Rocky and Bullwinkle* program spoofed the malleable adaptability of Hollywood to outside forces, "Peabody" did the same things to events of the past, exposing them all as part of an elaborate shell game which was fairly simple and easy for an outside force like Peabody to manipulate. It was fortunate for the "heroes" of the past that Peabody's intentions were always honorable: one thing he was *not* was a con man.

Significantly, the Peabody character was able to acclimate into the upper end of an affluent "white" society, unlike Hanna-Barbera's animal characters. He succeeds in ridiculing and marginalizing a different social stereotype related to white men—the college-educated, intellectual character. In spite of his intelligence and resourcefulness, Peabody is in many ways a negative portrait of the intelligentsia. "Humility" is not a word that exists in his extensive vocabulary. He does not hesitate to remind Sherman (and the viewers) that *he* is in charge, and quickly puts the other characters in their place if they have delusions of outwitting him. The writers actually reinforce this position by giving Peabody a deified status. This is accomplished not simply through his own portrait but also through the portrayal of the other figures. The supporting cast is drawn as narrow stereotypes with broad foreign and American regional accents that make them look and sound foolish, even if they were really brilliant scientists, artists, writers, etc. All of this is done primarily to increase our impression of Peabody, but it also does the job of stoking the flames of his ego, making him even more arrogant. He is a positive *and* a negative specimen of masculinity, and therefore his segments give off a different but equally satiric vibe from the other Ward characters.

The message here is that having some intelligence may help you see the flaws of other people and situations more easily, but having too much of it will turn you into a control freak. In this way, Peabody represents one of the ultimate ways in which Ward left his audiences not only laughing but thinking—questioning ideas about masculinity and wisdom.

❖ ❖ ❖

Another Ward series that accomplished this goal was "Dudley Do-Right of the Mounties," which made its debut relatively late in Ward's oeuvre, premiering on *The Bullwinkle Show* in 1962, but quickly established itself as a popular attraction in its own way. Like the "Rocky and Bullwinkle" segments, it was structured as a satiric rejoinder to an overused and heavily conventional Hollywood narrative—the Canadian melodrama. As historian Pierre Berton has noted, the image of Canada as created by Hollywood had little to do with the realities of life in the country. Instead, it was reduced to a snow-covered fairytale paradise full of shallowly defined dramatic stereotypes.[136] This was an image that was ripe for satire, and Ward took full advantage of the opportunity he was given. What resulted was a traditional "Canadian" melodrama, full of stock situations and stereotypes, played at the cranking speed of a bedroom farce, which made it much more humorous than dramatic. By heavily ridiculing his subject matter, Ward proceeded to expose Hollywood conventions for the shams that they were.

This was particularly true of the title character (Bill Scott) and his opposite number, "arch-villain" Snidley Whiplash (Hans Conreid). Both characters are prisoners of the mechanics of melodrama, unable to do or say anything that does not fit in with their respective "heroic" or "villainous" personalities. Dudley is thoroughly obsessed with his role as a "heroic" male, and living up to his surname. This limits his personality severely, since someone who always "does right" is not very interesting on a level of dramatic tension, and therefore he never rises above the stereotype he is desperately trying not to be. Likewise, Whiplash is a melodrama stereotype *par excellence*, perpetually leering and threatening from behind his black cape. He would be a threatening villain if, like Boris Badenov, he were not entirely aware of the fact that he *is* a villain, which allows him to banter with and threaten the narrator in ways similar to those of Boris. In addition, Whiplash is given a richer and deeper character than Dudley, heightening the irony of the fact that the "bad guy" has the audience's sympathy in a way the hero does not. This is particularly the case with his stereotypical obsession with tying women to railroad tracks, which he is seen doing even in the main title sequence. Like an alcoholic, Whiplash maintains that he wants to stop "this terrible thing" but is utterly incapable of doing so. The inability of both Dudley and Whiplash to transcend the narrow categories of "hero" and "villain" renders their constant conflict pointless because it will never be fully resolved due to their perpetual mechanical acting-out of old patterns. Whiplash even goes so far as to say, in one episode, that it is "a waste of my time," since he knows how things will ultimately end in a way Dudley never will, which is one of the program's most obvious subtexts.

The two other major characters add a greater level of subversion to the proceedings, since they are not as strictly bound to the plot mechanics as are Dudley and Whiplash. Inspector Fenwick (Paul Frees), Dudley's perpetually blustering commanding officer, represents one level of this. A middle-aged British stereotype, he speaks in a voice that doesn't inspire confidence, rendering almost everything he says amusing even when he is trying to be dead serious. (Frees patterned the voice after British character actor Eric Blore, who specialized in playing these kind of effeminate, foppish characters, and Ward's use of this character type in a command position in the supposedly ultra-masculine RCMP is therefore a highly subversive act.) This ends up not confirming his authority and ability to act, but makes him a figure of mockery instead, though Dudley, of course, hardly notices this. Added to this is the Inspector's projection of a rugged dignity that Dudley unintentionally (and Whiplash intentionally) wounds repeatedly, giving this unlikely "boss" figure, at least temporarily, the sympathy not given to either the "hero" or the "villain" simply because he has to repeatedly put up with both of their crazy antics.

An even more subversive element is provided by Nell Fenwick (June Foray), the Inspector's daughter and Dudley's love interest. Nell, unlike her previous role models, is not a paper-doll cut-out version of Canadian womanhood. She is, in fact, the most multidimensional character in the series. We are able to see her character develop and become refined in ways which are impossible for the men, and with that comes an ability to beat all of them at their own games. As a consequence, Nell achieves a status which is not supposed to be available to "mere" women in the past time period of the stories. She is able to convince the audience easily, for example, that she can be a capable and effective RCMP officer in one episode and a lawyer in another, but the men in the series are so firmly set in a stereotypical "male" view of the world that they cannot accept these achievements, and belittle them by attempting to deceive her into accepting their view of the world, which she somewhat reluctantly does. But this does little to defeat the satiric subtext Ward injects into these stories— that the best "man" in this rugged "masculine" country is actually a *woman*, and not simply a stereotypical sexpot, but a cunning creature against whom the supposedly "heroic" and "villainous" men are utterly helpless. Just like "Rocky and Bullwinkle," "Dudley" turns Hollywood from a glorification of supposedly "positive" masculine "virtue" into a cruel and bitter joke, and with it questions the ability of dramatic narratives to present men as "heroic" figures in the first place.

◆ ◆ ◆

As demonstrated by his programming, Ward was not one who was squeamish about promoting himself and his work. And it would be this off-camera promotion that would ultimately cause the decline and demise of his studio, as much, as if not more, than the irreverent attitudes actually exhibited within his programming.

At both ABC and NBC, and with his longtime sponsor, General Mills, Ward repeatedly put himself in the doghouse with an irreverent attitude toward censorship and a Barnumesque zeal for promoting himself and his work. In terms of his work, Ward noted that "we want to prove we're funny by doing something fresh, not because someone else has already been funny."[137] That was apparent to anyone who viewed his work, but not always to those involved with its censorship. As columnist Dwight Newton wrote in 1961, the networks censorship departments and advertising agencies were often "appalled by ... Ward's cartoon endeavors because he is a nonconformist, a great dissenter, a stinging satirist, a sort of modern day Mark Twain in an industry that forever trembles at the thought of possibly offending a viewer or an advertiser."[138] Though approval from these groups, notes Keith Scott, was a commonplace practice in these more conservative times, the "unique nature" of the product "caused much panicking and compromise."[139] The conflicts ranged from minor ones regarding dialogue and the content of the episodes, about which Ward and the censors often disagreed, to more serious ones that the networks felt undermined them. A case in point was the live-action Bullwinkle puppet Bill Scott operated and voiced to introduce the first 13 installments of *The Bullwinkle Show*. From mocking the pretensions of Walt Disney's *Wonderful World of Color*, to satirizing Red Skelton, to finally suggesting that children remove the control knobs from their television sets so "we'll be sure to be with you next week," this segment caused no end of headaches for NBC and no end of their resentment toward Ward. It was no surprise that this segment was ultimately dropped.[140]

Ward did not confine his irreverence to the screen alone. He was notorious for the lengths to which he went to promote his work, which were seen as extravagant even for the time.[141] One example: the use of a Salvation Army–like promotion to launch *The Bullwinkle Show* on NBC in 1962. This was minor in comparison to other elaborate stunts: the renting of Coney Island to launch *Fractured Flickers* (see below), the erecting of a statue of Rocky and Bullwinkle on the Sunset Strip and particularly the campaign to gain statehood for Moosylvania, a fictional island featured in two "Rocky and Bullwinkle" installments, of which Bullwinkle was the hereditary "governor." Ward went so far with this as to have his longtime editor, Skip Craig, actually go to Minnesota and purchase an island that was within one of the state's many lakes to effectively serve as the real-life equivalent of the fictional island. Ward and publicist Howard Brandy next went to the White House for the president's approval of the statehood maneuver, only to be abruptly turned away. They had arrived in the midst of the Cuban Missile Crisis.

Further publicity gimmicks took the less elaborate form of humorous "mailers" sent out to network executives, regulators and publicists.[142] One invited these groups to promote the premiere of *The Bullwinkle Show* by spending the entire week before the premiere going around naked. The "How to Kill Yourself" campaign offered large sums of money to contestants willing to assault world leaders such as Fidel Castro and Mao Tse-tung if they would promote *The Bullwinkle Show* while doing it. And, in response to FCC Chairman Newton Minow's desire for TV programming that was less "violent," Ward offered a package of "non-violent" programming, including "Championship Hopscotch" to replace boxing, and "Hamlet" with a mandated "happy ending."[143] Minow, the target of the joke, seemed to understand it: he went so far as to request Ward produce additional material in the same line.

Not surprisingly, the program's on-camera baiting of censorship, and its producers flouting of conventional promotional mores, created considerable conflict with NBC, but, initially, good ratings prevented them from completely foreclosing on Ward. Eventually, though, the conflicts proved to be too much for the network. After one season in prime time, the program was demoted to a Sunday afternoon slot, where it managed to produce a final blast of irreverence with the "Wotsamatta U" sequence, satirizing college football in spite of the fact that its host network reaped considerable revenue from the broadcast of same.[144] By 1964, the program was history, and Ward was forced to turn to other venues to continue producing material with his trademark irreverence.

◆ ◆ ◆

Ward's post–*Rocky and Bullwinkle* career was checkered, marked more by an inability to realize desired projects than an actual availability to produce them. His burning of bridges with networks and sponsors during the *Rocky and Bullwinkle* era and beyond hampered him commercially, and prevented him from producing work that was of the same caliber as what had come before. Nevertheless, he was still able to create some products in the old line before he and his studio and staff were effectively exiled to the less financially threatening world of commercial advertising.

During 1963, Ward and Scott concentrated production on *The Nut House*, a series of blackout comedy skits airing on CBS that failed to be picked up as a series, and the aforementioned *Fractured Flickers*, picked up for syndication in the fall of 1963.[145] Hosted by Hans Conreid, the series was based on a simple premise: "Vintage [silent] films would be re-edited into crazy new stories, with the writers creating incongruous material to be read in funny voices over the mute images."[146] Thus, for example, Lon Chaney's characterization of "The Hunchback of Notre Dame" suddenly became the humorous saga of a cheerleader, and Rudolph Valentino's character in *Blood and Sand* became an insurance salesman rather than a matador. Linking this material was an extended interview segment between Conreid and a celebrity guest. Despite the success and the uniqueness of the project, it lasted for only one season in syndication.

Ward returned to animation with *Hoppity Hooper*, which aired on ABC during the 1964-65 season.[147] The storylines were very much in the fashion of the earlier *Rocky and Bullwinkle* series, but with a catch: this time, by sponsor fiat, the show was written specifically for a child audience. As a consequence, part of the program's ability to appeal to an adult audience was lost. This may account for the relative obscurity of this program in comparison to the rest of Ward's *oeuvre*. Based around the fictional community of Foggy Bog, Wisconsin, the title character (Chris Allen) was a naïve amphibian who had been hoodwinked into assisting the vulpine con artist "Professor" Waldo Wigglesworth (Hans Conreid) after the con artist somehow managed to convince Hoppity he was his long-lost "uncle." Further helping (or hindering) them was Fillmore Bear (Bill Scott), a genial idiot who dressed in Confederate soldier clothing and punctuated events by blowing his bugle at inopportune times. Though there was a high quality to some of the segments, such as "The Traffic Zone"[148] (a parody of *The Twilight Zone*[149]), the general attitude regarding the program was that it was inferior to Ward's previous work. The series was supplemented by previously produced Ward products and entered syndication briefly later in the 1960s.

By this time, Ward had begun a lucrative relationship producing commercials for Quaker Oats, particularly for Cap'n Crunch and other cereals, which kept the studio afloat into the 1980s.[150] Only one other series was produced, composed of three projects in development for some time at the studio, and contained in a series consisting of 17 episodes aired on ABC between 1967 and 1970. Each of the segments was notable for having a memorable theme song as well as a high component of the bizarre humor that remained the studio's hallmark. In this sense, it was the exception rather than the rule for the time and place at which it entered the television schedule. But, rather than being a return to form for the producer, it ended up being his swan song as a producer of narrative-based television animation.

The lead (and title) segment was "George of the Jungle," a parody of the "Tarzan" stories with "the flattest-sounding, non–Jungle name in the world"[151] for the lead character. Our hero (Bill Scott) was an incompetent, Tarzan-like figure who lived with his attractive wife, Ursula (June Foray), who had been raised in the outside world, and several animal friends. These included an ape named (appropriately) Ape (Paul Frees), whose speech was reminiscent of Ronald Colman; Shep, an elephant that George erroneously believed was a large puppy; and the Tooki Tooki Bird, who served as "the Mbwebwe Valley's answer to AT&T"[152] in spite of the fact that its vocabulary was limited to quoting its own name. George, a clumsy but well-meaning idiot, was unable to swing through the trees uttering his Tarzan-like yell without crashing at least once, which occasioned the use of the admonition "Watch out for that tree!" in the show's theme song. His lack of intellect was further emphasized by his regular referral to Ursula as "that long-haired fella who never shaves." In spite of this, George, along with his friends, managed to come out on the winning end against the likes of the trappers Tiger and Weevil; Jerry Mander, a "property developer, sub-divider and general contractor"; the powerful tycoon (or, to George, "typhoon") Seymour Nudnik; mad scientist

Dr. Chicago; and an eccentric big-game hunter known as the Duke of Ellington, who wanted George's head for his trophy room.

Similar absurdities were present in the two other segments of the program. "Tom Slick" was the saga of an ultra–good-guy car racer (Bill Scott) who apparently "made Dudley Do-Right look like one of the Manson family."[153] Accompanied by his girlfriend Marigold (June Foray) and his feisty grandmother/mechanic Gertie Growler (Scott), Tom raced his "Thunderbolt Grease Slapper" against a variety of opponents, most notably the Teutonic villain Baron Otto Matic (Paul Frees), and in a variety of ways, not only on land but also in the air and underwater. He ultimately won the races, more by accident than design. Although a "vast crowd" was always present, Hal Erickson[154] points out that it never seemed to sound like more than three people at one time, whose reactions were decidedly unenthusiastic whether they were saying "Yay" or "Boo."

The final segment was the longest one in gestation, dating back to a 1960 pilot film.[155] "Super Chicken" was perhaps the most absurd of the later group of Ward programs, focusing on the adventures of Pittsburgh-based, playboy rooster Henry Cabot Henhouse III (Bill Scott), who assumed the identity of the title character by drinking a mysterious "super sauce." Assisted by the timorous lion Fred (Paul Frees impersonating Ed Wynn), the surprisingly feeble fowl encountered a wide variety of absurd foes, including the Laundry Man, Dr. Gizmo, the Fat Man, Rotten Hood, The Muscle, and a gigantic mass of hair which, when reduced to baldness, became the Houston Astrodome. Fred's perennial complaints led to Super Chicken's admonition, "You knew the job was dangerous when you took it...," a line featured in the theme song that took on a popular life of its own.

One key difference between these segments and Ward's earlier work was the fact that the producer was not allowed by the network to continue the serialization format used before. As a consequence, Ward "was forced by running-time restrictions to go for quick reaction laughs rather than the subtly interwoven satire"[156] that had distinguished his earlier work. Still, the programs remained more effective in their more limited formats than many of their contemporary programs were in their original broadcast periods.

George of the Jungle was Ward's last original animated series to see production, though several ideas were developed, with some even managing to reach the stage of pilot films.[157] However, as a wave of conservatism struck television animation, Ward found himself increasingly relegated to the sidelines. In an interview, he blamed the process of operations at the networks as one of the main reasons for his slowing down:

> The real trouble with TV is that everyone is trying to please someone else. We've stopped going to the networks. They're friendly and nice, but we never get an affirmative answer. I really can't blame [them] ... they go the safe route. Any idea you take to a network has to go through fifteen guys. Fourteen of them may like it, but if the fifteenth says no, they all want to hedge and take a second look. If it's something wild, they back off.[158]

Ward concentrated much of his activity from the 1970s forward on honoring his commercial commitments to Quaker Oats, developing new pilot ideas, and operating a variety of sideline businesses, the most successful being Dudley Do-Right's Emporium, a souvenir shop opened in 1971.[159] But, facing increasing censorship and the loss of key talent, particularly through Bill Scott's death in 1985,[160] Ward's activity as a producer ceased entirely in the 1980s.

◆ ◆ ◆

Jay Ward died in 1989. Had he survived into the 1990s, however, he would have found that his ideas related to television animation production would have gained a receptive audience once again. He had effectively been forced out of business in the 1970s by a decline in interest and support for the manner in which he produced and promoted television animation. Yet the final decade of the 20th century found his *zeitgeist* very much present among the new generation of television animators, especially those using humor as their primary means of narrative expression.

Ward's humor had fundamentally been based on iconoclasm and irreverence, things that television in his prime was not fully prepared to incorporate into its narratives. The comedy in much of his programs depended entirely on the disjunction between the overused formats his characters were presented in and the manner in which they reacted to them. Certainly, following the Vietnam War and Watergate, with increasing numbers of the American citizenry becoming dyed-in-the-wool cynics, the stock of these tactics as humorous devices rose extensively. The live-action comic programming of the 1970s and onward employed this to a great degree, but it was not until the 1990s that television animation was able to do so. *The Simpsons*, for example, was very much the kind of program Ward would have made had he thought of applying his irreverent attitude toward the family situation comedy: the mildly jaded attitude of this program's humor owes much to Ward's house style.

Yet Ward's approach to narrative storytelling, as a fluid, flexible form rather than something written in stone, was something that would endure in the industry to an even greater degree. There are few television animation programs after the 1990s that do not employ in some way the deconstructionist, post-textual narrative style he introduced in his programs, even those of his one-time rivals at Hanna-Barbera/Cartoon Network and Disney and their associates at Nickelodeon. Characters often refer to the fact that they are "merely" cartoon characters, protest the aging mechanics used to propel their plots, describe others as representative of "stock" character types, and explain (for the benefit and amusement of the audience) the manner in which stories will unfold. And, like Ward's characters, they refuse to stand idly by and let events overwhelm them: they insist on being active participants in the development of their fictional lives.

Ward also pioneered and legitimized the parodying of other media forms. He was both a producer and a viewer of television, and Ward and his staff felt television could do a great deal better than it was doing. His characters' self-parodying attitude toward the medium in which they appeared echoes in the mouths of later characters, including those of *The Simpsons*. Even more indebted to Ward in this light are the works of Seth Macfarlane (whose series utilize Ward's formula with even more corrosive, Rabelaisian humor at their core) and Craig McCracken (especially in the critical portrayal of weak male authority figures in *The Powerpuff Girls*). The producers have secured this connection by paying Ward direct homage in their work: Ward characters have made cameo appearances in episodes of these series, while an entire episode of *The Powerpuff Girls* was conducted in the fashion of a typical "Rocky and Bullwinkle" installment. Ward was heavily criticized in his heyday, and driven out of television because he would not conform to the set standards of his time. Little did his critics know that he would have the last laugh.

Other Voices

While Hanna-Barbera and Jay Ward were the dominant voices in television animation production during this time, a number of other studios were also operating, some of them producing work that was equal in merit and influence to these two dominant studios, albeit, for many of them, far less in terms of total production output. This chapter concludes with a brief overview of some of these producers and studios and their output.

TOTAL TELEVISION PRODUCTIONS

The other major client of the Mexico-based Val-Mar/Gamma studios, Total Television's work is often confused with that of Jay Ward for precisely that reason. Nevertheless, this company's product was significantly different. As Hal Erickson notes, Ward's series were "classic[s]," whereas most of Total Television's work "merely filled up the room."[161] Much more focused on innocuous humor than satire, Total Television's work stands on its own merits today as materials of lasting significance in its own right.

A collaboration between ad men Buck Biggers and Chet Stover, the principal writers, along with art director Joe Harrington and sound recording artist Treadwell Covington, Total Television began operations in the early 1960s.[162] The first program to emerge from the alliance was *King Leonardo and His Short Subjects*, debuting on NBC in 1960 and running there for three seasons.[163] Set in the fictional African realm of Bongo Congo, it focused on the adventures of the titular leonine monarch (Jackson Beck) and his erudite, "true blue" skunk aide Odie Cologne (Allen Swift), as they dealt with the villainous aims of Biggy Rat (Beck) and Itchy Brother (Swift). These adventures took on the serialization format of Jay Ward's work but never equaled them in terms of length or content. Supporting these segments were "The Hunter," a dog detective voiced by Kenny Delmar in the style of the "Senator Claghorn" character he had created for radio's *Fred Allen Show* in the 1940s; and "Tooter Turtle," the tale of a milquetoast turtle who wanted to better himself and enlisted the magical services of Wizard the Lizard in order to achieve his aims, which inevitably backfired on him. Although the series managed to achieve the entertainment value that its network (NBC) and sponsor (General Mills) wanted, it was poorly plotted and staged, often repeating material and ideas with few variations. This would became the studio's Achilles heel in later years. Nevertheless, this program established Total Television as a credible producer, and helped Biggers and Stover to gain additional assignments from the networks, who were seemingly eager for what they could provide.

The second Biggers/Stover collaboration was slightly more successful. *Tennessee Tuxedo and His Tales* debuted on CBS in 1963 and ran there for three seasons.[164] Featuring more of an educational component than the previous series, the title segment focused on a "cynical" penguin (Don Adams) and his walrus companion Chumley (Bradley Bolke) as they sought adventure beyond the Megopolis Zoo in which they were housed. The educational component was provided by the all-knowing Mr. Whoopee (Larry Storch), who would illustrate essential information via a collapsible "three dimensional blackboard" when Tennessee and Chumley asked for his aid. As a consequence, this series serves as one of the first cartoons to combine education and entertainment—something that would become more commonplace in the following decade, albeit with less skill and subtlety. The supporting segments were the same as before, with the exception of a new feature, "The World of Commander McBragg," the limping saga of a boisterous, boastful army officer (Kenny Delmar) that failed to add any luster to what the company had already presented.

The third series highlighted what was by far the most famous product of the studio. *Underdog* debuted as the title segment of a popular series on NBC in 1964, switching to CBS in 1966 and returning to NBC in 1968.[165] Our hero (Wally Cox) was a mild-mannered canine shoeshine boy who, when trouble loomed, transformed himself into the title character, who spoke entirely in rhymed couplets. He was frequently forced to rescue his female friend, TV reporter Sweet Polly Purebred (Norma McMillan) from peril in the course of his seven-minute serialized adventures, which were structured in four parts each. The principal villains were the underworld kingpin Riff Raff and the mad scientist Simon Bar Sinister, though other, minor ones abounded as well. Memorable for its theme song, the series was chiefly marred by repetitious writing and dialogue, though this helped it endure with a younger audience. Initially supported by new episodes of "The Hunter" and "The World of Commander McBragg," the show in its CBS incarnation took on two new features. "Go Go Gophers" was a Western parody focusing on the incompetent efforts of Colonel Kit Coyote (Kenny Delmar) to rid the west of the surviving members of the Gopher Indian tribe; one writer went so far as to refer to it as "a comedy about genocide."[166] (The series nevertheless headlined a Total Television rerun package broadcast on CBS in 1968.) "Klondike Kat," meanwhile, focused on the incompetent title character, a member of the "Klondike Kops" who frequently tried and failed to arrest the cheese-stealing, *Quebecois*-accented mouse Savoir Faire.

After one final, minor series, *The Beagles*, airing on CBS in 1966,[167] the saga of Total Television came to an abrupt end with the closure of the Val-Mar/Gamma studio in 1969. However, the series the company produced, particularly *Underdog*, would endure in cable and syndication reruns for many years to come, ensuring the presence of Total Television among the "classic" television animation programs of the past.

Rankin-Bass

Another long-lasting partnership that emerged out of the advertising industry, Arthur Rankin, Jr., and Jules Bass produced an enviable body of work that has remained as influential as the work of their contemporaries. Working both in traditional animation, and in a new, stop-motion process known as "Animagic," they all but single-handedly helped to pioneer a new venue for television animation—the holiday special—while also producing a sizeable body of work in other ventures during the 1970s and 1980s. However, it was during this period that they produced many of the works that shaped their reputation in the coming years and would establish their studio as a power broker in the animation industry.[168]

New York native Rankin had a background in design and art acquired on the heels of his graduation from high school. Following service in the navy during World War II, he worked briefly at RKO before moving to ABC in 1948. He spent five years there, advancing to the role of art director while working on numerous broadcasts, before leaving in 1952 to form his own company. Work with the Gardner Advertising Agency led him into contact with Philadelphian Jules Bass, who worked his way up from mailroom clerk to become a partner in the agency. They eventually decided to strike out on their own, on a business model designed to, as Rankin later noted, combine "his advertising know-how with my television and artistic know-how."[169] By 1955, they established their own company, Videocraft International (later to become Rankin-Bass Productions in the early 1960s), along this model, with the two partners alternating between handling administrative and artistic duties while sharing a corporate byline. Initially concentrating on advertising, they diversified into fictional programming in the early 1960s with felicitous results.

Historian Rick Goldschmidt observes that the studio produced a number of interesting series during this period.[170] The first Rankin/Bass production was *The New Adventures of*

Pinocchio, which aired as a collection of five-minute segments on local children's programming during the early 1960s. Setting the template for a number of future projects, it adapted and updated a children's classic using the "Animagic" format to depict the adventures of the title character and his sidekick Cricket as they dealt with the conniving Foxy Q. Fibble and Cool S. Cat. The following year, a similar format was used for *Tales of the Wizard of Oz* to adapt L. Frank Baum's classic to the screen. (They would also produce a television special, *Return to Oz*, based on the same characters in 1964.) Later in the decade, they produced *The King Kong Show* for ABC in 1966, a cel animation program featuring the giant ape in two segments, and one segment of the supporting feature, "Tom of T.H.U.M.B.," regarding a diminutive secret agent and his Oriental sidekick. The decade ended with the *Smokey Bear Show*, produced for ABC in 1969. It was a cel animated series based on the "Animagic" special produced in 1966. More series would be produced in the 1970s and 1980s, as the company expanded beyond animation and television into producing new forms of entertainment.

But it was in a new area—the holiday special—that the company came to produce some of its most popular work.[171] The first project in this line was *Rudolph the Red Nosed Reindeer*. Based on the popular song, the program was an elaborate Christmas special debuting on NBC in 1964 and rebroadcasted regularly ever since. Financed chiefly by General Electric, an advertising client of Rankin-Bass, at a cost of $500,000, the lively production showcased the charms of the stop-motion "Animagic" process to its greatest lengths. The story of how the title character (voiced by Billie Mae Richards) was transformed from a "misfit" to a legendary figure was effectively told, and charmingly narrated by Burl Ives as Sam the Snowman, setting a clear pattern for other projects to follow in the same line. After the broadcast of this groundbreaking work, the studio suddenly became "very, very hot!"[172] to use Rankin's words, and other projects soon followed in its wake, using similar narrative and musical formulas. Using both "Animagic" and traditional cel animation to tell the stories, the work included the aforementioned "Wizard of Oz" and "Smokey the Bear" specials, a failed pilot for Edgar Bergen and Charlie McCarthy, an adaptation of Charles Dickens's *Cricket on the Hearth* starring Danny Thomas (NBC, 1967), the Thanksgiving-themed *Mouse on the Mayflower* (NBC, 1968), and an "Animagic" take on another Christmas standard, *The Little Drummer Boy* (NBC, 1968). The decade closed with the cel-animated tale of another "misfit" made good, *Frosty the Snowman* (CBS, 1969), based on another popular song and narrated charmingly by Jimmy Durante, which joined *Rudolph* in the pantheon of recurring Christmas favorites. The fact that these specials enjoyed high ratings on their original broadcasts, and remain popular to this day, are testament to the enduring quality of Rankin and Bass's work and the high standards they set for those who chose to follow in their

Rudolph, the Red-Nosed Reindeer, Rankin-Bass's 1964 holiday special (Classic Media/Photofest).

pioneering path. This would be a reputation that they would only enhance in the forthcoming years.

DePatie-Freleng

The partnership between legendary animation director Isadore "Friz" Freleng, whose career stretched back to the silent era and included many noteworthy productions at Warner Bros.,[173] and veteran businessman David DePatie, lasted 17 years and produced numerous animated productions along the way for both film and television. While not always of a high quality, the work of DePatie-Freleng Enterprises that has stood the test of time remains noteworthy, while even the less ideal projects have some interest historically.

Initially, and oddly, the studio's first major client was Freleng's former employer, Warner Bros., who hired the studio to produce new theatrical cartoons under its own masthead. This relationship lasted for four years until the studio re-organized its own animation department again. The general consensus is that these cartoons were inferior to what had been produced before, with Leonard Maltin going so far as to call them "abysmal."[174] This could not be said for the Pink Panther series, debuting in 1964 and featuring what became the studio's trademark character. A commission to produce the title sequence for the motion picture *The Pink Panther* led to the creation of the title character, who became, in effect, the studio's mascot. A long running, Academy Award–winning series of animated short films followed,[175] supplemented by several companion series, including "The Inspector," an animated take on the Inspector Clouseau character from the films; "The Ant and the Aardvark," an unorthodox animal conflict series; "Roland and Ratfink," an idealized good and bad guy; and "Hoot Kloot," a stereotyped Southern "redneck" sheriff. Though the series all started out well, the quality of the writing declined rapidly. By 1969, it was apparent where these products now belonged, and *The Pink Panther Show*, a repackaged version of these and other short films, began airing on NBC, where it remained under various names and formats throughout the 1970s.

By then, however, DePatie-Freleng had joined the ranks of television animation producers, producing work that was no better and no worse than what had come before.[176] The first series to be produced by the studio was *Super Six*, debuting on NBC in 1966, focusing on a bunch of bizarre characters working for the "hero for hire" service Super Services, Inc. Also featured were the inept cowboy hero Super Bwoing, and the ethnically jumbled characters the Brothers Matzoriley. It was undistinguished in the ratings, but was kept around until 1969 mostly due to a lack of a desire to replace it. The second series was far worse in quality. *Super President and Spy Shadow* aired on NBC only during the 1967-68 season. The former segment focused on U.S. President James Norcross, who possessed superpowers and moonlighted as a superhero, while the latter focused on private investigator Richard Vance, who had an independently functioning shadow that helped him in his job. The National Association for Better Broadcasting, a social activist group, went so far as to call it "[a]n all time low in bad taste," while David DePatie himself made it clear that it was "the worst thing we've ever made."[177] So much for the quality of that series. A far better reflection of the studio's abilities was *Here Comes the Grump*, airing on NBC beginning in 1969,[178] a "quest"-oriented series focusing on the youthful Terry Dexter's efforts to free a faraway land and its leader, Princess Dawn, from the gloom-inducing title character. Comic slapstick and capers abounded, but were not always present in the studio's later work.

Although DePatie-Freleng's work was not always of the highest quality, the studio had established its reputation as an effective if uninspired producer of television animation, and would remain so during the 1970s.

KING FEATURES

Under the leadership of Al Brodax, the syndication arm of the Hearst newspaper group entered the field of animation production initially to take advantage of the increasing stock of its owned properties as animated features. However, it briefly expanded beyond this to produce some of the most diverse and interesting television animation of the 1960s.

The studio's first venture into television animation production came in 1960, when Brodax engineered a deal to produce a new series of Popeye cartoons for television, effectively continuing the recently expired, long-running theatrical animation series (see Chapter 1). However, no one animation studio of the time was able to meet Brodax's demand that all of the required material be produced within a two- to three-year span, so King Features subcontracted much of the work to a variety of different studios. Involved in this work were Popeye's original home base, the Paramount studio, as well as Larry Harmon Productions (see also below); Jack Kinney Studios; Gene Deitch Studios; Rembrandt Films, TV Spots; and the British firm Halas and Batchelor, who completed the animation based on storyboards devised at King Features itself. Paramount also distributed its productions in the series for theatrical release. As Leonard Maltin observes, "To say that the results were inconsistent would be a mild understatement."[179] Hal Erickson was more to the point: the use of this practice of multiple studios with different approaches created "the most schizophrenic cartoon series on television, one character in search of a style."[180] Nevertheless, the program's production as color films ensured their value as a syndicated package for many years, in spite of the internal differences in production and style resulting from the variances in studio origins.[181]

The success of the "Popeye" package led to the bundling of adaptations of three other King Features–owned properties—"Beetle Bailey," "Snuffy Smith" and "Krazy Kat"—under the umbrella title of "The King Features Trilogy" for sale to local stations.[182] Produced under the same conditions as the "Popeye" cartoons, they resulted in the same types of stylistic inconsistencies that had marred the earlier package, although "Krazy Kat" in particular did attempt to retain the flavor of its original source. Nevertheless, the program was a disappointment artistically and, ultimately, in the ratings as well.

More successful artistically and commercially were the two other major productions from the studio during the decade. *The Beatles* (ABC 1965–69) cleverly depicted the Fab Four in animated form, though their voices were imitations done by Paul Frees and Lance Percival. Aping the style of the Beatles films directed by Richard Lester, the series possessed a humorous ambiance that compensated for its flaws. Much of the work was done by the British-based TVC studios, later to produce the Beatles animated feature film *Yellow Submarine*.[183] More conventional in style and tone was *Cool McCool* (NBC 1966–69), devised by *Batman* creator Bob Kane, about the adventures of an incompetent secret agent who nevertheless manages to succeed; a supporting feature showcased the title character's equally inept policeman father, Harry McCool, and his partners Tom and Dick.[184]

UNITED PRODUCTIONS OF AMERICA (UPA)

The story of UPA in the television era demonstrates the destruction of the influential "limited animation" style the studio developed for theatrical animation in the 1940s and

1950s. Though initially able to present work on a par with previous achievements, the later work of the studio, under less sympathetic management, was less distinguished.

The first UPA venture, and, in fact, one of the earliest network television animation programs of any kind, was *The Gerald McBoing Boing Show*, which began on CBS in 1956, and featured the sound-effects-speaking boy who had starred in the studio's landmark Academy Award–winning short of 1950.[185] Produced by studio veteran Robert "Bobe" Cannon, with Bill Scott as associate producer and chief writer, the series, in addition to the title star, included features such as the child entertainers The Twirlinger Twins; Dusty of the Circus, who could communicate with animals; illustrated vignettes animated by Ernest Pintoff; and segments such as "Meet the Artist" and "Meet the Inventor," which proved to be the blueprint for some of Scott's later work with Jay Ward (see above). The problem was that, while visually distinguished in the UPA fashion, it was simply not so in any other way. As Leonard Maltin notes, "The show had definite merit, but the parts were greater than the whole[,] and the program's gentle spirit endeared it more to PTA groups and television critics than to children."[186] That the program managed to survive in its Sunday afternoon timeslot for nearly two years was more a goodwill gesture than anything else.

Internal friction and the departure of much of the original UPA staff in the following years finally led UPA co-founder Stephen Bosustow to throw in the towel, selling the studio to the much less artistically inclined producer Henry Saperstein in 1959. The Saperstein era saw the studio concentrate much more aggressively on television production, but in the process it "discarded its reputation for quality in one fell swoop."[187] The focus of production during the remainder of the decade would be on two characters: Mr. Magoo (voiced by Jim Backus), the nearsighted, crochety old man who had essentially become the company's star character, and Dick Tracy, Chester Gould's legendary police detective of comic strip fame. Magoo first starred in 130 short cartoons and some more ambitious projects, made between 1960 and 1962, marketed by the studio on a barter syndication basis to local stations.[188] Although formulaic and repetitious due to the nature of its production process, the series survived, as many television animation properties of this time did, because of the fact that it was produced in color, making it more valuable than earlier black-and-white properties. This was not the case with an ambitious 1962 holiday special telecast on NBC. *Mr. Magoo's Christmas Carol* perfectly cast Magoo in the role of Scrooge, and benefitted from the presence of a talented cast of performers, as well as a memorable score by veteran songwriters Jule Styne and Robert Merrill. The increasingly elastic nature of the character was fully exploited in his last major vehicle, *The Famous Adventures of Mr. Magoo*, airing on NBC during the 1964-65 season, which saw him ambitiously and often effectively cast as the likes of Dr. Watson, Cyrano De Bergerac, Don Quixote, Ishmael in *Moby Dick*, Gunga Din, and others.

The lavishness of the later Magoo projects was absent in the far less plush approach taken with the 130 *Dick Tracy* cartoons, even though Chester Gould himself was involved in the production of the initial films.[189] Packaged as a series of wraparounds for local stations to provide host inserts, the cartoons did not actually feature much of Dick Tracy himself. Instead, Tracy would farm out much of the actual work to one of his four major deputies: corpulent Heap O'Calorie, police dog Hemlock Holmes (paired with the comical "Retouchables"), or, more troubling, two very visible ethnic caricatures: fast-running Latino Go Go Gomez and Asian martial arts expert Joe Jitsu, who dispatched opponents while uttering such things as "so sorry" and "excuse, please." Gould's villains—Flattop, Mumbles, Pruneface, The Brow, et al.—came off considerably better in the limited format. The program benefitted from being in color and managed a long run in many markets until the 1980s, when controversy over the Gomez and Jitsu characters helped force it off the air.

For much of the remainder of its existence, UPA concentrated its efforts on marketing rather than production, a sad end to a studio whose work had once been influential and lasting in its impact on both animators and viewers.

TERRYTOONS

After Paul Terry sold his studio to CBS in 1955 for a total of three and half million dollars the new owners began turning production away from theatrical animation toward that of the television variety, and sometimes both simultaneously, for another decade before finally forcing the closure of the studio for financial reasons.[190] The reason for his sale, Terry claimed, was primarily financial, but also because the new medium helped make his properties valuable again:

> We never made a great deal of money [in theatrical animation]. The great boon, as far as I'm concerned, was when television came along and made all this old stuff valuable again. Otherwise, you never would have heard of Terrytoons. It was just a hand-to-mouth business. You made a living. Sure, you paid your bills and had enough to go ahead for another year, like most businesses do. But we kept laying these negatives up, and then television came along; they were hungry for material. They've done better in television than they ever did in the theatres.[191]

The irony of the situation, however, notes Leonard Maltin, was that Terry could have earned much more money out of his library and characters, considering the large amount of money CBS, and its syndication arm, Viacom, would earn from them in the years to come, both from the older projects, and from newer projects made directly for television.[192]

CBS's employment of Terrytoons took two distinct forms. The first was to create packages of older material for rebroadcast in new ways. One form of this was demonstrated by *CBS Cartoon Theater*, a package airing in prime time during the summer of 1956 and hosted by the little-known Dick Van Dyke, which could be considered one of the first of its kind.[193] Far more long-lasting and successful was a series top-lined by the studio's most famous character, Mighty Mouse, though again for the most part these were simply reruns of earlier theatrical cartoons. Television audiences did not seem to mind this, however. *Mighty Mouse Playhouse* debuted on CBS in 1955 and continued until 1966, with as high as a 11.6 rating and 45.8 percent share of the audience during its run.[194]

Original productions were not ignored. Under the leadership of Gene Deitch, the studio produced the stylistically ambitious "Tom Terrific" series, which aired as a segment of CBS's *Captain Kangaroo* during the 1950s and 1960s. Leonard Maltin considers it "one of the finest cartoons ever produced for television,"[195] but the limitations of its format, coupled with the fact that it was filmed in black and white rather than color, meant that it has not received much play in recent years.The title character was a young boy with a funnel-shaped hat that allows him, chameleon-like, to assume a wide variety of guises. Using these quasi–super-heroic abilities, Tom, accompanied by his dog, Mighty Manfred, dealt with a variety of foes in a cliff-hanger format, particularly Crabby Appleton, cheekily described as being "rotten to the core." Drawn in an artistically spare fashion but with good scripting, the show possessed appeal to both children and adults.However, studio business manager Bill Weiss fired Deitch in 1958, meaning that later productions of the studio would mostly be less distinguished. The relationship with *Captain Kangaroo* continued through another, minor series, *The Adventures of Lariat Sam*, which aired on the program during the 1960s.[196]

Subsequent projects from the studio fulfilled the double-duty requirements of exhibition on film and television while forcing the studio to expand its limited staff to meet these requirements. *Deputy Dawg*, debuting in 1960, focused on a slow-witted Southern-accented canine law officer, and was distinguished by the voice work of the talented and versatile comedian Dayton Allen. This series, initially made for television, was popular enough with Southern audiences that it was, in fact, released to theaters in those areas.[197] *The Hector Heathcote Show*, airing on NBC between 1963 and 1965, focused on the title character, a bumbling inventor who nevertheless changed the course of history with his work; he was supported by Hashimoto, a judo-skilled Japanese mouse, and Sidney, a profoundly neurotic elephant.[198] All three characters also appeared in theatrical series. The syndicated *Astronut Show*, airing in 1965, focused on the friendly alien title character and his relationship with the human Oscar Mild; this series, like *Deputy Dawg*, was filled out by cartoons from the studio library.[199]

The last major television project to emerge from the studio came courtesy of new studio head Ralph Bakshi, who had begun working at the studio as a teenager in 1956 and came into a leadership role ten years later.[200] Commissioned by Fred Silverman, *The Mighty Heroes*, airing on CBS during the 1966-67 season, was a superhero program that spoofed the genre at the same time as it enacted its clichés; in that sense, it predated similar approaches taken during the 1990s and 2000s. The group consisted of Diaper Man (a talking baby, and thus a clear, if milder, forerunner for *Family Guy*'s Stewie Griffin [see Chapter 6]), Tornado Man, Rope Man, Strong Man and Cuckoo Man, whose personalities were as one-dimensional as their names implied. Similarly designed were the villains, including the Junker, the Stretcher, the Shrinker, the Enlarger, etc. Although the premise seemed limited, Bakshi's emerging skills as a director distinguished it. "While hampered by the severe limitations of movement imposed by short schedules and tight budgets," notes Leonard Maltin, "Bakshi still managed to give these cartoons life and zest."[201] The project, unfortunately, ended after 26 episodes, after which Bakshi went elsewhere to further a distinguished but controversial career in both theatrical and television animation.

Production gradually slowed after that point, with no future projects for television in spite of some planning, and the studio doors were closed after the 1960s. However, the studio's work remained visible and profitable as syndication packages, and, despite the artistically mixed quality of the total product, have remained so.

Lee Mendelson and Bill Melendez

These producers—documentary filmmaker Mendelson and veteran animator Melendez—are known chiefly for one thing: their animated adaptations of Charles Schulz's *Peanuts* comic strip, which appeared periodically for the better part of four decades, from the 1960s to the 2000s. Yet, given the quality of this work, that is enough to secure them a significant position in television animation history. Working directly and closely with Schulz, they preserved the integrity and simplicity of the artist's work, and therefore ensured their own work would achieve the same cultural immortality as Schulz's strip.[202]

The relationship between Schulz and the producers began in 1963, when Mendelson approached Schulz about producing a documentary about him,[203] which initially went unaired. For the special, some original animation of the characters was commissioned. This was produced by veteran animator Jose "Bill" Melendez, who had gained Schulz's trust through animating his characters in a series of commercials for the Ford Motor Company in the late 1950s. Melendez, born in Mexico, moved to Arizona as a teenager, and then to California, where, while still a relatively young man, he joined the staff of the Walt Disney studio in 1938. He remained until the divisive strike in 1941, having become an active union member by this time. He spent the balance of the 1940s at Warner Bros., moving to UPA in 1948 and then briefly back to Warner Bros. By the 1950s, he had begun focusing his energy on commercial production, working for John Sutherland Productions and Playhouse Productions, producing over a thousand commercials and industrial films and winning numerous international awards along the way. By 1964, he had established his own eponymous firm for this purpose, around the time he was first approached by Mendelson and Schulz for work on the documentary special.[204]

Schulz had long resisted turning his comic strip characters into animated figures, believing that they would be corrupted in the process, but Mendelson and Melendez were able to convince him otherwise. While the documentary failed to sell, it did result in a beneficial side project. In May of 1965, John Allen, an executive with the McCann-Erickson advertising firm, noted to Mendelson that one of the agency's clients, Coca-Cola, was interested in sponsoring a special for Christmas featuring the *Peanuts* characters. Could this be produced? Mendelson agreed, even though it gave Schulz, Melendez and himself only six months of lead time.[205]

Fortunately, the trio had already developed a strong working relationship based on mutual trust and respect. As Schulz biographer David Michaelis has observed, "Theirs was a highly productive collaboration, each bringing something characteristically valuable to the work."[206] The pattern for subsequent projects was set: Schulz scripted, Melendez storyboarded, directed and supervised the voice recordings, and Mendelson oversaw production. Some immediate decisions were made that would have major impacts on the final product. The characters were to be voiced by real child actors rather than adults.[207] At Schulz's insistence, there was to be no pre-recorded laughter on the sound track, then considered to be a staple of prime-time television animation production. And, in particular, Schulz's desire to have Linus recite from the Bible for an entire minute for a climactic scene posed particular problems: the special was to air on network television via CBS, and the general attitude toward religion in network television at that time was largely to pretend that it simply did not exist. Schulz, however, stood firm on this point, and the scene remained as a critical part of the story—in which the perennially disappointed Charlie Brown attempts to discover the true meaning of Christmas within the increasingly vapid commerciality surrounding the holiday.

CBS executives were initially unimpressed with the results; indeed, Mendelson and Melendez, due to some technical errors in the initial film print, felt they had failed as well. "If the show hadn't already been scheduled to air in six days," Mendelson later observed, "it might not have been broadcast."[208] But broadcast it was, in December 1965, as *A Charlie Brown Christmas*. Bolstered by its humorous, powerful storyline, as well as the innovative musical score provided by jazz musician Vince Guaraldi, the special was an enormous success, both critically and in the ratings. The minimalist approach to animation evocatively recreated Schulz's trademark drawing style without compromising it, and the final work betrayed no artistic sacrifices. The ultimate rewards came late in the following year when the special won an Emmy for "Outstanding Children and Young People's Program"—one of several the cumulative series would win over the following years—as well as a Peabody award for its creative excellence. It has since become a Christmas holiday tradition of sorts, broadcast annually to appreciative audiences.

The Mendelson/Melendez/Schulz team soon became an active partnership, producing additional specials at network request. In particular, *It's the Great Pumpkin, Charlie Brown* would become as much of a Halloween-themed TV staple as its predecessor became for Christmas, as would *A Charlie Brown Thanksgiving* for its eponymous holiday. Eventually, they expanded into producing feature films about the characters, as well as some limited, short-run television series. Yet, regardless of what form they took or what subject matter they dealt with, the trio ensured that the essential heart and themes of Schulz's comic strips remained intact. Indeed, it would be these specials, as much as Schulz's own comics, that helped to secure for his characters the legendary status they have achieved and—regarding their depiction of children and childhood-related themes, in particular—their lasting and continued influence within the seemingly limited confines of television animation.

Chuck Jones at MGM

Although he was one of the harshest critics of the "limited" aspects of television animation, Chuck Jones was still able to make his mark as a producer of television animation in the 1960s through his short association with MGM. While his work at the studio was largely a footnote to his successful earlier career at Warner Bros., he was, through the sustained artistic quality of his product, able to make a significant impact upon audiences.

After Warner Bros. shut down its animation department in 1963, Jones, along with producer Les Goldman, established Tower 12 Productions. After producing some projects on their own, MGM approached the company about reviving the studio's "Tom and Jerry" series, in the process absorbing the Tower 12 concern. Jones accepted "solely because the budgets I submitted would allow me to continue with full animation,"[209] which was essential to his vision of animation. Although he had the services of many of the animators he had worked with at Warner Bros., this series of films were uneven at best. Jones had far more success with an animated adaptation of Norton Juster's book *The Dot and the Line*, narrated by Robert Morley, which won an Academy Award in 1965.[210]

It was perhaps this success that most convinced the noted children's book author and illustrator, Dr. Seuss, to begin work with Jones on the first major animated adaptations of his work,[211] something that he had largely resisted until this time. Under his "true" identity of Theodore "Ted" Geisel, the author had worked with the animator on "Private Snafu," a wartime series of short films intended for soldiers,[212] and an ongoing friendship resulted. The mutual assurance between the pair was most evident in their adaptation of the author's Christmas-themed morality play, *How the Grinch Stole Christmas*, originally broadcast in 1966. Narrated by Boris Karloff, whose voice accurately captured both the moralistic sentiments of the fable-like story and the cunning personality of the Grinch, the special cost its broadcast network, CBS, approximately $350,000, thanks to financial assistance from the Foundation for Commercial Banks, the sponsor of the original broadcast.[213] In spite of the lavish cost, an outgrowth of Jones's determined attitude to maintain full animation, the program was a success, winning a Peabody Award and remaining a holiday staple on both network and cable television. The commitment to quality was also evident in the second Seuss/Jones collaboration, *Horton Hears a Who!*, released in 1970 and also a Peabody winner, which was equally effective in defining the theme of personhood in spite of size. The previous

Chuck Jones at the drawing board in 2000 (Warner Bros./Photofest).

year also saw the release of Jones's collaboration with another highly individualized artist—Walt Kelly, creator of the *Pogo* comic strip—for *The Pogo Special Birthday Special*, broadcast on NBC, which was equally faithful to its source material, down to the fact that both Kelly and Jones provided voices for some of the characters.[214]

In spite of these successes, MGM, in the process of going through some difficult executive upheavals, was unable and unwilling to continue to support Jones's lavish approach to animation, largely because they were losing interest in the art form altogether. "[They] saw no future in $100,000 a year net from every TV special," noted Jones, "so that was that."[215] Consequently, Jones resigned from the company in 1970.

Through his company, Chuck Jones Enterprises, Jones produced a number of other acclaimed specials during the 1970s and 1980s, as well as working on periodic revivals of his characters at Warner Bros., and remained active until his death in 2002. Yet, although his MGM period was an abbreviated one, it was a latter-day highpoint in a sense of his long and distinguished career, and proved to others active elsewhere in the field of television animation that the application of higher than average standards to the art form, though costly, was still effective in presenting stories. This attitude and approach would become more definite and influential as the decades progressed, a tribute to Jones's lasting influence on the field of animation as a whole.

BOB CLAMPETT

An animator and producer known for his bizarre sense of humor and vividly conceived characters, Clampett began his career as one of the major architects of the zany Warner Bros. studio style of the late 1930s and 1940s.[216] While he pursued avenues in a variety of ventures, animated and otherwise, during his career, his stylistic approach was always unique and identifiable. His one major venture into television animation in the 1960s was no exception.

Born in San Diego, California, in 1915, Clampett grew up in Hollywood obsessed with the burgeoning film industry. At an early age, he assisted his aunt Charlotte Clark in designing and marketing the first Mickey Mouse dolls. He also displayed an early talent for drawing, and, after having drawings published in the *Los Angeles Times*, the rival *Examiner* recruited him on a part-time basis. Through his school career, he regularly contributed to the school papers and other artistic ventures.

Following his graduation in 1931, Clampett began pursuing a full-time career as an animator at Harman-Ising Studios, remaining with their distributor, Warner Bros., when the producers left in 1933. By 1937, he was made a director, after an apprenticeship with Tex Avery, who shaped his comic style. During this time, he showed himself to be an innovative and highly gifted director. Highlights of his career included the bizarre classic *Porky in Wackyland* (1938) as well as more controversial fare, such as *Coal Black and De Sebben Dwarfs* (1943), a blackface parody of the "Snow White" story. Yet whether he was working on one-shots or films featuring the studio's soon-to-be iconic characters (many of which he played a major role in creating), Clampett's bizarre, brash and original form of humor was always evident in his work.

Leaving Warner Bros. in 1946, Clampett worked briefly for Columbia and Republic before setting his sights on the then-new medium of television in 1949. Initially airing locally on a daily basis in Los Angeles, *Time for Beany* was a 15-minute puppet show that gained a national audience before ceasing in 1955. The lead characters were colorful in the typical Clampett fashion: propeller-wearing Beany Boy, his devoted friend Cecil the Seasick Sea Serpent, and Beany's uncle, tale-spinning Captain Horatio Huffenpuff, who commanded the *Leakin' Lena*. Villainy was supplied in the form of the black-clad Dishonest John, prone to exclaiming "Nya Ha Ha" to establish his presence. The series combined thrilling adventures directed at children with inside jokes directed at adults. Clampett's love of wordplay and puns was evident in many of the settings featured on the show—the Jingle Jangle Jungle, the Ruined Ruins, and the Schmoon (the moon of the Moon)—as well as in the names of the supporting characters, such as Tearalong the Dotted Lion and the Terrible Three Headed Threep. Given the quality of this series, it was not surprising that it acquired two Emmy Awards during its run; prominent fans included Lionel Barrymore, Groucho and Harpo Marx, and Albert Einstein.

In 1959, Clampett converted the series to animation, through a production deal with television distributor Associated Artists Productions, which had achieved success with distributing "Popeye" and early "Bugs Bunny" cartoons. A total of 104 productions were planned in the series, all of which Clampett claimed to have produced in one weekend! United Artists, the parent company of A.A.P., distributed the earliest cartoons in the series internationally, beginning with *Beany and Cecil Meet Billy the Squid*. Soon afterwards, Mattel Toys took over sponsorship of the series, with the theatrical cartoons mixed in with new made-for-television productions. Beginning in 1962, *Matty's Funnies with Beany and Cecil* began airing on the ABC network, where it remained for six years, and then entered syndication, where it remained successful for many years. The series retained most of the characters, situations and satire that had contributed to the success of the original puppet show, though, for the most part, it was adapted to changing times and the differences between puppet shows and television animation.

It was not entirely smooth sailing for Clampett, though. Much like Jay Ward (see above), he had a definite, ingrained approach to humor that did not endear him to critics and sponsors, even if it did succeed in helping him gain and maintain a loyal following of fans. He later complained that he was very much constrained by the conservative nature of sponsorship during that period.[217] In spite of that, much like Ward as well, the series regularly featured humor that attacked advertisers, celebrities (particularly Walt Disney) and authority figures, as well as approaches to humor that were overblown or even anachronistic at times. As Hal Erickson observes, "If Clampett thought a Jewish Indian was funny, he'd have a Jewish Indian, and hang the consequences."[218] It was likely for this reason that the show's production was limited to the 26 original episodes produced, in spite of the program's popularity. This popularity, much like Jay Ward's, ensured the enduring appeal of the characters to more than one generation of television viewers.

Clampett spent much of the remainder of his life producing commercials and making well-received personal appearances across the country, as well as reaping the rewards of domestic and overseas rerun sales of the *Beany and Cecil* series. This culminated in the release of the entire series on home video by RCA-Columbia in 1983. Unfortunately, Clampett died of a heart attack in Detroit in 1984 while undertaking promotion of this very package. However, his groundbreaking work in theatrical animation, television, and television animation had begun to be rediscovered at this time and remains appreciated. *Beany and Cecil*, in particular, retains a devoted cult following, much like the work of Jay Ward, precisely because it understood that television animation could attract a more sophisticated (read: adult) audience. Its approach, and its example, would be extensively emulated in future years by a new generation who understood exactly what they had to offer.

Art Clokey

Traditional cel animation was the dominant art form within television animation, and has largely remained so. Other forms of animation, particularly in terms of the experimental variety, were noticeable more for their absence than their presence. One notable exception during this period was the clay animation of Art Clokey, who demonstrated that there was a place for his chosen art form for commercial and didactic use. However, a variety of personal and business problems prevented Clokey from fully exploiting the potential of the art form which he initiated, and from establishing a solid business.

Born on October 12, 1921, in Detroit, Clokey had a difficult childhood. Essentially abandoned by his mother after his father's death in an automobile accident, he was adopted by a nationally known composer, Joseph Clokey, and relocated to the West Coast.[219] After service in World War II, he initially studied for the Episcopal ministry before drifting into the study of film at USC. He was attracted to the dimensions of clay animation because it provided him with more of a multidimensional canvas to work on, and because, as he later remarked, "It was cheaper than getting actors."[220]

He taught at the Harvard Military Academy, where he earned the chance to exhibit his pet character—Gumby, a green humanoid boy figure—for 20th Century–Fox executive Sam Engel, who thought the character had considerable potential for exhibition as a children's property. Beginning with the short film *Gumbasia*, in 1953,[221] the character and his various sidekicks—most particularly his orange horse friend, Pokey—were sold as a series to NBC in 1956. It first appeared as a segment of the popular children's program *Howdy Doody* before it became a series in 1957. It later entered syndication in 1959. A second series of Gumby adventures would be produced for syndication in 1966 and 1972, while a third, "all-new" series would be produced in 1988.[222] Clokey worked on a deliberate and rudimentary schedule, particularly initially, when his budget was around $700 per minute. The full-color six-minute films, structured as two to three part adventures, were meticulously filmed on a frame-by-frame basis with only slight character movement. The episodes were distinguished in particular through the elasticity of the characters. Gumby would "stretch, shrink, disintegrate, roll into a ball, multiply, and in general glide weightlessly from gag situation to plot point to visual non-sequitur with the brisk nonchalance of a two-year-old who fully accepts the absurdities of the world with the innocence of the untaught."[223] The character drew his eternal optimism and appearance in part from Clokey's adopted father, while the innocent nature of the episodes came from Clokey telling the stories to his children prior to putting them before the cameras. "The love I had for them would be translated onto film," he later said.[224]

In 1961, Clokey turned his now-established "pixilation" technique to another, slightly more realistic form of animated storytelling. *Davey and Goliath* was unique among television animation programs in that it was financed by a religious organization—the United Evangelical Lutheran Church of America.[225] However, despite its religious origins, it was never overtly ecclesiastic. The series focused on 11-year-old Davey Hanson and his dog Goliath, who could talk, but only to Davey. The 64 15-minute episodes were adventures designed to test the heroes' faith in their community, friendship, and faith, only to have all doubts resolved by the end. Despite the religious nature of the series, and the lack of additional episodes beyond the initial group due to lack of funding, the program was successful, and remains an attraction particularly toward religious-minded television programmers. Clokey himself, however, found his own Episcopalian views coming into conflict with those of his Lutheran sponsors, and he ultimately left the series for this reason.

In the mid–1960s and early 1970s, Clokey's career was damaged by fallout from his personal life. Divorce from his wife, and the sudden death of his daughter, caused him to undergo extensive psychotherapy, while career opportunities diminished.[226] Eventually, however, he remarried and resurrected his career, producing the short art film *Mandala* in 1975, reflecting his growing interest in Eastern spiritual philosophy. Establishing Premavision Studios, he produced the aforementioned "all-new" Gumby series in 1988 and a feature film with the same characters in 1995, while also producing a new Davey and Goliath special in 2004. Since that time, while being honored for his past achievements in the field of clay animation, he has continually sought new opportunities to bring his now-legendary characters to the attention of new generations.

JOE ORIOLO

A native of Union City, New Jersey, Oriolo was one of many animators whose career began with drawing as a child.[227] He attended Union High School and Cooper Union and worked as a show card writer for Sears Roebuck before beginning his career in animation. He began at the Max Fleischer Studio as an errand boy in 1933 and gradually worked his way up to animator, moving with the Fleischers when they relocated to Miami in 1938. In turn, when the Fleischer studio was re-organized as Famous Studios in 1942 in New York, Oriolo went back. It was during this time that he created the now-familiar character of Casper the Friendly Ghost, only to lose artistic and financial control of the character to Paramount and end up fighting losing battles over the years to gain it back.[228]

Oriolo left Famous Studios in 1945 to work as a freelance animator and cartoonist. Under this arrangement, he was recruited by Otto Messmer to become his assistant and ultimately his successor on the "Felix the Cat" comic strip. Recognizing that animation and merchandising possibilities still existed in the old character, Oriolo, in the 1950s, made arrangements to bring the character to television by arranging for a television production unit to be established under the umbrella of the company managing the merchandising of the character. Oriolo ran into opposition from those who considered Felix a dated character, and he was only able to interest Trans Lux Studios in financing a series after putting up his own money to produce a pilot film.

Beginning production in 1958, but not released to television until 1960, the *Felix the Cat* series consisted of 260 color episodes, most divided into cliff-hangers.[229] While it was eventually to achieve success in syndicated distribution, the series suffered from a number of creative and technical flaws that prevented it from being a success in execution. The limited budgets—$5,000 per episode—were but one cause of this. Another reason was the fact that Oriolo's staff consisted mainly of former Fleischer and Famous colleagues, who were uneducated in the new creative and economic realities. As John Canemaker notes, Oriolo chiefly educated them through a soon-to-be famous dictum in the industry: "Scenes that could not fit under his office door ... held too many drawings."[230] These exercises in traditional "full" theatrical animation were sent back for revisions.

Still another problem was the slow pace at which the series generally moved, as noted by historian Hal Erickson:

> The stories moved at a pace that made a snail look like Speed Racer. The lethargy was emphasized by the incongruously peppy background music ... and by ... Oriolo's insistence that [the] voice actor[s] speak v-e-r-y s-l-o-w-l-y [sic], one syllable at a time, in order to consume film footage which would otherwise have to be more elaborately animated and thus push the project over its already skintight budget.... Complaints that the cartoons were overly violent ... were perhaps mitigated by the fact that the series' sluggishness couldn't remotely build up any tension or suspense, but that's small compensation for the overall mediocrity.[231]

In spite of these flaws, the series, and its memorably infectious theme song, remained a saleable property throughout the 1960s. Yet Oriolo only produced one series of episodes due to the fact that Trans Lux was unwilling to provide more funding.

Oriolo would produce two more series in the 1960s based on the *Felix* formula, without a noticeable increase in quality.[232] *The Mighty Hercules*, produced again for Trans Lux and based on the legendary Greek hero, debuted in syndication in 1963. While there was an increase in the quality of the animation, the series was marred by the repetitious elements of its format, and, in some cases, its dialogue. In all, 130 five-minute episodes were produced. *Johnny Cypher in Dimension Zero*, produced for Seven Arts in 1967, followed a similar outer-space formula through 130 six-minute episodes.

Oriolo spent much of the remainder of his career working on television commercials and the occasional longer creative piece on a freelance basis, while continuing to supervise his company, Oriolo Film Studios, and overseeing the licensing and merchandising related to Felix the Cat. He died in 1985.

STEVE KRANTZ

Much like Al Brodax at King Features, Krantz was a producer of animated programs as opposed to an animator, and thus his work lacked the finesse and expertise of programming done by actual animators. Like Brodax, he farmed out animation work to a variety of studios, with the same results: a disparate and often appallingly poor quality. Still, as a producer, his work retains some historical importance, chiefly as a pioneer of the field of syndication within television animation as well as one of the first producers to employ Canadian animation production companies.

The first series to feature the Krantz Films imprint was *Marvel Superheroes*, which debuted in syndication in the fall of 1966.[233] Each of the segments was devoted to one of the famed comic-book company's major characters: Sub-Mariner, Captain America, The Incredible Hulk, The Mighty Thor and Iron Man. The services of the Paramount Cartoon Studio, then headed by Shamus Culhane, were employed,[234] but the dominant studio influence was that of Grantray-Lawrence, a decade-old animation firm operated by Robert Lawrence, Grant Simmons and Ray Patterson primarily to produce advertising. Because Krantz wanted to get the series on the air with 195 six-minute installments produced by September 1966, and on a budget of only $6,000 per segment, the animation producers were forced to cut corners in drastic ways. Lawrence ultimately hit on the process of Xerography as a solution to the problem—a relatively new process that allowed a direct transfer of pencil sketches to animation cels. The Disney studio had begun using this method for their features. Similarly, a cliff-hanger format was used for the scripts, affording the animators the luxury of using only one script for every three installments. Though some of the segments, particularly Culhane's *Mighty Thor* contributions, stood out for their good draftsmanship, the excellence of these segments could hardly compensate for the paucity of the whole. As Hal Erickson notes, the idea that this series was "animated" was "perhaps too grandiose a term for a technique which frequently utilized camera pans and hand-jiggled cutouts to convey "movement,"[235] a bare-bones technique that dropped television animation to its lowest ebb as an art form. The fact that many Marvel fans, and ultimately Stan Lee himself, came to disown the series as part of the characters' canons is perhaps the greatest testament to its lack of artistic quality.

A greater commitment to the animation end of the product, at least, was demonstrated by the immediate follow-up, a full-length series adaptation of the one major Marvel character absent from the previous project: Spider-Man.[236] The eponymous series debuted on ABC in 1967 and ran for three seasons. This project was equally divided between different producers: Grantray-Lawrence was the credited animation company for most of the episodes, though the bankruptcy of the firm during the production process ultimately caused veteran animator Ralph Bakshi to take over at Krantz's insistence. The principal voice cast—Bernard Cowan, Paul Soles, Paul Kligman and Peg Dixon—were Canadians, and had been employed on many Rankin-Bass projects (see above), giving the series an enduring appeal in Canada because of this "Canadian" content. Though the series avoided the deeper psychological elements that writer Stan Lee and artist Steve Ditko had used in the comics, it was still able to construct action-filled narratives in spite of the limitations of its scripts, animation and budget. There was also a surplus of humor, and an infectious, melodious theme song (co-authored by Academy Award–winner Paul Francis Webster), that, along with continual rebroadcasts in later years, kept it within the public's consciousness.

Krantz's final two productions, both chiefly collaborations with Shamus Culhane, suffered from the same limitations of the animation processes used, though both featured highly imaginative concepts at their centers. *Rocket Robin Hood*,[237] debuting in syndication in 1967, was a translation of the Robin Hood mythology to a high-tech science fiction future, keeping the essential elements while adapting others to the new surroundings, such as relocating Sherwood Forest to an Asteroid, having Prince John now command the National Outerspace Terrestrial Territories (or N.O.T.T., for short) and having the characters employ "a powerful new weapon—the electro-quarterstaff" in the course of their adventures. The segmented cliff-hangers were interspersed with interesting biographical profiles of the lead characters, but unfortunately not enough to create true variety. The animation retained its sub-par quality, with lengthy segments of animation and short bits of dialogue recycled endlessly in the narratives whether they belonged or not. What distinguished this series was that it was even more Canadian in nature than *Spider-Man*. The Canadian firm Trillium was the distribution partner, and the voice actors (Cowan, Kligman, Carl Banas, Chris Wiggins and others) were also Canadians. As well, the Toronto-based Al Guest studios were the original animation staff,[238] until they had a falling out with Krantz, forcing him to turn to Ralph Bakshi again to rescue the series. These "Canadian" elements have ensured an afterlife in Canada for this series that has far exceeded its original run in the United States.

The final project for Krantz Films, before Krantz permanently turned his attention away from television animation, was another project produced in association with Culhane. *Max, the 2000-Year-Old Mouse*[239] featured an animated rodent claiming to be an eyewitness to history, who periodically wisecracked while a solemn-voiced narrator intoned the truth about the historical events to the audience. It offered absolutely no competition to "Peabody's Improbable History" as a distinguished form of its historical sub-type.

KENNETH SNYDER

Little is known about this producer, who died in 1989, save for the information related to the four programs he produced during the 1960s. Each in its own way was forward-looking to later trends in television animation production.

Snyder's first animation venture was *The Funny Company*, a co-production with Mattel which debuted in syndication in 1963.[240] Focusing on a gang of kids operating from an underground clubhouse, the series was a pioneer in "educational" television animation, with the "educational" elements cleverly balanced with entertainment. At the center of each episode was a massive, UNIVAC-like computer called the Weisenheimer, which produced the "educational" content via pre-existing live-action film clips culled from short industrial and promotional films. The sense of humor possessed by Snyder and his staff (or its lack thereof) is demonstrated simply through the names of the characters: Buzzer Bell (the group's leader), Jasper National Park, Polly Plum, Merry Twirter, Shrinkin' Violette (who literally "shrank" when frightened), Dr. Todd Goodheart (a kindly adult inventor), Super Chief (a Native American who "spoke" via a railroad horn), Terry Dactyl (a lizard who served as the club's mascot), and token villains Belly Laguna and Cheese Lasagna (a mad doctor and mobster, respectively).

Given the state of his previous program, it was therefore a surprise that Snyder's second venture was as uproariously funny as it proved to be. *Roger Ramjet*,[241] which debuted in 1965, was a stunning parody of the superhero genre, very much the equal of Jay Ward's series in both the quality and quantity of its gags. Like Ward and Bob Clampett's prior work, it would provide a clear-cut example both for enacting and satirizing its genre of choice, forming a clear bridge to later programs in this sub-genre with similar intent. Ramjet himself (voiced by Gary Owens) was a scientist, aviator and *uber*-patriotic American depicted as a paragon of American virtue. He led the American Eagle Squadron, chiefly consisting of the four youngsters Yank, Doodle, Dan and Dee. (This and other elements of the series clearly indicated what was being made fun of here.) Ramjet's chief super-heroic abilities came from his use of short-acting "proton pills," which imbued him with superhuman abilities. This supposed "reliance" on drugs by the main character, an exaggerated accusation given the actual content, helped the series into undeserved obscurity in later years. The program's structure as a series of short films rather than half-hour narratives, and the disinterest of station executives toward playing it, were also at play here. This was unfortunate, considering the humor in the scripts, chiefly written by Gene Moss and Jim Thurman, was far above that of the average non–Hanna-Barbera/Ward work of this period and quite comparable to these two studios at times. Yiddish and showbiz style humor abounded, as well as a use of written sound effects during fight scenes predating the live-action *Batman* series of the mid–1960s, and goofy character names were common—Noodles Romanoff, Jacqueline Hyde, Lotta Love, General G.I. Brassbottom, Lance Crossfire, and the like. Fortunately, VHS and DVD reissues and frequent replaying on Cartoon Network in recent years have managed to pluck this underrated but often brilliant series from obscurity.

Snyder's final two series, again produced in collaboration with Mattel, were a sharp departure from his earlier, humorous work in favor of a more neo-realistic approach that barely disguised the salesmanship of the plotlines. Debuting on ABC in 1969, *Hot Wheels* was a blatant exploitation of Mattel's famed miniature automobile line, distinguished by a new realistic approach to character animation that Snyder termed "Anamorphism."[242] While in narrative intent it was clearly another pioneering "educational" series—the series focused on a group of teenage auto racers who strictly observed traffic and safety regulations in contrast to the more reckless opposition—it was also, according to the FCC, a half-hour commercial for Mattel. The regulatory body thus ordered ABC to remove the program from the air, as it insisted "program-length commercials" had no place on the network airwaves. (This attitude would change in the 1980s, as we will see.) ABC, after initially contesting the ruling, complied, thus making it clear to producers and advertisers what kind of behavior was expected. A similar fate ultimately awaited the next (and final) Snyder/Mattel collaboration, *Sky Hawks*, which aired on ABC at the same time as *Hot Wheels*, and applied the same tactics to aviation that *Hot Wheels* had already done for the open road.[243]

Format Films

This firm was established by three former UPA animators—Julius "Jules" Engel, Buddy Getzler and Herbert Flynn—in 1959, and was active only during the following decade. The company's chief product was television commercials, although it also did sub-contract work for Warner Bros. on some theatrical cartoons, as well as producing two notable television animation programs, which, though some hold out for their "cult-classic" status, are more interesting historically than as works of art in their own right.[244]

The first of these programs debuted on CBS in October of 1961, in prime time, in order to appeal to the new attraction to television animation that Hanna-Barbera had ignited with *The Flintstones*. It was unique in that it latched onto a trend in popular music that had started three years earlier with two #1 hit records on the *Billboard* charts on the Liberty label. They also won three Grammys at that inaugural ceremony. Ross Bagdasarian, the brains behind both of the recordings, was a Californian of Armenian descent who had been working as an actor, singer, songwriter and musician in his native state for nearly a decade, after choosing not to submit to his father's wishes and enter the grape-growing trade. He had developed a new approach to recording that was certainly unique for the time and exploited the unexpected pliability of the recording process. His voice would be recorded at half-speed (16 rpm) and then played back at normal speed (33⅓ rpm) which resulted in a distortion of the voice, making it appear to be higher than it actually was.[245] The first record, "Witch Doctor," was credited to Bagdasarian's nom-de-plume, "David Seville," but he took a different approach for the second song. It was a Christmas-themed release, and was the first incarnation of a fictional rodent trio that was soon dubbed "The Chipmunks" collectively, and Alvin, Simon and Theodore individually (as a tribute to Liberty executive Alvin "Al" Bennett, label co-founder Simon "Sy" Waronker, and studio recording engineer Theodore "Ted" Keep, respectively).

For the series, dubbed *The Alvin Show* in honor of the most prominent and troublesome of the trio, the three voices were given cartoon form, with David Seville as their protector and manager. Narrative segments were alternated with music video–type segments where the trio performed and promoted their latest recordings. Yet, in spite of the project's presumed "adult" appeal, the overwhelming tone was a juvenile one, and it proved to be most appealing to a younger and less critical audience. Bagdasarian's heirs (Bagdasarian himself died in 1972) would have more success later on converting the project to animated form (see Chapter 5). More successful in execution was a made-for-TV creation featured by Format: the exploits of Clyde Crashcup (Shepard Menken), a pompous scientist who, with the assistance of the nearly mute Leonardo, claimed to have "invented" a variety of things, from baseballs to housewives. The program failed in prime time, but its value as a marketing vehicle for its stars, and their continued popularity, ensured that CBS would later feature it prominently in its Saturday morning lineup.

The second and final Format project was another project imported from another medium. The legendary Lone Ranger had been a radio attraction since 1933, and, at Fred Silverman's request, it was rebooted for television animation by Format in 1966,[246] in a format that included three brief segments per episode as opposed to one long one. Walt Peregoy's background art stood out against the limited character movement, as did the storylines, which focused far more on the Lone Ranger and Tonto confronting a variety of costumed villains and aliens than the more down-to-earth Western villainy they were used to, a symptom of the times. Nevertheless, it lasted three seasons on CBS's Saturday morning lineup. Again, another studio team would handle the material more faithfully to the source in the following decade (see Chapter 4).

Hal Seeger Productions

Seeger, a native of Brooklyn, New York, began his career as an animator at the Max Fleischer studio during the 1930s and 1940s. After some time working away from animation during the 1950s, he returned to the field in television during the 1960s, producing a small but diverse body of work during that time which had some lasting impact on audiences.[247]

Seeger's first production was, in a sense, a return to his career's beginning, as it was an updated version of the project that had first launched the career of his former employer, Max Fleischer. Debuting in 1962, *Out of the Inkwell* was a clear response to the continuing popularity of Koko the Clown, Fleischer's silent star, as an attraction on local children's programming.²⁴⁸ The modern nature was stressed by its being filmed in color, but the ancestry was affirmed by having Max Fleischer himself appear in the pilot, interacting with Koko as he had in the earlier series. A link to the past was further secured by the fact that the series was directed by Fleischer veteran Myron Waldman. The final results, however, due to production restrictions, were extremely mediocre.

Seeger's next venture into television animation was more diversified and successful. *The Milton the Monster Show* debuted on ABC in 1965 and ran for three seasons there.²⁴⁹ Whereas most television animation programs of the period featured no more than three segments per episode, this series presented no less than six during its run, which benefitted at times from direction by the likes of Shamus Culhane and Myron Waldman, and writing by Jack "Popeye" Mercer, among others. In order, the segments were as follows. The title segment, set on Horror Hill in Transylvania, focused on the title character, a would-be Frankenstein figure who, through an inadvertent overdose on "Tincture of Tenderness," became an overgrown softy, causing no end of problems for his creators, Professor Weirdo and Count Kook. "Fearless Fly," up next, was a superhero parody à la Hanna-Barbera's *Atom Ant*, in which mild-mannered Herman Fly became the heroic title character by donning his "atomic-powered" glasses. "Penny Penguin" was a segment focusing on a little "brat" of a girl who inadvertently caused considerable problems for her parents. "Flukey Luke" was an undistinguished Western parody, while "Muggy Doo" was an equally undistinguished retread of Hanna-Barbera's animal con-artist formula. The last segment is generally considered to be the best of the group. "Stuffy Durma" focused on a hobo who, upon inheriting a fortune, was installed in a lavish manor and forced to contend with a private secretary, Bradley Binkley by name, intent on turning him into a "gentleman." Nevertheless, the former hobo insisted on continuing to live his life as he had always done. While the program's diversified approach did lead to some entertaining features, few of the segments came close to equaling the better-executed material of the period.

The last project from Seeger was far more derivative in nature. *Batfink*, released in 1967, was essentially an early adaptation of the "Batman" franchise, but with a difference: rather than being a man disguised as a bat, this hero actually *was* a bat.²⁵⁰ Assisted by a Japanese martial arts expert named Karate, the hero focused on fighting the likes of Hugo a Go Go and other colorfully named villains. The series consisted of one hundred films edited together in groups of five to create half-hours. Though the music score was a cut above average, as it involved veteran animation composer Winston Sharples borrowing the familiar tunes of Raymond Scott (which Carl Stalling had used in his scores for Warner Bros.), the rest of the series was not, causing the Seeger studio's history to close on a poor note.

SAM SINGER PRODUCTIONS

Singer, who died in 2001, is another marginal figure in animation history about whom little is known, save for the information about his programs. As with others working in this period, his work has received limited exposure due to its structure as a segment of other programs or being dropped into obscure timeslots where it could not be seen. In Singer's case, as well, there were more troubling issues of racial and social stereotyping that have further obscured it. A case in point was his first major series, *The Adventures of Pow Wow*, first airing on *Captain Kangaroo* in 1956 and then syndicated two years later by Screen Gems, predating Hanna-Barbera's more successful relationship with that firm.²⁵¹ Focusing on a small Native American boy, the dialogue-free series attempted to teach both the hero and his audience important and valuable life lessons through each five-minute episode. Though a favorite with its intended audience, and based in part on Native American folklore, the poor animation and troubling racial elements have largely sent this program into obscurity.

Even more obscure, and more racially troubling, was Singer's next project, *Bucky and Pepito*, airing in syndication in 1959.[252] Twice as long as the *Pow Wow* episodes, the series focused on Bucky, a cowboy-hat–wearing American kid, and Pepito, his Mexican friend. The stereotypical nature of the latter character was emphasized by the theme song describing him as "oh so lazy and oh so very, very slow," in spite of the fact that he was actually an inventor, albeit a bad one. Poor animation and cliché-ridden writing further reduced the quality of the series.

The last major project by the Singer studio was its most inventive in nature, *Courageous Cat and Minute Mouse*, airing in 1960.[253] This was an exercise in self-parody for series creator Bob Kane, as he was effectively recasting his already-legendary Batman character in comic terms. The lead characters were anthropomorphized versions of Batman and Robin, and their opponents—notably the Edward G. Robinson–like Flat Face Frog—resembled Gotham City's rogue's gallery. Kane also parodied Batman's extensive use of gadgetry with Courageous Cat's Catgun, which was capable of transforming into nearly anything, *except* a gun. While the idea seems funny on paper, it was less so in execution, as the Singer studio simply stuck with the initial gimmick of the property and did little to advance it. Other studios, notably Hanna-Barbera, would come to refine and expand on this idea in later years, with far more success.

The Singer studio produced only one other series, *Sinbad Jr.*, in 1960, though this project was soon shelved and was taken over by Hanna-Barbera five years later.[254]

Larry Harmon Productions

Harmon (ne: Lawrence Weiss) owes his fame to one thing: he originated and popularized the character of Bozo the Clown, which he fashioned into a nationwide franchise during the 1960s.[255] An energetic man who earned the nickname "The White Tornado,"[256] Harmon worked extensively to expose his character in as many ways and as many media as possible. A side effect of this was his establishing a studio to produce animated films featuring the character, to be shown during the local "Bozo" programs. Between 1958 and 1961, Harmon produced 156 five-minute Bozo cartoons, featuring the clown and his sidekick Butchy Boy, which were remarkably inane in their content. More important historically was the fact that they provided an important training ground for Lou Scheimer and Hal Sutherland, the founders of Filmation Studios, which would become one of the most dominant television animation production firms in the genre's history (see Chapter 4). The Harmon studio was a contributor to King Feature's "Popeye" package (see above), and closed out its existence in 1966 by producing a series of cartoons featuring animated doppelgängers of the legendary comedy duo Laurel and Hardy.[257]

Ed Graham Productions

This studio, primarily an advertising firm, is known for producing only one animated series: *Linus the Lionhearted*, first airing on CBS between 1964 and 1966; reruns later aired on ABC between 1966 and 1969.[258] The program was a blatant example of a series with its roots firmly in the field of advertising, as it was an outgrowth of a series of commercials Graham had produced for General Foods and its Post line of cereals. Each of the lead characters of the animated segments had been a spokes-character for one of those cereals, and was now "rewarded" by being featured as a star in a program segment. The title character (voiced by character actor-turned-TV-production tycoon Sheldon Leonard) was a leonine monarch with a Runyon-esque *patois* accompanied by a coterie of loyal subjects (most voiced by Carl Reiner). Sugar Bear (Gerry Matthews), the still-familiar spokes-character for Sugar Crisps, was also featured, as were So-Hi (Bob McFadden), a caricatured Chinese boy who read fables to the audience; the dapper Rory Raccoon (McFadden); and Lovable Truly (McFadden), a surprisingly effeminate (for the time), Southern-accented mail carrier. The lavish budget of $87,000 per installment was luxurious by the standards of the time, and the program clearly looked it, although the quality of the writing varied from episode to episode and segment to segment. Eventually, the program was forced off the air by the FCC for the same reasons Kenneth Snyder's Mattel-derived series were canceled at the same time (see above); it returned to syndication only after virtually all the characters were no longer being used in advertising.

KAYRO PRODUCTIONS

This firm produced only one animated series as well: *Calvin and the Colonel*, airing on ABC during the 1961-62 season.[259] Essentially, this was a rebooting of the popular (but highly racist) radio and television program *Amos 'n' Andy* in animated form; it was unable, unlike its contemporary *The Flintstones*, to disguise its roots in any effective way.[260] This was most apparent in the fact that *Amos 'n' Andy*'s creators and stars, Freeman Gosden and Charles Correll were directly involved with the series, as were former series writers Joe Connelly and Bob Mosher (famous as the creator/producers of *Leave It to Beaver*, and, later, *The Munsters*). Essentially, what this series did was repeat the con-artist formula at the heart of *Amos 'n' Andy* in a supposedly more "neutral" setting. Taking the central roles were Colonel Montgomery J. Klaxon (Gosden), a threadbare vulpine realtor modeled on *Amos 'n' Andy*'s "Kingfish," and Calvin J. Burnside (Correll), a dimwitted bruin patsy based on Andy. Other characters followed the pattern of those on the prior series, such as the shyster weasel lawyer Oliver Wendell Clutch (Paul Frees). But the borrowing did not end there: many of *Calvin and the Colonel*'s scripts were, in fact, exact replicas of earlier *Amos 'n' Andy* episodes! The animation, at least, was above average, thanks to the efforts of the veteran firm Creston Studios. However, production problems, heavy negative criticism, and, ultimately, less than desirable ratings forced the series off the air after less than one season.

FILMATION

See Chapter 4.

Conclusion

The era between 1957 and 1969 can be seen clearly as the period when television animation came into its own. Producers entered the field who were capable of using the artistic materials at hand, and their own creative resources, to produce material that continues to have value today, even if only as a historical curiosity. In the hands of a particularly versatile and gifted studio, such as Hanna-Barbera, or a producer with a highly individualized and clearly articulated sense of humor, such as Jay Ward, the genre was able to provide the medium of television with some of most endearing and enduring programs, characters and moments. It would be the programs of this halcyon era that television animation producers of a later era would draw from as a source of inspiration, and their programs would serve to confirm that link. In the more immediate future, television animation would face increasingly rigorous internal censorship, and vigorous external demands for a product that displayed less irreverence than in the past. This would come to limit television animation's newly gained artistic liberation, and make it appear even more incredible to historians that the producers active between 1957 and 1969 were able to achieve what they did given the circumstances within which they existed.

Chapter 4

House Arrest (1970–1979)

As the 1970s began, the United States of America was enduring one of the most heated and divisive political periods in its history.[1] In ways unseen for over a century, the country's name became increasingly ironic, as social, racial and political issues caused it to become a patchwork quilt of splintered, idealized concerns. It was inevitable, therefore, that the country's mass media would find itself confronting its own ideological conflicts. This was particularly evident in the field of television animation, as the artistic and creative abilities of those involved in this enterprise were almost permanently compromised in a repressive cultural atmosphere in that decade.

Television animation, an artistic form still seen as an entertainment enjoyed primarily by children, was made the most prominent scapegoat of the debate over "violence" in the mass media in the late 1960s and early 1970s. As a consequence, it was subjected to an unprecedently high level of censorship. What resulted was a period in which the old ideals and storytelling practices of theatrical animation, where the majority of the original television animators had been baptized by fire, were suddenly and irrevocably made irrelevant and "dangerous." Much of this came at the hands of external censorship groups who had no understanding of animation as an art form, nor the means by which it had traditionally communicated messages to its audience. Television animators, in this "new normal," were no longer expected to be mere entertainers. If they were to continue to remain in business, they were expected to enlighten their audiences as well as entertain them. With its traditional production ethics tested and heavily scrutinized, television animation was, for the most part, robbed of its ability to be genuinely humorous and entertaining. It was, instead, sacrificed on the altar of public service by its television-network patrons. Relief from this repressive system, set in place to put social advocacy groups and concerned U.S. government officials at bay, would take nearly two decades to achieve.

Part of the problem with television animation lay in the fact that, in spite of its demonstrated ability to appeal to a wider audience, it was still seen as a field whose chief appeal was to young children. Therefore, it was increasingly examined in ways that suggested that entertaining, and, increasingly, enlightening the children in its audience was not only a necessity but an obligation. To reinforce this fact, the television networks began employing educational consultants to examine ways in which educational messages could be inserted into television animation programs. Furthermore, they twisted the arms of their chief animation suppliers by suggesting that they would be put out of business if they did not comply with this new dictum. Such demands could be made only in a televisual world still controlled largely by three major networks. The entrance of cable television in the 1980s would slowly begin to erode this power even as the structures for enforcing it remained. The escapist storytelling abilities of television animation were, understandably, severely compromised by this new education dictum.

An even greater and, for television animation, more limiting concern was continual conflict between the producers and the networks over the issue of "violence." An ongoing concern with television since the early 1960s, the debate heated up considerably toward the end of the decade, with the war in Vietnam, the frequent rioting by African Americans in American cities, and the assassinations of Martin Luther King, Jr., and Robert F. Kennedy in 1968 serving as major catalysts for change. In particular, one grassroots protest group, Action for Children's Television [ACT], began fighting to make television a "safer" place for children.[2] Bowing to both political and economic pressures, and unwilling to sacrifice the lucrative commercial benefits of their prime-time programming, television executives responded by lowering the boom on television animation. Anything that was remotely perceived as violent in animation scripting thus became highly suspect. As a result, intense levels of conflict began emerging between television animation producers, on the one hand, and network executives and social advocates on the other—one group trying to execute their creative freedom, the others desperately trying to rein in a group they considered, rightly or wrongly, to be responsible for "corrupting" the youth of America. It was no wonder, under these circumstances, that the creative quality of television animation, largely well done in the 1960s in spite of the conditions under which it was made, began to drop considerably as a whole during the 1970s.

The "necessary evil"[3] of censorship resulted in conflicts between producers and censors that did relatively little to affirm the value of television animation as a programming genre. Indeed, it did just the opposite, stripping it bare of the elements that had allowed it to appeal to audiences in the previous decade in the name of "protecting" children from its "harmful" elements and effects. With careless but efficient accuracy, the basic elements of dramatic narratives (fistfights, kicking, gun and swordplay, etc.) and comic stories (most of the basic elements of slapstick) were purged from the storylines and replaced with shallow and well-intentioned platitudes and ideologies. This increased the marginalization of television animation that had existed in the 1950s and 1960s and made it easier for its opponents to view it as a "waste of time." Ironically, although prime-time television was, arguably, far more "violent" in character and intent than television animation was at this time, it was much less affected, presumably because its audience was more diverse, "mature" and affluent than the perceived one for television animation.

There were those, however, who were capable of walking the censorship line with considerable ease. In the early 1970s, the animation studio Filmation, founded and headed by Lou Scheimer, took over from Hanna-Barbera at the head of the industry, in part because it was better equipped to deal with the production processes involved with the new environment. Unlike most of his contemporaries, Scheimer had never worked in the theatrical animation industry. His background was, instead, in commissioned, non-commercial filmmaking, where the demands of backers and sponsors *always* had to be met. He was, therefore, well equipped to treat his television animation programs as a tailor would his clothing: made to measure for a wide variety of customers. Yet, at the same time, Scheimer was very aware of his obligations to be both entertainer and educator, a fact that ultimately made him more successful at perpetrating this unwieldy and unlikely marriage than his contemporaries. Like

Jay Ward, Scheimer also demonstrated a liberal political philosophy in his work, as demonstrated by his depictions of female and African American characters in particular. But, unlike Ward, he often found persuasive—and even subversive—means of presenting his message through purely subtle means.

The story of television animation in the 1970s is a study of a transitional period, a time in which an old way of making animation was severely challenged and tested, and a new way of making television animation asserted itself for a new environment. How these two forms met different fates—and different levels of acceptance—in the brave new world of 1970s television is the subject of this chapter.

The Crackdown: Its History, Its Effects and Its Legacy

The debate over children's understanding of violence is one that predates the existence of television by a considerable period of time.[4] Yet television, because it was directly accessible to children within the home and not isolated in the outside world, was a danger that many American parents felt almost obligated to confront.

The evolution of the mass media and public entertainment in America was something that had never gone opposed. Most commonly, opposition came in the form of socially, politically and religiously conservative people, who feared that the "corruptive" influence of these entertainment forms—perceived and actual—would cause consumers of them to deviate from cultural and social norms. Opponents of the American circus in the 19th century, for example, feared that the shows would entice innocent young people to abandon normality and "run away" with the shows, which some actually did.[5] Opposition to the most prominent popular literary form of the day—the dime novel—was based on similar pretexts. To Brander Matthews, a prominent academic and literary critic of the time, dime novels were "villainous sheets which pander greedily and viciously to the natural taste of young readers for excitement, [whose] irreparable wrong ... is hidden from no one."[6] Variations on this theme of "irreparable wrong" cited by Matthews would be replayed and revised in the forthcoming years, as new and ever more threatening forms of media and entertainment worked their way into American life.

This is not to say that the practitioners of live and literary entertainment were entirely negligent toward their obligations to their audiences. As noted in Chapter 1, in vaudeville, the pre-eminent live media form of the time, the reverse was true. The founders of the influential Keith-Orpheum vaudeville circuit, in particular, demanded a strict mode of decorum that forbade, among other things, profanity, broad sexuality in dress and speech, and anything perceived to have the potential to offend the audience "on pain of instant discharge," though this did not include, significantly, the racist and sexist forms of humor prominent in the era's comedy. And, as vaudeville became the essential training ground for the founding entertainers of film, radio and, ultimately, television, these sentiments attached themselves to those media as well.[7]

The advent of visual culture, exemplified by the rise of motion pictures and then television, gave force to arguments against the "corruptive" influences of the mass media. As historian Robert Sklar has demonstrated, the ascension of the motion picture coincided with the rise of the Progressive political reform movement, which "drew much of its energy from the middle classes' discovery that they had lost control over—and even knowledge of—the behavior and values of the lower orders; and the movies became prime targets of their efforts to reformulate and reassert their power."[8] As the industry grew, concern over its conduct widened, culminating in the Payne Fund and Study Experiments of the late 1920s, whose results were published in 1932.[9] The first systematic study of a mass media of any kind, the Payne Fund studies examined what motion picture narratives were capable of "instructing" people in, particularly the young. In response, the Hollywood studios, with the strong influence of interested parties in the American Catholic Church, set up a doctrinal system of filmmaking regulation, which became known—within the industry, and later historically—as the Production Code.[10] Adopted in 1934, and in force until the mid–1960s (with the advent of the modern "rating" system), the Code locked American filmmaking into a narrow doctrinal system, forbidding the use and display of profanity, overt sexuality and scatology on the screen while, at the same time, encouraging and supporting an idealized portrayal of American life and the Christian faith. In the short term, this served the purpose of limiting the growth of ideologically threatening ideas in filmmaking, including in animation. These values were carried over into the early days of television, as so many of television's pioneers were filmmaking veterans well aware of the prior media's code of ethics and behavior.

When commercial television broadcasting began in the United States in 1948, therefore, reactions to it and attempts to limit its influence already had just over half a century of incubation. The severe backlash toward it from critics, particularly with regard to its impact on children and youth, thus had traceable roots. Yet nothing could have prepared television producers for the three-decades-plus of criticism they would receive and endure simply for being part of this nascent industry.

♦ ♦ ♦

As historian Lynn Spigel has noted, television's rise as a commercial medium coincided with the postwar "baby boom," and it was in a perfect position to be characterized as a "family" medium.[11] As with the movies before it, efforts to create regulation and monitor use of television were predicated on the middle classes' desire to "educate" and "enlighten" members of the lower classes.[12] This was coupled with efforts to keep women in the home, and to regulate the leisure time of their children.[13] Television was a prime target for these "experts," and for the critics who suggested that television viewing was unhealthy and, essentially, a waste of time. This was a biased view that denied both the intelligence of the individual viewer, as well as the efforts of the medium itself to enlighten and entertain, but it is a viewpoint that persists to this day. It was certainly the attitude expressed in a 1950 illustration from *The Ladies' Home Journal* by artist Munro Leaf. The drawing featured an emaciated girl "typed" as a TV addict, and the accompanying caption encapsulated many of the then-current viewpoints, and stereotypes, related to television viewing:

> This pale, weak, stupid-looking creature is a Telebugeye, and, as you can see, it grew bugeyed by looking at television too long. Telebugeyes just sit and sit, watching, watching. This one doesn't wear shoes because it never goes out in the fresh air anymore and it's skinny because it never gets any exercise. The hair on this Telebugeye is straggly and long because it won't get a haircut for fear of missing a program. What idiots Telebugeyes are.[14]

To modern readers, this view of the average youthful TV viewer is distorted. It exaggerates the addictive capabilities of television, and suggests that viewers who watch no longer have the freedom to stop watching once they start. Yet this argument, in various forms, would be the weapon television's critics would use to wage war on the medium.

As Spigel has suggested, children were in a difficult position. Efforts at regulating their behavior and thoughts dated back to the days of the Puritans, with efforts at regulating the mass media with which they engaged lasting nearly as long.[15] Yet the intensity of social, political and media change in the mid–20th century brought these debates too close to home, especially for a generation of parents who had already endured the hardships brought on by the Great Depression and World War II, and had no intention or desire to allow their children to go through similar deprivations.[16] This explains the social and political means by which they aimed to "protect" their children, in particular from the "animalistic" sounds of rock and roll music, and the flurry of sounds and images emanating from television sets. "Corruption" of their children, and its abrupt halting, was their primary—and, often, only—concern. Given this opposition and scrutiny, the fact that the animation studios of the 1950s and 1960s as discussed in Chapter 1 (particularly Hanna-Barbera and Jay Ward) were able to achieve what they did is somewhat miraculous. However, even the goodwill created by those projects was not enough to prevent persistent negative scrutiny of television animation, largely due, as has been discussed, to philosophic beliefs that predated television animation but were, nonetheless, forced upon its producers.

The Censoring of Television Animation

In searching for the word "violence" in a dictionary, a reader comes across six alternate definitions:

1. Swift and intense force.
2. Rough or injurious force, action or treatment...
3. An unjust or unwarranted exertion of force or power.
4. A violent act or proceeding.
5. Rough or immoderate vehemence, as in feeling or language.
6. Injury, as from distortion of meaning or fact.[17]

These definitions do much to explain what violence is—or may be perceived to consist of. What they *cannot* do is illuminate the degrees to which violence may be used justifiably as part of a fictional narrative. They also fail to capture different degrees of violence, from harmless childlike clowning, to murder, to genocide, and all points in between. This was and is a fundamental, flawed problem with the ongoing campaign against media "violence." Since no single, clear and uniform definition of the term exists, it can be used freely by anyone wishing to use it to refer to almost anything the individual user considers to be "violent," whether or not it may actually be so according to a dictionary definition of the term. This is where controversy exists within the study of "violence" in television animation, in the historical period covered in this chapter and beyond.

As suggested earlier, the concern over violence in television animation was a concern that predated television animation itself, but was brought into sharper focus by both the immediacy of the television-viewing experience and the supposedly "irrevocable" effects this brought on. As a consequence of social and political activism undertaken against them in relation to this, the television networks felt that they had no alternative but to reshape television animation—the primary target of the attacks, justified or not—to placate their critics and protect their economic investments.[18] What resulted from this was a system of censorship that was, at the very least, overzealous, resulting in the citation of even minor on-screen activities as acts of "violence" rather than flowing from the creation of a more acceptable, uniform definition of the term.[19] Because a lack of cohesion existed on the issue, the disputes and complaints about "violence" in this era ring hollow to contemporary viewers—as does the networks' almost dictatorial response to reining it in.

In their defense, the animators consistently reminded their critics that animation was, first and foremost, a fantastic art form that was never intended to be viewed on the diametrically opposed terms of "realism." Indeed, the acts many earlier animated films and programs had depicted were, by any logical viewing, impossible to undertake in real life (as was the case for most theatrical animation films), or were executed by beings with unrealistic powers and abilities (i.e., superheroes). But, as will be discussed shortly, this was a position that network and advertising regulators did not accept, causing them to either cut or censure these acts in both exhibited theatrical and television animation.[20]

For their part, animation producers were quick to contend that, contrary to what their critics believed, even child viewers of television animation *were* capable of telling the difference between "real" and "fake" violence[21] but, at the time, no one in charge seemed to care. Walter Lantz, a producer whose work was heavily censured through this system, made his concerns about the arbitrary nature of the system clear in an interview with film historian Danny Peary in 1980:

> I never considered any cartoon I produced too violent. I thought of them as slapstick comedies. I didn't know what slapstick was until I came out here [to Los Angeles] to work for Mack Sennett. Then I realized it took pratfalls and socks on the head and being shot at to get big laughs in the theatre. The pies in the face and so forth. *So we just went one step further and exaggerated the gags* [emphasis added]. It takes a physical gag to get a belly laugh. In cartoons especially, you don't get it very often with just dialogue.
>
> I wouldn't say that the ... [cartoons of the theatrical animation era] ... were violent. They used the same techniques that I used. *Nobody really bleeds or dies* [emphasis added]. If someone is shot full of holes, he [*sic*] is back to normal in the next scene; if his teeth fall out, he has a full set an instant later. The trouble today is that *these groups have set themselves up as censors, and they don't know what they're talking about,* because *they don't look at these cartoons through the eyes of children* [emphasis added]. They should be home taking care of their kids instead of setting themselves up as critics.[22]

Lantz's contention that the biases against television animation stemmed from an essential lack of knowledge on the part of censors was reinforced by his contemporaries, William Hanna and Joseph Barbera, who reiterated this point in interviews by indicating that the "fantasy" violence they specialized in was unfairly and unjustifiably lumped together with the more "realistic" violence of live-action programming and was therefore made indistinguishable from it.[23] But, in spite of the force with which they made this argument, and the fact that additional studies suggested that there was, in fact, no direct causal linkage between television animation and real-world violence,[24] network television sided with the regulators in a blatant attempt to maintain its social and economic control over the children's programming market. As a consequence, notes historian Jason Mittell, the indirect labeling of animation as a "children's" medium resulted in its effective "exile" to Saturday mornings in the mid–1960s:

> The most vital effect of establishing Saturday morning cartoons as a cultural category was filing the *entire genre* under a "kid-only" label [emphasis added]. This was accomplished less through targeting a children's audience and more by driving away the adult audience. Cartoons had been on Saturday morning since the 1950s, but it was only in the 1960s that they became harder to find anywhere else on television schedules. Likewise[,] sponsors moved to

Saturday mornings not because they could reach *more children* in that timeslot, but because they could actually reach *fewer adults*, thus raising the percentage of children per rating point and advertising dollar [emphasis in original]. The appeal of cartoons for children *was always considered a default*—what changed in the mid–1960s was the assumption *that adults could like cartoons too* [emphasis added]. Following the creation of the Saturday morning enclave, cartoons became stigmatized as a genre *only* appropriate for children, removing the traditional affiliations with a mass audience [emphasis in original]. This was accomplished partially by [the] networks latching onto an existing phenomenon—adults watched the least amount of television on Saturday mornings. But the industry furthered this association by marketing Saturday morning cartoons *solely to children*, by forgoing the visual complexity and adult humor that marked earlier animation, by sponsors advertising only to children during the timeslot, and by isolating cartoons from all other genres and timeslots to maintain tight associations between all the texts within the generic category [emphasis added]. The marginalization of cartoons also served to further its appeal among its target audience—one of the appeals of Saturday morning was the very fact that *adults did not watch the shows and the programs (and the ads) were aimed primarily at them* [emphasis added]. Parents accepted the generic timeslot's role as "baby-sitter" and yielded media control to children, furthering the industrial commitment to defining the genre narrowly.[25]

Thus, television animation was marginalized both as a creative programming genre and an economic factor within the television animation industry *specifically* because it was targeted at a narrow social and economic group—children—who did not possess the political means to protest the way it was marketed at them. This, by default, was left to their parents, whose concerns—in particular regarding the use, definition and interpretation of "violence"—frequently differed from their own.

◆ ◆ ◆

As with concerns over corruption, concerns over violence in animation predated television but were amplified by it. The marginal status of theatrical animation within the filmgoing program of the 1920s, 1930s and 1940s in particular had much to do with this. Though, as demonstrated in Chapter 1, some studios were able to achieve ongoing success with star characters, the genre as a whole was seen to have only marginal appeal, directed chiefly at the younger members of the audience. As a consequence, concerns over animated films' effect on younger viewers were often exaggerated, and met similarly exaggerated responses from censors. Not even the key pioneer of modern theatrical animation, Walt Disney, and his star character, Mickey Mouse, were exempt from this, as journalist Terry Ramsaye noted in the *Motion Picture Herald* in 1931:

> Mickey Mouse, the artistic offspring of Walt Disney, has fallen afoul of the censors in a big way, largely because of his amazing success. Papas and mamas, especially mamas, have spoken vigorously to censor boards and elsewhere about what a devilish, naughty mouse Mickey turned out to be. Now we find that Mickey is not to drink, smoke or tease the stock in the barnyard [anymore]. Mickey has been spanked.
> It is the old, old story. If nobody knows you, you can do anything, and if everybody knows you, you can't do anything—except what every one [sic] approves, which is very little of anything. It has happened often enough among the human stars of the screen and now it gets even the little fellow in black and white who is no thicker than a pencil mark and exists only in a state of mind.[26]

Mickey was far from the last animated character who would be "spanked" for enacting bad behavior in front of a youthful audience. In fact, censorship would only escalate in the following years. The studios differed in their approaches, but, with the exception of the odd maverick figure (e.g., Tex Avery; see Chapter 1), Hollywood animators were well aware of the perceived limits of taste and tolerance, and, while exaggerating and often defying reality, they stayed within its moral limits.

The violence issue became more of a concern when these animated films were first exhibited on television in the 1950s and beyond. The problem was, simply, that animation producers and the censors with which they were forced to work came from two different worlds. In both film and television, animation operated within a highly internalized culture which its censors did not even attempt to understand. Likewise, animators, who were not used to the extreme levels of censorship television now demanded of them, saw censors not as people trying to help them but as beings who threatened the continued existence of their art and craft—and, therefore, a personal threat to themselves as well. Frequent and often heated conflict between them was inevitable. Yet, what was ironic about this whole situation, notes historian Stefan Kanfer, was that while television animation (now typed as the resident "children's" genre) was undergoing the bulk of the scrutiny, the vast majority of the real "violence" on television was occurring elsewhere—in the considerably more lucrative and prestigious realm of prime-time programming.[27] But the assumed correlation between television animation and violence was by now far too entrenched in both the television community as a whole, and, worse, in the outside world, for it to be countered or reversed by this point. Confirmation of this was made clear in then–FCC Chairman Newton Minow's now-infamous "Vast Wasteland" speech of 1961, in which he indelicately placed the words "violence" and "cartoons" side by side at the end of a long sentence decrying the "deplorable" situation of the television industry of the time.[28]

One significant producer who protested the manner in which the television establishment had mistreated him was Walter Lantz, the longtime head of the animation department of Universal Pictures. In bringing his work to television, Lantz discovered that his sponsor and their advertising agency were prepared to force him to go through an even stricter form of sponsorship than the Production Code:

> The first thing that happened was the elimination in one swoop of all my films that contained Negro [sic] characters; there were eight such pictures. But we never offended the colored race [sic] and they were all top musical cartoons, too.
>
> The [advertising] agency reasoning was that if there was a question at all on a scene, why leave it in? It might cause some group or other to bring pressure, and if there's one thing the sponsor doesn't want, it's to make enemies.
>
> The next thing we cut out en masse were all drinking scenes. In one cartoon, we showed a horse accidentally drinking cider out of a bucket and then, somewhat pixilated, trying to walk a tightrope. On TV, you'll see the tipsy horse on the screen, but since we cut out the scene showing his drinking the cider, the TV audience won't understand why he is groggy.
>
> The agency censors also kept a sharp eye out for any material which could be construed as risqué. The entire "About Ben Boogie" cartoon was rejected on the grounds that it showed a little harem girl [sic] wriggling her hips.
>
> Mental health and physical disabilities weren't overlooked either. In "Knock Knock," Woody [Woodpecker]'s activities eventually lead him to a nervous breakdown. When we got through cutting this one, what was left didn't make much sense.[29]

What happened to Lantz, unfortunately, was *de rigeur* for the treatment of theatrical animation in the television era. As a consequence, its creative value, and its makers' original artistic intentions, were lost. In the 1990s, for example, viewers watching vintage Warner

Bros. cartoons might have mistakenly believed that they were seeing the films as they were originally exhibited in theaters, when, in fact, they were likely watching the versions of these cartoons censored for television nearly three decades earlier.[30]

A Significant Parallel Case

A preamble to the concern over television animation, and the extreme results of attempted or imposed outside censorship, was displayed in the early 1950s in the scrutiny toward animation's creative cousin, the comic book, which proceeded to confirm the marginalization of that genre as a literary form. Originally developed as reprints of newspaper comic strips in the early 1930s, the comic book had become an artistic force in its own right, inventing the character of the superhero and pioneering numerous new breakthroughs in visual storytelling.[31] Its popularity peaked during World War II, but after the war its audience became increasingly limited to children and young adults. This is where the problem began. Because of the nature of the audience, as well as the graphic, realistic manner in which many stories were told, it was easy for outsiders to accuse comic books of contributing to the prevailing perceived ill of the moment—juvenile delinquency.[32] This, at least, was the assertion of the German-born American psychiatrist Frederic Wertham.[33] In his then-landmark but now-suspect study, *Seduction of the Innocent*, Wertham systematically—but with limited actual proof—indicted comic books as a principal contributor to juvenile delinquency. Among other things, he accused superheroes of being latent homosexual figures, and comic-book crime stories of helping to spur on the trend toward real-life crime.[34] As historian David Hajdu has recently suggested, the strength of Wertham's argument was given unnecessary force by the McCarthyite political ideology of the times, as well as his own status as a so-called "expert" on the youth of America. In more clear-headed times, he would have simply been dismissed as a voice in the wilderness.[35] However, it was the comic-book makers who proved to be the subjects of criticism and attack, to the extreme of having their products immolated by incensed mobs of citizenry in highly publicized public burnings.[36] They were also the ones who were called in front of a U.S. Senate commission on juvenile delinquency to rationalize their actions. In this setting, they dug their own graves by defending their actions. Such was the case with EC Comics founder William Gaines, who insisted that the high levels of exaggerated violence portrayed in his comics were simply a reflection of the things his audience wanted.[37] As a result, just as the film industry set up the Production Code to clean up their house and avoid the influence of the government, so too the comic book industry founded its own in-house regulatory group, the Comics Code Authority (CCA). The CCA's function and mandate was similar to the Production Code's: it served as a means of limiting what could be respectfully addressed within comic-book narratives to avoid outside regulation. However, similar to the Production Code's imposed moral limitations on movie narratives, the CCA also served to limit the further artistic growth and experimentation of the comic-book medium.[38] Gaines, pointedly, did not join the organization. Instead, he abandoned the comic book industry altogether, but remained active as a publisher through converting one of his best-selling books, *Mad*, into a well-regarded humor magazine, one that is still in existence today.

The dispute over comic books and their content, along with the industry's response, had many parallels to the later, more protracted, dispute over violence in television animation. First, in both cases, opponents of the form were able to proceed by fiat or threat of action from the American government on the basis of what was clearly limited evidence. The word of supposed "experts" such as Wertham was valued and considered far above those provided by the actual creators of the work, whose opinions should have been taken more seriously than they were. Second, in neither case were the factors thought to be contributing to perceived problems arising from the works themselves clearly and firmly articulated. Third, regulations designed to solve "the problem" were put in place not by the government, but by factions within the industries themselves. As a consequence, both the creators of comic books and the creators of television animation had their ability to tell stories severely compromised for an extended period of time. With regard to the "violence" issue, the enduring influence of these debates became increasingly apparent in the late 1960s and early 1970s, when both television animation and America were fundamentally reconsidering a number of complex issues and practices.

How Television Animation Was Censored (and Persecuted)

As noted in Chapter 3, the traditional placement of television animation on Saturday mornings truly began in 1965, with the advent of Fred Silverman's "superhero morning" format on CBS. Three years later, however, the freewheeling nature of television animation was reined in by the imposition of new and restrictive censorship requirements. The King and Kennedy assassinations, the war in Vietnam, and the rise of social protest groups such as ACT forced a change in the censorship atmosphere that severely limited the artistic mobility of television animation. To use Joseph Barbera's words, an "excessive amount of fear and terror"[39] on the part of network television executives would force unwilling producers to reconsider the way they not only did business, but also the manner in which they constructed stories for their intended audience.

The heart and soul of the conflict was the issue of "violence," particularly in the superhero genre. But a closer look at the program narratives of this time shows that violence was actually used, if at all, as a last resort. The limitations of television animation technology at this time prevented the staging of the kind of well-choreographed, "violent" fight scenes the producers were often accused of creating. These would become much more evident only *later* in television animation's history, with improved technology and storytelling, in programs such as *The Powerpuff Girls* (see Chapter 6). Greater emphasis was placed, instead, on the mental acuteness of the heroes, and how they used this aspect of their abilities as much, if not more than, their physical abilities to defeat the villains (as would also be the case later on). As with their theatrical predecessors, the main thing these programs were guilty of was being in the right place at the wrong time—or even, in some respects, being ahead of their time. Regardless of the merits of these programs, the majority of them were either canceled or moved to less-accessible timeslots as a salve against criticism, which nevertheless continued unabated.[40]

It was understandable that television animation programs should have been constructed to make them both entertaining and a source of potential profit for producers, executives and advertisers. Contemporary newspaper articles suggested that it was possible to reap fortunes from television animation via advertising directed at children[41]—which would hardly have endeared television animation series to hassled parents. It did not help, of course, that many critics of television as a whole wrote disparaging, ageist newspaper articles regarding television animation's primary audience during this period.[42] The majority of these articles, in fact, did little but parrot the fears and opinions of the opponents of television animation, giving little if any space to supportive opinions. Occasionally, though, some token attempts were made to allow all the parties involved to speak their minds, but these supposedly "objective" discussions of the matter were still weighed heavily in favor of one side only. Robert Windeler's 1968 *New York Times* article, "Violence in TV Cartoons Being Toned Down," provides an example of this practice. Mrs. Irvin Hendryson, said to represent the national Parent Teachers Association, voiced the case for the "establishment," saying that television animation was "worse than immoral" and "full of horror and violence and negative values."[43] Significantly, the reporter did not ask her to explain exactly *what* made television animation "worse than immoral," or what the "horror and violence and negative values" she cited actually *were*. In contrast, Joseph Barbera was quoted as saying that his studio was being "victimized" by the violence trend and that the networks were basically forcing the studio to fall in line with the network's plans for solving the "problem." "Saturday mornings are so competitive now," Barbera stated, "that we have script meetings and we talk about character analysis and motivation—for cartoon shows!"[44] Viewed in the context of the article, the quote suggests that not only was Barbera unaccustomed to subjecting his animated series to such supposedly "deep" critical analysis (as implied by the reference to "character analysis and motivation"), but that somehow, via the unstated implications of the article, he believed that television animation was not *worthy* of this kind of analysis. This attitude would persist with critics of television animation well into the 1990s, when it actually *was* becoming worthy of it. The manner in which Windeler—and the *Times*—ultimately take the side of the critics and regulators is made readily apparent when Windeler cites the opinions of a resident "expert," Beverly Hills–based psychiatrist Dr. Murray Korengold, to affirm, albeit loosely, the baseless accusations of Mrs. Hendryson and others like her. Dr. Korengold began his remarks by referring to the series as simply "quickie cartoons,"[45] a cheap shot that establishes his opinion of television animation immediately and directly. He went on to say that superhero characters, in particular, were responsible for "desensitizing ... children—to social and personal violence, to pain and compassion for other people's suffering."[46] As well, the characters served to represent "the American ethic of hegemony and supremacy; he [*sic*] uses violence without explicit application and arrogates himself very radically into everybody else's life."[47] This attitude—and, in particular, this statement—is remarkably similar to the negative attitude toward superheroes that Wertham had articulated in *Seduction of the Innocent* over a decade earlier, suggesting how heavily his erroneous statements about the entire superhero genre had tainted "establishment" views of both comic books and television animation. But, as with Mrs. Hendryson, Korengold offers no direct citations of narratives and actions within the narratives to support his statement; he does not explain *what programs* convey this viewpoint, *how* they do it, and *why*. Equally significantly, Windeler does not ask him to do so, just as he had not asked Mrs. Hendryson to clarify her remarks. In Windeler's article, the "expert" status of Mrs. Hendryson and Korengold is clearly and quite obviously held over and above Joseph Barbera's complaints about excessive negative regulation chiefly because Barbera was a television animation producer—and, therefore, it seems, not to be trusted. This biased, and often contemptuous, attitude toward television animation persists in a close reading of articles related to the subject in the *New York Times* throughout the 1970s in particular.

Equally significant was the fact that figures in other aspects of the animation industry did not even attempt to defend their "sibling" producers in television animation. Some surviving pioneers of theatrical animation, such as Chuck Jones, took a contemptuous, "My kid could paint that" attitude toward television animation that further limited the ability of outside viewers of the situation to see the programs' individual merits.[48] As a means of defense, the producers insisted that they were simply being forced to follow marching orders from outside sources. "Do you think we put into the story boards [*sic*] what *we* want?" producer David DePatie rhetorically asked reporter Digby Diehl in 1967. "The networks control our material [emphasis in original]."[49] Despite the producers' implicit and explicit explanation of the censorship situation they were forced to endure, however, negative attitudes toward television animation would continue to become amplified. The following years would only create further problems from the producers as a result.

Clearly, no one could have foreseen how prolonged the conflict in Vietnam would be when 1968 began, nor the after-effects of the King and Kennedy assassinations. Yet these events and their side effects added considerable fuel to the fire burning over the supposedly "close" relationship between television animation and the actions of America's children. Violence, rather than being used sparingly to indicate realistic areas of concern, became a buzzword closely related to the genre of television animation. It was used heavily but loosely to refer to the supposed contents of television animation programs. This was in spite of the fact that, while many studies had been conducted to determine the relationship between television and children, the majority of them reflected children's reactions to the *process* of broadcasting—specifically, whether or not they were able to identify and interpret *static images* shown to them via the mechanics of television broadcasting—as opposed to the actual *content* of narrative-based television animation programs,[50] which would have thrown a greater degree of truth and light on the matter. Again, however, this factual evidence was patently ignored, especially after Washington became involved with the threat of external censorship, which plainly strengthened the opposition's case even further. The U.S. government's involvement came via the 1969 U.S. Senate Subcommittee Hearings on Communications, headed by Senator John Pastore of Rhode Island, which supported the idea of legislation that would create exactly this outside censorship. As noted at the time, Pastore's views and actions were a subliminal indictment of the entire television medium which, by proxy, would result in the creation of intensive censorship on the network level. His opponents challenged the arguments made by Pastore, saying he was using the issue of the "manipulative" nature of television simply as a way to ensure his own re-election.[51] Nevertheless, Pastore's commitment to the television issue was a real one. He headed further Senate Subcommittees on Communications in 1972 and 1974 which came much closer to indicting the supposedly negative effects of television animation and condemning the actions of those who produced and supported it.[52] Put simply, television animation was being made to pay a form of penance for the actions of television as a whole. The imposed regulatory actions of the networks stemming from the Pastore hearings would almost exclusively be focused on programming directly aimed at children or felt to be so (i.e., television animation), with little thought put into attempting to impose similar regulatory action on the rest of the production end of the industry.

◆ ◆ ◆

It was understandable, in these turbulent times, that certain interested people would attempt to influence television producers, network executives, and regulators to create a more "constructive" viewing environment for children. This is where the parents came in. Action for Children's Television (ACT) was a group that was begun with good intentions, but, through the course of their actions and the related side effects, they would come to take the blame, particularly in the eyes of television animation producers and their successors, for the eventual "dumbing down" of the entertainment aspects of television animation.

Founded by Peggy Charren, a housewife/social activist from the Boston suburb of Newton, the original stated intent of ACT was to "[eliminate] commercials from children's viewing hours and [clean] up the program content."[53] The first goal was the more ambitious, considering how heavily commercials dotted the TV landscape, then and now. It was also the more daunting, requiring years of testimony in front of Congressional and FCC hearings, as well as expensive campaigns in the public media. Nevertheless, ACT's membership quickly jumped into the 8,000-plus bracket, a testimony to how widespread its anti-commercial, anti-violence stance had become.[54] As an organization consisting largely of middle-class parents, ACT articulated its arguments with a clear social and political consciousness through presenting itself as concerned citizens acting chiefly on behalf of their children.[55] Its influence over advertising issues was quickly felt, as the networks rapidly reduced the amount of advertising available for Saturday morning broadcasts, particularly related to ACT's greatest concerns—candy-coated cereals, vitamins aimed at children, and toys perceived to be sexist in nature.[56]

Changing the actual content of the programs was another matter. Since, as Charren herself noted, political action to force parents to watch television with their children at all times (and thus have a direct understanding of its impact upon them) was out of the question, it was therefore up to the networks to exercise greater control over both advertising and program content on Saturday mornings.[57] The implication of this statement was clear: if the networks were held *directly accountable* for what they presented to audiences on Saturday morning, they could more easily become the targets of social and economic boycotts for presenting "damaging" material to child audiences. While ACT chose not to follow through on this threat, as they would in their long campaign against the sugar industry during the 1970s,[58] this issue was something that the networks were now being held accountable for, in ways they certainly did not like. Needing a convenient scapegoat, antagonists naturally focused on the producers of children's television, particularly television animation.

These changes were gradual but noticeable throughout the 1970s. If the decade had opened with an overemphasis on super-heroic action, it ended with this material either exiled from the air entirely or heavily hamstrung. Comedy was put under similar restraints. Satirical critiques, snappy dialogue, and other examples of the more creative uses of television animation narrative construction were largely abandoned. In their place came a highly starched and narrowly defined format, focused as much, if not more, on edification as entertainment. Where vibrant storytelling once existed, moralized ideology, focused on proper hygiene, comportment, and other concerns, became the norm.

It should be noted that, at this time, the producers of television animation had, effectively, no choice but to undergo this severe process of change. The market for animation in prime time had vanished, not to return until the 1990s. Syndication on a daily basis, which provided a viable basis for the production of material outside of network control, would not emerge as an option until the 1980s, as would the financial and cultural viability of cable television. The *only* marketplace that existed for television animation in this period, with the exception of the occasional prime-time holiday special, was Saturday morning. In this new, restrictive realm of operations, producers would have to abide by a stringent set of regulations if they wished to remain in business. Those who would not or did not (such as Jay Ward; see Chapter 3) simply were frozen out of the market. And, first and foremost, they had to be wary of the boogeyman-in-residence: the ever-changing network definition of "violence."

The problem with the networks' definition of "violence" was simply that it was too broad and elastic for the producers to understand fully what it meant for them, as it frequently included both comic and dramatic actions undertaken in the name of the plot and for no other reason. As they were strongly influenced by commissioned sociological studies of the relationship between children and violence (which, as historian Hal Erickson significantly notes, *always* managed to provide the results desired of those who funded them[59]), the networks arbitrarily drew lines in the sand for producers and blatantly warned them *not* to make the characters act "violently" at the least provocation. This was an act of self-preservation on the part of the networks, one which was clearly designed to divest themselves of responsibility for a situation they themselves had created in the first place. As historian Stefan Kanfer notes, the networks "had already miscalculated the moral climate, and they had no intention of compounding their error."[60] That the producers collectively were unhappy with this turn of events was, at the very least, an understatement. Joseph Barbera, in particular, argued that this excessive form of network censorship simply amounted to "legislated television." "It's as if they had legislated football and said you couldn't tackle anymore," he told writer Gary Grossman in 1981. "I can guarantee that we could still have a product that would have kids screaming their heads off with laughter, but we'll never be allowed to do it again on Saturday morning."[61] But, for all the complaints they made about the new order of things, the producers were definitely not in control of the situation. Nor were they able to control the escalating production costs that were a central reason their product came to look increasingly "cheap" in comparison with the past.[62]

Just like the plotlines of the programs they regulated in the 1970s, television animation censorship strategies ranged from conventional to absurd. Typical of the attitude was a memo circulated at Filmation Studios during this period:

> Program Practices [i.e., the censorship department] at CBS has ruled that a character that has been hit in a fight [c]an not have: 1] eyes at half-mast 2] eyes twirling 3] tongue hanging out 4] dazed or hurt look 5] closed eyes 6] circles around head. No Expression Of Pain Or Dazed Expression! [*sic*] The characters [c]an react with frustration at being foiled again. Camera: Do not shoot scenes you find with the no-nos in them.[63]

Significantly, these "no-nos" threw out the staple conventions of half a century of animation storytelling. Anyone familiar with American theatrical animation in its prime period is aware of just how important both vibrant animation *as well as* storytelling and characterization was for the genre's earliest, as well as many of its ongoing, successes. As a consequence, it was not surprising that television animation's creative qualities, in particular its freewheeling storytelling abilities, began to suffer under the new regime. This was particularly the case at the more established studios, such as Hanna-Barbera, whose staffers resented the increasing network interference—especially if they were veterans of the less regulated atmosphere of theatrical animation. Regulation was not helping creative quality; it was, instead, hindering it. As Hal Erickson later observed, "How could you create anything with impunity when the tongue-cluckers kept changing the rules?"[64]

Ironically, "the rules," which had been imposed as a "solution" to a highly ill-defined "problem," had become a problem in and of themselves, one seriously jeopardizing the continued creative freedom and integrity of television animation as both a programming genre and an economic entity. The networks had simply imposed them on the producers based solely on economic and political leverage, with no thought to consulting the producers, ACT or anyone else in the process, to distance themselves from the "violence" and censorship debates as quickly and—for them—painlessly as possible.

The networks varied in their approaches to the issue, but NBC's response was the most basic and reflective of its time. In 1975, it established a "Social Science Advisory Panel" to define what to do about the matter of "violence" in children's programming.[65] Predictably, a prime focus of attention was the "comic adventure full of gag strings and pratfalls," where the story supposedly served the needs of the action rather than the other way around.[66] In an effort to curb the existence of "violence" in its programming, the network insisted that the Panel be directly involved in the development and production processes for series, during which it would voice the network's mandate and ascertain whether or not programming was being produced to meet the network's specifications.[67] This served to shape the definition and scope of television animation broadcast on NBC until the early 1990s, when the network abandoned television animation *in toto* in favor of early-morning news programming and late-morning live-action programs aimed at young adults.[68] Similar restrictive covenants also served CBS and ABC well until both of those networks abandoned or limited their traditional Saturday morning programming formats, the former in the late 1990s, the latter in the late 2000s.

Along with the actual and fabricated concerns about "violence," the networks also mandated that programming now contain an additionally ill-defined and limiting programming idea. This was something called "pro-social values," a term that was loosely defined as a mandate for educational content to be placed, often in the most unsubtle ways, within the narrative content of the programs.[69] Joseph Barbera once again serves as an example of how his generation of animators reacted to a network-mandated program content imposition. With bitter wit, Barbera announced that he could no longer even produce cartoons where cats chased mice unless the characters "suddenly stopped to give lessons in basket weaving or glassblowing."[70]

Given the immense volume of programming his company was now producing, and the way in which it was being heavily censored, Barbera had much to complain about. This was a type of scrutiny and interference that he and his staff heavily disliked. Because it had operated in a comparatively censorship-free environment during the 1950s and early 1960s, Hanna-Barbera was unable to completely adapt to the "new normal," and its product suffered as a result. One only needed to look at some of what the company was producing at this time to understand how this change drastically affected it. In terms of comedy programming, it was forced largely to rest on its laurels, trading on the name-brand recognition and goodwill created by its star characters to create programming whose chief purpose was simply to sustain a production schedule. A key example of this was *Yogi's Gang*, broadcast on ABC between 1973 and 1975, in which Yogi Bear and a large posse of characters from the studio's heyday traveled together on a floating, airplane-like "ark," and confronted the actions of a wide variety of transparent villains. The names of the villains alone revealed their character and intent: Mr. Waste, Mr. Cheater, Lotta Litter, The Envy Brothers, Mr. Pollution and the Greedy Genie.[71]

The studio's straightforward, action-oriented programming suffered even more under the new regime. The most popular and representative of this new sanitized format was *Super Friends*, broadcast on ABC in various incarnations between 1973 and 1986.[72] It was based on DC Comics' popular *Justice League of America* series—the name change, as Hal Erickson significantly notes, was a symptom of how badly the network wanted to avoid even the idea of militarism in its programming.[73] *Super Friends* was a series that was truly remarkable—at the time and now—in a number of ways. While theoretically an action-oriented superhero program, its narratives were carefully constructed to avoid any actions that even remotely connoted combat of any kind.[74] No personality or ideological conflicts existed between the lead characters, and some of the "villains" went so far as to apologize for creating havoc in that week's episode or segment. Instead, the lead characters: Superman, Batman and Robin, Aquaman, Wonder Woman, and the made-for-TV Wonder Twins, proceeded to lead the viewers through what was essentially "a caped and cowled learning seminar, wherein [they] would stress and practice teamwork, trust and cooperation," as well as other network-mandated "virtues."[75]

The presence of popular psychologist Haim Ginott, another supposed "expert," as a technical advisor simply reinforced this ambience. Later in the program's run, in an effort to alter the traditionally lily-white ranks of the superheroes, several "ethnic" heroes were added to the lineup: they included the African American Black Vulcan, the Native American Apache Chief, the Asian Samurai, and the Latino El Dorado. Yet this effort was equally limiting, and in some respects, almost racist; these characters, rather than being full-bodied individuals, were wooden tokens whose very presence debased the ambience of goodwill they were supposed to provide (though one could also say that of the other characters as well). It was their ethnicity, rather than their abilities, that was their *raison d'etre*, and even the viewers knew it.[76]

If *Super Friends* deserves to be remembered, it is chiefly for the fact that it was a monumental contradiction in terms: a superhero program with hardly any super-powered conflict in its narratives.[77] In the context of its time, it represents exactly the ideological currents defined in the network content imposition period, as well as the fact that its producing studio was not entirely willing or able to adapt to them.[78]

We cannot, however, say that television animation as a whole was without value or merit at this time. Some studios, such as Filmation (see below) were perfectly capable of producing work that balanced the necessary educational mandate with entertainment value, while others, such as Hanna-Barbera, found the situation more challenging. Yet, oddly enough, the series that managed the balancing act in perhaps the most resourceful and entertaining fashion was not a series *per se*, but a collection of short musical vignettes sandwiched between the programs. *Schoolhouse Rock*, as this project was known, was a staple element of ABC's schedule during the 1970s and early 1980s, and was revived with equal success in the early 1990s. Created by advertising executive David McCall, the project was an innovative attempt to produce educational messages through the beats and rhymes of contemporary pop, rock and jazz music.[79] Broken down into various sub-groups ("Science Rock," "Grammar Rock," "America Rock," etc.), each segment focused on a musical number on the theme *du jour*, with basic but effective and occasionally innovative animation, and lively vocal performances by the likes of Blossom Dearie, Grady Tate, Bob Dorough, Jack Sheldon and others. The segments served their functions quite well, educating memorably on their intended subjects while at the same time enthralling the audience with both the vocal performances and the visual imagery accompanying them. A multiple Emmy Award winner, the project spawned sound track albums and CDs and a stage presentation, as well as being honored later with video and DVD reissues. Despite its assets and credits, even the *Schoolhouse* had its detractors, who felt its efforts were simply "too little too late" to redeem all of Saturday morning in their eyes. Annenberg communications scholar Aimee Dorr went so far as to call it "shlock."[80] Nevertheless, *Schoolhouse Rock* convinced many, in the industry and outside of it, that television animation could indeed be successfully used for educational purposes, and its ideal and example would be extensively adapted and modified during the 1970s and 1980s.

Animation by Filmation

While some producers found the new environment of television animation censorship difficult to adjust to, there were others who found the new methods and approaches quite acceptable. The ascension of Filmation, and the ideals of its founder, Lou Scheimer, provide us with a representative example of a producer and studio that were able to work well within the confines of a restrictive creative environment.

Lou Scheimer was not a part of the original generation of television animators. He had not been apprenticed during the era of theatrical animation, nor had he been forced out of it by the contraction of the theatrical animation industry into television. Prior to establishing his studio, Scheimer had done as much non-commercial as commercial filmmaking, and was therefore well accustomed to working within the prescribed limits set for him by those who commissioned his work. He guided Filmation through the 1970s and 1980s by concentrating on its strength as a producer of comic and dramatic narratives and making them appealing to both audiences and programming executives. Most significantly, however, Scheimer engaged and respected his audience in a way most television producers in his time did not. Knowing full well that children and young adults were his primary audience, and that it was his duty to make sure that they came away from his programs both entertained and enriched, Scheimer harnessed himself and his studio's product to the new pro-social dictums. He made his lead characters people relatable, with obtainable goals. His treatment of women, African Americans, and child and young adult characters put other producers of his time to shame, and set a clear standard for his successors to follow. Though he may have been a businessman/animator as much as William Hanna and Joseph Barbera were, Scheimer proved himself more capable than they in being aware of who his audience was and what his obligations to them were during the 1970s and 1980s. This was one of the major reasons his studio remained in business as long as it did, and why his programming played a guiding role in re-inventing the manner in which television animation undertook even the basic telling of stories.

Born in 1926, and raised in Pittsburgh, Pennsylvania, Louis Scheimer (as he was billed on his earliest productions) was the son of German-Jewish immigrants to the United States. (His father, a World War I veteran, had shortened the family name from the more cumbersome "Gunderscheimer" upon immigrating.)[81] Displaying artistic talent from an early age, Scheimer refined his abilities as a student at Carnegie Tech (now Carnegie Mellon) University, where the young Andy Warhol was a contemporary. Like many artists from the Eastern states, Scheimer was forced to travel to the West in the 1950s in search of work, though he eventually returned East briefly before permanently settling in Los Angeles in the 1960s. His chief employers during this time were advertising agencies and non-commercial filmmakers, who employed him to produce animated ads for Ford and other clients, along with commissioned religious films. Ironically, he also worked briefly at Hanna-Barbera during the late 1950s. During this time, he met and first began working with Hal Sutherland, a gifted animator who would become Filmation's principal director for most of its existence.

Scheimer gave some perspective on himself and his background in an interview with writer Edward Palmer in 1987:

> I came out here [to Los Angeles] in 1955 hoping to get a job in the animation industry.... [B]asically to get a job in the animation industry you're talking about programming for young people ... and it was the heyday of the animation industry. It was when UPA was ... doing terrific stuff.... [U]nfortunately, it also was the end of the animation industry as it was then known because just about that time was when the major ... [film studios] were starting

to close their animation studios.... And television had not really started to pick up the pieces.... [W]hen I first came on ... the only thing around was doing animation for commercials.... [T]here was a bunch of studios around that fortunately kept the animation industry alive in those early days doing commercials.... [I]t was not until ... the early sixties that television [animation] really started to become significant.... In those days sponsors were really buying shows and placing them and bartering them and hiking back time and stuff like that.... [I]t wasn't until the very early sixties that television [animation] really became important with network television.... I started ... [Filmation] ... in 1962. The first three or four years were dreadful. We'd pick up a job now and then, but it was difficult.[82]

The most significant of these early "jobs" was *Rod Rocket*, a syndicated series broadcast in 1963, which Scheimer co-produced and co-directed.[83] Largely obscure today, the series involved "serialized space adventures with a soft-pedaled educational slant,"[84] setting in place the basic template that would come to be a trademark of Filmation's production process. For this project, Scheimer recruited a number of animators at one of his former employers, Larry Harmon Productions, and this group, headed by Sutherland as animation director, formed the basis for the Filmation production staff. Soon afterward, Scheimer took on as his business partner Norman Prescott, a veteran executive in the radio and popular music fields whose contacts would become increasingly valuable to the studio.

The studio's big break came in 1965, when DC Comics approached it to bring their star character, Superman, to television animation as part of Fred Silverman's "superhero morning" concept at CBS. The result was a vibrant program which stayed true to its source material even within the limitations of the six-minute episode format. With *The New Adventures of Superman*, as the series was titled, "Filmation established its future *modus operandi*."[85] First of all, while many of its future productions would be adaptations from other media sources, Scheimer and company were still able to infuse the material with personal touches. Superman, in this series, was kept entirely within a fantasy context. There were no references to the then-incipient war in Vietnam, unlike when, as noted in Chapter 1, the Max Fleischer–produced Superman theatrical cartoons directly involved the character in World War II.[86] He did intervene occasionally in military affairs, as when American military installations were threatened by alien invaders in "The Force Phantom," although episodes like these were rare. As well, Filmation, unlike Fleischer, used Superman's comic-book enemies heavily in the narratives,[87] and proved capable of constructing highly original and compelling narratives on their own. One example: "The Pernicious Parasite" episode, wherein Superman is nearly defeated by a petty thief who, through exposure to radiation from a mysterious chemical, becomes capable of draining the strength from the body of anyone he touches—and consequently targets the Man of Steel as a potential mother lode. Narratives like these focused clearly on a polarized, Manichean depiction of the forces of good and evil, another studio hallmark.[88] Another regular development began with the employment of figures involved with Superman's prior media incarnations to ensure a level of accuracy and fidelity rare in media adaptations of outside sources. The studio employed writers from DC Comics (George Kashdan, Leo Dorfman, and Bob Haney) for the scripts, and the stars of the long-running radio series (Bud Collyer as Clark Kent and Superman, Joan Alexander as Lois Lane, and Jackson Beck as the narrator) to reprise their roles for the animated version. While, to some critics, the animation itself may have left something to be desired,[89] Filmation clearly established itself as a credible producer of superhero animation, and television animation as a whole, with this series. In the coming years, the studio would become so identified with superhero narratives that it became known within the television industry as the "superhero company."[90]

Yet, to its credit, Filmation proved itself to be equally effective at producing other kinds of television animation. One example of this came in 1968, when Fred Silverman commissioned it to produce a series based on the popular "Archie" comic-book line as a perceived "antidote" to the concerns over "violence" in television animation.[91] *The Archie Show*, debuting in the fall of that year, and its successor programs, became an immensely successful franchise for the studio. While it certainly traded on the name-brand recognition of the characters, the series was produced in a manner that made it equally appealing to both children and young adults. Each episode of the original program, for example, concluded with a "dance party" segment, after the fashion of those included in NBC's live-action series *The Monkees*, aimed at the same audience, which had just concluded its original run. Through the involvement of Prescott and CBS, music publication tycoon Don Kirshner, who had previously worked on *The Monkees*, was contracted to supply original music for these segments. These songs, written by Kirshner's stable of songwriters, were then presented on the show and issued on Kirshner's record label as if they were "performances" by the fictional characters' band, "The Archies." Surprisingly, one of these recordings, "Sugar, Sugar," proved to be popular enough to become a #1 hit on *Billboard*'s pop music chart, which certainly must not have hurt the TV show's popularity.[92]

As the program cycle continued during the 1970s, the formats within came to vary considerably. As Prescott once explained in an interview, the studio was in a position where it had to constantly "look for other ways to utilize the characters in new forms to regenerate interest. Sometimes we succeed, sometimes we fail."[93] Where they succeeded was in expanding to an hour-long format in 1969 and featuring a giant "jukebox" at the center of the action in 1970–71. Where they failed was in taking the format beyond the scope of its original focus. *Archie's TV Funnies*, running between 1971 and 1973, found the characters operating a TV station which presented animated adaptations of archaic comic strips such as "The Katzenjammer Kids," "Nancy," and "Dick Tracy," whose appeal to television audiences in the 1970s was questionable at best. Likewise, the well-intentioned *U.S. of Archie*, airing between 1974 and 1976 to coincide with the build-up to the American Bicentennial, suffered from poor ratings and uneven execution. On the positive side, the series helped to bring attention to then-neglected figures in American history, such as Harriet Tubman.[94] This was a demonstration of yet another enduring Filmation studio trait: its socially progressive politics. While the *Archie* programs did not always succeed in their aims, they kept the studio active, and, like Hanna-Barbera's productions of the previous decade, showed that Filmation was a company capable of investing television animation with a unique, idiosyncratic quality absent in its competition's work. The studio's successful and varied work in the 1970s reinforced this position to an unquestionable degree.

Fat Albert and the Cosby Kids

The idiosyncratic nature of Filmation, and the best example of its methodology and ideology during this time period, is seen best through the lens of the studio's most popular and famous program of the 1970s: *Fat Albert and the Cosby Kids*. This groundbreaking and enduringly influential series debuted on CBS in 1972, and ran there and in syndication for over a decade, an unusually long run by the limited lifespan standards of television animation. From the first announcement of its production in April of 1972,[95] *Fat Albert* was heralded as a revolutionary program, and, to a degree, it delivered on this promise. To begin with, there was the presence of the star performer and his definite vision for the program. Bill

Fat Albert and the Cosby Kids. Center: Rudy; clockwise from top: Fat Albert, Weird Harold, Bill Cosby, Bucky, Russell, Mushmouth, Dumb Donald (Bill Cosby/Filmation Associates/Photofest).

Cosby was (and is) one of the most influential African American figures in the history of American media, and one who has repeatedly made numerous, if subtle, political statements in the name of his art.[96] *Fat Albert* was no exception. In many ways, it fundamentally altered the methodology and means by which television animation communicated with its young viewers, creating a template for numerous "pro-social" narratives to follow in the 1970s and 1980s.

Fat Albert differed from the majority of child-directed programming at this time, animated or otherwise, in two important ways. First, it had a major and important cultural figure (as Bill Cosby had already proved himself to be at this stage in his career) as its guiding spirit, and, second, it was intended to educate viewers even more than entertain them. Having risen from growing up in poverty in Philadelphia to becoming an Emmy Award–winning actor and Grammy Award–winning stand-up comedian, Cosby was already a great success story to many. Yet he was not entirely satisfied with this. Having dropped out of high school and then college to pursue his entertainment career (much to the disappointment of his mother, who had always insisted that "education is a must!"[97]) Cosby, in the early 1970s, embarked on a quest to better himself and become a good example to people who identified with him. His commitment to education led not only to his becoming involved with educational TV programming, for example by appearing on PBS's *The Electric Company*,[98] but also to his pursuing academic degrees in education. The climax of this quest came in 1976, when Cosby received a doctoral degree in education from the University of Massachusetts.[99] *Fat Albert* proved to be the centerpiece of this quest. It was a series that, in Cosby's mind, would be "more than simple entertainment for a Saturday morning."[100] Its deceptive, and almost subversive, purpose was to educate children, particularly African American children, in the reading, writing and behavioral skills they seemed to lack. Cosby used the development of the program as fuel for his doctoral studies, insisting that the program's mandate be weighed heavily to the study of educational issues.[101] The most significant step in this light was his recruitment of a panel of advisors, headed by Dr. Gordon Berry of UCLA, who provided input to ensure that each episode's intended purpose conformed with Cosby's educational mandate.[102] As a consequence, it is clear that Cosby played a key role in ensuring that the program was used as a vehicle for the illustration of pro-social narratives, as clearly demonstrated by the structure and content of the program episodes themselves.

Whereas other programs before and after would simply pay lip service to the mandate of educational content, *Fat Albert* made it a key and essential part of its storylines. As executive producer (the first African American to hold this position on an animated television program) and live-action host (innovatively cut into the animation footage to set up the stories and provide commentary on them for the audience's benefit), Cosby put his identifying marks on the series and, with them, provided an implicit guarantee that the program would have substance as well as entertainment value. This was made most clear in his greeting to the viewer during the program's main title sequence: "This is Bill Cosby coming at you with music and fun, and if you're not careful, you may learn something before it's done." Yet, as much as Cosby contributed to the program's success, he likely would not have been able to produce the show as he wished had Lou Scheimer and Filmation not been completely willing and able to support him in his aims. In other hands, even with Cosby's presence, the results might have been disastrous, but Filmation was a studio that was just as committed to diversity and education in television animation as Cosby was. When he was asked why he was supportive of positive portrayals of minority groups in his work, Scheimer responded with a simple but revealing statement: "It had to be done" simply because his contemporaries were *not* doing this. Scheimer's political thinking was thus progressive enough to allow Cosby to structure the show as he wished and create the educational mandate for it that he wanted. The presence of this educational mandate, as well as the inventiveness of the studio's writing staff, would ensure that both the educational and entertainment aims of the series were met, often in extremely felicitous ways.[103]

Fat Albert was one of the first programs in television animation history to depict African American characters *without* the condescension or racism that had clearly been present in media depictions of the race in the past.[104] Indeed, Cosby and Filmation went to great lengths to ensure that their characters, despite their obvious racial characteristics, would appeal to people from a wide variety of backgrounds. As they were based on people Cosby had known in his childhood and had immortalized in his stand-up comedy routines, they displayed real emotional behavior even as they engaged in slapstick comedy antics.[105] Like Walt Disney's Seven Dwarfs, they were constructed both as a unit concerned with mutual goals and as individuals with finely honed personalities. The title character, Fat Albert (voiced by Cosby himself), was not only the group's gravitational center, but its moral one as well. Bill and Russell Cosby (Cosby and Jan Crawford, respectively) were distinguished by their fraternal loyalty, with Russell further distinguished by his small size, distinctive voice and quick wit. Guitar-playing Rudy (Eric Suter) was portrayed as an arrogant braggart, and, therefore, the resident "bad" example for the audience—as well as being a regular target of his friends' wisecracks. Mush Mouth (Cosby) displayed a personalized speech pattern focused around repeated use of the letter "B." Dumb Donald (either Cosby or Lou Scheimer or both, depending on the source) lived up to his name with the insertion of the odd inane comment into the dialogue. Mudfoot (Cosby), an elderly African American man, frequently gave the boys counsel, whether they wanted it or not. These characters were supplemented by a wide range of others, most of whom only appeared in a single episode, and whose chief function was to help the Cosby Kids illustrate the theme/issue of the week for the viewing audience.

According to historian Christopher Lehman, the show's distinctive sense of both time and place was directed clearly at urban youths, its primary target:

> [The series] present[ed] scenery that illustrated the cost of the Vietnam War to urban America. After President [Lyndon] Johnson began spending more on the war than combating poverty in the 1960s, cities nationwide fell into disarray. Likewise, [the series] include[d] dilapidated buildings and garbage-filled junkyards in it backgrounds. In addition, the role of the junkyard as the space for the juvenile black characters to play represents the absence of community centers or public playgrounds—facilities frequently sacrificed by cities confronted with shrinking funds for public play areas. The [characters] make toys [and, in many of the closing segments, musical instruments] out of junk, showing not only creativity but also the financial inability to purchase toys. Such imagery was on par with contemporary movies focusing on urban African-American hardship[s].[106]

Lehman makes a key point here when he indicates how significantly the show drew on contemporary urban, and particularly urban African American, experiences to create its milieu, one that many in its target audience could easily relate to.[107] Though somewhat passively by the standards of the modern media, the series brought major social issues of its time, including racism and gender relations, as well as slightly more minor ones (such as the consequences of lying, cheating and judging others solely on the basis of their appearance) into sharp focus for its audience, allowing them to confront these concerns on a remarkably realistic level.[108] This was, in and of itself, a significant political statement. Up until this time, the vast majority of television animation's narratives had been solely focused on escapism and magical realism. By setting the program in a real and recognizable setting, Cosby and Filmation were making it clear that what was going on in the series was *not* the product of fairy-tale–styled imagination, but the bare bones of real life itself. This was a significant departure for the genre of television animation, and an approach that in the coming years would be regularly imitated to help give needed realistic depth to television animation storylines. With Cosby's assistance, Filmation proved that it was a studio that could set trends as well as follow them with this series. Further grounding this realistic atmosphere was the studio's employment of African

American street slang in the dialogue, such as the insult game "The Dozens,"[109] and the ultimate statement of un-coolness—"no class!"[110]

The narratives reflected the seriousness of the program's intentions. Every episode was firmly grounded in exploring issues of hygiene, comportment or morality universal to all children, or issues specifically concerning lower-class and African American children. One of the Cosby Kids or a close acquaintance would experience a problem, which would then be explored in depth. Coupled with Cosby's live-action commentary on the action, the results could be humorous, harrowing or often both. In the early episodes, at least, the theme of the episode was further emphasized at its ending by the gang "performing" a song based on the moral on their manufactured junkyard musical instruments.

An examination of one of the early episodes, "Dope is for Dopes," indicates how significantly these various elements of *Fat Albert* tied together to create a compelling television experience. Franny Bates, an acquaintance of the gang, has been treating them to a variety of expensive presents paid for, apparently, with money from Franny's brother, Muggles, who is a "businessman" of some nature. When Fat Albert accidentally damages Franny's motorcycle while riding it, he goes to visit Muggles (who has the experience of an urban criminal, or a "blaxploitation" film villain),[111] and offers to work for him to pay for the damages. Muggles gives Albert a package to deliver, but, before he can deliver it, he is arrested by the police. They inform the naïve Albert that the package contains drugs and that Muggles is a notorious drug dealer. Albert is forced by the police to participate in a sting operation, which results in Muggles being arrested. Franny promptly loses his money, and bitterly ends his friendship with Albert as a result. Albert worries that he has also lost the friendship and respect of the gang, but they are, in fact, proud of what he has done and tell him this. All is resolved.[112]

The very idea that a television animation program could and would be built around such a contemporary, hot-button issue as drug dealing and drug use illustrates just why *Fat Albert* was such a groundbreaking program for its time. Few other programs, animated or live, would have even remotely considered tackling the topic as subject matter, despite the fact that the drug culture was epidemic in urban centers of the time, and young kids like Albert were being used as "runners" for "pushers" such as Muggles. In the series' approach to the issue, however, it was not red-flagged as a topic of grave national concern, but situated in purely human terms by focusing on Franny's reaction to discovering how his brother was really making his money. Like many of the characters placed in similar positions in the program's narratives, he does not like it, but he chooses not to allow the gang to help him confront the situation realistically because he has become emotionally overwhelmed by it. Narratives such as these—which allowed "real world" narrative arcs to be examined effectively and constructively in the otherwise "fantasy" realm of television animation—are a major component of *Fat Albert*'s legacy to the programs that chose to follow its pro-social narrative path.

Other episodes of the series similarly grounded real, relatable problems in the fantastic context of animation to ensure they were addressed and examined in ways that could be grasped constructively by the audience. "The Newcomer," for example, focused on Dumb Donald's reaction to the news that his parents are going to have a baby. Initially, he is emotionally shattered by the news, fearing that his parents will no longer have any use for him once the baby arrives. However, when the baby does come, he becomes interested in, and protective of it. The sensitive manner in which the show examined the scenario underlined its message—that older brothers and sisters should be grateful for the chance to be involved with younger siblings, and should not consider them annoying nuisances or usurpers of parental attention. Yet the series also presented issues and storylines that could *not* be solved easily within the timeframe of a half-hour television program. A very prominent example of this is the episode "Talk, Don't Fight," which deals with the touchy subject of inner-city gang warfare and its impact on the families of the gang members. The Cosby Kids' friend, Tito, is confronted with this situation when his older brother becomes a member of a gang. At the climax of the episode, Tito is killed by a bullet aimed at his brother, in a highly dramatic sequence that involves a rising heartbeat on the sound track and visual evidence of a (literal) smoking gun.[113] As historian Heather Hendershot has noted, such a blatant depiction of a person's death was unheard of at this time in Saturday morning television; if death occurred in the narratives at all, it happened off-screen, presumably to shield the audience from the effects of seeing it. Hendershot contends, justifiably, that it was only because of Cosby's influence and the program's stated educational mandate that such a program could have even been made in the first place.[114]

Episodes such as these provided a clear ideological challenge to the prevailing view that television animation did not, and could not, present material with redeeming social values. It was through their production, in fact, that Cosby and Filmation's attempt to present the programs as educational narratives was seen at its most effective level. By constructively dealing with issues that children and young adults, especially (though not exclusively) in the African American community, dealt with on a regular basis, *Fat Albert* towered above its contemporaries, and remains one of the most powerful examples of how a television animation program can effectively present educational narratives without being forced to compromise its creative storytelling in the process. As well, in outlying issues related to the "urban crisis" facing the majority of African American children, the series stood out from other animated and live programs of the era, which often pretended African Americans did not exist to avoid discussing social and political issues of concern to them. The stories in this program were not escapist fairy tales. They were inescapably *real*—which added immensely to their impact.

This commitment to social realism was something the series maintained throughout its run. In one of the later episodes, "Busted," the boys become involved with a "Scared Straight"–styled program after accidentally witnessing a crime in progress. Just as their real-life counterparts in the now-famous program would have done, a group of menacing convicts "assaulted the terrified boys with threats, profanity, and sexual invitations."[115] Few other television animation characters had encountered such a psychologically damaging scenario before the Cosby Kids were placed in this position, and few would again until the advent of more liberal-minded programming strategies in the 1990s. Cosby prefaced this episode with a warning about its content, but that could not have been enough to prepare some viewers for the kind of visceral experience that was to come. Presenting this kind of material was a calculated risk on the part of Cosby and Filmation, but only *Fat Albert*, among television animation programs of its time, was realistic enough to present this material as effectively as it did.

One might believe that CBS, the program's home for much of its original run, would have been pleased with *Fat Albert*'s pro-social agenda, and would have encouraged its producers to continue making material in the same vein. In actuality, the relationship between producers and network was far more complex than that. Initially, CBS took pride in the series, describing it as an effective and new form of televisual discourse when defending itself against John Pastore, ACT, and others who opposed television animation.[116] Yet, at the same time, given its status as a "mere" television animation program, it was also considered disposable. When Cosby and Filmation approached the network for funding to extend the show's production run, they were refused on at least one occasion. CBS's argument was that reruns of the shows were doing as well in the ratings as the original broadcasts, so there was, as a result, no reason to waste money on the production of new episodes.[117] As a consequence, although it ran for over a decade on the network, *Fat Albert*'s production run on CBS was limited to 54 episodes. During some seasons, CBS would not allow the production of any new episodes at all.[118] This was hardly a fit way to treat such a socially constructive program, and it likely would not have happened if it had not been a television animation program, and one aimed, specifically, at an underprivileged group of consumers whom the network could not profit from directly. At least Cosby and Filmation seemed to believe this, and, as a consequence, when the potential came to revive *Fat Albert* as a syndicated program in 1984, with full production resources and support now available, they jumped at the chance.

By this time, the series had already undergone a drastic cosmetic change. In the late 1970s, the title of the series was changed to *The New Fat Albert Show*, and there was also a change in the show's atmosphere. The early *Fat Albert* episodes had been presented within the confines of a world made up almost entirely of African Americans, which, despite its realistic trappings, had seemed to almost be hermetically sealed off from the larger (read: white) world.[119] In the later episodes, the characters began attending a primarily white school, and seemed to be almost the only African American people in existence there. The storylines began focusing on the Cosby Kids' friendships with the white characters, whom they often had to rescue from difficulty. As well-intentioned as this may have been, this tended to mute the impact of the storylines of some of the later episodes, as the more complicated sphere of race relations began intruding, both directly into the narratives and indirectly into the character relationships. In such a context, the program's formula became more limited—and limiting.

Nevertheless, the Cosby Kids were still allowed to keep their junkyard and dilapidated clubhouse, to which they frequently adjourned to watch television. The subject of one of their favorite programs, whose adventures were depicted extensively in each of these later episodes of the series, was one of the few positive changes to the show's format in this period. The Brown Hornet (Cosby) was an African American superhero with a clearly defined altruistic attitude toward life. Although his adventures were written and drawn comically, in a bizarre visual approach reminiscent more of the early Looney Tunes than the rest of the show they accompanied, the Hornet and his sidekicks Stinger and Tweeter (Lou Scheimer and his daughter Erika, respectively) were treated in plainly human terms, as were the bizarrely conceived extra-terrestrials they dealt with, in roaming the galaxy. In contrast to the "ethnic" superheroes on *Super Friends* in particular, the Hornet was a strongly conceived and purposeful character who provided a positive example for the Cosby Kids—and *their* audience. He could be related to in a way others of his kind could not, in part because he displayed a streak of self-deprecating humor along with his other abilities. The Hornet segments were placed at the beginnings of the episodes they appeared in, so that they could serve as something of a mini-preamble for the actions in the main episodes to follow, as the Hornet's unique brand of justice was enforced on a wide variety of space tyrants, crooked salesmen and other ne'er-do-wells who needed to be shown the error of their ways. They minutely copied the issues that would be dealt with in the main story, and often handled them, given their more limited running time, better than the main stories did themselves. It was perhaps no wonder that, in these episodes, Fat Albert would cite the Hornet as a precedent for the actions he took to resolve his own problems. The Brown Hornet stories functioned well as a show-within-a-show, and could easily have provided fodder for a spinoff series had Cosby and Filmation been so inclined. Even with the emerging trend to depict ethnic superheroes in a more realistic manner, the Brown Hornet still stands out as one of a kind.

In spite of the limitations placed upon it, *Fat Albert and the Cosby Kids*, in its various incarnations, was still able to produce material of a nature never before seen in television animation. By doing this, it was able to establish itself as a lasting and enduring influence on future television animation storytelling. It fundamentally reshaped the manner in which television animation dealt with African Americans, treating them as human beings rather than stereotypes and bringing the unique urban social issues they faced to the attention of a diverse national television audience. Yet the most important part of its legacy was the fact that it was instrumental in changing the relationship of television animation programs *vis-a-vis* their intended audience, in ways that continue to resonate, directly and indirectly, in modern television animation programs. After this series, television animation programs could no longer simply take their audiences for granted. Their narratives, characterizations and plots would have to conform to more realistic models, and they would now have to engage the viewers as active participants in the ongoing narratives if they wished to retain their attention and loyalty. After *Fat Albert*, television animation characters, particularly in programs aimed directly at children and young adults, would have to be both enlightening and entertaining figures if they wished to survive in the competitive television marketplace. And, as we will see, this was not a task at which all of them proved capable.

Despite *Fat Albert*'s phenomenal success, it proved to be lightning in a bottle rather than the beginning of a long-term trend. The extreme censorship of the era, coupled with the interest of the networks in following short-term popularity trends rather than establishing brand loyalty as television animation providers, did much to decrease the value of even the most well-intentioned projects during the decade. Filmation found this out the hard way, as it struggled (and occasionally succeeded) to balance the education/entertainment mandate Cosby and Scheimer had established with *Fat Albert* with the esoteric production style that had become the studio's trademark.

OTHER FILMATION INITIATIVES

As noted earlier, Lou Scheimer was already accustomed to balancing his needs and desires with those of the television executives who employed him. If he was handed lemons in terms of what he could do, he could still make lemonade. He had already demonstrated this with his 1960s superhero programs, the "Archie" series and *Fat Albert*, and kept his company in operation during the 1970s and 1980s on similar principles. In addition, just as Hanna-Barbera had achieved financial security after being sold to Taft Broadcasting in 1967, Scheimer achieved this for Filmation with its sale to the TelePrompter Company in 1969. (It was later sold to Westinghouse Broadcasting in the early 1980s, and was then acquired, and shut down, by L'Oreal in 1988; see Chapter 5.) This freed Filmation to experiment, and it began to produce a wider variety of both animation and live-action programming under Scheimer's guidance.

One of his more notable experiments predated *Fat Albert* by one television season. Debuting on CBS in 1971, *The Groovie Goolies* re-invented the traditional "monsters" of horror films of an earlier era in a "harmless" comedy setting.[120] While Frankenstein, Dracula, the Wolf Man, the Mummy, etc., had once been the key names in terror, World War II, and particularly the advent of the atomic bomb, had robbed them of their ability to truly scare people, and so, in the postwar era, they had simply become caricatures of their former selves.[121] Consequently, *The Groovie Goolies*, especially since it was aimed at children, was much more of a horror-themed version of *Rowan and Martin's Laugh-In* than a genuine horror narrative. The presence of defanged monsters from an earlier era was certainly symbolic of how much the "monsters" of Saturday morning had themselves been defanged. Yet even this proved to be not enough for critics of the form.

More directly related to the educational aims of the studio was *Mission: Magic*, broadcast on ABC during the 1973-74 season. The educational portion of the program was mainly accomplished through the presence of its protagonist, Miss Tickle (Erika Scheimer), a teacher who was able to transport her students to a world of fantasy—where adventure and learning awaited—simply by having them take a step through her chalkboard. Accompanying them was an animated version of actor/singer Rick Springfield (an imposition on the part of the network),[122] who regularly performed musical numbers related to the story at hand. This concept seems harmless and inoffensive today, but not so to critics of the time. As historian Hal Erickson has noted, the National Association for Better Broadcasting (NABB), a conservative, hard-to-please advocacy group that sprang up in the wake of ACT, complained about the program's "eerie settings and music," as well as its supposed use of "robbery, gangs and other sordid ingredients in cheap mediocre animation."[123] One has to question the motive of the NABB's comments here, given Filmation's already established track record for quality, but this harsh criticism was par for the course in this era.

It should be said that the NABB's comments mark it as a member of the group which comprised television animation's fiercest critics, then and now: conservative-minded social activists, religious leaders, and narrow-minded academics such as Annenberg communications scholar George Gerbner, who simply did not "get" what television animation was (in the eyes of its creators and producers) *supposed* to be about.[124] Mistaking what was intended as harmless fun as "threatening," "negative" or (as in the above case) "sordid" situations that supposedly had the potential to create "irrevocable" harm for children, ignoring and deemphasizing the positive aspects of the genre, and making baseless claims for its lack of creative value, these individuals and organizations criticized television animation programming without proper reasoning or, indeed, without offering any legitimate justification for the words and actions they proffered to defend their position. As with Drs. Wertham, Korengold and Ginott, and Mrs. Irvin Hendryson (see above), these individuals and groups used their self-imposed "expert" status as a shield that allowed them to belittle television animation from afar, and to argue that they knew what was best for the children of America. The hawk-like manner in which they monitored, and distorted, the actual content of television animation programming did much to prevent the finer examples of the programming produced in this period from being seen in a purely objective light, and went a considerable way toward the continued creative regression of the form in the 1970s and 1980s.

Yet, to viewers and television executives alike, Filmation remained a studio committed to quality in spite of this spate of baseless criticism. There was no better example of this than the studio's acclaimed animated version of the popular live-action science fiction series *Star Trek*, which debuted in 1975, six years after its prototype ended. This program had much to recommend it, and showed just how effective Filmation was in transferring narrative forms from other media into animation. In a unique form of support, the original series' creative team was actively involved with the animated version. Series creator Gene Roddenberry served as executive consultant on the storylines, while D.C. Fontana, one of the live series' principal writers, served as story editor and associate producer, making her one of the first women to hold this position in television animation. In addition, nearly all of the original cast members reprised their roles for the animated version. When preparing the series, Scheimer and Prescott went so far as to solicit the opinions of hard-core *Trek* fans at a 1972 convention. To ensure that the program would be able to be seen by this fan base, the producers convinced NBC (which had also broadcast the original series) to air the program in a late-morning timeslot, even though this would mean a significant decline in the overall audience share.[125] The result was a series that managed to reproduce and, at times, even enhance the appeal of its live-action predecessor, the latter coming chiefly because of the nature of its presentation. The series could provide materials, characters and plots that its studio-bound, financial-resource-dependent predecessor could not, simply for the reason that animation could provide visual effects and enhance plot and character illustrations without additional expense. Thus, this version of the program provided a wider range of non-human alien beings, and provided the supporting characters, particularly Lieutenant Uhura (Nichelle Nichols), with more instrumental roles than before. As well, many of the episodes were sequels, revisions or updates of earlier live-action episodes that felicitously exploited the animation medium. The effort ultimately paid off in the eyes of both critics and audiences. In 1976, the series received an Emmy Award for "Outstanding Children's Entertainment Series," the only such award the Filmation studio received during its existence.[126]

Nevertheless, the future beyond its initial broadcast period was not kind to the series. When noted science fiction author Alan Dean Foster was hired to adapt the animated series' scripts into prose form for book publication, he apparently did not even watch the series for reference purposes. Likewise, there has been considerable, vociferous debate among fans of the franchise about whether or not the animated series should officially be considered part of the program's "canon." Although Paramount (the producer) included the series in its issuing of the franchise on DVD, several otherwise well-researched books on the franchise simply leave the animated series out of the chronology—a fact that demonstrates the strength of the position against it. What is undeniable for our purposes, however, is that the animated *Star Trek* had, in many ways, just as strong an impact on its genre as the original live-action series had on its own.

Like *Fat Albert*, *Star Trek* was a significant and groundbreaking program for a number of reasons. As with the earlier program, it was the result of an outside producer (in this case, Gene Roddenberry) trusting Scheimer and Filmation with presenting an accurate animated version of a concept originally successful in another format, and finding that the producers were more than up to the challenge. In the case of *Star Trek*, the portrayal of the characters and their relationships with one another was to have an even more significant impact on the future of television animation than *Fat Albert*'s portrayal of white/black and inter-black race relations. In the original *Star Trek* series' design, Roddenberry had shaped character relationships in as democratic a way as was possible, given the show's militaristic undertones. The mere presence of a group of people from a wide variety of different races and backgrounds working together on relatively harmonious terms was a significant departure from the traditional focus on the "superiority" of the white American male in earlier media narratives (including, as shown in Chapter 3, some television animation programs). By choosing to respect Roddenberry's vision for the series and bring it to television animation intact and, in some ways, enhanced, Scheimer and Filmation were striking a major blow for a similar showing of democratic values in television animation narratives, which their forthcoming work would emphasize even further. In addition, by choosing to follow the original series' lead by respecting the intelligence of the audience, the series earned the favor of even the most hard-to-please critics of television animation, and clearly made it possible for further "highbrow" approaches to television animation to have a chance to succeed.[127]

Filmation proved equally successful at adapting several other existing media properties at this time. In its adaptation of *Tarzan*, in various incarnations between 1976 and 1982 on CBS, Tarzan (played by Robert Ridgely) was restored to Edgar Rice Burroughs's original conception of him as erudite and articulate, a version shattered by the MGM/RKO films starring Johnny Weismuller in the 1930s and 1940s. His "mate," Jane, was conspicuously absent from this series as well. There were a number of possible reasons for this change, but the severe censorship of the times explains most of them. Likewise absent from this series were the dramatic action sequences, graphic fights, and creatively portrayed African peoples of the Weismuller films, which, like the often inaccurate subject matter of the Burroughs novels, could not have been faithfully or fully reproduced in the conservative production environment of the 1970s. Nevertheless, the program, which chiefly involved Tarzan in relatively minor plot trifles (such as mediating a truce between two warring tribes of miniature human beings after becoming small himself), was notable for its high-quality background art, as well as for its clever and careful use of rotoscoping.[128]

For much of its original broadcast run, *Tarzan* was sandwiched among other Filmation products within a joint timeslot, as it appeared that the mythical King of the Jungle, in his new, more benign form, could not carry a timeslot on his own. During the 1977-78 season, it shared a timeslot with a new *Batman* series, whose chief asset was the fact that Adam West and Burt Ward, the stars of the popular mid–1960s live-action series, reprised their roles as Batman and Robin, respectively. The Caped Crusader received top billing in this combination. Then, between 1978 and 1980, Tarzan headlined *Tarzan and the Super Seven*, a mammoth 90-minute extravaganza designed by CBS to directly compete with another program of similar length produced by Hanna-Barbera for ABC. Tarzan and Batman were both retained, but of greater historical interest were the supporting characters—superheroes of an incredibly diverse and unique nature—who reflected the studio's growing confidence in its progressive political stance. "The Freedom Force" was Filmation's answer to *Super Friends* (see above) and consisted of the Egyptian goddess Isis (Diane Pershing) (also the subject of a popular live-action series produced by the company at this time); the legendary Greek hero Hercules (Bob Denison); Merlin (Michael Bell), the powerful magician and kingmaker of Arthurian lore; Sinbad (Bell), the famed mariner from the *Arabian Nights*; and a new character, Super Samurai (Bell), "the giant of justice" and alter-ego of a young Asian boy named Toshi. "Microwoman and Super Stretch" featured a husband-and-wife team, Chris and Christy Cross (Ty Henderson and Kim Hamilton, respectively). She could shrink to the size of a doll, while he was able to contort his body in a variety of elastic ways. Significantly, both characters were African American, a subtle reflection of the studio's ideals. Meanwhile, "Web Woman" focused on Kelly Webster (Linda Gary), a scientist who was gifted with the powers of all insects by Scarab (Lou Scheimer), a mysterious alien who served as her mentor. "Manta and Moray" concerned the last survivor of an Atlantis-like underwater society and his human friend (Joe Stern and Joan Van Ark, respectively). The program concluded with a live-action serial, *Jason of Star Command*, similar to the full-length live-action series the studio was then producing. Anyone who wanted a clear sense of how creatively diverse and politically progressive the Filmation studio was in its heyday needed only to see a *Tarzan and the Super Seven* broadcast to be convinced.

Between 1980 and 1982, the Tarzan series continued alongside two other adaptations of bygone media productions, *The Lone Ranger* and *Zorro*, which used animation to bring a new vitality to their antiquated ideas and structures. The Lone Ranger, the legendary masked rider of the plains who starred on radio between 1933 and 1954 and in films and an early live-action television series between 1949 and 1957, was an ideal adaptation choice for the times, owing to the fact that the character already abided by the high moral standards television animation's censors now demanded of it. As noted in Chapter 2, the Ranger and his faithful Native American companion, Tonto, had already appeared in television animation in the late 1960s via Format Films, but that version had played fast and loose with the original radio format. In Filmation's version, the Ranger was brought firmly back to his roots. The radio program's original opening narration ("A cloud of dust and a hearty 'Hi-Yo, Silver!,' etc.) and its powerful theme music (Rossini's "William Tell Overture") also opened the animated program. Animation veteran William Conrad (working under the pseudonym J. Darnoc) added further weight as both the narrator and the voice of the Ranger. In keeping with the changing times, Tonto (played by Ivan Naranjo in this version) was upgraded from a one-dimensional stereotype to a character with a broader range and wider vocabulary, yet one who continued to remain a loyal assistant and friend to his "kemosabe." The necessary educational component was provided in two ways. First of all, the narratives allowed the Ranger and Tonto to encounter historical figures from their indigenous time period, such as President Ulysses S. Grant, Buffalo Bill Cody and Annie Oakley (the latter pair making a memorable joint appearance that treated them with far more dignity and respect than Jay Ward had done when he featured them in separate segments of "Peabody's Improbable History" more than a decade earlier), and fictional characters from the era as well (e.g., Mark Twain's Tom Sawyer). The second component was something that was fast becoming part of Filmation's house style: when the narrative proper concluded, the Ranger would deliver a 30-second public-service announcement on a topic related to the episode's subject matter.

A similarly effective job was done with the adaptation of *Zorro*, the pulp-fiction hero of old California created by writer Johnston McCulley. Zorro, like the Lone Ranger, was a well-traveled media property when he came to animation, having been portrayed effectively by the likes of Douglas Fairbanks, Sr., and Tyrone Power in the movies, as well as by Guy Williams in a live-action TV series produced by Walt Disney, which aired in the late 1950s and early 1960s on ABC. Filmation's Zorro (Henry Darrow) resembled Williams physically, while his nemesis, the ruthless Spanish army officer Captain Ramon (Eric Mason), resembled actor Basil Rathbone, who had played the villain in the 1940 version of *The Mark of Zorro* (which starred Power).[129] Keeping with the censorship of the era, however, significant changes were made to the way Zorro performed his heroics in this format. For one thing, he never instigated swordplay with his opponents, simply saying that Captain Ramon's soldiers were "doing their duty" when they engaged in duels with him.[130] Filmation also provided new additions to the traditional cast of characters, most notably through the presence of Miguel (Julio Medina), the faithful retainer of Don Diego (Zorro's foppish secret identity), and Lucia (Socorro Valdez), an attractive but dangerous female pirate who shared Zorro's antipathy for the Spanish army but significantly lacked his altruistic attitude. Another important departure for the times was that the voice cast consisted primarily of Latino actors; in earlier versions of the story, non–Spanish Anglophones were typically cast in the leading roles. This was a progressive move on Filmation's part. Zorro followed the Lone Ranger's lead in providing public-service announcements after the narratives about the time and place he came from—explaining, in one instance, that the Pacific Ocean got its name because the explorer Balboa thought it was so "peaceful" (explaining the Spanish origins of the word "pacific").

The *Lone Ranger* and *Zorro* series represented Filmation's great strength at keeping the action-adventure sub-genre of television animation alive at a time when its creative integrity was most threatened, and, indeed, introducing these heroes of earlier times to a brand new audience. But while many of these projects were successful, the company also produced its share of badly conceived misfires as well. Overt comic material à la Hanna-Barbera was a particular Achilles heel. A case in point was *Uncle Croc's Block*, airing on ABC during the 1975-76 season. The live-action framing sequences of this series featured the title character (Charles Nelson Reilly), a children's show host who was, in fact, a bitter misanthrope who hated his boss, his job, and his audience, in that order. (In this light, he is a clear antecedent of *The Simpsons'* Krusty the Klown; see Chapter 6.) While it was an interesting concept on paper, in execution it was simply too little, too late. The live-action children's television series, the primary target of the series' satire, was a dying genre by the 1970s, humbled and reduced by changing audience tastes, imposed educational mandates, and ACT-sanctioned bans against program hosts touting products in commercials. Consequently, the program's true potential was minimized. Further reducing the quality were the presence of poorly conceived animated features, showing how inept the studio was at producing purely comic narratives. *Fraidy Cat* focused on a cat living on the last of his purported "nine lives." He had to avoid uttering the words one to eight (as doing so would result in the reincarnation of past versions of himself, who were scheming together to kill him) or nine (as doing so would result in his death). *Wacky and Packy* was the mirror image of *The Flintstones*, featuring a prehistoric caveman and his pet mastodon set loose in a modern city. Finally, there was *M.U.S.H.*, an incredibly uninspired parody of *M*A*S*H* (CBS 1972–83), whose sole novelty came from transforming the characters into dogs and then moving the action from war-torn 1950s Korea to "a god-forsaken snowbound outpost."[131] (It was also the only segment retained when the series was cut from an hour to a half-hour due to a decline in ratings.) ABC was so unimpressed by this fiasco that it vowed that it would not do any more business with Filmation, an act that slightly tarnished the studio's reputation as well as its ability to gain a wider audience for its work.[132]

Some of the studio's attempts to reinvent older media heroes for a newer, younger audience were simply not successful, in conception, execution or in the ratings. One notable failure in this vein was *Lassie's Rescue Rangers*, airing on ABC during the 1973-74 season. In this series, the legendary canine heroine was reincarnated as an aide to Forest Ranger Ben Turner and his family, who were active in protecting the natural environment from those who would threaten it. Significantly, this foreshadowed many of the ecology-themed plotlines of television animation in the 1980s and beyond, but, at the time, the series was unappreciated simply because the animation did not do the character or concept justice. Rudd Weatherwax, the trainer of the live-action Lassie, felt it was unworthy of the character's mantle, and referred to it simply, and ironically, as "trash." The ever-hostile NABB put it even more simply and bluntly: in their eyes Filmation had "incorporated violence, crime and stupidity into what is probably the worst show for children of the season."[133] Nothing displays the NABB's biases and attitudes better than statements like this. If well-intentioned programs like this did not please them, then what would?

There were additional misfires in the same flawed line, such as the self-explanatory vehicle *Will the Real Jerry Lewis Please Sit Down?* broadcast between 1970 and 1972 on ABC. (While Lewis created the series' format he was not directly involved with the production, which might explain its deficits.) However, the studio was able to produce comedy in a gentler vein, rather than with broad farce, as with *The Secret Lives of Waldo Kitty*, broadcast on NBC between 1975 and 1976. An adaptation of the central idea of James Thurber's story "The Secret Life of Walter Mitty," this underrated but charming program focused on an underdog, milquetoast cat (Howard Morris) who dreamed of heroically rescuing his female friend (Jane Webb) from the clutches of the bulldog (Allan Melvin) who frequently threatened them both. Opening and closing with live-action footage of the two cats and the dog with their off-screen voices dubbed in, the narratives proper consisted of Waldo's heroic "dreams," and allowed the studio to poke gentle fun at some of the properties it had already adapted to animation (especially Batman, Tarzan, The Lone Ranger and *Star Trek*) with gentle, unobtrusive comedic results. Thurber's estate, however, was less amused, actually suing Filmation for copyright infringement![134]

By the end of the 1970s, in spite of their past successes, Filmation was finding that its established approaches to material were starting to wear thin under network censorship. Further attempts to adapt heroes from the past (such as Mighty Mouse, in a series airing from 1979 to 1982 on CBS) to the "pro-social" present were increasingly spotty creatively. Clearly, a change of venue was needed. With that in mind, Scheimer engineered in the early 1980s to have Westinghouse, an influential station owner and syndicator, become Filmation's new parent company. The larger production demands (five shows a week instead of one for daily syndication) suited Scheimer and his team fine, and Westinghouse offered far less production interference than the networks. As a result, the deal came as something of a relief. Filmation would continue as an innovative television animation producer into the 1980s until it came to something of a tragic end toward the end of the decade (see Chapter 5).

Hanna-Barbera in the 1970s

As noted earlier, Hanna-Barbera, which remained the dominant producer by volume in terms of production during the 1970s, was the studio whose creative integrity and identity was most severely compromised during this decade. The dictatorial censorship of the time, which Joseph Barbera came to speak against, was a large factor in the decline in the quality of the studio's product during the decade, but there were other factors as well. In an effort to meet an increasingly high level of production demands, the studio was forced into radically changing the way it did business, in ways that came to anger and alienate the animation staff and gradually to erode the collegial, bucolic atmosphere under which the studio had done its classic work in the 1950s and 1960s. In addition, Barbera, like Walt Disney before him (and like contemporary Lou Scheimer's Filmation studio) eagerly began to spread the studio's creative wings into non-animation and non-television ventures, with decidedly mixed results. The consequences of this were obvious: while Barbera remained committed to creating and producing new television animation, he was not nearly as devoted to the projects as he had been earlier, and the projects which had made it to air suffered from his increasingly *laissez-faire* attitude. Most directly and obviously, the combination of extreme censorship and creative decline resulted in a rehashing and restructuring of earlier formats in the hope of gaining new success, an approach that became increasingly unpalatable over the course of the decade.

Put simply, nobody could rip off Hanna-Barbera better than Hanna-Barbera itself. If anyone knew how to produce things cheaply, it was they. The sad thing was, they did not have to.

◆ ◆ ◆

The rapid expansion of the television animation industry over the course of the 1950s and 1960s had helped Hanna-Barbera grow from a small cottage industry into a multi-million dollar enterprise—growth that was bolstered by the rapid rise of its principal characters into iconic "star" figures. Yet this process was not without its growing pains. Increasing demands for the studio's time and services necessitated first an expansion beyond the small team chiefly responsible for the studio's greatest hits, and, eventually, beyond the United States altogether, through the controversial process of "runaway" animation—the process of using foreign animation studios for animation labor as opposed to domestic ones, due to labor and economic issues.

William Hanna, who oversaw production at the studio's Cahuenga Avenue base of operations while Joseph Barbera globe-trotted to nail down deals for series, recalled that the studio's need to expand was simply necessitated by the way it was now doing business:

> Our facilities had become extended to the bursting point. We literally had every qualified animator in town busily engaged in some production or another. Joe and I had seen this coming for some time. For years we'd maintained a frenetic pace of production and business development as our studio and company had thrived along with the industry it had fostered. But now[,] events had reached a point where the animation business had, in true cartoon fashion, become the orphaned elephant that threatened to outgrow the house of its adopted parents.
>
> Expansion was clearly imminent. We would simply have to build a bigger house for the critter. In order to do that effectively, we would have to go farther than across town. The largest expanse of elbow room that beckoned was in fact waiting for us overseas.[135]

As Hanna saw it, the need to "build a bigger house for the critter" outweighed any concerns that might have arisen, and did arise, in many of the countries where he subsequently set up subcontracting arrangements for Hanna-Barbera productions—some of which did not even speak or trade in English, the language and audience for which they were produced. His Los Angeles–based employees, however, saw it in quite a different fashion.

As animation historian Tom Sito has so fully chronicled in his excellent book, *Drawing the Line*, the establishment of unions in animation had been achieved through as bloody and costly a fight as that undertaken to establish unions in other American professions over the course of the 20th century. By the late 1970s, however, unions had effectively become a fact of life for the Hollywood-based animation industry, but their demands frequently struck studios such as Hanna-Barbera as excessive. The central motivation for the switch to "runaway" production for these studios was simple and obvious: animators in other parts of the world, such as in Asian countries, worked under governments where unions were in more politically limited conditions than in the United States or, in extreme cases, effectively forbidden, and studios could, therefore, get away with paying these animators considerably less than their American counterparts for doing the same work.[136]

Local union leaders Harry "Bud" Hester and Morris "Moe" Gollub (both Disney veterans) had anticipated the shift by trying to force television animation studios to include a clause in their contracts that specifically insisted production on television animation programs not be moved away from Los Angeles "unless ... sufficient employees with the qualifications to produce a program or series are unavailable."[137] Filmation and other studios that never employed "runaway" tactics to begin with easily acceded to the demands, but Hanna-Barbera was different. They were supremely confident in the fact that they, and the union, "took care" of their employees well enough, which proved to be their undoing.

In August 1979, the dispute between producers and union came to a head when the

Motion Picture Screen Cartoonists (MPSC), the principal Hollywood-based animation union, went on strike, with Hanna-Barbera as its primary target. Studio production manager Jayne Barbera (Joseph's daughter) supposedly reacted to the news in what was "typical" behavior for her: "screaming epithets through the still hallways, throwing chairs, and kicking empty desks in impotent rage."[138] In contrast, Hanna, to his credit, seemed to keep his own formidable temper (the partial basis, as he admitted later, for Fred Flintstone's) in check. "I understand exactly what you are going through," he reportedly told one animator, "and [I] sympathize completely."[139]

The strike, nevertheless, occurred at a critical time—chosen to disrupt the current crop of productions so they would not be ready for their September TV schedule debuts and, therefore, to jeopardize the studios' relationships with the networks, who "were not very understanding about missed air dates."[140] Hanna-Barbera and the other studios employing "runaway" animation quickly capitulated and began employing the Hester-Gollub clause in their contracts, but the studio got its revenge in other ways by ramping up its "runaway" production in response. When a similar, industry-wide strike broke out in the summer and fall of 1982, the response of the three dominant television animation producers in the area was reflective of how much they favored or disliked "runaway" animation. DePatie-Freleng, a studio that did little "runaway" work, allowed picketers to march out in front of its closed offices. Lou Scheimer did them one better by marching outside the Filmation offices with a picket sign *himself* along with his employees. ("It was crazy," he later recalled.[141]) William Hanna and Joseph Barbera did no such thing. Their studio, it seemed, was the one that appeared to be most resistant to keeping its production operations entirely within America, and was targeted accordingly.

The damage of the 1979 and 1982 strikes, which publicly aired grievances that had built up gradually over the previous decade, did incalculable harm to morale at the Hanna-Barbera studio. Given this slow-building tension, it is perhaps no wonder that, during the 1970s, the truly innovative aspect of the studio's animation production almost ceased to exist.

◆ ◆ ◆

Union problems were one thing; creative problems were another. As far as he was concerned, Joseph Barbera increasingly felt that limitations were being placed on what he could do in terms of creative development because of the excessive demands of television censors, whose "or else" attitude he bitterly came to resent. With this in mind, just as Hanna began to expand the animation operations of the studio beyond America, Barbera began expanding studio operations into fields where he could be free of the network censorship bailiwick and produce creative material more worthy of the studio's commitment to quality. And, just as Hanna's expansion plans met with resistance in the animation industry, Barbera's plan to expand the creative scope of the company met with resistance, even within the company itself.

As Barbera saw it, his relationship with Hanna had evolved to a point where they were no longer working together directly. Barbera would supervise the creation of new characters, or, increasingly, acquire the licensing rights to established ones, and then he would simply trust Hanna and the animation staff to provide the final product where and when it was needed:

> Bill's job began precisely where mine left off. As the pace continually intensified very early on during the television years, we didn't even sit down to discuss characters or story ideas.

> There was no time. I came up with the characters and the stories, and Bill just took them from there, as completely confident that I had done my job as I was certain he would do his.
>
> We never-ever-got in each other's way.[142]

The mutual confidence in each other, honed over several decades' joint work, remained evident. But, increasingly, the partners were working in remote isolation from each other, rather than in the lockstep fashion employed during their theatrical cartoons and early television animation productions—yet another reason the creative quality of their studio's product of the 1970s and 1980s would suffer in comparison with the past.

As he was now less directly involved with the animation production aspects of the studio, Barbera became interested in making it less of a purely animation-centered concern and more of a diverse multi-media provider, much as the Disney studio had moved beyond its original animation-centered production operation toward becoming a multi-media powerhouse (though not yet the corporate monolith it would become in the 1980s). Naturally, his partner, and their business associates, viewed this attitude with horror, until Barbera, in his usual style, eloquently defended his mindset:

> The real problem was that most of my colleagues, Bill Hanna included, just did not want our studio to be in the live-action business.
>
> *We're a cartoon studio* [emphasis in original], they all said, and they couldn't understand why in the world I wanted to go into live-action.
>
> *What's wrong with cartoons?* [emphasis in original], they asked.
>
> The answer was—and is—*nothing* [emphasis in original]. There's *nothing* wrong with cartoons [emphasis in original]. I love doing cartoons. But why should that mean I can't do live-action, too—or, for that matter, write a play and get it produced on Broadway?[143]

Barbera was a highly—and uniquely—creative man but, as even his colleagues and friends could note, when he wanted to do something he felt would be really *great*, he could become persistently stubborn about it, refusing to abandon the idea until he had firmly proved to himself, rather than others, that the project truly lacked potential. Hanna recalled that there were times when even he riled Barbera's "good Sicilian blood" and they had "some real set-tos." They both humorously stated, on other occasions, that their relationship—and their opposing views on what constituted "the good life"—could, in fact, provide the basis for a rollicking situation comedy à la *The Odd Couple*.[144]

This being said, Barbera's position did have some precedents. During the 1960s, the company had set up its own music-publishing firm (Anihanbar) to control its copyrights in this area, and this logically expanded into starting its own eponymous record label which, after a brief flirtation with the rock-and-roll mainstream,[145] focused chiefly on sound track releases. So, in some respects, the studio was already a diversified business. Barbera simply wanted it to become more so.

His expansion of the studio's production slate, however, was a decidedly mixed affair. He developed too many ideas at once, and did not have the time to adequately supervise them all. "The bigger you get [as a company,]" he later admitted, "the less personal control you have over everything you produce."[146] Some projects, however, suffered more from this than others.

On the television end, there was, for example, *The Hanna-Barbera Happy Hour*, a live-action comedy/variety series which aired on NBC during the spring of 1978. The gimmick behind it was that the "stars" of this series were two life-sized female puppets, a blonde named Honey and a redhead named Sis, each animated by a six-man team invisible to the audience due to the then relatively new "chroma-key" electronic masking system. This project lasted a mere four episodes.[147] On the other hand, the studio also began producing a small group of live-action films for television with some success. *The Gathering*, a sensitive, Christmas-themed family drama starring Edward Asner, was the most successful of these, winning an Emmy Award for Best Drama Special in 1977.[148]

Barbera was likewise eager to expand into feature-film production. The studio had already produced two successful animated feature films based on their hit television characters,[149] and Barbera believed they could succeed just as well in live-action. He developed a live-action film project called *C.H.O.M.P.S.*, about a robot dog-cum-security system, which he persuaded American-International Pictures to distribute. However, the project proved to be star-crossed. In Barbera's original story for the film, the lead character was portrayed as a Doberman pinscher with a variety of super-canine abilities, but, in a meeting with AIP's executives, they "convinced" him that Doberman pinschers were not a very popular breed of dog, and that a more "lovable" breed would have to be used instead. Although Barbera felt that this defeated the entire purpose of the concept, he went through with it and saw the film through production. The film was modestly successful, but not nearly the hit Barbera envisioned it as, and with that, Hanna-Barbera's attempt to become a live-action film producer came to an abrupt end via a veto from the studio staff.[150]

Even when the studio returned to its natural production terrain (animation, as fodder for feature-film production) there were mixed results. After a lengthy period of negotiations with humorist E.B. White, Barbera secured the adaptation rights to his classic children's story *Charlotte's Web*, in tandem with Canadian financier Edgar Bronfman, who provided monetary backing.[151] Distributed by Paramount, the resulting film project, released in 1973, was, unquestionably, one of the studio's greatest achievements. Freed from the grind of producing for tight TV deadlines, the studio staff were able to produce some of the most realistic yet graceful background art and character designs they would ever create, under the expert direction of studio veterans Charles "Nick" Nichols and Iwao Takamoto. A brisk but entirely faithful script by Earl Hamner, Jr. (creator of the hit television series *The Waltons*) preserved the book's integrity amid a brace of original music, and some superb vocal performances (Henry Gibson as Wilbur the pig, Debbie Reynolds as Charlotte the spider, and especially Paul Lynde as the feckless con-man rat Templeton) served as the clincher. It was nearly entirely faithful to the spirit and intent of its source, and audiences responded accordingly, making it a box-office hit as well as a creative success.[152]

Unfortunately, Hanna-Barbera was never able to recapture, even modestly, *Charlotte's* box-office success. Their next feature film venture, *Heidi's Song*, again distributed by Paramount, was released in 1982 after an extensive incubation period. While this adaptation of Johanna Spyri's classic children's story, directed by Robert Taylor (who also co-wrote) was clearly cut from the same lavish cloth as *Charlotte*, it was simply tossed away by its distributor and thus ignored by audiences. This in spite of a fine screenplay (which Barbera also co-wrote) and the presence of star power similar to *Charlotte*'s (Lorne Greene played Heidi's gruff but tender grandfather, while Sammy Davis, Jr., portrayed the antagonistic Head Ratte [*sic*]).[153] Hanna-Barbera would produce only one further animated feature film while Hanna and Barbera themselves were still at the helm—an adaptation of *The Jetsons*, distributed by Universal and released in 1990.

Despite Barbera's flirtations with other media, television animation remained the studio's primary breadwinner, and the studio concentrated most of its efforts here in the form of both series and specials during the balance of the decade.

◆ ◆ ◆

The television animation productions of Hanna-Barbera in the 1970s took several forms, most of which demonstrated the company's tendency to follow, rather than set, trends.

The first group of programs was a mostly lead-footed attempt to reprise the family-sitcom mold of *The Flintstones* and *The Jetsons*. Though seemingly well thought out, they mostly proved to be disappointments. *Where's Huddles?*, a prime-time series airing on CBS during the summer of 1970, was unique chiefly due to the fact that its lead character, Ed Huddles (voiced by Cliff Norton), was a professional football player. In the *Flintstones* mold, Ed's chief on-screen associates were his wife Marge (Jean Vander Pyl), his best friend, teammate and neighbor Bubba McCoy (Mel Blanc), and Bubba's wife Penny (Marie Wilson). Also involved in the action were Ed's snotty neighbor Claude Pertwee (Paul Lynde); Ed and Bubba's African American teammate Freight Train (former Duke Ellington band singer and movie cowboy Herb Jeffries); and Mad Dog Maloney (Alan Reed), the coach of the Rhinos—the team for which Ed, Bubba and Freight Train played. The potential of this series was squandered almost immediately by the fact that most of the plotlines were recycled from earlier Hanna-Barbera efforts. Ed and Bubba's profession, as well, was shoved in the audience's face through the studio's by-now-standard comic overkill, as represented most blatantly by the presence of Ed's dog Fumbles (a giant orange mongrel who walked around in a helmet and cleats), and by Ed and Marge's Pebbles-like daughter, improbably named Pom Pom. On the plus side, the programs usually climaxed with some well-animated football games, called with expert precision by Emmy-winning sportscaster Dick Enberg.

The next effort in this realm was a little more successful. Airing in syndication between 1972 and 1974, *Wait 'Till Your Father Gets Home* would be the closest thing to an "adult"-oriented sitcom à la *The Simpsons* that Hanna-Barbera's new production and censorship mindset would allow it to produce during this period. Developed chiefly to take advantage of the new opportunities provided by the Prime Time Access Rule,[154] *Father* was very much structured in the fashion of the most popular live-action sitcom of the time, Norman Lear's *All in the Family*, in that it literally dramatized the almost anthropological culture clash between the straight-laced "establishment" (usually defined as the generation of people who lived through the Great Depression and World War II) and their more open-minded "hippie" offspring. Yet, as was common with Hanna-Barbera, there were some strategic differences between their product and its role model. The "Father" of the title was Harry Boyle (Tom Bosley), who worked as the manager of a restaurant-supply company and then came home to confront the activities of his dysfunctional family (though it was not nearly as dysfunctional as their equivalents in the 1990s and 2000s would prove to be). Harry's wife, Irma (Joan Gerber), was broadminded enough to be supportive of everyone in a way Harry was not, but his oldest children, Alice (Tina Holland) and Chet (Lennie Weinrib), were unquestionably, and stereotypically, "shaggy-haired liberal[s]"[155] after the fashion of *Family*'s Mike "Meathead" Stivic, though they made their points much more quietly than he did. Youngest child Jamie (first Jackie Haley, later Willie Aames) was more supportive of, and deferential toward, Harry—up to a point. The central difference between Harry and his live-action role model, Archie Bunker, was that Harry was not an intolerant bigot, but a relatively nice person who did not seem to deserve the abuse the other characters heaped on him. A more Bunkeresque presence was provided by Harry's neighbor Ralph (Jack Burns), a communist-hating acolyte of the late Joseph McCarthy, who "wore survivalist-style camouflage and a full magazine of bullets, and who constantly hid in the bushes for fear of enemy reprisal."[156] (In this sense, he is clearly the direct ancestor of *King of the Hill*'s Dale Gribble; see Chapter 6.) Ralph's fearsomeness was further emphasized by the fact that he ran the local Neighborhood Watch group as if it were his own private militia, with the assistance of his chief adjutant, a nearly mute old woman known only as Whittaker.

Given the comic potential of the series, it was surprising that much of it was squandered by poor execution. The studio often seemed to be hedging its bets, folding in the face of even *trying* to do something adult and satirical, which it no longer seemed capable of doing. If anything, a lawsuit filed by a prominent California used car dealer who felt he had been mocked by the studio in *roman a clef* fashion, made them even less eager to trouble the waters.[157] As a consequence, *Father*'s two-season run, half of which many stations chose not to air at all, chiefly consisted of restrained plots and storylines, along with gratuitous guest appearances by the likes of Pat Harrington, Jr., Don Adams, Jonathan Winters, Monty Hall, Phyllis Diller, Don Knotts and Rich Little. However, the example of its existence as an "adult"-oriented sitcom was clearly something that was not forgotten by the generation of television animators to come.

Other attempts at the genre produced worse results. *Roman Holidays*, airing on NBC during the 1972-73 season, was yet another feeble kick at the *Flintstones/Jetsons* can. Here, the setting was the Roman Empire (likely, the pagan BC version rather than the Christian AD one), but the anachronistic juxtaposition process that had helped the prior series to succeed simply made this one flounder. Family patriarch Gus Holliday (David Willock) was structured as a typical mid-century American in Roman clothing (toga, sandals, and a Caesarian laurel wreath on his head), with the others following the same path. Gus worked as an engineer with Forum Construction (Hal Erickson notes that he simply would have been a slave in the "real" Rome[158]), and then came home to his family at the Venus de Milo Arms. The other members of the Holliday family included Gus's mild-tempered wife, Laurie (Shirley Mitchell); his aptly named pre-teen daughter, Precocia (Pamelyn Ferdin); his teenage son, Happius (Stanley Livingston), better known as "Happy"; and Brutus (Daws Butler), the family's pet lion. A regular visitor was Happy's girlfriend, Groovia[159] (Judy Strangis), who often became involved in the episode plots. Once again, Hanna-Barbera chose to use this series as a charter course in the School of Bad Comedy Writing. The Venus de Milo landlord, for example, was named Mr. Evictus (Dom DeLuise), while Gus's boss was dubbed Mr. Tycoonius (Hal Smith). And it went on from there. Like George Jetson (whom he resembled in more than one way), Gus Holliday was a good natured *schlub* who had a surprising knack for getting himself into stereotypically exaggerated sitcom situations (such as impersonating a much younger man in order to be the "escort" of Mr. Evictus's hard-to-please teenage niece, specifically so the old man wouldn't act on his persistent threats to eject the family).

The last venture in this line, *These Are the Days* (ABC 1974–76), was another blatant imitation of a popular live-action TV hit, in this case *The Waltons*. However, it was successful in conveying the truly nostalgic feelings of the past engendered by its live-action predecessor, which was pretty much all that was asked of it. It was also very well animated, and scripted with a sense of taste and realistic restraint: something that could not be said for other studio productions of the era.

Another category of programming could simply and bluntly be referred to as "milking the cash cow," i.e., retreating into the creative and financial security seemingly provided by the studio's now-iconic cast of cartoon characters. *Yogi's Gang* (see above) was one example of this, but there were others as well. *Scooby Doo* and *The Flintstones* were the primary beneficiaries (if that is the right term) of this process. For the former, the process began with *The New Scooby Doo Comedy Movies*, airing on CBS between 1972 and 1974. This was essentially the earlier *Scooby Doo* format expanded from a half-hour to a full hour, and, if that was not enough, there was the additional blandishment of guest stars. While some of these choices were inspired (casting Don Knotts, a comic actor famous for acting cowardly, as a foil for the equally cowardly Scooby and Shaggy) and some seemed logical (Batman and Robin), others were totally bizarre (Sonny and Cher?). After a two-year layover, during which he moved from CBS to ABC,[160] Scooby was featured as part of *The Scooby-Doo/ Dynomutt Hour* in 1976 (see below for the latter component), and then as a principal part of *Scooby's All-Star Laff-A-Lympics*, airing in various forms between 1977 and 1979. The series (essentially an elaborate and self-congratulatory retooling of *Wacky Races*) showcased a varying group of athletic competitions featured in far-flung settings. (In this sense, it and *Wacky Races* can be cited as very distant ancestors of the modern "reality show" genre—in particular, competition-oriented series such as *Survivor* and *The Amazing Race*.) The competitors consisted of three groups: the "Yogi Yahooeys," headed by Yogi Bear and featuring the studio's star characters of the late 1950s and early 1960s, the "Scooby Doobies," headed by Scooby Doo and featuring most of the studio stars of the late 1960s and early-to-mid 1970s, and the "Really Rottens," the sole original characters, who functioned as the token, toothless villains-in-residence, à la Dick Dastardly. This group included the colorfully named likes of Mr. Creeply, Dread Baron, Dinky Dalton and Daisy Mayhem.

The Flintstones was similarly and just as extensively strip-mined during this time. This began with *Pebbles and Bamm Bamm*, airing on CBS in 1971-72, which magically converted the Flintstones' and Rubbles' offspring into teenagers and paired them with like-named and like-minded peers. The following year, the project was expanded to a full hour and re-titled *The Flintstones Comedy Hour*, with some new material included. In 1979, the characters were resurrected in the old format on NBC as *The New Fred and Barney Show*, with Pebbles and Bamm Bamm being depicted once again as young children. However, there was very little in this that was "new," save for the fact that Canadian actor Henry Corden replaced Alan Reed (who had died two years earlier) as Fred, and would essay the role until his own death, in 2005.[161] As part of a different programming strategy, reruns were coupled with the adventures of two newer characters (a teenaged version of *The Fantastic Four*'s Thing, and the Shmoo, a boneless, amorphous character originally created by cartoonist Al Capp for his legendary comic strip *Li'l Abner*). Although the titles suggested that Fred and Barney "met" the Thing and the Shmoo in the episode narratives, they only did so in the "bumpers" leading up to commercial breaks.

Both *Scooby Doo* and *The Flintstones*, in their original incarnations, were creatively discredited by these cheap resurrections, and neither program would ever truly regain any measure of the original enthusiasm they had once gathered from television audiences. The creative dissolution of the properties, in both new series and as a brace of new, independently aired "specials," would continue throughout the 1980s, as the studio over-relied on them to disguise their increasing creative impotence (see Chapter 5 for additional programs featuring the characters).

One might conclude from the above examples that the studio had simply run out of new ideas for series and was running entirely on creative auto pilot. But this was not entirely the case. A number of far more entertaining examples of the studio's series product also existed during this period, even though they were few and far between.

In an effort to compete with Filmation's *Archie* franchise, Hanna-Barbera began another category of production: series featuring teens for teens, as *Scooby Doo* was originally supposed to be. The most direct imitation was another set of characters in the same line, who would ultimately become part of the *Archie* comics line as well. Developed with input from Fred Silverman, *Josie and the Pussycats* ran in its original incarnation between 1970 and 1972 and "in outer space" between 1972 and 1974. The series concerned an all-girl rock group: red-haired Josie (Janet Waldo), African American Valerie (Barbara Pariot),[162] and Melody (Jackie Joseph)—a stereotypical "dumb blonde" whose ears wiggled at any forthcoming danger. Joining them were their principal acquaintances: Alexander Cabot III (Casey Kasem), their wealthy, bespectacled and cowardly manager; his perpetually angry sister Alexandra (Sherry Alberoni), who functioned as the principal antagonist (and was, according to Timothy and Kevin Burke, "a complete bitch"[163] to boot); blond and benign Alan M (Jerry Dexter); and Sebastian (Don Messick), Alexandra's cat, who functioned as the Muttley to her Dick Dastardly. The show—which featured an encounter with a villain (necessitating the now-ubiquitous chase sequence, cued by the phrase "Let's get out of here!"), and a group of musical numbers, every week—was perfectly fine when viewed as individual installments. Collectively, however, it highlighted what was clearly the problem with the studio during this time: the writers appeared to be able to think of only one good plotline for the characters, and then recycled it endlessly for the rest of the program's run, with only minor variations in theme and setting.

Similar ventures in this vein followed the same repetitive format, even though some had truly imaginative ideas at their core. *The Funky Phantom*, broadcast during the 1971-72 season, was a good example. It was, in many ways, an Americanized version of Oscar Wilde's "The Canterville Ghost." The principal character, disembodied spirit Jonathan Muddlemore (Daws Butler, reprising his Snagglepuss voice), was a Revolutionary War–era American who had hidden inside a grandfather clock to escape British soldiers and ended up stuck inside—until three early-'70s era teenagers (Skip [Micky Dolenz], Augie [Tommy Cook] and April [Tina Holland]) released him. "Mudsy," as he was nicknamed, promptly became their companion on a series of *Scooby Doo*–like adventures, which also depicted the recurring conflict between Mudsy's equally ghostly cat, Boo, and Skip's pet bulldog, Elmo. They traveled from place to place in a dune buggy named the "Looney Duney," which inadvertently suggested the kind of comedy the show tried, and ultimately failed, to produce.

There was still more in this line. In spite of its title, *Butch Cassidy and the Sundance Kids* (NBC 1971–72) bore absolutely no resemblance to the popular Paul Newman/Robert Redford movie from 1969. Instead, it focused on (you guessed it) a teenage rock group which traveled around the world while (you guessed it again) solving mysteries. They also had the now-requisite pet companion, who was named (oddly enough) Elvis.

Clearly not knowing when to quit, the studio trotted out two other blatant *Scooby Doo*-type mystery/comedy series during the 1970s. *Goober and the Ghost Chasers*, airing on ABC between 1973 and 1975, was the more noteworthy of the pair, mainly due to the presence of the title character (Paul Winchell)—a blue-furred, orange-toque–clad mutt who was able to make himself invisible at will and also had a way with a wisecrack. He was assisted by his teenage companions Gilly (Ronnie Schell), Ted (Jerry Dexter), and Tina (Jo Ann Harris), and by some gratuitously inserted celebrity "guests" (including members of the Partridge Family, who starred in their own series for Hanna-Barbera around the same time; see below). Other than Goober's contributions, the plots and dialogue were, unfortunately, blatant *Scooby Doo* rip-offs, right down to the "if it hadn't been for you meddling kids" monologue by the unmasked villains at the conclusion of each episode.[164] Even more derivative was *Clue Club*, airing on CBS between 1976 and 1977, whose stars were a pair of semi-humanized bloodhounds—egotistical Woofer (Paul Winchell) and lethargic Wimper (Jim MacGeorge).

Their associates were Larry (David Joliffe), Pepper (Patricia Stitch), D.D. (Bob Hastings), and Dotty (Tara Talboy)—the latter a 13-year-old "computer expert," and thus something of a fictional peer of two fellow "computer experts" who began their work in this period and would make it big in the forthcoming years—Bill Gates and Steve Jobs.

The most bizarre variant of this sub-genre, however, was *Jabberjaw*, airing during 1976–77 on ABC, whose "funny animal" protagonist was, of all things, a shark. Frank Welker voiced the character in a manner that was unquestionably based on the voice of Jerome "Curly" Howard, arguably the most famous member of the legendary comedy team, The Three Stooges. He was wont to complain, à la Rodney Dangerfield, that he never got "no respect" from anybody. As might be expected, this series was set underneath the ocean, with "Jabber" serving as the drummer of a teenage rock group called the Neptunes, who consisted of Biff (Tommy Cook), Bubbles (Julie McWhirter), Shelly (Pat Parris), and Clamhead (Barry Gordon)—a direct clone of Shaggy. The usual story patterns were repeated ad nauseum here.

There were, however, some projects that were more effective at combining laughs and thrills, even if they tended to wear the influence of the films and TV series that begat them on their sleeves.

Inch High, Private Eye, for example, which aired on NBC during the 1973-74 season, spotlighted a private investigator who was, as the title implied, only an inch tall. But that was the sole thing about it that could truly be considered novel. The title character's personality was quite clearly modeled on that of Maxwell Smart, the protagonist of the satirical sitcom-cum-spy drama *Get Smart*, which had aired on NBC in the previous decade. This was simply reinforced by the fact that his voice actor, Lennie Weinrib, portrayed him through a blatant imitation of *Smart*'s star, Don Adams. (Adams himself did more effective voice work prior to the series, as noted in Chapter 3, and would do more in the following decades; see chapters 5 and 6.) Because Inch was so small, he could only accomplish his job with the aid of normal-sized confederates, who consisted of his niece Lori (Kathi Gori), her boyfriend Gator (Bob Luttell), and their dog Braveheart (who wore a brandy cask, like that of a St. Bernard rescue dog, that held Inch's arsenal of weaponry). Inch's boss, Mr. Finkerton (John Stephenson), was head of the Finkerton detective agency and was routinely driven "to hair-pulling despair"[165] by Inch's inept antics—until Inch inevitably lucked out and solved the case of the week.

A far more imaginative character, one of the few inventive ones coming from the studio at this time, was spotlighted in *Captain Caveman and the Teen Angels*, airing during the 1977-78 season on ABC. "Cavey" (memorably voiced by Mel Blanc) was a prehistoric superhero who had been freed from glacial imprisonment by a trio of teenage investigators cast in the mold of yet another popular live-action TV series: *Charlie's Angels*. They consisted of the vivacious African American Dee Dee (Vernee Watson), the cowardly blonde Taffy (Laurel Page), and brunette Brenda (Marilyn Scheffler). But it was the Captain who provided the laughs, some artificially gathered from a laugh track (now an annoyingly persistent presence at the studio) and others, fortunately, genuine. Speaking in delightfully accented pidgin English ("Me make wrong turn"), Captain Caveman was, in Ted Sennett's words, "a genuine original"[166] addition to the studio's lineup at a time when it desperately needed one.

◆ ◆ ◆

An even more genuinely "original" concept was the subject of the sole creatively successful series produced by Hanna-Barbera during the 1970s, whose inventiveness and entertainment value made it stand out head and shoulders above the rest of the studio's dire product of the decade.

During the 1970s, there were two film genres that achieved enormous popularity from out of nowhere, and would have lasting influences on both film and television (including television animation) for decades afterward. Both genres focused, at their core, on the need for individuals to empower themselves in order to gain justice, and, also, on elaborate, almost ritualistic displays of violence. The "blaxploitation" genre was the first of the two. Begun with Melvin Van Peebles's 1970 underground hit *Sweet Sweetback's BADasss Song* [sic], and continuing through such hits as *Shaft* (Gordon Parks, 1971) and *Superfly* (Gordon Parks, Jr., 1972), these projects focused on heavily empowered African American protagonists—a quantum leap from earlier film portrayals of African Americans—who gained revenge on "The Man" (i.e., the "white" establishment) for the wrongs done to African Americans socially and politically.[167] While enormously popular, the genre shared, significantly, an Achilles heel similar to the Hanna-Barbera product of the '70s, namely the endless repetition of a few simple plot points. This was also the problem with the other popular genre, a series of Asian films based around the use and abuse of martial arts, which came to be collectively known as "chop socky" films. Produced overseas by the likes of the Hong Kong–based Shaw Brothers studio, these films, particularly those featuring the now legendary Bruce Lee, developed just as large a following as the "blaxploitation" films, and likely for the same reason—the immediate and visceral gratification felt by the audience at seeing "good" so blatantly and effectively triumph over "evil." The following grew despite many flaws with the presentation of the films, in particular the fact that the dubbing of the films' dialogue into English was often horrendously bad. Hollywood, nevertheless, was quick to exploit "chop socky" on its own in 1973's *Enter the Dragon* (Robert Clouse, 1973, featuring Lee in his last major role before his sudden death), and to combine it with "blaxploitation" in ways that highlighted both their essential similarities and their joint weaknesses. By far the most obvious example of this was *Black Belt Jones* (Clouse, 1974), featuring Lee's African American *Enter the Dragon* co-star, Jim Kelly, as an inner-city based karate expert who, in typical "blaxploitation" fashion, hunts down and kills the mobsters who murdered his mentor.

It was likely this latter film that most inspired Hanna-Barbera to come up with a similar hybrid product of its own later that year.

Debuting in the fall of 1974 on ABC, *Hong Kong Phooey* was a rollicking farce that managed to effectively spoof both "blaxploitation" and "chop socky" in a way that connected it directly to two earlier projects that had also spoofed "invincible" heroes—*Atom Ant* and *Secret Squirrel*. The first genre was spoofed by casting an African American (character actor Scatman Crothers) in the canine title role, and giving him an exaggerated self-confidence in line with a typical "blaxploitation" hero, while the second was spoofed by making him a supposed martial arts "expert." All the studio's writers had to do was take it from there, which they managed to do very well in spite of the now-established handicaps they were having to deal with internally and externally.

The series focused on laconic Penrod (or "Penry") Pooch, who worked as a janitor at a local police station, and where his bumbling ineptitude frequently exasperated the resident cop on duty, Sergeant Flint (well played by veteran comic character actor Joe E. Ross). (This produced some memorable dialogue exchanges: for example, when Flint sarcastically asks Penry if he has taken "stupid lessons," the latter replies, with genuine sincerity, that his stupidity "just come[s] to me natural.") The sole ally he had was Rosemary (Kathi Gori), a dim-witted blonde whose dialogue chiefly consisted of answering the phone in the fashion of the old "You Don't Say" vaudeville routine (which involves someone repeating the title phrase into a phone three times, and then, when asked who had called, simply responding, "He didn't say"). Penry, however, like many of his prototypes, was merely hiding his light under a bushel. When trouble loomed, he would retreat to the basement of the station, jump into the bottom drawer of a file cabinet, and assume the identity of the title character when he emerged. Wearing a black mask and a red-and-white gi with a yellow belt, Hong Kong Phooey would then exit to capture that week's criminals.

The comedy of the series derived chiefly from the fact that HKP was not nearly as competent at his job as he (or many others in the program) imagined himself to be. Many criminals spoke of him with the same kind of awed reverence that the residents of Frostbite Falls gave Rocky and Bullwinkle, and in both cases it was nearly undeserved. Although he presented himself as a "master" of his art (and reinforced this through constant use of an "inner" non-vocalized dialogue with the audience), he was constantly having to check his "Kung Fu Book of Tricks" to make sure he was doing things right. His nearly mute, cynical feline assistant, Spot (Don Messick), was frequently frustrated with him (to the point of smacking his forehead repeatedly in exasperation) and was often forced to bail him out. Coupled with a group of exaggerated villains in the line of earlier projects, the result was a series that, for once during the studio's 1970s dry spell, managed to deliver on what it promised.

There were, of course, limitations in the narratives, though in this case they say more about censorship restrictions of the time than they do about the quality of the series. HKP never engaged in direct combat with his adversaries, which is just as well because they probably knew more about martial arts than he did. More often than not, he attempted to demonstrate his "expertise" through elaborate showboating, which did little more than reduce his enemies (and the audience) to laughter. In the established Hanna-Barbera tradition, he succeeded more by luck or accident than anything else, but his gloating, cocksure attitude remained intact, continuing the humor even when he had returned to the far more servile role of Penry.

In *Hong Kong Phooey*, Hanna-Barbera had a genuinely comic narrative, and a genuinely comic hero, for the first time in quite a while, and they made sure he was treated in the manner he should have been treated—that is, as a walking joke—rather than as the overtly moral knight-in-shining-armor he imagined himself to be. The results were incredibly felicitous, and, for once, the studio chose to leave a good idea alone rather than repeat it to death through formulaic reproductions.

◆ ◆ ◆

Hong Kong Phooey aside, the studio seemed desperate for ideas, and, especially, for ways of executing them that respected the essential integrity of the stories and characters *as well as* the blatant censorship of the time. This was made most apparent when Hanna and Barbera attempted to resurrect their original star characters, Tom and Jerry, in 1975. By network fiat, the chase sequences that had been the original cartoons' bread and butter were *verboten*, so the cat and mouse were made friendly enemies instead of out-and-out villainous enemies, and simply trotted through a series of ineptly written, impotent comic narratives. Similar problems existed with Tom and Jerry's new made-for-TV neighbors in their timeslot. *Grape Ape* focused on an enormous, King Kong–like, purple-hued ape (Bob Holt), whose dialogue consisted chiefly of rumbling his own name and apologetically uttering "Sorry!" when he inadvertently caused damage. The Ape was accompanied by Beegle Beagle (Marty Ingels), a con-man/hustler of the Top Cat/Yogi Bear school, through a variety of settings and formats, which only occasionally produced the laughs they were intended to.

Similar problems existed with *Dynomutt*, airing on ABC in 1976–77 in tandem with new episodes of *Scooby Doo*. Developed and written by studio veterans Joe Ruby and Ken Spears, the series transplanted much of the original intent behind Barbera's *C.H.O.M.P.S.* project into animation, albeit in very broad comic form. This robotic dog (Frank Welker) was a dimwitted idiot (is there any other kind?) who was paired with The Blue Falcon (Gary Owens), a superhero taken straight from the studio's '60s heyday, although his chief function in the stories seemed to be acting as the dog's straight man. Oriented toward slapstick rather than straightforward super-heroics, the series placed Dynomutt and "B.F." into conflict with the usual gang of villainous idiots. Although he always lucked out and won in the end (of course), Dynomutt was too caught up in his own self-confidence, not to mention his bumbling ineptitude, to be taken seriously as a hero, which alarmed his straight-faced partner. ("When will that dog ever learn?" he would repeatedly say to himself, with just cause.[168])

A trio of series during the period focused on the seemingly novel device of humanized automobiles, which was, predictably, run dry through repetition. *Speed Buggy* (CBS, 1973–74) was yet another *Scooby Doo* retread, with the novelty coming chiefly from Mel Blanc reprising his "portrayal" of Jack Benny's Maxwell in the title role. The following year, on NBC, Hanna-Barbera offered *Wheelie and the Chopper Bunch*, whose entire cast consisted of humanized automobiles, led by the title character (Frank Welker) and his girlfriend Rota Ree (Judy Strangis). This trilogy was concluded by *Wonder Wheels*, airing on CBS in 1977–78; the title character was a "supermotorcycle"[169] used by high school student Willie (Micky Dolenz) as part of his journalistic enterprises.

One of the more felicitous programs to come out of the decade was an update of the classic Yogi Bear con-artist formula to the anti-establishment "hippie" mindset of the youth of the late 1960s and early 1970s. *Help! It's the Hair Bear Bunch!*, airing on CBS between 1971 and 1972, was the title of this offering. The title trio lived in Cave Block No. 9 at the Wonderland Zoo, where they frequently outwitted their typically dimwitted captors. They consisted of the leader, Hair Bear (Daws Butler), whose name clearly derived from the enormous Afro he sported on his head; Bubi Bear (Paul Winchell), a more level-headed confederate; and Square Bear (Bill Callaway), one of the studio's now-patented dimwitted idiots. Opposing them were the short-tempered zookeeper, Mr. Peevely (John Stephenson, impersonating character actor Joe Flynn, of *McHale's Navy* fame[170]), and his incompetent assistant, aptly named Botch (Joe E. Ross). As it incorporated some of the "flip, sophisticated"[171] style of the early animal con-artist formula, the series (while a throwback to the studio's earlier style of comedy) maintained a distinct connection with the time and place in which it was produced.

But another sign of the studio's desperation manifested itself in its decision to adapt pre-existing media properties to television animation, in an attempt to both gain viewers and draw laughs. The first of these was *The Addams Family*, airing on NBC between 1973 and 1975. Based on the popular live-action 1960s sitcom (which, in turn, was based on the macabre art of cartoonist Charles Addams), the animated series departed from the sitcom by featuring the family touring the country in a recreational vehicle, which, predictably, was actually a traveling haunted house. A level of authenticity was maintained by having original cast members Jackie Coogan (Uncle Fester) and Hanna-Barbera veteran Ted Cassidy (Lurch) reprise their parts.[172] *The Partridge Family: 2200 A.D.* (CBS 1974–75), meanwhile, "announced its premise in the title"[173] and simply reprised the family-oriented humor of its live-action counterpart in space, while of necessity also borrowing from *The Jetsons*. *The Amazing Chan and the Chan Clan* (CBS, 1972–74) was equally derivative, focusing on the animated exploits of legendary fictional Asian detective Charlie Chan (Keye Luke, who played "Number One Son" Lee in the Chan movies of the 1930s) and his large, like-minded family.[174]

Arguably the most creative use of a pre-existing group of characters at this time, however, was *The Harlem Globetrotters* (CBS 1970–72), spotlighting the legendary basketball-cum-comedy team as they "score[d] points against teams made up from everything from robots to kangaroos."[175] (They would be revived later in the decade as *The Super Globetrotters*, which, as the name implied, featured them in super-heroic form, following the set studio pattern in this sub-genre.)

Straight forward, non-humorous super-heroics was far more limited in terms of production than it had been during the 1960s, with only three real attempts made at it. *Sealab 2020*, airing on NBC during 1972–73, had an imaginative idea at its source: a self-contained city at the bottom of the ocean. Predictably, this was done for scientific purposes, with Dr. Paul Williams (Ross Martin), a "Chinook Indian [*sic*] with extensive knowledge of oceanography,"[176] as the leader. (One might argue that Dr. Williams, based on his identified ancestry, was the first lead character in television animation with such a background.) *Devlin*, airing on ABC during 1974–75, was slightly more Earth-bound, as it focused on "three orphaned young people, aged 11 to 20, who performed as a daredevil motorcycle team with a small traveling circus." Predictably, the series focused on both the family's domestic issues and on issues involving the circus, while the characters "dispensed an occasional safety tip."[177] More ambitious in tone and design was *The Godzilla Power Hour*, airing on NBC between 1978 and 1979. The title project was a variant on the popular "Godzilla" film series from Japan's Toho studios, which dated back to the mid–1950s, and it followed the pattern of the more recent films in the series by making Godzilla a heroic figure instead of a villainous one. In this series, Godzilla ("voiced" by Ted Cassidy) befriended a scientific expedition led by Captain Carl Majors (Jeff David) and Dr. Quinn Darien (Brenda Thomson) after they saved his miniature, comic "relative" Godzooky (Don Messick) from peril. From that point on, as the team "investigated mysterious phenomena" across the world, Godzilla would inevitably come out of the ocean to rescue them from whatever monster was imperiling them at the climax.[178] The second half of the hour featured "Jana of the Jungle," the saga of a female Tarzan (B.J. Ward) searching for her lost father, in the company of a magically endowed Native chief (Ted Cassidy).

The last major category of production for the studio was the production of half-hour and hour-long "specials" for network broadcast, some of which aired in prime time, and others as part of daytime and Saturday morning omnibus series, such as ABC's long-running *Weekend Special* and *Afternoon Special* programs. (The other studios discussed in this chapter also contributed their fair share to these projects.) The first major project for the studio in this line aired in 1966. *Jack and the Beanstalk* reunited Hanna and Barbera with Gene Kelly, with whom they worked on sequences from MGM musical films in the 1940s and 1950s. This project derived its success and charm from the juxtaposition of live footage of Kelly with animated backgrounds and characters, and was impressive enough to win an Emmy for Outstanding Children's Special.[179]

Few of the other projects in this line were as ambitious or as successful. Chiefly, they were literary adaptations (*Alice in Wonderland, Gulliver's Travels, The Count of Monte Cristo, 20,000 Leagues Under the Sea, Five Weeks in a Balloon, Last of the Mohicans, Black Beauty, Cyrano De Bergerac*), excursions into American history (*Davey [sic] Crockett on the Missis-*

sippi), or vehicles for the studio's stars (*Yogi's First Christmas, Scooby Doo and the Ghoul School*, etc.). By far the most distinguished of these was *Last of the Curlews*, an adaptation of a book by Canadian nature writer Fred Bodsworth, which aired on ABC in the fall of 1972. Focusing on the ultimately tragic tale of a bird from an increasingly vanishing species as he attempts to find a mate, the film was lyrically and realistically animated in a way that presented its subject matter with the respect and dramatic restraint needed to present the story effectively. It deservedly won an Emmy for Outstanding Achievement in Children's Programming the following year.

◆ ◆ ◆

While Hanna-Barbera remained a financially and creatively viable entity during the 1970s, it was increasingly undergoing a creative identity crisis that was, in part, its own creation. Its inability to consistently recapture its old standards of excellence, despite the great isolated success noted above, was something even its most ardent followers were coming to grips with. This would only deepen during the 1980s, as the founders of the company, and those most loyal to them, struggled to maintain a position in a changing industry that was threatening to pass them by altogether.

Other Voices

The boom in television animation production that had occurred during the 1960s slowed to a small trickle during the 1970s. With many of the studios that had operated during the previous decade having gone bankrupt or being otherwise out-of-business, only a small group of producers, headed by Filmation and Hanna-Barbera, was now serving the marketplace. But four other studios—two veteran operations and two relative newcomers—were still able to make their own unique marks during this time, in ways significantly different from the industry leaders.

RANKIN-BASS IN THE '70S

Unlike the troubled environment of Hanna-Barbera, the 1970s were largely "business as usual" for Rankin-Bass. Because they focused primarily on specials as opposed to series, and consequently built their stories around more family-friendly narrative patterns than the other studios, they were far less affected by the imposition of draconian censorship on television animation. It certainly did not hurt that the primary market for their products was not Saturday morning, but prime time itself. Still, like Hanna and Barbera, as the decade evolved, Rankin and Bass began to struggle with creating variance within a formula they themselves had initiated.[180]

The Rankin-Bass specials of the 1970s varied little from their predecessors of the previous decade, which continued to receive constant exposure during this period (as they still do today), and for the most part they did not depart from that successful formula. By now, the elements were in place: typically a holiday setting, charming stories and characters, and at least one celebrity lending their voice to a project. All the producers needed to do was fill in the blanks.

The decade began with an impressive cavalcade project, *The Mad, Mad, Mad Comedians*, airing on ABC in 1970. A cel animation project, it featured a large group of veteran comics, both contemporary (Flip Wilson, The Smothers Brothers) and classic (Jack Benny, George Burns, George Jessel, W.C. Fields, The Marx Brothers) performing some of their best bits in front of a similarly animated audience. Impressively, nearly all of the comedians provided their own voices for the project. The exceptions were W.C. Fields and Chico Marx, both of whom were deceased by this time. Paul Frees, who was becoming as much of a regular at Rankin-Bass as he had been at Jay Ward's, executed convincing impersonations of those two legendary funnymen.

The holiday format was resurrected for *Santa Claus Is Comin' to Town*, broadcast on ABC during the winter of 1970. Fred Astaire served as the narrator figure, S.D. (for Special Delivery) Kluger, a postman who proceeded to inform the children in the audience about Santa Claus's *curriculum vitae*. Santa Claus himself was memorably portrayed by Mickey Rooney, and he was assisted in the same way by Keenan Wynn as the Winter Warlock, and by Paul Frees as the villainous Burgermeister Meisterburger. In addition to the standard title song, there were a number of equally tuneful numbers written by Bass and composer Maury Laws, who were becoming the studio's chief musical department.

For Easter 1971, the studio presented *Here Comes Peter Cottontail* on ABC, which offered a similarly fanciful take on the origins of the Easter Bunny. Danny Kaye (as Seymour S. Sassafrass) played the narrator and two other characters, and Vincent Price played the villain. Kaye was also the star of the studio's next project, *The Enchanted World of Danny Kaye: The Emperor's New Clothes*, airing on ABC in the winter of 1972. This combination of "Animagic" and live-action was intended as the pilot for a series which failed to sell. Imogene Coca and Cyril Ritchard co-starred. No celebrities were present in the voice cast of *Mad, Mad, Mad Monsters*, airing on ABC in the fall of 1972, which was an extended gag reel of classic movie monsters, much like the studio's earlier Animagic feature film *Mad Monster Party* (Embassy, 1967) and the more recent computer animation Hollywood offering *Hotel Transylvania* (Columbia, 2012).

Another animated special featured the presence of legendary baseball player Willie Mays, with the title, *Willie Mays and the Say Hey Kid* (ABC, 1972), incorporating Mays's famous catchphrase. In December 1972, the studio produced another special, *The Red Baron*, featuring the antics of an anthropomorphized canine flying ace, for ABC. That network was also the home base for *That Girl in Wonderland*, airing in 1974, which essentially served as a vehicle for the talents of Marlo Thomas (who had previously worked for the team on *Cricket on the Hearth* in the 1960s, in which she co-starred with her father, Danny Thomas; see Chapter 3).

Returning to the realm that had made them famous—Christmas—Rankin and Bass's next offered *'Twas the Night Before Christmas*—an elaborate cel animation adaptation (and significant expansion) of the legendary Clement Clarke Moore poem, which first aired on CBS in December 1974. The poem (also known as "A Visit from St. Nicholas") served as the climax of the narrative, which is based around an apparent rejection of the town of Junctionville by Santa, who has returned all the letters the townsfolk had sent him during the year. The main story is more complex than usual for Rankin-Bass, building as it does on two separate but distinct plotlines: the troubled business affairs of town clockmaker Joshua Trundel, and the exploits of Father Mouse, who lives in the interior of Trundel's house and tries to instill his son Albert with the proper Christmas spirit. Joel Grey (who had recently won an Academy Award for *Cabaret*) played Trundel, and veteran comedian George Gobel did the honors for Father Mouse; they shared the narrator duties. Tammy Grimes played Albert effectively, while John McGiver stole the viewers' attention as Junctionville's pompous, perennially befuddled mayor. Bass and Laws again did the music, a wonderful job that added much to the special's impact.

That same year, and that same Christmas season, the studio produced *The Year Without a Santa Claus* for ABC. Based on a children's book by Phyllis McGinley, the story concerns the confusion and difficulties caused when an ailing Santa (once again Mickey Rooney) decides to take a year off from his Christmas gift giving. The special was narrated by Shirley Booth, who also played Santa's wife, while Dick Shawn and George S. Irving were memorably featured as the feuding elemental spirits Snow Miser and Heat Miser, respectively. Among the more charming aspects of the special is the climax, where snow actually falls in the small Southern town where much of the action takes place—after Santa agrees to renege on his threat of retirement and resume his gift-giving ways. A more sober take on the holiday was featured in *The First Christmas*, airing in December 1975 on ABC, which was set in an abbey and starred Angela Lansbury in the lead role.

The First Easter Rabbit, a cel animation special broadcast in April 1976, reunited the producers with Burl Ives, who had starred in *Rudolph the Red Nosed Reindeer* (see Chapter 3). Robert Morse, Stan Freberg, Paul Frees and Don Messick had supporting roles here. The producers also reteamed with a fictional character from the past for *Frosty's Winter Wonderland*, airing in the winter of that same year. Jackie Vernon reprised his role as Frosty, with Andy Griffith as the narrator, Dennis Day as Parson Brown, Paul Frees as the villainous Jack Frost, and Shelley Winters as Crystal, the snowwoman who becomes Frosty's wife. Still more repetition occurred with the Animagic special *Rudolph's Shiny New Year*, which featured Rudolph (again played by Billie Mae Richards) saving Happy, the baby New Year, from peril. The cast of this one was top-heavy with stars: Red Skelton as Father Time and Baby Bear, Frank Gorshin as Sir Tenworththree, Morey Amsterdam as One Million B.C., Hal Peary as Big Ben, and Paul Frees as Santa Claus. Apparently not understanding when enough was enough, the studio also produced a sequel to *The Little Drummer Boy*, titled *Book II*, which also aired in the winter of 1976 on NBC. Greer Garson served as the narrator, with Zero Mostel stealing scenes in his usual fashion as a villainous Roman tax collector.

Fred Astaire, meanwhile, returned as S.D. Kluger for *The Easter Bunny Is Comin' to Town*, an Animagic special airing in the spring of 1977, which purported to tell the story of how the Easter bunny came to be, with the assistance of the affable Hallelujah Jones (Ron Marshall).

Thankfully, a major departure from the usual chain of programming came next. *The Hobbit*, a 90-minute cel animation feature, aired on NBC in the winter of 1977. It was the first major adaptation of any of J.R.R. Tolkien's work to any visual medium, and clearly pointed the way toward Peter Jackson's lavish live-action adaptation of the Tolkien canon during the 2000s. Rankin and Bass were at their most lavishly Disney-esque in terms of the animation here, which is remarkably faithful to the spirit, the intent, and, most importantly, the narrative of Tolkien's work (again pointing the way to Jackson's adaptation of *The Lord of the Rings* over three films, and *The Hobbit* itself over another projected three). As usual in a Rankin/Bass special, the voice cast was full of star performers. Comedian Orson Bean was well cast as Bilbo; also in the cast were Richard Boone as Smaug the dragon, Hans Conreid as the dwarf Thorin Oakenshield, John Huston as Gandalf the wizard, Otto Preminger as the Elvenking, and Cyril Ritchard as Elrond. Veteran voice men Paul Frees, Don Messick and John Stephenson filled out the ranks. Technologically and creatively, *The Hobbit* was the most stylishly impressive cel animation production Rankin-Bass would ever produce for television, and they were justly rewarded with a Peabody for it, as well as a Christopher Award.

It was back to business as usual, though, for the last three major specials produced during the decade. *Nestor, the Long Eared Christmas Donkey* (ABC, 1977) was another Animagic "misfit" tale, this one featuring the title character helping Joseph and Mary travel to Bethlehem. *The Stingiest Man in Town* (NBC, 1978) was a renamed musical version of *A Christmas Carol* done in cel animation, highlighted mainly by the vocal presence of Walter Matthau as Scrooge and Tom Bosley as the narrator—a cricket named B.A.H. Humbug! Finally, there was *Jack Frost* (NBC, 1979), the Animagic story of the spirit of winter, with Robert Morse in the title role and Buddy Hackett as the narrator, a groundhog named Pardon Me Pete.

Rankin-Bass also made an effort to continue its production of series, with animation subcontracted to foreign houses à la Hanna-Barbera, particularly the England-based studio of John Halas and Joy Batchelor and Japan's Mushi studios. The first series to emerge from the arrangement was *The Tomfoolery Show*, airing during the 1970-71 season on NBC and based around the bizarre "nonsense" school of children's literature, particularly the works of Edward Lear and Lewis Carroll. While well produced and well intentioned, it was never able to acquire the audience it deserved. *The Reluctant Dragon and Mr. Toad Show* (ABC 1970–72) similarly took its cues from the works of another English children's author, Kenneth Grahame, with lesser results.

Other studio productions were literally tailor-made for popular performers. *The Jackson Five Show* (ABC 1971–73) featured the enormously popular rhythm-and-blues singing group from Motown Records, who had had four consecutive #1 hits on the *Billboard* pop charts in 1970 alone. This series was produced very much along the lines of Hanna-Barbera and Filmation's efforts in the teen sub-genre at this time, down to the seemingly needed presence of "funny" animal companions. Future Disney boss Michael Eisner, then an ABC programming executive, played a major role in shaping the series and getting it on the air, according to Rankin.[181] Presumably, he was also involved in developing a similar series around the Osmond family (ABC, 1972–74), which achieved pop-chart success equivalent to the Jacksons' soon after them.

Two other series projects from the studio during the decade are also noteworthy. *Kid Power* (ABC, 1972–74) was based on the comic strip "Wee Pals," created by African American cartoonist Morrie Turner. The series was far ahead of its time in advocating racial and multicultural social alliances between children, symbolized by the fact that the characters belonged to an organization known as the Rainbow Club. Further underlying this belief was the notion, outlined in the theme song, that "Kid Power" would somehow be able to induce social change that adults, with their more limited worldview, could not create. (This was certainly an idea that television animators of the 1980s, 1990s, and 2000s would take to heart; see chapters 5, 6 and 7 for obvious indebted examples.) The last series project from the studio during the 1970s was *The Festival of Family Classics*, airing in syndication during 1972–73. The stories were taken from classic literature and international folklore, and executed and illustrated with the studio's requisite handsomeness.

While their competition was struggling to keep up with abrupt changes to the television animation marketplace, Rankin-Bass, for the most part, was able to keep up production on the same lavish levels they had instigated in the previous decade. Eventually, however, the same creative torpor that had hurt their competition would come to close in on them as well.

DePatie-Freleng in the '70s

Like Rankin and Bass, David DePatie and Friz Freleng saw no need to alter their business model with the change in decade, with the result that their studio continued going on its merry way in terms of production. Freleng, however, was increasingly disillusioned by the assembly-line nature of television animation production, and, at decade's end, he amicably split with his partner.

Freleng's increasingly disheartened attitude is understandable, in view of the studio's series productions over the course of the decade. In addition to the ongoing *Pink Panther* series (see Chapter 3), the studio's series began to suffer from increasing underachievement. The first of these was *The Further Adventures of Dr. Doolittle* (NBC, 1970–71), an adaptation of Hugh Lofting's children's character produced in conjunction with 20th Century–Fox, which had produced a film based on the character in 1967.

During 1972–73, two other lackluster adaptations graced the network airwaves. *The Barkleys* was an uninspired variant on *All in the Family* which, as Hal Erickson has justly noted, "brought the word 'derivative' to hitherto unscaled heights."[182] Much like Filmation's equally uninspired take on *M*A*S*H* (see above), the sole novelty here came from transforming the characters into dogs. The lead character was a bus driver, Arnie Barkley (Henry Corden, who was apparently instructed directly by the network to imitate *Family*'s Carroll O'Connor in his performance[183]); also in the cast were his wife, Agnes (Joan Gerber), and their children Terry (Julie McWhirter), Chester (Steve Lewis), and Roger (Gene Andrusco). The other production of that year was *The Houndcats*, airing on ABC. Deriving its concept chiefly from *Mission: Impossible*, as well as from a short-lived Western variation of that series called *The Bearcats*, this involved a mixed group of cats and dogs who performed by now standard secret-agent activities. The group consisted of the leader Stutz (Daws Butler); Muscle Mutt (Aldo Ray), a brawny strongman-type; Rhubarb (Arte Johnson), an electronics expert; Puddy Puss (Joe Besser), a master of disguise, able to contort his face into a variety of guises; and Ding Dong (Stu Gilliam), a Southern-accented daredevil.

The following season, for CBS, the studio produced *Bailey's Comets*, yet another retread of an established concept, in this case Hanna-Barbera's *Wacky Races*. Here, an element of novelty was introduced by having the stories focus on a truly all–American sporting institution, the roller derby, but otherwise things remained the same. The central character was Barnaby Bailey (Carl Esser), who captained the team mentioned in the title. Borrowing from the comedy film *It's a Mad, Mad, Mad, Mad World* (Stanley Kramer, 1963), much of the action surrounded the quest for a buried treasure worth $1 million, with clues repeatedly dropped in the narratives. Barnaby and company faced off in locations across the world against some colorfully named opponents, including the Roller Bears, the Broomer Girls, the Dr. Jekyll/Hydes, the Cosmic Rays, the Yo Ho Hos, and the Texas Flycats, but that was all the color that was provided to this otherwise drab series.

The derivative nature of the studio's series was further reinforced by the two studio offerings produced in 1975. *The Oddball Couple*, airing on ABC in 1975, was a broad, unsubtle variation on Neil Simon's popular comic play *The Odd Couple*, which had already been successfully adapted for film and television. The protagonists of this series were Spiffy (Frank Nelson), a Felix Unger–type neat cat, and Fleabag (Paul Winchell), an Oscar Madison–styled dirty dog. Goldie Hound (Joan Gerber) was their joint secretary. A more legitimized media adaptation was produced that same year. *Return to the Planet of the Apes* was an adaptation of another 20th Century–Fox film property, and was again produced in collaboration with the film studio. Set one thousand years after the action in the original film, the series focused on a trio of modern human astronauts who became marooned in the bizarre simian-dominated universe created for the original film and its sequels.

For 1977–78, on NBC, the studio produced *Baggy Pants and the Nitwits*, a series in line with the old Hanna-Barbera series in that it featured two components united only by a conjunction. The former was a pantomime series featuring a cat modeled on Charlie Chaplin's Little Tramp. Despite the iconic status of Chaplin and his character, as noted in Chapter 1, most attempts to translate him to animation were failures, and though Freleng, like many animators of his generation, was deeply influenced by Chaplin, he was likewise unable to do the job. The second segment featured comedians of a more recent vintage. The characters of Tyrone (Arte Johnson), an archetypal "dirty old man," and Gladys (Ruth Buzzi), the hairnet-wearing object of his "affections," had been regular features of NBC's popular revue comedy series, *Rowan and Martin's Laugh-In* (1968–73). In *The Nitwits*, this pair, with all the sexual subtexts of their relationship removed, were featured as a pair of unlikely, aging superheroes called back to duty, with predictable results.

Two more productions were collaborations with Marvel Comics who, interested in entering the animation business themselves, took over the studio's assets in the 1980s. *The New Fantastic Four* (NBC, 1978–79) was self-explanatory, effectively a continuation of the earlier Hanna-Barbera adaptation of the characters. There were, however, a few significant changes. The Human Torch was absent from this version, as Marvel was then planning a separate series featuring him in collaboration with Universal, which was never produced. In his place was a glib android known as Humanoid Electronic Robot-B Model (HER-B, or "Herbie" for short). In addition, the Four's creators were actively involved in the production of the series, which they had not been before. Stan Lee scripted a number of episodes of the series, deriving them from his own comic-book narratives, while Jack Kirby personally supervised the storyboarding of the series on a shot-by-shot basis to make sure the images conformed to his original drawings. Because violence was so out of favor by this time, the scripts instead emphasized wisecracking dialogue, one of Lee's strengths as a writer, to the extent that The Thing (played by Ted Cassidy in this version) came off, according to Hal Erickson, as "a mutant Rodney Dangerfield."[184]

The second Marvel series was *Spider Woman* (NBC, 1979–80), a feminized variation on one of Marvel's star franchises developed by Stan Lee himself. Like Peter Parker, Jessica Drew (Joan Van Ark) gained superpowers from being bitten by a spider, although in her case this was accentuated by her scientist father personally treating her with an untested serum known only as "Number 34." Now a successful magazine publisher, Jessica alternated her secret identity with flying (often literally) into action as the title character when she was needed. More emotionally secure than her predecessor, Spider Woman could also send out streaks of venom from her body like laser blasts, and had a telepathic range that encompassed nearly the entire world. Although the feminist attributes of the narrative were notable for their time, this was undercut by Jessica often having to rely on the assistance of the two key men in her life: Jeff Hunt (Bruce Miller), a photographer in her employ, and Billy Drew (Bryan Scott), her young nephew, who possessed genius-level intelligence.

The final series produced by DePatie-Freleng was *What's New, Mister Magoo?* (CBS, 1977–79) a typically uninspired resurrection of UPA's classic elderly myopic character.

DePatie-Freleng series were inevitable failures during this time, despite the studio's insistent use of high-production values. One could not, however, say that for the handful of specials they produced during the decade.

The most felicitous of these were the extended collaborations between the studio and Dr. Seuss, which continued the high-quality work he had done with Chuck Jones at MGM in the previous decade (see Chapter 3). Freleng, like Jones, was an old friend of the Doctor's from his World War II work under his real name (Theodor "Ted" Geisel), and the same mutual trust existed between them as had existed between him and Jones, with the results speaking for themselves.¹⁸⁵ Mostly directed by Hawley Pratt, a loyal Freleng lieutenant dating back to his days as Freleng's layout artist at Warner Bros., the specials fell into two categories. As with Jones, the studio produced lavish adaptations of the Doctor's books, specifically *The Cat in the Hat* (CBS, 1971) and *The Lorax* (CBS, 1972), both of which displayed a fidelity absent in later Seuss media adaptations. Three other books were condensed into one special in *Dr. Seuss on the Loose* (CBS, 1973). Increasingly, however, Seuss was beginning to develop original ideas for television animation products as well. *Halloween Is Grinch Night* (ABC, 1978) saw a young Who boy, Ukariah, confronting the now-evil-again Grinch, while *The Grinch Grinches the Cat in the Hat* (ABC, 1982) pitted Seuss's two great creations against each other. *Pontoffel Pock, Where Are You?* (ABC, 1981) focused on a misfit who acquires a magic piano that can transport him anywhere in the world, while *The Hoober-Bloob Highway* (CBS, 1975) focused on an imaginary ribbon of light which transports young children down to Earth, under the direction of the man for whom the highway is named. The specials were successful both creatively and critically. *Halloween Is Grinch Night* and *The Grinch Grinches the Cat in the Hat* won Emmy Awards for "Outstanding Children's Special" and "Outstanding Animated Program," respectively, of their original broadcast seasons, while *Pontoffel Pock* was nominated for an Emmy for "Outstanding Animated Program" in the first year of that category's existence.

Other specials from the company included a series featuring their star character, The Pink Panther; one of these, *Olym-Pinks*, was nominated for an Emmy alongside *Pontoffel Pock* in 1979–80. In collaboration with comedian Flip Wilson, the studio produced *Clerow Wilson and the Miracle of P.S. 14* for NBC in 1972, followed by a sequel, *Clerow Wilson's Great Escape*, for the same network in 1974.¹⁸⁶ Finally, in 1977, DePatie-Freleng produced *My Mom's Having a Baby*, an innovative live-action/animation combination featured on ABC's *After School Special* series, which earned DePatie and Freleng a third Emmy.

In spite of his success, however, Freleng was becoming disillusioned with both television and animation. This might simply have been a factor of his age; he was 74 years old in 1980. Like Joseph Barbera, he was becoming a critic of the industry of which he was a part. Although he had had a distinguished, award-winning career in both film and television, Freleng increasingly felt that he was being used by the networks to provide only what they wanted him to produce, rather than what he wanted to produce himself. He felt that, in being forced to steer his product toward a child audience, he was being forced to shortchange adult viewers:

> The adult audience today has been robbed of a certain amount of entertainment.... Kids keep getting [animation] on TV, but *you won't find an adult sitting down and watching a kid's show* [emphasis added]. I believe [adults] miss [the entertainment value in animation], and I believe there's a neglected audience [out there].¹⁸⁷

Freleng was correct. In their desperate overhauling of their programming to attract children—and to appease the ferocious temperaments of their parents—the television networks had minimized the potential role of television animation and completely ignored the fact that it was capable of attracting an audience *beyond* children. This blatant generalization, which had come to taint all network thinking on animation, would ultimately cost them dearly in the following three decades.

In any event, in 1980, at the completion of their current work cycle, Freleng and DePatie amicably dissolved their partnership. The company's physical assets were sold to Marvel

Comics, which began production of new animated series under DePatie's supervision. Freleng, meanwhile, returned to his old home base, Warner Bros., where, alongside his old colleague and former protégé Chuck Jones, he now attained the status of *eminence griese*. At Warners, Freleng produced compilation films and TV specials based around his classic cartoons and characters, assisted in the production of new material, and consulted on other projects (specifically, when Hanna-Barbera attempted to revive the Pink Panther unsuccessfully in the 1980s; see Chapter 5). Ever on the job, Freleng was creating limited signed editions of prints from his classic films at the time of his death in 1995.[188]

FRED CALVERT PRODUCTIONS

Like Kenneth Snyder (see Chapter 3), little is known about Calvert or his studio other than the two series he produced during the 1970s. He is notoriously hated by many veteran animators and fans for doing a re-edit of Richard Williams's long-in-gestation feature film, *The Thief and the Cobbler* in the 1990s, after Williams lost financial and creative control of the project.

Calvert's two television animation productions of the 1970s establish him chiefly as a journeyman artist with little personal creativity, but one who was clearly willing and able to go along with the decade's mandated program. *Emergency + 4*, airing on NBC between 1973 and 1976, was an animated version of the popular prime-time live-action series *Emergency!* focusing on the daily activities of Los Angeles–area paramedics, which was created and produced by *Dragnet* creator Jack Webb. Webb's production company, Mark VII, and his distributor, Universal, produced the series in collaboration with Calvert's studio. *Emergency!*'s stars, Kevin Tighe and Randolph Mantooth, reprised their live-action characters here, but, rather than the rest of the live-action cast, they were supported, in typical television animation fashion, by a group of children and a brace of "funny" animals. The series was both produced and ultimately canceled for expedient, exploitative reasons, as noted by historian Hal Erickson. NBC discovered that the biggest chunk of the live-action series' fan base was children, so an animated version of the series logically seemed in order. Likewise, the program was canceled chiefly because its live-action counterpart seemed doomed in the same way, although it managed to survive another year after the animated series' run ended.[189]

The second Calvert series was equally exploitative, but in a different way. The full series title announced its premise exactly—*I Am the Greatest: The Adventures of Muhammad Ali*. The legendary boxing champion portrayed himself in the series, which was about the only remotely positive thing about the program. Accompanied by a fictional niece and nephew, as well as his real-life PR man, Frank Bannister (also playing himself), Ali—said to be acting as a "modern Robin Hood"—went through the usual basic tropes of 1970s Saturday morning TV. The flaws in the series were obvious: as pointed out by Hal Erickson, the animation made Ali "look more like a movie lobby display than a real human being," and this was compounded by the fact that earlier fictional film and TV appearances had revealed that Ali was hardly what could be called a gifted actor. The series stumbled through the 1977-78 season, more through its stunt casting and spotlighting of "minority" concerns than anything else.[190]

SUTHERLAND LEARNING ASSOCIATES

This company's one notable achievement was *The Most Important Person*, a series of broadly educational vignettes first seen on CBS's *Captain Kangaroo*, and then in its own timeslot on the network during 1972-73. The regular cast consisted of three animated animals, Fumble, Hairy and Bird, paired with two animated children, Mike and Nicola. Very much in the vein of *Sesame Street* and *The Electric Company*, the series was sponsored by the Department of Health, Education and Welfare—making it the first television animation series to receive this kind of direct endorsement by the U.S. government.[191]

Nelvana

One of the most dominant forces in the Canadian animation industry, the legendary Nelvana studio has also been one of the few to have a consistent foothold in the American market. The studio's skill, diversity and quality has been apparent from its earliest productions, which were syndicated in America during the 1970s.

For most of its existence, the studio has been directed by a trio of ambitious animator/businessmen—Belgium-born Michael Hirsh, Canadian Patrick Loubert and transplanted Englishman Clive Smith—whose noteworthy work would come to gain them considerable attention in Canada and beyond. As studio historian Daniel Stoffman has noted, the trio were hoping to build a film studio in Canada at a time when no such thing existed.[192] But the three young men were ready, willing and able to make it happen, at least when it came to animation.

The studio was established in 1971, taking its name from a fictional superhero, Nelvana of the Northern Lights, who had appeared in Canadian-produced comic books in the 1940s at a time when an export ban existed on their American counterparts. It established a beachhead with the CBC by producing "filler" material, short pieces to fill out a half-hour when a program ended unexpectedly. Soon the Canadian public broadcaster, impressed by their work, was commissioning full-length specials from them, which were syndicated in America by the powerful Viacom group to make up their production costs. An equal blandishment, much like other high-end animation projects of the era, was the presence of both American and Canadian celebrities in the voice casts.

Under the umbrella title of *Nelvanamation*, this series of specials aired in syndication between 1977 and 1980, chiefly in the local station prime-time "Access" slot of 7:30–8:00. Each of the specials started with an imaginative presence, and then proceeded along with ambitious animation far above the standard TV norm, a reflection of the fact that Nelvana was outside of the Hollywood mainstream and had not yet been co-opted by it as it would be in later years, as its reputation grew.

The first project, *A Cosmic Christmas*, was a variation on the traditional Christmas story, with three aliens assuming the role of the troika of "wise men" to analyze modern-day celebrations of the holiday. Its success encouraged more projects in the same line, which became increasingly ambitious. Next up was *The Devil and Daniel Mouse*, a Halloween-themed modern variation on the story of "Faust," already immortalized by the likes of Goethe, Turgenev and Christopher Marlowe in literature and theater. The novelty here came from the story's portrayal of the then-contemporary world of popular music. Featuring anthropomorphic characters, the tale focused on Dan and Jan, a male/female pair of folk-singing mice, whose lives and careers are threatened when Jan sells her soul to the villainous B.L. Zebub (guess who *he* really is), a stereotypical Hollywood agent type, who promises to make her into a rock singing star. But, as always, all ends well. The story is notable for enacting the divide between the musically "pure" realm of folk music as opposed to the more "corporate" atmosphere that had come to taint mainstream pop/rock in America during this time. It is equally significant that Canada, through the Canadian government's passage of "Canadian content" regulations for radio stations, was beginning to build its own homegrown popular music industry during the time the special was produced and aired—one that would eventually develop a conflict-ridden relationship with its American counterpart not unlike the situation presented here.

Romie-O and Julie-8 came next. As the title implies, this was a bizarre variant of Shakespeare's *Romeo and Juliet*, with the title characters turned into robots and the setting an inspired sci-fi styled universe. The humor level here was evident by the closing punchline: "Oil's well that ends well." The principal villain was named Spare Partski, reflecting an enduring popular-culture obsession of the Cold War in its constant demonization of the Slavic race.[193]

At this point, Viacom, who felt that the lack of presence of "star" (i.e., American media) performers in the specials was causing them to underperform, began insisting Nelvana include them in the voice casts, and the studio complied. The first project to feature this element was *Intergalactic Thanksgiving* (*Please Don't Eat the Planet*, in Canada), which starred legendary TV comedian Sid Caesar in one of the principal roles. The humor in the project was thus mainly built around the borscht-belt style featured on Caesar's 1950s variety series, while the main story focused on a variation on Aesop's "The Ant and the Grasshopper"—a hardworking and a slothful pair of alien settler families in conflict, with the former bailing out the latter when their "food making machine," designed to prevent them from farming their own crops, goes berserk.

The next project was even more "American" in nature. *Easter Fever* (*The Jack Rabbit Story* in Canada) focused on a Friar's Club–style Roast for the Easter Bunny (although done in the relatively cleaner style that Dean Martin was then regularly presenting on television). The star attraction here was Garrett Morris, one of the original stars of *Saturday Night Live*, as the Bunny, but he was upstaged by the talented Canadian voice cast, including *SCTV* veteran Catherine O'Hara and a young impressionist named Maurice La Marche, who provided excellent vocal impressions of Steve Martin and Don Rickles for anthropomorphic versions of those two veteran comics. La Marche would come to be a regular, respected and rewarded member of the extended international animation voice actor community, as will be noted later in this book.

The special cycle came to a close with *Take Me Up to the Ballgame*, which starred Phil Silvers (whose wisecracking con-man act had been the inspiration for many a cartoon equivalent in the 1950s and 1960s in particular, but also beyond) as an interplanetary sports entrepreneur trying to promote a galaxy-wide all-star game. His character may have been inspired by the late Abe Saperstein, who built the Harlem Globetrotters (see above) into a worldwide, dynamic force through similar Silvers-esque *chutzpah*.

Though the specials were not without their flaws—they were often weakly written in spite of their impressive visuals and voice casts, and frequently featured intrusive musical numbers à la Disney animated features—it was undeniable that Nelvana was providing a breath of fresh air to a genre and industry that was rapidly becoming stale. It helped, of course, that Nelvana at this time was producing specials, not series, and that it was Canadian, a distinction that kept it free from the draconian American censorship of the era. As Hal Erickson observes, "At a time when animated TV specials were chiefly confined to paste-up collections of old theatrical cartoons ... [the specials were] a warm, welcome gust of creative originality."[194] The American television industry was quick to recognize that originality, and Nelvana and other Canadian animation studios emerging in its wake would soon find themselves with a large and growing list of demands for their services, both at home and abroad, in the following decades.

SHAMUS CULHANE

After severing his relationship with Steve Krantz (see Chapter 3), this veteran animator produced two more short "fill in the gap" series during this decade. *The Wonderful Stories of Professor Kitzel*, airing in syndication in 1972, was similar to his earlier *Max, the 2000 Year Old Mouse*, in that it combined a Yiddish-flavored animated character with illustrated historical vignettes. Culhane had originally intended it for use in schools, but, after acquiring sponsorship from Bristol-Meyers, he agreed to television distribution through Worldvision, the television syndication arm of Taft Broadcasting (and thus the off-network syndicator of Hanna-Barbera, which Taft also owned).[195] Three years later, Culhane produced *The Spirit of Freedom*, which was similar to *Kitzel* in its intent, with a Yankee Doodle–type figure at its center.

Conclusion

Because of fear of external disapproval and heavy internal censorship, television animation in the 1970s in America was certainly not all it could have been, given who was producing it. The remaining members of the old guard, personified by Hanna-Barbera, were finding it harder to live up to their established standards of creative excellence in the new decade because of this censorship. Other studios, notably Rankin-Bass, Filmation and newcomer Nelvana, had fewer problems. They had already geared their product to the changing marketplace, and were far better able to conform to the new standards demanded of them. However, issues of conflict and control between the animation studios and the television networks, and even between the studios and their own animators, continued to simmer under the surface. With both the further retrenchment of old, outdated standards in the network environment and the development of entirely new forums for exhibition of animation on television asserting themselves, the following decade would display both the advantages and the liabilities of the "old" and "new" way of doing things in a rapidly changing industry.

Chapter 5

Sweet and Sour (1980–1990)

The 1970s had been a period of struggle and change for television animation, one in which fundamental creative and production ideas were severely tested. During this time, the struggle for creative and political control over the final product manifested itself in conflicts between studios and networks and within studios. These conflicts persisted in varying degrees across the 1980s, especially at Hanna-Barbera, the sole remaining edifice of the pioneer days. In other respects, positive change was being introduced—slowly. This took the form of a plethora of new, younger studios entering the field, as well as ambitious new ways of exhibiting the product outside of the traditional television network channels.

Still, the poor treatment of television animation in the 1970s did continue during the 1980s. In fact, in many ways, it intensified, in spite of the growing economic changes in the television landscape. The election to the U.S. presidency in 1980 of Ronald Reagan, who in his early years had been a Hollywood film star, marked a major shift in American corporate policies, including those of the media. Reagan, nicknamed "The Great Communicator" for his oratorical skills, would remain in office for the majority of the decade, his benign, patriarchal public image effectively masking the drastic manner in which he reshaped American corporate, social and political discourse during the decade.[1] Thanks to the president's economic deregulation policies, the 1980s would be remembered as a period when the deadly sin of greed took greater hold in American corporate life. No sector of the economy was greedier than that of the media, which underwent the greatest series of acquisitions, mergers and bloodless corporate takeovers it would ever see during this decade. Although television had arguably helped Reagan win the election, the industry supporting it was somehow seen to be disposable. No one put this better than Mark Fowler, Reagan's appointee to chair the Federal Communications Commission, who infamously noted that television was simply "a toaster with pictures."[2]

Along with the philosophical and economic changes, as they applied specifically to television animation, the creative and economic underpinnings behind series began to become blurred, creating the fusion between art and commerce groups such as ACT had long been protesting about. Toy companies, particularly Mattel and Hasbro, the two industry leaders, needed not simply to produce advertisements for their toys; they could now build entire series around them. As journalist Tom Engelhardt would write in 1986, this resulted in creative stagnation that came to be an industry-wide concern:

The actual serie[s] revolve[d] around a series of evil plans to loose havoc on innocent [people], or to trap the hero [or heroine] and deny him his [or her] transforming powers, or stop the mighty robots from being assembled, or to kidnap a friend of the superheroes, or to steal something so powerful, dangerous, radioactive [or] death-dealing that it will destroy the ... universe or alternately turn into a world of slave/zombies at the service of the Evil Force [sic].

All of which results in a series of chases and battles with techno-wonder weapons—space stations, laser beams, harnessed black holes, assorted yet-to-be invented and never-to-be-invented mega-weapons—and a final withdrawal by the forces of evil, muttering curses and threatening to return, followed by a pro-social message, often not obviously related to the show, or perhaps a "safety tip" by the show's hero.

Such a summary only begins to touch on the similarities among these shows. To the extent that they are driven at all, the forces driving them are three—the introduction of new characters with their accompanying weapons, castles and other accoutrements; the necessity for "teamwork"; and the displaying of the show's techno-weaponry through special effects. Each is a larger imperative linking the show into the energy field of licensed-character marketing.[3]

In many respects, Englehardt's analysis conveys exactly what the artistic problem was with television animation in the 1970s and 1980s: dry, repetitive storylines, shallow characterizations and little, if any, effort made to provide anything deeper along those lines. It would be exactly this set of clichéd narratives and situations that would come to dominate television animation in the 1980s—and it would be exactly these clichés that the television animators of the 1990s and 2000s would be directly rebelling against in their work.

For the network overseers and censors of television animation, the 1980s was roughly the same as the decade before, with the same entrenched attitudes toward "violence" and "pro-social" material still very much present. The entry of new, more ambitious producers into the television animation industry did not change this attitude one iota. Stan Lee, the legendary comic-book writer and editor who was beginning to shepherd Marvel Comics into television animation, found this out the hard way when he made his first programming pitch to a network:

> I'll never forget my first encounter, in 1981, with a network VP to whom I was pitching an idea for an animated series. Since it was our first meeting [,] she acted as though she really wanted to get to know me, to learn how I felt about Saturday morning cartoons. I was genuinely pleased when she asked for my opinion of the cartoons appearing on network TV at that time.
>
> Trying to be as candid as possible, I told her that I thought most cartoons were beautifully drawn and well animated. The only thing I couldn't understand, said I, sincerely trying to be helpful, was why the stories themselves were, for the most part, so unintelligent, with characters speaking in cartoon-speak rather than with real dialogue.
>
> If you shut your eyes, I told her, and turn on the TV, you could always tell when a cartoon series was playing [,] because the dialogue was so unnatural and "cartoony-sounding."
>
> At that point, she looked me straight in the eye and said, "We don't want our [animated] series to consist of talking heads."
>
> Still thinking I had a chance to reach her, I replied, "I'm not advocating 'talking heads,' or using more dialogue. I'm only suggesting that whatever dialogue you use be better written."
>
> I was hoping for a chance to give her some concrete examples. But she immediately snapped back, "We're not looking for talking heads."
>
> It was like a scene from *Alice in Wonderland*. I felt like I was at a mad tea party. No matter what I said, her only retort was, "We don't want talking heads."

> However, I did learn a lesson. I realized that [,] when some executives ask what you think of anything, it's purely a rhetorical question.
>
> She repeated the talking heads bit three or four more times [,] and, since I don't need a bridge to fall on me, I eventually gave up.... Nor did I ever pitch her another show.
>
> When I related that little incident to my friend David DePatie [a seasoned veteran television animation producer by now], he simply smiled and told me, "Welcome to Hollywood."[4]

If gifted newcomers to the field like Lee—or, for that matter, veteran producers like DePatie, Joseph Barbera and Lou Scheimer—could not change established network mindsets, then it simply revealed the increasing ideological fissures between the networks and television animation producers. This attitude on the networks' part, which remained intact even as new forces of television production and distribution began to erode their "ownership" of the American viewing public, would ultimately cost them dearly.

In the 1980s, one major new way of producing programming outside network control began to manifest itself: syndication. From the beginning of television's history, this way of selling and marketing programming to individual stations, in a fashion that sidestepped the network chain of command, had long been used to establish programming among audiences in ways the networks could not have conceived possible.[5] What was notable about the process was that it allowed programs to be "stripped" (i.e., aired on a daily weekday basis as opposed to simply once a week). As a necessity, it required the production of far more episodes for series than weekly network projects. Not surprisingly, highly creative studios such as Filmation, which had begun to chafe under network restrictions, would blossom in this format.

Yet the major tipping point for the industry during the decade was the entry of one particular studio into the field. Walt Disney Pictures, the "eight-hundred-pound gorilla of animation,"[6] had long believed that television animation was an inferior species, and that if it entered into the field, it would somehow tarnish the value of the sacred Disney "brand." (This, in spite of the fact that since the 1950s the studio had been producing live-action series and omnibus programs hosted by Walt Disney himself—a man who was deeply aware of the growing cultural importance of television.) What changed their mind was a change in management, as well as the television marketplace. The arrival of Michael Eisner, a seasoned veteran of both film and television management, marked a major shift in the studio's attitude toward television animation. Eisner, who had been deeply involved (as noted in Chapter 4) in creating television animation programming at ABC, now invested studio resources in developing television animation programming at Disney, for both creative and financial reasons. With Disney's new commitment to television animation soon evident, the entire television animation industry suddenly gained a patina of respectability. It was as if the simple presence of the Disney "magic" in television animation could now atone for the industry's past "sins."

Disney was only one of a growing group of new animation houses that were beginning to challenge, if only subliminally, the old way of doing things in the television animation business. Most of the new organizations, such as Film Roman, Ruby-Spears and Nelvana, were companies run by veteran hands in the field. Others, such as DIC and Saban, were run by European investors eager to tap the financial resources of the American market. What all of them created collectively, however, was a new wave of commercial and creative credibility for television animation, at a time when such new thinking was required for the genre to advance artistically.

Hanna-Barbera in the 1980s

The final decade of this now-iconic studio under the leadership of its storied founders, William Hanna and Joseph Barbera, was marked by a mixture of old ideas and thinking, attempts to modernize the product by bringing in outside sources, and, ultimately, by the beginning of the 1990s, an effort to bring in new management to bring a halt to the growing creative *ennui*. Changes in ownership during this period did not help, as the faltering fortunes of Taft Broadcasting caused it to sell the company at the end of the decade, making it vulnerable to turbulent economics for the first time in two decades.

For the most part, the studio seemed content to continue onward and upward as before. The first productions of the new decade reflected this. In 1980, for CBS, the studio debuted *Drak Pack*, yet another attempt to turn the fabled Universal Pictures monsters of the 1930s and 1940s into God-fearing "good guys" for television animation consumption. The series and character names reflected this attitude. Drak, Jr. (voiced by Jerry Dexter), Frankie (Bill Callaway) and Howler (Callaway) were descendants, respectively, of Dracula, the Frankenstein monster, and the Wolf Man. When trouble loomed, the trio would clasp their hands together, shout "Wacko!" and then would be magically transformed into their ancestors. Significantly, as studio historian Ted Sennett points out, they were "not the fearsome demons of legend but fighters against evil and injustice."[7] Inevitably, they were assigned missions by Drak's great-grandfather, Big D (Alan Oppenheimer). The gang's enemies in this one were the Organization of Generally Rotten Enterprises (OGRE), headed by a madman named Doctor Dred (Hans Conreid), who traveled the Earth in his Dredgible. Since this was a Hanna-Barbera program, the Doctor was assisted by a brace of comically inept hench-people: Toad (Don Messick), Fly (Messick), Mummy Man (Chuck McCann) and Vampira (Julie McWhirter).

Even more derivative in nature was the second major 1980 series, produced for ABC. *Fonz and the Happy Days Gang* was based on the network's enormously popular live-action sitcom, *Happy Days*, and followed that series in transferring the adventures of Arthur "Fonzie" Fonzarelli and company to animation. Original cast member Henry Winkler lent his voice to this enterprise, as did his co-stars Ron Howard and Donny Most. The wild card characters were Cupcake (Didi Conn), a "girl from the future" with a wide variety of supernatural powers and space-age themed exclamations, and Mr. Cool, Fonzie's pet dog, who minutely copied his master's mannerisms. The following season, the studio also created a series based on *Happy Days*' equally popular spinoff series, *Laverne and Shirley*. The title pretty much said it all: *Laverne and Shirley in the Army* (later changed to *Laverne and Shirley with the Fonz*, when the latter character joined the lineup). Live-action series star Penny Marshall voiced her role in the animated version.

◆ ◆ ◆

Another 1981 series, *The Smurfs*, would prove to be far more enduring. In fact, this Big Blue Machine would become NBC's longest-running Saturday morning series ever, win its studio multiple Emmys and other prizes, and prove to be one of the most influential of its kind ever to see broadcast on television.

As with many noteworthy aspects of the Hanna-Barbera story, this one begins with the legendary programming boss Fred Silverman. Having left CBS in the early 1970s, Silverman was recruited by ABC to reverse its traditional third-place ranking in the ratings. Within a few years of his arrival, ABC was the ratings leader of the industry, sparked by a brace of popular sitcoms (*Happy Days, Laverne and Shirley, Mork And Mindy, Three's Company*) and lightweight dramas (*Charlie's Angels*). This was not without controversy, as many of his successful programs focused on the use and abuse of "jiggle" elements—the prominent display of attractive young women in as little clothing as needed for propriety, for which *Charlie's Angels* and *Three's Company* became particularly (in)famous. Naturally, NBC, the new number three, was envious of the results, and they promptly recruited Silverman, in a very obvious gesture, to right their ship. The results were ultimately disastrous. Silverman invested huge amounts of money in what were ultimately flawed, hollow concepts, such as *Supertrain*, an ambitious anthology series set on an enormous train that boasted one of the more realistic—and expensive—settings in TV history. By 1981, Silverman had been shown the door, but his younger disciples remained, and they ultimately transformed the network into a ratings powerhouse for the rest of the decade and well into the next one.

One major bright spot of Silverman's time at NBC came while he was attending an industry meeting in 1979 in Aspen, Colorado. Accompanying his daughter into a toy shop, he found a group of toys that impressed him. "I had never seen them before," he later recalled. "I was so taken with them that I went ... to Hanna-Barbera and said, 'Get the rights to the Smurfs, and you have an on-the-air commitment.' [That meant the studio could be guaranteed a timeslot without having to go through the typical rancorous process of developing projects for network approval.] The rest, as they say, is history."[8]

The characters that impressed Silverman were a group of miniature blue dwarfs—said to be only "three apples high"[9]—who lived in mushroom-shaped homes in a forest glade. Despite the obvious similarities, they were not creations of mythology, but rather of a Belgian cartoonist, Pierre Culliford, who wrote and illustrated his work under the pen name "Peyo." In 1947, the artist had launched his career with *Johan*, a comic book set in medieval times. Soon afterward, after beginning work for *Spirou*, a popular weekly comic book based in Brussels, Peyo revised the concept of Johan by giving his lead character a sidekick named Pirlouit. In 1957, these characters first encountered the creatures originally known as the "*Schtroumpfs*" (later re-dubbed the Smurfs for English speaking countries), a name derived from a nonsense term invented by Peyo and his *Spirou* colleague Andre Fraquin. By 1960, these characters were popular enough to be featured in their own comic books, and a total of nine theatrical feature films were produced featuring them between 1960 and 1966, as well as a previous television animation project produced in Europe in the late 1970s.[10]

However, they were virtually unknown in the United States, in comparison to their European popularity. Silverman clearly saw their potential to become stars of the same magnitude in America, and he was counting on Hanna-Barbera to make it happen for him.

The studio, however, was initially unsure what to do with the concept, as Joseph Barbera would later recall in his autobiography:

> To be perfectly honest, I was hardly blown away by the characters: little blue guys, all looking alike, each wearing a kind of white diaper and sporting sort of floppy cones for headgear. But if Fred was ready to make a commitment, well, who needs more enthusiasm than that?... We secured the rights and put the series into development.
>
> At one point early in the development, an NBC executive named Mickey Dwyer vigorously championed the notion of making the Smurfs all different colors in order to distinguish them one from another. Fortunately, I was able to argue this down. Not that there was any particular genius behind my position. To begin with, I just didn't want to complicate production by introducing a lot of different colors, and, even more important, I was sure Peyo [who was given final approval over every aspect of the subsequent series as well as the

opportunity to write scripts for it] would object and that would throw a monkey wrench into the whole licensing deal. However, as I look back on it, maybe I should claim to have been moved by brilliant poetic insight. A big part of the Smurfs' charm—and staying power—is that, while they all look basically the same and, indeed, are almost nondescript, they each have unique personalities that kids quickly recognize and identify with. Making them all different colors would have given them nothing more than superficial identities— "This is the red one, he's the green one, she's the pink one"—which, really, would have been no identity at all. Making them all look pretty much alike forced us to develop characters with genuinely distinctive personalities.[11]

It also served, as a result, to make the animation of the characters go considerably more smoothly than usual. "All the [Smurfs looked] alike," recalled animator Gordon Clark. "They just [wore] different hats."[12]

Barbera's major contribution to the series was to insist that the characters be featured in a one-hour format as opposed to a half-hour. He believed that the series concept, languid as it was, needed to flow slowly in order for the audience to understand and appreciate it. This was, as usual, a unique concept that he had to fight the network to get:

> I pulled a real coup when I managed to get the show upped from the standard half-hour format to a full hour. I congratulated myself on this, and we forged ahead until, near the end of production of the first batch of shows, I learned that NBC's new daytime programming director, Irv Wilson, had raised a protest with Fred, telling him the hour format was a big mistake. In response, I wrote a long letter to Fred, who finally asked me to come to a meeting in New York to argue my case in person.
>
> Well, what, exactly, *was* my case? [Emphasis in original.]
>
> I searched my soul and searched it some more, and all I could think of was that my reason for wanting to make the show an hour instead of a half-hour was that it meant twice as much business for Hanna-Barbera Productions. But I knew I couldn't quite present it that way. There was nothing to do but get on the plane and hope that something better would occur to me.
>
> What it came down to[,] was me at one end of a long conference table in NBC's Rockefeller Centre offices, Fred at one end, and Irv Wilson and the other execs along the sides.
>
> "Why don't you go ahead, Joe, and tell us why we need an hour," Fred began.
>
> "Well," I said, "look. This is a new show, right? And what is in this new show? Little blue characters.... Okay. So you're a kid, right? And you happen to be flipping around the channels and you catch part of the first hour of the show. Now, if you've only got a half-hour show, by the time you get to it—this show with the little blue characters—you've only got a few minutes left. You watch it for a few minutes, it's over, and you forget about it. But, if you've got another half-hour to go, you stay with it, because you've got thirty more minutes to figure out what's going on. You get wrapped up in it, you hang in, and you stay with the show."
>
> Don't think for a minute that a person can babble something like this and fail to believe that it is absolute, unadulterated double-talk.
>
> The thing of it is, though, it worked.... [W]e made more money than we would have made with half-hours, and NBC—well ... [t]hose little blue guys were like the cavalry riding in to the rescue.[13]

"Riding in to the rescue," even for the loquacious Barbera, was an understatement. NBC, frustrated with the perennially meager ratings of the Saturday morning division, had long been toying with expanding its lifestyle/news franchise, *Today*, to the weekend hours as a replacement for television animation. Thanks to the immediate success of *The Smurfs* (the first real "hit" show NBC had seen on Saturday morning in over a decade) those plans were, at least temporarily, scrapped. Ironically, Fred Silverman, the instigator of the program's development, had already packed his bags and left by the time it debuted; it would thus remain as the major legacy of his time with the network. A season later, the series would expand to an unprecedented 90 minutes before returning to an hour for the balance of its run.

Produced in association with the Belgian studio Sepp International, *The Smurfs* was a reflection of the new processes of production at Hanna-Barbera. Hanna and Barbera themselves were credited as executive producers, a reflection of the fact that their now-advanced ages prevented them from supervising all aspects of the production as they had in the past. Instead, production, direction, voice-acting supervision and writing were now entrusted to an increasingly long string of deputies. For *The Smurfs*, for example, Gerald Baldwin served as producer and story editor for the entire existence of the series, and it is to him that we can credit the uniform excellence of the show during the series' unprecedented nine-year run.

The series itself was far more simplistic than the circumstances that spawned it. As Ted Sennett notes, "The Smurfs, like the Seven Dwarfs, had names that characterized them immediately,"[14] saving the audience the trouble of trying to tell them apart visually. The names also served the purpose of identifying what roles they had in the community, as well as the essential nature of their personalities. Papa Smurf (Don Messick), the white-bearded, Reagan-esque patriarch, was set apart by his tough but kind personality, his practice of "white" magic, and, particularly, the fact that he dressed in red clothing while the others were uniformly clothed in white. Likewise, the bespectacled Brainy (Danny Goldman) was the resident intellectual. Much like Jay Ward's Mr. Peabody (see Chapter 3) he was portrayed as a negative character, continually spouting his opinion when it was neither required nor needed. This often resulted in the other characters simply telling him to shut up, or, in extreme cases, bodily throwing him out of Smurf Village. In the village structure, Brainy effectively functioned as the Alexander Haig to Papa Smurf's Reagan—i.e., he believed he was in charge, when, in fact, he was not.

Other Smurfs were cast in the same one-dimensional mode. Hefty (Frank Welker) was a muscular strong man. Handy (Michael Bell) was the resident handyman. Greedy (Hamilton Camp) was the resident cook, who typically wanted all the food for himself. Vanity (Alan Oppenheimer) was the resident narcissist.[15] Grouchy (Bell) was the misanthrope in residence, continually prefacing everything he said with "I hate...". Smurfette (Lucille Bliss) was the lone female in the group, with her thatch of long blond hair and stereotypically "feminine" behavior. And so on and so on. Their very name was used as an all-purpose noun, verb, and adjective in their discourse (e.g., "That's not Smurfy!"), which added a bit of levity to the often slow-moving proceedings.

Oddly enough, the most interesting character on the program was its chief villain. His name was Gargamel (an excellent vocal performance by Paul Winchell), and he was a wizard by trade. Sporting a balding dome, a prominent, jutting nose, and incredibly unkempt, patched and disheveled clothing, this gentleman, for reasons known only to him, was intent on capturing the Smurfs in order to use them for his own purposes, chiefly to enact the spells in his *Great Book* on them. "So many uncast spells!" he would declare. "So many uncaught Smurfs!"[16] With the assistance of his equally vicious cat, Azriel (Don Messick), and, later, his apprentice, Scruple (Brenda Vaccaro), he would boldly enter Smurf Village whenever he felt like it and pluck a couple of Smurf specimens out of the blue. Naturally, the Smurfs, in spite of their small size, put up ample resistance and eventually set their comrades free. Inevitably, episodes like these would end with Gargamel screaming, crying, and beating his hands, feet and body on the stone floor of his decrepit castle or the forest floor, in genuine anguish, at his repeated inability to capture and do away with his miniature enemies. Not that he was *completely* incompetent, though. Smurfette, for example, was originally his creation, developed for evil purposes until Papa Smurf used *his* magic to turn her over to the good side.

The fact that the series was an hour or 90-minutes long during its original broadcast run prevented it from assuming the problems apparent in Hanna-Barbera productions of the previous decade—the milking of a good premise dry through banal repetition. The stories of Gargamel's attempted capture of the Smurfs were alternated with interesting stories of life in Smurf Village and, in the 90-minute version, with episodes featuring Peyo's pre–Smurfs characters, now known as Johan and Pee Wee (the latter sporting an atrocious singing voice). Later seasons would feature more characters joining the cast. In 1985, the miniature Smurflings and the tomboyish Sassette (Julie Dees) were added to provide more "kid" and "female" characters in the mix. This was balanced by the development of the heavily patriarchal Grandpa Smurf (Jonathan Winters) to oversee them. The Smurfs' neighbors, the Wood Elves, particularly the deaf Laconia,[17] also began playing roles in the series and its related specials. The final season saw the most drastic shift in the formula, as the Smurfs were torn away from the village setting to make trips around the world as well as backward and forward in time.

Though the series won two Emmys and a variety of other awards during its run, acclaim was not universal. Timothy and Kevin Burke, in their sociological study of the Saturday morning experience during the 1970s and 1980s, have little good to say about it, particularly regarding what they see as its obvious political subtext:

> Smurfs were not independent autonomous individuals, but instead were specialized units of a greater Smurf whole, like army ants.... The Smurf hive-mind is pretty chilling once you look at it closely.
>
> A lot of kids liked *Smurfs*, and so did some of Saturday morning's most persistent critics, largely because the show was cloyingly pro-social. Smurfs always learned, by the end of the episode, that cooperation was good and rugged individuality was bad. However, *Smurfs* [was] ... deeply loathed by many Saturday morning veterans, including us....You couldn't really avoid [watching] it [because of the manner in which it was structured and scheduled], and it was just good enough in technical terms that you could watch it without suffering too greatly. But the Smurfs themselves were so malevolently cute that we kept hoping Gargamel would manage to boil them down into their component atoms.
>
> Their most Smurfy crime, however, was simply that their success spawned legions of imitators.[18]

Indeed it did, and you will likely meet all of them before this chapter is through. But it must be said that, in spite of the mercenary nature of show business, imitation, no matter how bold and transparent, remains the sincerest form of flattery. And what was imitated was not simply the characters themselves, but the generally bucolic nature and setting of the program, which was exactly the tonic needed for both networks and producers weary of fighting battles over "violence" in the narratives of stories. *The Smurfs*' ultimate legacy for the genre of television animation was the establishment of a newer, gentler approach to storytelling and characterization than what had occurred before. This measured and far less frantic approach to television animation storytelling would continue to run across the 1980s, 1990s and 2000s as a gentler tributary to the more explicitly "cartoony" storytelling of yore, and would influence the storytelling of the genre in entirely unexpected ways over the course of that time.

◆ ◆ ◆

While the Smurfs were busy serving as the saviors of NBC's Saturday morning lineup, Hanna-Barbera was also continuing with other, similar productions on its docket. Some of these were as lavishly produced as the Smurfs, and drank from the same artistic cup, while others were simply a continuation of the established retread process at the studio.

In 1979, the studio secured a major coup when Hanna and Barbera persuaded their old MGM colleague Tex Avery to come out of a self-imposed retirement and work on developing series projects for them. Avery promptly came up with a suitable project, but the restrictions of American television network censorship disgusted him. With Hanna-Barbera's hopeful blessing, Avery hoped to film "Quicky Koala," as he originally titled it, in Canada to save on costs, and to have it air in syndication, to sidestep network regulation so it could be presented as he wished.[19] This, unfortunately, was not to be. In the summer of 1980, Avery died of a heart attack in the Hanna-Barbera parking lot.

The studio, however, thought the idea was too good die with its creator, and put it into production as the centerpiece of an omnibus project similar to most of the studio's product of the 1950s and 1960s. *The Kwicky Koala Show*, as it came to be known, debuted on CBS in the fall of 1981. While the studio animators were unable to duplicate Avery's hilarious, impudent pacing and quicksilver timing ("He was faster than the eye," remarked Joseph Barbera[20]), the influence of Avery was still clearly felt. The title character (Robert Allen Ogle) was an innocent-looking but secretly sly figure in the mode of earlier Avery creations, such as Droopy and Chilly Willy. His nemesis was Wilfred Wolf (John Stephenson,) who went to extraordinary lengths to catch him for the usual predatory reasons. Also featured were similar zany ideas that worked chiefly because they were only expected to carry a single segment rather than a whole show, and were paced accordingly, creating far more humorous results than usual. "Dirty Dawg" resurrected the old animal con-artist formula in a gritty inner-city setting, with lead characters who looked surprisingly like modern homeless people. The lead character (Frank Welker) spoke "like Groucho Marx crossed with Howard [Cosell],"[21] and was abetted by his diminutive assistant, Ratso (Marshall Efron). Their opponent was Officer Bullhorn (Matthew Faison), who, as Hal Erickson observes, was clearly "a goofy [retroactive] caricature of the cops who'd busted hippie heads during the 1968 Chicago Democratic Convention."[22] The third segment was a wild variant on the chase cartoons Avery and others had produced at Warner Bros. and MGM in the 1940s and 1950s, set in Hanna-Barbera's old *Yogi Bear* territory. "Crazy Claws" focused on the title character (Jim MacGeorge,) a lynx-like wildcat, as he perennially foiled the efforts of the insane-looking mountain man Rawhide Clyde (Robert Allen Ogle) and his sycophantic dog, Bristletooth (Peter Cullen), to capture him. Attempting to referee the ensuing bouts was the mild-mannered-sounding Park Ranger Rangerfield (Michael Bell), who, to his horror, often got caught in the crossfire. "I should have gone into an easier line of work," the Ranger observed in one installment, "like wrestling sharks."[23]

Other programs obviously played the "cute" card, instigated by *The Smurfs* and fed by competing programs from other providers. *The Shirt Tales*, debuting on NBC in the fall of 1982, was based on a line of greeting card characters from Hallmark, whose principal *shtick* was the fact that, periodically, things that they said were displayed on their shirts. A collection of small animals living in an oak tree in a park, they would emerge to do some good. They could communicate with one another by way of Dick Tracy–styled wristwatch communicators, and traveled in the Shirt Tales' Super-Sonic Transporter (or, mercifully, the "STSST"), which could expel a laser-like beam. Their rallying cry was, not surprisingly, "It's Shirt Tale time!" whereupon "SHIRT TALES" would flash on their chests. The group consisted of Rick Raccoon (Ronnie Schell), Pammy Panda (Pat Parris), Digger Mole (Robert Allen Ogle), Bogey Orangutan (done by master impressionist Fred Travalena as a dead-on take on the late Humphrey Bogart, as the name implied), Tyg Tiger (Steve Schatzberg), and, later, Kip Kangaroo (Nancy Cartwright). The other series regular was the park superintendent, Mr. Dinkle (Herb Vigran), who "was sometimes an ally, sometimes an opponent, but always the basically decent protector."[24] of the group.

As the cute animal sub-genre was made to order for television animation in the 1980s, Hanna-Barbera naturally went to great lengths to get as much mileage out of it as it could. One example was *The Biskitts*, debuting on CBS in 1983, which featured lead characters who were essentially canine Smurfs, as they were all "as tall as a dog biscuit."[25] This group was made up of the guardians of the crown jewels of Biskitt Castle in the name of its monarch, whose recent death had created a power vacuum in the realm. As expected, the characters were imaginatively named. Waggs (Darryl Hickman) was the leader; his associates included the likes of Lady (B.J. Ward), Scat (Dick Beals), Sweets (Kathleen Helppie), Spinner (Bob Holt), Wiggle (Jennifer Darling), Mooch (Marshall Efron) and Downer (Henry Gibson). Their nemesis was King Max (Kenneth Mars), brother of the late monarch and king of a neighboring realm, who, predictably, sought his brothers' jewels. His associates were his guard dogs Fang (Peter Cullen) and Snarl (Mars), and his incongruously named court jester, Shecky (Kip King). A wildcat named Scratch (Cullen) also possessed predatory instincts toward the tiny heroes.

Another series was noteworthy chiefly because it tried to do what had been done elsewhere less successfully. In a pact similar to the one made earlier with Avery, the studio convinced the now-semi-retired Friz Freleng to help them bring the Pink Panther back to television animation in a new series. The results were less than spectacular. *The Pink Panther and Sons*, airing on NBC in 1984, showed the character as a single father interacting with his two young sons, Pinky and Panky, with predictable results.

During the 1986-87 season, the studio went back to the canine realm—not to mention the pre-established character well—for two much more entertaining series. *Foofur*, airing on NBC, was another collaboration with Sepp International, focusing this time on a good-natured, blue-furred bloodhound (Frank Welker) who had inherited the estate of his late master. With the assistance of his young niece, Rocky (Christina Lange), he converted the building into a residence for themselves and a variety of colorfully designed associates. Among these were Louis the bulldog (Dick Gautier), a former "street gang" member; Annabel (Susan Tolsky), a vain sheepdog; the aristocratic Fritz-Carlos (Jonathan Schmock) and Hazel (Pat Carroll); and Fencer (Eugene Williams), a "jive-talking"[26] alley cat. Their principal nemesis was Mrs. Escrow (Susan Silo), a real estate agent who was unaware, for some reason, that the group was living there, and was always trying to sell it as a result, necessitating defensive action from the group in response. An undeniably "cute" vein ran through the stories, but the writers managed to insert bits of humor to prevent it from being dry.

Pound Puppies, airing on ABC during the same season, was a far more elaborate take on the humans-vs.-animals theme, which was becoming a readily apparent part of the "cute" sub-genre. Based on an established line of stuffed toys from Tonka, who co-produced with Hanna-Barbera, the series was an outgrowth of a television special produced for ABC, which first aired in the fall of 1985. This special, in turn, became a massive hit on the nascent home video market; VHS and DVD issues in this and subsequent decades would become a major source of ancillary revenue for television animation producers.[27] Be that as it may, the series itself only bore a surface similarity to the special that spawned it. Led by the aptly named Cooler (Dan Gilvezan), the title characters operated what amounted to "a computer operated underground network in order to match deserving doggies with loving families" under the guise of a "pound," which was "actually more of a sanctuary for homeless hounds"[28] than an animal-control facility. The parallels to prison movies, in particular *The Great Escape* (John Sturges, 1963), were fairly obvious; in fact, that film had supplied the special with both its name and theme. Not surprisingly, in both special and series, the incompetent dogcatcher in charge of the pound, Dabney Nabbit (Frank Welker), always had his hands full with his would-be charges. The series differed from the special in that it moved the setting from the Wagga-Wagga dog pound to the estate of Millicent Trueblood, a wealthy millionaire who could communicate with dogs via "Puppy Power," a second-sight–styled possession. When Millicent died at the ripe old age of 101, her villainous grand-niece, Katrina Stoneheart (Pat Carroll), hoped to tear down the mansion and erect condos to be used only by—wait for it—cat lovers. In this, Katrina was foiled; she inherited only the mansion and not the pound and its related properties. That was given to Millicent's young ward, Holly (Ame Foster), who also possessed the ability to talk to the dogs. As a consequence, the stories once again were built on a paper-thin Manichean dynamic, with Cooler, Holly and company against Katrina, her daughter Brattina (Adrienne Alexander), and her pampered cat, Cat Gut (Welker). Assisting Cooler were Howler (Robert Morse), an eccentric inventor who stored a huge backlog of inventions in his hat; young, impressionable Bright Eyes (Nancy Cartwright); Whopper (B.J. Ward), a young disciple of Baron Munchausen; and Nose Marie (Ruth Buzzi), a caricatured Southern belle. While obviously not subtle in stating its good-vs.-evil story outline (as evident by the character names listed above), the program was much more entertaining and enjoyable than its more cloying counterparts in the "cute" sub-genre. Much of this had to do with the injection of new blood into the studio's writing staff, particularly story editor Tom Ruegger, who would distinguish himself further in the following decade at Warner Bros. (see Chapter 6).

Other projects reflected the same levels of creative desperation evident in the 1970s. During the late 1970s and 1980s, the studio on two separate occasions attempted to revive another old cartoon warhorse, Popeye, for the new television animation era. *The All-New Popeye Hour*, as the first project was called, aired on CBS between 1978 and 1983; in later seasons, it was cut to a half-hour and re-titled *The Popeye and Olive Comedy Show*. In addition to new, mostly non-violent adventures of the old gang, highlighted chiefly by a more feminist-minded Olive Oyl than in earlier incarnations, there were new features, such as "Private Olive Oyl," which replicated the theme of *Laverne and Shirley in the Army*. It featured Olive (voiced by Marilyn Scheffler here) and another E.C. Segar creation, the hulking, non-verbal Alice the Goon, as army privates under the command of the typically loudmouthed Sergeant Bertha Blast (Jo Anne Worley). Four years later came *Popeye and Son*, in which Popeye and Olive had married and had a son named Junior, who *hated* spinach. Bluto, who was now married and with a son himself, remained the chief antagonist.[29] Poor results also came from similar products in this line. *The Gary Coleman Show* (NBC, 1982–83) featured, in animated form, the star of the popular live-action sitcom *Diff'rent Strokes* as an apprentice angel sent to Earth in the guise of a normal kid. (The Mexican animators working on the project had apparently never seen *Diff'rent Strokes*, because they initially drew the diminutive African

American actor as a *white* child.³⁰) *The Little Rascals* (ABC, 1983–84) was an animated take on Hal Roach's classic *Our Gang* comedy films, while *The Dukes* (CBS, 1983–84) was a similar adaptation of the popular Southern U.S.–set action-comedy series *The Dukes of Hazzard*.

There was a bit more imagination employed in the studio's straight drama offerings of the decade. *Challenge of the Gobots* (Syndicated, 1984) focused around some competitors of the Transformers (see below) who were in competition with the villainous Renegade Robots. *Galtar and the Golden Lance* (Syndicated, 1985), was a lush sword-and-planet spectacle, focusing on the taciturn hero Galtar (Lou Richards) as he rambled in search of the villainous Tormack (Brock Peters), who had been responsible for the death of his parents. *Sky Commanders* (Syndicated, 1987) took a leaf from *G.I. Joe* (see below) in focusing on the renegade soldier Mike Summit (Robert Ridgely) and his associates as they fought the vicious General Plague (Bernard Erhard). By far the most imaginatively conceived of this group was *Wildfire*, which debuted on CBS in the fall of 1986. Sara (Georgi Irene), a 12-year-old horse-loving resident of Montana, found her life irrevocably changed when she befriended the supernaturally gifted horse Wildfire (John Vernon). He promptly took her into the fairy-tale realm of Dar-Shan, where Sara discovered that, much like the lead characters of *He-Man* and *She-Ra* (see below), she was actually a princess of this realm; her mother had sent her to Earth to protect her from the forces of evil. Sara, Wildfire and company then proceeded to engage in predictable good-vs.-evil battles with the sorceress Diabolyn (Jessica Walter), who sought control of the realm via possession of the amulet that Sara wore around her neck at all times.

The formula of *The Smurfs* was repeated in a number of other series "in which fantasy characters, living happily in their own environment, were menaced by outside forces."³¹ *Pac-Man*, debuting on ABC in 1982, was an adaptation of the enormously popular arcade video game, a nod to that medium's growing popularity. It focused on the title character (Marty Ingels) as he faced off against the Ghost Monsters, intent on destroying his race and home, Pac-Land. For the same network the following year, the studio offered *Monchichis*, a collaboration with Mattel based on their "Happiness Dolls" line. The monkey-like title characters lived in the kingdom of Monchia under the leadership of a benign wizard, and were threatened by the Glumplins, whose leader, Horrg (Sidney Miller), was referred to by his underlings as "your loathsomeness," "your nastiness," and other such honorific titles. *The Trollkins of Trolltown*, airing on CBS in 1981, focused on a race of diminutive beings who seemed to reside somewhere in the American South, given their mannerisms and accented speaking voices. Under the leadership of the spoonerism-spouting Mayor Lumpkin (Paul Winchell), Sheriff Pudge Trollsom (Alan Oppenheimer) and his deputy, Flake (Marshall Efron), managed to keep the peace in a most comical fashion. Also involved in the escapades were the dog Flooky (Frank Welker); Blitz (Steve Spears), son of the mayor, and Pixlee (Jennifer Darling), daughter of the sheriff.

The series that displayed the strongest roots in the Smurf tradition, however, was *The Snorks*, yet another collaboration with Sepp International, which debuted on NBC in 1984. This was the creation of another Belgian cartoonist, in this case Freddy Monnickendam, who shared the executive producer credit on the series with Hanna and Barbera. He would later do the same duties on *The Smurfs*, and also was responsible for the creation of *Foofur* (see above). The back-story was unusually elaborate. When a merchant ship was sunk by pirates in the 1643, the captain was saved from drowning by an air pocket in one of the cabins. During his submersion, the normal-sized man came upon the spectacle of "a microscopic underwater civilization, populated by strange, tiny creatures who seemed human save for their fishlike facial features and the snorkels emanating from their heads."³² He dubbed these characters, who were no bigger than the thumb of a man, "Snorks," and, upon his return to dry land, spread the legend of them to anyone who would listen. In a parallel situation, the Snorks spread through their own folklore the legend of giant alien surface dwellers from "Dry Space" who posed a persistent threat to their existence.

Reference to this prologue was chiefly contained in the main title sequence. The series depicted life in the Snork community circa 1984, where they had developed a society comparable to the human one it was contrasted with, including schooling, split-level homes, and such gastronomical delights as "kelp burgers." Our hero was Allstar (Michael Bell), a high-school-age Snork; his chief associates were his gal pal Casey (B.J. Ward), and their friends Dimmy (Brian Cummings), Daffney (Nancy Cartwright), and Tooter (Frank Welker), who communicated only via sound effects. The pompous Governor Wetworth (Frank Nelson) ran the operation, while his self-centered son, Junior (Barry Gordon), was a regular fly in our heroes' ointments. While the series' plotting was fairly routine, going so far as even to borrow from *The Flintstones*, the draftsmanship was of unusually high quality by '80s television animation standards. A high level of contrast was provided by drawing the Snorks themselves as traditional cartoon characters, while drawing the sea life around them—and the occasional "Dry Space" antagonist—as realistically as possible.[33]

In spite of these successes at animating the creations of other people, the studio was increasingly floundering when it came to their own properties. It was simply a case, in this regard, of not knowing when to leave well enough alone.

The key cases in point here were the continuation of variations on *The Flintstones* and *Scooby Doo*, although these new versions were handled with a bit more taste and a bit less repetition than before. Regarding the former, the first product for the new decade was *The Flintstones Comedy Show*, which first aired on NBC in 1980. A 90-minute offering, it was an omnibus divided into six separate but equal segments. "The Flintstone Family Adventures" effectively updated the old sitcom format for the 1980s, rather than simply rehashing old '60's plotlines, as had been the case for the '70s versions. "Captain Caveman" resurrected the star of *Captain Caveman and the Teen Angels* (see Chapter 4) in what was presumably his original super-heroic environs, while also, neatly providing him with a secret identity in the form of a bespectacled, meek copy boy named Chester, who worked at the *Daily Granite*—presumably named in honor of its editor, Lou Granite (Kenneth Mars). Wilma Flintstone and Betty Rubble also worked there, and were often cast in the Lois Lane–like position of having to be rescued by the Captain, who was as bumbling as ever. "The Bedrock Cops" was a loony variation on contemporary TV cop shows, with Fred and Barney cast as inept reservists under the command of Sergeant Boulder (Lennie Weinrib) and assisted by a brace of Shmoos (see Chapter 4). "Pebbles, Dino and Bamm Bamm" was a prehistoric variant on *Scooby Doo*, with the Flintstone and Rubble kids now teenagers once again. "Dino and The Cavemouse," a project devised by Tex Avery, provided a similar take on "Tom And Jerry"–styled "chase" cartoons. Finally, there was the most bizarre, and, arguably, the funniest segment of the project—"The Frankenstones." Based on characters who had appeared in some of the prime-time specials the studio produced featuring the Flintstones, these characters provided a refreshing prehistoric take on existing "horror" and "monster" stereotypes in television animation. Charles Nelson Reilly brought his trademark snooty act into animation as the Frankenstone patriarch (who was named, rather predictably, Frank), while Ruta Lee was likewise well cast as his wife, Hidea. The segments were linked with a variety of animation "drawing tips" and guessing games conducted by Fred. NBC was impressed enough with the results to air selected edited reruns of the series on its schedule between 1981 and 1984.

The next chapter in the saga came in 1986, on the series' old home network, ABC. It was a project that was literally conceived on the fly; Joseph Barbera contends that he dreamed it up just as a deal to make a Cabbage Patch Kids series fell through, in order to save the hour timeslot he had bargained for with the network.[34] *The Flintstone Kids* was based on the concept of what would become known in the industry as "babyfication"—taking established cartoon or media characters and reducing them to childhood or infantilism, the ultimate example of which was the earlier *Muppet Babies* (see below) on CBS. Thus, in contrast to earlier narratives related to the series, which contended that Fred and Barney had not met Wilma and Betty until they were young adults, this series' main segments were built around the idea that they were all childhood pals instead.[35] In addition to childhood versions of Fred, Barney, Wilma, Betty, Dino and even the future Mr. Slate, there were some new characters added: stereotyped bully Rocky Ratrock (Marilyn Scheffler), rich girl Dreamchip Gemstone (Susan Blu), and Philo Quartz (Bumper Robinson), who was the first African American character in the saga's history. The parents of the leads were Ed and Edna Flintstone (both voiced by Henry Corden), Robert and Flo Rubble (Mel Blanc and Marilyn Scheffler) and Wilma's mom, Doris Slaghoople (Jean Vander Pyl). The burden of the project's length was once again eased by dividing it into segments for easier consumption. In addition to regular segments featuring the newly reduced-in-age characters, there were also "Dino's Dilemmas," vehicles for the now pint-sized dinosaur dog, and "Flintstone Funnies," wild personalized flights of fancy à la those in *Muppet Babies* and elsewhere in the sub-genre. But the true highlight of the series was "Captain Caveman and Son," providing new adventures of the Captain (Mel Blanc), now assisted by his son, Cavey Jr. (Charlie Adler), under the pretext of being the Flintstone Kids' favorite TV show. Clearly pointing the way to further cartoon parodies and satires of the superhero genre, in particular *The Powerpuff Girls* (see Chapter 6), this segment was highlighted by over-the-top humor, such as the Captain shattering the traditional "fourth wall" between audience and performers to remonstrate with his young viewers if he felt they were reacting too strongly to his antics! A more serious spinoff from the project was a prime-time anti-drug special airing in 1988, called, rather obviously, *The Flintstone Kids "Just Say No" Special*. The series proper lasted four years on ABC.

Scooby Doo was also relentlessly tinkered with during this time. The most prominent addition in terms of the cast of characters during this period was Scrappy Doo, a miniature nephew of our hero who was his total opposite in terms of personality, first introduced in 1979. Where Scooby was more likely to run from danger, Scrappy was more likely to embrace it, as his name implied. He was wont to run directly into a fracas, therefore, boasting that he had "Puppy Power!" as he did. However, his addition served simply to weaken the essential formula of the series and highlight its obvious flaws. As Timothy and Kevin Burke have noted, if Scrappy was so eager to attack the so-called "monsters" because he recognized how vulnerable they *really* were, "Why didn't the whole gang just kick the crap out of the monster the first time they saw it?"[36]

The answer to that question was simple: Hanna-Barbera had a valuable franchise going on here, and they weren't about to acknowledge the weaknesses in their storylines simply because they bore little resemblance to reality.

That being said, the studio continued to trot the characters through increasingly inane story sequences and storylines throughout the 1980s. The first production of the decade was *The Richie Rich/Scooby Doo Hour*, airing first in 1980, which paired Scooby with animated adventures of Harvey Comics' fabled "poor little rich boy," who dated back to the

1950s. The majority of the '80s, though, saw reruns of the property being repeatedly trotted out under new names. There were three exceptions. *The New Scooby-Doo Mysteries* (ABC, 1984–85) were the same as before, save for the fact that they were newly produced episodes. Far more imaginative was *The Thirteen Ghosts of Scooby Doo* (ABC 1985–86), an astonishingly well produced real-life ghost chase spread over the course of 13 episodes, and given weight by the voice and presence of Vincent Price as occult specialist Vincent Van Ghoul. This was the work of Tom Ruegger and other new-breed animators, whose talents would blossom later elsewhere. *A Pup Named Scooby Doo*, airing between 1988 and 1993 on ABC, was a "babyfication" take on the series that was highlighted by a surprisingly strong streak of humor, in particular its ability to burlesque the entire "Scooby Doo" franchise. One component of this was manifested by a character who was repeatedly wrongfully accused of perpetrating the crime by the youthful sleuths. He was appropriately dubbed Red Herring.

There were other attempts to adapt similar classic characters to the "new" environment of the times. *Yogi's Treasure Hunt*, debuting in 1985, was a self-explanatory update of the *Yogi's Gang* format, featuring most of the same characters from the prior series (see Chapter 4). This series was one of the featured components of *The Funtastic World of Hanna-Barbera*, a syndicated 90-minute block airing on Sunday mornings, which proved to be a success in that underutilized timeslot. Far more ambitious in nature were the series collected under the umbrella title *Hanna-Barbera's Superstars*. These were full-length feature films that, for the most part, were effective in showcasing the stars featured, many of which had not received such full-scale treatment by the studio in some time. First airing in syndication, the projects have been successful on home video and DVD reissues. For the record, the titles were: *The Good, the Bad, and the Huckleberry, Rockin' with Judy Jetson, Scooby Doo and the Ghoul School, The Jetsons Meet the Flintstones, Scooby Doo and the Reluctant Werewolf, Scooby Doo Meets the Boo Brothers, Top Cat and the Beverly Hills Cats, Yogi and the Invasion of the Space Bears, Yogi and the Magical Flight of the Spruce Goose,* and *Yogi's Great Escape*. The prominent featuring of *The Jetsons* dovetailed nicely with the studio's revival of that project in syndication in 1985, combining reruns of the older programs with newly produced and updated material, and, ultimately, the feature-film version.

The last major series project produced by Hanna and Barbera themselves aired during the 1988-89 season on NBC. As was so often the case by now, it was an adaptation of someone else's idea rather than a project developed by the studio itself. *The Completely Mental Misadventures of Ed Grimley* was an adaptation to animation of the pointy-haired "nerd" character created by Canadian comedian/actor Martin Short and portrayed by him on both *SCTV* and *Saturday Night Live*. Short shared executive-producer duties with Hanna and Barbera, and supposedly undertook the project to gain the attention of his children.[37] Given the nature of the character and his origins, much of the series was targeted toward the character's adult fans rather than the traditional child-centered fan base of Saturday morning TV animation, so its position in that timeslot ultimately hurt it in the ratings. Short's Grimley was surrounded in animated form by his neighbor, Miss Malone (Catherine O'Hara), his hostile landlords, the Freebuses (Andrea Martin and Jonathan Winters), his pet rat Sheldon and his goldfish Moby. The fraternal twin brothers Roger and Wendell Gustav (Winters and Danny Cooksey) interpreted the stories for the audience in animated form, while Count Floyd (Joe Flaherty), another star *SCTV* character, did much the same (although less successfully) in live-action film inserts. The failure of the series said as much about the realities of the television business in the 1980s as it did about the series' actual creative quality, which was higher than average for the decade. Had it debuted in the 1990s and 2000s on cable, or been scheduled in a more adult-directed timeslot, it likely would have been more successful. Regardless, the failure of the series put the kibosh on similar plans to bring other comedians, such as Whoopi Goldberg and Rodney Dangerfield, to animation, and stands as a sad closing note to the distinguished animation careers of Hanna and Barbera.

◆ ◆ ◆

Just as the most ambitious projects of the 1970s at Hanna-Barbera had little to do with television animation, their most ambitious project produced during the 1980s ultimately had little to do with television at all, even though it was originally intended for that market. As with the projects of the previous decade, it was the result of Joseph Barbera having perhaps too much faith in what he considered to be a good idea.

It sounded simple enough: Barbera wanted to produce an animated version of the Bible.

He first conceived the idea in 1969, and remained committed to it for a total of 17 years until he could convince skeptics in the industry of its value. One attempted alliance with Mattel to produce it fell apart when the company, which had been attempting to start its own television animation subsidiary, abandoned the notion. Barbera's attempts to animate the Bible, in fact, became something of a running joke in the industry, one which, as with most jokes, had a basis in truth. "Let Joe Barbera in the door," it was said, "and he won't leave until you've heard the good word for the Good Book."[38]

Eventually, it was Hanna-Barbera's own parent company, Taft Broadcasting, impressed by the amount of research and background art that Barbera had collected over the years, as well as his extreme dedication to the project, that allowed it to go into production for release as a series of home-video cassettes. Although some of the staffers were resistant to the project (Hanna himself reportedly told Barbera that he wouldn't have touched it "with a ten-foot pole"[39]), it nevertheless proceeded. Working closely with the writers and animators in a way he had not for years, Barbera conceived the series as being utterly faithful to the original Biblical narratives while still adding touches of animation filmmaking to the way in which it was presented.[40]

The project was collectively known as *The Greatest Adventure: Stories from the Bible*, and it was enormously successful from the time of its 1986 debut onward. Barbera was committed to the project chiefly because he understood the enduring, eternal value of the narratives presented in the Bible, and his commitment was evident in the final production. It was almost immediately certified as "the most successful original animated videocassette series for children," with sales well past the one-million mark.[41] Religious organizations showered it with awards for excellence in broadcasting as a reflection of its creative excellence.

The Greatest Adventure's success was a watershed moment in the history of animation and of that of Hanna-Barbera. For most of television animation's existence, it had been organized religious groups, particularly evangelical and Baptist organizations, which had been among its most vociferous enemies. These groups would continue to be thorns in the industry's side, but, with this series, Hanna-Barbera had proved that the television industry could be used as a force for "good" as well as for "evil." Even those who condemned the industry as a whole could not deny the excellence of the project—nor the sincere intentions of Barbera in presenting it.

Such all-encompassing good intentions were becoming rare at the studio. First, the studio founders were aging and gradually withdrawing from full oversight, saving their energies for work on projects that more specifically required their direct involvement. Hanna underwent open heart surgery in 1990 (Alzheimer's disease would disable him further toward the end of his life) and limited his involvement with the company after that, and, though Barbera remained personally involved with projects involving the star characters, he, too, lightened his workload. Another factor was the financial decline of Taft Broadcasting, which forced the sale of Hanna-Barbera to the Great American Broadcasting organization in 1989. The final establishment of the new guard came in 1991, with the enveloping of the studio into Ted Turner's burgeoning cable TV empire, at which time Hanna and Barbera, now sharing the title of Chairman, allowed others to take full creative control of the studio for the first time in its history.[42] The rest of the studio's story, however, will be addressed in the following chapters.

◆ ◆ ◆

In August 1988, at the annual Emmy Awards ceremony, William Hanna and Joseph Barbera were presented with the Governor's Award for Lifetime Achievement by the Academy of Television Arts and Sciences. They were the first (and, are so far, the only) television animation producers to receive this honor.[43] Five years later, they were also the first and only television animation producers to be inducted into the Television Hall of Fame.

William Hanna died in 2001, at the age of 91. Joseph Barbera, still active to the end, passed on in 2006, at the age of 95. With the exception of Walt Disney, no other individuals had so utterly transformed the art and commerce of animation over the course of their careers.

The Hanna-Barbera studio was the one company that helped to secure television animation's place in animation history as a programming genre. The importance of its pioneering achievements can never be overstated. Although its creative quality declined during the 1970s and 1980s, this was due to interference and censorship at the network level, rather than any lack of commitment to or understanding of the art of animation on the producers' part. When given full reign, the studio under its founders was capable of producing an astonishing virtuosity and range of productions, from *The Flintstones* to *Last of the Curlews*, that fully demonstrated that television animation was a legitimate form of art and deserved to be respected as such. That the studio endured during this period in spite of financial and creative disputes with networks, sponsors, syndicators, and even its own staff, when its competitors were being felled by similar disputes, is an enduring tribute to William Hanna's film direction, organizational and management skills, and Joseph Barbera's fluidity at developing original characters and stories and seizing the potential of outside characters for animation adaptation.

The greatest legacy Hanna and Barbera ultimately left was establishing which formats would work for animation in television and which would not. Their earliest work was produced in short forms, between seven and 11 minutes, that could easily be inserted into whatever timeslot was allowed. With *The Flintstones*, they pioneered the concept of a self-contained half-hour as an effective format for television animation. It would be their pioneering work of the 1950s and 1960s that future television animators would draw from for inspiration, both in reverential and mockingly critical ways. In terms of laying down the time-length formats for which television animation was most effective, there was no greater influence than Hanna and Barbera. The effective, continued use of television animation in both individualized segments (e.g., *The Powerpuff Girls*) and full-length narratives (e.g., *The Simpsons*; see Chapter 6 for both) is, even more than their platoon of legendary characters, Hanna-Barbera's greatest legacy to the television animation business.

William Hanna and Joseph Barbera were survivors, managing to weather problems in both the film and television animation business with surprising ease, and, in the process, to establish themselves as the most prolific and influential producers in television animation history. It is unlikely that the business of television animation, turbulent as it is, will ever see two more inventive, thoughtful, successful and, above all, perennial personalities in its ranks again.

Animation by Filmation: Part Two

Much like Hanna and Barbera, the 1980s also marked Lou Scheimer's swan-song period as a television animation producer. However, in his case, this was due to forces beyond his control more than a simple desire to retire, as it had been with his longtime friendly rivals.

In the period just prior to the sale of the company to Westinghouse (see Chapter 4), Filmation remained hard at work creating television animation product for the networks as it had in the previous decade. *The Tom and Jerry Comedy Show*, debuting on CBS in 1980 and produced in collaboration with MGM, was another attempt to resurrect the latter studio's venerable creations for a new time period. Repudiating the Hanna-Barbera "friendship" concept imposed five years earlier, Tom and Jerry were again rivals, though in "safer" contexts such as athletic and workplace competition. Supporting them were Droopy, his old nemesis The Wolf, and Tom's bulldog enemy Spike, and his lookalike nephew, Tyke. Something about working with the high-energy MGM characters must have created similar manic energy in the Filmation staff, for the usually weak-on-comedy writers were suddenly able to come up with the laughs needed to make the show work. The working environment came to resemble that of the theatrical animation studios of yore, as "many artists [developed] unscripted sight gags right on the storyboards as part of a genial rivalry with the writing staff."[44] While no latter-day imitators could fully recapture the feel and style of the old MGM cartoons, the Filmation staff certainly did its best.

Increasingly, the studio was beginning to forsake comedy in favor of super-heroics, something it had always seemed to execute more effectively than humor. Yet, even here, they were running into the same sort of troubles other studios were facing during the decade— how to present something truly original. *Blackstar*, airing on CBS in 1981, focused on the title character (George DiCenzo), an astronaut who found himself on a distant planet, sucked into a black hole, where he became involved in a rebellion against the typically despotic Overlord of the Underworld. (The character's name, according to Hal Erickson, was a reflection of the fact that he had been originally created as an African American, a notion the network promptly rejected.[45]) This ambitious setup foreshadowed many of the later projects of the studio during the decade, but was itself mostly undistinguished. Writer/producer Tom Ruegger and artist Bruce Timm, both of whom would go on to better things (see Chapter 6), got their start here.

Over at NBC the same year, the studio produced *The Kid Super Power Hour with Shazam*, a 60-minute live-action/animation mix similar to the earlier *Tarzan and the Super Seven* for CBS (see Chapter 4). Half of the program was devoted to the short animated feature *Hero High* and live-action bumpers related to it, featuring the animated characters as a real-life rock group. *Hero High*, as the name implied, focused on a specialized educational facility for super-powered teenagers, heroes and villains alike. The former group consisted primarily of Captain California, Gorgeous Gal, Misty Magic and Weatherman; the latter was comprised of Rex Ruthless, Dirty Trixie and Punk Rock. The second half of the program was devoted to the adventures of the hero formerly known as Captain Marvel during the golden age of comic books in the 1940s, created by writer/artist C.C. Beck. In these stories, Billy Batson, a young orphan boy, was able to turn into the Captain by uttering the totemic phrase "Shazam!" an acronym for the ancient deities from which he drew his powers—Solomon, Hercules, Atlas, Zeus, Achilles and Mercury. Later joining the cast of characters were Freddie Freeman, another young boy adopted by Captain Marvel, who became "Captain Marvel, Jr.," by uttering the Captain's name. Billy's long-lost twin sister, Mary, became "Mary Marvel" also by shouting "Shazam," although her powers derived from a group of feminine deities whose names formed the same word. Fawcett Publications made the series into a money spinner until legal problems with industry leader DC Comics forced them out of business, with DC taking over the characters. When DC itself revived the character in the 1960s, another Captain Marvel (working, appropriately, for Marvel Comics) had been created in the interim. This revived superhero worked under the name of his old catchphrase—Shazam—for Filmation, both in an earlier live-action series and a new animated one. Many of the elements of the series, as noted already, were holdovers from the comics, as were many of the primary villains, such as the bald, bespectacled super-villain scientist, Dr. Sivana and the malevolent worm, Mr. Mind. However, there were also differences. The comic books were extremely violent; the animated series, compliant with 1981 TV regulations, was anything but. Likewise, the 1940s comics prominently featured Nazis as the bad guys; there were none to be seen in the animated version. Still, the project clearly complied with the studio's established reputation for fidelity in media adaptations, and, along with its live-action counterpart, made a new generation aware of Captain Marvel/Shazam—a generation, pointedly, who had never even heard of him as a comic-book character. As demonstrated by a later generation of TV superhero animators, the influence of these classic characters could not easily be dismissed.

The two final network series from Filmation were somewhat more routine. *Gilligan's Planet* (CBS, 1982–83) was, as its name implied, an adaptation of the iconic '60s sitcom *Gilligan's Island* to television animation, something the studio had done in the mid–70s for the same network with *The New Adventures of Gilligan*. The new series' chief gimmick was that it was set in outer space rather than the deserted island of the sitcom. The live-action cast members voiced their roles in both versions of the animated program. *Sport Billy*, although primarily running in syndication during its 1982 run (it had originally been produced during 1979–80), also managed a brief engagement on NBC during the summer of 1982. Based on a West German sport organization's mascot, the story focused on an interplanetary Frank Merriwell type (voiced by Lou Scheimer's son, Lane) committed to fair play and clean living. He had been dispatched by the ruler of Olympus, Sporticus XI (Frank Welker) to protect the world's athletes from the entreaties of the corrupt Queen Vanda (Joyce Bulifant), who "committed every underhanded foul-play trick short of bribing basketball players to shave points."[46] As was often the case, Billy was accompanied by his girlfriend, Sport Lilly (Bulifant), and his dog, Willie (Welker).

◆ ◆ ◆v

Sport Billy set the template for the remainder of the studio's output. It was syndicated, often underwritten by outside sponsorship, and was, for the most part, structured as battles between good and evil—a clear reflection of the real-world influence of President Ronald Reagan, who had ramped up the Cold War during his first term by referring to the Soviet Union as the "Evil Empire." The proliferation of similar "Evil Empires" across the television animation landscape during the 1980s, and similar forces of "good" to oppose them, was a clear indication of how television animation was now influenced by real-world politics, as opposed to ducking and covering as it had done before. Filmation, however, did not so much replicate the era's political divides in its work as use them as a vehicle for presenting its own, more progressive, politics to the era's most impressionable viewers.

The two most successful series of this period reflected this policy acutely, even though, to some critics, they were tainted by the fact that they were a collaboration with one of television animation's most persistent and controversial advertisers. The Mattel Toy Company, founded in the late 1940s by Elliott and Ruth Handler and Harold Mattson (the company deriving its name from Mattson's surname and Elliott Handler's first name), had prospered through the application of television advertising to its line of products, particularly the now-iconic Barbie doll.[47] Now that the separation between advertising and animation programming was becoming blurred, Mattel approached Filmation with an offer the studio couldn't refuse. To counter its rival Hasbro in the boys' action figure department, Mattel, via designer Roger Sweet, had developed the character of He-Man, a handsome blond-haired strongman type, paired with a group of comrades known as the Masters of the Universe.[48] It was an enormous financial success, spawned in part by DC Comics featuring the characters as part of their products.[49] As a further extension of the brand, Mattel sought to feature the product in television animation. ABC, conscious of earlier issues with Mattel-based material (see Chapter 3), turned down the project. However, Richard Weiner, Inc., Mattel's PR firm, proceeded on a promotional blitz that lined up an enormous number of stations on a barter basis, proving the enduring commercial viability of syndication as an option for television animation distribution.[50]

Mattel had done its part in developing the characters and selling the show. All Filmation had to do was produce it, with far more *carte blanche* than it was used to at the networks—so long as it creatively employed the various members of the action figure line and its ancillary products. On viewing Mattel's concept of the series, Lou Scheimer immediately recognized that it was somewhat thin dramatically. He later explained that, to him, it looked simply like "a barbarian running through the forest," and, consequently, he called on his writing staff (which included such future heavyweights as Tom Ruegger, Larry DiTillio, J. Michael Reaves, Paul Dini and future *Twilight Zone* historian Marc Scott Zicree) to supply the needed weight for a series airing on a daily basis. That they did.

The program's power—not to mention that of its hero—was clearly evident from its main titles, beginning with the colorfully redesigned Filmation logo. The hero, Prince Adam of Eternia (John Erwin), introduced himself, his mission, his friends and his foes in a direct, effective way, so the audience was immediately aware of what the show was all about without needing to see any more. The centerpiece was his transformation into He-Man. "Fabulous secret powers were revealed to me the day I held aloft my magic sword and said…. BY THE POWER OF GRAYSKULL!" Upon saying this, he was transformed into the super-powered hero, proclaiming to all and sundry in hearing distance that "I HAVE THE *POWER*!!!" That power was demonstrated by his dramatically throwing a fist at the camera, after which Lou Scheimer's name (now rendered as a Walt Disney–style signature) heralded his executive-producer credit. The sequence climaxed with a shot of He-Man's mortal enemy Skeletor (Alan Oppenheimer), laughing threateningly. Many other television animation programs have heralded their characters, setting and themes effectively in similar ways in their own main title sequences over the course of the genre's history, but few have done it more intensely and dramatically.

The parallels and sources—from fairy tales, Robert E. Howard's sword-and-sorcery stories of the 1930s, and *Star Wars*—were immediately obvious. *Too* obvious, to some detractors. Prince Adam and He-Man were clearly one and the same, though most of the other characters never found that out, for dramatic reasoning more than anything else.[51] Likewise, the villainy was typically inept. Skeletor could be scary if you were a small child, but, to everyone beyond that age, he was simply a comic-opera blusterer, even though he *was* able to carry out a threat once in a while. The general consensus among the most vocal critics, such as ACT's Peggy Charren, was that the episodes were nothing more than "program-length advertisements ... created to sell things. Accessories of the toy line must be part of the program." New Jersey senator Frank Lautenberg, an advocate of educational children's television, went further, calling them "a violation of good taste and good judgment." But Charren went even further than that in her comments: "These shows are not thought up by people trying to create characters or a story"[52]

Charren and Lautenberg had clearly not actually *viewed* episodes of the series, because *He-Man* was much better written than many of its contemporaries, and its characters more memorable. The studio was extremely conscious of its target audience—a necessity borne out of years of experience. Thus, while *He-Man* delivered heavily on the action-adventure components required to sustain the audience's attention, it was also capable of a unique, subtle, philosophical bent rarely seen in television animation, much like Scheimer's and Bill Cosby's earlier work on *Fat Albert* (see Chapter 4). There were multiple examples of this, which fleshed out the characters. "The Problem with Power," for example, details the enormous weight of guilt that comes upon He-Man when he mistakenly believes that he has killed an innocent bystander; he relinquishes his Sword of Power by throwing it away into an abyss. Likewise, He-Man's female companion, Teela, and his patroness, the Sorceress (both Linda Gary), were memorably featured in stories that explored their origins and displayed their physical and mental abilities. Stories like these included the studio's old tradition of indicating the moral at the end of the story, most of which were delivered by Orko (Lou Scheimer), a comic relief, partially visible wizard character who was entirely incompetent during the narratives proper. Mostly, these morals were well done and inoffensive and did not interfere with the messages of the narratives, only reiterating them. But sometimes, as Timothy and Kevin Burke note, they did more than that:

> Preachy morals [were stuck] on the ends of episodes, largely to get ... critics off [the producers'] backs.... In some cases the morals actively contradicted the events of the episode. In "Like Father, Like Daughter," Teela finds a loophole in ... [an] order not to follow.... He-Man—and manages to save ... [him] as a result. The moral of the episode, according to the conclusion? "Obey your parents." Huh?[53]

Incidents like these, however, were more the exception than the rule. Once again, Filmation had, with *He-Man*, managed a tricky divide: they had produced a series that was both entertaining and educational without compromising its creative integrity in the process. Given the larger number of episodes they were required to produce in their syndication contract, the studio took ample advantage of the opportunity it was given. While they could produce straightforward, uncompromising action-adventure when needed, Scheimer and the studio staff were far more interested in producing more dramatically challenging narratives, and it is these stories that are *He-Man*'s legacy to the action-adventure-oriented programs that would follow it. It was no longer enough to produce simple fight stories to be repeated ad nauseum. Characters after *He-Man* would have to fight their own fears and insecurities as much as they did their villainous enemies, a fight that was far more complicated and ongoing in nature. The program's legacy in this regard would endure much more in the programs influenced by it than in the property's non–Filmation animated revivals of 1990 (DIC) and 2002 (Mike Young), which were more grim and mercenary in nature.

In some respects, another, more lasting legacy would be established with a spinoff series, one designed following *He-Man*'s success to support a toy line now designed to appeal to the feminine section of the market.

Debuting in syndication in 1985, *She-Ra: Princess of Power* focused on the adventures of Prince Adam's heretofore-unknown twin sister, Princess Adora (Melendy Britt), who, upon transforming herself into the title character via a similar sword, possessed powers and abilities akin to his. On the surface, it seemed to offer little that was new. Hal Erickson provides the case for the prosecution: for one thing, "the opening credits on both [series] were virtually the same, shot for shot," for another, "the villains had shared traits," and for a third, She-Ra herself, in his view, came off "more like a drum majorette than a superwoman."[54] But there is actually a lot about the series that is notable and deserves defending. Erickson himself quotes a Filmation executive saying that "we always wanted to do a series with [a] resourceful [woman] in the lead, [a woman] who did not need men to save [her]."[55]

And therein lies the rub.

Prior to the advent of feminism, American film and television animation's record at portraying positive female role models was negligible at best. The image of female characters in any art form in a given period of time is, by default, a reflection of how women were seen during the social and geo-political period in which the work was produced. In the early part of the 20th century, women were rarely seen in narratives in which their characters did not play a direct role and, even then, the roles were restricted to a specific, narrowly defined set of character traits, which included passivity and seeming physical and emotional fragility. Conversely, in the 21st century, there are very few fictional narratives that do *not* feature women prominently in some fashion, a reflection of how far they have advanced socially, politically and economically during this period of time.

The 1980s, a period in which the ramping up of the masculinized Cold War was paired with a backlash against the first wave of the modern feminist movement, was an important transition period in television animation's portrayal of girls and women. The influence of toy industry sponsors was carefully calculated. While their thinking was as narrow as that of network television executives in terms of what boys and girls would "like" or "get," they took the key step of separating the genders instead of treating the audience as a vast homogenous mass, as had been the case in the 1960s and 1970s. By doing this, toy companies underwriting television animation productions made television animation producers think along similar lines for the first time. As a consequence, the *She-Ra* series was aimed directly at girls in a way *He-Man* and other series were aimed at boys, which necessitated the creation of an active female hero to maintain the structure it had inherited from its predecessor.

Thus, She-Ra became one of the first true female action heroes in television animation ("a woman ahead of her time," according to critic Kathleen McDonnell[56]), blazing a trail that would be followed by a veritable army of female characters in the 1990s, 2000s and 2010s in both dramatic and comedic forms. Her abilities—enormous physical strength, as well as cunning and mental logic that allowed her to often beat her foes *without* having to rely on her strength—were tools she was not afraid to use, albeit in a restrained, rational, "feminine" way. Likewise, she was treated as an equal—and, more often than not, a superior—by both male and female characters, friend and foe alike. This was clearly a trait borne of necessity. Rather than functioning as a glorified palace guard, as her brother and his friends did, Adora, She-Ra and their colleagues were *rebelling* against the unjust rule of the Evil Horde, and they needed all the friends and allies they could get. Compared to the circumscribed positions held by earlier female characters in television animation, She-Ra was an active, powerful and heroic figure, and an admirable role model for her audience, even if that audience consisted of (or was *conceived* to consist of) the often dismissed, ignored and politically powerless sector of the audience that is prepubescent girls. It is equally notable to remark that she held this position at a time when the backlash against feminism was at its height in the mass media.[57]

The narratives of the series proper confirmed this feminine empowerment while continuing with the action-plus-enlightenment format introduced by *He-Man*. It also rendered, thankfully, the secret identity issues of the earlier series redundant by clearly demarcating Adora and She-Ra as two different people in dress, manner and, especially, voice. (In keeping with a tradition from earlier female dual identity heroes, She-Ra's voice was deeper and more "masculine" than Adora's to confirm her greater power.) In spite of the obviousness of many of the morals presented, the rebellious nature of the stories of *She-Ra*, paired against the Orwellian state control of the Horde, stood out even more than that of their predecessor. The titles of some of the episodes alone ("Friendship," "Book Burning," "The Price of Freedom" [one of He-Man's many guest appearances], "The Greatest Magic," "A Lesson in Love") only hint at the virtuosity and power of this underrated series.

But, despite the rebelliousness in many of the characters and storylines, there were still many ways in which the series and its star were limited by their format. "The Xena of the eighties,"[58] as she was dubbed by Timothy and Kevin Burke, was aimed at an explicitly feminine audience as an action figure and the commercials related to it, and the television series had to conform to this portrayal. Consequently, there was an abundance of usage of "feminine" narrative traits, such as caring and kindness, that were not explicitly addressed in the more male-oriented *He-Man*.

Yet She-Ra was clearly embodying feminist traits at a time when such characters did not exist in television animation. This characterization would consequently become an important part of the inheritance of later television animation narratives. It would be one of the relatively few things from that decade that later producers would choose to continue rather than destroy.

◆ ◆ ◆

For the rest of Filmation's existence, in spite of its continued success, there was a sameness in the studio product. The uniqueness of *He-Man* and *She-Ra* was not repeated in the studio's later offerings, and undoubtedly contributed to the studio's demise.

Filmation's two final series offerings, apart from the 1984 syndicated revival of *Fat Albert*, were *Ghostbusters*, released in the fall of 1986 by Tribune Broadcasting, and *Bravestarr*, released in the fall of 1987. The former was an animated adaptation of *The Ghost Busters*, a live-action comedy series produced by the studio during the mid–1970s. This was not unnoticed by Columbia Pictures, which, trying to bring its own *Ghostbusters* film franchises to animation at the same time (see below), engaged in a heated legal battle with Filmation over which of their franchises was the "real" one.[59] Ultimately, this proved to be a moot point, as most viewers familiar with both series can easily tell you how different they were from each other. Filmation's series focused on the sons of the protagonists of *The Ghost Busters* (Patrick Fraley and Peter Cullen) and their simian associate, Tracy (Lou Scheimer), as they focused on combating a small army of spooks under the leadership of Prime Evil (Alan Oppenheimer), a bargain-basement Darth Vader type. The pro-social elements of the studio's storytelling were once again in force, but this series, like its earlier prototype, was played primarily for laughs, even if they were somewhat forced.

Bravestarr was somewhat different in concept, and more straight-faced. A hybrid science fiction Western, the series focused on the adventures of the title character (Patrick Fraley), a law enforcer with super powers and robotic abilities derived from the forces of nature. His primary assistant was Thirty Thirty (Ed Gilbert) a gun-toting "Equestroid," while his mentor was Shaman (Gilbert), an elderly Native American spiritual leader. Bravestarr was also conceived as a Native American character, making him one of the first Native Americans to star in a TV animation program.[60] Yet it was becoming apparent that pro-social moralizing was being overdone at the studio; this program's creative quality was the one that suffered the most due to this.

It is interesting to speculate what directions Filmation might have taken in the 1990s, as others began aping the programming trends it had originated. But that, due to an unfortunate chain of events, is something that we will never know.

As animation historian Tom Sito has noted, the 1980s was a period in which it became commonplace for larger companies to buy and sell smaller organizations under their control "for a quick buck and a tax-loss write off."[61] As a Filmation stalwart, Sito saw this firsthand at the company where he worked. Because the company was now offering year-round as opposed to seasonal work during the 1980s, it provided a home for animators displaced from other studios. However, when the Swiss conglomerate L'Oreal-Nestle purchased Filmation from Westinghouse in 1987, things changed. The cosmetics and food giant was only interested in acquiring the studio's backlog for distribution in the European television market, and had no interest in keeping the Reseda, California–based physical plant in operation. And so, without a word of warning, Filmation was shut down in February of 1988—a day before a federal law requiring 60-day notices prior to plant closures was scheduled to go into effect.[62] Scheimer, who had initially agreed to the sale, was shocked and appalled by the decision, and remained so regarding the subject when this author interviewed him nearly 20 years later.

Happily, however, much of the studio's product, long out of circulation, has been issued on DVD during the 2000s, so the enormous legacy of Scheimer and Filmation, much like that of Hanna-Barbera, will now be available to a new generation of viewers who will, undoubtedly, appreciate the series as much as their predecessors did.

◆ ◆ ◆

The greatest legacy Lou Scheimer and Filmation left to American television animation arose from their efforts to make programming more socially inclusive than it had been before. Scheimer knew that racial minorities, women and young people were underrepresented and often falsely portrayed in the media, and he used his work to make a difference in that regard. *Fat Albert and the Cosby Kids* alone helped to broaden the image of African Americans in the mass media, while at the same time helping to show that the marriage of entertainment and education need not be of the shotgun variety. It is only a small step from *Fat Albert* and *Zorro* to the African American and Latino characters of modern television animation, and an even smaller one from Microwoman, Web Woman and She-Ra to the powerful, ultra-feminist heroines of *The Powerpuff Girls*, *Kim Possible* and *My Life as a Teenage Robot* (see chapters 6 and 7).

Filmation also rode the crest of the "pro-social" wave of the 1970s and 1980s to sow the seeds for the programming operandi created by the "Educational/Information" protocols of the Children's Television Act of 1990, and the programs which followed in its wake. Scheimer's pioneering work at portraying children and young adults as multi-dimensional beings, as well, set a clear benchmark for the portrayal of such characters by the next generation of television animators, who clearly strove to develop these kinds of characters to appeal to both teen and "tween" audiences. Walt Disney Studios, being a relative newcomer to television animation, would find this approach extremely helpful in developing its own television animation series in the 1990s and 2000s (see chapters 6 and 7).

Lou Scheimer was often accused by outsiders of manipulating his audience, but this was never something he consciously intended to do. If anything, he wanted to make sure his audiences came away from his programs enlightened as well as entertained. Quite often, he succeeded at this. As a result, he provided a clear-cut example for other television animation producers to follow.[63]

Enter Disney

The major event of the 1980s regarding the television animation industry was the entry of Walt Disney Pictures into the field, an act that came to marginalize other television animation producers, especially on-the-ropes concerns such as Hanna-Barbera and Filmation. It was a remarkable turnaround for a studio that had long shunned the television branch of the art form that had made it famous, and it was an act that came to redefine, for many critics, the social and political position of television animation. The "Magic Kingdom," with a large legacy of family-oriented animation and live-action film products behind it, seemed to many the perfect candidate to provide a more rationalized sensibility to the production and planning behind television animation. But those able to see behind the smiling corporate façade were soon able to recognize the true motives behind the decision, and they were troubled by the direction chosen by the newly conceived enterprise—as they would be by most of the corporate and political decisions made by Michael Eisner during his 22 years as head of the company.

For all the trumpeting of Walt Disney Television Animation as a new and innovative venture, the truth of the matter was that, in the 1980s, their product was no better or worse than that of any other television animation studio. To fulfill production quotas, they were still forced to outsource nuts-and-bolts animation to overseas studios, now increasingly the norm for television animation.[64] And, while some innovative projects did emerge, they were often held in check creatively by excessive corporate oversight. Many other works, however, either directly or indirectly traded on the company's history and reputation to disguise their obvious weaknesses. It would not be until the 1990s, when the company began bringing in more outside producers and writers to supervise projects, that the creative quality of the projects began to truly improve.

Disney's entry into the television animation field sent one message to the outside world, but quite another to the animation industry itself. To better understand this, a brief corporate overview is in order before examining the shows themselves.

◆ ◆ ◆

As an independent film producer in Hollywood for most of his career, Walt Disney, in spite of a growing reputation, was as beholden to the major film studios to distribute his projects as anyone else working outside of the "studio system." In his youth, he had been roughly treated by distributors who openly stole his characters or his money from him, and he was determined not to allow that to happen to him again. With the aid of his older brother, Roy (a family loyalist who spent much of his life contentedly as Walt's CFO), he had negotiated distribution deals that increased in value as his star rose—first with Columbia, then United Artists, and, finally, RKO, which distributed nearly all of Disney's features until the early 1950s. At that point—when the notorious Howard Hughes took over the latter studio and ran it neatly into the ground—Walt and Roy agreed that the time had come for Walt to begin distributing himself. They certainly had the financial resources to do it by now, in spite of the large sums of money Walt was investing in developing the Disneyland theme park, which he viewed as a personal legacy akin to his films. And so, in the fall of 1954, the Disney studio announced it was ending its relationship with RKO and starting its own distribution company, Buena Vista (a Spanish phrase meaning "a good view"). In making the announcement, Walt claimed the project was Roy's idea, which "I hope works out as he has planned it."[65] It certainly did so. This decision marked the Disney organization's transition into film and television distribution as well as production, and markedly increased its size and economic power as a consequence.

But as Disney/Buena Vista grew over the course of the 1950s and 1960s, the original homey intimacy of the company began to vanish, even as it staunchly maintained its image as a purveyor of wholesome family entertainment. With the dissolution of the Production Code in favor of a ratings system, and the advent of more "adult"-flavored modes of production at the other studios, family-directed material became the rock the studio clung to in order to continue its existence. Even still, a mode of sameness and repetition came to emerge in the film and TV productions, something caused partly by Walt being distracted by outside projects, but mainly by an increasing reluctance on the part of the staff to change the way things had always been done.

Nobody understood this better, or felt the consequences of this more, than the man himself. "I'm not Walt Disney anymore," he noted toward the end of his life. "Walt Disney is a thing. It's grown to become a whole different meaning than just one man."[66] It was a significant statement concerning an artist who had begun simply as an animator and ended up leaving behind an enormous critical, cultural and economic legacy. This legacy had come to be one that those working at the company bearing his name would now eternally be forced to uphold and maintain—whether they liked it or not.

◆ ◆ ◆

Walt Disney was absolutely correct in foreseeing his fate. By the time of his death in the winter of 1966—and Roy's four years later—Walt Disney truly was a "thing" rather than a person. And, increasingly, it was becoming much more of a sterile, antiseptic "thing."

With the deaths of the elder Disneys, creative control passed into the hands of Ron Miller, a former professional football player who had become Walt's son-in-law (and whom Walt had persuaded to join the company so he would have a "safer" job), while economic control came under the jurisdiction of Card Walker, a studio loyalist who had worked for the company since the late 1930s. This administration, which lasted for the balance of the 1970s and the early 1980s, was moderated chiefly by the generational differences between the two men. Miller wanted to diversify the studio's productions into more adventurous avenues; Walker, who considered himself the primary custodian of the Disney legacy, did not. As a consequence, the studio's film productions (animated and live-action alike) kept essentially to the formulas Walt had initiated, though the results became progressively dire. The periodic reissues of older Disney product, and their appearances on the studio's television omnibus series, only served to show how creatively rudderless the company had become, despite Miller's best efforts to inject new creative blood into it.

Watching from the sidelines was a prominent, if often unheralded, member of the Disney board who felt things could be better than they were. Roy Edward Disney—Roy's son and Walt's nephew—was bothered by the perennial feuding between Walker and Miller, which he considered a deficit to the company's financial health. He hoped to find someone who could run the company who had considerably more drive than Miller and less resistance to change than Walker. And, in 1984, after Walker had retired and Miller had been fired, the right candidate came into view.

On the surface, Michael Eisner was the polar opposite of Walt and Roy Disney. The Disneys were impoverished WASP Midwesterners who had worked their way up to wealth through luck, spirit and fortitude. Eisner, on the other hand, was born into a wealthy Russian-Jewish family from New York, and he was precisely the stereotypical Hollywood "type" the Disneys had prided themselves on *not* being. He had grown up in a sheltered environment ("I just assumed that everyone lived the way we did," he would later write[67]) and early on set his sights on being part of the entertainment industry. After a failed attempt at becoming a playwright, he eventually became an executive at ABC where, supervising the daytime schedule, he gained a familiarity with television animation that would later serve him well (see Chapter 4). When his mentor, Barry Diller, left ABC to accept an executive position with Paramount Pictures in the late 1970s, Eisner followed him there. Soon afterward, he became Paramount's head of production, supervising the production of a number of hit films while substantially increasing the company's television production. At Paramount, Eisner began to develop the management style he would later bring to Disney. He would cultivate new talent and induce established ones to join the studio on advantageous terms, so long as the creative personnel were willing to do as they were told—including staying within assigned budgets. If they could not, would not, or did not, Eisner did not hesitate to remind them (sometimes extremely bluntly) exactly *who* was in charge.

Eisner might have reigned for many years at Paramount, but his job there fell to internal politics. When Charles Bludohrn, the chairman of Gulf and Western (Paramount's then-parent company), died suddenly of a heart attack in 1983, the management of the company changed, and Eisner was fired. Consequently, when Roy Edward Disney offered him the job of heading up the Disney company, Eisner jumped at the chance, and brought Jeffrey Katzenberg, his protégé at Paramount, along with him.[68]

As is so often the case when a corporation or government changes management at the top level, Eisner made his presence known immediately at Disney, and instituted the first of a number of sweeping changes that would radically transform the organization. Film production was increased, chiefly through increasing the volume of such for Touchstone Pictures—a Miller initiative that would allow the studio to produce and distribute "adult"-oriented movies without tainting the family-oriented Disney brand in the process. The studio likewise made an effort to increase its television production, something that had withered away during the Miller/Walker era. Eisner made inroads into the theme parks, overhauling Disneyland and Walt Disney World and establishing new parks in Japan and France, with mixed results. He also furthered Disney's media holdings, establishing the Disney Channel to give the company a presence in the rising cable TV business, and scoring a major coup by purchasing ABC and its properties in 1995.[69] (Ironically, but fittingly, ABC had aired Walt Disney's earliest TV productions, and, as noted above, was the place where Eisner first cut his media teeth.) Yet Eisner angered many at Disney, not simply because of his dictatorial management style, but because he so blatantly promoted himself as the public face of the company, reflected primarily through his role as the host of the company's re-tooled TV omnibus—a role only Walt Disney had held before him.[70] Katzenberg, who took on the Herculean task of successfully re-booting the studio's animated feature-film department during the late 1980s and early 1990s, took particular umbrage at this, and acrimoniously left the company for this reason.

For our purposes, however, it was during the Eisner era that Disney first entered the arena of television animation. And, as was typical of the way things were done during his watch, this was done slowly at first, but then with a vengeance.

◆ ◆ ◆

Because Walt Disney had assumed that the cost of producing animation directly for television distribution was too high, the studio had never done so before the 1980s. While Disney expressed admiration for the TV animation of Ozamu Tesuka in Japan, and thought that his system might work for the studio, he died before toying with the idea. However, under the Eisner regime, the problem of producing animation for television seemed to be solved.

Walt Disney Television Animation (WDTA), as it came to be known, would be based around a system that was a radical departure from the norms of television animation in the 1980s. Disney argued that the "cheapness" that had crept into the genre was the result of too many economic and creative shortcuts being taken by the established producers. What they would offer, instead, would be television animation produced on budgets comparable to their features, although the production process would be modified to account for the vagaries of the television industry. Any profit would come, not necessarily through initial broadcasts, but through rebroadcasts on other emerging Disney media outlets. This strategy, while a calculated financial risk, would come to be enormously successful, and secure the ongoing presence of Disney as an animation powerhouse in both film and television.

Disney did not get around to establishing in-house facilities for WDTA for some time, so the earliest TV animation production under the Disney name was subcontracted. Murikami-Wolf-Swenson, under the leadership of producer/director Fred Wolf, was the beneficiary of this contract, and this helped set up that studio as a reputable television animation producer (more on them below). The first series to go out on network TV under the Disney name was *The Wuzzles*, airing on CBS during the 1985-86 season and then on ABC during 1986-87. Set on the island of Wuz, the imaginative concept behind the series was that it focused on the day-to-day life of a bizarre group of illogical biological hybrids and their conflicts with one another and the outside world. The characters included the likes of Bumbelion (Brian Cummings), Eleroo (Henry Gibson), Hoppopotamus (Joanne Worley), Moosel (Bill Scott), Rhinokey (Alan Oppenheimer) and Butterbear (Kathy Helppie). "What could have been oppressively cute was refreshingly irreverent thanks to the comic expertise of the writing staff," notes Hal Erickson.[71] The most notable example of this was the casting of satiric comedian Stan Freberg as the narrator, and the use of his trademark deadpan delivery as an effective way of cutting through the treacle inherent in the essential concept and storylines.[72]

The second Disney program was built around a similarly imaginative idea, even if its debt to earlier programs, such as *The Smurfs* (see above), was thunderously obvious at times.

Based around a concept developed by the Heide candy company, *Adventures of the Gummi Bears*[73] was a unique combination of Tolkeinian mythology and sophisticated humor. It was successful enough to last for four seasons on NBC from 1985 to 1989, another on ABC from 1989 to 1990 (in partnership with *Winnie the Pooh*; see below) in syndication as part of "The Disney Afternoon" (more on this later) in 1990, and in repeated reruns on the Disney Channel, setting the production and syndication pattern for most subsequent Disney series in the process. The heroes were a group of "cute" little bears who were, in actuality, the heroic saviors of the mythical kingdom of Dunwyn, who gained super powers via consumption of Gummiberry juice (something not unlike the "magic potion" featured in the *Asterix* comic book series). By name, they included Gruffi (Bill Scott first, Corey Burton later), Chummi (Jim Cummings), Granni (June Foray), Sunni (Katie Leigh), Tummi (Lorenzo Music), Cubbi (Noelle North), and Zummi (Paul Winchell), among others. For variety's sake, there was also a brace of recurring human characters: Cavin (Christian Jacobs first, Brett Johnson later), a page boy who served as the principal intermediary between the bears and the humans; the surprisingly and strikingly rebellious Princess Calla (North); and the hammy, over-acting villain, Duke Igthorn (Michael Rye), who had his eye on taking the throne of Dunwyn à la Richard III, but was perennially stymied by the Gummis. As with the *Wuzzles*, the potentially leaden scenario was enlivened by a fresh sprinkling of humor, some of it of the self-deprecating nature that Disney critics often said was missing in that company's product. With this series, the Disney TV animation division was truly off and running. Many of the staff members who worked on this program would play important roles in later television animation projects at Disney and elsewhere in the future: they included producer/director Art Vitello, writer/producer Tad Stones, producer/director Alan Zaslove, writer Jymn Magnon, and actors Jim Cummings, Tress MacNeille, Rob Paulsen and Kath Soucie.[74]

Initially, the next series to come out of the studio, *Ducktales*, was supposed to have been a Saturday morning offering, as its two predecessors had been. However, Bob Jacquemin, who had been put in charge of Disney's new television syndication division, was extremely impressed by the idea and format of the series, and, sensing the potential for the series to be a big hit, he actively lobbied Eisner to have the series put under the jurisdiction of the syndication division. Eisner granted his request, and the result, according to studio historian Bill Cotter, "virtually reinvented television animation."[75]

The decision also resulted, eventually, in the creation of what became known as "The Disney Afternoon," a two-hour animation block airing in syndication on weekday afternoons during the late 1980s and most of the 1990s. This programming strategy, more than anything else before it, announced to the world and the television animation industry at large that Disney was truly in the TV animation business. By carving out a significant block of TV territory for its programming, Disney set itself up with an unprecedented economic position for a television animation studio, and it was not unnoticed by the competition. In response, Hanna-Barbera, Rankin-Bass, DIC and the nascent FOX network would come to establish blocks of their own in future years, in a mostly futile attempt to equal the wealth and prestige Disney would reap from this strategy.

In contrast to the statement made by the actual programming of the block, the programs within it were, for the most part, only modestly entertaining, drawing heavily as they did on the studio's entertainment heritage for their appeal rather than any original ideas of their own.

Ducktales, which aired in syndication from 1987 to 1992, was the most prominent example of this trend. In announcing the series, WDTA president Gary Krisel dropped the gauntlet to the competition by declaring the series to be "a high-quality [product] with ... characters and storylines [that] could almost single-handedly revitalize a floundering segment of the television business."[76] For the most part, the series delivered on its aim, at least on the technical end. Budgeted at over $100,000 higher per segment than the average series of the day, it looked far slicker than anything else on the air at the time, and set the standard for future Disney productions in this regard. Furthermore, the studio writers were clearly committed to infusing the narratives with a unique approach to humor—"not the [traditional] pretested, timid, derivative old jokes [of the past] ... but laugh-out-loud laughter."[77] This was not surprising, considering that the staff consisted of some reliable old pros in the field, including directors Fred Wolf and Bob Hathcock, and writers Ken Koonce and David Wiemers.

The narratives, characters and setting of the series were, originally, the work of Carl Barks, the prolific (but un-credited) comic-book writer and artist and former Disney animator, who had spent nearly 30 years establishing and refining a unique fictional universe within the umbrella of the Disney empire.[78] While Barks was not credited as the series' "creator," he should have been. The lead character, after all, was his creation. Scrooge McDuck (Alan Young)—"the World's Richest Duck"—was a generally good-natured, globe-trotting adventurer eager to find hidden treasures to increase his already-vast wealth. This was often done in the company of his young nephews, Huey, Dewey and Louie (all Russi Taylor), and dimwitted pilot Launchpad McQuack (Terry McGovern). When not doing that, they were residing in the community of Duckburg, where they had to contend with a brace of characters from Barks's *oeuvre* and some new creations, such as the crime-fighter Gizmo Duck (Hamilton Camp), the secret identity of mild-mannered Fenton Crackshell. In the former camp were the villainous Beagle Boys, who constantly had their eyes set on stealing part, or all, of Scrooge's fortune, and sorceress Magica De Spell (June Foray), who held the same lofty goals.

Despite the studio's commitment to providing high-quality animation and belly-laugh–filled scripts, the creative limitations of the series were obvious at the time, and remain so today, as a view of the storylines of the series provided by Cotter suggests.[79] In retrospect, it suffers from the same sort of problems as other 1980s producers' series: once it had established its central premises, it kept reproducing them in different ways simply to keep the series going. It might have been better served by being a simple Saturday morning series of 13 episodes as originally planned, rather than the 99 episodes that were ultimately produced in the syndication format.

Still, the studio, like Scrooge McDuck himself, had discovered a veritable pot of gold in the syndication market that it was unwilling to share with other people.

Before heading back to the syndication mill, however, Disney next produced a far quieter and gentler series for the Saturday morning market, one clearly aimed at a different demographic than its syndication factory. Once again, it was based on someone else's fictional universe, but, in this case, the debt was properly acknowledged.

The New Adventures of Winnie the Pooh debuted on ABC in 1988, and, in one form or another, ran on that network's schedule over an incredible 15-year period. That is a testament to the enduring appeal of the beloved characters featured within it more than anything else, although the producers did make the series very entertaining.

The characters were, in fact, created for a child audience of one. British humorist, poet and playwright Alan Alexander Milne (known simply as A.A.) had developed the world of the Hundred Acre Wood and its characters to entertain his young son, who served as the model for their human acquaintance, Christopher Robin. Although Milne had a reputation as a satirist in his adult-oriented work, a body that the Pooh saga has now effectively overshadowed, satire was not present here. Because Milne held proprietary and protective rights to his fantasy world, his Pooh books were not adapted to other media until after his death. Disney was the first studio to adapt it to animation, producing a group of acclaimed short films for theatrical distribution between 1966 and 1983, mostly under the skillful direction of distinguished studio veteran Wolfgang "Woolie" Reitherman.[80] The second of these, *Winnie the Pooh and the Blustery Day*, won an Academy Award in 1969. All of these films were distinguished by excellent, convincing voice work, particularly character actor and Disney veteran Sterling Holloway as Pooh, and Paul Winchell as the hyperactive, scene-stealing Tigger.

When the series debuted in 1988, as a result, it only had to follow the pattern set by the prior films in terms of narrative construction, and it did just that. What resulted, as Hal Erickson has aptly put it, was "a delightful eye of calm in a hurricane of Saturday morning slapstick."[81] There were some cosmetic changes behind the scenes, however. Sterling Holloway had died in the interim between productions, so Jim Cummings, one of the most versatile and talented voice actors of the late–20th and early–21st centuries, assumed the role of Pooh, very effectively; he would later do the same for Tigger when Paul Winchell died during series production interims.[82] The rest of Milne's classic cast—wise Owl (Hal Smith), timid Piglet (John Fiedler), and egotistical Rabbit (Ken Sansom)—was also present, as was the antagonistic Gopher (Michael Gough), a Disney studio creation. The series was entertaining and, to a degree, instructive for its target audience, as was its intention, but it also had outside admirers. This was clearly demonstrated by the fact that it was awarded two Emmys for "Outstanding Animated Program" during its lengthy run, and by the fact that it would set a benchmark for other similarly bucolic programs produced for its target audience in the future, by Disney and other studios.

The Disney studio's last production of the 1980s was a return to the syndication norm. As with *Ducktales* before it, and other programs after it, it borrowed from the studio's creative heritage while at the same time trying to present it in a more modernized context. *Chip 'n' Dale's Rescue Rangers* was an action-oriented series that followed the prior series' model in developing its characters and storylines; unlike the prior series, however, it was produced only over a single year. Costing a reputed $28 million,[83] the series starred the two mischievous chipmunks who had appeared, first as supporting characters and then as leads, in Disney short films between 1943 and 1954, when the shorts unit was disbanded. In the series proper, Chip (Tress MacNeille) and Dale (Corey Burton) were cast as Indiana Jones–like soldiers of fortune who intervened in criminal cases involving various uniquely designed members of the animal kingdom. Assisting them were Gadget (MacNeille), an intelligent female mouse whose skills as an inventor of weapons was always useful to the gang; Monterey Jack (Peter Cullen first, Jim Cummings later), an Australian-accented braggart mouse; and Zipper (Burton), a comic, non-vocalizing fly. A persistent nemesis was Fat Cat (Cummings), an oily feline gangster out to destroy them all. While, as with most animated programs of the time, the nuts-and-bolts animation of the series was done overseas in Asia, the Disney studio supervised every aspect of that process so that it would meet the exacting standards the studio was now setting for its television animation work. As a result, as with *Ducktales*, the animation was much better than the storylines, which, with the exception of a handful of imaginative pieces, were pedestrian. The flaws in the quantity-over-quality approach of Disney toward syndication were clearly becoming apparent. Yet the main concern of the studio seemed to be primarily to regain its financial investment in the property, which it managed to do in spades through what was said to be "the largest national marketing and promotional campaign ever to launch an animated television strip."[84] Who cared about the actual *artistic* quality of the work when so much *money* was at stake, anyway?

The Disney studio's increasingly bipolar approach to television animation in the 1980s (high production values in the animation content, but limited development of stories and characters) would continue during the first half of the decade, in both syndication and network broadcasts and sometimes in both simultaneously. Given the mercenary nature of the governance of the studio at this time, this was not entirely a surprise, but it was at odds with the traditional position of Disney as both a technological *and* creative force in the animation industry. Not until the middle of the decade, through changes in both the television and animation industries' approach to the production and distribution of television animation, would things change at Disney—for the better.

Other Voices

Even with Disney's entry into the television animation field, television animation was becoming too large and too diverse a platform for one studio or network to entirely control it. Even though the established studios, such as Hanna-Barbera and Filmation (see above) and Rankin-Bass (see below) were beginning to fade artistically and commercially, there were an increasingly large number of studios on the rise, the largest number since the 1960s. Some of these were American-owned, others operated by foreign entities, but they shared with the older shops the desire to produce quality material affordably—even if they were not able to fully accomplish one or the other as a result.

Ruby-Spears Enterprises

Of the many studios that emerged during the 1980s, Ruby-Spears had one of the most distinguished pedigrees, and much of its work showed this. During their nearly two decades working for Hanna-Barbera, Joe Ruby and Ken Spears had become one of television animation's most accomplished writing teams, and they hoped their new venture would bring them the kind of success their former employers had long enjoyed. Yet this, for a variety of commercial and artistic reasons, was not to be.

Established in 1977, the Ruby-Spears studio initially operated independently, but, the following year, the founders sold the company to Filmways, a film and television producer most famous for producing such classic shows as *The Beverly Hillbillies*, *Green Acres* and *The Addams Family* (see also chapters 4 and 6 for this) during the 1960s. However, Filmways had financially overreached in acquiring too many smaller organizations, such as Ruby-Spears and book publisher Grosset and Dunlap, and by 1981 the company was bankrupt. The main Filmways company and its film library was acquired by Orion Pictures (and then by MGM when Orion itself went bankrupt), and the satellite companies were sold elsewhere. In the case of Ruby-Spears, it was acquired by Taft Broadcasting, Hanna-Barbera's parent company. This put Ruby and Spears in an awkward position, competing against their former employers' firm for corporate patronage while each studio operated independently (although they occasionally collaborated on long-format projects, with each studio animating a separate property in an hour timeslot). This situation lasted until 1991, when Hanna-Barbera was acquired by

Turner Broadcasting. Ruby and Spears allowed Turner to acquire their product library, but chose not to continue to produce under Turner, as Hanna-Barbera would do. Instead, they spun off into RS Holdings, and continued production in a more minor vein for a few years afterward.

As producers, Ruby and Spears were simply not as accomplished as they had been as writers. In a sense, that may have been due to the fact that they were operating at their peak during what was arguably television animation's darkest period, when it was felt that projects coming in from outside the field had more potential for success than those gained from genuinely original sources. Given this handicap, their animators—many, like Ruby and Spears themselves, former employees of Hanna-Barbera—managed to make the shows *look* good, at least, in spite of the industry-wide handicap of genuinely uninteresting characters and storylines during the decade. And while there were a lot of projects that simply went along with the established program, Ruby-Spears, when given a project they genuinely believed in, could work wonders with the best of them.

The studio's first project set the bar for what was to come. *Fangface*, which aired during the 1978-79 season on ABC, was one of the few productions with characters developed within the studio itself, and its failure was what likely convinced Ruby and Spears to begin focusing on acquiring material from outside sources. The hero was Sherman Fangworth (Jerry Dexter), a teenager who turned into a werewolf at inopportune times. The title and the character's surname gave the premise away immediately to the audience, clear evidence of the fact that Ruby and Spears had not yet shed the influence of Hanna and Barbera. "Fang" was assisted by his friends Kim (Susan Blu), Biff (Frank Welker), and Puggsy (Bart Braverman).

A change in direction was needed, and it was provided in 1979–80 with *The Plasticman Comedy Adventure Show*. The title character was a superhero capable of twisting his body into a large variety of elastic forms. He dated back to the 1940s, when he was created and originally drawn by the underrated artist Jack Cole. Because "violent" action series were considered off limits, this series was played for laughs, just as Cole had originally conceived "Plas" as a comic figure more than a dramatic one. Consequently, the hero (voiced by Michael Bell) went through the motions, accompanied by Southern-accented lady friend Penny (Melendy Britt) and Hoola Hoola (Joe Baker), "a Hawaiian Lou Costello soundalike."[85] In later episodes, Plas and Penny would marry and have a son, Baby Plas (Bell), when the show was reduced from an hour to a half-hour. In its original hour format, the title character was supported by "Mighty Man and Yukk," featuring a miniature superhero and an incredibly ugly dog, respectively; "Rickety Rocket," an African American variation on *Space Kidettes* (see Chapter 3), and "Fangface and Fangpuss," new episodes of *Fangface* (see above). Although the series failed on Saturday mornings, it would later become successful in daytime syndication, securing Ruby-Spears's financial future for the time being.

In 1980, two dramatically different shows were produced for different markets. Toplining the first series was *Heathcliff*, the combative comic strip feline created by George Gately. The episodes were relatively standard fare, due to the fact that the character and his colleagues had to be modified to fit the non-violence standards of the time.[86] The main recommendation of the series was that Heathcliff himself was voiced by the legendary Mel Blanc, who also played several other characters. (Blanc would play Heathcliff again when he was revived by DIC in 1984 [see below].) In his first season, Heathcliff was supported by *Dingbat and the Creeps*, involving a vampire dog (Frank Welker, imitating Curly Howard) supported by a living pumpkin and skeleton (Don Messick, impersonating Jimmy Durante and Bela Lugosi, respectively). The following year, Heathcliff was joined by a fellow comic-strip refugee: Marmaduke, an overbearing and infantile Great Dane (Paul Winchell). Both Heathcliff series aired on ABC.

At the other end of the dramatic spectrum was *Thundarr the Barbarian*, airing initially on ABC from 1980 to 1982 and then on CBS from 1983 to 1984. Set in a future world destroyed by a comet, the title character (Robert Ridgely) was a freelance, Conan-like mercenary empowered by a supernaturally gifted Sun Sword. He was aided by the simpering Princess Ariel (Nellie Bellflower) and the lion-like mutant Ookla (Henry Corden). This, more than any other series produced by Ruby-Spears, reflected the exasperating duality of television animation in the 1980s: excellent animation and production values wasted on poor, underwritten scripts. While Ruby and Spears had proved themselves the equal of Hanna and Barbera at providing excellent animation for their series, there was still a paucity of dramatic development in the storylines.[87] That the show was a hit and spawned imitators says much about the creative state of the art during the 1980s.

It was back to more lighthearted fare for the next two entries in the studio canon. *Goldie Gold and Action Jack*, airing on ABC during the 1981-82 season, was an action-oriented series with minor comic touches. The title characters were a fabulously wealthy blond teenager (Judy Strangis) and a flamboyant journalist (Sonny Melendez) who worked for the magazine the former published. It drank deep from the James Bond and Indiana Jones wells, though it botched attempts at humor. The major asset this series had was that the legendary comic-book artist Jack Kirby was responsible for the character designs. *Mork and Mindy*, produced in 1982 for ABC, was an adjunct production to Hanna-Barbera's animated versions of other popular Paramount TV sitcoms (see above). The stars of this popular series—Robin Williams, Pam Dawber and Conrad Janis—voiced their roles in the animated version.

The year 1983 saw the release of the one project of Ruby-Spears that could be said to be an ongoing "franchise" hit. This was *Alvin and the Chipmunks*, airing on NBC from 1983 to 1990 and again as *Chipmunks Go to the Movies* in 1990–91. As noted in Chapter 3, Ross Bagdasarian had created the famous rodent trio in the late 1950s out of his experiments with tape recording, and had created a popular phenomenon in the process, including the aforementioned *Alvin Show*. The project lay dormant following Bagadasarian's death in 1972, until his son, Ross Jr., took it upon himself to resurrect the legacy in partnership with his wife, Janice Karman. Oddly enough, it was a joke feature on a radio program, where faster-than-normal-speed records were credited mockingly to the Chipmunks, which played a major role in the resurrection. A new Chipmunks record, *Chipmunk Punk*, was issued in 1980, and was followed by a Christmas special produced by Chuck Jones in 1981. Ruby and Spears used Jones's version of the characters for their basis, with Bagdasarian playing Alvin, Simon, Theodore and their mentor/father figure David Seville, and Karman portraying the boys' new female equivalents, the Chipettes. No longer folksingers, as they had been in the '60s, in this incarnation the boys were full-fledged rock stars. The stories were also full-length, unlike the fragmentary, performance-driven narratives of the earlier series. This allowed the writing staff, headed by story editors Cliff Ruby and Elana Lesser, to bring touches of parody and satire long absent from television animation back, albeit in muted forms, such as in an episode parodying *This Is Spinal Tap* and other rock mockumentaries. The final season took this one step further and concocted full-length Chipmunk-centric parodies for the gang. The cleverness of this series made up for what was absent in earlier Ruby-Spears product, as the Bagdasarians clearly gave the staff much to actually sink their teeth into. The series entered syndication in 1988 and has remained in reruns on cable TV providers practically ever since. The enduring appeal of the characters was further underlined in the 2000s, when 20th Century–Fox, in partnership with the Bagdasarians, produced a trio of successful live-action/animation hybrid films featuring the rodent stars.

Other 1983 productions showed a much more derivative side to the studio. *Mister T* (ABC 1983–86) starred the formidably sized, heavily muscled, tough-talking actor best known for his role as B.A. Baracus on *The A Team* (NBC 1982–87). Since the latter program scored high among pre-teens (the key demographic for Saturday morning), an animated series starring Mister T was seemingly in order. In this series, Mister T operated a gymnasium and provided assistance and guidance to a brace of neighborhood kids (a multiracial group, of course). Mister T voiced his character, and also delivered the closing pro-social morals in live-action form. *Mister T* managed to stay on the air for three seasons, even though that wasn't necessarily reflective of its artistic quality.

Likewise derivative was *Rubik the Amazing Cube*, initially airing in tandem with Hanna-Barbera's *Pac-Man* series (see above) in 1983–84 and then on its own in 1985. This was based on what was one of the most popular toys of the 1980s: a cube built with different-colored plastic blocks that users tried, often in vain, to coordinate by color. Here, the cube was made into a "person" (voiced by Ron Pallilo)—and a superhero, at that—but only if his squares were correctly aligned by color, of course. The one major asset of the series was that Rubik was assisted by a group of Latino kids "intensely involved in improving the standards of their neighborhood,"[88] one of the rare times this undervalued demographic was clearly acknowledged on screen by a TV animation producer prior to the 1990s.

For ABC, also in 1983, the studio produced something a little bit more heartwarming, if a bit more sugary. Back in 1978, the studio had produced a special for the network based on Catherine Woolley's children's book *The Puppy Who Wanted a Boy*. It was well produced by the standards of the day, and led to three sequels in the following years. Naturally, a series seemed in order, but somehow the property did not work as effectively as a series as it had as one-shot specials. *The Puppy's Further Adventures*, as the series was originally known, was another time-share project with Hanna-Barbera, bracketed with older episodes of *Scooby Doo* (see above) under the title of *The Scooby and Scrappy Doo/Puppy Hour*. Here, the canine hero, Petey (Billy Jacoby) searched for his lost family, in the company of the human girl, Dolly (Nancy McKeon), and doggy pals, Duke (Michael Bell), Dash (Bell) and Lucky (Peter Cullen). The sympathetic, sensitive *Puppy* episodes paired with the broadly comic *Scooby Doo* was as odd a pairing as anything else in television animation history; other than having dogs in the lead roles, they had nothing in common. The network soon came to realize this, and began airing the *Puppy* episodes separately in early 1984. A few more new episodes aired under the title *The Puppy's Great Adventures* before cancellation loomed, although it was briefly resurrected by CBS in 1986. Despite the ratings failure of the series, it demonstrated the dramatic chops of the studio as much as *Alvin and the Chipmunks* had its comedy skills, although, unlike the latter series, it has never been revived through reruns.

In the mid–1980s, the studio contributed its fair share to the action-oriented series market, for both network and syndication broadcasts. *Turbo Teen*, produced for ABC in 1984, involved a teenager named Brett Matthews (Michael Mish) who could transform himself into a racing car after crashing his car into a scientific lab. *Dragon's Lair*, airing in 1984–85 on ABC as well, was based on a popular video game from Cinematronics, and involved the medieval-styled adventures of King Ethelred (Fred Travalena), Dirk the Daring (Bob Sarlatte), Princess Daphne (Ellen Gerstel), and the supposedly "ferocious" dragon Cinge (Arthur Burghardt). While well written, the series' graphics were not up to the standard of the game's. *That* animation was done by Disney veteran Don Bluth, already in the process of establishing himself as a credible animated feature-film producer.

There was still more in this line, mostly confined to 1985 and 1986. In the former year, the productions were led by *The Centurions*, a space opera featuring Crystal Kane (Diane Pershing), a computer scientist who was responsible for the creation of the title characters, crime-fighting robots. Vince "Ben Casey" Edwards played Crystal's right-hand man, Jake Rockwell, while Jack Kirby was credited as a consultant. A brief reprieve was provided by *It's Punky Brewster*, airing on NBC from 1985 to 1987 and again during 1988–89. Like *Mork and Mindy*, it was based on a popular live-action sitcom, this one about an abandoned pre-teen living with an avuncular photographer. The only major concession to the new medium was the addition to the cast of Glomer, a magically powered gremlin-like creature, who helped to provide an element of fantasy missing from the original stage-bound live series. Original cast members Solelil Moon Frye, George Gaynes, Cherie Johnson, Ami Foster and Casey Ellison voiced their roles in the animated version.

Then it was back to the action grind in 1986. *Chuck Norris' Karate Kommandos* [sic] was a vehicle for the popular bearded karate expert-cum-film star, who voiced his animated likeness. The fictional Norris was a presidential agent charged with confronting Vulture, a mysterious Asian criminal cartel. He was assisted in his missions by the rag-tag "Karate Kommandos," which he had personally trained. While the series featured some good fight sequences, achieved partly through rotoscoping Norris from filmed images,[89] it was also undermined by the mandated insertion of pro-social messages at the end from the star's own mouth. Norris could not credibly get away with insisting that "violence is my last option"[90] if that was the cornerstone of the series.[91]

Even more problematic were the other studio productions of that year. *Rambo*, debuting in the fall of 1986, was another action-oriented property from the movies that, for some reason, somebody thought would make a good animated series. The character of John Rambo, originally a vengeful Vietnam veteran on the loose in a small American town, was created by Canadian novelist David Morrell in the 1972 novel *First Blood*. Ten years later, that novel was adapted for the screen, with Sylvester Stallone as Rambo. While the novel's original story involved Rambo being killed at the end, he proved to be too popular to die, and he was resurrected, now as an utterly heroic warrior, for two self-named sequels. These led to the series, which had only Rambo and his old commanding officer, Colonel Trautman, in common with the movies. (Neither Stallone nor Richard Crenna, who played Trautman, reprised their roles in the series; the characters were instead voiced by Neil Ross and Alan Oppenheimer, respectively.) Rambo was now the leader of what was unashamedly called the Force of Freedom, which was just your average bunch of military misfits. Their opponent was an organization called SAVAGE, led by a Douglas MacArthur clone named General Warhawk (Michael Ansara). Jack Kirby was again employed as a consultant.

Lazer Tag Academy, NBC, 1986–87, was another steal from a popular trend, a video game called, not surprisingly, *Lazer Tag*. The heroine was a 13-year-old named Jamie Jaren (Noelle Harding), who traveled from the war-torn year 3010 to confront evil time traveler Draxon Dreer, a.k.a. Silas Mayhem (Booker Bradshaw). Dreer, having escaped from prison in 2010, stole a time machine and returned to 1987 to stop Jamie's ancestor, Beth (Christina McGregor), from coming up with the machine in the first place. It was complex and convoluted—no surprise it lasted only a year. And, regarding Dreer/Mayhem, I'll let Hal Erickson have the last word: "Why do cartoon villains with dangerously descriptive names always choose even more conspicuous phony monickers when travelling in disguise?"[92]

After a year's absence, the studio returned with two new productions in 1988, featuring characters who were at completely opposite ends of the popular-culture spectrum. The first series was *Police Academy*, debuting in syndication. It was based on a surprisingly popular series of comedy films about life in a supposedly "average" police department, released by Warner Bros. (who co-produced the series) between 1985 and 1994, each one more inept, tasteless and vulgar than the last. The writers and directors of the films were interchangeable veterans of numerous average TV sitcoms, which testifies to its level of comic aptitude. The only consistent off-screen presence was producer Paul Maslansky, who shared executive-producer duties on the series with Ruby and Spears. The latter didn't have to do as much as usual in actually developing the characters except to make them animated. As Hal Erickson observes, "The blueprint for these characters was etched long before [in the movies] ... character development and nuance weren't part of the job description [for the animators.]"[93] Thus, anyone who has seen any or all of the movies can tell you what was going to happen in the series. This was underlined by the fact that the cast comprised essentially the same characters as the movies (although, in this case, the original actors did *not* reprise their parts in this version). Except for the skimming off of the dirtier aspects of the films' humor, for obvious reasons, the series offered little that was not in the films, presenting these modern Keystone Cops as being as bumbling as ever. The central difference was that, rather than the garden variety villains of the movies, the force was up against some colorful opposition. Yet, with names like Numbskull, Mr. Sleaze and Lockjaw, they were pretty much self-descriptive, like the show itself.

The second major production of the year was far more ambitious and far more successful. In fact, it is probably the most successfully conceived and executed series Ruby and Spears ever produced.

The year 1988 marked the 50th anniversary of the creation of Superman, and, as part of the celebration, DC Comics commissioned Ruby-Spears to produce a new animated version of the Man of Steel, which debuted in the fall of the year on CBS. At least on a creative level, the publisher got what it wanted. This exceptionally conceived, drawn and written program was one of the handsomest and most exciting television animation superhero sagas ever produced, and still stands up well, even against later versions of Superman produced by Warner Bros. in the 1990s and 2000s (see chapters 6 and 7).[94] "Superman hadn't moved this well since the Fleischer efforts back in the 1940s,"[95] notes Hal Erickson—high praise for a television animation series of the 1980s, which were more often called out for their creative shortcomings. As with the Filmation version (see Chapter 3), there were ties to the earlier incarnations of the hero, such as the featuring of a variation of John Williams's movie theme over the exceptional credit sequence, in tandem with the opening narration from the original 1950s television series (delivered here by veteran actor William Woodson). Superman (voiced in this version by Beau Weaver) underwent a fascinating series of adventures and battled equally fascinating foes, in a way much more reminiscent of his comic-book travails than his appearances on *Super Friends* (see Chapter 4). The program was much more entertaining and compelling for precisely that reason. Wonder Woman was featured effectively in one installment. The project was the victim of poor ratings and bad scheduling and expired after one season, but it deserves to be remembered for the exceptionally high quality of its images, characters and storylines. It was undoubtedly helpful to DC as well, by introducing the Man of Steel to a new generation of fans and admirers.

The last major Ruby-Spears production of the decade was, alas, back to the derivative norm. *Dink, the Little Dinosaur* was this series' self-descriptive name, and it ran on CBS from 1989 to 1991. It debuted following the success of the Steven Spielberg–produced, Don Bluth–directed feature *The Land Before Time*, released the previous year, and while considering the series on its own merits, that shadow is hard to escape. Like his filmic counterparts, Dink and his fellow dinosaurs lived and learned in a pro-social manner. While the studio employed consultants on the prehistoric era so that the show was scrupulous to actual dinosaur appearances, it also presented several different types of dinosaurs living together in complete peace—an action taken for the sake of narrative flow rather than realism. Consequently, the show was an average and predictable mixed bag.

◆ ◆ ◆

Joe Ruby and Ken Spears were never completely able to escape the creative shadow of their former employers, William Hanna and Joseph Barbera, as producers of television animation. Their independence as producers was further compromised by being forced to exist under the same corporate bailiwick as Hanna and Barbera, which tainted both enterprises with the brush of sameness. Furthermore, Ruby and Spears were never able to produce as varied a product as Hanna and Barbera did before them, and thus were never able to establish a reputation independent of Hanna and Barbera. But, given good material and a free reign, Ruby and Spears, like Hanna and Barbera, were able to produce excellent television animation with a lasting, venerable quality, and it is for these products that they should be remembered.

DIC

This Franco-American studio effectively replaced Hanna-Barbera as the major television animation combine studio during the 1980s and 1990s. While it was as capable as its contemporaries of producing large loads of undistinguished fare, it was also capable of the odd, more unique production, as with its first and most famous program, *Inspector Gadget*.

The company (whose acronym is typically produced *Deek*) was first established in France by Jean Chalopin in 1971 as a production division of a well-established media company. Eleven years later, Andy Heyward, a former Hanna-Barbera staffer, established a branch office in America. Heyward had originally been hired by Chalopin to translate the company's European productions into English, but he soon began to produce new material especially for the American market as well. In the early 1980s, Heyward, Chalopin and director Bruno Bianchi came to develop the firm as an effective, if sometimes restrained, producer of television animation, both for syndication and network broadcasts. They retained the original French name—an acronym for *Diffusion, Information et Communication*[96]—even though wags in the industry were soon to claim that it really stood for "Do It Cheap."[97] This was, in part, a reaction to the company's business practices, which included the outsourcing of non-creative work overseas, the hiring of staff on a per-program rather than year-round basis, and, specifically, its anti-union politics.[98]

In 1986, Heyward, with the aid of outside investors, purchased control of the company. Chalopin, Bianchi and line producer Tetsuo Katayama then left. Robby London and Michael Maliani served as Heyward's right-hand men from this point on. A year later, in an effort to neutralize a growing debt, the company sold foreign distribution rights to its productions to Saban Entertainment (see below), who then gave them to the now-independent Chalopin. This action permanently poisoned the relationship between Chalopin and Heyward. DIC and Saban settled this issue in 1991.

In 1993, after several years operating independently, Heyward sold the company to Capital Cities Communications, the then-parent company of ABC; two years later, when Disney purchased ABC (see above), DIC came along as part of the deal. In 2000, Heyward, with the aid of a brokerage firm, bought control of the company back; he bought the brokerage firm out four years later. In 2008, DIC was sold to and absorbed into Cookie Jar Entertainment, at which point Heyward formed his own new firm, A Squared.

◆ ◆ ◆

DIC's first production for American television, a Heyward creation, would unquestionably become its most famous, and set it on the course it would follow for three decades, mostly with less auspicious results.

The character in question was named Inspector Gadget, and he was the lead character in an enormously popular and enduring series which debuted in syndication in 1983. A bionic man powered by a vast amount of comically devised weaponry and tricks, Gadget employed them often through his work as a globe-trotting secret agent. What was unique about the program was that, while on the surface it appeared to be an action-oriented program, it was much more obviously played for laughs, managing to bridge the often chasm-like divide between the two sub-genres in a way that would clearly show others how to do the same. The status of Gadget as a comic bumbler was reinforced by the studio's choice of voice actor for him: Don Adams, who had effectively portrayed a similar live-action hybrid hero on *Get Smart* during the 1960s. Adams's involvement with the program got it attention in the press that at the time was rare for a television animation project, and this, along with his own creative portrayal, helped the show to become a profitable hit in the syndication market over the course of 86 episodes.

Gadget's effectiveness as a detective, predictably, was undermined by his innate stupidity, as well as his buoyant, Rocky-and-Bullwinkle–like optimism ("the sun always shines on [his] head," noted his creator[99]). Likewise, the villains had no more success getting rid of him than Boris Badenov had getting rid of the moose and squirrel, since they employed pretty much the same flawed methodology. The investigation of the motives behind the plots in the stories was, therefore, left to more competent characters. Gadget's pre-teen niece, Penny (Mona Marshall, Cree Summer Francks and Holly Berger, at different times), was usually the one who ended up doing the *real* investigations; in doing so, she showed herself to be one of the most resourceful and intelligent female characters of the 1980s, even if she got kidnapped quite often. Many of her solutions came as a result of her employing a "computer book," a prescient, if bulkier, ancestor of modern hand-held computers, electronic organizers and phones. Also on the Inspector's side was Brain (Frank Welker), a hyper-intelligent canine employed by Penny as something of a field operative, and who possessed an effective, if flamboyant, skill at disguising himself. Gadget's principal enemy was Dr. Claw (Welker), the villainous, disembodied, head of the criminal cartel MAD, who managed to run an efficient criminal ring in spite of the fact that nearly all of his hench-people looked and behaved like members of the Three Stooges. His wrath-filled voice, which sounded like someone shouting through a clogged drainpipe, was his most intimidating asset, as when he repeatedly threatened to "get" Gadget "NEXT TIME!" over the closing credit crawl. Watching from the sidelines was Gadget's boss, Chief Quimby (Maurice La Marche), who was inevitably and comically blown up by the *Mission: Impossible*–styled "self-destructing" paper messages through which he gave Gadget his assignments.

Although it was often only the geographic location of the episode that changed for each installment (and these, thankfully, were many and varied), the program was always capable of delivering on what it promised in terms of comic and dramatic content. This was no small feat, considering how *verboten* its brand of comic slapstick had become in network television animation during the 1970s and 1980s; *Gadget*'s status as a syndicated program allowed it to escape these taboos. However, while DIC hit a home run with this series, most of the studio's later product would, unfortunately, consist mainly of grounders, bunts and all-out strikeouts.

◆ ◆ ◆

Flushed with the success of *Inspector Gadget*, DIC plunged into full-throttle production of other series. *The Littles*, produced for ABC in the fall of 1983, took its cue from a series of books by John Peterson, focusing on a *Smurfs*-like race of miniature sprites. The year 1984 brought three more routine projects. *Heathcliff* was a new syndicated version of the George Gately feline character originally animated by Ruby-Spears (see above). *Kidd Video*, airing on NBC and CBS between 1984 and 1987, was a hybrid rock music/video game/adventure series, as the title character (Bryan Scott) struggled to escape the alternate reality Flip Side and defeat the evil Master Blaster (Pete Renaday). *Pole Position*, meanwhile, aired on CBS between 1984 and 1986. Based on a popular video game, the show took a cue from Hanna-Barbera's *Devlin* (see Chapter 3) by focusing on a traveling family of stunt motorcyclists and race-car drivers, with the extra-added attraction of two anthropomorphic supercars named, predictably, Wheels and Roadie. The year 1984 also saw the release of *The Get Along Gang*, based on a group of anthropomorphic animal greeting-card characters.

The Care Bears saw the studio bringing the enormously popular greeting card-turned-theatrical animation characters to television for the first time; Nelvana (see below) would take over the characters the following year. The Care Bears themselves were anthropomorphic beings who possessed supernatural powers, which allowed them to interfere in earthly doings if they felt people weren't "caring" enough. Logically, they then proceeded to right those wrongs. The project was incredibly tedious if you were older than, say, five, and there was the inevitable backlash from older viewers. "Most grownups," observed Hal Erickson, "emerged from ... viewing [the program] ... feeling as though they'd just been smothered in maple syrup."[100] Timothy and Kevin Burke's view of the characters has much more of a knife-thrust feel to it: they call the Bears "empathetic vampires" who "scoured the world for little children from whom they could suckle, operating with the cover story that they were just trying to 'help' the kids learn about their emotions."[101] This parallel to child molestation, however, would have been something the creators and producers of the show would have vehemently denied had they known about it then.

The studio's other 1985 productions were more routine. *Jayce and the Wheeled Warriors* was a syndicated space opera built around a hero living on an agrarian planet, who was in predictable conflict with an anti-ecological villain wanting to strip mine the place for profit. *M.A.S.K.*, another syndicated effort, was based on a toy line from Kenner. The Mobil Armored Strike Kommand [*sic*] operated under the leadership of Matt Tracker (Doug Stone), and engaged in derring-do heroics reminiscent of both *Mission: Impossible* and *G.I. Joe* (see below).

The later productions of the decade offered even less in the way of variety, and likewise bore the mark of being developed by outside sources rather than the studio itself. The year 1986 offered three such projects. *Kideo TV* was an ambitious syndicated block modeled on Disney's "Disney Afternoon" that ran for 90 minutes daily. Included were reruns of *The Get*

Along Gang, along with three new programs: *The Popples*, *Ulysses 31* and *Rainbow Brite* [sic]. The former and latter were doll/toy projects from American Greeting Cards and Hallmark, respectively, while the middle series was based on an established Japanese series. *Kissyfur*, airing on NBC on 1986–87 and again from 1988 to 1990, was the story of an anthropomorphized bear cub and his father, who had escaped circus life in favor of a slightly less hectic existence among their own kind in the Louisiana swamp–styled community of Paddlecab. The final project of the year was much more high profile and successful. *The Real Ghostbusters*, airing on ABC, was based on the popular 1984 film *Ghostbusters*; the adjective was used primarily to distinguish the series from Filmation's similarly named offering of the time (see above). As in the movie, the group consisted of bespectacled intellectual Egon Spengler, self-styled ladies' man Peter Venkman, laconic humorist Ray Stantz, mercurial African American Winston Zeddmore, and eccentric secretary Janine Melnitz. None of the film actors voiced their roles, though the film's producer and director, Ivan Reitman, and executive producer Bernie Brillstein served as consultants. As in the film, the characters offered what was essentially a high-tech extermination service for paranormal beings, and used a variety of scientifically devised means to combat them. The one standout in the cast was the team's mascot, Slimer, a green blob who had been a minor antagonist in the film. He received top billing in 1988 and kept it for the program's four remaining years on the air. Columbia Pictures, which distributed the film and its 1989 sequel, co-produced the series with DIC. Columbia would revive the project less successfully for syndication in 1997.

The year 1987 offered more of the same, competently animated series with little or nothing to offer in the way of story or character development. *The Adventures of Teddy Ruxpin* was based on a popular toy from the Worlds of Wonder organization, the idea being that a teddy bear would move and "talk" in sync with a pre-recorded cassette of narration. Though it sold well initially, a backlash was inevitable, and Worlds of Wonder was soon driven to bankruptcy. Before that happened, however, this animated project was produced, which involved Teddy (Phil Barron), his eight-legged caterpillar pal Grubby (Will Ryan), and kindly inventor Newton Gimmick (John Stocker) traveling in an airship to collect a cache of magic crystals. They were opposed by the comically flamboyant Tweeg (John Koensgen), head of the Monsters and Villains Organization (or, simply, MAVO).

Alf, airing on NBC between 1987 and 1989, offered more in terms of characterization and comedy, since it was based on a popular live-action sitcom airing on the same network between 1986 and 1990. This animated version was a prequel to the live-action series, and the connection was made further by the fact that the creator/producers of the live project—Tom Patchett, Bernie Brillstein, and Paul Fusco (also Alf's voice on both projects)—were the executive producers of the animated version as well. Here, the animated Alf (or, rather, Gordon Shumway) endured a stress-filled life as a resident of the alien planet Melmac. The series benefited from a satirical drive in the writing, another holdover element from the live version. A year later, the series expanded to an hour with the addition of *Alf Tales*, a storybook parody project in the vein of *Mad* and Jay Ward's "Fractured Fairy Tales" (see Chapter 3). This component aired on its own in 1989–90 when the parent series was canceled.

Also produced in 1987 was the usual quota of undistinguished action and comedy fare. *Beverly Hills Teens*, airing in syndication, was just as its name implied: the lifestyles and beliefs of wealthy California teenagers rubbed in the audience's collective face. *Dinosaucers*, another syndicated effort, focused on the ongoing feud between two groups of alien dinosaurs, predictably divided into teams of good and bad. More highbrow in intent was *The HBO Storybook Musicals*, airing between 1987 and 1993 on the pay cable service, an ambitious series of classic children's stories engineered chiefly by artist Michael Sporn. Other productions of the year were far less distinguished. *Lady Lovelylocks and the Pixietails*, airing in syndication, was essentially an infomercial for a toy line aimed at girls, while *Starcom: The U.S. Space Force* and *The Sylvanian Families*, two other syndicated efforts, were unable to hide their derivative plotlines and their thinly disguised toy advertising.

The final two years of the decade for DIC were business as usual. *The New Archies*, airing on NBC between 1987 and 1989, brought the *Archie* comic-book characters back to television animation after a decade's absence. The major difference in this version was that the teenage characters were now nine-year-olds, and there were some African American characters, one male and one female, in the mix. Other than that, there was not much that was actually "new" about the series. *Beany and Cecil*, which aired on ABC for an extremely brief period of time in 1988, was another revival of a 1960s property, this time produced by John Kricfalusi, who had cut his animation teeth working for Ralph Bakshi (see below). It is believed that Kricfalusi's perfectionistic—and slow—working methods, as well as his inability to meet scheduled deadlines, were a major reason the program was canceled.[102] This would also be his Achilles heel on his signature project, *Ren and Stimpy* (see Chapter 6). *C.O.P.S.*, airing in syndication in 1988, was an ambitious action-oriented series set in a corrupt future time city, and dealt with the conflict between the title force and some ruthless villains. Most of the lead characters were bionic, and bore flamboyant one-word nicknames like "Hardtop" and "Mainframe." The major notable thing about this series was that the C.O.P.S' leader, Baldwin "Bulletproof" Vess, was African American, which stood him in contrast to the Caucasian characters making up the rest of the cast.

Camp Candy, airing on NBC between 1989 and 1991 and in syndication during 1992, was a vehicle for the rotund Canadian comedian John Candy, who had gained fame as a cast member of *SCTV* and parlayed that into a series of roles in popular films. Candy portrayed himself, and also served as executive producer.[103] As implied by the series' title, Candy's fictional doppelgänger was a counselor at a summer camp (as Candy himself had been in real life) located on Lake Cacciatore. He balanced supervising his multi-ethnic gang of charges with dealing with the main antagonist, Rex De Forest, who was out to redevelop the camp property into condominiums. This underlined the series' potent slap-in-the-face attitude toward big business, an attitude in television animation first cultivated in the 1980s and further, more stridently, underlined in the following decades. While the series was mostly routine, it did win a Humanitas Prize in 1991 for an episode dealing with childhood leukemia. Some of Candy's *SCTV* associates contributed voices, just as they had for Martin Short's earlier, more directly *SCTV*–inspired NBC series (see above), which added to the fun. In the later syndicated version, Candy also appeared in live-action wraparounds (à la Bill Cosby in *Fat Albert*) to reinforce the pro-ecology nature of the project. The series was well intentioned, but it unfortunately ended up being bogged down in clichés. Tragically, it was one of the last major entertainment projects involving Candy, who died of a heart attack in 1994.

The same flawed storytelling styles were evident in some of the studio's other offerings that year. *Captain N: The Game Master*, produced for NBC, was an adventure-oriented series set in the world of video games, specifically those of the enormously popular Nintendo company. Later incarnations of the series paired the adventures of the Captain with those of Nintendo's star characters, the Super Mario Brothers. This amalgam lasted until NBC abandoned Saturday morning in 1992. Another media tie-in series was also produced for NBC in 1989. *The Karate Kid* was based on the popular 1985 film of the same name, and was co-produced with the film's producer, Jerry Weintraub. However, the series abandoned the revenge-on-the-bully theme of the film and its sequels (and a more recent remake) in favor of a more standard "quest" plotline. While this was a fresh approach, the ratings were poor, something DIC was rarely accustomed to, and it was canceled after a year. Neither of the film's stars (Ralph Macchio and Pat Morita) was involved here.

◆ ◆ ◆

As with its competition during the 1980s, DIC suffered from rushing to produce work to meet deadlines, and the creative end of its productions, with the exception of *Inspector Gadget*, suffered as a result. Yet this rarely, if ever, impacted its bottom line, and it remained very much in demand from outside producers to adapt their products to animation because of their graphic competency. Consequently, Andy Heyward and his company would remain a major television animation producer during the 1990s and 2000s, if only because, rather than developing their own ideas, they were extremely competent at illustrating the ideas of others.

SABAN ENTERTAINMENT

In a rare interview, Haim Saban described himself, likely with tongue in cheek, as a "cartoon peddler."[104] Whatever his tone might have been, it is nevertheless accurate in describing the business practices of the man. Like Steve Krantz in the 1960s (see Chapter 3), Saban was not himself an animator, but rather a middleman between animators and distributors, packaging series so they could be consumed both in English-speaking and foreign countries. His *modus operandi* was essentially to purchase popular foreign projects, both animated and live-action, and dub them into English for a wider audience, or, less regularly, to underwrite programming directly for those English audiences. While his company's work was mostly undistinguished creatively, it was financially effective. Yet his greatest success had nothing to do with animation whatsoever.

Born in Alexandria, Egypt, to Jewish parents, Saban was forced to leave the country of his birth when Egyptian president Gamel Abdel Nasser organized a formal campaign against Jews in 1956. He spent the majority of his youth in Israel, where he first became involved in business ventures. His first projects were in music management and production. After his attempts to manage an Israeli classical group were undermined by warfare, he switched his operations to Paris. There, Saban developed a service through which he produced music sound tracks for television series, and sold many of these in America, including to producers of several of the animated series already discussed in this chapter. By the mid–1980s, the ambitious producer had expanded from just music into all aspects of television animation production.[105]

Saban was soon successful enough to divide his company into two separate organizations, one handling domestic North American distribution; the other, foreign. In this light, he was involved in the conflict between Andy Heyward and Jean Chalopin over the DIC library (see above), although this did not affect Saban Entertainment directly.

Saban had developed a strong working relationship with executive Margaret Loesch, a former Hanna-Barbera and Marvel supervisor who became the driving force behind the Saturday morning division of the FOX network (more on her later).[106] The most notable success of this relationship was *Mighty Morphin Power Rangers*, a re-dubbed and edited Japanese children's live-action series, which became both a programming and a marketing phenomenon during the 1990s. As a recognition of this loyalty and success, FOX purchased Saban outright in 1996, with the company becoming the almost-exclusive Saturday morning supplier to the network.

In 2001, that relationship ended when News Corporation, FOX's parent company, sold Saban, along with the Fox Worldwide Cable group, to Disney. At this point, Saban's existence as an independent production company came to an end. Since that time, Haim Saban has remained active as a power broker in the media industry, although he no longer produces or distributes content directly. Disney, meanwhile, owns the Saban library, but has not issued much of it on DVD.

◆ ◆ ◆

During the 1980s, Saban was not so much a direct producer as a halfway house between the domestic market and foreign animation producers looking for work and exposure in America. This business model was retained for the majority of the company's existence, though it eventually did produce projects on its own in later years.

Other than co-production deals with DIC and Marvel (see above and below for details on those series), the production slate for the company in the 1980s was sparse and stale. *Macron 1*, debuting in 1985, was a re-dubbed Japanese animated program focusing on science fiction. *Sparktaus and the Sun Beneath Sea* [sic], debuting in 1986, was a French-Japanese co-production dealing with the mythical lost city of Atlantis. *Maple Town*, based on a Tonka toy line, featured a traditionally "cute" cast of anthropomorphic characters interacting after being introduced by the live-action host, Mrs. Maple. It first aired in 1987. The last two Saban productions of the decade were 1988's *Noozles*, a marsupial variation on the *Care Bears*, airing on the Nickelodeon cable network, and two 1989 projects: the self-explanatory *Grimm's Fairy Tales*, a Japanese import airing on Nickelodeon, and *Wowzer*, another Japan-Europe co-production, which aired on the Family Channel.

By tapping the foreign market for animation resources, Saban did his part to contribute to the glut of television animation in the 1980s, although he essentially was watering down the elements that made them appeal to the original audience by replacing the original audio tracks with synthetic English ones. The business model obviously worked for him, and eventually allowed him to concentrate more exclusively on the North American market during the 1990s.

FILM ROMAN

This organization, unlike much of its competition in this decade, was a house built on quality productions rather than quantitative volume. This was no surprise when you consider the résumé of company founder Phil Roman, who had cut his teeth working in similar quality-minded studios. Although Roman was essentially an adapter of other people's ideas to animation, as opposed to a genuine creator, he was gifted both with an ability to judge the strengths and weaknesses of his properties vis-à-vis the working components of the animation process, and the ability to present them in the clearest and most effective ways possible. Consequently, while his studio's production output was small in comparison with most of his contemporaries, it was a unique harbinger of quality in an industry seemingly lacking in it, a distinction underlined by the Emmys Roman and his staff would be presented with in the following years.

Roman had learned the value and reward of hard work from the beginning of his life. Born in Fresno, California, in 1930, he was the son of immigrant migrant farm workers who encouraged their son to "get ahead" in life rather than follow in their footsteps. Viewing Walt Disney's *Bambi* at the age of 12 encouraged his pursuit of the animator's trade, which he practiced by producing drawings for his high school paper and taking art courses by correspondence (*Peanuts* creator Charles Schulz served as his instructor). When he graduated from high school, he studied art at the Hollywood Art Center School, his studies being interrupted by military service during the Korean War.

When he graduated from the Art Center School in 1955, Roman was hired as an assistant animator at Disney, but, realizing that the prospects for advancement were limited, he quit two years later to become a full animator at Imagination Inc., a San Francisco studio specializing in commercials. The experience allowed him to familiarize himself with all aspects of animation production, which would become invaluable to him later on. In 1959, he returned to Hollywood, where his credits included working on *Calvin and the Colonel* (see Chapter 3). During the early-to-mid 1960s, Roman gained his animation stripes as a member of the MGM animation division headed by Chuck Jones, working on Jones's revival of *Tom and Jerry*, the Dr. Seuss specials and the feature film *The Phantom Tollbooth* (see Chapter 3 for more details of Jones's MGM work).

When MGM shut down its animation division again in 1970, Roman joined Bill Melendez in producing the long-running *Peanuts* series (see Chapter 3). He eventually succeeded Melendez as the line director of the series, as well as doing occasional freelance work for UPA, DePatie-Freleng and Ralph Bakshi. Roman left Melendez in 1984 to start his own company, Film Roman, which took over from Melendez as the producer of *Garfield* specials (see below). The success of this series allowed Roman to work on more lucrative ventures, such as becoming the animation house for *The Simpsons* and other prime-time animation projects (see Chapter 6) and establishing an international production pact with Russian animators, while continuing to produce series, specials and features on his own.

Roman took his company public in the late 1990s, which caused some personal setbacks for him. When events caused the investors to lose confidence in him, he was ousted as CEO in 1997, and then resigned. He formed a new organization, Phil Roman Entertainment, and continued to produce. Roman rejoined the Film Roman board in 2001, and, a year later, his new and old companies merged, with Roman continuing to remain active as a producer and director.[107]

◆ ◆ ◆

The sole series produced by Film Roman in the 1980s would be an outgrowth of the studio's earliest productions, a property inherited from Roman's earlier employer, Bill Melendez. Created by Indiana-born cartoonist Jim Davis, Garfield, an orange, black-striped feline (named in honor of Davis's grandfather, in turn named for former U.S. president James A. Garfield), became one of the most popular comic-strip characters in the world following his debut in 1978. How popular was he? Twenty-five separate paperback collections of reprints made the *New York Times* best-seller lists, for one thing. As Hal Erickson observes, "Either there were a lot of cat fanciers out there, or [the strip] fulfilled the non-feline fancier's long held suspicion [or stereotypical view] that all cats are worthless parasites who spend all their time eating, sleeping [and] arrogantly playing off affection they don't deserve and secretly plotting domination against both the human and canine races."[108] Whatever the reason for his popularity, taking Garfield into the realm of television animation seemed a logical next step, considering that the synergy between comic strips and television animation was at its height during the 1980s. Many diverse strips, from Cathy Guisewite's *Cathy* to Tom Wilson's

Ziggy, would get the TV treatment in specials in this decade; the *Cathy* and *Ziggy* specials were good enough to be awarded Emmys as the best of their kind during their original broadcast years. *Garfield*, however, with the exception of *Peanuts*, would be the only one to become a recurring broadcast feature.

Peanuts and *Garfield* shared a comic-strip syndicator (United Media), so it was logical that they would also share an animation house. Consequently, Lee Mendelson and Bill Melendez would be the producers of the first few specials before ceding the job to Roman in 1984. Everything about the later series, from its subversive comic tone to the voice casting, was present from the first special, *Here Comes Garfield* (1982), and would be continued in the brace of specials that followed. Cast in the voice of Garfield was a particularly inspired choice—Lorenzo Music. He was a veteran comedy writer and television producer who was a prominent architect behind the success of the MTM live-action sitcom factory during the 1970s. For one of these series, *Rhoda*, he essayed a role because he could not find an actor suitable for the part. This was Carlton, the disembodied voice of the doorman in the title character's apartment building, whose arrogant, indolent behavior was very similar to Garfield's. (Music was no stranger to animation; he'd already adapted Carlton to animation in the special *Carlton Your Doorman*, which he won an Emmy for producing in 1980, and he became a much in-demand voice actor following his Garfield work.) Music claimed the role was tailor-made for him: "[Garfield is] a selfish, lazy, arrogant, conceited, gluttonous slob—and I know how to do that."[109] It proved to be the truth, and provided much of the charm in the character for both the specials and the series that would follow. Music would voice the character off and on until his death in 2001; no other actor would be able to fully convey the character's essence in later years, though others, such as Bill Murray, would try.

That being said, the ongoing success of the specials (the cumulative series of which would win five Emmys between 1983 and 1989) made the series concept much more of a possibility. CBS announced such a project for Saturday morning consumption in 1987, but it wasn't until a year afterward that Garfield made his Saturday morning debut, as the star attraction of *Garfield and Friends*. Initially a half-hour, it expanded to a full hour in 1989 and remained as such until it came to an end in 1995. (When the series entered syndication in 1993, the hour episodes were edited into half-hours to meet timeslot requirements. Only 73 of the original 121 episodes are available in the syndication package.)

The main "Garfield" segments were essentially like the comic strip, except writ large. Garfield's main supporting cast were his "master," "sanctimonious, idealistic"[110] Jon Arbuckle (Thom Huge), whose occasional displays of temper belied his essentially neurotic personality; and Odie (Gregg Berger), a dimwitted dog. Occasional visitors included Nermal (Desiree Goyette), "The world's most cloying cat, whose very existence was reason enough for Garfield to plot revenge against Nature [*sic*]."[111] In spite of the obvious limitations that existed within the framework of the comic strip, the series was multifaceted and versatile in its plotting and also (unlike most of the efforts of its time) genuinely and engagingly funny. Much of that humor was of the satirical and self-deprecating nature—two underplayed hands in the 1980s. In fact, many of the most effective episodes played off the obviously vast gulf between Garfield's essentially anti-social loner personality and the reigning pro-social culture of network television censorship at the time.

The "Friends" of the title provided their own fun in a different way. They were the stars of *U.S. Acres*, a barnyard-flavored strip also created by Jim Davis, which was far shorter lived than *Garfield*. Much like those of their companion project, the characters in this series were not stereotyped, prettified or otherwise portrayed simply as mere "livestock."[112] The principal protagonist was Orson (Berger), a surprisingly intelligent pig, who was usually seen reading or dreaming about what he read (something that likely would have endeared him to the intellectuals and educators in the audience). When he wasn't doing that, he was dealing (politely, for the most part) with the competing egos around him. These included Roy (Huge), a bellicose, perpetually scheming rooster; Wade (Howard Morris), an inner-tube-wearing duck, who displayed an overstated level of panic and hysteria; Lanolin (Julie Payne), a bitchy sheep; and Sheldon (Frank Welker), a chick stuck in his shell! By far the best episodes of the segment were the ones that allowed Orson full range to indulge in his literary-derived fantasy daydreaming, with the other characters playing well-chosen supporting parts. These were effective chiefly because the roles Orson cast himself in—such as the Roman strong-pig Hogcules, the James Bond–styled secret agent Double Oh Orson, and particularly the flamboyant (and tragically underemployed) superhero Power Pig—were such blatant movie hero he-men, in contrast to his "real"-life Caspar Milquetoast personality.

Much of the program's success can be attributed to veteran animation and comic-book writer Mark Evanier, who co-authored every episode with Sharman DiVono, and also directed the voice-recording sessions. Evanier would recall that this series was one of the rare occasions in television animation history that nearly everything was exactly as the creators wanted it to be, as opposed to being heavily tinkered with by the network or other supplier. He gave ample credit to his colleagues: "The cast was terrific, the ... animators did a splendid job, the network left us completely alone [,] and Jim Davis..., Lee Mendelson [and Phil Roman] somehow managed to infuse the project with a touch of class and excitement."[113]

I can think of no higher praise for a television animation series produced between 1970 and 1990, when the happy alchemy between producers, cast and especially network was usually absent.

Garfield has since been revived in computer animation form, for feature films and new animated TV projects. But none of these projects have the essential comic soul and wit of his 1980s–90s animated incarnation. If one wishes to understand the character at his best, and the equally entertaining world of *U.S. Acres*, you had best stick with *Garfield and Friends*. Accept no substitutes.

Marvel Entertainment

Marvel Entertainment was, essentially, the television animation division of the already-legendary comic-book company, which had radically reshaped that medium's rule book during the 1960s and 1970s. The company's involvement in animation had been engineered by its creative driving force, Stan Lee, who saw it as a logical step toward expanding Marvel's corporate bottom line beyond the low-profit comics industry and into areas where it could reach more diverse audiences. Ironically, the company found its greatest success in the 1980s with animating comic-book–styled characters from other sources.

As noted at the beginning of the chapter, Lee found the network censorship and promotion system not to his liking, so his oversight related to the series was chiefly limited to the comic-book characters he had helped to create. Day-to-day operations were left to a more seasoned industry veteran. Margaret Loesch had worked both sides of the producer/network divide, first as an NBC administrator and then as a production supervisor at Hanna-Barbera. As Marvel's executive producer in the 1980s, she first displayed the balanced governance that would allow her to supervise the meteoric success of the new FOX network's children's division in the 1990s.[114]

Still, the company's production line replicated that of DePatie-Freleng, whose assets it had effectively taken over: mostly routine and undistinguished fare, with an occasional surprise.

The first series to come under the Marvel brand was *Pandamonium*, which aired during the 1982-83 season on CBS. The series was the joint creation of Fred Silverman, who had become an independent producer after being fired by NBC, and Hanna-Barbera veteran Jerry Eisenberg, but that was about all it had to recommend it. It involved a group of superpowered pandas and their human friends confronting a Central Casting bad guy named Mondraggor.

The year 1983 saw the debut of *Dungeons and Dragons* on CBS. Based on the popular role-playing game, this was a relatively standard quest series in which "six young people ... embarked on an amusement park ride which turned out to be a one-way trip into the fantasy land of Dungeons and Dragons."[115] Each of the kids was assigned a particular role to play during the course of the ongoing game, which allowed them to survive the confrontations with the villain-in-residence, the Venger. Despite debuting during a year when *Newsweek* vetted the opinion that television animation was "a national disgrace," this series managed to last for three seasons and later be revived in reruns.

The year 1984 provided the Marvel studio with its biggest hits in both syndication and network broadcasts. That the two series involved were so diametrically opposed in tone and content suggested exactly how broad-minded and versatile the studio was actually becoming.

The first of the two series was *Muppet Babies*, which debuted on CBS in 1984 and remained there for the balance of the decade and into the 1990s. For the few people unfamiliar with Jim Henson and his legendary marionette/puppet hybrids (the name resulted from a portmanteau of the two words), a brief explanation is in order. A native of Mississippi, Henson began experimenting with puppetry as a child. By the late 1950s, he had become a successful TV show performer in Washington, D.C., and the following decade saw him making regular appearances with his growing troupe on network television variety shows. The iconic status of the characters was sealed in the 1970s in two ways: first, through their appearances on the legendary PBS educational series *Sesame Street*, and then, the syndicated variety program *The Muppet Show*, produced by England's ITC studios. Both programs won numerous Emmys for Henson and his colleagues, and remain in broadcast, syndication and on DVD to this day. Henson built an empire around his funny and engaging characters, making three feature films featuring them (four more would follow after his death) and expanding his company into more ambitious projects, such as the fantasy films *The Dark Crystal* (1982) and *Labyrinth* (1985). Tragically, however, he died of a streptococcal infection in 1990, just as he was on the verge of negotiating the sale of his company to Disney.

Henson was a stickler for quality in his work, and if he was associated with any product bearing his or his characters' names, it had to deliver. *Muppet Babies* did. In the process, it became as much of an Emmy magnet as its parent programs had been, and, mostly, those awards were well deserved.

The central premise of the series involved regressing Henson's star Muppet characters (Kermit the Frog, Miss Piggy, Fozzie Bear, Gonzo, Scooter, Rowlf, Animal, et al.) to babyhood and theoretically "restricting" them to the four walls of their nursery. (Skeeter, a twin sister for Scooter, was added, at the suggestion of the network, to provide a second major female character for the project.[116]) I say "theoretically" because the characters had unlimited imaginations, and their marvelously produced daydreaming fantasies were the glue that held the show together. The only intruder into this world was the group's Nanny, seen only from the legs down. (She was portrayed, somewhat fittingly, by Barbara "June Cleaver" Billingsley.) The program was far more effective than any others in the "babyfication" school it came to foster in the following years. First, although the Muppet characters were portrayed by impersonators rather than Henson and his crew, they kept the established personalities of the characters, providing continuity for those familiar with the "adult" versions of the characters. Second, Henson never treated his audience with condescension as other television animation producers employed unconsciously in their stories, so educational components in the narratives were developed organically in the stories rather than superimposed in the middle or end. Thirdly, the production of the series itself was highly unique. Not only was the animation look of higher quality than the average series, but the producers also incorporated live-action footage to make the fantasies of the characters seem more "realistic," from well-chosen movie clips to new footage of celebrities such as John Ritter and Whoopi Goldberg.

CBS knew a good thing when it saw one, and thus the series' life span was longer than average for most Saturday morning programs. Originally a half-hour when it debuted in 1984, it was expanded to a full-hour format the following year and was re-titled *Jim Henson's Muppets, Babies and Monsters*. This was due to the inclusion of the "Little Muppet Monsters," live Muppet characters who tried to stage an amateur theatrical version of *The Muppet Show* every week. After three episodes, this feature was scrapped due to high costs. The series remained an hour until 1987 when it became a 90-minute feature—the result of CBS's decision to cancel the controversial *Garbage Pail Kids* series before it was even broadcast. It was back at an hour for 1988, and remained at that until ending in 1992. By that time, it had proved its value in syndication, and later in reruns on both FOX and Nickelodeon.

Muppet Babies was a fine series on its own, and a fitting valedictory to the multi-media appeal of Jim Henson's iconic troupe. It was something Loesch herself would take pride in on reflection. "We put a lot of money and time into [the series]," she would later recall. "But I believed [that] it would make TV more imaginative. Maybe I made kids laugh and stirred their imagination.... Maybe I did make a difference."[117]

As one impressed viewer of the show, I can tell you that she was absolutely right.

◆ ◆ ◆

The other major 1984 series from Marvel was far different in tone and intent. *Transformers* was based on a line of toys from the Hasbro company, eager to enter the same competitive animation arenas as its longtime rival Mattel. The company (originally Hassenfeld Brothers) was a family concern that had begun pencil manufacturing in the early 20th century, gradually adding a toy-manufacturing adjunct. The toy and pencil companies then separated, with each remaining in the hands of the Hassenfeld family. Under the leadership of Stephen Hassenfeld, and, after his death, his brother Alan, Hasbro had become a major power broker in the American toy industry, with only Mattel as a challenger.[118] Converting its characters to animation, for Hasbro, however, was simply a means of keeping up with the Joneses, rather than producing anything truly original. Consequently, while Mattel gave Filmation enough rope to hang itself, Hasbro kept a tight leash on Marvel, preventing them from doing anything innovative with the characters that did *not* allow them to plug the toys. It was this excessive corporate interference that, by her own admission, ultimately caused Margaret Loesch to leave Marvel.[119]

The Hasbro/Marvel alliance lasted through several series, each relentlessly selling a Hasbro toy line with little thought to creative content. The aforementioned *Transformers* debuted in 1984, and focused on two groups of super-powered robots able to disguise themselves as cars. Predictably, one group was good, the other evil. The good group consisted of the Autobots, led by the pragmatic Optimus Prime; the evil ones were the Decepticons, led by Megatron. Given that both sides had little in the way of character, the conflicts depicted in the series were mostly meaningless. But Hasbro was clearly aiming at young viewers (specifically, boys) who had less discriminating tastes, and so the series was a hit. The surprising appeal of the characters continued through the 1990s and 2000s into several more follow-up series, as well as several movies, one animated failure and several live-action successes, all of which—not surprisingly—were produced by Hasbro.

Even more troubling to some viewers was *G.I. Joe*, debuting in 1985, which spawned an entire mini-canon of war-themed shows during the decade. Based on one of the longest lived toys in the Hasbro arsenal, whose fortunes have risen and fallen with the popularity of the American military itself, the title referred not to an individual, but a fighting force in conflict with the evil Cobra organization. If any series in this book can be said to be a product of its time, it is this one. Although the series did feature ethnic minorities and women prominently among the heroic cast, a reflection of new realities in the world, it otherwise bore little factual resemblance to reality.[120] Given the extensive warfare that America would engage in during the 1990s and 2000s and the media coverage related to it, it is important to stress this point. The failure of two later versions of the project in 1990 and 1995 were a reflection of the property's decline in value since its '80s heyday.

The final toy synergy project was no less disturbing, even though it was milder in tone and intent. If *Transformers* and *G.I. Joe* were clearly aimed at boys, *My Little Pony and Friends*, debuting in 1986, was likewise aimed at girls, and was as successful with its target group as the earlier series. The title characters were anthropomorphized female horses who, in the tradition of other '80s characters, embodied varied personality traits. The educational consultants, Robert and Anne Selman of Harvard University, were employed to ensure that the right emotional and educational tone was present. (Oddly enough, they performed the same function for *G.I. Joe*.) The main *Pony* segments were interspersed with ones plugging similar Hasbro products: Glo Friends, Moondreamers and Potato Head Kids. These were dropped in 1993, when the property moved to the Disney Channel, and new episodes further entrenched the sticky sweet ambience of the project.[121]

◆ ◆ ◆

Marvel was in no way neglecting its own characters during this period, however. The first of these projects was *Spider Man and His Amazing Friends*, debuting in 1981–82 on NBC. It was succeeded by *Amazing Spider Man and the Incredible Hulk*, airing during 1982–84 on the same network. In this version, "Spidey" was accompanied by two college-age superhero chums, Angelica "Firestar" Jones and Bobby "Iceman" Drake. Other than that, it basically took up where the 1967 series left off, except that it was better animated, with the hero once again walking a fine line between mild-mannered photographer and flamboyant superhero. *The Incredible Hulk*, absent since the ill-fated *Marvel Superheroes* project in the 1960s (see Chapter 3), made a triumphant return to animation on the strength of being the star of a popular live-action series on CBS. He was later given his own series in 1984, while the Spider-Man episodes continued in reruns.

The studio's commitment to the action-filled legacy of Marvel Comics was further confirmed by two popular syndicated projects. *Super Sunday*, airing in 1985, featured a block of new, derivative programs, headed by *Robotix*, a saga of warring reptilian aliens, and *Bigfoot and the Muscle Machine*, the story of adventurous monster truck driver Yank Justice. Two other segments, *Inhumanoids* and *JEM*, were popular enough to air on their own, and will be discussed in that context below. *The Marvel Action Universe* was more self-explanatory. It consisted of reruns of the earlier *Spider-Man* project coupled with two new projects: *Robocop*, a cleaned-up version of the popular action film about a cyborg law enforcer (Orion Pictures, which produced the film, co-produced this segment with Marvel) and *Dino Riders*, a group of modern human adventurers in prehistoric times.

Elsewhere, the company continued to honor its syndicated and network commitments. *Defenders of the Earth* featured resurrected characters from the King Features comic strip syndication archives, including Flash Gordon, The Phantom and Mandrake the Magician. The aforementioned *Inhumanoids* were an evil subterranean race opposed by the ultra-good Earth Corps. *JEM*, on the other hand, was a surprisingly flinty update of the rock star-cum-superhero formula of Hanna-Barbera's earlier "Impossibles" (see Chapter 3). The title character was a rock singer who was, in reality, the secret identity of Jerica Benton, music executive-cum-orphanage patroness, with the transformation made possible through her late scientist father's apparatus. This allowed the show to balance the fantasies of its pre-teen audience with a sometimes bitter, unflinching look at the state of the American record business circa 1986, which gave it a substance other rock-and-roll–oriented television animation programs had lacked. *Visionaries: Knights of the Magical Light* focused on a science fiction universe in the guise of the middle ages (à la Frank Herbert's novel *Dune* and its sequels). The fact that this, like other Marvel product, was based transparently on a Hasbro toy line was only partially mitigated by playing the show as much for laughs as thrills.

Marvel's last three productions of the decade also did little to hide their origins or their intent. *Little Clowns of Happytown*, airing on ABC during 1987–88, focused on a group of miniature clowns whose pro-social intent was to show the children in the audience the benefits of a positive personal attitude and laughing at least once a day. Given that this show failed in the ratings, they didn't get that laugh from this show. *Fraggle Rock*, airing on NBC during 1987–88, was a mostly futile attempt to repeat the magic of *Muppet Babies* by adapting another Jim Henson puppet franchise to animation. *Rude Dog and the Dweebs*, airing on CBS during 1989–90, was based on a line of clothing from Sun Sportswear, but managed to be entertaining in spite of its pedestrian storylines. Rob Paulsen, one of the most talented and versatile of the new generation of voice actors to emerge in the 1980s, had a perfect showcase for his skill at wry, sarcastic dialogue delivery in the title role. He'd have many more such opportunities—in better shows—in the following decades.

◆ ◆ ◆

Marvel's entry into television animation was a mixed bag. As a television animation provider, it was much more of a work-for-hire operation, in contrast to its sister company. Particularly regarding its relationship with Hasbro, it operated on a strict "we were just following orders" policy that belied the studio's creative expertise. When that expertise was paired with someone with a genuine creative vision, such as Jim Henson, the results could be magical. Likewise, the relationship with Marvel's comics served the company better than most of the outside projects it took on, and the studio wisely began to focus on reaping the rewards from working directly with them instead of with outsiders in the following decades.

NELVANA

As noted in the previous chapter, the Canadian company, Nelvana, had first distinguished itself in the late 1970s with the *Nelvanamation* series of syndicated specials. Through this, they gained the attention of American media programmers who were attracted to it both for the high quality of its images and the fact that its geographic location made for economic advantages. In the 1980s, Nelvana began to focus more directly on the American market, with mixed results both creatively and technically.[122]

The decade started out ambitiously for the company with an extravagant music-themed feature film, *Rock and Rule*. Finally released in 1983, the project was a misfire at the box office and taxed the company's financial resources as much as its artistic ones. To absorb the loss, the company rapidly expanded both its animation and live-action filmmaking divisions to create product. Nelvana engaged in a relationship with DIC that allowed it to do subcontracting on *Inspector Gadget* (see above), and that, in turn, led them to succeed DIC as the producers of the *Care Bears* series (see above), including the feature films featuring the latter characters. It also was engaged to produce the TV specials featuring Strawberry Shortcake, who, like the Care Bears, had originated at the American Greetings Company. This led to further American TV assignments.

The first of these was an outgrowth of the American Greetings relationship. *My Pet Monster* was the story of a toy that came to life when it was released from a pair of handcuffs with a key in the possession of its owner, Max. The stories revolved around Monster's mischief and Max's attempts to prevent it. The series was well animated but underwritten, and lasted only for the 1987-88 season on ABC.

The studio's later productions of the decade, all coming at the end of that time, were more successful, and established the future *modus operandi* of Nelvana, like many of its peers, as a producer-for-hire rather than a creative originator or innovator. *Beetlejuice*, airing on ABC from 1989 to 1992 and on FOX from 1991 to 1993, was based on a darkly comic film released in 1988 that had been a major box-office success. Tim Burton, the film's director, and David Geffen, the producer, were the executive producers here, making sure the vision of the original property was maintained, although the plotting was altered for television. This was recognized with an Emmy Award in 1990 in the Daytime Emmys' animation category.

The title character (voiced by Stephen Ouimette) was an otherworldly confidence man who was the confidant of Lydia Deetz (Alyson Court), a moody young lady with more than a passing interest in the occult. Stories alternated between the "real" world where Lydia resided and the bizarre "Netherworld" from which Beetlejuice hailed, with felicitous dramatic and comic results. As Hal Erickson notes, this was "one of the few animated series [based on an outside source] to equal and even occasionally improve upon its source material."[123] Just as they had in the 1970s, Nelvana's made-in-Canada product was beating the American competition at its own game.

Nelvana solidified its position with a milder project, an adaptation of a European storybook character. *Babar* was based on the stories of an elephant monarch and his similarly anthropomorphized subjects, created by artist/writer Jean De Brunhoff and later continued by his son, Laurent. The stories were an outgrowth of a movie project featuring the characters produced in 1989, and the series retained the format: Babar would relate adventures of his past in a simple way. The project was drawn and written simply in line with the De Brunhoff formula, and was effective for that reason. It ran on the HBO cable service between 1989 and 2000, and earned a Cable Ace award in the first of those years.

From its precipitous position at the start of the decade, Nelvana had, by the end of the 1980s, firmly established itself as a quality provider of television animation. In the following decade, it expanded on this position.

Murakami-Wolf-Swenson

Murikami-Wolf-Swenson was first established in 1965, as a collaboration between veteran animators Jimmy Murakami and Fred Wolf; Charles Swenson was added as a partner in 1971.[124] Initially, the company focused on experimental, non-commercial filmmaking but, after Murakami relocated to Ireland in the early 1980s, Wolf began to take the company in a decidedly commercial direction. This would produce good commercial results in turn.

The major source of this revenue came from one source: *Teenage Mutant Ninja Turtles*. These now-well-known characters originated in a comic book produced in 1983 by artists Peter Laird and Kevin Eastman, which became an underground cult hit. After being picked up for mainstream distribution by the Archie Company and franchised by the Playmates Toy Company, the Turtles became animation stars in 1987 with the production of the series by Murakami-Wolf-Swenson. In bringing the characters to television animation, they were streamlined and made less violent, and while there was an adventure component to the series, it was played primarily for laughs. Indeed, the invisible line between audience and characters known as "the fourth wall" could sometimes seem as nonexistent here as it had been during Jay Ward's heyday.

Put briefly, this series concerned four turtles who, through exposure to radiation, became humanized ninja fighters, under the guidance of their master, Splinter (Peter Renaday), a mutated rat. The quartet consisted of Leonardo (Cam Clarke), the designated leader; Donatello (Barry Gordon), the intellectual; Raphael (a scene-stealing Rob Paulsen), the wit; and Michaelangelo (Townsend Coleman), the California-styled "party dude." The opposition consisted chiefly of Shredder (James Avery), the villainous, masked master of the Foot Clan, and Krang (Patrick Fraley), a disembodied brain from Dimension X. These two, much like other TV animation villains of the '80s, took their frustrations out on each other as well as their opponents, but here it was done in such a way that Hal Erickson has compared Shredder and Krang to Neil Simon's crochety "Sunshine Boys" in terms of their verbal antagonism.[125] Assisting the Turtles was television journalist April O'Neil (Renae Jacobs), one of the more resourceful and intelligent female characters of the era.

Originally aired in syndication, the property was added to the CBS Saturday morning lineup in 1990, in the wake of two successful feature films featuring the characters. They remained there until being canceled in 1996. The following year it was briefly revived as a live-action series on FOX, and then in animation again in 2003. This version was co-produced by Laird and Eastman's Mirage company, and was more reflective of their original comic-book vision of the characters—dark and mercenary—than the earlier animated series had been.

The success of the project led to Wolf setting up his own animation company after breaking with Murakami and Swenson. The only other animation project produced by the studio in the 1980s was *The California Raisins*, airing on CBS during 1989–90. Based on Will Vinton's popular "Claymation" characters from television commercials and TV specials, the series failed to convey what had made the original characters so popular, and lasted only a season. Vinton would have more lasting success as a producer on his own terms, at the time and later.

Calico

Calico was, similar to Saban, a distributor of programs rather than an actual producer. It was headed by Peter Keefe, who later ran Zodiac (see Chapter 6).

The three series bearing the company's name were: (1) *Denver, the Last Dinosaur*, created by Keefe and released in syndication in 1988, a "comedy of errors" resulting from a dinosaur living in the modern world; (2) *Saber Rider and the Star Sheriffs*, released in 1987, a re-dubbed science fiction/Western hybrid from Japan; and (3) *Vytor*, released in 1989, a more generalized science fiction series.

Ralph Bakshi

The re-entry of this man (one of the most controversial figures in the history of animation) into television was enough to raise alarm bells among purists and regulators in the field. Bakshi, by the late 1980s, was simply wishing to keep his company active, and he seized with a vengeance the one opportunity that came his way. However, his past reputation, along with a horrifically misinterpreted act in one episode of his comeback series, served to deny that project, one of the best of its kind during the decade, the broadcast run it deserved.

Following his earlier TV work at Terrytoons (see Chapter 3), Bakshi left what, to him, was the confines of television animation for the feature-film arena. Working initially under the patronage of the controversial Steve Krantz (see Chapter 3), Bakshi produced two highly adult-oriented features—*Fritz the Cat* (1972), based on Robert Crumb's X-rated comic book, and *Heavy Traffic* (1973), a *cinéma vérité* portrait of his native Brooklyn. After splitting with Krantz over financial issues, Bakshi became his own producer, but found it difficult to access funding for future projects. It didn't help that one such project, *Coonskin*, a modernized take on Joel Chandler Harris's Uncle Remus stories, was denounced as racist by the NAACP, and disowned by its original distributor, Paramount. Still, Bakshi was able to fund projects throughout the 1970s and early 1980s, including a condensed feature-film version of J.R.R. Tolkien's *The Lord of the Rings*; *Wizards*, an original take on similar fantasy material; and *American Pop*, a musical history of the United States. Though reception for his work ranged from tepid to hostile, Bakshi unquestionably had established himself as the reigning *auteur* of American theatrical film animation—one of the few (besides Walt Disney) deserving of that title in that conservative-minded field.

However, by the mid–1980s, Bakshi was burned out. No longer able to get funding for features, he was scrounging for work wherever he could find it, including television. During a meeting with CBS executive Judy Price, he pitched her the idea of doing a new series of films starring Mighty Mouse, the star character of his old employer, Terrytoons. Bakshi, it turned out, did not own the rights to Mighty Mouse, but that was fine with CBS: they did. After all, CBS had owned Terrytoons since Paul Terry sold his company to them in 1955 (see Chapter 3). Consequently, Price approved the series, and Bakshi, after expanding his skeleton staff, got it into production.[126] The series debuted on CBS in 1987 and ran until 1989.

For the new project, Bakshi substantially redefined the character, giving him an introspective alter ego, Mike Mouse, who worked at an assembly line under the leadership of his love interest, Pearl Pureheart. The format of the new program—three short films per half hour—allowed for the resurrection of the fast-paced timing of old theatrical cartoons, and the show's directors and writers (including Bakshi protégé John Kricfalusi [see above and Chapter 6]) responded accordingly. Parody and satire abounded in this environment much more than any other animated program of the decade. Bakshi even managed to take shots at the lead character's corporate heritage in an episode in which Gandy Goose, the venerable 1940s Terrytoons warhorse, was resurrected from a 40-year period of "suspended animation" and was driven to madness by the changed world he now encountered.

But it was another episode, "The Littlest Tramp," that got the series into trouble. In one segment, Mighty Mouse, after being temporarily weakened, renews his strength after sniffing a flower which supposedly was "doctored with health-inducing vegetables."[127] However, according to the Rev. Donald Wildmon, one of the most prominent foot soldiers of the Religious Right movement of the 1980s, that was *not really* what he was sniffing. The reverend, head of the ultra right-wing American Family Association, viewed the episode in response to a complaint a Kentucky mother had filed with him, and did not like what he saw. Here are the reverend's own words:

> This woman had phoned our office a few days earlier. And [,] to be honest, I thought she was just another crank caller trying to play a joke on us. The incredible charge she made against CBS was so ludicrous, I found it impossible to believe. Sensing I thought she was off base, she offered to send me her video tape [sic] so I could see for myself.
>
> As the tape she sent rolled [,] I focused my eyes on a furry little mouse with big ears and a cape. The animated rodent, who was depressed because the lady mouse had not been responding to his affections, was reclining next to a campfire at the end of a long day. A few moments later [,] the melancholy mouse reached under his cape and pulled out a powdery looking substance. Then [,] I noticed that the powder suddenly disappeared right up the creature's nose.
>
> "Please tell me I didn't actually see what I just saw," I said to my co-workers, who appeared to be in a state of shock. "Let's see that again."
>
> When the tape rewound, we again watched the TV screen in incredulous wonder as the scenario repeated itself. Into the cape went the cartoon character's hand. Out came a powdery substance. Up his nose it went.
>
> "Our Kentucky friend wasn't kidding," I finally said, breaking the sober silence in the room. "It's as plain as day. They've really got Mighty Mouse snorting cocaine."[128]

From this conclusion, Wildmon put forth the argument that CBS and Bakshi were essentially promoting the use of cocaine among children, the show's intended target audience. The fact that cocaine was then freely circulating among the Hollywood elite, and that Bakshi himself, based on his earlier work, was considered to be little more than a pornography merchant in the eyes of Wildmon, et al., added fuel to this argument. Bakshi, for his part, compared Wildmon to the Nazis when he finally did speak about the incident.[129]

Regardless of that controversy, it was actually poor ratings that did *Mighty Mouse* in. It marked the twilight of Bakshi's career as a commercial creative artist. In the following decade, he would produce only a TV special for Nickelodeon (*Tattertown*), a hybrid live-action/animation feature film (*Cool World*) and an adult-oriented series for HBO (*Spicy City*), before retiring to pursue painting, a pursuit in which he was indeed free to experiment.

GILLIS-WISEMAN

The Canadian firm Gillis-Wiseman produced only one series, but what a series it was.

Kevin Gillis, a former folksinger turned television personality, had initially developed the series and characters in collaboration with a friend, newspaper columnist Gary Dunford, based on an incident they had observed at a cottage near Ottawa. Dunford chose not to pursue development of the project, so Gillis instead engaged the assistance of Ottawa lawyer Sheldon Wiseman to realize the project. This resulted in the creation of *The Christmas Racoons*, first broadcast on the Canadian Broadcasting Corporation's television service in

1980. Three more such projects followed, and this led, in 1984, to the CBC underwriting a regular prime-time project featuring the characters—the first of its kind on CBC and one predating *The Simpsons* (see Chapter 6) by several years. Disney assisted in providing funding, and so the series, which remained in production until 1992, was first seen in America on the Disney Channel.

Wiseman was credited as the executive producer of the series project, simply titled *The Raccoons*, but in nearly every other respect the project was definitely Gillis's baby. He was the principal writer and director of the program, as well as the composer of both the musical score and the numerous songs featured in the project's episodes. This attention to detail and direct control of the project had not really been seen in television animation since the glory days of Hanna-Barbera, and contributed immensely to making both the specials and series the enjoyable products that they were. Like Nelvana before them, Gillis and Wiseman injected a unique Canadian sensibility into what had previously been an American-dominated marketplace. This was reflected in the measured tone of the stories, the subtlety with which their message was reinforced, the relaxed quality of the voice acting, and, above all, the absence of violence for the sake of violence. When Gillis and Wiseman were asked by Japanese syndicators to make the show more "violent," in fact, they pointedly refused to do so.[130]

Bert Raccoon (Len Carlson) was the lead, as underlined most prominently in the opening credit sequence, loudly enjoying himself at a variety of pursuits. A well-meaning slacker, Bert tended to search for adventure where there was none to be found, and that, as would be expected, got him into trouble. He was frequently rescued by his more sober-minded pals, Ralph (Bob Dermer), and Melissa (Susan Roman), who operated the *Evergreen Standard*, a newspaper whose politics were clearly both left and green (at a time when both of those philosophies had gone under the radar in America). The primary target of the paper's wrath was Cyril Sneer (Michael Magee), a cigar-smoking patrician businessman in the guise of an anteater, who was a clear prototype for *The Simpsons'* Mr. Burns (see Chapter 6). This created a conflict for Cyril's bespectacled, mild-mannered son Cedric (Marvin Goldhar), who was Bert's best friend.

One can easily describe how the plots of this series flowed, but it is difficult to completely capture its tone in words. *The Raccoons* was the most "Canadian" television animation program ever seen in America, both in the sense of the way Canadians stereotype themselves and the way Americans stereotype them in turn. It was rare for a character to even slightly raise his/her voice, even in what would be played as an out-for-blood conflict in an American series. Whereas American characters were firmly structured as "heroes" and "comedians," these characters were not. Stories concerned logical problems, issues and solutions, and were resolved in ways understandable to the viewer. Gillis and Wiseman were, in a sense, reinforcing their Canadian audience's view that diplomatic conflict management is better than a militaristic response to the same problem. "Your way of living doesn't work the same way ours does," was part of the message. There was an implicit assumption of openness and freedom existing in the Canadian wilderness, even if this was more a fantastic elaboration on the producers' part than the actual truth.

Gillis and Wiseman ended their partnership amicably when the series ended in 1992. Both men remained involved in the Canadian animation business—Wiseman as the founder of Lacewood Productions and Gillis as a freelance creator/writer/producer of such programs as *Atomic Betty* (see Chapter 7). Little of what they produced apart equaled what they had produced together.

Rankin-Bass in the '80s

Just as the 1980s marked the effective end of the creative partnership between William Hanna and Joseph Barbera (see above), it likewise marked the end of the equally fecund partnership between Arthur Rankin, Jr., and Jules Bass. While the decade began with the continuation of their high-quality run of specials, it ended with the producers becoming involved in production of syndicated series, a task for which they proved ill-equipped. Consequently, they amicably parted ways at decade's end, concluding the run of a formidable creative organization.[131]

The first special of the new decade was *The Return of the King*, a cel animation adaptation of the concluding volume of *The Lord of the Rings*, which effectively served as a follow-up to the studio's earlier adaptation of *The Hobbit* (see Chapter 4). It aired on ABC in May 1980. Orson Bean, who had voiced Bilbo Baggins in *The Hobbit*, now portrayed his heroic nephew, Frodo. John Huston reprised his role as Gandalf and also narrated. They were joined by Theodore Bikel as Aragorn, William Conrad as Denethor and Roddy McDowall as Sam Gamgee. The special was as highly effective as *The Hobbit*, but has unfortunately been overshadowed in recent years by Peter Jackson's lavish live-action full adaptation of the entire *Lord of the Rings* trilogy.

Next was a new Animagic special, *Pinocchio's Christmas*, airing in December 1980 on ABC. The story is pretty much self-explanatory, as it bears similarities to both Walt Disney's 1940 feature film and Carlo Collodi's original book, not to mention Rankin and Bass's earlier treatment of the material (see Chapter 3). Headlining the cast were Rankin-Bass veteran George S. Irving as kindly old Geppetto and veteran comedian Alan King as the villainous puppeteer Maestro.

Another self-explanatory special was *The Leprechaun's Christmas Gold*, which aired on ABC in December 1981. This Animagic portrayal of some elements of Irish folklore likely would have worked better as an hour rather as the half-hour it was upon airing. Art Carney portrayed the central protagonist, a leprechaun named Blarney Killakilarney.

The Coneheads, airing on NBC in 1983, was something of a departure for the studio. It was based on the popular series of comedy sketches featured in the early days of *Saturday Night Live*, and was intended as the pilot for a series that never got off the ground. *SNL*'s footprints were all over the project. Lorne Michaels, *SNL*'s inventive creator, served as executive producer, and the special was scripted by veteran *SNL* writers Tom Davis and Al Franken. Dan Aykroyd, Jane Curtin and Laraine Newman, who had played the bizarre aliens from the planet Remulak on *SNL*, voiced their parts. Although Don Duga, who served as continuity artist, suggests that there was behind-the-scenes friction between the writers and producers (unusual for a Rankin-Bass project), he also indicates that Aykroyd, who had played a major role in developing the characters, assisted him with ensuring that the animated characters duplicated the unique mannerisms of their live counterparts.[132] The sitcom-style structure of the plot and gags (reinforced by the presence of a pre-recorded laugh track on the audio feed) didn't really work at times, given the characters' origins in the world of sketch comedy, but it proved to be a better showcase for them than did the overblown 1993 live-action feature film, also produced by Michaels and starring Aykroyd and Curtin.

Rankin and Bass did much better with their next project. *The Wind in the Willows*, airing on ABC in the summer of 1985, was a zesty and flavorful adaptation of Kenneth Grahame's beloved children's novel. According to studio historian Rick Goldschmidt, the project is closer to its source than any previous animated version (including Walt Disney's 1949 take on the material), presenting "the entire story without any significant plot changes."[133] That alone should be enough to recommend it, but there are other positive elements as well. Jules Bass and Maury Laws wrote a wonderful group of original songs, highlighted by the title number, performed by Judy Collins. The vocal performances here are some of the best in the studio's history, highlighted by Charles Nelson Reilly's excellent portrayal of Toad, and including Roddy McDowall as Ratty, Jose Ferrer as Badger, and Eddie Bracken as Mole.

Coming full-circle, the last Animagic special had the same theme, characters and subject matter as its earliest ones. *The Life and Adventures of Santa Claus*, airing on CBS in 1985, was based on a novel by L. Frank Baum, and essentially follows the same origin-of-Santa story as the earlier *Santa Claus Is Comin' to Town* (see Chapter 3), albeit in a far slower and more somber fashion. No big names were in the voice cast, unless you count Alfred Drake, the voice of the Great Ak; he originated the role of Curly in the original Broadway production of *Oklahoma!*

The final special produced by Rankin and Bass together was *The Flight of Dragons*, airing in the summer of 1986 on ABC. This was a fantasy opus borrowed from two separate texts involving dragons, one by the Canadian-born science fiction writer Gordon R. Dickson, the other by British children's writer Peter Dickinson. Romeo Muller and Jeffrey Walker's script admirably managed to link the two disparate works into an exciting whole. John Ritter played the lead; supporting roles were enacted by Harry Morgan, James Earl Jones, Victor Buono and Larry Storch.

With the exception of a lavish feature film version of Peter S. Beagle's *The Last Unicorn*, distributed by Lord Lew Grade's ITC organization in 1982, Rankin and Bass's last major efforts in the field of animation were three syndicated series, all distributed by the company's new corporate parent, Lorimar-Telepictures. The first of these, *Thundercats*, debuted in 1985, and was very much in the vein of other outside-property derived series of the era. While Rankin and Bass's reputation for and commitment to quality made the show *look* good, at least, they could not hide its fundamentally derivative nature. The stories, involving the title characters' conflicts with the forces of evil led by Mumm-Ra, were derivative of *He-Man*. Just as boldly derivative was the fact that the lead Thundercat, Lion-O, was powered by a sword, and called his associates into battle with a ringing cry much like He-Man's. In essence, this series was an enjoyable waste of time—and space.

Silverhawks, debuting in the fall of 1986, was more of the same. It involved a group of super-powered androids who, not surprisingly, were in conflict with science fiction–derived forces of evil, headed by the creatively named Mon-Star. The program, like *Thundercats*, was inspired by a line of toys, and aired back-to-back with the former series in many markets, reinforcing their connections to each other.

The most innovative of the three projects was *The Comic Strip*, debuting in 1987, whose emphasis, as the title implied, was primarily comedy doled out in 11-minute installments. "Karate Kat" featured an anthropomorphic cast of characters, headed by a would-be martial arts expert who bumbles his way through assignments for the McClaw Detective Agency. *Street Frogs* followed the exploits of some African American–styled amphibians, and was notable for the use of hip hop culture and rap music at a time when the mainstream media was largely ignoring it. *Mini Monsters*, according to its producer, featured "a cast of kids that were actually the kids of the famous monsters everybody knows [i.e., Frankenstein, Dracula, The Mummy, The Invisible Man, The Wolf Man, etc.] and they were away at camp."[134] Conclusions about episode content can be drawn from this statement. Finally, there was the relatively straight forward *TigerSharks*, which repeated the *Thundercats/Silverhawks* approach under water.

It was at this time that Rankin decided to throw in the towel. "We made so many pictures [during the 1980s] that I don't remember the individual titles at this point," he later recalled. "After doing that for five years, I was absolutely, totally exhausted.... When it came time to renew contracts, I said to Jules ... 'I think I want to take a long breath and I don't know what I want to do next.' Jules felt more or less the same way."[135]

And so, a partnership that had revolutionized television animation came to an entirely reasonable end.

Bass has, for the most part, retired from the animation business, instead launching a profitable new career as a children's book writer/illustrator. Rankin has returned to production in a limited form under the Rankin/Bass name, now working with writer-producer Peter Bakalian, who served as line producer of company productions during the 1980s. The revived company produced a lavish feature-film version of *The King and I* in 1999, released by James G. Robinson's Morgan Creek company through Warner Bros., and a Christmas special, *Santa Baby!* for FOX in 2001. Rankin currently lives in Bermuda, where he works as a university film instructor and stage play director.[136]

The Nadir Moment: "Cartoon All-Stars to the Rescue"

This chapter cannot conclude without mention of this 1990 project. Without question, it marked a turning point in the history of television animation, showing how fast and how far the creative quality of the genre as a whole had declined during the 1980s, and how easily pro-social messaging had co-opted it. Yet, inadvertently, it marked the close of one era of television animation and the dawn of another.

With financial aid from McDonald's, the project was produced by the Academy of Television Arts and Sciences (the organization responsible for presentation of the Emmy Awards). Essentially, it was designed by the U.S. government as a step toward combatting the increasing rates of drug abuse in America, something to which many children were exposed in real life. To that end, it seemed logical to use the characters of Saturday morning television (who were already being used to put forth pro-social messages) as a means of communicating to the children of America the all-caps message that DRUGS ARE BAD FOR YOU. Nearly every major television animation studio donated time, money and characters to what was essentially a simple story and message against drug abuse.

Introduced by President George H. W. Bush and First Lady Barbara Bush (overseas broadcasts used local heads of state in their place), the special aired on *every available* network, syndication and cable outlet available to it *at the same time*, an unprecedented situation that has never been replicated. This block-booking strategy had its intended effect: the total audience numbers were 30 million, higher than any other program in Saturday morning television history.[137]

Conclusion

While television animation gained more exposure during the 1980s than ever before, the quality of much of the actual work obscured the potential understanding of the genre in creative terms. While there were many good programs produced, they were outnumbered by an avalanche of poorly produced and ill-conceived hackwork. Consequently, the few productions during the decade that had genuine merit were often ignored and overlooked, and the genre as a whole was marginalized by critics. That the producers could easily contend that they were being *forced* to produce material this way was something those critics did not want to hear.

Things would not stay this way, however. At many television animation studios, a new generation of animators, writers, directors and producers were cutting their teeth. They were increasingly frustrated during the 1980s because they were prevented from doing so many of the stories and ideas they *wanted* to do because of network, studio, and government bureaucracy. Some wanted to reinvent the medium, whereas others wanted to do things the way they had been done in the past.

And, to echo William Lloyd Garrison, they WOULD be heard, in the 1990s and beyond.

Chapter 6

Songs of Innocence and Experience (1990–1999)

It is often said that media consumers in individual countries "get the culture they deserve." Nowhere is that saying more justified than in America, in terms of the culture of television animation during the 1990s.

It is important to make this point because of the seismic shifts made creatively, culturally, economically and politically by television animation during this decade. What were the causes of this change?

They were many and varied, and need some attention before we can fully discuss the programs and their creators that sparked and participated in this revolutionary change.

First and foremost, the television industry itself went through a number of difficult changes during the decade. One of the most significant of these predated the decade itself. These were the effects of the entry of the FOX television network, launched in 1987.[1] This network's impact first became truly apparent in the 1990s. Rupert Murdoch, a cagey Australian newspaper publisher, had slowly built his organization, News Corporation, into a formidable presence in the American market. FOX was the result of the merger of two company acquisitions, 20th Century–Fox Film Corporation and Metromedia Television (an established chain of independent stations), and it was a major part of Murdoch's plan to establish a firm foothold in the affluent American marketplace. FOX was not the first network start-up to attempt to challenge the hegemony of ABC, CBS and NBC, nor would it be the last. It was, by far, the most successful and lasting, however, and its mere presence on the airwaves—to say nothing of its more liberal programming stance in comparison to the older networks—marked a major change in the way things were done in the network television business. Murdoch's cut throat business methods, which included openly poaching stations from the established networks, made for formidable business opposition. The high quality of the network's programming, geared chiefly at the lucrative 18–49 demographic, provided creative competition as well. As we will see, television animation would prove to be a major building block of the strategy, not only during the daytime hours, but in prime time as well, with the enduring success of landmark programs such as *The Simpsons* (see below).

Just as important was the rapid mushrooming of the cable TV industry, which further eroded the economic and viewing power of the older networks. Cable, after a slow start in the late 1970s, had grown rapidly during the 1980s, to the point that there seemed to be a channel marketed to each distinct market and demographic. In this new atmosphere, television animation, like so many other marginalized genres, was given a specific place to thrive. Nickelodeon, an established network oriented toward children, and Cartoon Network, a newcomer whose mandate was obvious from its name, both began producing large quantities of original animated programming (in addition to providing safe harbor for reruns of older material), and competed strenuously for the children's market. This had the happy result of producing a considerable number of exceptional shows between them (see below). Disney, after entrenching its position in the media landscape with the purchase of ABC in 1995, rushed to keep up with the two new cable Goliaths. Gradually, Disney abandoned the strategies that had characterized its work in the 1980s in favor of programming with a tone and spirit more like its competitors.

In 1990, Congress passed the Children's Television Act (CTA), which brought with it sweeping reforms to the way network and syndicated programming engaged with child audiences. It effectively ended the syndication boom of the 1980s by banning toy-centered programming, and also by insisting that character behavior be "legitimized." In other words, there should be no fighting or warfare without a firmly defined, just cause. Where network television was concerned, it simply legislated the pro-social dictums that had been unofficially enforced for two decades, under the new banner of Education/Information (E/I) criteria. Some producers were able to produce effective narratives within the E/I mandate, but the effect on others was utterly poisonous. The implication of the CTA and the E/I criteria, coupled with eroding ratings numbers, eventually forced the networks to abandon traditional Saturday morning programming as it had existed since 1965, and, ultimately, nearly all of their children's programming, to the cable channels. NBC was the first to fold and walk away from the table, in 1992; the others would follow gradually over the course of the 1990s and 2000s.

There was also social and political change that had to be dealt with, both in the world at large and within the industry itself. The end of the Cold War—signaled by the collapse of the Berlin Wall in 1989, and confirmed with the demise of the Soviet Union in 1991—was a dilemma for America. It had been their desired result of the conflict, but it also meant the demise of one of the key justifications of their military-industrial complex. For nearly half a century, the United States had used the existence of the "Evil Empire" as both a carrot and a stick with its population, cowing them with the persistent "threat" of "nuclear war" while encouraging scientific experimentation, development of intelligence capabilities, and other forms of patronage as a way of "beating" the "Commies."[2] With the enemy gone, however, many Americans began to openly question the country's role in world politics. The battle for control of the public agenda began with groups turning on one another, and this spread into the media, including television animation. Once a home chiefly for mild ripostes and unthreatening sweetness, television animation became a home across the dial for vicious, uninhibited, and toxic satire, which, whether politely or otherwise, began showing the true colors of America in a way it never had before. It could not simply be written off as a "children's" medium any longer.

The television animation industry changed drastically. Whereas in the 1970s and 1980s programming at the larger studios, such as Hanna-Barbera, Filmation, DIC, etc., had been produced according to a model of bureaucratic *realpolitik*, there was now a new system of production at play. During the 1970s, a model of media production emerged in opposition to the traditional studio system that stressed the rights of the creator of a work to control the destiny of his/her product. "Hyphenates"—artists who combined their acting, writing or directing skills, or sometimes all three, with the financial acumen of producers—became all the rage. This system came belatedly to television animation in the 1990s, as a means of allowing uniquely creative individuals to remain within the fold of a studio or to be lured away to another by better remuneration. The majority of the best programs of the 1990s and 2000s were produced by hyphenates, and their quality was always immediately apparent. The hyphenates generally ran looser ships than their predecessors, encouraging their subordinates to make extensive contributions to the way the show was planned and developed, with faster, funnier, more exciting and more satisfying programs being the result. The advent of the hyphenate marked a major change in the process of television animation production, mostly for the better.

Even more drastic, however, was the rapid reversal of a decades-old bias against the "weaker" sex. The presence of women and girls in the narratives, and their portrayal, had always been reflective of the position of women in both society and the animation industry. Since women had largely been relegated to the non-creative ends of the business in the past, the vast majority of portrayals of women in the medium had been conceived under sexist biases. This, however, changed in the 1990s. The change was not simply a reflection of how the role of women had changed in America since the feminist-minded 1970s. It was the increased presence of qualified and gifted women behind the cameras in the animation industry itself, not only as animators but also as writers, producers and directors, with many managing to obtain hyphenate status. Concurrent with this was an avalanche in the number of female characters, the majority of whom were protagonists in their narratives rather than observers, as they had been in the past. These characters were strong in both body and mind, and spoke their minds well and often, and they came to rapidly redefine the construction and theory behind television animation narratives at all levels of production across the 1990s and 2000s. "Baby" simply could not be put in a "corner" any more.

The Simpsons

The Simpsons, out of all the myriad series discussed in this book, is the One That Changed Everything.

It was unprecedented when it debuted in 1990, and remains frustratingly difficult to categorize today. If you lived during the 1990s and 2000s, you were undoubtedly confronted by the series in both original broadcasts and reruns, in the successful feature film, and in the comic books featuring the characters.

For the uninitiated, here are some facts to demonstrate the magnitude of the importance of *The Simpsons* on the television animation landscape of America.

The Simpsons is the longest-running television animation series in existence, at 23 years and 500+ episodes and still counting, an eternity in a genre where most series are lucky if they get a second-season pickup. It is also the longest-running prime-time sitcom in TV history, live-action or animated, and prime time is a far more competitive marketplace than the animation sector. It has won more awards than any other animated series, including numerous Emmys. It has produced enough written analysis and critique to fill a library.[3] It has always been produced with higher budgets and more exacting creative and artistic standards than any other series before it, and that has resulted in a project that is nearly always able to deliver on what it promises, even if that may seem to be the moon.

Even more staggering has been its influence over the entire television animation community. As the first of its kind, it effectively served as the laboratory for entirely new forms of discourse between television animation and its audience. Not since the glory days of Jay Ward (a major influence on the series' creator) had an animated series so deliberately engaged and enraged its audience at the exact same time, fueling both heated support and heated enmity in the wider world. The brazen assertiveness of the characters, writers and animators alike was a wake-up call to the television animation industry. As the show leaped from strength to strength throughout the 1990s, the rest of the industry would struggle to keep up with its innovations. In any event, as innovative as many television animation programs would be on their own terms during this period, there were certainly many moments where the *Simpsons*' producers could easily exclaim, "We did that first."

Few who study television animation would dispute that claim. For there is one further inescapable fact about this unique program: once a viewer is caught in Springfield's web, it is nearly impossible to get out.

Matt Groening, creator of *The Simpsons* (20th Century–Fox/Photofest).

◆ ◆ ◆

The history, structure and evolution of the program over the years, as well as the backstage shenanigans behind it, have already been explored in depth in numerous texts that are directly or indirectly about it, but some background information is required to understand the series' history and evolution.

Let us begin at the beginning...

Matt Groening, born in Portland, Oregon, in 1954,[4] was the son of a freelance filmmaker and writer, and grew up in a home environment that encouraged creativity. A talented artist, he attended Evergreen College, a progressive, liberal-arts college in Washington, and then headed to Los Angeles, where he worked a series of menial positions. In 1978 he created the popular comic strip *Life in Hell*, seen first in underground magazines and then, beginning in 1980, as a nationally syndicated newspaper strip. Over the course of the decade, the strip built up a wide following, including lucrative merchandising spinoffs. It wasn't long before Hollywood came calling.

If Groening had been actively searching for a patron for his art, he could not have found a better or more influential one than James L. Brooks. Born in Brooklyn, New York, in 1940, Brooks had begun his professional life working in the mailroom at CBS, an experience which would fuel his later professional work.[5] After briefly working for David Wolper, Brooks began to concentrate his efforts on creating fictional television programs of his own. He first made his mark creating *Room 222*, a comedy/drama hybrid set at an inner-city Los Angeles high school, which ran on ABC between 1969 and 1974. He had far greater success as a creator of straightforward comedy. With Allan Burns, an established animation and live-action comedy writer, he created *The Mary Tyler Moore Show*, which became one of the most popular and iconic sitcoms of the 1970s, and he remained a principal writer and producer of the series for its entire seven-year run. When the show's run ended, Brooks and several colleagues established the John Charles Walters company, distributed by Paramount, and produced another classic sitcom, *Taxi*. Brooks won multiple Emmys for writing and producing both programs. His television success gave him entrée into a new field of endeavor, the movies, as a writer-producer-director. Here, he achieved equal success; in 1984, his adaptation of Larry McMurtry's novel *Terms of Endearment* (1983) dominated the Academy Awards, garnering acting awards for Shirley MacLaine and Jack Nicholson and three awards for Brooks: Best Picture, Best Director and Best Adapted Screenplay. Brooks was then able to set up Gracie Films, an independent film and television production company, through which he produced another popular film, *Broadcast News* (1987), which earned him further Oscar nominations.

Later in 1987, Gracie Films, which was initially distributed by 20th Century–Fox, entered into an agreement to provide the infant FOX network with programming. The chief offspring of this arrangement was a variety program starring British comedian Tracey Ullman. As a way of providing smooth transitions between scenes, the idea of providing short animated "bumpers" was tabled and ultimately accepted. Brooks was an admirer of Groening's work and suggested that they approach him about using his *Life in Hell* characters for the bumpers. This, too, was accepted.

Groening, however, was wary of giving up control of his lucrative comic-strip characters to Gracie Films and FOX, and, before meeting Brooks about the potential deal, decided not to give them away. Instead, on the fly, he conceived the idea for "a sort of anti-sitcom"[6] about a monstrously dysfunctional[7] family. "Racing against the clock, he gave them a good old generic American surname—Simpson—and then assigned them first names stolen from his own family."[8] It was this project that Groening ended up pitching as the bumper feature, and this project which Brooks accepted. The Simpsons thus spent their first three years—what program historian John Ortved has justly called their "Cro-Magnon"[9] period—as a bumper feature on *The Tracey Ullman Show*, and they were pretty much expected to be just that and nothing more.

As animation historian Hal Erickson has noted, the bumpers, whose original quality was sluggish at best, gradually developed into one of the more engaging aspects of the program.[10] The logical conclusion seemed obvious: make the characters into a series of their own. Groening and Brooks promptly worked toward this goal, recruiting distinguished live-action sitcom veteran Sam Simon to serve as the initial "show runner,"[11] and the talented animation firm Klasky-Csupo (see below) to produce the animation content. The actors who had voiced the Simpsons in the bumpers—Dan Castelleneta, Julie Kavner, Nancy Cartwright and Yeardley Smith—were recruited to reprise their parts in the series, and were joined by two other talented veteran actors—Hank Azaria and Harry Shearer—who between them would portray the majority of the members of the program's ever-expanding and diversified supporting cast. The program first aired as a Christmas special in 1989, and as a series proper the following year.

As is often the case with a series, the earliest episodes of *The Simpsons* are certainly not their best. They are crudely written, drawn and sometimes voiced, and are very much responsible for the initial and visceral negative reactions the series received in the press. There was a good reason: the staff of the program was often at odds—in the same way the Simpsons were with each other and the world at large. Groening and Simon were immediately at loggerheads about the program's direction, and the animators were attacked for their less-than-stellar work. The writing staff, used to the fast-paced world of live-action sitcoms, had difficulty adjusting to the time-delay process required in animation construction, and particularly hated the fact that they did not have the luxury of making revisions to the material as quickly as they would have liked. One thing led to another, as it does where creativity and money are concerned in Hollywood, but things ultimately resolved themselves. Labor issues caused the producers to dump Klasky-Csupo in favor of Film Roman (see below), who managed to do the unthinkable by making the characters more physically attractive than they had been in the past. Meanwhile, Simon, who many believe was the true architect behind the show's success, acrimoniously left the program in 1995 in a dispute over creative control and financial compensation. He retains an executive producer credit and a share in the program's revenues, however, as part of a litigated settlement with FOX.[12] Other creative individuals, including David Mirkin, Bill Oakley, Josh Weinstein, Mike Scully and Al Jean, would take over Simon's position as show runner in the following years, with varied degrees of success. There would also be further behind-the-scenes skirmishes, mostly between Brooks and his colleagues on the Ullman project (including Ullman herself) over the "ownership" of the property, and between the actors and studio over money. Yet these, unlike the earlier ones, have done relatively little damage to the series, primarily because its creative track record has remained relatively unaffected.

Once the craft was righted, it was unstoppable. Collectively, the program's episode log is the most formidable work of art in television animation history, and it has an impressive track record with its individual episodes, the majority of which are gems. It has managed to weather all sorts of changes in the television landscape, and the curses of sameness or deterioration that typically affect long-running series, by always managing to surprise viewers.

Chiefly, this has been done through a small but noticeable chain of actions. First, the writers have always remained on the pulse of their audience, always aware of what is going on in the world and always ready to mock it savagely—in a way that it is rarely expected. This includes the seemingly endless parade of celebrity "guest voices," most of whom have performed surprisingly well for people with virtually no experience working in animation voice acting. Second, they never take the series' position in the world of animation and television too seriously, frequently using those media as a means of caustically accusing the series itself of being part of a problem rather than a solution—though not in the same way as its detractors. By not holding themselves superior to their subject matter, the writers are better able to relate to the feelings of their audience, and are better equipped to translate those feelings into relatable jokes and narratives. Third, and most importantly, the series has continued to develop its characters in a way that is unprecedented in media narratives, and remains relatively exceptional today. Detractors may complain that the series is shallow, but, looking at the series episodes chronologically, we see that the characters, while retaining their physical appearances, have gradually developed richer and deeper personalities, which make them easily able to juggle conflicting internal beliefs and ideas. No matter how long or short a time a character is in a scene, they all play memorable, important parts in both advancing and enriching the narrative. As the series has grown and developed over the years, it has taken on the character of a soap opera, without the melodrama or continuous narrative. Characters can be absent from one or more episodes, but then return with a flourish, their place in the ongoing story never in question. No other television animation program has really achieved this, and the fact that it continues to grow makes it all the more impressive an achievement. In the world of television animation, *The Simpsons* is a novel among smaller colonies of short stories.

As impressive as it is collectively, however, the series remains even more effective when broken down into its individual components. The individualized segments have taken on every major issue under the sun in America between 1990 and 2013, and have hit the mark nearly every time. At their best, they display the comic satirical skill of Dickens, and the reflective, America-turns-on-itself anger that fueled the likes of Mark Twain, Sherwood

Anderson, Sinclair Lewis, H.L. Mencken and John Dos Passos. This series displays the same caustic approach to its subject matter, while enlivening it with often-unexpected reserves of humor.

◆ ◆ ◆

The engine of any television series, animated or otherwise, is its lead characters. They are responsible for maintaining the attention of the audience, engaging us in the seriousness or frivolity of their activities, and, ultimately, ensuring that the viewer returns. In this respect, *The Simpsons* is blessed. Rather than putting all of its energies behind one lead character, it alternates quite effectively between four, and in the process manages to create many different ways of telling stories around them. The enormous group of supporting characters adds to this, creating an unprecedented reservoir for the writers to draw from.

Homer (Castalleneta), the *paterfamilias*, comes first, for he is the focus of the majority of the storylines and the origin of the manic comic energy of the series. Almost entirely bald, with a seemingly permanent five-o'clock shadow, he is, in the fitting words of historian Gerard Jones, a "paunchy slob, not yet forty but already skidding downhill, slaving away in Springfield's nuclear power plant."[13] While the roles of husband, father and employee would be enough to soften most men into compliant domesticity, this process has never occurred in Homer, simply because he possesses epic levels of both stupidity and arrested development in his intellect. He also possesses a complicated emotional track record, making him able to turn from friendly and easy going at one moment to vicious and intimidating at another. The program's writing staff have nearly always used him as the bully pulpit for ridiculing the most ignorant and uninformed intellectual views ever produced by America. (His vicious shifts in tone and attitude, thus, neatly mirror those of the program as a whole.) Homer is, effectively, a boy in a man's body, repeatedly behaving and acting at a level far below his chronological age. He is thus Springfield's equivalent of the "village idiot" often seen in depictions of the towns of provincial England, or its American equivalent, the "town drunk"—as typified by Huckleberry Finn's ne'er-do-well father in that novel. Nevertheless, while many complain about or ridicule him, he is not entirely a lost cause. In many episodes, he displays a surprisingly entrepreneurial zeal, much like Ralph Kramden or Fred Flintstone before him, but, as with theirs, his ventures are all doomed to failure, simply because, in his stupidity, he has bitten off more than he can chew, and suffers the consequences. His failures only seem to drive him further toward his beloved Duff beer.

The common belief that women mature faster biologically, emotionally and intellectually than men is amply demonstrated in the Simpson matriarch, Marge (Kavner). Her appearance is dominated by an enormous blue beehive, which seems to be a symbolic reflection of the intellectual gulf between her and her husband, and her voice (which is the natural, unaccented one of her voice actor[14]) is raspy enough to command attention even when whispering. Marge has, by default, stepped into the power vacuum established by her husband's ineffectiveness, working as both nurturer and disciplinarian even when the conflict between those roles is obvious. Even though the ship of her family is not entirely seaworthy at times, Marge is persistently and determinedly confident in her ability to make sure it does not sink. This is reflected in her occasional efforts to file down the family's dysfunctional horns. In many respects, she resembles the perennially frustrated housewives profiled by Betty Friedan in *The Feminine Mystique*, able to function well in what could be considered her "natural" habitat, but both angry at and fearful of the world at large for what it has so clearly done to those closest to her.

Bart (Cartwright) is another kettle of fish entirely. He is clearly the star of the bumpers and the earliest episodes, and the major factor in the series' earliest popularity, but certainly not in its enduring success. A ten-year-old ball of perpetual energy, he is clearly out for a good time in life regardless of what anyone else thinks of him, his family included. As M. Keith Booker notes, "He embodies the most subversive energies of the series and is probably the character whose point of view is closest to that of ... Groening [himself]."[15] Hardly his sister's more studious type, he is much more attuned, like his father, to activities that do not require high levels of intelligence, such as the orchestration of epic acts of mischief—something he executes well, and often, with the diligence a veteran criminal might give to a robbery or heist. Bart's character has changed over the years, however, and the later generation of series writers have invested him with more clear-headed intelligence and emotional comportment than did their predecessors, although he is still allotted an occasional backslide now and then. Bart's contemptuous attitude toward established forms of authority remains at the core of the series itself, although he himself is no longer the focus of the main action.

Lisa Simpson (Smith) is, in many respects, Groening's most incendiary, formidable and enduring creation. Utterly belying her physical appearance as an eight-year-old girl, with the red dress and white pearls to signify this, she is, in fact, an intellectual titan, able to express feelings and opinions that the other characters dare not. While she is often ignored and mocked, her words are often those of reason, and proven in retrospect to be immensely wise.

She seems to be the only person in her family—not to mention the entire town of Springfield—with rational intelligence. She may be belligerent at times in pursuit of a goal, but is she more capable than the other characters of seeing the flaws within the narratives, characters and situations. There is, thus, much of the "child-is-father-to-the-man" to her, especially vis-à-vis her father and brother. She is able, and required to be, far more mature mentally than she is physically, and the toll that this takes is repeatedly made clear to the viewer—no matter how successful she is in achieving a goal.

I interpret Lisa is as a late–20th/early–21st-century proponent of transcendentalism, the most formidable intellectual discourse of the 19th century. As practiced by the likes of Ralph Waldo Emerson, Henry David Thoreau and Margaret Fuller, transcendentalism's core beliefs—the value of nature, the danger of capitalism, and the sensibility of peace—are close to the sentiments close to Lisa's heart. Moreover, Emerson's depiction of the ideal transcendentalist is as close to a description of Lisa as you are likely to get:

> [She] believes in miracle, in the perpetual openness of the human mind to new influx of light and power; [she] believes in inspiration, and in ecstasy. [She] wishes that the spiritual principle should be suffered to demonstrate itself to the end, in all possible applications [,] to the state of man, without the admission of anything unspiritual.[16]

Lisa takes it entirely upon herself to be the social and political conscience of her community,[17] a Herculean task considering the amount of ignorance she has to confront on a daily basis, and manages to come out right in the end. She frequently takes a stance that make her an active, important character in the show's narrative, and codes the show as implicitly supporting her stance on the issue at hand.[18] This is a remarkable stance for a genre and a medium that, as demonstrated earlier, has often ignored female characters and their opinions. In particular, it reflects this program's ability to attract both adults and children to its messages and ideas, and its ability to intellectually engage the whole audience without alienating either group in the process.

Though Lisa is clearly an adult figure in terms of her spirituality and intellect, she is still limited, physically and socially, by her status as a "child." Her difficulty at negotiating this divide—sometimes successfully, sometimes not—is important due to the fact that she was one of the first major female characters in television animation to confront these issues head on and resolve them on her own terms, providing a model for countless others in the process,

Thus, there are four different roads, four different entryways into the most powerful and complex television animation series ever produced. Which of them you most respect and admire says much about what, if anything, you admire about this series and, likewise, who you are as a person.

◆ ◆ ◆

There has never been a television animation program like *The Simpsons*, in terms of continuing creative quality, episode quantity or enduring cultural influence. No other series has been as continual a presence in American culture, nor so constantly on its cutting edge. And no other series has so repeatedly made itself so openly available to so many layers of analysis, as animation, television, film and literature. There is simply nothing else like it in the culture of America, and there is likely nothing else that will ever equal or better its stature. In television animation, its influence is totemic. So many of the series of the 1990s and 2000s owe so much to it—in characterization, plotting or general anti-authoritarian attitude—that they cannot be fully listed here. Just as Ernest Hemingway said that all modern American literature is descended from *Huckleberry Finn*, all post–1990 television animation is descended, in one way or another, from *The Simpsons*.

FOX Beyond The Simpsons

The success of *The Simpsons* sparked a mini-revival of television animation as a prime-time attraction at the other networks, just as *The Flintstones* had done during the early 1960s (see Chapter 3). And, as before, viewers saw through the copycat intent and shallowness of the projects and spurned them violently, in spite of some of their impressive pedigrees. *Capitol Critters*, airing on ABC during the winter of 1992, was a collaboration between Hanna-Barbera (see below) and distinguished prime-time TV drama producer Steven Bochco, whose credits include *Hill Street Blues*, *L.A. Law* and *NYPD Blue*. The thin premise—rodents living within the walls of the White House—and the appalling, realistic violence of its pilot episode, were enough to turn most viewers off immediately. *Fish Police*, another Hanna-Barbera project, aired for nearly the exact same time on CBS during 1992. Based on an underground comic-book series created by Steve Moncuse, it relentlessly drubbed its under-the-sea premise with typical Hanna-Barbera overkill until the viewers were sick of it. This was in spite of an impressive cast of voice actors, including John Ritter, Edward Asner, Jonathan Winters, Buddy Hackett, Robert Guillaume and Tim Curry. The most appalling of these failures, however, came the following year, again on CBS. The product of a star-crossed creative marriage between famed film directors Steven Spielberg (see below) and Tim Burton (see Chapter 5), *Family Dog* was based on an animated short film that had aired as a segment of Spielberg's TV anthology *Amazing Stories* six years earlier. The nominal creator of the series was Brad Bird, later to gain fame as the director of *The Incredibles* and *Ratatouille* on the big screen, but his intentions for the series were marginalized in favor of those of Spielberg, Burton and "show runner" Dennis Klein, whose background in live-action proved to be more a hindrance to the series than an asset. What resulted was a project that was woefully underwritten, badly animated (in spite of attempts made to repair the damage by the producers, which heavily ballooned the per-episode cost) and featured shallow, ill-conceived characters (save for the title character, who was mildly entertaining). It was no surprise that this project, too, limped its way to cancellation.

The fact that such distinguished producers had tried and failed to replicate the success of *The Simpsons* not only underscored the uniqueness of that series, but also illustrated one of the major Achilles heels of the television animation business: truly innovative projects are few and far between, and vulnerable to being "ripped off" in one way or another in a quick attempt to grab cash and/or prestige. Fortunately, in this case, viewers were able to see these flawed projects for what they were, and put them out of sight and mind as soon as possible.

◆ ◆ ◆

In the end, it was the FOX network, which had started the whole prime-time animation trend, that ended up resurrecting television animation as a prime-time genre, sustaining it as such for an astonishingly long time period. The network's objective in gaining audiences in the 18–49 demographic dovetailed nicely with the fact that it was this demographic that was most likely to appreciate the presence of animation in prime time. Likewise, as a programming service that prided itself on providing edgy, unconventional fare to its viewers, FOX was more than willing to consider programming material from producers unwilling to play by the conventional "rules" of prime time. In the late 1990s, it gave chances to three producers with three unconventional series concepts that, along with *The Simpsons*, helped it to earn ratings, prestige and awards while building each series into an attractive property.

The first such series debuted in the winter of 1997, and, while often marginalized in poor timeslots, managed to eke out an impressive 12-year run.

Mike Judge was born in Guayaquil, Ecuador, in 1962, and raised in New Mexico. A self-described "skinny kid who got pushed around [a] lot"[19] in his youth, he initially pursued a career as an electronics engineer after gaining a university degree in physics. After attending an animation festival in Dallas, he chose instead to pursue animation as a career. His early projects, done in a primitive, realistic drawing style, attracted the attention of MTV, through which Judge produced his early signature series, *Beavis and Butthead* (see below). This series and the following one gained Judge a foothold in the film business, both as an animation producer and a live-action film director, with such films as *Office Space* and *Idiocracy* to his credit.

For his first prime-time network project, Judge developed a series that would focus on everyday life in the kind of Southwestern community where he had grown up. He teamed with former *Simpsons* writer/producer Greg Daniels to develop it, with Daniels managing to file down the unsavory aspects of Judge's MTV programs, though Judge's neorealist drawing style and approach to subject matter largely remained intact. In spite of the haphazardly manner in which it was conceived (Judge, much like Matt Groening before him, waited until the last minute to give his lead character a proper name[20]), the program, which was dubbed *King of the Hill*, soon developed a strong following in the ratings. Its low-key, slow-burn approach was, however, a high contrast to the manic, high-energy *Simpsons*, which it followed on Sunday nights for most of its run.

Like Springfield before it, Arlen, Texas, the program's setting, is a typical example of an American "tank town"[21] where, it might be assumed, "nothing" goes on. Yet this was not the case. Judge, Daniels and their writing team managed to unearth a large cache of subject matter, humorous and otherwise, to fuel their setting and characters, and to present it in the fashion of such established Southwestern tale spinners as Mark Twain, O. Henry and William Faulkner. In confronting the issues specifically relating to small-town America during the time of its run, the series was particularly bold and effective, its realistic graphics and acting adding weight to the messages presented in this regard.

Again, the direction of the series is shaped by its lead character. His name is Hank Hill (Judge), and he is as simple and direct as the cadences of his name suggest. Hank is the mirror image of Homer Simpson, doggedly devoted to his successful career as a propane salesman while, at the same time, presenting the proper patriarchal image for his wife and son. An arch-conservative, and a self-identified Republican and Dallas Cowboys fan, Hank is thin-skinned despite his outwardly stoic manner, and easily offended by the increasingly liberal-minded world around him. Those who offend him are often threatened with having their asses kicked, but this talk is essentially for show, to blow off steam and to cut off discussion when he does not want to go somewhere. So long as he is allowed to do his job, cut his lawn, and drink beer with his friends in the back alley of his house in peace, he is relatively harmless.

Hank is sensibly paired with a wife who knows exactly how to keep him in line. Peggy (Kathy Najimy) resembles her husband in temperament, not showing indignation on a topic unless provoked. An award-winning substitute teacher when the series begins, and later successful at other ventures, Peggy is "a sharp-tongued, no-nonsense woman, smarter than anyone else in her family and unafraid to say so."[22] If Hank is, as the title implies, the "king" of the house, Peggy is the "queen," but she tends to take her "royal" imperatives more seriously than he. Both of them, however, share an unshakeable stubbornness in their conviction that they are "right" about the correct way to deal with each episode's main problem, which is the major source of tension in their otherwise successful marriage.

One major bone of contention between them is the behavior of their son. Bobby (Pamela Segall Adlon) is "a corpulent, self-absorbed, over-sensitive underachiever."[23] He is not the boy Hank wanted him to be, prompting Hill Sr. to exclaim often that he "ain't right," mainly because Bobby aspires to be a professional comedian. Hank's efforts to convert his son into a "real man" always meet with failure, and Peggy's continued indulgence and protection of her only child does not help matters any.

To focus exclusively on the main characters will eventually drain away viewer interest, so a successful series must also have an interesting group of supporting characters.

The major supporting characters are Hank's aforementioned drinking buddies, Dale Gribble (Johnny Hardwick), Bill Dauterive (Stephen Root), and Boomhauer (Judge). Each of these men brings his own particular comic and dramatic hang-ups to the table. Dale, who wears sunglasses and an ever-present baseball cap to hide both his identity and his extensive baldness, works as an exterminator, but devotes more of his time to being a freelance conspiracy theorist. His bizarre theories and activities related to this provide a great deal of the program's comedy. Bill, on the other hand, contributes *gravitas* to the scenarios. He is the most Faulknerian character in television animation history. While going about his business as a barber for the U.S. Army, he is an immensely emotionally scarred and troubled man, deeply obsessed with his past, including the wife who abandoned him. His inability to find the social security of his friends, despite many attempts, further damages his already-thin emotional veneer. Boomhauer, in contrast, is mostly a minor player in the stories. A self-styled ladies' man with a seemingly effortless approach to attracting women, he speaks in a rapid-fire, Southern-accented cadence that only the other characters in the program can understand and interpret.

Other supporting characters in the series are cut from the same dramatic-comic cloth. Rather than artificially sweetening the conflicts between these characters and Hank, however, the producers wisely milk them for all the drama they can. This is particularly apparent with two important recurring characters, each of whom have shaped Hank's Oedipal feelings about his manhood. One of them is his father, Cotton (Toby Huss). A distinguished World War II veteran (he claims to have served in both the European and Japanese theaters, though only the latter is confirmed by the program's history), Cotton is white-haired, beady-eyed, and diminutive, the consequence of having his shinbones blown off during a battle. He is an old-school patriarchal figure, used to having his own way all the time, which causes conflict with his son and daughter-in-law. In the relationship between Cotton and Hank, we can see the roots of Hank's insecurities about Bobby, for Cotton likewise thinks that his son is not nearly the "man" he could have been. This point is made clear toward the end of the series, when Cotton marries the nurse he befriended while in the hospital and they have a child together. The boy is named "Good" Hank, in contrast to Cotton's grown son, who becomes known to his father as "Bad" Hank.

The other "father" in Hank's life has a similarly complex relationship with him. Buck Strickland (Root) is the founder and owner of the propane company that Hank has spent most of his adult life working for, and of which he is currently the assistant manager. Buck is a hard-drinking, womanizing son of the Texas soil, and prone to embarrassing himself and his company at inopportune times, at which point Hank is forced to play the diplomat and smooth things over with aggravated actual or would-be customers. Although Hank has made it clear in the past to his boss the potentially damaging aspects of this behavior, and Buck has made at least token attempts to reform himself, it has proven to be a vicious circle. It is chiefly the fact that Hank feels an enormous sense of loyalty to Buck for employing him when no one else would, as well as the fact that, at the core, they share similar attitudes toward life and work, that keeps Hank working with the Strickland company as long as he has. This loyalty is rewarded at the end of the series' run, when both men are inducted into the Texas Propane Sellers' "Hall of Flame."

As with *The Simpsons*, a number of "guest voices" passed through the series over its run, but the manner in which the two shows used their performers says as much about the differences between them as it does the similarities. Whereas many *Simpsons* guests simply played themselves, in a calculated attempt to grab attention and ratings, the majority of *King of the Hill*'s guests simply played characters who were as enmeshed in the program as were the regulars—one might not have even realized their involvement in the series unless you saw their names in the closing credits. The one exception to this rule was an unlikely one— jazz musician Chuck Mangione, who was a semi-regular during the early years, and used his presence to jokingly promote himself. ("Take it from me, Chuck Mangione. Unplugging the iron *feels so good...*")

In all aspects, *King of the Hill*, like *The Simpsons*, was certainly not your average, run-of-the-mill animated series, which was FOX's point in putting it on the air in the first place. What was noticeable about it, however, was not what was present in the narratives but what was absent. There was no fantastical element about the series at all, save for an occasional "dream" sequence. There was no relentless clowning and mugging for the camera, as is now commonplace in animated series; rather, the characters were realistically depicted in their thoughts and behavior, and reacted and behaved entirely within the confines of the situations in which they were placed. The stories were anchored on realistic places, people and activities, with a firm, grounded sense of place and time. Whereas most television animation series and characters smack of fantasy and artificially enhanced views of life, time and space, there was not a single narrative or character featured on this program that could not conceivably occur or exist in real life. With this series, which won two Emmy Awards during its run, Mike Judge transcended the prejudice directed toward his earlier work to create the only successful neo-realist program in the history of television animation. He did for rural Texas nearly the same thing that Vittorio De Sica and Roberto Rossellini had done for postwar Italy in the 1940s: he translated a complicated place and situation into purely human terms to which viewers could easily empathize and sympathize.

FOX, however, chose not to continue the realist route, as Judge did in his less successful animated sitcom, *The Goode Family*, produced for ABC after the demise of the earlier project.

◆ ◆ ◆

It was clear when the first episode of *Futurama* debuted, in March of 1999, that there were both similarities and differences with Matt Groening's earlier work. While he sold the series to the network by essentially saying it would replicate his prior series (over which he had lost creative control) in the future,[24] it proved to be that and more. A product of both heavy background research and a collaboration with *Simpsons* veteran David Cohen, *Futurama* resembled its parent series in comic tone and manner, but looked completely different. Rather than the stylized look of *The Simpsons*, which caused all the Caucasian characters to look like they were suffering from jaundice, the series felt and looked like the science fiction parody it was, thanks to handsome digital animation from Korea's Rough Draft Studios. However, it did not last, chiefly because of increasingly heated conflict between Groening and network management, which was not as supportive and open-minded toward him in 1999 as it had been in 1990.[25]

Behind the scenes conflict aside, *Futurama* was exceptionally well produced, and was an excellent addition to Groening's already-vast creative legacy. Though FOX buried it for the most part in out-of-the-way slots where it was prone to pre-emption, especially during football season, it still was able to develop a devoted following. The fact that it repeatedly cleaned up at the Emmys, outpacing Groening's older project, could only have increased the tension between network and producer, who saw each other's position as inflexible and insulting. This, no doubt, contributed to the program's removal from the network schedule in 2003.

Philip J. Fry (Billy West), Groening's protagonist, was a typical 20th-century slacker who made his living delivering pizzas. Accidentally, while visiting a cryogenics lab, he becomes frozen for a thousand years, during which the world, and his native New York, changes. When he awakens, he is at first a square peg in a round hole, but eventually settles into an advanced version of his old job for the Planet Express company. His principal companion at work is Leela (Katey Sagal), a purple-haired, Cyclopean female alien; very typically, she is more intelligent and competent than any of the male characters in the series. Likewise, in typical romantic comedy fashion, she is initially hostile, but then gradually warms toward him. The resident troublemaker is the amoral Bender (John DiMaggio), a finagling robot who is perpetually drunk (because he needs alcohol for fuel). His dirty deeds are a principal source of many stories, and contrast him with his (slightly) more moral colleagues. Each of them is employed by the spaceship company's owner, Professor Farnsworth (West), who is actually Fry's great-nephew.

Just as *The Simpsons* gleefully dislocated the clichés of the sitcom, *Futurama* cut like a buzz saw through the even greater level of clichés associated with both literary and mass-media science fiction. It particularly redressed one over-utilized metaphor: that it would be Earth (read: America) that would lead the rest of the universe into space colonization and effectively dominate it. This made sense during the Space Age, but not so much in the 1990s. No character embodied this more than Zapp Brannigan (Maurice La Marche), a dimwitted, blond Adonis of a spaceship captain, who typified the James T. Kirk–style of interplanetary social and sexual arrogance that was the major grist for the writers. Other science fiction clichés similarly bit the dust. In this universe, many 20th/21st-century celebrity figures were not dead, but still implausibly present, their still-live heads preserved like museum specimens in jars. Former U.S. president Richard Nixon, in this condition, was able to reclaim his old job, with the now-headless body of his old vice-president Spiro Agnew at his side.

Likewise, another beloved sci-fi warhorse—the company that owns everything and everybody in the world—was also given the gears. It was under the control of Mom (Tress MacNeille), an elderly woman who projected a grandmotherly image to the wider world, but was a Joan Crawford–styled tyrant behind closed doors. The principal targets of her anger, predictably, were her three sons, who looked and acted like the Three Stooges. Her character effectively served as a feminine mirror image of *The Simpsons*' Mr. Burns, who held similar economic and political leverage over Springfield. Like him, she served as an excellent vehicle to showcase the communication skills of her underrated voice actor, which could truly be said for all of the characters in this series vis-à-vis their vocal performers.

FOX's decision to cancel the program did not mean the end of the series. Bargaining based on the program's strong fan base, Groening's Curiosity Company, while still remaining tied to its old network's parent studio, was able to take the project over to Comedy Central in the mid–2000s, first in a set of new feature-length films featuring the characters, then in a new series of half-hour episodes, which earned yet more Emmys for the series. Clearly, by this time, it was evident that Groening had gained his artistic revenge, not simply on the wider world and media clichés he had so brazenly mocked, but also on the television network that had once embraced and then constrained him.

◆ ◆ ◆

A similarly spirited and invective-filled approach was evident in the third and final animated series that joined FOX's prime time lineup during the 1990s. While it, too, has had a complex and contradictory relationship with its network over the years, it would also, like its predecessors, establish itself over the course of its run as a unique and principled work of art.

Like Matt Groening and Mike Judge before him, Seth Macfarlane is not only a talented animator, but a figure gifted in other fields, including, as demonstrated recently, a Sinatra-styled vocal performer, a film director, and a nationally televised awards show host. Macfarlane is thus not merely a television animation producer; he is also one of the few true *auteurs* in the field. While seemingly undisciplined, his work, once one is able to see past the vulgar effrontery that dominates it, is capable of true and distinguished parody, satire, political statements and human drama, even if these come in unexpected ways. The surest sign of Macfarlane's control over his material, however, is the fact that he is the voice of nearly every lead male character on his programs. Yet the fact that he is a gifted and diversified actor prevents this aspect of his work from achieving sameness, and, in fact, enhances it.

Macfarlane was born on October 26, 1973, in Kent, Connecticut, and raised in the

Seth MacFarlane, executive producer and creator of *Family Guy*, is surrounded by characters from the show (shown from left): Chris, Lois, Stewie, Peter, Brian, and Meg (Fox/Photofest).

kind of small-town New England atmosphere he would later gleefully satirize in his work. He attended Kent School and the Rhode Island School of Design, where he produced his first animated short film, *The Life of Larry*, in 1995. The film introduced many of the essential elements of his later signature style. Upon his graduation, Macfarlane was hired as a writer/animator at Hanna-Barbera/Cartoon Network Studios (see below) during the time that many similarly single-minded individuals were converging artistically there. Working on such series as *Dexter's Laboratory*, *Cow and Chicken* and *Johnny Bravo* for Hanna-Barbera, *Ace Ventura* for Nelvana, and *Jungle Cubs* for Disney (see all below), Macfarlane was able to make his own singular mark on the material, in particular with the peculiar, confrontational style of comic and dramatic anthropomorphism that would come to be one of his trademarks.

Macfarlane gained a higher level of visibility for his work in 1996, when Cartoon Network aired *The Life of Larry* as part of its omnibus series *World Premiere Toons*, and its success led to a follow-up film. The title character, a dimwitted middle-aged man named Larry, and his associate, an intelligent dog named Steve, are clear prototypes for two of the prominent characters in his signature series. But nothing further might have become of the idea had FOX not approached Macfarlane about developing the characters further under their auspices. Originally set to air as a bumper feature on the network's comedy-variety series *Mad TV*, it was instead developed as a stand-alone series, which debuted following FOX's telecast of the Super Bowl in 1999.[26]

The title of the series was *Family Guy*.

This program has two distinct incarnations, the first being its initial broadcast period between 1999 and 2003, the second its resurrection between 2006 and the present. In the earlier version, the humor is rapid-fire in the style of *Laugh-In* or *Monty Python's Flying Circus*, employing the quick cuts between material and the confrontational style of approach to subject matter characteristic of both programs. Although there is the odd dramatic moment, the onus seems to be on fitting as many jokes as possible into the half-hour. The second version of the program is far different in approach and tone. It is paced more slowly, with the emphasis on character rather than jokes. In this version, we are allowed to see the characters in much more human terms than before, even including some of the melodramatic narrative approaches that would not have been acceptable in the original version. The change in tone is not reflective so much of higher artistic aims on Macfarlane's part (although it is more ambitious satirically than its predecessor); rather, it is a reflection both of changes in its creator's outlook—the ultimate driving force of the series—as well as changes in America during this period.

In both versions of the series, as well as Macfarlane's two later projects for the network (see Chapter 7 for both), there are essential linking elements at work. The first and most prominent is Macfarlane's approach to the central personality elements of his characters. None of these beings, quite frankly, can be mistaken as candidates for sainthood. They are extremely candid about every aspect of their lives, prone to physical and verbal violence of the worst kind, and to abusing their minds and bodies. The characters behave like members of the Friars Club, repeatedly mugging and clowning for the invisible audience, and trying to "top" each other repeatedly. As with *The Simpsons*, we see only the stoic, emotionally unfriendly side of the local terrain depicted, with the more "caring" aspects hidden away. More obviously, Macfarlane includes a whole host of social deviants, including an obvious sex addict and an unrepentant pedophile among his supporting cast, and presents them in such a way that the audience is implicitly and unsympathetically told to "deal with it." This absolute brazenness in comic tone and approach mark Macfarlane more directly as an heir to Jay Ward and Bob Clampett than William Hanna and Joseph Barbera, though even Ward and Clampett would have drawn the line at what some of Macfarlane's characters have done or said.

This leads into another defining aspect of Macfarlane's approach: the spasmodic shifts in tone, attitude and approach even within the context of individual episodes. At one moment, things can get extremely down and dirty, with blood and vomit used whenever and wherever needed to prove a point. Other than perhaps the creators of *South Park* (see below), Macfarlane is the most Rabelaisian television animator ever to produce content. Like Clampett, he has a "hang the consequences" approach, meaning that he simply does not care if the audience is offended by his attitude so long as things work for him and the network. Naturally, he has been excoriated in the press for doing this. Yet he is also capable of doing extremely effective dead-on parody similar to Mel Brooks, in such a refined way that it belies the frat-house nature of his usual humor and reflects a serious student of film, television and other media. If he decides to do a parody of the *Star Wars* movies, for example, it actually *looks and feels* like the *Star Wars* movies, with only the presence of his characters in the iconic roles and his iconoclastic humor ensuring its recognition as his own work.

Macfarlane's vulgarity has offended many people, and prevented him from being taken seriously. However, others have supported him to such an extent that it seems to vindicate him. This utterly polarizing behavior regarding his actual and potential audience, more than anything his characters actually do or say, makes Macfarlane one of television animation's toughest nuts to crack.

◆ ◆ ◆

Let us consider, briefly, the main characters in *Family Guy*, because they serve as the central vehicles for the show's manic energy, and, even more directly than in *The Simpsons*, the mouthpieces for their creator's view of the world.

Peter Griffin (Macfarlane), the father, is another classic example of the "man-child" who has been burdened with responsibilities beyond his mental capabilities and responds to them by retreating into irresponsible and childish behavior. His Boston-Irish accent and working-class demeanor mark him as a "regional" character, like *King of the Hill*'s Texans, but that is as close as the series gets to depicting life in any "realistic" way. As Hal Erickson observes, his "efforts to be a good husband [are] mitigated by his sloth, insensitivity [which borders on physical and mental cruelty at times], and addiction to creature comforts."[27] That he is capable of the odd bit of mental lucidity, humanitarianism or sympathy is chiefly because of the inconsistent nature of the program in terms of plot and character development. This was particularly the case during the program's early years, but, even in the later version of the series, an understanding of who Peter and the other characters truly are is sacrificed repeatedly in order to keep the laughs coming. The tendency of Macfarlane and the writers to abandon traditional plotting and characterization at a moment's notice is most evident in the regular shifts in Peter's character and behavior, which are not unlike Homer Simpson's at times. Peter, however, is, unlike Homer, entirely aware that he is a fictional character, which manifests itself in his comic mugging and eye-rolling directed at the camera, the odd line uttered directly at the viewers, and the blasé manner in which he repeatedly dismisses the consequences of his often highly destructive behavior in the episode narratives. These behaviors tend to reinforce Macfarlane's intended sub-text: that his program is simply a mere "cartoon," and should not be judged as a higher form of art, however it might merit this consideration.

As expected, Peter's wife is his mental opposite, and the only person capable of seeing who the real person behind his flamboyant megalomania actually is. In this case, Lois (Alex Borstein) is not simply a mental mirror image but one in many other ways as well—attractive where he is homely, rail-thin where he is stout, Protestant where he is Catholic, and from an affluent background (although one would never know it from her Brooklyn-styled accent) as opposed to his sturdy working-class roots. Even more than her husband, Lois can be cavalierly manipulated by the writers for the sake of a joke, with stunningly contradictory results. One minute, she is lecturing "Peetah," fairly firmly and competently, about the stupidity and ill-conceived thoughtlessness behind whatever he has done or plans to do this week. The next one, she is telling incredibly bawdy tales of her past lives, often under the influence of liquor, tobacco or harder drugs. As a consequence, it is impossible, even for a regular viewer of the series, to determine exactly what her true identity and attitude toward life actually is, because the manner in which the series was and is still produced does not seem to allow for anything resembling actual consistency in character growth and development—which is the closest thing Macfarlane really has to an artistic Achilles heel.

The wild card element of the series, as noted by M. Keith Booker, comes in the form of the two most prominent members of the supporting cast.[28] Stewie (Macfarlane), Peter and Lois's youngest child, is, depending again on the whims of the writers, a megalomaniacal genius bent on world domination (though his more homicidal tendencies, including his Freudian obsession with killing Lois, from the earlier years, have now largely been curbed) or an effete sophisticate in the manner of Rex Harrison, on whom his voice is clearly patterned. Stewie represents the more *outre* aspects of Macfarlane's humor. He is given license to act and think more bluntly and violently than any other character in the series, and the level of "comedy" that these acts and sayings take on is increased strictly because of whence they came. In the earliest episodes, when his megalomania was at its height, these were played almost strictly for shock value, but, more recently, his character has grown mentally and emotionally and become more diversified and active in the storylines. Either way, his being a nursery-school–aged boy behaving like a full grown "man" is the most obviously and bluntly realistic aspect of the series, which adds a heavy and reflexive irony to it.

The other major supporting character is cut along the same lines, even though he represents the closest thing the show—and Macfarlane's entire *oeuvre*, for that matter—has to an actual "voice of reason." Brian (Macfarlane, using his normal speaking voice), the family dog, is, ironically, the "most normal and best adjusted member of the household."[29] That does not mean, however, that he does not have his own problems. A Lisa Simpson–styled liberal democrat (emphasis on the small l and d), Brian is repeatedly incensed by the injustices of American society (and not simply the ones perpetrated upon his "race"), and infuriated by the *laisse-faire* attitude of the other characters toward them. Yet Brian, unlike Lisa, is far more likely to be hoisted on his own petard when he actually tries to do something about them, which repeatedly and rapidly erodes his self-confidence, and further causes him to join Peter in solace over alcohol—the value of which being one of the few things they truly agree upon. Brian's persecution by the society he lives in, and the insults and humiliations he has to endure as a member of a "minority" group, add a further political edge to his character. Though a published author, he suffers from a lack of sales; when unsold copies of his book are delivered to the Griffin house, they number in the thousands. Likewise, he has dealt with the fiascoes of numerous disastrous love affairs. His strongest relationship, oddly enough, is with Stewie; several of the most enjoyable episodes have depicted them effectively as comic globe-trotting adventurers, à la Bing Crosby and Bob Hope in their popular Road pictures.

Stewie and Brian's prominence in the narratives does much to marginalize the presence of Peter and Lois's two older children in the stories, whereas if the show were live-action they would be more prominently the focus. Meg (Lacey Chabert first, Mila Kunis later), the bespectacled, high-school–aged daughter, is, in many ways, the family's resident whipping post, the target of many physical and verbal attacks by the other characters due to what they and the writers (though not necessarily the audience) perceive as her innate stupidity and homeliness. (She was, however, spectacularly able to effectively turn the tables on the other characters in one episode, when she excoriated them in terms similar to the ones I have used to describe them above.) Junior-high–aged Chris (Seth Green), on the other hand, is a dim-witted cretin who, like his father, embodies much of the worst behind Macfarlane's low-brow geared humor. He is so stupid, in fact, that he fails to notice the blatant flirting by the above-noted pedophilic character with him as such.

Like *The Simpsons*, *Family Guy* has a rich bounty of supporting characters, and to describe them all in full detail is simply beyond the mandate of this book. But, as you can expect, each of them is perverted in body, mind or spirit in the way we have now come to expect from Macfarlane. From Glen Quagmire (Macfarlane), the aforementioned sex addict, to Joe Swanson (Patrick Warburton), the surprisingly competent paraplegic policeman, to local mayor Adam West (played by the former Batman portrayer of the same name[30]), each of these characters supplements and sometimes exceeds the Griffins in terms of adding to the absurd/ribald quality of Macfarlane's comedy, and each, like them, is capable of adding dramatically to the program's storylines in unexpected ways. Once again, however, character development and growth can always be easily chucked if a good joke takes precedence.

The one consistent element in Macfarlane's storytelling style is, quite plainly, never to expect any sort of "conventional" storytelling approach in any way, because he simply doesn't "do" that. *Family Guy* defines these attributes directly and plainly, and his later animated projects, despite their own individual merits as comedy and satire, would essentially grow on these benchmarks.

Nickelodeon

This now-iconic brand began its existence humbly, as "Nick Flicks," a local television program airing out of Columbus, Ohio, in 1977. Two years later, it expanded into a full-length daytime programming service via the Warner Amex cable distribution company where MTV would later originate in 1981. Originally a non-commercial project, it later reversed this policy through changes in management, which led to its current existence as an outpost of the Viacom media empire. In the summer of 1985, it expanded into the evening hours with "Nick at Nite," a package of classic TV reruns designed to attract nostalgic adults rather than children. By 1989, it was available in more than half of the measured TV households in the United States.

Nickelodeon has built its success on providing what can be described as a kid-friendly environment, with programming that largely evades the realities of life in favor of fine-tuned escapism.[31] Television animation has, naturally, played a major role in this strategy, although the company did not begin to become involved in producing its own in-house series until the 1990s. However, once they began doing so, they never stopped. Nickelodeon's animated series are now one of its trademarks, and are unique, due to the fact that they have always fully maintained the artistic desires and sentiments of their creators, even when they clash with the company's engineered mandate. Along with its longtime rival, Cartoon Network (see below), Nickelodeon has kept the torch burning, with great success, for both traditionally oriented program strategies and more ambitious rule-breaking projects, in television animation when other programmers have largely abandoned it, creating an impressive and staggeringly diverse body of work in the process.

Because the company's product is so heavily the result of the intentions of their producers, they can only really be discussed on a per-show basis, and that is what I will do here.

REN AND STIMPY

The first Nickelodeon-underwritten series was an important and visceral test case for what the network was willing to accept in terms of content and authorial control, and this would come to set the standards for future network projects. The network's experience with the production of this series would define the limits of the creative latitude it would give its producers.

John Kricfalusi, the series creator, is a Canadian, born in Chicoutimi, Quebec, in 1955. Drawing was a passion for him, as it was for most of the artists who entered the field of animation, and from an early age he was both writing stories about and drawing pictures of the Hanna-Barbera and Warner Bros. characters he admired. (The influence of these cartoons is very easily felt in his own work.) He studied animation at Oakville, Ontario–based Sheridan College, where he came under the thrall of Bob Clampett, whose idiosyncratic gag writing and narrative patterns Kricfalusi soon would come to emulate. Other influences included

Mad magazine founder Harvey Kurtzman, Chuck Jones, Jack Kirby, and Hanna-Barbera character designer Ed Benedict.

In 1980, Kricfalusi began working as an animator at Filmation, where he was baptized by fire in the practices of modern television animation production, which he quickly came to resent. He then moved to Hanna-Barbera, where he supervised production in Taiwan for a brace of episodes of the revival of *The Jetsons*, making his directorial debut with the episode "Hi-Tech Wreck." When he returned to the United States, he was hired by the equally idiosyncratic Ralph Bakshi (see chapters 3 and 5), who employed him as an animation director. In this capacity, Kricfalusi oversaw the ill-fated *Mighty Mouse: The New Adventures* (see Chapter 5) while directing eight installments himself. Later, Kricfalusi would employ Bakshi as a voice actor on his projects.[32]

After working on the *Tattertown* special for Bakshi and the short-lived *Beany and Cecil* revival for DIC (see Chapter 5 for both), Kricfalusi struck out on his own with a vengeance. He established his own company, Spumco (named, depending on the source, for a sardine can, an animator named Raymond Spum or the Danish word for "quality"), and began shopping his newest idea around. When all of the broadcast networks vetoed the idea, he went to Nickelodeon. After an energetic pitch session and a decision to allow Kricfalusi to produce the series along the lines of old-fashioned cartoons, with no written scripts and orchestral rather than synthetic music,[33] the series went into production, debuting on the network in 1991.

It was almost immediately apparent to the network, however, that Kricfalusi had simply bitten off more than he could chew, artistically and financially.

The central characters of the series were Ren (Kricfalusi first, Bob Camp and Billy West later), an anemic but sadistic Chihuahua with a Peter Lorre–styled voice, and Stimpy (West, imitating the vocal inflections of Three Stooges' member Larry Fine), a dimwitted cat. Both characters shared an unhealthy obsession with their bodily functions, which had an unpleasant habit of driving the stories. While theoretically based on the adventure and job-hunting formulas of earlier cartoon series, it was nothing at all like them, simply because of Kricfalusi's own bizarre obsessions and peccadillos. Though it looked simplistic, the budgets soon escalated to a shocking $400,000 per episode, and that might have spelled the end—had it not been for the fact that the series developed a strong following among students on college campuses, turning it into a ratings hit, with merchandising spinoffs proliferating.

This led to an increased level of tension in the relationship between Kricfalusi and Nickelodeon. Although he received a percentage of the merchandise sales related to his characters, he had not authorized these projects; the network had. Furthermore, the network dug in its heels when it felt that Kricfalusi was becoming too creatively far out, demanding cuts to offensive material prior to broadcasts. Kricfalusi might have averted trouble had he not developed a reputation as both "the Slowest Drawer on the West Coast,"[34] unable to produce material to fit the deadlines required of him as a television animation producer, and as a man forever surrounding himself with "yes men [who thought he was] a genius."[35]

The end result was inevitable. Nickelodeon exerted its prerogative as the property's legal owner and fired Kricfalusi, forcing his lieutenant Bob Camp to take over, in the face of resentment from "John K.'s" supporters. The series production moved far more quickly under the later regime, and overall, managed to retain the flavor of the original series without repeating Kricfalusi's indulgences to the same degree. Obviously, considering the series ultimately ran for seven years, the issues the network had with the series were purely with its creator, not with his characters. The network—and other animators, as well—learned from this experience: the network would never again allow a series creator to intimidate them as Kricfalusi had, while other animators learned that Nickelodeon would respond strongly if they tried to push the limits of what was required of them, and most of them would come to behave accordingly.

After withdrawing from television for a number of years, Kricfalusi returned briefly to television in 2001 with *The Ripping Friends*, a superhero spoof that continued the ribald scatology of his earlier project. Then, in 2003, he returned again to his signature series with *The Ren and Stimpy Adult Party Cartoon*, in the process also resuming the vocal chores for Ren. For acolytes of Kricfalusi who disliked the milder version of the show produced without him, it must have been joyous. For others who had trouble with his approach, including his still needlessly complex production methods, it was simply déjà vu all over again, and this version of the program quickly and quietly disappeared.

Doug

While *Ren and Stimpy* typified the free-wheeling edge of Nickelodeon's comedy approach, and would be followed by other series in the same vein, the two other studio projects of 1991 were much more in line with the simpler, kid-friendly intentions of the network. In far quieter ways than Kricfalusi's series, they would come to define television animation's treatment of their lead characters over the next two decades.

Born in Virginia in 1953, Jim Jinkins worked in advertising before developing Doug, the character that would become the star of the property he would bring to Nickelodeon in 1990. He had first developed him as the lead character of a children's book, "Doug Got a New Pair of Shoes," which went unpublished. However, Nickelodeon executive Vanessa Coffey was impressed enough with the project that she wanted Jinkins to produce an animated series based on it. This, in turn, led Jinkins to establish his own production company, Jumbo Pictures, to produce the project.[36]

The series, in the words of the usually hard-to-please Peggy Charren, was "nice, warm and funny," and pointedly, did not "talk down" to its audience in the worn-out fashion of the 1980s.[37] Our hero was the mild-mannered Doug Funnie (Billy West first, Thomas McHugh later), an 11-year-old *nebbish* whose fears and concerns, as well as his elaborate heroic fantasies, were the driving force of the program. Associates of Doug included his would-be girlfriend Patti Mayonnaise (Constance Shulman), his best friend Skeeter Valentine (Fred Newman) and bully-in-residence Roger Klotz (Billy West first, Chris Phillips later), along with Doug's scene-stealing dog, Porkchop. Jinkins, who had previously worked for the Children's Television Workshop, knew how to tell stories with subtlety and a universality that would attract a wide audience, and this stood *Doug* in good stead in comparison with its more frantic competition. The visual approach of the series, however, was more experimental, with many of the characters drawn with only one eyebrow as representative of their (limited) thought patterns, and colored in a variety of hues that were used to imply their individuality as people, in contrast to established cookie-cutter designs at other studios.[38] It soon became a popular asset to Nickelodeon's schedule.

Nickelodeon lost that asset in 1996, when Jinkins and his business partner David Campbell sold Jumbo Pictures to Disney. Under this arrangement, they would produce *PB&J Otter* and the animated series version of *101 Dalmatians* (see both below) for the new boss, as well as producing a revised version of *Doug*, which ran for several years on ABC. While some cosmetic changes were made to make the animation look more professional, and the storylines were at times heavily modified to meet network E/I requirements, Jinkins and company did not sacrifice their heartfelt storytelling style, which likely satisfied fans of the Nickelodeon version while still entertaining those encountering it for the first time. The combined *Doug* series ultimately lasted 166 episodes, and the separate versions continue to play on the cable outlets owned by their respective copyright holders. This is an extremely good testament for a series with modest origins, aims and achievements, which easily managed to achieve what so many animated series of its time have failed to do: entertain its target audience while offending no one in the process.

RUGRATS

The third of the trilogy of original "Nicktoons," *Rugrats* was the most commercially successful of the three, not only in its own original incarnation, but in several films and a sequel series as well. It served as both the trademark series and the launching pad of the remarkable Klasky-Csupo organization, which, producing content for Nickelodeon and other providers, became one of the most influential television animation producers of the 1990s and 2000s before financial and personal problems halted its growth.

Gabor Csupo, born in Hungary in 1952, spent the first part of his life as a music and art student before joining his native country's major film studio, Pannonia, in 1971. Four years later, after fleeing the Communist government in Hungary, he moved to Stockholm, Sweden, where he produced that country's first major animated feature film. In Stockholm, he first met Arlene Klasky, another Hungarian-born animator. Klasky had attended Chouinard Art School in Los Angeles, and then developed an impressive track record as a graphic designer. Csupo and Klasky became personal and professional partners, and, although their marriage ultimately ended in divorce in 1999, they have maintained a professional relationship.

In 1981, Klasky and Csupo moved to Los Angeles, where they established their eponymous firm, originally running it through their apartment. By 1983, they were able to establish themselves in a studio on Hollywood's Seward Street, and built up a successful business in graphic design and animation. This led to their entry into the television animation business, animating *The Simpsons* (see above) from the time of the earliest bumpers until 1992, when conflict with the program's creators and labor problems within the studio itself led 20th Century–Fox to replace them in that position.

By this time, Klasky and Csupo were eager to become producers on their own terms, and developed a concept for a series with animator Paul Germain, with whom they shared creator credit. *Rugrats*, based on a six-minute pilot film, was the result. Originally running from 1991 to 1997, the series also spawned a brace of specials, and three feature films based on the characters released in 1998, 2000, and 2003, becoming a franchise worth $1 billion. It led to further projects, not only for Nickelodeon (those are discussed below and in Chapter 7) but occasionally from other networks. The two most notable of these were *Duckman*, airing on the USA network between 1994 and 1997, based on the comic-book character created by Everett Peck and produced in association with veteran live-action writer/producers Jeff Reno and Ron Osborn; and *Santo Bugito*, a Latin-flavored anthropomorphic insect project airing on CBS during 1995–96.

Klasky and Csupo's business hit a professional snag in 2002, when, during negotiations with Viacom, Klasky demanded that the company receive a share of the profits of the program episodes they produced for Nickelodeon instead of taking the upfront upkeep payment then customary. A decision to contract for smaller jobs outside of the company added to the conflict, with the result being that Nickelodeon reduced its commission levels from the studio, and the studio, in turn, was forced to reduce its staff. The studio has never fully recovered from this action. In the interim, Gabor Csupo has developed a successful, parallel career as a live-action film director.[39]

◆ ◆ ◆

As the creators of the series would later remark, *Rugrats* was based on a remarkably simple but elastic premise: the world according to young children, specifically infants.[40] Using their own children and their childhood memories as models, they constructed characters and narratives that conformed to this worldview. Neither overtly hip nor pretentious, this program went about its business in a manner that was attractive without lapsing in and out of coyness, and adding the occasional dose of satire for flavor. The background and character designs—Klasky and Csupo's signature element—were far more influenced by European than American modes, giving the program a unique visual look to complement its unique concept. Klasky and Csupo also developed a creative gestation process for the series that was unique in the time-conscious world of television animation. No less than six drafts of a particular episode script would be written, which were further refined during the three months required for the animation of the episode, and then finally ironed out by the producers themselves.[41] This control extended to the animation, produced in Korea, through measures such as the then-novel "animatic" process of digitally encoding essential elements of the series.

The focus of the series, as clearly noted, was on its child protagonists, who could communicate verbally among themselves but largely remained mute when addressed by their parents and other adults. One-year-old, diaper-clad Tommy (E.G. Daily) was the nominal star; his infant colleagues included Chuckie (Christine Cavanaugh first, Nancy Cartwright later) and the twins Phil and Lil (both Kath Soucie). Life was made difficult for them, to say the least, by their older non-infant cousin, Angelica (Cheryl Chase), a tyrannical, blonde bully who fulfilled the traditional dramatic role of antagonist, and is likely the most memorable Klasky-Csupo character for precisely that reason. From this simple children-in-conflict premise, along with the issues related to the adults surrounding them, Klasky and Csupo mined humorous domestic gold. As co-creator Germain later put it, the series was "an intelligent show for intelligent kids," trying to deal with the issues faced by real children in the real world, without doing it in the "preachy" fashion of too many pro-social programs of the 1980s.[42] In this, it succeeded, and since this was all its creators and audience wanted of it, it was an exemplary success besides. It was also influential, in terms of initiating a new way of communicating with its intended audience, with the subtle, realistic depictions of child characters coming to be emulated by others. If only for this series, Klasky and Csupo deserve to be remembered as one of the most idiosyncratic production teams in the history of television animation.

ROCKO'S MODERN LIFE

Of the original group of television animation programs to emerge during the early 1990s at Nickelodeon, this series was arguably the funniest and most creatively accomplished of the group. This was because its creator was not only a tactical expert in the traditional field of cartoon belly-laugh comedy, but also an original-minded and effective satirist in a field whose humorous aims, admittedly, are rarely raised above the level of slapstick.

Joe Murray, born in 1961, grew up in southern California, and managed to survive the trauma of having a television set fall on his head when he was five years old. ("No harm done physically, but it may explain the slightly dislodged view my brain later had of the world," he later wrote.[43]) Art from an early age came to embody not simply a future career, but also a rebellious (if moderated) view of the world that would come to dominate his television animation. While still a teenager, his gift for creating visual caricatures led him into a wide variety of enterprises, including political cartoons for the *San Jose Sun* newspaper. From this, he was able to establish a small illustration business, but he retained an interest in animation and dabbled in it. In 1989, he was honored by the Academy of Motion Picture Arts and Sciences in their student animation program for his first animated film, *The Chore*. A second, more ambitiously produced short, *My Dog Zero*, brought him to the attention of Nickelodeon. Liking the tone the network was setting for its audience, Murray sent them the proposal for *Rocko's Modern Life*, partially based on some earlier, rejected comic-strip and animation ideas, and, in 1993, after some time had passed, was informed that Nickelodeon was accepting the project, in spite of the fact that Murray had no prior experience in producing television animation. Production was instead entrusted to Games Animation, a network-owned subsidiary set up to continue production of *Ren and Stimpy* after the firing of John Kricfalusi (see above).

Some detractors voiced the opinion that the show was a loose rip-off of that prior series, but I maintain, along with Hal Erickson, that this claim is baseless.[44] While Murray was inexperienced as a television animation producer, unlike Kricfalusi, he made up for it, first with a skilled approach to his art and, secondly, a refined sense of humor lacking in his predecessor. Though he was able to come up with Tex Avery/Looney Tunes–styled humor to "punch things up" every once in a while, Murray stressed character, dialogue and satire more than his contemporaries. His work was played with a deft combination of wacko and intelligent comedy that is not seen elsewhere in television animation; one has to go outside the field entirely, to such live-action comedy geniuses as Billy Wilder and Preston Sturges, for adequate comparison. For Murray, like Wilder and Sturges, was able to put his protagonists through multiple kinds of hell, but always rewarded whatever virtue they possessed by the end of the story.

The program, according to its creator, was designed as "a satirical view on everyday living ... and each show dealt with relatable life issues.... Every episode ... is based on a personal experience of mine, or one of the directors' or writers.'"[45] This, in many ways, was one of the secrets of Murray's success. No matter how absurd things got (and given the nature of the character and setting designs, they certainly *did* get absurd), it was always possible to understand and sympathize with the characters and their motivations within the context of the individual episodes. While many of his contemporaries abused the new freedoms given to them by luxuriating in vulgarity, Murray and his colleagues, whose later output would mark them as one of the most influential crews in television animation history, did not. Murray was interested, chiefly, in stories and characters, not cheap jokes and off-color gags, and his audience admired and respected him for that.

The structure of the program was pure, classic sitcom. Rocko (Carlos Alarazaqui), the title character, was a wallaby rarely out of his trademark Hawaiian shirt and brown loafers. Friendly and approachable unless pushed too far (as he often was), Rocko was a classic case of an immigrant trying to adjust to a new life in a new country that was often at times as alien to him as it was to the viewers themselves. In the classic model of Jack Benny, Bob Newhart and Jerry Seinfeld, he was not so much an instigator of action as he was a reactor to—

or often unwilling accomplice of—those around him. Most commonly, this consisted of his bovine pal Heffer (Tom Kenny, a great performance at the beginning of a great career), whose over-affectionate attitude toward life and destructive behavior masked the genuine affection he had for Rocko; and Filbert (series director Doug "Mr." Lawrence), a bespectacled, archly defensive terrapin cynic in the manner of *Seinfeld*'s George Costanza. Also playing roles in many of the stories were Rocko's immediate neighbor, Ed Bighead (the peerless Charlie Adler), a cane toad who appeared to be a reincarnation of that stern opponent of sitcom mischief, Gale Gordon; and his wife, Bev (also Adler), who sounded like a female version of Harvey Fierstein. It would be this group plus one that would carry the majority of the storylines and the hilarity that inevitably ensued from them. The "plus one" was a response to a network request for a "positive female role model." ("Are there any positive MALE role models [in animation]? ... [sic]" was Murray's initial response.[46]) From these discussions emerged the recurring character of Dr. Paula Hutchinson (Linda Waller), a feline medico whose area of specialization seemed to mysteriously change with each appearance. She became firmly anchored later in the series, when she and Filbert became engaged and then married. One prominent physical characteristic of the Doctor was the fact that she had a hook in place of one hand, a satiric Murray response to the demand that his "positive" female character have an appropriate metaphorical "hook" to her.

Murray's delightful universe utterly rewarded viewers, and, in spite of it having the longer-than-average running span of five years (1993–98), it was good to the last drop. With both this series and his later *Camp Laslo* (see Chapter 7), Murray assured himself a permanent place in the history of television animation, not simply because his own work was so highly crafted, but because he employed so many like-minded people in a spirited world of collaboration all its own. Though many people employed on this series, animators, directors, writers and actors alike, would go on to do other work in the television animation industry, they would often only rarely equal or better their work on this series.

Aaahh! Real Monsters!

A Klasky-Csupo product reputedly sold on the basis of a few on-the-fly drawings by Gabor Csupo,[47] this series centered around a school for monsters and its students and staff. Ickis (Charlie Adler), Oblina (Christine Cavanaugh) and Krumm (David Eccles) were the three principals, with the intimidating Gromble (Gregg Berger) as their teacher. The show, which featured the same European-derived artwork as other Klasky-Csupo products, lasted for 52 episodes between 1994 and 1997. During this time, the monsters, who were presented as being in the same age range as the show's target audience, dealt with the growing-up issues that were becoming a commonality at Nickelodeon, as well as learning the tricks of the "monster" trade. It was a pleasant diversion, but nothing exceptional.

Hey Arnold!

At the same time as some Nickelodeon producers were exploring the comedic and technological possibilities now open to them, another one, beginning in 1996, was redefining the manner in which it actually portrayed the members of the network's target audience. This series was unique due to its subtle form of humor, its quiet but approachable narrative style, and, most importantly, its multifaceted portraits of the child characters who were at its center, in a manner that managed to be sympathetic without being either preachy or moralistic in the process.

Series creator Craig Bartlett has stated quite clearly that this was a project intended to "reach into my own subconscious and create a film about my origins."[48] He had first made his mark as an animator producing clay animation (or "claymation") films for *Pee Wee's Playhouse*, the same manner in which the first films featuring the lead character of his signature series emerged. After working as a story editor on *Rugrats* for three years, Bartlett gained the opportunity to present a pitch to network executive Mary Harrington, who suggested the idea of a series revolving around Arnold. After deciding to produce the series as a cel product rather than clay, and ditching the original angle of Arnold being a Walter Mitty–styled daydreamer, the show as it came to be took shape. As Bartlett later recalled, it came to be "a sensitive and emotionally realistic show about the trauma of being a kid—about the highs and the bummers."[49] Few other television animators would so successfully orchestrate the conflicting emotions of childhood.

This became the focus of the series, along with a gritty urban ambience not truly seen in television animation since the glory days of *Fat Albert*. Arnold (Toran Caudell first, Philip Van Dyke and Spencer Klein later) was a unique specimen in design, since he possessed a head shaped like a football, anchored by his blond hair.[50] He lived with his grandparents (Dan Castalleneta and Tress MacNeille) in a boarding house whose tenants provided a second line of stories. Occasional queries about the fate of his parents were evaded by the older couple, though the narratives of the series suggested they had been globe-trotting explorers who had been killed. Forced by circumstance to rely on his own wits more than he would have liked, nine-year-old Arnold developed into an "old soul" who served as a leaning pole against which his peers at PS 118 could vent their feelings. Most prominent among these was the blonde, sour-faced, uni-browed Helga Pataki (Francesca Marie Smith), who alternated between tomboy-styled bullying of Arnold (such as her frequent use of the obvious epithet "football head" in his direction) and others, and a secret, spectacularly played but ultimately unrequited crush on Arnold—something that, perhaps, helped distance herself from her own troubled home life. Others in the group included Gerald Johansen (Jamil Smith), Arnold's African American, cylindrically headed best pal; the super-intelligent Phoebe Heyerdahl (Anndi McAfee), Helga's buddy; the supremely unlucky Eugene Horowitz (Christopher Castile first, Jared Lennon and Ben Diskin later); bully-in-residence Harold Berman (Justin Shenkarow); Sid (Sam Gifaldi); Stinky Peterson (Christopher Walberg); and rich girl Rhonda Wellington Lloyd (Olivia Hack).

As with Arnold and Helga, we as viewers were occasionally witness to moments that showed these characters as having to deal with problems for which there were no easy solutions, a prime example of Bartlett's *cinéma vérité* approach to television animation and how well and truly it paid off for him. Another was his decision to (as Lee Mendelson and Bill Melendez had done before in the *Peanuts* specials) use actual children to play the children in his series. This lent the spoken dialogue in the program a heavy level of *gravitas* and required even casual viewers to pay attention to it in order to truly understand the stories. The finest compliment to the series' skill and approach, however, came in 2002, when Nickelodeon chose to make the show and its characters the subject of a theatrical feature film.

If Seth Macfarlane was television animation's Rabelais, and Joe Murray its Billy Wilder, then Craig Bartlett was its equivalent to John Cassavetes, depicting his world and its people in a way that they truly were without resorting to the comic and dramatic embellishments other producers might have used. And *Hey Arnold!*, as a humorous and occasionally moving work of art, was all the better for it.

KABLAM!

The creation of veteran animators Will McRobb, Robert Mittenthal and Chris Vicardi, this program can be best characterized as an animated variety show, using a variety of disparate forms and techniques that were rarely showcased on television. The centerpiece of the project was "Action League Now!," a stereotypical action-oriented series conducted through puppets. This project ultimately took on a life of its own as a separate Nickelodeon series in 2003.

THE ANGRY BEAVERS

Created by Mitch Schauer and debuting in 1997, this bizarre exercise in sledgehammer slapstick comedy unexpectedly developed a cult following among adults akin to that behind *Ren and Stimpy*—not surprising considering that it was, in many ways, cut from the same antagonistic, vulgar cloth. "Cartoons are typically soft, everything's happy," said Schauer. "I just went in the opposite direction."[51] That pretty much explains everything about the series itself.

The story, if it can be called that, concerned two adolescent beavers who were trying to make it on their own after their parents ejected them from their family lodge. Norbert (Nick Bakay) was bossy, hip and lazy, serving as the abusive Bud Abbott to the dimwitted Lou Costello antics of his brother Daggett (Richard Horvitz). Others in the all-animal cast included Bing (Victor Wilson), Big Rabbit (Scott Weil), Barry the Bear (John Garry), Truckee (Mark Klastorin), and Treeflower (Cynthia Mann), the lone female.

CATDOG

This series, created by Peter Hannan and debuting in 1998, was based on a rather one-dimensional idea: a cat and a dog implausibly sharing the same body. Likewise derivative were the personalities of the leads: Cat (Jim Cummings) was sophisticated and cultured, while Dog (Tom Kenny) was an ignoramus. Also in the cast were Winslow Oddfellow (Carlos Alarazqui), a blue mouse who lived with CatDog; Cliff (Kenny), Lube (Alarazqui) and Shriek (Maria Bamford), a trio of 1950s–styled "greaser" canines; the finicky Rancid Rabbit (Billy West); and the ironically named Mr. Sunshine (West). What the show lacked in terms of creative originality in its characterization and plotting was balanced by its impressive artistic design, which would come to be the saving grace of many a future series in this period, from Nickelodeon and other providers.

OH YEAH CARTOONS!

This omnibus project was essentially Nickelodeon's answer to Cartoon Network's earlier *What a Cartoon!/World Premiere Toons* project (see below) and served the same purpose: a tryout vehicle for ideas that had the potential to be series. Not surprisingly, the same man who had engineered the earlier project served at the helm of this one as well. After he resigned as president of Hanna-Barbera/Cartoon Network Studios (see below), Fred Seibert established his own production company, Frederator, under the auspices of which this series and its spinoffs were produced.[52] Under Seibert's direction, a total of 99 short films were produced between 1998 and 2002, each of which bore the unique sensibilities of the people responsible

and Little Beeper were *supposed* to be, but this road was not ventured down too often. The two major "human" characters chiefly were designed to provide their animal co-stars with opposition at one end and annoyance on the other. Wealthy, obnoxious Montana Max (Danny Cooksey) fulfilled the former role with aplomb; Elmyra (Cree Summer) filled the latter role with open and straight-faced displays of exaggerated affection.

What truly set the series apart from its contemporaries was its creators' willingness and ability to engage in controversial and experimental storylines. Few other series of the time would have even thought of including a full-length parody of *Citizen Kane* in one episode, nor would they have executed it as cheerfully and successfully. Other episodes did the same with environmentalism, censorship (via an antagonist who was a thinly disguised Peggy Charren), the history of animation (the aforementioned "Fields of Honey"), and the manner in which the show itself was produced, complete with the characters interacting with caricatured versions of the studio staff! In the old tradition of Looney Tunes, even the Boss himself was not safe. Spielberg was depicted in several episodes wearing his trademark baseball cap, glasses and scraggly beard, giving Buster and Babs guidance in between playing video games (a real-life Spielberg passion). In similar fashion, real-life stars were repeatedly given the gears, as were Michael Eisner and Jeffrey Katzenberg, who were shown wearing Mouseketeer hats!

The quality of the product varied from show to show and sometimes within the individual segments; it was impossible, after all, to maintain consistently high levels of quality even on a series like this. But, when you visited Acme Acres on a good day, you were amply rewarded for your efforts. Originally airing in syndication from 1990 to 1992, it later aired on FOX from 1992 to 1995 and the nascent WB network (of which, more later) from 1995 to 1998. Altogether, it was well received, and set a standard to beat for all future studio productions, especially after becoming an Emmy magnet during its run.

◆ ◆ ◆

The inevitable question, however, soon came to pass. *What do we do next?*

"We all wanted to do something new" Ruegger later recalled, "but there was reticence to launch another comedy series without another 'marquee' name involved."[111] That is, a group of characters who could serve as the effective anchor for another project along the lines of *Tiny Toons*—disparate segments linked on very loose terms.

Inspired by his young children, Ruegger came up with a concept that he thought might work. Spielberg, however, was unimpressed, believing that the original concept of the characters as three young blue ducks had already been "done." Undeterred, Ruegger retooled the concept. A chance glance at the giant water tower, emblazoned with the company logo, overlooking the Warner Bros. studio, gave him the inspiration that he needed. Soon, the project, dubbed *Animaniacs*, had the "marquee" characters it needed as well.

Unlike its predecessor, *Animaniacs* was built around attracting the adult audience which *Tiny Toons* had managed to attract more by accident than design. As a consequence, this series was structured in a far more fast-paced and frenetic manner. While *Tiny Toons* allowed you a chance to reflect on what you saw when you saw it, the pace of *Animaniacs* was far too fast to allow for such reflection. As studio historians Jerry Beck and Will Friedwald have noted, "Seemingly every moment contains some kind of wisecrack, pun (both verbal and visual), or slapstick gag—sometimes simultaneously—all the while driving the loosest of stories."[112] In other words, if you liked to laugh loud, long, clear and often, this was definitely the show for you. Given the audience it attracted, a lot of people felt it was.

The series concept itself was quite simple, a contrast to the hyperbolic nature of the main-title sequence (a trademark element of this and all future Spielberg/MacCurdy/Ruegger comedy-oriented projects). It focused on the trials and tribulations of a new generation of Looney Tunes characters. They were characterized as being between the ages of seven and 14, the same as their intended target audience, as they learned the tricks of the "toon" trade at Acme Looniversity [sic] in between starring in their own short features. The project was fluidly flexible in length: one episode would be devoted to a variety of shorts, the next to a full-length story. Fortunately, the writers and animators were entirely up to the challenges they faced in this regard. The underlying separation of the characters from their older counterparts was particularly underscored by studio publicity that insisted that they were not "related"[108] and watching the program made it abundantly clear that these "toons" had their own distinctive personalities. They were, in fact, some of the most memorable creations of the decade.

Leading the charge in the main-title sequence, and in most of the storylines, were the two Bunnys, blue-furred and red-shirted Buster (Charlie Adler first, John Kassir later) and pink-furred and yellow-sweatered Babs (Tress MacNeille). They were, as they frequently insisted, *not* related, but they made an effective team in all other respects. This was in part due to the fact that they were a study in contrasts in terms of their personalities. Buster was an appealing mix of manic and mellow, and therefore a perfect choice for the role of directly interacting with the audience. He was a skilled, effective performer, but he knew when it was appropriate to be "on" and when to be "off." Babs, on the other hand, had extreme difficulty with this. A spirited, opinionated, slick ball of fire in the manner of many great female comedians of the past, she embodied the female trickster at her most dangerously unpredictable. As critic Kathleen McDonnell has noted, her appeal stemmed from the fact that she was "a good girl [who was] funny because she [allowed] herself to be bad."[109] Her manic, intimidating personality makes her an affront to traditional attitudes toward femininity, although it is totally in line with the traditionally aggressive Looney Tunes comedy philosophy. Moreover, as McDonnell further notes, she has absolutely no intention of assuming the subservient female role. "Babs is constantly getting into mischief.... She [is] not the least interested in being just a girlfriend, confined to secondary straight-man or love-interest roles.... She [is] Buster's wisecracking equal, his partner in mayhem. Her right to be bad, wild and funny [is] not in question."[110] Nor, for that matter, is her confident and assured acting ability, which allows her to effectively play anything and everything, from a sex goddess to a cheerleader to a superhero. She redressed, effectively, a decades-long imbalance against female characters in theatrical and television animation, especially in the Warner product, not only through her own actions but those she takes to help her fellow female 'toons. The epicenter of this came in the Emmy-winning episode "Fields of Honey," in which she single-handedly helps to resurrect the career of a long-neglected female 'toon. In her words, deeds and actions, Babs, like Lisa Simpson and The Powerpuff Girls, made it possible for a new generation of female cartoon characters to step forward, cut up and rule.

Other characters in the show were cut from the same cloth, although they tended to be a bit more derivative of the characters that inspired them in most cases. Plucky Duck (Joe Alaskey), for instance, clearly derived his egotistical, scheming personality from forebear Daffy. Hamton Pig (Don Messick, in one of his last great roles), on the other hand, was very different from Porky: for one thing, he was more outspoken, and he didn't stutter. This reflected the fact that the writing of the series was more curve-ball oriented than the standard sledgehammer-comedy style. It was quite clear, however, who characters like Calamity Coyote

the prestige and money; his affection and understanding of the genre and medium was real, and all of the television animation series bearing his name in the 1990s reflected this.

Thus, when *Tiny Toon Adventures* debuted in 1990 expectations were high.

Spielberg and his production lieutenants Kathleen Kennedy and Frank Marshall, for one thing, had wrangled from the Warner brass the astonishingly high production figure of $350,000 per episode—or about $100,000 *more* than Disney was then spending on its efforts.[101] But this was just the beginning. They then assembled a gifted group of writers and artists, mostly disenchanted veterans of other, more conservative studios, to create and develop the characters with relative *carte blanche*, and an equally talented and eclectic group of actors to portray them. The most important members of this group would be producer Tom Ruegger and production executive Jean MacCurdy, who would become the guiding hands behind all of the classic Warner products, Spielberg-derived and otherwise, during the 1990s.

As noted in the previous chapter, Ruegger, born in 1956, spent much of the 1980s toiling at Hanna-Barbera and Filmation, where he helped to bring touches of class to some of those studios' otherwise moribund productions. Under Spielberg and Warner's aegis, Ruegger was able to fully develop his talents as a writer, producer and songwriter. He was marvelously inventive in his own work, and he encouraged his staff (including writer Paul Dini and artist Bruce Timm, who both became studio lynchpins) to do much the same, with positive results. Ruegger, who won an astonishing 14 Emmys during his Warner tenure, left the studio in 2004 to form his own independent firm. The company's product has never been truly the same since. He was assisted by MacCurdy, another Hanna-Barbera veteran, whose open, supportive management style truly allowed Ruegger and company to present their material with minimal corporate interference. This has earned her praise from many television animators not accustomed to this style of governance. MacCurdy and Ruegger would share executive-producer credit on most of the studio's non–Spielberg product during this period. Spielberg, of course, took the title for himself on the projects in which he was directly involved.

With the staff firmly established in the former Lorimar Building in the San Fernando Valley,[102] it was time to begin production on their new series. And what series they were.

◆ ◆ ◆

The first series production was the aforementioned *Tiny Toon Adventures*, which debuted in syndication in the fall of 1990. It originated with a feature-film production pitch that Spielberg had brought to Warner's door two years earlier and which had lain dormant. MacCurdy, sensing its potential as a television property, convinced Spielberg and Warner to bring it to television instead. She then called on Ruegger to develop it. In a span of two weeks, Ruegger and his hand-picked team had a concept, characters and a "bible"[103] ready for the cameras.[104] Spielberg's only major intervention in the creative process was to assist in the character development and to have "last call" on the scripts and animation before they were filmed; otherwise, he left the staff to their own devices[105]—a good call on his part.

What emerged was a series, the first of several, that was very much able to stand on its own creative legs. Ruegger's insistence on using newly developed characters in the old mode rather than merely recycling the old characters paid enormous dividends for both engaging and attracting new audiences.[106] It was also, quite surprisingly, one of the first trials and proving grounds for the newly emerging realm of often sexually explicit "fan fiction" on the Internet, a testament to its loyal following.[107]

times was another factor in gaining the company's product visibility it might otherwise have failed to gain on its own terms, and also legitimizing the studio's work in the eyes of the cost-conscious Hollywood bureaucrats its work often mocked.

The 1990s were an exceptionally solid creative period at Warner, but the following decade would see the studio rocked by economic turbulence at its parent company. Mediocrity inevitably resulted, which made it quite clear who was truly responsible for the studio's classic 1990s work.

THE SPIELBERG/WARNER ALLIANCE

Unlike many of his peers, the presence of Steven Spielberg's very name in a project credit list is enough to guarantee even passing interest for that project in the media. His decision to provide economic and creative guidance to the nascent Warner product, by adding his name and presence to it, was a major factor in raising the acceptability level of television animation to new heights. Yet, for all the publicity that his involvement created, and all the personal input he provided, the success of the series that Amblin Entertainment would produce in collaboration with what would come to be known as Warner Bros. Television Animation (WBTA) had as much to do with the uniquely creative and diverse individuals which Spielberg gathered under his wing, and what they produced under his auspices, than anything the man himself could have provided on his own.

Spielberg was accustomed, from the beginning of his filmmaking days, to having authorial control on his projects and, on the rare occasions when he directly intervened, it was strictly for these reasons. These occasions were predictable if you knew something about Spielberg.

The facts and figures about Spielberg's life and career have been outlined in great detail elsewhere.[100] Suffice it to say, Spielberg was and is, from his early youth, a supporter of the art of animation. His veneration of the Looney Tunes canon, in particular, manifested itself through his including clips from them in his first major theatrical feature, *The Sugarland Express* (1974), as well as his career-defining smash hit *Close Encounters of the Third Kind* (1977). As his stature in the industry grew, moreover, so did his support for the medium of animation. By far, the most ambitious and successful of these ventures was the highly successful animated feature film *An American Tail*, released in 1986. Spielberg was hardly an impartial financier on this project. He played a major role in shaping the story, which mirrored the story of his Jewish ancestors on their journey to America, and went so far as to name the young rodent lead, Fievel, in honor of his grandfather. The success of this and subsequent projects ultimately led Spielberg to establish his own London-based animation studio, Amblimation. He also played a major role in producing and developing *Who Framed Roger Rabbit?*, an overtly affectionate cinematic valentine to the theatrical cartoons of the pre-television era, which won several Academy Awards in 1988. Nobody could accuse Spielberg of being in the animation business just for

Steven Spielberg in 2002 (Sci-Fi Channel/Photofest).

under the watchful eyes of the school's unsympathetic principal (Don Adams, an unusual but surprisingly effective choice for the part). Series creator Rose was determined to create "a positive and believable role model for girls mired in that awkward period between adolescence and the teen years," to "address feminist issues without overstressing them," and allow "young girls to express their inner-most feelings, rather than leave them bottled up inside."[99] In all of these respects, she succeeded, especially considering the majority of the series' fans were girls much like Pepper Ann herself. Rose's lessons were particularly inspiring to series writer Scott M. Gimple, who went on to explore similar pre-teen issues on more starkly dramatic terms in his later Disney series, *Fillmore* (see Chapter 7).

Creator-driven series tend to vary from project to project, depending on whether the titular "creator" has strong enough control over the project. This proved to be the main problem with *Nightmare Ned*, which aired only for a brief period of time on ABC in 1997. This series focused on the nightmare dreams of Ned Needlemeyer (Courtland Mead), who, by all appearances, seemed to be an intensely troubled young man. However, the project was marred by tension between the visions of its titular "creator," Walt Dohrn, later to join the creative team of *Spongebob Squarepants* (see above), and its producer-director, Hanna-Barbera veteran Donovan Cook. The failure of the project was such that Disney effectively disowned it, never reviving it on cable as it did other studio properties. Perhaps it was simply too dark a subject for Disney's traditionally optimistic creative mindset. That was something of which *PB&J Otter*, a kid-friendly, Jumbo Pictures–produced series airing on the Disney Channel in 1998, could not be accused. Set in the swampland world of Lake Hoohaw, it was more or less a Disneyfied version of Walt Kelly's *Pogo* comic strip, minus Kelly's satirical approach. The title trio (whose names stood, respectively, for Peanut, Baby Butter, and Jelly) engaged in their community and with their fellow citizens in a manner reminiscent of numerous "cute" character shows of the 1980s. While having the required education component, the series was, unlike its predecessors, entertaining without being nauseatingly moralizing in the process.

◆ ◆ ◆

From this point on, television animation at Disney would be almost entirely dependent of the strength of the ideas, characters and concepts that individual artists and producers brought to the company table. And, for the most part, during the late 1990s, and early 2000s, those producers would consistently deliver high-quality material.

Warner Bros.

Much as they had initially followed rather than led as a theatrical animation provider, Warner Bros. did not truly enter the television animation business until Disney had proven that the field was ripe for growth and experimentation. Yet, just as it had come to dominate Disney creatively in short theatrical animation by the 1940s, Warner came to overshadow Disney during the 1990s as well. Although Warner, like Disney, aggressively borrowed from its esteemed corporate heritage for much of its productions (including not only Looney Tunes, but also its corporate siblings, DC Comics, Hanna-Barbera and Turner-owned MGM cartoon properties), it had the advantage of having access to characters and concepts that were far less stodgy than Disney's, and that made their series more dynamic and attractive. An advantageous alliance with the most commercially successful film director of modern

in almost anthropological terms, the schoolyard culture of American children, in much the same way Iona and Peter Opie did for their British counterparts in *The Lore and Language of Schoolchildren*, in less academic and more dramatic terms. There was a great deal of humor there besides, particularly in the comparison of the noble deeds, behaviors and acts of the featured children to the heavily stereotyped, antagonistic and morally flawed nature of the adults looking after them.

Drawing on a wide variety of film clichés, particularly those of prison and World War II POW–themed movies and television series, to create the proper them-vs.-us feeling for the main series, Germain and Ansolabehere then proceeded to encode these attitudes into their characters themselves. Leading the kid contingent was T.J. Detweiler (Ross Malinger first, Andrew Lawrence later), a self-styled anti-authoritarian rebel in the well-worn model of Colonel Robert Hogan (Bob Crane) of *Hogan's Heroes* fame (and *his* likely role model, Sefton [William Holden] from the 1953 film *Stalag 17*). T.J.'s sentiments about the unfairness of the world of adults were echoed in some ways but modified in others by those of his pals. They were: Vince LaSalle (Rickey D'Shon Collins), the token African American, a smooth-talking athlete; Gretchen Grundler (Ashley Johnson), the homely brain; Mikey Blumberg (Jason Davis), who looked like a stupid oaf but was actually a skilled poet (an effective metaphor for this show's own disarming, unexpected creative approach); Ashley Spinelli (Pamela Segall), a tough tomboy; and Gus Griswald (Courtland Mead), an easily dominated army brat. They and all the other children were, during the context of recess, in thrall to "King" Bob (Toran Caudell), who ruled his "realm" with properly "regal" capriciousness. The adults who governed them during the contexts of their classes were little better. Peter Prickley (the perfectly cast Dabney Coleman), the principal, was an officious bureaucrat who, given his open disdain for his charges, was clearly in the wrong line of work. Muriel Finster (April Winchell), the recess supervisor, seemed to possess the spirit of every "mean" elderly teacher every child has ever encountered in their elementary school career. Fourth grade teacher Alordayne Grotke (Allyce Beasley), meanwhile, was an unquestionable "hippie" who unsubtly reinforced the anti-authoritarian tone of the series by not being able to conduct classes "without sweetly and offhandedly condemning Evil Industrialists, Evil Land Developers and Evil Everyone Who Doesn't Agree with Me [*sic*]."[96] The possibilities for satire in all the show's myriad contexts was endless, and, to their credit, Germain, Ansolabehere and their colleagues milked every storyline for all it was worth.

The series was an unqualified hit, and even managed to spawn a feature-film version, subtitled *School's Out*, in 2001. Altogether, it ran for six years, from 1997 to 2003, and managed to stay relevant and innovative for much of its run, in spite of the enforced "educational" element required by E/I regulations. Its success confirmed the rationality of continuing creator-driven production at Disney if it was to remain "relevant" to the children who remained its core followers.

Pepper Ann, which ran from 1997 to 2001, reflected the strengths of the new "off-site" production strategy. The creation of Sue Rose, who had invented the lead character in a comic strip for *YM Magazine* in the early 1990s,[97] it was the first of a number of series of the late 1990s and 2000s that would achingly explore the inner lives of their lead characters in highly exacting terms—a sub-genre that Hal Erickson has dubbed "pre-teen angst."[98] The title character (Kathleen Wilhoite), a 12-year-old student at Hazlenut Middle School, was, not being able to be part of the highly rigid "Cool" faction due to her independent, optimistic nature, went through her days associating with other friendly misfits like herself and trying, but failing, to gain the kind of "popularity" that would make her "Cool." This was done already, so they need not be repeated here. Suffice it to say, the project revolved around the title characters, living under the protection of the Dearly family, and threatened by the machinations of the malevolent Cruella De Vil (here played by April Winchell). However, the approach of the producers was decidedly different, and that proved to make all the difference for the series. As Hal Erickson notes, "The producers ... drew selectively from all previous ... adaptations [of the property] and added several of their own original grace notes."[95] The most "original" of those "grace notes" was Cadpig (a brilliantly sly, insinuating vocal performance by the perennially underrated Kath Soucie), based on a "runt" character in Dodie Smith's original novel on which the films were based. Tiny in size but massive in intellect and cunning, Cadpig was a ruthless scene stealer who effortlessly dominated the stories in which she was featured, and inspired both affection and awe in the audience. Soucie's marvelous way with words allowed multiple levels of meaning in even the most banal E/I–sanctioned dialogue the seemingly "innocent" and undeniably "cute," little "Dal" was forced to deliver. This skill helped to make Cadpig, with her free-spirited, New Age–derived manner, the Lisa Simpson–styled rose that grew out of what was otherwise a largely airless strip of creative concrete. The presence of such a liberal-minded character in such a conservative setting was a clear sign of how, increasingly, the Disney programming ethos was changing.

◆ ◆ ◆

Increasingly, Disney was biting the bullet on the strategy of deriving its television animation product solely from its feature film archives. Consequently, the remainder of the studio's television animation product was produced solely on creator-driven terms. The results were felicitous, and set in motion an entirely new area and production mindset for WDTA.

In addition to the Nickelodeon-imported *Doug* series (see above), the series that most boldly announced this change was *Recess*, which debuted on ABC in 1997. Both in terms of creative and technical orientation, the change was pronounced. From this point on, Disney would focus more on serving as an independent contractor and banker for independent productions à la Nickelodeon and Cartoon Network, with only rare excursions into mining its own past, although it stubbornly insisted on keeping its name in the "official" names of the programs. Nevertheless, the program concepts themselves would, from now on, reflect the individual mindsets of their inventive producers as opposed to traditional studio groupthink.

Recess was a prime example of this strategy at its most effective. Blazing a path that would be followed numerous times over the following years, the series was a product of a new vision linking up with the Magic Kingdom's animation staff, with the result being a more creatively innovative and technically sound product. In this case, the outsiders were Paul Germain and Joe Ansolabehere, both veterans of the Klasky-Csupo studio; Germain had, in fact, co-created that studio's signature hit, *Rugrats*, with the proprietors (see above). In a sense, Germain and Ansolabehere (both graduates of the UCLA film school), working with children's book illustrator Dave Shannon, simply applied the kid's-eye-view approach of the earlier series to an older demographic group.

As the title implied, the series focused on the twice-daily ritual of outdoor activity that occurs in nearly every elementary school in North America on a daily basis. Here, the outdoor activities of the kids of Third Street Elementary were allowed to be presented, in documentary realist fashion, as an effective metaphor for the follies of the outside world. And that was just in the main title sequence. The stories proper more radically and deeply explored,

ing cat and dimwitted dog (Jason Marsden and Frank Welker, respectively) who behaved like John Kricfalusi (see above) characters while still remaining Disney-standard friendly—an achievement in and of itself. The two other segments were also bizarrely conceived, but were just as poorly executed. Pith Possum (Jeff Bennett), was an egotistical, incompetent, anthropomorphic superhero, while Tex Tinstar (Bennett, using the same Elvis-derived accent he employed for *Johnny Bravo* (see above) tried and failed to make hay in the same sledgehammer process with the clichés of the Western.

AFTER ABC

Disney's takeover of ABC, as noted above, necessitated changes in the way the company did its television animation business. Now, WDTA was responsible not just for the Disney Afternoon (which gradually withered on the vine from this point on) and the odd Saturday morning program; it was now required to produce an entire network's Saturday-morning lineup! Such an unprecedented situation carried with it an enormous amount of inborn stress, and the more directly in-house product initially suffered from the strain. This burden was ultimately met by bringing independent contractors such as Jim Jinkins into the mix, and by gradually and more directly invoking the Nickelodeon/Cartoon Network model of creator-driven production, which had already proven itself via *Gargoyles*. It was not an easy transition by any means, but it would come to lead, in the 2000s, to a stunningly innovative era in production at WDTA.

The remainder of the 1990s, however, was chiefly devoted to maintaining the status quo, with one or two notable exceptions.

Product divided from this point into the series that continued to lap from the company's established creative stream, which was rapidly becoming a declining tributary, and those which chose to blaze their own paths under the studio's auspices. We will consider the former briefly before moving on to the trailblazers who would become the dominant influence at the studio by the 2000s.

The studio's feature-film and animation product, past and present, gave birth to a group of series which wore its prior existences so directly on its sleeves that most viewers could not take them seriously. Most need to be discussed only briefly. *The Lion King's Timon and Pumbaa* is self-explanatory to those familiar with the 1994 feature film. *Quack Pack* was another theatrical reboot, featuring Donald Duck as a television cameraman, Daisy Duck as a stereotypically egotistical TV reporter, and Huey, Dewey and Louie as "grown-up" teenagers. *Jungle Cubs* featured the main animal characters of the 1967 *Jungle Book* feature film in youthful fashion. *Hercules* was a similarly uninspired series version of the 1997 feature.

101 Dalmatians: The Series, which doubled in syndication and on ABC between 1997 and 1999, had the potential for being another corporate-minded "downer" in line with its predecessors, but it was not. This was due, in part, to the fact that the series was produced by Jumbo Pictures, not the main Disney TV animation unit, and the fact that the executive producers—Jim Jinkins and David Campbell, plus Hanna-Barbera and Disney veterans Tony Craig and Roberts "Bobs" Gannaway—were determined to do things *their* way, not the "Disney" way. Their efforts resulted in a series that, while not always able to transcend its corporate origins, was something the other studio-derived product of the period was not: genuinely entertaining.

Once again, if you are familiar with the original animated feature film (1961) or its live-action remake (1996), you probably know the characters and conflicts of the project

rather than a prequel. The one major change in the lineup was making Iago (Gilbert Gottfried), the quarrelsome parrot who had been villain Jaffar's henchman in the movie, one of the heroic characters, which no doubt had those familiar with the movie scratching their heads. Robin Williams, who had truly stolen the film as the chameleon-like Genie, was not involved in the series, although Dan Castalleneta did a serviceable job of replacing him in the role. Otherwise, it was the same adventure-oriented format as before, but the Arabian Nights–styled gimmickry that had worked so well in the movie did not transfer well to series TV, given the repetitive nature of the storylines.

Seemingly getting the message that the process of cannibalizing the parent company's products was not working anymore, WDTA next proceeded to do something truly and boldly original. *Gargoyles*, debuting in 1994 as part of the Disney Afternoon, was the kind of straightforward action-adventure program that had been the bread-and-butter of many syndicated animators in the 1980s, but it was drawn and written with the graphic handsomeness of one of the company's animated feature films, and that, as it turned out, made all the difference. Setting a precedent for many future studio projects, it was the product of an outsider—in this case, writer Greg Weisman—who brought a much-needed interjection of panache into a tired, run-down, assembly-line production system. Weisman's concept for the series was far more elaborate than anything WDTA had produced before, with art clearly created to match it. The central characters, led by the forebodingly mannered Goliath (Keith David), were a supernaturally gifted crew of heroic warriors who guarded the world from evil by night and assumed the rigidity of statues during the day. The Scottish castle where they resided was moved to New York City by the malevolent billionaire David Xanatos (Jonathan Frakes), who placed it on top of his base of operations. As a result, a thousand-year-old spell rendering them permanently in stone was broken, allowing them to become alive at night. They were then able to continue their old work again, with the aid of the sympathetic human police officer Elisa Maza (Salli Richardson). Their chief enemies included not only Xanatos (who later changed sides and became their ally), but also the villainous gargoyle Demona (Marina Sirtis), Goliath's vengeful ex-lover, who, contrary to the others, was human (under the alias Dominique Destine) during the day and turned to stone at night. The once-a-week show operated under a serialized format, which gave it the flavor of a supernaturally flavored soap opera, much to the delight of more discriminating viewers. Shakespeare and Faerie mythology were prominent influences on the show's story arcs, while the voice cast was dominated by veterans of the *Star Trek* universe (along with Frakes and Sirtis, Paul Winfield, Kate Mulgrew, Avery Brooks, LeVar Burton, Nichelle Nichols, Brent Spiner and Michael Dorn all lent their voices to the project). Given all of this, the final project had a satisfying dramatic element of *gravitas* absent in many TV animation projects of the 1990s. It ultimately lasted three years in syndication, and spawned a sequel series, *The Goliath Chronicles*, which aired during the 1996-97 season on ABC.

Even at Disney, however, old habits tended to die hard, and it would still be some time before the new direction for the studio's television animation that *Gargoyles* had suggested would be fully enacted upon. In the meantime, it was business as usual.

Nothing said that better than the last product of the company prior to the ABC takeover. *The Shnookums and Meat Funny Cartoon Show*, debuting in syndication in 1994, was a poorly executed exercise in full-blown slapstick comedy. The brainchild of the underrated Bill Kopp, who had been one of the major driving forces of Savage Steve Holland's equally underrated *Eek! The Cat* (see below), this series' three components paled in comparison to their creator's earlier, better work. The main attraction was the title duo, a schem-

chief by-product of this was the cleverly named *Raw Toonage*, an omnibus project that again aired on CBS, also during 1992–93. As studio historian Bill Cotter points out, the company went to great lengths to imply that this series would have "an edge, with promotional clips suggesting that viewers would be treated to something new and different from Disney."[94] That, as it turned out, was exactly what the problem was with the series; by Disney's conservative programming standards, it was *too* new and different. For that reason, the studio ended up ceasing production of it after 12 installments. Most of the episodes featured a host whose segments linked the rest of the show (e.g., Goofy talking about the Olympics, Scrooge McDuck demonstrating his "money bin" security system, and so on), à la Rod Serling in *Night Gallery* mode. The main segments were *He's Bonkers* and *Marsupilami*, both later airing as series on their own (see below for details), and *Totally Tasteless Video*, a series of short parodies, which were not nearly as "tasteless" (in the vulgar sense) as their name implied, although most were "tasteless" in the sense that they were unavoidably bland.

Hoping to salvage something from the *Raw Toonage* fiasco, Disney expanded the two major short features of the series into projects of their own. *Bonkers*, which first aired on the Disney Channel in 1993, was an outgrowth of the "Toontown" universe first developed by the studio with the feature film *Who Framed Roger Rabbit?*, produced in collaboration with Steven Spielberg (see below) in 1988. The series had, to its credit, a clever premise and better than average execution for a Disney show of this period. The premise was simple: After cartoon star Bonkers D. Bobcat (the ever-reliable Jim Cummings) lost his job, and inadvertently rescued Donald Duck from peril, he was given a full-time position in the Tinsletown Police Force (i.e., the LAPD) in the newly-created "Toon" Division. The satirical edge of this decision came through the fact that Police Chief Kanifky (Earl Boen) was eyeing the mayor's chair, and he believed putting Bonkers on the force would help him secure the "Toon" vote. Sergeant Lucky Piquel (Cummings again, more sober sounding this time), Bonkers's human detective partner, didn't think this was such a good idea, considering that he was more prone to being seriously injured during their assignments in a way the manic Bonkers was not. Nevertheless, they managed to be effective together. Aping the scattershot machine-gun approach of the Warner Bros. product of the period (see below), the show was successful in portraying the often-conflict-ridden relationship between human beings and "'Toons," but only up to a point. If another studio or creator of the time had managed to get their hands on this concept, it might have been an edgier and more successful project.

Marsupilami, the other *Raw Toonage*–derived show, was a bit different. Airing on CBS during 1993–94, it was an anthology series consisting of three cartoon shows that couldn't be any more disparate. The top-lining project was created by Andre Fraquin, a Belgian cartoonist whose work famously shared space in *Spirou* magazine with *Smurfs* creator Peyo (see Chapter 5). Marsupilami himself (voiced by Steve Mackall) was a cheetah who possessed an enormously long tail, which, in typical cartoon fashion, could be used in whatever fashion its owner desired. His closest associate was Maurice (Jim Cummings), a muscle-bound, non-verbal gorilla, who came in handy when hunters came calling for the cheetah. The middle segment featured Sebastian (Samuel Wright), the Jamaican-accented crab from the *Little Mermaid* film and series (see above), recast as the concierge of a lavish resort hotel. The third segment concerned the wacky adventures of the cat-and-dog duo Shnookums and Meat, who would soon get a series of their own (see below).

The next addition to the Disney Afternoon lineup came in 1994, with the premiere of *Aladdin*. Not surprisingly, this was based on the highly successful animated feature film that debuted in 1992, although this series, unlike the *Little Mermaid* series before it, was a sequel

key (Jim Cummings) became a barkeep who eagerly and gullibly supported Baloo, while Shere Khan the tiger (Tony Jay) became the Sydney Greenstreet–type who owns everything in town, save for Baloo and Rebecca's business. The ongoing plotlines and stories were, thus, as easy to figure out as the main characters.

There was a little bit more effort applied to the next series project, but only a little. *Darkwing Duck* trod the fine line between straight super-heroics and comedy that would later be followed more successfully by *The Tick* (see below) and *The Powerpuff Girls* (see above). On its own, it was a clever idea, but it was heavily marred by creatively uneven and morally fatuous execution. The title character (voiced in fine style by Jim Cummings) was a masked crime-fighter quite reminiscent of the old pulp-fiction and radio hero, the Shadow, in dress and manner. However, he did not possess his predecessor's ability to "cloud men's minds," or any level of competence in his job. This is where the comedy in the show originated. In "real" life, he was the ultra mild-mannered, middle-aged Drake Mallard, perennially trying to set a good example for his adopted daughter, Gosalyn (Christine Cavanaugh). His sidekick, imported from *Ducktales* (see Chapter 5), was the still obliviously clueless Launchpad McQuack (Terry McGovern). His principal nemesis was Steelbeak (Rob Paulsen), head of the Fiendish Organization of World Larceny (F.O.W.L.), and he had a feminine aide/love interest in the form of the attractive, supernaturally gifted Morgana Macawber (Kath Soucie). Need we say more? Darkwing himself, whom his voice actor credited with having "an ego the size of Montana"[92] was a clueless idiot in spite of his theatrical panache, and thus, much like Inspector Gadget (see Chapter 5), he tended to succeed more by accident than design. That about sums up the show itself as well.

Much more derivative in nature, and not simply in its borrowing from company roots this time, was *Goof Troop*, which debuted in syndication in 1992. A haphazardly inept situation comedy, it showed the increasing desperation coming to taint the Disney TV animation unit, and its stubborn unwillingness to adapt to more contemporary trends in the TV animation genre. Some 78 episodes were produced for syndication, with an additional 13 airing exclusively on ABC. As the title implied, the star of the show was Goofy (Bill Farmer), one of the studio's marquee animation characters from the old days, but it really wasn't a fit vehicle for him, in comparison to his classic Jack Kinney–directed cartoons of the 1940s and 1950s. In this project, he was the father of 11-year-old Max (Dana Hill), who typically wanted little to do with him. The majority of the storylines tended to focus on Goofy's relations with his neighbor, a retooled version of the ages-old cartoon villain Peg Leg Pete (Jim Cummings), who now wore a prosthetic leg instead of what had once earned him his name.[93] The cast was filled out by Pete's family: his wife Peg (April Winchell), whose placid exterior concealed a tempestuous inner core; his son, P.J. (Rob Paulsen), Max's best friend; and his inquisitive young daughter, Pistol (Nancy Cartwright). The writers shamelessly pillaged every live-action sitcom ever made for material, and the lack of effort in their work clearly showed. Any success the program had, unlike its slightly more imaginative predecessors, was entirely due to the prestige of the company name behind it.

Disney's The Little Mermaid, which aired on CBS during 1992–93, is self-explanatory, if you happen to be familiar with the 1989 animated feature film of the same name. Using the same character designs and settings as the film, and using the same voice actors, it was set up as a prequel to the film. You can imagine the series storylines if you already saw the film, which was strictly what the show was being built around.

To its credit, WDTA's management had noticed the emerging sameness in the product, and did attempt to try to retool it briefly to make it more in line with the competition's. The

But, by 1995, Disney seemed to understand what was changing, and its own work began to become modified to meet the new standards and programming criteria as a result.

This happened for two specific, distinct and parallel reasons. The first of these was economic in nature. In 1995, as noted in the previous chapter, Michael Eisner engineered a deal by which Disney acquired ownership of Capital Cities Communications, an influential force in the television industry primarily because of its ownership of the ABC television network. The fear in the television industry stemming from the purchase was that Eisner and his team would re-make ABC in their image. In regard to the network's Saturday morning lineup, at least, this was exactly what happened. Disney had already placed programming on the network, but, after it acquired the network in toto, virtually all non–Disney programming was promptly purged. This complete monopoly situation would last for the better part of a decade and a half, until corporate changes and redirections led Walt Disney Television Animation (WDTA) to focus exclusively on programming only for the network's cable channels, leaving ABC Saturday morning a wasteland.

WDTA at this point was given a much-expanded mandate, and its programming strategy changed rapidly as a result. The parent company engineered contracts with independent producers, such as Jim Jinkins's Jumbo Pictures (see above), to ease the main TV animation unit of some of the burden. The older strategy of recycling the older Disney characters had run dry by this point, and a new solution had to be found. That solution came in mimicking the creator-driven production model employed by Nickelodeon and Cartoon Network, which was engaged in giving creators of series much more control over their work than would be expected of a collectivist-oriented concern (as Disney was often portrayed as in the outside media). But, if Disney expected to keep up with the Joneses creatively and technically in the burgeoning world of television animation production, what choice did they really have?

Fortunately, Disney was able to attract some of the best and brightest minds in the television animation business, often poaching them from the competition with the offer of better production deals or the possibility of running their own series. Again, as with Nickelodeon and Cartoon Network's employment of the creator-driven process, Disney struck gold with the concept during the late 1990s and well into the 2000s. Granted, there was still the odd piece of work that reminded viewers too much of the company's storied past, but that could be endured to get to the truly good work. ABC Saturday morning after 1995 may have been a creative monopoly held by one studio, but it was a well-functioning, entertaining, and creatively diverse monopoly nonetheless.

Before ABC

In the early years prior to the ABC takeover, WDTA's main objective was keeping the pipeline flowing for the Disney Afternoon syndication block (see Chapter 5). It did this, competently animating series in spite of the fact that there was little that was truly innovative or imaginative about them. A case in point was *Tale Spin*, debuting in syndication in 1990. Compared by Hal Erickson to "the old Richard Arlen–Chester Morris "soldier of fortune" B-pictures of the 1940s,"[91] the focus here was on Baloo the bear (Edmund Gilbert), of *Jungle Book* fame, re-imagined as a barnstorming bush pilot based in the port city of Cape Suzette. Here, he verbally sparred with Rebecca Cunningham (Sally Struthers), the equally ursine business manager of the shipping company he worked for, in between jetting off for adventures with his young sidekick, Kit Cloudkicker (R.J. Williams). The borrowing from *Jungle Book* included re-imagining two other characters from that film as well. King Louie the mon-

elements of the series should be noted. The villains of the series, for example, are formidable and diverse, much like Chester Gould's equally bizarrely designed gangsters from the *Dick Tracy* comic strip. Among them: Mojo Jojo (Roger Jackson), a super-intelligent, Japanese-accented monkey who frequently speaks in extended, run-on sentences; Fuzzy Lumpkins (Jim Cummings), a mutant hybrid of a Muppet and one of the degenerate hillbillies from *Deliverance*; Him (Tom Kenny, who doubled as the William Conrad–styled narrator), an underworld figure clearly patterned after the Devil; Princess Morbucks (Jennifer Hale), an arrogant, obnoxious rich girl, whose chief aim in life seems to be to try to become the fourth Powerpuff Girl; the Gangrene Gang, a green-hued group of young male juvenile delinquents; and Sedusa (Hale), a conniving, flamboyant, succubus-styled villainess. These and other similar villains made for formidable competition for the Girls, and underlined the action-oriented nature of the program, as well as McCracken's idiosyncratic approach to both character and setting design.

Of course, the Girls would be nothing without their literal creator and figurative father, Professor Utonium (Tom Kane), as he is prone to reminding them. The Professor is as conflicted a figure as his three creations, embodying the stereotypes related to men as they do those of women. An enormously talented scientist, he has very little skill in relating to the outside world, particularly women, and that is a major handicap in relating to his Girls. Nevertheless, he is a capable father—much more so than most of the other "dad" characters discussed in this book. He is able to be kind, affectionate or stern when it is required of him, but he can take this too far. In his devotion to his "children," he resembles Charlotte Baum's depiction of the stereotypical Jewish mother: "[His] children's achievements belong to him, for [he] has lived [his] life for—and through ... [them]. [They] succeed not to please [themselves] but to satisfy [him], the fear of [his] displeasure intensifying [their] own anxieties about failing."[90] Once in a while, he may find a way to equal the Girls, but this is inevitably destructive. Then, the Girls—and others—have to tell him, respectfully, to back off, and he is able to do so without complaint.

The joy that so many people found in the series was amply represented by the fact that it developed an enormous cult following, as well as a spectacularly successful parallel life in licensed merchandising. Cartoon Network was confident enough in it to commission a feature-film version of the series in 2002, which told the origin of the Girls in a way that the opening credits of the series glossed over. However, although the film was technologically superb (including an astonishing inter-cut montage sequence reminiscent of Sergei Eisenstein) and contained an engagingly moving storyline, it was a financial failure.

The series is still with us, in reruns and on DVD, and it will no doubt continue to be seen in one form or another for many years to come, a sure sign of the fact that it truly is a television animation masterpiece.

Disney in the 1990s

Disney, like Hanna-Barbera/Cartoon Network, went through a variety of phases during the 1990s. At the beginning of the decade, the emphasis was essentially a continuation of the programming trends of the previous decade (see Chapter 5 for examples), with only minor variations. The attitude in this period seemed to be simply to continue what had gone before, regardless of the manner in which television animation itself was changing during the period.

The Powerpuff Girls symbolize, in different ways, how girls and women have been stereotypically drawn by the mass media, but their behavior confounds those stereotypes. The "childish glee"[89] they display on the outside is merely a mask for the individuals within. Judging them solely on their appearance is often the undoing of their enemies, and is a lesson that should not be lost on the viewer, either.

Blossom (Cathy Cavadini), the self-defined but largely accepted "leader," represents one facet of this. A strong-willed figure who is equal parts diplomat, intellectual, general and politician, she often speaks in tones that reinforce the commanding nature of her personality, and is spectacularly taken aback when anyone questions her. Still, there are times when her chronological age reveals itself behind her iron will, and she displays the vulnerability usually hidden to the public. She is the group's superego, serving as public conscience and private mediator alike. However, her assumption that she is the superior member of the group is a flaw as well as an asset. In battle, she often assumes a stern, "I don't want to hear it" demeanor regarding any challenge to her plans, particularly from the pugnacious Buttercup. Likewise, she occasionally displays tactless arrogance toward friends and foes alike by rubbing her "superiority" in their faces. But McCracken and company never allow her to go too far. The consequences of her arrogance are often depicted severely, forcing Blossom to retrench into a moving contrition.

Bubbles (Tara Charendoff Strong) exists in an opposite sphere, seemingly paper-doll fragile on the outside but, in reality, forceful and determined to make things right. She is the humanist ego of the group, displaying a high level of sensitivity and kindness, as if she were trying to make up for that lack in her colleagues. Moreover, she speaks in irresistibly sweet vocal tones that, combined with her blonde, blue-eyed good looks and often incredibly naïve personality, make her, unquestionably, the most stereotypically "feminine" of the group. In spite of being in a "profession" that requires physical and verbal violence, she displays an aversion to it when she feels it serves no purpose. In more than one instance, witnessing highly charged displays of violence drives her to tears. This sensitivity is one reason why the villains often make her the centerpiece of their attacks on the group; she appears to be the weakest of the three. However, Bubbles is far more than she appears, and when she chooses to assert herself, chiefly as a response to verbal or physical slights, it is a vindication of the sympathy of the audience.

The aggressive, Id-focused element of the group is, therefore, almost entirely contained in Buttercup (E.G. Daily), the tomboy. Buttercup would rather "kick the hell" out of her opponents than even give a token attempt at hearing their side of the story first. At her worst, she is a quarrelsome, snarling gutter punk who would crush all evil in her powerful, fingerless fists, and is someone Blossom and Bubbles themselves can barely control. Even in moments of repose, she can be sullen, unfeeling and volatile in her temper. Blossom is her regular physical and verbal sparring partner, and their quarrels underline what is best and worst about their respective characters. In spite of her outward displays of James Cagney–styled street toughness, however, Buttercup is fiercely loyal to Blossom and Bubbles, because only they can understand, with her, what it is like to be a super-powered little girl. Likewise, it is only to them that she can confide her vulnerabilities, due to her ultra-macho "public" image. Buttercup is the least "sensitive" of the three, but her sensitivities are displayed in the same volcanic fashion as her fisticuffs.

As with the leads of *The Simpsons*, the one of the three heroines that you most identify with says much about you as an individual.

The length and format of this book prevents an in-depth discussion, but some other

of Cartoon Network executives, particularly Linda Simensky, eventually got the project on the air, and aimed at the appropriate demographic.

Unlike many of his contemporaries, McCracken guided the series with a firm authorial hand, although he also encouraged experimentation on the part of his staff. He supervised every story session, providing the needed guidance for the storyboard artists, writers and directors. In this context, they would "throw ideas around" until they came up with story ideas that "felt good," which were then subdivided into "beats." The story sessions were then converted into outlines, of approximately three to four pages, based on the material coming from the story sessions. When this was done, McCracken would then proof read the material, with "really detailed notes ... how I [wanted] the sequence to be [storyboarded] ... what the goal of the sequence [was] ... from whose perspective it's supposed to be drawn." The story material was then transferred to the storyboard department, which would take six weeks to script and plan the 11-minute segments. Each particular member of the writing staff was allowed platforms for experimentation within reason. After revisions were made to the storyboards, a process involving the entire team, McCracken would re-draw and re-script material he was unsatisfied with, sometimes for entire sequences. "It's just in the nature of the business ... to get the shows right," he would later remark.[88]

They ended up getting the show "right" very often.

◆ ◆ ◆

McCracken's authorial control over his series, more dominant than most of his peers, is most evident in the boldness of the graphic quality of the drawings. Displaying a host of influences, from vintage UPA, to Japanese *anime*, to the child portraiture of Margaret Keane, each episode draws the viewer effortlessly into a created world and manages to convince us, through a chain of interlocked, perspective-based camera movements, that we are experiencing the events along with the protagonists. The team experimented in particular with camera angles, placements and effects that are rarely seen in more conventionally structured television animation programs. If a zip pan, montage, deep focus close-up or quick cut is required, it is employed without hesitation. The fact that McCracken makes his images graphically simple instead of overcomplicating them makes them easier to follow, and more engaging.

In contrast to the graphic sensibilities, the actual stories run the gamut from simplistic to complex. They are occasionally heartbreaking stories of childhood innocence coming into conflict with a domineering outside world. Other times, they are played simply and obviously for comedy. Still others follow some of the conventional playbooks of the superhero genre, most notably the earth-shaking battles between the heroines and the numerous villains. In this latter category, McCracken was particularly deft in the variety of foes he provided for his heroines, some designed to provoke laughs more than fear. Nothing set McCracken's approach toward the series apart more than his heroines themselves. No other female television animation characters have been so prominently featured in a series. Their delight is to be savored, their rage feared. Even at their most helpless, the viewer is never allowed to forget what they are capable of doing at their most powerful, benevolently or otherwise, and we are never allowed to assume, likewise, that because they are "heroes," all of their actions are therefore just. Indeed, their patience is frequently tested, and their wrath brought out, by the epic levels of stupidity they have to confront. When H.L. Mencken famously referred to America as a "glorious commonwealth of morons," he clearly had in mind the citizens of Townsville—not to mention numerous other television animation communities.

◆ ◆ ◆

Craig McCracken was born in Charleroi, Pennsylvania, in 1971. After attending high school in his native state, he moved to California to attend California Institute of the Arts. During his studies, he met Genndy Tartakovsky, who would become a close creative collaborator. He first made his mark with a character named No Neck Joe, who appeared in a series of films exhibited as part of Spike and Mike's Twisted Festival of Animation, a national event featuring independently made short films. But it was another project that would help him make his mark on the animation world.[85]

As he later explained to Joe Murray, another film featuring the characters who would become his visual signature, originally called the Whoopass Girls, helped him to get in the door at Hanna-Barbera:

> I had just started the first semester of my third year at CalArts when I got a call from my friend Paul Rudish, who was working at Hanna-Barbera at the time. Paul said they were looking for an art director for this new show called *2 Stupid Dogs* [sic]. So I brought in my portfolio, showed it to the producer [,] Donovan Cook, got the job and never went back to school. I had never worked a day in the industry, I had never art directed anything other than my own films, and here I was designing the look of this new show. Actually, the whole *Dogs* crew was made up mostly of a bunch of young kids who were just starting out in the industry. When Donovan asked me if I knew any storyboard artists, I recommended my friends from school, Genndy Tartakovsky and Rob Renzetti [both later producers in their own right; see above and Chapter 7]. [Hanna-Barbera] crammed us all into this funky trailer on the parking lot[,] and we learned on the job how to and how not to make TV cartoons. We were really lucky to start out at [Hanna-Barbera] because they had [series] production down to a science. There were a lot of really helpful and experienced people there who took their time to show these punk kids the who, what, where, how and why of TV animation.
>
> A while later, word got around that Fred [Seibert], the president of [Hanna-Barbera] at the time, was looking for new ideas for shows, so I took my *Whoopass* film and pitched it to development. They really liked it. They showed it to Fred and he really liked it, so we started negotiating for a series pickup.[86]

This occurred in 1993, but, following the launch of the *What a Cartoon!* series, the project was redirected there in the form of two short subjects instead of becoming a series in its own right. At the same time, Tartakovsky pitched *Dexter's Laboratory* (see above) to the same development group, with McCracken as part of the creative team, and short films of this were commissioned as well. In the process of development, *Whoopass* gave way to *Powerpuff*, likely to avoid offending the intended audience and their parents. When *Dexter* became a series in its own right, McCracken became its art director and effective second-in-command to series creator Tartakovsky. When production ended on *Dexter*, the same unit began production on *The Powerpuff Girls*, with McCracken as executive producer and principal director, and Tartakovsky as a supervising animation director. The close collaboration between McCracken and Tartakovsky in these years explains the visual similarities between *Dexter* and the early *Powerpuff* episodes. When Tartakovsky stopped directing for the series to pursue his own projects again, the look of the series changed, albeit only slightly.

As animation historian Allan Neuwirth has noted, McCracken is perhaps one of the most driven individuals ever to produce television animation, and that drive has been largely sustained through all the phases of his television animation career.[87] Initially fearful that Cartoon Network was not interested in the project, he had tried to take it elsewhere during the interim between the short films and the series, to no avail. The fact that it did not initially test well with network-commissioned focus groups was also a problem. However, the support

to be produced within its boundaries. Often, it is not possible to view the merits of such works until some years have passed beyond the initial period of production. It is usually only then, when we can view the work objectively both within and outside of the social and cultural contexts under which it was produced, that its value can be assessed.

Under these considerations, *The Powerpuff Girls* is one of the most exceptional series in the history of television animation.

It was a game-changing project. Few other television animation directors before Craig McCracken had displayed such a dynamic level of artistic control in terms of both camera control and character construction. Nor had any displayed such a nuanced understanding of the history and gender politics of the superhero genre and its underlying ideals. Much like the *auteurs* of modern cinema, McCracken was able to create a unique personal vision within a much abused sub-genre within television animation, and he was able to do so in a way that immediately garnered a strong cult following. Like Fellini, Kurosawa and Bergman in their nations' respective cinemas, McCracken may be seen in the future as a figure of enormous power and influence within his field of endeavor. He was literally taking television animation places it had never gone before, and doing a great deal to show how effective an art form it could be, particularly in terms of his innovative applications of live-action photography and cinematography.

What was even more remarkable than the series' technical virtuosity was the fact that its tone was decidedly feminist. In putting young girls forward as his superhero characters, McCracken was fundamentally challenging the age-old value structure of this media genre, which had long been often corrosively masculine in nature. His heroic trio, in addition to battling the seemingly endless array of formidable villains they faced, was often forced to confront the sexism of the wider world regarding how girls and young women are "supposed" to act in manner, dress and speech. The conflict between their gender's and their "profession's" stereotypical intentions and ideals made for both impish comedy and drama. But, somehow, they always managed to come through and "save the day," to a surprisingly diverse chorus of fans.

And all in the space of deftly handled doses of 11 minutes apiece.

The Powerpuff Girls not only saved the world from evil, but they also made the world safe for girls to believe that they, too, had the capacity for heroism. And that, along with the series' technical innovations, will likely be their greatest and most enduring legacy.

The Powerpuff Girls. **Shown from left: Buttercup, Blossom, Bubbles (Warner Bros. Pictures/Photofest).**

◆ ◆ ◆

work but, after his Loyola professor, Dan McLaughlin, showed *Mess o' Blues* to a friend who worked at Hanna-Barbera, the studio hired him to develop it into a series. Rechristened Johnny Bravo after a character who had appeared in an episode of *The Brady Bunch*, the central character retained his Elvis-like mannerisms from the short and was a given a similarly conceived voice by Jeff Bennett, one of the talented generation of young voice actors who sprang up in the industry in the 1990s. The scene was set from the beginning of a high contrast between expectations and reality; whereas Elvis, in his movies, was inevitably able to charm his leading ladies off their feet, Johnny definitely was not.

Part of his problem lay in his very obvious self-delusion. As Michael Mallory notes, he too often relied "on body language that consis[ted] of rapid-fire, hilariously over-dramatic posings, all the while mumbling pick-up lines that must have been culled from the walls of a frat house."[83] The effect was to make him a joke to everyone except himself. Even when he succeeded, he still ended up failing. In an episode penned by Seth Macfarlane (see above), for example, Johnny manages to make a date with an attractive woman over the Internet, only to discover on meeting her that she is, in fact, an antelope who is merely using him to make her lobster boyfriend jealous![84]

There are, however, two women in Johnny's life who *are* interested in him, though not in the way one might expect. His beloved "Mama," Bunny (Brenda Vaccaro), is one of them. Johnny is a Mama's boy in classic Oedipal fashion, and constantly tries to please her, even if that requires altering some fundamental component of his personality and behavior. As would be expected, these attempts to change himself are fundamentally flawed and ultimately fail. The other female is regarded more as a nuisance by Johnny: eight-year-old Suzy (Mae Whitman), who harbored a crush on him but had the bad luck to appear in the context of his life at the least opportune times—particularly when Johnny was trying to woo some older woman.

While the series' storylines were simplistic, and played very obviously (though quite effectively) for laughs, the design of the program was something else. In his attempts to provide a properly retro feel for the series, Partible recruited Joseph Barbera to consult on the stories and iconic studio artistic specialist Ed Benedict to assist with the design. (Though he was not directly involved, William Hanna's influence is also felt in the direct cuts between character poses.) This gave the program a distinctive visual feel that set it apart from the competition. The directors used a deeper focus approach than was common for television animation, emphasized most directly by the many times Johnny poked his finger in the direction of the camera. There was also a high degree of stylized violence, ranging from Johnny's overplayed macho posturing to his would-be paramours repeatedly and soundly beating the living tar out of him. ("She wants me," was his inevitable, clueless response to this.) A further solidification of the retro feel of the series was the presence of several 1960s and 1970s-era celebrities who appeared in vocal form, most often as themselves.

The series, though its concept was weak, was handsomely mounted, and managed an impressive run, from 1997 to 2001. (Partible was not involved in the second or third seasons.) What it may have lacked in substance, it made up for in style, just like Johnny himself. And perhaps that was the reason it kept the audience laughing and entertained as long as it did.

THE POWERPUFF GIRLS

Television animation, like most things related to television, is based on a quantity-over-quality production model, which often seriously negates the capacity for exceptional work

the concept, Feiss decided to make the characters into animated ones after the *What a Cartoon!* call went out. The reason for the choice of characters? "A chicken because they're such funny little creatures, and ... a cow because it looks so foolish with that udder under her body." He named them, simply, Cow and Chicken. "I thought it was stupid to name them Fred or something like that," he later explained.[80]

The pilot cartoon, "No Smoking," set the surrealistic but hilarious tone of the project directly and immediately. Amiable schemer Chicken (voiced, as were most of the characters on this series, by the one-of-a-kind Charlie Adler) and his more dimwitted but innocent "sister," Cow (Adler), are threatened by the flamboyant (and unquestionably "gay") villain-in-residence known only as The Red Guy (Adler) for his resemblance to a certain underworld deity. As the title implies, the Red Guy abducts Chicken by offering him contraband cigarettes. With the aid of her "blankie," Cow is able to transform into Super Cow, a purple union-suit–wearing super-heroine who communicates verbally only *en Español*, and promptly makes things right, as you would expect.[81] Subsequent programs would build on this, most notably by featuring Cow and Chicken's "parents" as caricatures of the traditional from-the-waist-down-only portraits of parents and other adult figures in animation—in this case, they have *no* upper torsos whatsoever! The manic, high-energy writing was very good, done by writers who would eventually mine this wacko-humor territory further at Cartoon Network and elsewhere, but the real star here is the amazingly versatile Charlie Adler, whose work on this series, is, as Michael Mallory justly puts it, "nothing less than a tour-de-force."[82] Not since Mel Blanc's glory days at Warner Bros. had there been such a virtuoso display of voice acting. Adler's work here, along with his many other credits as voice actor and director, surely qualifies him for a hall-of-fame position in an astonishingly under-examined field of artistic endeavor.

Feiss also developed a companion series, *I Am Weasel*, which served as a bridge between *Cow and Chicken* segments. The focus here was on the enigmatic but highly successful I.M. Weasel (Michael Dorn) and his efforts to do well in the world, and the comparable efforts of his self-declared enemy, I.R. Baboon (Adler) to interfere with such. These were played and developed at the same speed as the main feature, in part because the Red Guy was also the main antagonist here. *I Am Weasel* was spun off into its own series in 1999, although this consisted chiefly of reruns.

Since the end of the series, Feiss has concentrated on working independently, developing and winning acclaim for a variety of short features. Whether or not he ever returns to television animation is anybody's guess, but, judging by what he accomplished with *Cow and Chicken*, he would have a lot to live up to.

JOHNNY BRAVO

He considered himself God's gift to women, but most women he met considered him worse than poison. He was Johnny Bravo, and he was the star of an immensely funny series that combined a satire on modern gender relations with an affectionately, aggressively retro look that added to its appeal.

The series was created by Van Partible, a Filipino born in Manila in 1971. An avid artist from childhood, he did not consider animation as a career until he was older. As a student at Loyola Marymount University, he produced an animated short film, *Mess o' Blues*, about an Elvis Presley–styled musician unaware of how much of a has-been he is. Due to his lack of experience in the field, Partible was initially turned down when looking for animation

thought: "What's the opposite of a little girl who likes art and dance? A little boy maybe likes science; then he can have a big [laboratory] in his room." Things started to escalate from there.[73]

The little girl, a blonde, gawky, would-be ballerina, was named Dee Dee, and the little boy (patterned in part on Tartakovsky's own brother) was dubbed Dexter. The central conflict between them—Dexter being super-intelligent, Dee Dee being dumb as a post—was played for all the laughs that could be mined from the concept. Cartoon Network executive Mike Lazzo was impressed enough with Tartakovsky's original pilot that he green-lighted a series immediately. To assist him in producing the project, Tartakovsky recruited a like-minded peer, Craig McCracken, to serve as the art director and chief character designer. They became an effective team, and the mutual trust between them was maintained when McCracken later got his own series (see below).[74]

The animation of the series was sophisticated, combining American and European art disciplines in unexpected ways. Constant movement, a departure from the static "illustrated radio" approach of earlier Hanna-Barbera series, and gutbucket slapstick comedy in the writing of the program added to its appeal.[75] The formula of the series, in contrast, was simple enough: child genius Dexter (Christine Cavanaugh first, Candi Milo later) was forever trying to improve himself and the world, only to have his dimwitted sister Dee Dee (Alison Moore first, Kat Cressida later) somehow botch up his work with her stupidity and cluelessness. Although they were at opposite ends of the gray-matter spectrum, the characters were still affectionate and loyal to each other, part of Tartakovsky's intention for the program,[76] and that set them apart from many of the other sibling duos of their era. The program ran in its initial form from 1996 to 1998, and was revived briefly in 2001.[77] Initially, two comedy-minded superhero-themed series—*Dial M for Monkey* and *Justice Friends*—were featured as supporting series until Tartakovsky decided to centralize the project's focus.

Acclaim was quick to come for the series, which earned three Emmy nominations and other honors during its run. *Variety* even named Tartakovsky one of its "Fifty to Watch" for in 1995.[78] Yet, as impressive as Tartakovsky's debut series was, and how truly accomplished its animation in particular was in comparison to its competition, both Tartakovsky and McCracken were just at the beginning of what would be amazing careers.

COW AND CHICKEN

This series also focused, in a way, on a brother-and-sister duo, but that was about all it really had it common with its predecessor.

David Feiss (pronounced *Feace*) was born in Sacramento, California, in 1959. He began animating as a child, producing his first amateur films in the early 1970s. At the age of 19, he launched a professional animation career by joining the staff of Hanna-Barbera. Developing skills as a character designer, animator and animation director, he later left the studio, working briefly for DIC and then assisting John Kricfalusi with the *Ren and Stimpy* pilot, before returning. In his second stint at Hanna-Barbera, he began directing TV specials while at the same time working as an inker on the last Hanna-Barbera feature film, *Jetsons: The Movie*, as well as *Once Upon a Forest*, an ecological-minded feature produced by William Hanna for 20th Century–Fox, which was released in 1993.[79]

The origin of his now-noteworthy series project came out of his frustrations with trying to read bedtime stories to his young daughter. The protagonists of the story he improvised were "a 460-pound cow and a chicken with an attitude." When his daughter approved of

and relative newcomers alike, began developing and pitching projects to Seibert and Cohen. As studio historian Michael Mallory notes, "Well over a thousand artists presented storyboards, sketches, [art] school projects, or privately produced 'seed' cartoons to a studio selection panel, each hoping to land a development deal, which carried with it access to studio production resources."[70] The lucky chosen few would bring with them projects that would literally transform the theory, art and practice of television animation overnight, helping to bring new blood to a studio and industry desperately needing it.

Among those who had their material presented and accepted were Butch Hartman, Michael Rann, Eugene Mattos, George Johnson, Pat Ventura, David Feiss, Genndy Tartakovsky, Craig McCracken, Van Partible, and John Dilworth. Feiss, Tartakovsky, McCracken, Partible and Dilworth eventually saw their projects turned into series (the details of which are in Chapter 7 and below), while Hartman, after toiling as a director on some of these projects, eventually became a producer in his own right for Nickelodeon (see Chapter 7 for his work there). But there were also some surprises. The ever-controversial Ralph Bakshi produced two shorts for the project, and the legendary Italian animator Bruno Bozetto also contributed. Fittingly, William Hanna and Joseph Barbera, now working separately, also produced material, and were the only animators omitted from the selection process due to their obvious stature. Hanna, working alone as an animation director for the first time in decades, produced the short *Hard Luck Duck*, while Barbera produced two films revolving around Dino the dinosaur from *The Flintstones*.[71]

To say that *World Premiere Toons*, and its two counterpart projects supervised by Seibert at Nickelodeon (see above and Chapter 7) were successful would be an understatement. Viewers were suddenly able to see what television animation and its creators could do when allowed to be fully and truly *themselves*.

The original four series launched by Cartoon Network were products of Seibert's vision for Hanna-Barbera, but, as he had intended, they more directly reflected the outlook and intentions of their creators, and these are the only terms on which they can be truly understood.

DEXTER'S LABORATORY

Genndy Tartakovsky, born in Moscow in 1970, was the son of a prominent dentist whose clients included the Russian national hockey team and members of the country's cabinet. Consequently, by the standards of postwar Communist Russia, he grew up, initially, on comfortable terms. However, the family was Jewish by descent and, fearful of anti–Semitic attacks, the Tartakovskys relocated to the United States after an extended stopover in Italy. It was here that Genndy first developed the skills as an artist that would come to serve him well. (His father was unable to continue practicing dentistry in the United States because of a non-transferable dental license, so he took other jobs to support the family.)

Living first in Columbus, Ohio, and then in Chicago, Illinois, Tartakovsky developed an interest in animation which complemented his developing skills as an artist. He attended Columbia College and California Institute of the Arts, where he made his first films as an animator. After working overseas briefly, he joined the staff of Hanna-Barbera around the time of the call for *World Premiere Toons*.[72]

As he later recalled, the origins of his series came to him in a rather round-about way:

> I basically came up with [the series] ... because I wanted to animate a little girl dancing.... I came up with this character and liked her, and I thought, instead of doing one scene of her dancing, I'll do a little show about it. I needed something for her to interact with and I

on them. This could have been conducted fairly straightforwardly in line with the past, but Kirschner was aiming as much, if not more, for the older viewers rather than children in terms of his tone, and made for that reason most of his characters shady and complicated rather than good-and-evil strictly.[67] The animation, chiefly farmed out to Fils Studios, based in the Philippines, was also of a higher quality than expected from the studio at this time, which added to its appeal. Unfortunately, while the project was impressive artistically, its high costs precluded the production of additional episodes, and, after being buried in the ratings by less dramatically complicated material, it was summarily canceled.

Kirschner had better luck with his one comic success. *The Addams Family*, previously mounted in animation by the studio during the mid–1970s (see Chapter 4), was brought back to television animation in 1992, following the success of the 1991 live-action feature film featuring the Charles Addams characters. This version, much more faithful in spirit to the characters, mindset and tone of the mid–1960s sitcom than its predecessor, was an enormous success in the ratings, drawing 3.5 million viewers at its peak.[68] It was a success that was deserved given the high artistic quality of the project, in terms of its animation, writing and particularly the voice acting. John Astin, who had played family patriarch Gomez in the original sitcom (but was not present in the first television animation version) returned to the role with his customary theatrical panache. This served to provide a sense of cunning energy into even the most banal storylines (just as it had in the original sitcom). Astin was matched step for step by veteran comedian Rip Taylor as Uncle Fester, who cut up mercilessly in the part he seemed born to play. The major additions were in terms of its setting: the town of Happydale Heights, in which the Addams mansion was incongruously placed, seemed to have the flavor of a conformist religious commune rather than an actual town, making it a clever satire of religiously oriented conservative America. The most prominent of the supporting characters were the Normanmeyer family, represented by underwear manufacturer and obsessive devotee Norman (Rob Paulsen, sounding shockingly like then-president George H.W. Bush), and his hysterically repressed wife, Normina (Edie McClurg). The series was a clear highlight in a dire period in the studio's history.

Kirschner had accomplished something during his time at the studio, but not enough to completely reverse the creative decline of much of its product. That would left to Fred Seibert to fix, with spectacular results.

The Seibert Era and Its Legacy

As noted above, Seibert's major innovation as the head of Hanna-Barbera was the encouragement of the development of new ideas. The central vehicle for this was the now-celebrated *World Premiere Toons/What a Cartoon!* project, which, in defiance of the now-outdated, calcified standards of network television, brought television animation back to the format in which it had first appeared and flourished in the new medium. Composed exclusively of seven- to eleven-minute cartoon segments commissioned by Seibert and his initial counterpart at Cartoon Network, Betty Cohen, it revealed a hitherto-hidden wealth of young talent. When let loose, these writers and artists produced works of high quality despite their variance in tone and approach, works that truly reflected the intentions of their creators.[69]

The original plan was to produce 48 short films over a three-year period, which would then air on Cartoon Network with a two- to three-week interval between projects. But, as word of the project spread through the animation community, numerous animators, veterans

tors and producers, series creators would be given the full autonomy to devise, develop and refine their concepts as they saw fit, with only largely nominal interjections from the bureaucracy. The prime reflection of his attitude were the anthology series *What a Cartoon!* and *World Premiere Toons*, from which the series (discussed below) emerged. The change in the studio's creative outlook, and the intended use of Cartoon Network as its launching pad, was almost immediately apparent to both viewers and industry insiders. Seibert's willingness to develop and encourage talent launched a vivid, infectious, engaging new golden age in television animation.

Seibert left Hanna-Barbera in 1996, following Turner Entertainment's acquisition by Time Warner. The following year he launched Frederator Studios (see above and Chapter 7), which produced some of the most innovative television animation programs of the late 1990s and 2000s. He spent much of this time expanding the company's base beyond television animation into feature-film production and Internet distribution, with mostly felicitous results.[66]

The Kirschner and Seibert eras at Hanna-Barbera really constitute two separate creative and ideological periods at the studio, and will be discussed below as such.

THE KIRSCHNER ERA

Although David Kirschner had an impressive-enough track record as a producer when he came to Hanna-Barbera in 1989, he was, essentially, expected to stay the course commercially and artistically, and that he basically did. Thus, the pre–Cartoon Network-era Hanna-Barbera product of the early 1990s mostly resembles what the studio was producing in the previous decade, although, to his credit, Kirschner was able to bring an occasional surprise to the table.

Under his leadership, the studio continued the franchises of the past with *A Pup Named Scooby Doo* (see Chapter 5) and the badly conceived and executed *Yo, Yogi!*, which reimagined select members of the classic Hanna-Barbera gang as modern "tweens." Kirschner also ventured disastrously into prime time with *Capitol Critters* and *Fish Police* (see above). Other productions similarly ventured down retread road, as implied just by their titles (e.g., *Young Robin Hood*, *Bill and Ted's Excellent Adventures*, etc.) *Gravedale High* was a similarly uninspired variant of the monsters-as-kids school of earlier decades, only partially redeemed by the presence of *SCTV* veteran Rick Moranis in the lead role. (He was, in fact, given above-the-title billing: a rare occurrence indeed for an animation voice actor.) Even the studio's reunion with the classic MGM characters created by the founders and their contemporaries, thanks to their now being part of the same corporate family, did not come off as well as they should have, with both *Tom and Jerry Kids* and *Droopy, Master Detective* being only minor chips off the old block. Then there was *SWAT Kats*, a derivative action series set in an all-feline future universe, which suggested that the 1980s action cycle had truly run its course.

The Kirschner era did, however, produce two exceptional series, one dramatic and one comic, and these deserve further discussion.

The Pirates of Dark Water, a project of Kirschner's own invention, originally aired in syndication as a miniseries in 1991, and then on ABC during 1991–92. Inspired in part by the fictional universes of science fiction author Frank Herbert and fantasy author J.R.R. Tolkien, this series was set on Mer, a planet which, as its name implied, was almost exclusively made of water. Ren, prince of the kingdom of Octopon, was entrusted with recovering the 14 treasures of the kingdom before the evil, all-consuming entity Dark Water got its hands

(which included cartoon properties owned or inherited by the studio, including vintage MGM, Warner Bros. and Paramount material) would serve as the fulcrum of Cartoon Network in its earliest years, until it began to follow Nickelodeon's lead in producing new material. As Turner saw it, what he was doing was simply doing for animation what he had already done for news via CNN: making it available to the television audience whenever they wanted it, rather than at the set, non-negotiable times of network television.[65] Many viewers came to agree with this line of thinking, and are grateful to Turner for providing this option.

William Hanna and Joseph Barbera were no longer in direct creative control of the studio bearing their names by this time, although the name was retained until 2001, when, in reflection of its new mandate, it became Cartoon Network Studios. They were, however, retained in honorary positions, most notably as members of the cable channel's board. (John Kricfalusi also served here before and after being fired by Nickelodeon.) The corporate destiny of the company in the 1990s was instead entrusted to two men, each with different views and ideas for the future of the genre of television animation. They were David Kirschner, who was largely unable to accomplish his aims at the studio, and Fred Seibert, who was.

Kirschner, born in 1955, came to animation, like Arlene Klasky and Gabor Csupo, from the world of graphic design. A graduate of USC, he illustrated album covers and other commercial products until 1983, when he created the successful *Rose Petal Place* children's book series. The franchise's adaptation to animation was his introduction to the medium, and he liked it enough to stay there. His major achievement in the field of animation came in 1986, when he wrote and co-produced *An American Tail*, a phenomenally successful animated feature film orchestrated by Steven Spielberg (see below) and directed by Don Bluth. Three years later, he was appointed chairman of Hanna-Barbera on the strength of this success. However, despite some impressive individual series, he was unable to halt the growing *ennui* on the part of the staff, a holdover from the later days of the actual Hanna-Barbera era. He resigned in 1992 and has since pursued his own career with some success, including the long-running *Child's Play* horror-film series and the animated feature film *Cats Don't Dance*, as well as the television animation version of the *Curious George* children's book series.

Seibert, unlike Kirschner, had enough media experience to revive the Hanna-Barbera brand successfully, and the good sense to allow the staff to begin executing their own ideas, both to fulfill their own desires and provide programming for the then-burgeoning Cartoon Network. Born in New York in 1951, Seibert attended Columbia University, first in pharmacology, then in history. While still attending college, he worked at a radio station as an engineer, which led to a career as a recording engineer and producer in the jazz field. He worked in these capacities, as well as artist management, for the balance of the 1970s. Based on his music-industry experience, he became one of the founding executives of MTV in 1981, and played a major role in cultivating that channel's early success. Later in the same decade, he and associate Alan Goodman (his partner in the media/branding firm Alan/Fred, Inc.) did much the same for Nickelodeon, helping to introduce the Nick-At-Nite concept and developing the now-famous advertising identity still in use by the channel, although it was not producing its own television animation at this time.

Thus, when Seibert assumed the helm of Hanna-Barbera, he had accumulated enough experience to bring new life to the struggling studio, and he began to do so in spite of the fact that he had no prior experience working in the animation industry. He was, however, a devoted animation fan, and that made all the difference to the attitude he took toward his new job. Under his watch, the studio shifted from the collectivist philosophies of Hanna, Barbera and Kirschner to a more creator-oriented approach. Much like live-action film direc-

commercial success of the network, as reflected above and again in Chapter 7, marks this strategy as both commercially successful and aesthetically wise. The same could be said of its greatest rival in the cable sweepstakes, as well, for between them, over the course of the 1990s and 2000s, they would come to "own" much of television animation in the same way DC and Marvel still largely "own" the comic-book business.

Hanna-Barbera/Cartoon Network in the '90s

Just as the FOX network came into being as the result of the boardroom piracy of one media tycoon, so was Hanna-Barbera creatively revived, and Cartoon Network born, out of similar creative business acumen on the part of another. However, unlike his predecessor, the founder of Cartoon Network was not simply interested in expanding his economic web of interest, but also in expanding the sphere of influence of the product lines he controlled. The channel's support of older forms of animation in reruns, as well as the creation of innovative homegrown product, allowed it to attract an audience immediately and profitably, and, to its credit, despite changes in its on-screen lineup and its off-screen ownership and management, it has managed to survive credibly. As in the case of its rival Nickelodeon, this has been done both by highlighting and targeting the uniqueness of its viewers' intent in seeking it out and the uniqueness of the creative products themselves.

Robert Edward ("Ted") Turner III is one of the most controversial, yet enormously successful, figures in American media history. One of the founders of the cable renaissance of the 1980s and 1990s, he has utterly transformed the way television viewers interact and engage with several formerly marginalized television genres, including television animation. The Cincinnati-born Turner spent much of his youth in military schools before joining his father's Atlanta-based advertising firm, taking it over completely when the older man committed suicide. Seeing that billboards, long the basis of the firm's operations, were becoming an outmoded form of communication, Turner switched the company's focus to radio and television. After purchasing a local Atlanta television station, he took its signal national as the anchor of the Turner Broadcasting Service. At the same time, he pursued a successful parallel career as a yachtsman, winning the America's Cup in 1977. In his mind, having full control in both business and yachting was essential, and he governed his affairs accordingly. ("I ran my company the same way I ran my boat," was how he later put it.[62]) Eager to expand his company's operations, he acquired sports franchises (notably the Atlanta Braves baseball team) and developed new outlets for his cable programming. The most famous and enduring of these was Cable News Network (CNN), the first 24-hour news channel in television history, launched in 1980. Yet he also had setbacks, failing in his bid to acquire CBS in the 1980s, and, some thought madly, acquiring MGM later in the decade. He sold the film studio shortly after buying it to its previous owner, but, wisely, kept the film library for use on his cable stations, notably Turner Classic Movies.[63] In the mid–1990s Turner sold his company to Time Warner, becoming a large shareholder and influential board member of that company until the aftershocks of its controversial takeover by American Online in 2003 led him to resign and pursue other ventures.

Turner purchased Hanna-Barbera from Great American Broadcasting in 1991, in part to halt Michael Eisner and Disney from launching a hostile takeover.[64] A big attraction for him was its programming archives, although he was also eager to continue production of new materials on a gradual basis. The Hanna-Barbera archives, along with that of MGM

Roach, and that is really how it should be viewed. The segments rise and fall on their own merits, even within the context of the individual episodes in which they are placed. There are certainly some gems among them, but there are also clunkers, to be sure. In playing so broadly, and for such aggressive intent, the series seems to confirm rather than defy the traditional "cartoon" stereotypes other series of the 1990s and 2000s have tried desperately to avoid, but that was likely Hillenburg's intent. On the other hand, there has been the odd bit of satire, and the odd bit of adult-oriented confrontational material (e.g., the suggestions that Sandy is, in fact, bisexual), but this has been done so unobtrusively that only those familiar with the source material of the joke can truly "get" it.[59] Also unique is the show's employment of live-action footage and characters, such as Patchy the Pirate (also portrayed by Tom Kenny), a cheap-laughs kid-show host in the tradition of *SCTV*'s Count Floyd.

After producing 60 episodes, and a feature-film version of the series, in 2004, Hillenburg distanced himself from the series to pursue other ventures, although on terms that were more amicable and less publicized than John Kricfalusi's exodus from *Ren and Stimpy*. Since that time, Nickelodeon has produced new episodes of the project in partnership with Hillenburg's production company, United Plankton, and has managed successfully to maintain the happy/bizarre ambience at the heart of the program in spite of its creator's absence.

Rocket Power

Yet another Klasky-Csupo product, this one is centered around the youth-oriented world of extreme sports: bicycling, skateboarding, roller-blading and what have you. Inspired by Arlene Klasky's interest in her children's activities in this area,[60] this series is set in the California town of Ocean Shores, and, not surprisingly, centered on young children involved in extreme sports. Leading the charge were 11-year-old Regina "Reggie" Rocket (Shayna Fox), and her nine-year-old brother, Oswald "Otto" Rocket (Joseph Ashton), as well as their pals Maurice "Twister" Rodriguez (Ulysses Cuadra) and Sam "The Squid" Dullard (Sam Saletta first, Gary Leroi Gray later). Providing the requisite fun-but-firm adult presence required for pseudo-realistic television animation programs are Reggie and Otto's father, Ray (a.k.a. "Raymundo") Rocket (John Kassir), operator of the local restaurant known as the Shore Shack, and his Hawaiian buddy Tito Makani, Jr. (Ray Bumatai). Legendary extreme skateboarder Tony Hawk appeared in the pilot episode in animated form, which lent the project the *gravitas* it needed to succeed. Although the show was a hit with its target audience, the producers admittedly walked a fine line with what they were doing, trying to present the sports in realistic fashion while at the same stressing the importance of safety in the old pro-social way.[61] One thing it failed to exploit effectively, however, was the uniqueness of its California setting—*that* would be done far more successfully by Doug Langdale and Disney with *The Weekenders* (see Chapter 7).

◆ ◆ ◆

From having no identity as an animation producer at the start of the 1990s, Nickelodeon suddenly ended as one of the great power brokers in television animation, effectively taking over a field that network television now thought of as yesterday's news. While it did not grant its creators *carte blanche*, and could fight back if pushed (as in the case of John Kricfalusi, and, later, Klasky-Csupo), Nickelodeon was far more willing than its predecessors in television animation to allow its creators to govern their creations as they saw fit, rather than constantly interfering in the production process. The consistent creative and

he was hired by Joe Murray as an animator for *Rocko's Modern Life* (see above), ultimately rising to the positions of writer, story editor and creative director on that series.[55]

Though initially unwilling to produce a series of his own after observing the frustrations Murray encountered helming *Rocko*, Hillenburg soon changed his mind. Never having completely abandoned his love of marine biology, he developed a series concept that combined his interest in that field with the warped, wacky "cartoon" feel of the series on which he worked. Following a flamboyant pitch session, Nickelodeon accepted the idea. However, Hillenburg surprised the executives when they ordered 40 episodes of the project by saying that he didn't think he could make that many, a reflection of his quality-over-quantity approach to animation.[56] Nevertheless, the show entered production and was an almost-instant hit. Just as with *Ren and Stimpy* before it, college-aged viewers were a sizable block of the audience, immediately ramping up the merchandising possibilities of the potential in the eyes of the network, which took full advantage of the opportunity.

Much of the series' success can be attributed to the unique nature of the title character (Tom Kenny at his most theatrically flamboyant). Spongebob is a provocatively and aggressively infantile man-child, very much in the mode of Jerry Lewis in his 1950s and 1960s movie vehicles.[57] He is, in the words of his creator, a "well-meaning, naïve dork,"[58] whose good intentions typically cause much more trouble than they solve. However, his in-your-face characterization, along with the series' sledgehammer approach, have largely been turn offs to viewers seeking more subtle comedy. The fact that the series remains in circulation is proof of the fact that this part of the audience has been outvoted.

Hillenburg's supporting cast and their characterizations further inform the bizarre unreality of the project. Patrick Star (Bill Fagerbakke), Spongebob's best friend, is a dimwitted starfish whose limited intellect and slow-burn delivery make him the perfect foil. Squidward Tentacles (Rodger Bumpass), Spongebob's neighbor and co-worker, is a snobbish intellectual who wants nothing except to play his clarinet in peace. To his chagrin, he spends much more time playing James Finlayson to Spongebob and Patrick's Laurel and Hardy, and ends up taking nearly as many lumps in the process as did "Fin." Other characters play foil to Spongebob in different ways. The furthest reaches of the concept were expressed through the character of Sandy Cheeks (Carolyn Lawrence), a Texas-accented squirrel who lives in a biodome and interacts with the other characters chiefly by donning an atmosphere-conditioned suit. Typically, she seems to be the only one of the characters to have anything approaching an above-average IQ, with physical skills to match. At the other end of the spectrum is Eugene Krabs (Clancy Brown), owner of the Krusty Krab (where Spongebob and Squidward both work), a crustacean whose obsession with money (gaining and keeping it both) approaches the classic levels of Jack Benny (the fictional version). Watching jealously from the sidelines was Plankton (Doug "Mr." Lawrence), a red-eyed protozoa who perpetually schemes, with the aid of his super-computer Karen (who is also his *wife*), to drive Krabs out of business, rather than maintaining his own meager one. More minor players include Mrs. Puff (Mary Jo Catlett), Spongebob's eternally flustered would-be driving instructor; Pearl (Lori Alan), Mr. Krabs's daughter, a teenaged whale; and Mermaid Man and Barnacle Boy (Ernest Borgnine and Tim Conway, both well cast), a pair of aging superheroes. (Mermaid Man looked suspiciously like an elderly version of DC Comics' Aquaman, who may very well have been his inspiration.)

This series does not have a consistent internal narrative in terms of its structure, which is one of its greatest flaws. However, it stands up well when viewed chiefly as a series of loosely interconnected short comedy films in the grand tradition of Mack Sennett and Hal

for creating them. Seibert's mentality, as it had been for the earlier project, was to produce creator-driven product in line with the classic theatrical cartoons of the 1930s, 1940s and 1950s, and, again as with the earlier project, he succeeded with flying colors.[53] Only three of the projects eventually became series, but these three—*The Fairly Oddparents*, *Chalkzone* and especially *My Life as a Teenage Robot*—would rank among the network's finest achievements, a testament to the worthiness of Seibert's conception for this project. (See Chapter 7 for the above-named series.)

THE WILD THORNBERRYS

Another Klasky-Csupo enterprise, also debuting in 1998, this series had an imaginative concept at its core, as well as an unlikely heroine. The story concerned a family of globe-trotting documentary filmmakers and their adventures in far-flung corners of the world. The heroine was 12-year-old Eliza (Lacey Chabert), a homely, bespectacled and braces-wearing girl who possessed the Dr. Dolittle–like ability to talk to the animals, which played a major role in driving the plots of most episodes. (Series creator Gabor Csupo was insistent on maintaining her awkward appearance despite pressure from the network to make her "cuter.[54]) Eliza's father, Nigel (Tim Curry), a British expert in the world's wildlife in the tradition of Sir David Attenborough, was, however, at the center of the actual films. Others in the cast included Marianne (Jodi Proznick), Nigel's level-headed wife, who functioned as the de facto cinematographer and producer of the docs; Eliza's apathetic older sister Debbie (Danielle Harris), whose long hair, oversized denim shirt and ripped jeans marked her as something of a satirical commentary on the "grunge" music scene of the late 1990s; youngest child Donnie (Flea of the Red Hot Chili Peppers), who behaved in the manner of a "feral" child; and Darwin (Tom Kane), an intelligent British-accented chimpanzee in the manner of *George of the Jungle*'s Ape (see Chapter 3), who served as Eliza's principal companion and confidant. The characters became the subject of a popular feature film in 2002, and the following year entered into a more star-crossed collaboration with Klasky-Csupo's other franchise in *Rugrats Go Wild*.

SPONGEBOB SQUAREPANTS

A television program's commercial success is not necessarily equivalent to its creative quality. This is simply because the audience at large, whom television producers are desperately trying to grab, vastly outnumbers the number of people who can judge the project on its artistic merits. The disparity between commercial success and creative quality in the television animation business is no better demonstrated than with this series. It has been in continual production and rotation since 1999, due to its popularity with both young and adult viewers, in spite of the fact that its creative quality has always been something of a hit-or-miss proposition.

The creator of the series, Stephen Hillenburg was born in Fort Sill, Oklahoma, in 1961. After relocating to California, he developed a passionate interest in the sea, and marine biology in particular. This naturally extended to his professional life. After graduating from Humbolt State University in 1984 with a degree in natural resource planning and interpretation, he spent three years as a marine biology teacher at the Orange County Marine Institute. However, this career was soon displaced by another, in animation. He enrolled in a master's degree program at California Institute of the Arts, graduating in 1992. Afterward,

The stars of the main segments were the Warners—fast-talking, wisecracking Yakko (Rob Paulsen), Liverpool-accented Wakko (Jess Harnell), and unbearably "cute" Dot (Tress MacNeille)—who were quite clearly unrelated to studio founders Jack, Harry, Albert and Sam. They were, in fact, a trio of cartoon characters created back in the 1930s whose antics were apparently far too much even for audiences then, necessitating their being locked away in the aforementioned studio water tower. They stayed there, as something of a skeleton in the studio closet, until escaping at the time of the program's premiere in 1993. Much to the horror of fictional studio boss, Thaddeus Plotz, who thought them the worst thing to happen to the studio since it released the (real) film *Don't Tell Mom the Babysitter's Dead*.[113] He promptly demanded studio psychiatrist Otto Scratchandsniff (Paulsen) bring a halt to the trio—a fruitless quest that consumed the better part of the program's run.

The Warners' comic antics betray them as products of the time that they were created— the 1930s. The comparisons to another funny family of the 1930s—The Marx Brothers— are most obvious, as are the influences of numerous other comics, male and female, of that decade. Ruegger and company effectively used the formula of most comedy films of the decade (that is, insert the comedians into an otherwise-placid setting and let them wreak havoc within it) in a hilarious way. Good comedy strategies, it appears, never age. For all their outward displays of adult, sophisticated mannerisms, however, the Warners still possessed the outward emotional views of children, particularly in regard to the utter contempt they held for the Margaret Dumont–styled figures of authority they often encountered.[114] That, no doubt, helped endear them to the children in the audience. As with the Marxes, chaos frequently ended up giving order a sound thrashing by the fadeout.

The Warners may have been the theoretical "stars" of *Animaniacs*, but they were merely the gateway to other inspired silliness from the Spielberg/MacCurdy/Ruegger gang. Unlike *Tiny Toons*, a firm group of regular, rotating features was presented on the program. The most prominent of these was *Pinky and the Brain*, which proved to be so popular that it eventually became a series of its own when the studio-owned WB network was launched in 1995. (The main series, originally broadcast on the FOX network, relocated there that same year, as did *Tiny Toons*.) This concept was simple enough in description: two laboratory mice, the super-intelligent Brain (Maurice La Marche, channeling his inner Orson Welles) and the Cockney-accented dimwit Pinky (Paulsen) repeatedly schemed to "try to take over the world" every night. Their efforts, however, were always doomed to failure, in spite of Brain's rigorous planning, chiefly due to Pinky's bungling, underscored by the latter's frequent exclamation of the nonsense syllable "Narf!" What had the potential to be dull, dreary and repetitious proved instead to be highly effective within the context of *Animaniacs*, and later—more elaborately—on its own. With its warped, satirical intentions and marvelous vocal performances by La Marche and Paulsen anchoring it, it was one of the highlights of the Spielberg/Warner collaboration.

The other characters and ideas were no less silly or funny in concept or execution. They included Slappy Squirrel (Sherri Stoner), an aging theatrical cartoon star eager to get back in the game; Rita (Bernadette Peters) and Runt (Frank Welker), an unlikely cat-and-dog duo; Buttons (Welker), an inept canine "hero" who took plenty of punishment in "protecting" his young owner, Mindy (Nancy Cartwright); and "The Goodfeathers," an outrageous avian parody of the gangsters featured in Martin Scorsese's 1990 film *Goodfellas* (distributed, not surprisingly, by Warner Bros.). These segments rose and fell on their own merits, as did the main Warner segments, but the fact that they were generally successful added to the merits of the full-length programs in which they were featured. Undoubtedly, *Animaniacs* and *Pinky and the Brain*, which both survived in one form or another until the end of the decade, were two of the animation highlights of the 1990s, and the fact that many comedy-oriented series of that time and beyond would try to replicate what they had done is a testament to how truly funny and engaging they were.

◆ ◆ ◆

By this time, the Warner studio had expanded to produce projects outside of Spielberg's influence (those are noted below) and it was becoming quite clear who was really doing the innovating at the studio.

Freakazoid!, a frenetic superhero parody, was clearly intended to do for that genre what the earlier series had done with the Looney Tunes canon. Although it also won Emmys in the manner of its predecessor, it ended up showing not what was right but what was wrong about the Spielberg/Warner relationship. This was a shame, because the stylistically flamboyant concept behind it deserved to be executed better than it was.

Bruce Timm, who had become the guiding force between the Warner superhero product (see below) just as Tom Ruegger had guided its comedy material, had originally conceived the series to be played straight. Unfortunately, Spielberg overruled this, insisting that the concept be played for laughs instead, and, as usual, he got his wish.[115] What resulted was a series that was neither fish nor fowl, not completely serious, but not completely funny either. The series focused on the then-burgeoning world of the Internet. Dexter Douglas (David Kaufman) was a young computer expert who, when abruptly absorbed into his computer during a power failure, became the frenetic yet neurotic title character (series writer Paul Rugg), who used his abilities to fight evil the old-fashioned way. Other characters featured included the Huntsman, a fellow superhero facing unemployment (!) because no one was committing crime in his neighborhood, and Lord Bravery, a blatant caricature of Jonny Quest (see Chapter 3). The methodology and ideas that had worked so brilliantly in *Tiny Toon Adventures* and *Animaniacs* failed the staff here, however, simply because the show was unable to maintain the delicate balance between comedy and straightforward action that a humorous superhero series desperately needs. Zany, madcap humor (Rugg maintained that the show was "basically about being silly"[116]) and straightforward super-heroics had worked well—separately—for the Warner studio; together, they did not. The show's ratings failure on the emaciated WB network must have darkened the relationship between Spielberg and Warner. That, along with Spielberg increasingly devoting his attention to launching the ill-fated Dreamworks studio in collaboration with Jeffrey Katzenberg and David Geffen, helped to bring an end to what had been a highly creative and successful animation partnership.

Warner Without Spielberg

The success that Spielberg and the Warner studio had achieved together was underscored by the fact that neither completely achieved the same level of competency, at least in terms of comedy, alone. Spielberg, apart from Warner, converted two features he produced, *Back to the Future* and *Casper*, into animation in partnership with their distributor, Universal. The former was mostly uninspired; the latter, in spite of considerable input from some Warner studio veterans, showed the dregs of the *Animaniacs*-styled approach to humor Spielberg instigated, in spite of the occasional inspired bit of satire within it. His 1998 series, *Toonsylvania*, was his first (and last) under the Dreamworks imprint. Trying to do for horror movie clichés what the earlier series had done for Looney Tunes, it largely failed, in spite of skilled input from the likes of Bill Kopp and Mike Peters (see both below). The jokes were there in spades, but the mad scientists, monsters, hunchbacks, zombies, hack actors and requisite angry mob simply didn't possess the engagement level, skill with dialogue delivery or especially the physical attractiveness of the Spielberg/Warner product.

Warner, for its part, was having difficulties of its own trying to produce Spielberg-styled comedy without Spielberg, and their efforts, or lack thereof, showed. *Taz-Mania* was a case in point. Here, the focus was on the Tasmanian Devil (the ubiquitous Jim Cummings), a.k.a. "Taz," in what was supposedly his native terrain, along with his family (they, unlike him, spoke English perfectly and behaved as if they were human). There was a typically bizarre assortment of supporting characters, of which the most dominant was the unprincipled canine grifter Didgeri Dingo (a brilliant, scene-stealing performance from Rob Paulsen), but there was little more to recommend the series other than good animation. Nevertheless, it managed a five-year (1991–96) run on the strengths of its origins. What really ended up scuttling the MacCurdy/Ruegger comedy ship for good, however, was *Histeria!*, airing on the WB network between 1998 and 2001. A sarcastic and satiric retort to newly imposed "educational" guidelines enforced by the FCC, the project put history itself, as the title implied, through the now-rusty studio comedy mill. A group of time travelers, including Father Time (Frank Welker), Aka Pella (Cree Summer), Miss Information (Laraine Newman), Cho Cho (Tress MacNeille), Lucky Bob (Jeff Bennett), Lydia Karaoke (Nora Dunn), and Mr. Smartypants (Rob Paulsen), served as our guides through the events of world history. The variety-revue humor approach of MacCurdy and Ruegger was by now starting to run thin, due to senseless comedy overkill (as reflected by the character names listed above). If Spielberg's solo efforts in the comedy field were desperately needing good jokes to sustain them, MacCurdy and Ruegger's were practically giving them away. *Histeria!* was as sad a footnote to MacCurdy and Ruegger's Warner animation career as *Toonsylvania* had been to Spielberg's.

But, if time had run out for the Warner studio in terms of comedy, they still had an ace in the hole in dramatic form.

◆ ◆ ◆

The corporate relationship between Warner Bros. and DC Comics dates back to 1968, when Kinney National Services, the then-parent company of the film studio, purchased control of the famed comic-book company from its surviving co-founder, Jacob "Jack" Leibowitz, who then became a board member of the new company.[117] Through restructuring engineered by the now-legendary executive Steve Ross, Kinney was reborn as Warner Communications in 1971 and, a decade later, became Time Warner through a merger with the Time-Life publishing and visual media concern. Along with the company's extensive holdings in the sound recording industry and growing influence in televisual and Internet concerns, Warner Bros. Pictures and DC Comics became tent poles for the organization's prestige and financial health in their respective industries. This created corporate synergy for both companies; Warner turned DC's characters into film and television properties, while DC turned Warner's animation properties (including those of Cartoon Network) into the most kid-friendly aspects of its increasingly pessimistic property lines. Animation, of course, was a major part of this crossover strategy.

Since Warner Bros. had closed its original, classic animation production division in 1963, DC's first ventures into television animation production had been simply to lease its properties to established studios in the field, such as Hanna-Barbera and Filmation (see chapters 3, 4, and 5 for examples). However, the establishment of the new Warner Television Animation division offered DC the chance to produce animation material in-house for the first time. It was not an opportunity they took lightly, by any means. Over the course of the 1990s and early 2000s, Warner would produce animated versions of nearly every DC property available to them, some of which dated back as far as the 1950s. In some cases, as with their versions of Batman and Superman discussed below, they were the near-definitive version of the characters possible. Yet with other projects, in spite of always handsome animation, they had less success.

The project, originally known as *Batman: The Animated Series* and later *The Adventures of Batman and Robin*, was one of the most graphically complex and emotionally compelling superhero sagas ever produced for television animation. Rather than the cheerful optimism of earlier adaptations of Batman and other multi-media heroes, there was an all-encompassing sense of dread, terror and darkness. The villains truly were *villains*, and Batman, for all of his stoic nobility, could be mistaken for one. Jean MacCurdy was absolutely correct when she dubbed the show's approach "Dark Deco," as it borrowed from both the growing pessimistic mood of the comics that spawned it along with sweeping stylistic touches of the Fleischer *Superman* cartoons of the 1940s. "What we really have here is an animated drama" she noted. "I think it may be the only animated series that takes a dramatic, rather than strictly action-adventure, approach."[118]

Truer words were never spoken.

In all aspects—design, characterization, plotting, direction, editing, acting—there was a unified sense of mood and purpose rarely seen outside of creator-driven properties. It was handsomely drawn, richly plotted and featured highly nuanced vocal performances. Devoid of any aspect of humor—especially the campy kind that had dominated the mid–1960s live-action series—the series producers, directors and writers went back to creator Bob Kane's original conception of the character—"a shadowy, unknown creature of the night who strikes out in the darkness."[119] From its debut in 1992 and throughout the decade, the series cast a wide artistic shadow; its definite influence on the super-heroic cartoons that came after it is particularly profound.

Unlike the character himself, the series had many parents, each of whom contributed in a particular way to its success. The original concept dated back to 1984, when producer Alan Burnett, then working at Hanna-Barbera, first mapped out his own take on it. Six years later, while working at Warner on *Tiny Toons*, he combined his vision for the series with that of his colleagues, Bruce Timm and Eric Radomski, who, like him, shared a genuine affection for the character and a desire to do the story justice. Timm then proceeded to fine-tune the series design, which, as he recalled, was a clear reaction to the restraints he and others had been forced to operate under during the 1980s, and even under the studio's own comedy-oriented product:

> Earlier in my career ... I was frustrated that the producers and directors always insisted on a design approach that actually worked *against* the strengths of animation: the characters always had to be drawn "realistically," with "realistic" facial features and anatomy ... every little line had to be redrawn *thousands* of times.... Result: crappy animation....
>
> We felt it was our duty to make the shows as high-quality as possible, by whatever means. If the dialogue was too corny and typically "Saturday morning," then *boom*! Quick rewrite at the recording session. If an action sequence didn't make sense, or could be done in a more exciting, cinematic way, then *boom*! Let the director and [storyboard] artists wing it. If a sequence was illogical, too goofy or superfluous, *boom*! *Cut* it! [Emphasis in original].[120]

Burnett, Timm and Radomski supervised the production of the episodes with such exacting care that they, especially Timm, would come to supervise further DC-oriented projects from Warner in the future. Executive producer Tom Ruegger and writer/producer/director Paul Dini, meanwhile, supervised the creation of the characters—both reboots of Batman's classic rogues gallery and entirely new creations, such as the humorous but malevolent villainess Harley Quinn (Arleen Sorkin). Dini, in fact, proved to be so effective in his Emmy-winning work on this project that DC Comics would later recruit him to reprise his work on their comic books.

The stories, as Jerry Beck and Will Friedwald justly note, dealt "with themes seldom touched upon by animated TV shows,"[121] which added immensely to their appeal. The most noteworthy of these was the Emmy-winning episode "Heart of Ice," which re-imagined one perennial Batman foe, Mr. Freeze, as acting villainously, in part, as a reaction to the death of his wife. "It had a surprisingly touching and human story amid the action," noted Dini, who scripted it, and this can very easily be applied to the series as a whole.[122] Under this new structure, villains who had been created decades earlier were given full and complete backstories for the first time, as were, to a degree, Batman and Robin. Topping this was a group of uniformly excellent vocal performances from a surprisingly diverse group of veteran actors as heroes and villains alike. Mark Hamill as The Joker and John Glover as The Riddler particularly stand out, but all of the performances were a notch above most of their contemporaries' work, given the quality of material they had at their disposal. Holding it all together was Kevin Conroy as Batman, who personified the grim, mercenary nature of the series perfectly. All in all, it was a very fine project, deserving of its many Emmys.

Given the success that they had with Batman, it was no surprise that the team moved on to doing a similarly excellent job with DC's *other* marquee star. Superman had been ignored since his excellent but attention-malnourished Ruby-Spears series of 1988 (see Chapter 5). The character re-emerged in spectacular form in 1996 under the direction of MacCurdy (sole executive producer this time), Burnett, Timm and Dini. Once again, the excellent Fleischer-derived artwork and moody character studies were there, but it wasn't nearly as dark as its predecessor. That was chiefly because Superman, in all his media incarnations, has always been a positive, optimistic character, unlike his corporate stable-mate, and it was that aspect of his character that dominated the tone of the series. What was different this time, however, was that what had been strengths in the Batman series were weaknesses here. The writers relied too much on Superman's comic-book nemeses to provide conflict, and these, with the formidable exception of the ever-present Lex Luthor, were largely joke figures who provided little true opposition to the Man of Steel. The truly memorable opponents proved to be figures of the writers' own invention, such as the flamboyant, electricity-charged villainess Livewire (Lori Petty), but, alas, these innovations were few and far between. Tim Daly and Dana Delany's largely wooden performances as Superman and Lois Lane, respectively, didn't help matters any. Still, the property was handsomely animated, and that distracted the viewer. It lasted 65 episodes in its original form, and was later seen in combined formats with Batman and other heroes.

Warner and DC had established a winning formula here, and they continued to plow the field well for the better part of the next decade. Yet, while the graphics always remained glossy and top of the line, the genuinely creative innovations in the writing would become increasingly fallow. This aspect of the story, however, will be saved for the next chapter.

◆ ◆ ◆

In the period between 1990 and 1999, Warner Bros. produced an exceptional group of dramatic and comic television animation programs that will forever remain among the cleverest examples of their kind. This was the product of a truly gifted group of individuals who came together to produce this exceptional work at a particularly fecund period in television animation history. And it was not destined to last. In the following decade, as its parent company was severely damaged by corporate warfare, Warner Bros. Television Animation retreated from the innovations into colorless formula. This only makes what was accomplished by the studio under Jean MacCurdy and Tom Ruegger's leadership stand out even more as the truly superb work that it was.

Other Voices

Besides the studios already profiled in this chapter, a number of other outlets, major and minor, were involved in the production of television animation during the decade. A small boom occurred in the number of houses active in the field, in part due to the increasing visibility and level of acceptance television animation was enjoying. Some of the studios had begun activity during the 1980s, and simply continued to produce mediocre material with no visible changes in creative quality or philosophy. Others were simply created in response to a perceived need, and perished soon after. But while their output was small and largely undistinguished in comparison to the major players of the decade's story, once in a while someone would produce something that was truly worth watching—if you could *find* it.

DIC

As noted in the previous chapter, Andy Heyward's company occupied a nebulous position in this decade, first independent, then part of Disney, then independent again. This corporate shuffling, and the new trends in television animation production and construction, had little impact on the creative end.

The year 1990 began with a rebooted version of *G.I. Joe* (see Chapter 5), along with an animated version of the pop stars of the moment, New Kids on the Block. In addition, the studio was initially entrusted with the animation for Ted Turner's overhyped pro-environment project, *Captain Planet and the Planeteers*. This was prior to Turner's acquisition of Hanna-Barbera, at which point production reverted to that studio instead. Rebounding from that loss, the company then produced several critical and commercial flops during 1991. *Hammerman* rather bizarrely presented rapper M.C. Hammer as a superhero. *Prostars* tried and failed to turn the unlikely star athlete trio of Wayne Gretsky, Michael Jordan and Bo Jackson into animated heroes; *Where's Waldo?* was a likewise unsuccessful attempt to turn the popular children's book series into a program; and *Wishkid Starring Macaulay Culkin*, which would be one of the last original television animation projects commissioned by NBC, was largely self-explanatory. That same year, DIC also animated the DC Comics property *Swamp Thing* with none of the flair Alan Moore had brought to the original graphic novels.

From that point on, the syndication and network television markets on which it had long relied began to dry up. DIC's productions became fewer in number, but there still remained quality-control problems. More and more, whether or not the project worked was based on whether the studio had anything of substance to work with, and, in most cases, it didn't. But this didn't stop it from trying.

The year 1992 saw the debut of *Super Dave*, the company's first product for the FOX network. Based on the exploits of the notoriously incompetent fictional stuntman Super Dave Osborne (portrayed, as always, by actor/writer/producer Bob Einstein), the series did little to elaborate on his act except to animate it. Thus, we were still subjected to Osborne nearly killing himself repeatedly in the name of "entertainment," but, since he was now animated, we didn't feel nearly as sorry for him when it happened. The studio had far better luck exploiting other pre-fabricated characters the following year. *Madeline*, based on the Ludwig Bemelmans children's books, was well executed and extremely pleasant by studio standards, and it managed to eke out a respectable run on ABC for that reason. The studio also got a good two-for-one proposition out of the Sega video game character Sonic the Hedgehog, programming him both in a syndicated daily strip with the emphasis on comedy, and in a weekly *Star Wars*–indebted adventure on ABC.

Further studio productions in the decade remained a mixed bag that rose and fell on whatever merits they happened to possess. *Where on Earth Is Carmen Sandiego?*, launched in 1994, was derived from a popular series of computer games from Broderbund Software; its educational mandate was smashed in the audience's face so effectively that it ended up winning an Emmy for its troubles. *Ultraforce*, from 1995, was a routine action-adventure saga. That same year, however, produced *What-a-Mess*, one of the more engaging studio products of the decade. Based on a series of children's books by Frank Muir, this project about an innocent but optimistic Afghan puppy deserved far more visibility and respect than it actually got.

The Wacky World of Tex Avery, which debuted in 1997, was purportedly based on the comic mindset of the legendary theatrical animator; in fact, it was simply an insult to his memory. Likewise, *Mummies Alive!*, from that same year, was a one-note series based on a one-note toy line. There were some more imaginative projects in 1999, but not by much. *Sabrina* was based on the popular live-action sitcom of the same name, itself based on characters from Archie Comics. The only major difference, other than its being animated rather than live, was that the "teenage" witch was now a junior-high pre-teen. *Sherlock Holmes in the 22nd Century*, meanwhile, was utterly self-explanatory in title and nature.

The studio was also responsible for bringing the popular Japanese *anime* series *Sailor Moon* into North American circulation during the decade, but, other than editing it to conform to North American standards of propriety, it could lay no claim to having influenced its production in any way. Given the scattershot nature of its productions during the decade, that was likely a good thing.

Film Roman

Like DIC, Film Roman was a studio that preferred to stay the course with what it was best at than attempt anything new. However, the similarities between the two shops end at this point. As noted in Chapter 5, Phil Roman, unlike Andy Heyward, was a producer who put quality above quantity, and his studio's product during the 1990s reflected that mandate handsomely.

In addition to producing animation for other programmers, notably for the producers of *The Simpsons* and *King of the Hill* (see above), Roman maintained production on his remaining '80s programs while venturing into new areas as well. Sometimes he succeeded here, but at other times he failed.

Roman was one of the first animators to provide animation content for the FOX network's children's division, but his 1990 production *Zazoo U*, a series set at a school for anthropomorphic animals, was an unqualified failure. He had far better luck when, in 1991, he returned to CBS, where his work in the previous decade had largely been shown. *Mother Goose and Grimm*, based on Mike Peters's lunatic fringe-styled comic strip, was extremely well drawn and written, managing to transfer its creator's artistic sensibilities very well to animation, just as Roman had already done with Jim Davis's Garfield (see Chapter 5). The trouble is, this time not enough people were watching, and, after a brief name change to *Grimmy*, after the lead canine character, the series was unjustly terminated.

Roman had a bit more luck with the pact he struck with the Soviet animation house ASK (see Chapter 5 for more details), which resulted in two syndicated projects. *Film Roman Presents Animated Classic Showcase*, launched in 1993, featured vintage Russian cartoons from the Soyuzmultifulm studio concern, which Roman dubbed in English and re-mastered in partnership with the Russian firm Films By Jove. Undoubtedly, this was the first time English-speaking viewers had ever seen this material, but it did better on video release than in syndication. A second package, hosted by Russian ballet dancer Mikhail Baryshnikov and released in 1996, did little better. That same year saw the production of *C Bear and Jamal*, an African American–centric series developed by rapper Tone Loc, who also voiced the teddy bear lead character.

However, to sustain his studio, Roman was also being forced to take on some levels of uncharacteristic hackwork. *Mighty Max*, based on a popular toy line, from 1993, can only be described as such. *Cro*, from the same year, was produced in collaboration with the Children's Television Workshop for ABC, and the problems with that relationship were evident from the start. Although Roman and company produced an engaging prehistoric world, and some talented actors to voice the characters, the CTW held far too much veto power over the on-screen content, and the results were neither educational nor entertaining.

The later years of the decade were mixed for the company. *The Critic*, created and produced by *Simpsons* veterans Al Jean and Mike Reiss for Gracie Films (see above) and Columbia Pictures, with James L. Brooks as executive producer, had some promise. Debuting in 1995 on ABC, it was an animated sitcom that focused on the travails of a popular TV film critic (Jon Lovitz) who was far less secure or opinionated in his off-camera life. Given its origins, it was no surprise that the series proved to be a comic gold mine in its written content, and the Roman animators produced visuals to match, especially in the numerous film parodies that were presented. Unfortunately, the ratings were not good enough for ABC, who canceled it after a few installments, nor for FOX, who resurrected it only for the same length of time. That same year, the studio resurrected Felix the Cat for Saturday morning consumption on CBS in *The Twisted Tales of....* Appropriately, Don Oriolo, whose father, Joe, had been responsible for Felix's comeback during the 1960s (see Chapter 3), shared executive-producer duties with Roman, although the sparely inked backgrounds and squash-and-stretch character designs were far more reflective of Felix's halcyon days during the 1920s, albeit with sound and music added. Once again, a delightful Roman series went largely unnoticed by the viewing public.

By 1996, the studio was serving more as a vehicle for the ideas of others than its own. *Bruno the Kid* was based on a series concept by film star Bruce Willis, who voiced the lead and co-produced, but that was about all it had to recommend it. *The Mask*, for CBS, was based on the popular Jim Carrey movie of the same name—minus Carrey, although the-ever reliable Rob Paulsen did a very good job standing in for him. More despairing in nature were two more pre-existing media properties of that year: *Mortal Kombat*, based on the graphically violent arcade video game, and *Richie Rich*, the Harvey Comics character previously adapted by Hanna-Barbera in the 1980s (see Chapter 5). The decade's work culminated in 1998 with *Bobby's World*, an adaptation of the comic routines and persona of Canadian-born comedian/actor Howie Mandel, who interacted with his animated alter ego, Bobby, in linking segments. It could be imaginative at times, but not enough to ignore the fundamental weaknesses in its concept.

Film Roman's nature changed, as noted in Chapter 5, when Phil Roman himself was ousted from the company he founded (he later returned). The new management was simply more interested in maintaining the existing contracts for outside animation supplying than it was for producing new, original animation, and that, for better or worse, has been the path the company has chosen since, with only a couple of exceptions. Given what Film Roman was capable of producing on its own, it is truly the viewers' loss.

SAVAGE STEVE HOLLAND

This veteran live-action filmmaker and television producer was responsible for one of the most engaging yet underrated television animation projects of the 1990s. Born in 1960, he was, like many of the other animators profiled in this chapter, educated at California Institute of the Arts. But while he achieved some acclaim as an animator, his first success came as a live-action filmmaker, with such 1980s films as *Better off Dead*, *One Crazy Summer* and *How I Got into College*. Switching to television and animation in the 1990s, he teamed with a friend and colleague, Bill Kopp, to create the deliciously demented *Eek! The Cat*, which ran on FOX between 1992 and 1997. Kopp, a native of Rockford, Illinois, born in 1962, was, like Holland, a graduate of California Institute of the Arts, who had won two Academy Awards for his student shorts. Together, they produced the *Eek* series and wrote most of the scripts, inspired by Holland's bad luck with pet cats, and with Kopp voicing the lead character. Both men would go on to produce other projects separately (those are noted elsewhere in this book) but, as with many other similar animation teams, what they produced apart didn't equal what they did together.

As Hal Erickson aptly describes it, the series "was a bizarre, dreamlike animated series best described as the misadventures of a neurotic cat—a compulsive do-gooder whose efforts always ended in catastrophe."[123] It was also nonsensical, extreme and completely illogical in its narrative and character portrayals, making it utterly hilarious. Eek spent much of his animated existence avoiding being utterly destroyed by a brace of violent enemies, that is, when he wasn't trying to romance his enormously fat girlfriend, Annabelle (Tawny Kitaen). Other characters included Sharkey, the "sharkdog" ever intent on killing Eek; The Incredible Elmo, a bulbous-red-nosed elk stuntman forever trying to raise money "for my brother Timmy's operation"; and the Squishy Bears, a Care Bear–styled group who frequently got violently abused by the animators. The aggressive approach of Holland and Kopp was most thoroughly manifested, however, in the on-going battle between the producers and their own network's censorship department, arguably the most heated conflict between producer and censors since the contentious 1970s.[124] Two other lesser components, *The Terrible Thunderlizards* and *Klutter*, alternated with the main feature in later years, under the umbrella title *Eek-stravaganza*.

Whatever your feelings may be about the excesses of animation violence, *Eek*, in spite of its relentless and shameless employment of it, was a one-of-a-kind cartoon gem. It deserves far more recognition than the purgatory to which it has been relegated by cable programmers.

Saban Entertainment

As noted in the previous chapter, Haim Saban's company became the principal supplier of content to the FOX network's children's division in the late 1990s, primarily on the strength of the live-action hit *Mighty Morphin Power Rangers* (until it was sold to Disney in the early 2000s). The majority of what it produced during the decade was workman-like and ill-distinguished hackwork, with a couple of noteworthy exceptions.

The decade began, blandly enough, with *Kid 'n' Play*, a vehicle for the then-popular rap duo, which aired on the soon-to-be-extinguished NBC Saturday-morning lineup during 1991–92. Most of the remainder of the studio product was similarly undistinguished, with only the Disney-styled presence of the company name in the "official" titles piquing interest in the fare. Saban was, in fact, a thorn in Disney's creative side during this period, creating series that were clearly derived from some of Disney's features, which might explain why Disney was so eager to take it over. The product itself included adaptations of *The Little Mermaid* (1991), *Pinocchio* (1992) and *Oliver Twist* (1996). These were central to the Disney/Saban conflict. Other series included an adaptation of *Gulliver's Travels* (1992), and an educational series called *The Why Why Family* (1996).

The other two major Saban productions were far more successful, at least artistically. *X Men*, a collaboration with the animation division of Marvel Comics (see below), was a lavishly produced adaptation of the famed comic-book series. Benefitting from the presence of Marvel editor *emeritus* Stan Lee as an executive producer, the series was structured very much in the same soap-opera fashion that writer Chris Claremont had brought to its comic-book counterpart. However, since the show was aimed chiefly at children, the emphasis was squarely on action. Those familiar with the characters from their comic-book (and, later, live-action movie) incarnations need only fill in the blanks, but the series also served as a faithful introduction to the characters for newcomers.

The other Saban product of the decade, likewise, stood head and shoulders above the rest of the company's product. In fact, it is one of the largely unnoticed highlights of television animation in the 1990s. Developed by future best-selling children's book author Jim Benton, *The Secret Files of the Spy Dogs* was a witty and highly entertaining send-up of the spy genre. Airing between 1998 and 2000 on FOX, it was a breath of fresh air in the increasingly stagnant world of network television animation.

Benton's simple but highly workable premise, which he refined in collaboration with veteran animation comedy specialist Michael Ryan, was this: the dogs of the world comprised a highly successful and disciplined Interpol-styled spy force that repeatedly saved their theoretical human "masters" without the latter group (who, predictably, were portrayed as being somewhat thin on the gray matter) ever noticing. Chief among the group were the intelligent, resourceful and witty Ralph (Micky Dolenz, in his best television animation performance) and the diminutive but cocksure "pink terrier" Mitzy (Mary Kay Bergman, in a career-defining role), while the mysterious but omnipotent Dog Zero (Adam "Batman" West) supervised things from afar. That the series managed to avoid repetition was due to the great writing of Benton and Ryan, as well as the superb, award-winning animation direction of Will Meugniot. Like their characters, the writers and director were seemingly willing to do anything to get the job done, and the efforts paid off in spades. Thus, while most of the series was played with a seriousness that prefigured the later, similar live-action series *24*, certain episodes threw stunning curve balls at the audience. One episode implied that TV programmers were using voodoo-practicing witch doctors to goose their ratings (and featured a Ted

Turner-styled network official, to boot); another was done as a parody of the live-action law-enforcement series *COPS*, while yet another was done as a *musical*! The mischievousness of the writers also manifested itself in some of the one-shot gags, including a hair-growing formula being redirected from its intended target to a convention of *bald* people![125]

Like *Eek! The Cat*, *Spy Dogs* was a gem that deserves to be seen and appreciated by many more people than it was at the time of its original broadcast. Hopefully, Disney, the current owners of the Saban library, will see fit to issue the series on DVD, with Benton's new status as the author of the best-selling *Dear Dumb Diary* books for adolescents serving as a drawing card.

MGM Television

This represented Metro-Goldwyn-Mayer's third go-round at operating an animation studio (see chapters 1 and 3 for the others) and was the least successful—commercially and artistically—of the three. Like Columbia/Tristar/Sony and Universal (see both below), MGM was clearly envious of the success of Disney and Warner (see both above) in the animation field, or else why would they have ventured back into the fray? Consequently, as with Columbia and Universal's similar ventures, MGM was not in the game to stay; it simply played a couple of hands at the table before walking away from TV animation again, having learned little from its experience.

Since Ted Turner had acquired the classic studio library, including the animation studio creations of the 1940s and 1950s, MGM was forced to rely on the properties it *did* own to create new animation, chiefly for syndication. Some of the characters they created or used merited the decision, while others did not.

The most successful series came as a result of the company acquiring United Artists, financially crippled by the colossal failure of Michael Cimino's philosophical Western, *Heaven's Gate*, in 1980. *The Pink Panther*, the old warhorse of the DePatie/Freleng studio, was resurrected in new adventures in 1993, with his ailing creator Friz Freleng now providing only nominal input (he would die two years later). This time, the normally silent Panther was given a speaking voice (Matt Frewer), although this detracted somewhat from his appeal. The series, supervised by Hanna-Barbera veterans Paul Sabella and Mike Young, was still very well produced, and gained bonus points for the variety of non-Panther shorts also featured, some revivals of classic DePatie/Freleng characters, others entirely new inventions.

This success did not extend to the other "branded" properties MGM underwrote during the 1990s. *James Bond Jr.*, produced in collaboration with Fred Wolf (see below) and based blatantly on a line of toys, was utterly self-explanatory. Similarly, *All Dogs Go to Heaven*, based on Don Bluth's 1989 United Artists–distributed feature as well as an MGM-produced sequel in 1996, wore its origins too cozily on its sleeve, in spite of some interesting voice casting and performances. But the desperation of the unit for material was most shockingly displayed by 1998's *The Lionhearts*, which purported to tell the behind-the-scenes life story of MGM's leonine mascot, Leo, and his family, most of whom were named blatantly after stars from MGM's golden age. That series—along with MGM's entire television animation unit—disappeared after a single year on the air, save for *Robocop*, a similarly uninspired take on the action movie series MGM had acquired after buying out the bankrupt Orion Pictures earlier that year.

Once the most powerful studio in Hollywood, MGM fell fast and hard during the

1970s, 1980s and 1990s, more so than any of its contemporaries. The paucity of its television animation product only served to indicate exactly *how* far the mighty had fallen.

COLUMBIA TRISTAR/SONY TELEVISION

As noted in Chapters 1 and 3, Columbia Pictures' earlier ventures in animation came in three forms: their in-house Screen Gems facility of the 1930s and early 1940s, their distribution of the products of the UPA studio in the late 1940s and early 1950s, and, finally, their distribution of the early work of William Hanna and Joseph Barbera through their Screen Gems television division in the late 1950s and early 1960s. In the interim, Columbia had twice become a corporate subsidiary like its peers, being first acquired by the Coca-Cola company in the early 1980s, and then, in 1989, taken over by the Japanese electronics giant, Sony. It was under the sphere of this ownership that Columbia once again entered the field of animation production directly, both by bankrolling independent television animation production and later setting up its own CGI-based feature-film production division. However, their television animation division's productions in the 1990s and 2000s, under both the Columbia/Tristar and Sony Pictures banners, were a mixed bag, not at all benefitting from its centralized production focus.

For the most part, the company's product during the 1990s was unashamedly derived from what the parent film studio was doing. Prominent examples include *Jumanji*, derived from the Chris Van Allsburg children's book and the film it inspired, as well as *Men in Black*, based on the company's astonishingly popular film franchise. *Godzilla*, clearly inspired by filmmakers Dean Devlin and Roland Emmerich's recent take on the legendary Japanese monster (their company, Centropolis, co-produced the series) also smacked in many ways of derivation, although it had the advantage of being well produced and staged. Where comedy-oriented product was concerned, the studio fared little better. *Dilbert*, based on the popular Scott Adams comic strip, was a much-hyped addition to the fledgling UPN network's lineup, but, despite being "run" by *Seinfeld* veteran Larry Charles, it failed to live up to the expectations of both viewers and programmers. *Dragon Tales* proved simply to be another action-oriented disappointment.

The two wild cards in the lineup failed to produce results, although that was the result of bad programming rather than a lack of creativity. *Channel Umptee-Three*, for one thing, had the advantage of being conceived and produced by legendary sitcom maestro Norman Lear (*All in the Family, Maude, The Jeffersons, Sanford and Son, Mary Hartman, Mary Hartman, Fernwood 2 Night*, etc.), who was re-entering production of series after a long absence. That generated some publicity, but the series didn't entirely deserve it. The concept was a clear echo of Jay Ward and Alex Anderson's unproduced *Frostbite Falls Review* from the late 1940s (i.e., animals operating a TV station; see Chapter 2), albeit retooled to fit the new 24–7 programming model of contemporary television. The title operation was a "pirate" station which operated from a moving van, and beamed its content to viewers entirely in "the white space" between existing cable channels.[126] The operators were Ogden (Rob Paulsen), an ostrich; Holey Moley (Neil Ross), a mole; and Sheldon Cargo (David Paymer), a snail. Opposition came in the form of Stickley and Pandora Ricketts (Jonathan Harris and Alice Ghostley). With the input of Lear and *Garfield and Friends* writer Mark Evanier (see Chapter 5), the series should have done well, but, at least in the ratings, it did not.

The other major venture into original concept programming fared about as well, although it was far more interesting. *Project G.E.E.K.E.R.* was created by Douglas TenNapel, also the brains behind *Earthworm Jim* (see below), in collaboration with the underrated but highly skilled Doug Langdale (see below and Chapter 7). A stylized science fiction series, the focus was on the title character (Billy West), a humanoid robot with destructive powers he could not control. Kidnapped by professional thief Lady Macbeth (or, informally, "Becky") (Cree Summer) and the talking dinosaur Noah (Brad Garrett), Geeker struggled to remain one step ahead of his vengeful creator, Moloch (Jim Cummings), who, typically, wanted to have him destroyed. It was by far the most artistically accomplished product produced by Columbia in the 1990s, and therefore its cancellation by a network (CBS) then engaged in a purge of all its animated series, is all the more unfortunate.

Unlike its peers, MGM and Universal, Columbia/Tristar/Sony would continue production of television animation into the 2000s, although, for the most part, there would be little change in the routine nature of their methodology.

Universal Pictures

Like MGM and Columbia, Universal was a relative newcomer to the television animation business, but, like its film studio peers, it had a historical background in the art, although it had been largely restricted to the output of one artist: Walter Lantz (see Chapter 1). The studio's ventures into television animation, however, were chiefly connected to the launch of a cable channel, the Universal Family Entertainment Network, supervised by industry veteran Jeff Sagal. Like the latest products from MGM and Columbia, Universal's new animation output was, for the most part, undistinguished.

The chief productions of the Universal TV animation unit were ideas raided from the theatrical film division, with little or no thought given to whether the properties were actually suitable. *Beethoven* was based on the film series about a mischievous St. Bernard, and the animators did a good job of converting the dog into an anthropomorphic character, complete with some similarly designed pals. Unfortunately, the writing staff simply lacked the ability to do anything truly innovative with them; the presence of Ivan Reitman (who had also produced the original feature film) in the credit list ensured that the content would be as inane as the live-action film. Similarly, *Problem Child*, based on a feature-film series about a preteen delinquent, was a project that was simply designed to fill space and kill time. Equally troublesome were the more action-oriented properties, both produced by Sagal. *Exo-Squad* was an ornately produced but largely ignored series involving warring tribes of humans and robots, while *Monster Force* resurrected the central idea behind Hanna-Barbera's *Drak Pack* (see Chapter 5), played straight this time, to little effect.

Apart from the studio's association with Steven Spielberg (see above), the most effective Universal product ultimately came from an outsider. *Earthworm Jim*, based on a popular video game, was supervised by the game's creator, Douglas TenNapel, though much of the witty dialogue was the work of Doug Langdale, who would later create the superlative *Weekenders* for Disney (see Chapter 7). The premise: a mere earthworm gets possession of a supersuit which gives him supernatural abilities. The stories follow the title character (flamboyantly voiced by Dan Castalleneta) on his "heroic" adventures, to considerably humorous effect. Jim was aided in his efforts by the youthful, idealistic Peter Puppy (Jeff Bennett, who doubled as the Westbrook Van Voohris–styled narrator) who, like his video-game counterpart, could change into an Incredible Hulk–styled monster at a moment's notice when he was injured. The other characters on the program, mostly Jim's opposition, were an equally colorful lot: Queen Slug-for-a-Butt (Andrea Martin), Princess What's-Her-Name (Kath Soucie), Professor Monkey-for-a-Head (Charlie Adler), Evil the Cat (Edward Hibbert), Psy-Crow (Jim Cummings) and Bob the Killer Goldfish (Cummings again). With good scripts, and some old pros doing the voice work, along with interesting character and background designs, the show was genuinely entertaining and appealing, but, running on the weak WB network, the series did not receive the wide circulation it deserved.

Given the resources it had at its disposal, it was highly surprising that Universal was unable to produce better shows. Ultimately, the staff of the Universal Cartoon Studios would be punished for their failure by being forced to produce numerous direct-to-video sequels to the company's earlier animated feature films—which, in the highly innovative 1990s, was a comedown.

Nelvana

Just as it had in the previous decade, this innovative Canadian production house continued with the acclaimed high-quality product it had done in the 1970s.[127] However, it was increasingly clear that the company was succumbing to the same sort of creative *ennui* of its American-based predecessors, as it increasingly began framing itself as a house-for-hire more than actually continuing with the truly innovative, individualized work that had distinguished it in the past.

The problems with trying to please both Canadian and American investors were reflected in the scattershot projects the company engaged in across the decade. *Little Rosey*, based on the comedy antics of Roseanne (Barr/Arnold) as a young girl, failed to attract interest on both sides of the border. *Ace Ventura*, meanwhile, was, like Film Roman's contemporary *Mask* (see above), an insipid animated version of a Jim Carrey movie vehicle minus Carrey. (Hanna-Barbera produced a third, *Dumb and Dumber*, around the same time.) Even worse was another film-derived product, *Free Willy*. The studio retrenched by producing the animation for the excellent *Eek! The Cat* (see above), but it seemed to be spinning its own creative wheels. The poorly conceived *Wildcats* clearly reflected this.

The company recovered some ground in the late 1990s. *Stickin' Around*, for instance, was an inspired children's series, with the characters and setting presented in the basic chalk-outline style of many a young child's drawings. Other series from this time reflected a similar basic approach in either graphics or storytelling, part of a new effort to redirect their programming directly at children. *Pippi Longstocking*, based on the Swedish author Astrid Lingren's legendary super-girl, was charming at times, although it suffered from undue coyness. Two other children's book series that benefitted from TV animation treatment were William Joyce's *Rolie Polie Olie* and Maurice Sendak's *George Shrinks*. *Donkey Kong Country*, on the other hand, was a largely haphazard attempt at adapting a Nintendo video game, with only the CGI-derived graphics providing interest.

During the decade, Nelvana also produced the self-explanatory *Dumb Bunnies*; *Blazing Dragons*, a stylized medieval comic farce from Monty Python's Terry Jones; *Birdz*, a dire exercise in avian anthropomorphic antics; and *Blaster's Universe*, an overtly educational science fiction project.

Nelvana was sold to the Canadian cable provider Corus Entertainment, and that company's platforms increasingly became the focus by which future projects from the company would be seen. In that sense, they would have to truly matter to be seen outside of Canada, and that, increasingly, would not be the case.

CINAR

Another Canadian-based animation firm, CINAR began to penetrate the American market during this time with some success. Unfortunately, that success was limited by financial problems that ultimately became its undoing.[128]

Like Klasky-Csupo (see above), CINAR was the work of a husband-and-wife duo, Micheline Charest and Roland Weinberg, who founded the company in America in 1976. Originally merely content distributors, in 1984 they relocated to Montreal and became producers as well. Much of the studio's work involved producing animated content in-house, with separate vocal tracks in French (for francophone audiences) and English. In 1993, the company went public, and over the next few years experienced its greatest success in cracking the American market.

However, in 2000, an internal audit revealed that over $100 million of company funds had been re-directed to an offshore bank account in the Bahamas, without the knowledge or consent of the board. Likewise, the company had also been paying American writers to do scriptwriting for them, while still crediting Canadians with the work for tax purposes. These revelations were dire for the company's future. While no formal criminal charges were ever made, and Charest and Weinberg denied knowledge of the illegal activities, they were still forced to pay heavy settlements to the Canadian and Quebec governments and were banned from economic activities for several years afterwards. CINAR, its stock delisted from the Canadian stock exchange, effectively ceased to exist as a corporate entity after that time.

These unfortunate events, however, should not taint the creative success of the studio's product, which was, for the most part, quite exceptional. While not all of the work was broadcast in or directed toward the American market, what was shown there garnered acclaim.

The primary beneficiary of CINAR's work was PBS, which, after years of resisting programming television animation among its distinguish children's show ranks, started biting the bullet in the mid–1990s. The first successful test case for the public broadcaster's new mandate was a CINAR product. *Arthur*, based on the long-running children's book series by Marc Brown (who contributed to the production of the series), immediately attracted a large audience with its simple, effective educational storylines, winning Emmys as well. Soon, animation began making further inroads at PBS (see Chapter 7 for more). Other projects of CINAR seen in America included a series based on the works of another famed children's author, Richard Scarry; *Little Lulu*, based on the noted comic-book character; *The Legend of White Fang*, based on the writings of Jack London; and *Stop the Smoggies*, a colorful pro-environment saga strongly reminiscent of *The Smurfs* in character, content and tone.

Bad financing aside, CINAR was capable of producing genuinely entertaining animation for television, and it is unfortunate that it could not produce more of it.

MARVEL

Due to corporate restructuring and bureaucratic infighting, the noted comic-book company's role in the television animation industry changed.[129] With the network and syndicated bases of operation upon which it had relied in the 1980s starring to disappear, and the loss of Margaret Loesch to the FOX network, original programming gradually came to an end, replaced simply by new incarnations of the famed organization's established comic-book superheroes. Still, the company was able to provide some interesting original projects before resigning itself to corporate hackwork.

In the early 1990s, the company basically continued as it had during the previous decade, though its true successes were becoming few and far between. Some ideas showed promise, but these were botched by poor, uneven execution. *Spacecats*, airing on NBC in 1991, was a collaboration with Paul Fusco, creator of *Alf* (see Chapter 5). A mixture of animation and live-action puppetry, it focused on a race of feline aliens who traveled to Earth to perform altruistic acts. While it didn't always work, the pieces that did, included a self-conscious narrator with a style modeled on William Conrad's, stood out. Charles Nelson Reilly, who portrayed the feline race's leader, the Disembodied Omnipotent Ruler of Cats (D.O.R.C.), effortlessly stole the show. *Dog City*, a similar animation/puppet hybrid airing on FOX between 1992 and 1995, had the benefit of being a collaboration with the Jim Henson Company. (Henson had conceived the series idea and aired a "pilot" episode on his eponymous short-lived NBC variety project, which aired shortly before his death.) While the central idea of using animated dogs in a parody of traditional film noir gangster films seemed interesting at first, it was unable to transcend the writers' obsession with stereotyped "dog" interests (e.g., fire hydrants, bones, etc.) to be truly meaningful in its content. Based on a graphic novel from the 1970s, *Bucky O'Hare and the Toad Wars*, in syndication in 1991, was pre-programmed to line up with a toy package from Hasbro, and was unable to transcend this corporate intent to be meaningful on its own. *Attack of the Killer Tomatoes* was a bizarrely conceived project based on a cult film from 1979, and, save for John Astin's performance as the main villain, was largely routine. *Biker Mice from Mars*, a syndicated "action" show developed by Loesch's replacement, Rick Ungar, had the misfortune of being at the wrong place at the wrong time. The action cycle of the 1980s had screeched to a halt by the time it debuted in 1993, due to the new restrictions of the Children's Television Act, and the all-too-obvious similarities to *Teenage Mutant Ninja Turtles* (see Chapter 5) hurt it further, even though Marvel had managed to secure wide circulation for it. *Little Shop*, inspired by the 1960 Roger Corman horror film *The Little Shop of Horrors* (and its 1986 musical remake), was utterly derivative of its source material, and therefore not very good.

It was at this point that Marvel decided to re-trench and concentrate on its strengths. In 1994, it produced a handsomely mounted version of *Spider-Man*, which was far more faithful to the spirit and intent of the original comic books than the previous TV animated versions (the character's celebrated co-creator, Stan Lee, was an executive producer). Featuring vivid animation and a surprisingly top-drawer vocal cast (including Edward Asner, Joseph Campanella, Martin Landau, Efrem Zimbalist, Jr., Roscoe Lee Browne and Jeff Corey, among others), the series was an engaging winner in all respects. It was enjoyed by veteran fans and newcomers alike, although it would ultimately be overshadowed by the live-action movie series of the late 1990s and early 2000s. Alongside the *X Men* series produced with Saban (see above), it reflected the new direction taken by the Marvel studio. Emulating Warner's illustration of the DC catalogue (see above), it produced new versions of *The Fantastic Four*, *The Incredible Hulk*, *Iron Man*, and *The Avengers*, plus new versions of *Spider-Man*, which, while technically sound, were only mildly interesting creatively unless you happened to be a truly devoted Marvel fan.

A footnote to the Marvel studio story was the brief independent operation of Sunbow Studios, its financial and creative partner during the 1980s. The sole major product to come from this arrangement was *The Tick*, a hilarious superhero parody which aired on FOX from 1994 to 1997 (and also, briefly, on Comedy Central). Based on a hit underground comic-book series created by Ben Edlund, it benefitted from having its creator on staff as a writer/ producer. The adventures of the dimwitted title character (Townsend Coleman), and his moth-suit-wearing sidekick, Arthur (Micky Dolenz first, Rob Paulsen later) were wickedly funny parodies of most of the major clichés of the superhero genre (both comic book and animated forms) and featured enormously *outre* characters on both sides. (Chairface Chippendale, to cite one example, literally had a *chair* for a *face*!) Like the later *Powerpuff Girls* (see above), it took a refreshingly humorous stance on a media genre full of puffed-up self-importance on both sides of the good-and-evil divide, and the viewers truly appreciated it.[130] Sunbow, however, was unable to continue the creator-driven production model it initiated here.

Fred Wolf Studios

After splitting from the Murakami-Wolf-Swenson organization, through which he had produced *Teenage Mutant Ninja Turtles* (see Chapter 5), Fred Wolf continued production under his own name during the 1990s. However, the majority of his work was largely tired action fare, with none of the skill that had been seen in his earlier projects. Some examples include *Barnyard Commandos*, *Fantastic Voyages*, *Dinobabies* and *Toxic Crusaders* (the latter based on a toy line), whose titles were largely self-explanatory. Other projects included a new version of the *anime* series *Speed Racer*, a revival of *Zorro*, and *Budgie the Little Helicopter*, an educational series based on a series of children's books by Sarah "Fergie" Ferguson (a.k.a. the Duchess of York).

Zodiac

The successor to Calico (see Chapter 5), this company, under Peter Keefe's leadership, managed to place a couple of moderately successful series in the syndication market before finally being forced to bow out. By name, these series were: *Mr. Bogus*, the tale of a good-natured "gremlin"; *Widget the World Watcher*, a pro-environment project with an empowered alien title character; and *Twinkle, the Dream Being*, a wish-fulfillment fantasy on the order of the later—and more entertaining—*Fairly Oddparents* (see Chapter 7).

A.K.A. Cartoons

This Canada-based company, run by Canadian-born animator Danny Antonucci, was responsible for two of the more eclectically produced series of the 1990s. *The Brothers Grunt*, produced for MTV in 1994 (see below), reflected the company's philosophy—"producing animation for everyone whether they want it or not"[131]—as it focused on a group of brothers who communicated chiefly through inarticulate vocalizations and by breaking wind. Antonucci showed himself to be slightly more refined a few years later for Cartoon Network (see above). *Ed Edd 'n' Eddy*, debuting on that provider in 1998, focused on a Three Stooges–like trio of misfit boys and their peers: the first Ed was a dimwit, the last a schemer, while the middle one seemed to possess something approaching a brain. Largely plot-less, with an emphasis primarily on scattershot gags and hand-drawn animation, the series gained a large following, especially among young boys, and thus it managed to remain on Cartoon Network, in new episodes and reruns alike, during the 2000s.

MTV

The surest sign of the increasing mainstream acceptance of television animation during the 1990s was the fact that it was turning up in highly unlikely places on the dial. For youth-oriented channels like MTV and Comedy Central (see below), animation was something that could and did lure audiences that did not normally watch them. However, since both channels were geared to young (particularly male) audiences, the animation they commissioned was built around the stereotypical "interests" of this group.

In addition to the previously mentioned *Brothers Grunt*, animation programming at MTV was largely lowbrow humor. The signature MTV animation series was *Beavis and Butthead*, created and produced by Mike Judge in 1993 (see above), which focused on two adolescent slackers to whom nearly everything in the world "sucked." The characters' repulsive physical appearances, and their ne'er-do-well activities (the pilot saw them beating frogs with a baseball bat on the pretense that they were playing "baseball" with them), led to anti-violence activists calling for Judge's head. Judge later revived them, briefly, when his more successful *King of the Hill* (see above) ceased production. He authorized a spinoff, *Daria*, starring the boys' lone female friend, but this was developed and produced by Glenn Eiffeth. Meanwhile, the company also produced two anthology series, *Liquid Television* (from which *Beavis and Butthead* first emerged) and *MTV Oddities*, as well as *MTV Downtown*, which was essentially an animated version of the channel's long-running "reality" series, *The Real World*.

The other major series to emerge from *Liquid Television* was somewhat different in intent and tone. *Aeon Flux*, debuting in 1994, was created by Peter Chung, yet another California Institute of the Arts graduate making his mark during the decade. The title character, a scantily clad secret-agent type, existed in a futuristic universe, spoke little, and was typically killed off at the end of each installment, only to be resurrected in the next one. Chung reluctantly developed the character into a series from the original short films at MTV's insistence, only to part company with the network after the production of ten installments. Both *Beavis and Butthead* and *Aeon Flux* later became feature films, the former in animation, the latter in live-action.

COMEDY CENTRAL

Even more than the rest of the Viacom empire, this channel has derived its success chiefly by engaging specific members of the television audience while severely irritating and alienating everyone else. Its major ventures into television animation are no exceptions to this rule.

Dr. Katz, Professional Therapist, based on the stand-up comedy routines of Jonathan Katz (who starred in the lead role), debuted in 1995 and ran for four seasons. Featuring a Bob Newhart–like psychiatrist and his desperate clients and family, the animation was the work of Tom Snyder (not the noted talk-show host), whose studio pioneered the use of "Squigglevision," an ultra low-tech animation process which favored the aural aspects of the broadcast over the visual. The dialogue was largely improvised (which attracted several high-profile guest stars), but animation purists cried foul when the series was praised in the press while other, more elaborate animated series were not.[132]

However, this series was dwarfed in public exposure and reception by another network project which, considering its relatively poor creative quality, became a surprisingly successful phenomenon. It was the product of Randolph "Trey" Parker and Matthew "Matt" Stone, who teamed up while studying filmmaking at the University of Colorado.[133] A 1992 Christmas-themed short film, featuring the limited-animation construction-paper technique that would become their trademark, led to a formal 1995 commission of similar material for a visual Christmas card presented by a Hollywood executive. That, in turn, led to the creation of the pilot for what eventually became *South Park*.[134]

Based on the adventures of four young boys (voiced by Parker and Stone themselves in the fictional town of Fairplay, Colorado, *South Park* is perhaps one of the most shockingly indulgent television animation programs ever produced. If the 1980s represented the limitations of television animation within a culture of censorship, *South Park* grossly and vulgarly represented an entirely opposite extreme. Mirroring the seemingly low-tech (but actually sophisticated) animation techniques used, the series, which has run almost consistently on its network since 1997, uses the most direct and foul means to attack the producers' targets. This crass approach has drawn a surprisingly large and devoted demographic, which has allowed the series to go on, largely unchanged, as long as it has, and even spawned a feature-film version in the early 2000s. The series served to establish the media credibility of Parker and Stone, who have since taken on additional projects, including the satiric, Tony Award–winning Broadway musical *The Book of Mormon*.

Conclusion

To employ an over-utilized expression, the 1990s was the "game-changing" decade for television animation. While its old homes and vehicles declined due to intrusive outside censorship and inside neglect, newer places on the cable and network television spectrum made themselves available to television animation. What resulted was an unprecedented level of creative and technological achievement, with a host of new, vibrant creative talent, hitching their wagons to a newly resurgent star. There was now no doubt that television animation could be virtually anything and everything its creators desired it to be. The people who produced television animation in the 1990s were, for the most part, well versed in classic animation, and their efforts to replicate the work of their predecessors, while ignoring the narrative, character and thematic clichés that had characterized some of those earlier efforts, resulted in some of the finest achievements in the history of television animation.

However, there was a price that had to be paid for this growing freedom. In the fragmented world of television in the 1990s, it was rarely, if ever, possible for a single series (with the unique exception of *The Simpsons*) to achieve the kind of across-the-board visibility that had once been possible in network prime-time and Saturday morning schedules. Programs produced for cable providers in particular would become increasingly yoked to the intended mandates of those providers, just as protective of their wares as the network officials before them. Living up to the mandates of a provider's intentions would become an increasingly thorny problem for animators as the first decade of the 21st century began.

Chapter 7

Dreams Deferred (2000–Present)

In the first decade of the twenty-first century many programs from the previous decade continued or were revived, and excellent new shows were produced. Many of these were "run" by distinguished veterans of 1990s programming, while others marked the rise of new talents at all levels of the industry. The television animation industry had never had such diversity in programming before. Animation was more direct and forceful in its storytelling, and more vivid in its cinematic control. However, it remained frustratingly elusive to define as a single entity.

The decade was one of turbulent change, which the genre felt obliged to confront. The election of George W. Bush to the presidency of the United States in 2000, followed by the destruction of the World Trade Center on September 11, 2001, resulted first in the return of conservative politics to power, and then to an astonishingly vicious cycle of hysteria, persecution and warfare unseen in America since the 1960s. As political rhetoric heated up over the course of the decade, leftist and right-wing politics polarized, with the former increasingly enraged at the latter's vicious "defense of freedom" of other nations via warfare. The tone of television animation, already critical during the 1990s, became even more so. Quite unlike the Vietnam era, television animation was an active participant in the war of words of the decade, with its direct and indirect satirical portraits of Bush and other right-wing politicians revealing the political colors of many of the people producing the series. Those who claimed irony, in the wake of 9/11, was "dead," were making a vastly exaggerated claim.

The new political tone of television animation was underscored, however, by the number of series that stressed the incompetence or ignorance of authority figures, and, in turn, the empowerment of their lead and supporting characters, the majority of them legally and socially "children." Whether or not this was a consequence of these programs being aimed at children is debatable, but it represented how much the genre had changed since the largely conformist apolitical programming of the 1970s and 1980s. The producers of these new series were simply not as beholden to the needs of sponsors, networks or cable providers as had been their predecessors, and their programs were increasingly reflective of how they and their audience saw the world. Even in more innocent-seeming programming aimed at young audiences, there were mild kernels of satire popping up. What is undeniable was the fact that the producers of television animation were no longer taking any of their audiences for granted. They were, instead, treating them with the utmost respect.

As with the prior decade, much of this rebellion was feminist in nature on and off screen. Female animators and executives were ever more assertive in shaping the genre's creative destiny, while ever-growing numbers of female characters wore their intelligence, physical strength and agility, and brazen verbal assertiveness like badges of honor and courage. They were often much more intelligent and savvy than their male counterparts, who, more often than not, were used to simply fill out the comedy quotas of the program. It was a swing of the pendulum away from the masculine 1950s and 1960s.

Although network television animation on Saturday mornings died a slow, painful death across the 1990s and 2000s, television animation has now become firmly anchored in cable television. This is particularly true at networks directly aimed at young people, such as Nickelodeon, Cartoon Network and the Disney cable family, who have, in effect, become the new standard bearers for the genre. Fortunately for fans of television animation, they are capable and effective stewards. The diversity and creative excellence of their product will be addressed in the following pages, and serve to remind us that television animation is going to be with us for a while. There is, however, another element to this. The cable networks, in developing their own individual "brands," have limited access to their products so they can maximize profit from them. Their cutthroat competition for ratings means that good quality-projects will still be sacrificed if they cannot draw viewers. Even with network television no longer a major factor in television animation distribution, some circumstances remain the same.

FOX in the 2000s

The 2000s, at FOX, chiefly represented the period in which Seth Macfarlane, the multifaceted creator of *Family Guy* (see Chapter 6), increasingly came into his own as the dominant creative voice of the network's Sunday-night animation block, which was fittingly redubbed "Animation Domination" at the turn of the decade. This came not only through the resurrection of his signature program after a network-instituted exile, but also through the addition of two other programs that, while slightly different in execution and tone than his earlier work, retained the irreverence and vociferously voiced creative delivery that was now Macfarlane's hallmark.

The origins of the first series can, perhaps, be traced back to September 11, 2001. For, as historian Jeff Lenburg notes, Macfarlane "was one of the fortunate ones who did not perish" that day:

> [He] was scheduled to fly back to Los Angeles on American Airlines Flight 11 after being a keynote speaker at his alma mater, the Rhode Island School of Design. His travel agent had given the wrong flight time or he was late in arriving (conflicting stories for the reason have both been reported) at [Boston's] Logan Airport, several minutes after his plane had already boarded. He ended up having to wait for the next available flight. In the meantime ... one hour after the departure of his original flight ... [it] was hijacked ... [and crashed] into the ... World Trade Center....
>
> ....Macfarlane was unable to contact his family for several days, actually driving halfway across the country before being able ... to inform them that he was okay.[1]

Such a near-death experience would be sobering for anyone who experienced it, and it is particularly noteworthy in studying the changes in Macfarlane's creative work from this point on. As noted in the previous chapter, the later edition of *Family Guy* is far different in tone and comedic approach from its predecessor.

After several years of lackluster ratings, despite winning acclaim and Emmys, FOX canceled *Family Guy* after 50 episodes had aired in 2002, and repurposed it as a syndication package. Much to the surprise of both the network and its creator, the series became a hit in this format, doing particularly well in an adult-oriented slot on Cartoon Network. As a consequence, the network chose to bring the series back to its airwaves in 2005, a first in television-network history. Macfarlane, for his part, remained philosophical about the whole thing. As he explained to *IGN Entertainment*:

> Yeah, it's been very surprising. [The series] just seems to have built-in momentum the longer we've been off the air, which is really interesting.... I hope by the time we come back on the air, it will have continued to build. It'd be great to come back with stronger numbers than we've seen [before]—and I think that's what's going to happen.[2]

Indeed, that was what proved to be the case. The revival of *Family Guy* has lasted far longer than its original run, and it remains, along with the reliable warhorse *The Simpsons*, the backbone of the current FOX Sunday-night lineup.

The revival, however, came with a catch. In tandem with veteran *Family Guy* veterans Mike Barker and Matt Weitzman, Macfarlane had developed a new project, one stemming from his dissatisfaction with the increasingly unpopular Republican presidential administration of George W. Bush.[3] He insisted on the network taking this project on along with *Family Guy*, and the network agreed. The level of confidence it displayed in the finished project was demonstrated by the fact that it launched the series in the same fashion it had done with *Family Guy* earlier—in a timeslot following network coverage of the Super Bowl in 2006, followed by a regular schedule position after its predecessor on the network schedule.

That it could not fail to get attention in this heavily promoted way was undeniable. Yet, that it deserved what would become its ongoing success was unquestionable, given its creative quality.

◆ ◆ ◆

American Dad, as the series was called, represented a new and even more visceral phase of Macfarlane's comedy. The humor is so barbed and critical, the characters so seemingly innocent but terrifying at times, and the whole series so jagged in tone and experimental in structure that it defies easy definition. Whatever else might be said of it, few television animation series have been as starkly (and unashamedly) realistic.

As with the earlier series, the title gives a cursory suggestion of who the program is about. Stan Smith (Macfarlane) is, quite frankly, every liberal-minded American's worst nightmare. As M. Keith Booker notes, he is "a fanatically right-wing CIA agent, devoted to what he perceives as the enemies of the American way of life, which in his case includes women, gays, [racial, ethnic and religious] minorities, and anyone else who doesn't entirely accept his own paranoid agenda."[4] That he is willing and able to *kill* people who don't agree with him is established from the outset, and adds a chilling undercurrent to his outward persona as a "typical" sitcom patriarch. In many respects, in particular regarding his obsession with attacking "terrorists" from other nations, he resembles certain television characters from the early-to-mid 1950s, who confronted communism in a similarly biased and distorted way. These included such communist-hunting heroes as the title character of *Biff Baker, U.S.A.* (CBS 1952–53)[5] and, in particular, the FBI agent who infiltrated the Communist party while maintaining the cover of an "average" citizen in *I Led Three Lives* (syndicated, 1953–56).[6] However, the 2000s are not the 1950s, and what were once thought of as virtues are now, through hindsight, seen as vices. *Biff Baker* and *I Led Three Lives*, as well, were dramatic series, and, therefore, their underlying messages were in complete support of their government and their audience's stereotypical assumptions about the "rightness" of the American way of life. *American Dad*, in contrast, is a comedy, and its intent is to satirize rather than support "official" government attitudes. Stan Smith might have been portrayed as a heroic figure if his character had been introduced in the 1950s, but in the 2000s, he is simply portrayed as a dimwit—albeit a highly dangerous one.

In the period prior to the demise of the Bush administration in 2009, Stan was frequently used by the producers as the butt of their caustic jokes about the political and religious right. Again and again, as Booker points out, he was employed in a fashion that caused him to be "essentially acting out the ideology of [the American political right wing], or at least of the Christian right [one of the political right's biggest sources of support, then and now]."[7] Of course, the end result of this real-life political paranoia, potently mixed with the unique exaggeration potential inherent in animation, was to make Stan and, by extension, the political right wing in America look incompetent. Since the inauguration of Barack Obama, however, real-world politics has played a much smaller role in the series, though it has continued to produce narratives that can seamlessly or awkwardly blend fantasy and reality. Stan's character has mellowed somewhat in these later episodes, in which he functions more as a "straight man" to the outrageous antics of the other, more highly-strung characters, but he remains as dangerous as ever when provoked.

Fittingly, one of the more intense characters in the cast is Stan's wife, Francine (Wendy Schaal), who typically reacts to her husband's behavior with a blend of horror, anger and sexually charged admiration. They are one of the oddest couples in a genre that is full of bizarre marriages and inter-sexual friendships. While Stan has often boasted of being a temple of physical and moral purity, Francine, like Lois Griffin before her, can be stunningly candid about her past and present behavior. She was an extremely enthusiastic rock music groupie before her marriage, and her attitudes have not changed. Therefore, although she seems very much the left-in-the-background right-wing political wife at times, she can be as potent as her husband. "I may be blonde and have great cans," she says in one episode, "but I'm pretty smart when I've had my eight hours."[8]

The disparity between Stan and Francine's personalities plays itself out most notably in the high degree of difference between their two children. College-aged Hayley (Rachael Macfarlane, the real-life sister of Seth) is the program's house liberal, and thus functions as a sounding board against Stan's views, making her akin, in some ways, to Mike "Meathead" Stivic of *All in the Family*. Particularly rankling to her ultra-religious father is the fact that she regards Christianity as "a farcical con game."[9] The two were perennially at odds during the Bush-era episodes, when it seemed that they had only their hair color (coal black) and family relationship in common. However, in the post–Obama era, Hayley has faded into the background of the episodes, as the series' political tone has changed. High school-aged Steve (Scott Grimes) is another matter. A bespectacled, underachieving nerd, he would much rather retreat into fantasy than face reality, something his mother, friends and other characters on the program openly encourage, but which his father rejects entirely. Just as he is angered that Hayley has rejected his value system, Stan is angry with Steve much of the time for his supposed lack of "maturity," and he blames this deficit in Steve's character entirely on Francine—*without* considering how his own paranoid, tyrannical personality may have influenced his son.

This would not be a Macfarlane program without some obvious sense of violation of reality, and the other two major supporting characters serve to fill this role.

Klaus (Dee Bradley Baker) is the first and more minor of these. A goldfish, he was the victim of a CIA experiment in which his brain was switched with that of an athlete from the former communist East Germany. His lack of mobility means that, for the most part, his role in the series has been somewhat smaller than his parallels in other Macfarlane series. However, the writers have been kind to him, giving him at least one good wisecrack per show that is usually relevant to the plot, as well as plenty of opportunities to gaze at Francine with what is unmistakably carnal lust.

It is the other major supporting character to whom increasing time and energy have been devoted, to the point that, in many of the more recent episodes, he has effectively replaced Stan as the program's lead. Roger (Macfarlane, brilliantly impersonating the late Paul Lynde) is a gray-skinned, bulbous-headed alien who was scheduled for destruction at the hands of the CIA. Stan rescued him, and he later saved Stan's life, creating a permanent—if somewhat rocky—friendship. As a consequence, the "effeminate"[10] alien has been holding court at the Smith house for a number of years, and the Smiths—whether they like it or not—always seem to be caught in the crossfire drawn by his actions. These are far more complicated and diverse than they may seem in mere description. A master of disguise, a brilliant Method actor, a ruthless con man, a shady trickster, but also—surprisingly—a loyal friend, Roger is the center of attention whenever he is on screen, and he is one of Macfarlane's most brilliantly executed characters. It is safe to say that the program would be far more limited in its narratives if he were not regularly featured.

Even the more minor characters in this series seem to have their crosses to bear. Authority figures in particular are portrayed in such a fashion as to suggest that they are morally and mentally unfit for their jobs. The most graphic example of this comes in the form of Avery Bullock (Patrick Stewart), the deputy director of the CIA, and Stan's boss. The casting here is quite effective, as Stewart's booming, Shakespearean vocal delivery belies the fact that his character is even more disconnected from reality than Stan's.[11] Even more disconnected from reality is Brian Lewis (Kevin Michael Richardson), principal of Pearl Bailey High School (which Steve attends), an African American who frequently behaves like an inner-city pimp or drug pusher rather than with the authority his job demands. This disjunction between established social and political roles and personally deviant behavior extends through all levels of the characterization pyramid, which serves to heighten the comedy and the subtext of the series.

Like Macfarlane's prior series, this program has a shifting narrative structure, in which, although the characters remain the same on a weekly basis, no two episodes are exactly alike in terms of their story structure. As with *Family Guy*, experimentation with the narrative expectations, character behavior, settings and story patterns is constant, as is the tendency to break the "fourth wall" to ensure the audience will "get" the jokes. Program episodes have ranged from conventional sitcom plots with the antes up, to projects that spoof the spy genre as a whole (including the James Bond films), to even more experimental work (such as a recent episode conducted as if it were a live stage play, complete with stage-bound special effects and an audience!). This is a series that, like its protagonist, is willing to go to great lengths to achieve its goals as entertainment. Whether that ends up shocking you or making you laugh depends chiefly of your understanding and tolerance of Macfarlane's idiosyncratic comedy.

◆ ◆ ◆

Macfarlane increased his dominance of FOX's Sunday night lineup with the debut of a third program in 2009, which had more direct roots to *Family Guy* than *American Dad*.

While this series was also very funny and viscerally shocking, it appeared viewers were tiring of constant exposure to this comedic approach. There were also signs that his "anything for a laugh" approach could backfire once in a while if his lead characters, like in this program, were of a racial minority group.

The character of Cleveland Brown, a stocky, mustachioed African American (voiced by Caucasian actor Mike Henry), was introduced in the earliest episodes of *Family Guy* as a good friend and drinking buddy of Peter Griffin. In these episodes, his Southern drawl was often the voice of reason, which was conveniently ignored. As the series evolved, however, Cleveland began to play a more active part in the narratives, and, at times, he upstaged the characters he was designed to support simply by doing the unexpected. Nevertheless, of the *Family Guy* supporting cast, this character seemed the least likely to be able to sustain a series as a lead, which made it all the more surprising when *The Cleveland Show* debuted on FOX in 2009.

Macfarlane and Henry shared the creator and executive producer credits (with another Macfarlane loyalist, Richard Appel). Macfarlane's increasing involvement with outside projects during this time is reflected by his more limited voice acting than in the earlier programs. He also seems to have yielded much of the creative direction of the series to the more inexperienced Henry, which undermines the project's creative credibility. That the series has become the weak link in the Macfarlane animation programming group has been reflected in its mixed critical and public reception, but, when it is empowered by a good script, it is of the same quality as its predecessors. This, however, did not happen often.

The series format reflects that of many sitcom "spinoffs," in which a prominent supporting character from a popular series is reconstituted as a lead character in another project. This is exactly what happened in the pilot episode. Tired of being the fourth wheel in Quahog, Cleveland decides to return to his old home town—Stoolbend, Virginia[12]—accompanied by his portly, bespectacled teenaged son, Cleveland, Jr. (Kevin Michael Richardson), who displays an astonishing level of arrested emotional development. Cleveland is reunited with an old high school acquaintance, Donna Tubbs (Sanaa Lathan), and they decide to get married. Based on this decision, Cleveland becomes the stepfather of Donna's two children: Roberta (Nia Long, later Reagan Gomez), a high-strung teenager, and Rallo (Henry), a preschool boy with the life skills and mindset of someone *far* older. Though Cleveland works as an installer for the Waterman Cable Company, the majority of the episodes develop far more elaborate plots, in which he is a frantic, destructive, African American mirror image of his old friend, Peter Griffin. The characters are cast in the same overblown fashion. These include Lester Krinklesac (Richardson), a stereotyped "redneck" who becomes Cleveland's friend and drinking buddy; Holt Richter (Jason Sudeikis), a diminutive, cryptically speaking ladies' man, another friend and drinking buddy; Tim the Bear (Macfarlane, later Jess Harnell), Cleveland's ursine co-worker, who also—you guessed it—becomes Cleveland's friend and drinking buddy; Tim's wife, Arianna (*Huffington Post* founder Arianna Huffington); Wally Farquhare (Will Forte), the flamboyantly effeminate principal of the local high school; Terry Kimple (Sudeikis), Cleveland's friend and co-worker; and Cleveland's parents, Cookie (Frances Callier) and Freight Train (Craig Robinson), who are, respectively, highly indulgent and viciously curt with him. Film director David Lynch, who pioneered the reality-bending approach Macfarlane later took, was appropriately cast here as Gus, the mercurial proprietor of The Broken Stool, where the guys typically did their drinking.

As with Macfarlane's earlier series, whether or not you enjoy the series depends on your capacity for absorbing and understanding dirty jokes, physical violence, mental cruelty, obsessive alcohol consumption and "riffs" on contemporary culture. In some cases, as in the contrast between Rallo's *uber*-worldliness and Cleveland Jr.'s Candide-like innocence, the character relationships are both funny and affectionate. The pure comedy sequences are staged well, and the use of popular culture as a source of parody and satire is quite effective. Some episodes, such as one that was supposedly staged "live," are hilarious. Yet there are troubling elements that are largely absent from Macfarlane's earlier series, and which undermine the comic impact of some episodes. We must remember that this series, while featuring African American lead characters, is produced by Caucasians, and reflects stereotypes of African Americans. This is seen in the irresponsible, immature behavior of the male African American characters, most prominently Cleveland himself, and in the loud voices and occasionally shrewish behavior of Donna and Roberta—two stereotypical images which go back to the ancient days of blackface minstrelsy. It might be said that much of *The Cleveland Show*'s failure to connect with its audience stems more from the unintended racism of the producers than it does from the creative quality of the series. That a white man voices two of the major African American characters might also be a political lightning rod (although Richardson, an African American, voices one of the white ones). Nevertheless, the series stands in sharp contrast to other contemporary depictions of African Americans in the media, which, with creative input from African Americans themselves, have succeeded in depicting them in more flattering and realistic terms.[13]

Macfarlane, Henry and Appel did not have racism on their mind when they created the program; they were simply trying to create a new vehicle for Macfarlane's distorted view of America and the world. And, in those terms, they succeeded.

◆ ◆ ◆

In recent years, FOX has been—desperately at times—trying to create a hit animated program alone, to avoid sharing credit and profits with Matt Groening, Mike Judge or Seth Macfarlane. These, for the most part, have been critical and commercial failures. In trying to come up with a new series, producers for the network have emulated the gas-producing, crotch-grabbing aspect of Macfarlane's approach—entirely forgetting that it was his finely developed characters and more sophisticated jokes that made his programs hits in the first place.

Star power was employed for some of these series, but this did little good in the final results. *Sit Down, Shut Up* was produced by Mitchell Hurwitz, the brains behind the Emmy-winning live-action sitcom *Arrested Development*, which it resembles. Unfortunately, Hurwitz seemed to think that producing an animated sitcom for adults meant writing for the lowest common denominator, so the result was a depressing parade of off-color humor, with horrifically bad puns used for some of the characters' names. The same problems affected two other series groomed for the Sunday-night lineup. *Allen Gregory*, the saga of an overly bright young man being raised by a wealthy gay couple, existed chiefly as a vehicle for the acting talents of its creator, Jonah Hill, while *Napoleon Dynamite*, a belated series adaptation of a popular mid–1990s cult film, was clearly trading on its studio's past glory. None of these series lasted beyond the year they were originally presented.

The one studio-produced project that has succeeded is chiefly the result of clever scheduling on the network's part rather than any level of creativity. *Bob's Burgers*, the creation of Loren Bouchard (formerly of UPN's *Home Movies* [see below]), has been, for the most part, an unappetizing return to the well-beaten dysfunctional family path. Set in the titular eatery, which has a habit of being repeatedly condemned for health-code violations (a bad omen for the program's creative quality), the focus is on Bob (H. Jon Benjamin), the mustachioed proprietor, and his family, who assist him in operating the restaurant. They include his wife, Linda (John Roberts), and their three children, bespectacled teenager Tina (Dan Mintz); dimwitted Gene (Eugene Mirman) and adventurous Louise (Kristen Schaal). Although the show has acquired a following, some defenders, and an Emmy nomination, it is hard to see why. The characters are drawn in a crude, blocky and unattractive style, behave in a rude and unrealistic fashion, and have none of the saving grace of the characters of Groening, Judge and Macfarlane. Bouchard and his team (which, depressingly, includes *King of the Hill* veteran Jim Dauterive) do not appear to be interested in doing anything experimental or risky with the characters, and the series suffers for it. It seems it was produced with the intention of offending everyone who watches it. The fact that it has done well in the ratings between *The Simpsons* and *Family Guy* may be the primary reason why it has succeeded. If it was removed from that slot, it might very well perish.

Nickelodeon in the 2000s

While FOX was struggling to maintain its creative integrity during this decade, its counterparts on the cable-television spectrum were continually moving from strength to strength, based on their ability to lure and retain the talents of both veteran animators and relative newcomers. Nickelodeon was a case in point. Although relations with Klasky-Csupo, its primary television animation provider of the previous decade, were on the decline due to growing financial conflicts, newer producers and studios (particularly Butch Hartman and Fred Seibert's Frederator concern) arrived to supplant them. Increasingly, programming came to represent the intentions of the producers rather than the network. No two Nickelodeon programs, or those of its rivals Cartoon Network and Disney during this decade, could be accused of resembling or "ripping off" each other in any way.

The channel's "brand," which now expanded to several accompanying specialty channels as well as feature-film production (with its corporate sibling, Paramount Pictures, as the principal distributor), remained an overpowering influence behind the scenes. Ratings, in addition, remained the primary factor by which series succeeded and became transcendent, almost untouchable, corporate "franchises," though this was exceedingly rare. Consequently, few of the producers who originated programming at the network stayed long after their pet projects were canceled due to network interference and/or low ratings. However, what they did manage to create, in spite of the internal obstacles they now faced, was rarely short of brilliant.

BUTCH HARTMAN

Like his one-time associates, Craig McCracken and Seth Macfarlane, this singularly talented writer/producer/director has, over the past decade, invested television animation with an artistic spirit that is entirely his own. His three programs—*The Fairly Oddparents*, *Danny Phantom* and *T.U.F.F. Puppy*—demonstrate a flair for skilled comedic timing and memorable characterizations, as well as a nuanced understanding of the often-conflicted and challenging positions of being "good" and "evil" in a fictional narrative. Yet Hartman's strengths can also be his weaknesses. His insistence on delivering his jokes and gags in a sledgehammer, Tex Avery-indebted–style robs them of their impact, while his tendency to repeat dialogue and plot points is annoying and unnecessary. Nevertheless, what appear to be weaknesses individually add up at the climaxes of his stories to create a satisfying whole.

He was born Elmer Earl Hartman IV in Highland Park, Michigan, in January 1965. "Butch" was a childhood nickname that he has retained for professional purposes. After his graduation from high school in New Baltimore, Michigan, he moved to California to attend California Institute of the Arts. His first animation work was as an in-betweener on the film *An American Tail* (see Chapter 6). Afterward, he worked at Marvel and Ruby-Spears before joining Hanna-Barbera in the mid–1990s. During this period, having advanced to the role of animation director, writer and storyboard artist, he worked in this capacity on many of the shows of the studio's halcyon period of the late 1990s. He also contributed two shorts to the *What a Cartoon!* project—*Pfish and Chips* and *Gramps*, neither of which was picked up for series development. At this time, he developed a friendship with Seth Macfarlane that extended into the latter's work—Hartman voiced the recurring character of Mr. Weed in the earliest *Family Guy* episodes, while another character—Dr. Elmer Hartman—received his name in Butch's honor.

Another friend from Hanna-Barbera was former studio president Fred Seibert, who had resigned from the company following its acquisition by Time Warner to found his own independent studio, Frederator. His first venture, after securing distribution from Nickelodeon, was *Oh Yeah Cartoons!*, a project similar to the earlier *What a Cartoon!* in the sense that it had the potential to be a vehicle for future series. That, along with growing internal problems at Hanna-Barbera, convinced Hartman that the time was right to jump ship:

> In 1996, I was working on *Johnny Bravo* ... having the time of my life. Then the first season came out, and [the network] didn't like it. Fred Seibert ... had moved over to Nickelodeon ... to develop a [new] series ... [so] I decided that I would make up a cartoon for Fred.[14]

Seibert, for his part, had recognized Hartman's talent, and was eager to have him aboard:

> I used to call Butch's agents [during this time] once a month and ask if he was free yet, and they would tell me he wasn't. By the end of the year[,] I stopped calling, because I was tired of being rejected. When his agents finally called me at the end of the year, I signed him, characters unseen.[15]

Not yet, anyway. But Hartman soon showed that he had a new, innovative trick up his sleeve:

> I wrote the pitch [for the project] in fifteen minutes. I wanted to do a show about a boy who could go anywhere, because I never wanted to be stuck for a story transition. I wanted to be able to just pop him from place to place. Magic seemed to be the best way to handle that. I drew the boy, and named him after my youngest brother, Timmy. Then I thought, Okay, how do I do the magic thing? I decided to give him a fairy godmother. So I drew Wanda. I thought it would be even better if she had a husband. I'd never seen a fairy god*father* before, but I drew Cosmo. Timmy is an only child—he's lonely—which is why his godparents show up to help him out in the first place. His enemy is his babysitter, Vicky. Once I mapped out the characters, the show developed from there, and one thing led to another.[16]

That "one thing led to another" is an understatement. Originally presented as a series of short films under the *Oh Yeah!* label, the project, which its creator dubbed *The Fairly Oddparents*, rapidly took on a life of its own. The program tested well with focus groups, and staggered Nickelodeon executives with its originality in concept and design. Debuting as a series in 2001, with Hartman and Seibert as executive producers, it has continued to run off and on in original episodes and reruns ever since. In the meantime, it has also become a licensing phenomenon, ensuring its durability as a property for years to come.

There is no doubt that *The Fairly Oddparents* is a unique show. Hartman's concept was relatively underutilized in television animation, despite its prevalent roots in both fairy tales and theatrical animation, and he took full advantage of the opportunity he had created. As the show has developed, Hartman and his crew have shown themselves to be both peerless and fearless in the creation and execution of gags, storylines and characters. Although the program is periodically unable to sustain the weight of these elements when it moves from 11-minute narratives to longer ones, it is usually entertaining, even though the jokes and dialogue are delivered more in the brassy, in-your-face manner of 1940s theatrical animation than would be expected of a modern television animation program.

As Hal Erickson notes, the series moves "about as fast as possible for a TV cartoon to move."[17] This is both a blessing and a curse; it is a fast watch, but any attempt to understand the characters except as walking joke machines is limited because of this practice. Nevertheless, we can typically understand just enough of the character's personalities and relationships with one another to help us follow along.

The majority of the elements of the original short films were retained, with additional touches that considerably expanded the show's comedic intent and Hartman's gift for staging both comedy and drama—his greatest asset as an animator. As is often the case with television animation programs, we are introduced to the program's concept and characters via a theme song, staged and sung with the verve of a number in a Hollywood musical. The protagonist is Timmy Turner (Tara Strong, though Mary Kay Bergman played the role in the pilot), an "average" young man "no one understands."[18] His otherwise dull existence is enlivened by the arrival of his "fairy godparents." These two—Cosmo (Daran Norris), a green-haired *dumkopf* who makes Homer Simpson look like a Rhodes scholar, and pink-haired Wanda (Susan Blakeslee), whose braying, Ethel Mermanesque voice hides her genuine affection for her young "sport"—were not only capable of granting Timmy his every desire, but also of treating him with the respect and concern denied to him by the other "adult" figures in his world. These included his biological parents (also Norris and Blakeslee[19]), chiefly portrayed as moronic ciphers, and Vicky (Grey DeLisle, one of the most dominant figures in TV animation voice acting during this period), the red-haired, foghorn-voiced Babysitter from Hell, who seemed to confirm the worst stereotypes of her "profession."[20] The persistent theme of the show, however, which was stated with more subtlety than most other aspects of the series, was "be careful what you wish for." Inevitably, in many installments, Timmy would be undone by his own vanity or greed, wishing for something that put him—or even the entire world—off-kilter, forcing him and the fairies to do what they could to correct the problem before the effects became permanent. This was accomplished with the emphasis on comedy, of course.

Gradually, with its ongoing popularity as a safeguard, the series expanded the length of its format—a half-hour, or longer—and the gag-happy formula of the series started to wear thin. There were exceptions (such as "School's Out!," an ambitious full-tilt musical), but both Hartman and Nickelodeon should have recognized that you can only push a good thing so far. (It did provide an example to other producers, at Nickelodeon and elsewhere, when they created full-length "specials" for their characters; see examples below.) These later, more ambitious episodes did provide Hartman with multiple opportunities to expand his dramatic canvas and show off his skills as a world-builder. Most prominent in this latter sense was the exploration of Cosmo and Wanda's homeland, Fairy World, which, predictably, bore very little resemblance to the Faerie realm of ancient English mythology. Rather than Titania or Oberon, the head Fae was Jorgen Von Strangle (Rodger Bumpass), a blatant and somewhat second-rate caricature of bodybuilder/film star/politician Arnold Schwarzenegger. Likewise, the connection between their world and ours was bluntly reinforced by such moves as naming the streets after contemporary magicians, such as Penn and Teller, and having the fairies being in frequent conflict with such beings as the nebulous Anti-Fairies and the gray-suited, highly bureaucratic Pixies (whose leader was wonderfully portrayed, in his trademark dry monotone, by actor/writer/game-show host Ben Stein).

Hartman stressed the connection between his work and the theatrical animators who had inspired him in a number of ways. The manic overacting of his characters and the unsubtle approach of his gags have already been mentioned, but there were other examples as well. Each segment began with a fully illustrated title card (proclaiming "*The Fairly Oddparents in....*"),[21] followed by the credits in a similar fashion. A similar "The End" title was used, often proclaiming proudly that the film was "made in Hollywood, U.S.A.," similar to a tag used on vintage MGM cartoons of the 1940s. Hartman also relied on a graphic handsomeness similar to that used by some of his peers, in which there was a level of beauty even in the more homely aspects of the character and setting designs, but which he executed and employed in his unique style. A standard design element exclusive to him, however, was the rendering of his characters' eyes as enormous white orbs with similarly large-colored circles for pupils—which has remained standard for all the characters in his series.

For all the flaws that became noticeable in the later editions of *Fairly Oddparents*, it was the series that made Butch Hartman's career, and the one with which he will be associated in television animation history, not unlike the situation with Craig McCracken and *The Powerpuff Girls* (see Chapter 6). Yet, like William Hanna and Joseph Barbera before him, Hartman was too talented an animator to restrict himself to one series, and, when Nickelodeon offered him the chance to produce new product under their auspices, he eagerly accepted.

◆ ◆ ◆

Having gleefully deconstructed one aspect of the world's fantasy universe with his first series, Hartman went on to another with his sophomore effort—the first for his own company, Billionfold. However, this time he kept much of the comedy in check in order to focus on the action/adventure component, with very satisfying results.

As with his first project, the series, as Hartman himself later admitted, came to be partly through his own experimentation and partly through serendipity:

> It all started in a moving van, while driving to Los Angeles with my mom. It was just after New Year's Day in 2001, and my other show ... was going along great. I knew that Nickelodeon was looking for a boy's action show. So I thought I'd try to come up with something, even though I really didn't have any ideas at the time.
>
> Well, that February, I went to pick up my mother in Las Vegas, because she wanted to move away from there. I told her she could stay with me for a while, so I went out to get her. Here I was in a moving van headed out of Vegas, and it's about an eight hour drive. Soon, Mom and I ran out of things to talk about. So, as I was driving, I thought, I'm just going to come up with a show, right here and now.
>
> The first thing that came to mind was Jonny Quest. I love that name! If I could come up with something that cool, just a name that neat, I'd be halfway there. I started thinking quest, thunder, lightning, power—just all these strong words. I finally fell on "phantom," which I thought was a very cool word. Now I needed a first name: Billy ... Jimmy ... Danny Phantom! That was it. By the time I got to L.A. ... I had my idea for a new show.[22]

Later that year, Hartman had a business dinner meeting with Nickelodeon executives Albie Hecht and Kevin Kay, who not only wanted to continue *Fairly Oddparents* but were also interested in any new series ideas Hartman had. Although Hartman would have preferred to pitch the series in a more professional setting, he still let them know about his "Danny Phantom" concept:

> Albie said, "No, no, just tell me what you've got," "Well, all right," I told him. "I've got this thing about a kid who's a ghost fighter. He's called Danny Phantom, and he's got ghost powers." Albie thought about it for a second and then asked, "Can you have it by March [2002]?" I said I thought I could, and he gave me a pilot right there over dinner![23]

The decision ultimately led not only to the creation of Billionfold to produce the series, but also to Hartman refining the idea further until it reached the final broadcasted version:

> So now, on top of the *Fairly Oddparents*, I've got to hire a whole new crew for *Danny Phantom*, and here's a guy who didn't even have a ... [series] two years ago. Originally, I was going to have Danny be a ghost detective with a team of kids working with him. *Danny Phantom and the Spector Detectors*! As we [the production crew] talked it over, though, we would make Danny a superhero, a kid who had the powers of a ghost.
>
> I kept drawing the character over and over, asking myself what unique visual thing this guy should have, and then I finally settled on the white hair. We ended up making him an insecure kid who doesn't know how to use his powers very well at first, so he starts out as kind of a nerd. Gradually, he becomes a confident hero. If you watch [the program]....all the way through, you can see him become more confident as ... [it] goes on.[24]

The casting of Danny as an insecure hero literally learning his "trade" on the job was a particularly masterful decision on Hartman's part. It made him much more relatable, especially to his peer group. Despite his supernatural trappings, Danny was not perfect: he had enormous personal insecurities, and often allowed his powers, and ego, to get the better of him. This disparity between who the characters were and what they had the potential to become also existed in most of the supporting characters, chiefly consisting of Danny's friends, family and foes. *Danny Phantom*, in rudimentary form, had every potential to be one of the stick-figure superhero shows of the 1960s and 1970s if it had not been executed properly. However, in the same fashion as its equally exceptional contemporary series, *My Life as a Teenage Robot* (see below), as well as *The Powerpuff Girls* (see Chapter 6), Hartman was able to present the project with the properly nuanced blend of comedy, action and drama. The series debuted in April 2004 and ran for four seasons, with several full-length "specials" produced as the series, like its predecessor, became one of Nickelodeon's most popular programs.

Again, the series premise is introduced through the theme song, which has a rap/urban rhythm and blues flavor to it, although Hartman uses pre-credit "cold openings" to establish the individual episode content. The protagonist, high school student Danny Fenton (David Kaufman), received supernatural abilities through an accident while fooling around with equipment used by his ghost-hunting parents. While learning how to best use his new abilities, Danny becomes an invisible superheroic defender of his hometown, Amity Park. He does this in spite of the fact that the local politicians and media (who insultingly refer to him as "Inviso-Bill") arbitrarily brand him as a villain, making him cautious about when and how he uses his new abilities. Danny's closest confidants (and the only ones who know the extent of his double life) are Goth girl Samantha "Sam" Manson (Grey DeLisle), the rebellious scion of a wealthy, conformist Jewish family, and Tucker Foley (Rickey D'Shon Collins), an African American digital-technology expert. These two are also his closest allies in the fight against evil.[25] In contrast, Danny is forced to keep his abilities secret, for the most part, from his family, for fear that they would not understand. This likely would have been the case with his father, Jack (Rob Paulsen), who, despite his expertise in ghost hunting, is, in every other respect, a typical cartoon dimwit. Danny's still youthful-looking mother, Maddie (Kath Soucie), is, however, far more intelligent and resourceful than her husband, although she remains unaware of her son's super powers. Danny's only real confidant in the family circle is his sympathetic older sister, Jasmine, or "Jazz" (Colleen O'Shaughnessey). Jazz is a Lisa Simpson–styled intellectual, perennially at work on a "thesis" involving something or other from the world around her. Naturally, she is able to logically piece together what has happened to Danny, but she is too loving and sympathetic to expose him. Jazz becomes an additional ally, in spite of the occasional bout of sibling rivalry.

These "good" characters are opposed by a variety of major and minor antagonists. In the latter category is Mr. Lancer (Ron Perlman), the bald, bearded, highly intellectual[26] jack-of-all-trades high school teacher, who is forever glowering menacingly at his students—particularly Danny—and trying ineptly to "relate" to them. Far more threatening is the parade of otherworldly menaces Danny is forced to confront. These malevolent beings from a parallel universe known as the Ghost World include: Skulker (Matthew St. Patrick, then Kevin Michael Richardson), a big-game hunter who targets Danny; Penelope Spectra (Tara Strong), a succubus type who remains youthful by feeding on the energy of young human beings; Ember (Strong), a rock-and-roller who hypnotizes the populace into glorifying her; Johnny 13 (William Baldwin), a motorcycle-riding rebel with an independently functioning shadow; Walker (James Arnold Taylor), the Clint Eastwood–type "sheriff" of the Ghost World; Desiree (Peri Gilpin), an enormously powerful female genie capable of granting anyone's wishes; and Freakshow (Jon Cryer), the ringmaster of a highly unorthodox circus. Most of these paled in comparison to the man who became the central "bad guy" of the series: Vlad Masters, a.k.a. Vlad Plasmius (Martin Mull). A university classmate of Jack and Maddie Fenton, who was spurned by Maddie, Vlad spends much of his time trying to kill Jack and get Maddie to accept him as his replacement. Danny, of course, is forced to stop him, and usually does, although this is complicated by the fact that Vlad is a human-ghost hybrid (and far more accomplished and experienced than Danny). Later in the series' run, he also becomes the mayor of Amity Park. In the climactic battle sequences, Hartman proves that he is as skilled at this form of expression as he is at comedy; he is, in fact, a peer of Craig McCracken [see Chapter 6 and below], Rob Renzetti [see below] and Genndy Tartakovsky [see Chapter 6 and below]. In both character and conflict, the series benefitted immensely from keeping Hartman's comedy sensibilities in check so that the dramatic elements of the series could fulfill their potential.

As with his prior project, Hartman underlined the unique sensibilities of the series through the use of highly imaginative title cards. Rather than replicating the methods of theatrical animation, the *Danny Phantom* cards resembled the *mise en scène* of many science fiction, fantasy or horror film ad posters from the 1950s and 1960s. As before, there is an identifying element ("Danny Phantom in..."), but it was smaller than that of *Fairly Oddparents*; the dominant element was the episode title itself, coupled with a tag line reminiscent of those films. The title card for "Pirate Radio," for example, featured the line "It will shiver your timbers!," while "My Brother's Keeper" was suggested to be "presented in Phantomation."[27]

Danny Phantom was a highly engaging and entertaining series, though in an entirely different way than *Fairly Oddparents*. With these two unique projects, Hartman showed himself to be one of the most versatile television animation producers of the decade. Unfortunately, his third project would be weighed down by his decision to go with an idea that emphasized his weaknesses rather than his strengths.

◆ ◆ ◆

Fairies and ghosts were unique elements to bring to television animation narratives, and Hartman clearly thrived by piloting his boat in unknown waters. Spies and humanized animals, however, were things that had already been "done," and Hartman's third series, *T.U.F.F. Puppy*, was weakened by his efforts to make these two old dogs do new tricks. Periodically, he was able to produce an installment that could recreate the thrills and the gales of laughter produced by his other two projects, but, more often, than not these elements were forced and inept.

Debuting in the fall of 2010, the series was indebted for its format, by its creator's own admission, to *Get Smart* (NBC/CBS 1965–70), though it substitutes typically "cartoonish" manic energy for the latter's dramatic restraints. This connection is reinforced through the action-oriented title sequence, with a theme echoing that of many popular spy-themed songs of the 1960s, particularly P.F. Sloan and Steve Barri's "Secret Agent Man." Set in an all-animal universe, anchored by the city of Petropolis,[28] the focus of the series was Dudley Puppy (Jerry Trainor), an agent for the crime-fighting agency known as the Turbo Underground Fighting Force (T.U.F.F.). Dudley, a big, broad-chested white dog in a black turtleneck, is, like his role model, Maxwell Smart, an incompetent who succeeds chiefly by accident. Awarded his position on a whim of the agency staff, he is more of a hindrance than an asset to the organization, though his ability to "save the day" in unlikely ways frequently redeems him. Nobody knows this better than his colleague and frequent partner, Kitty Katswell (Grey DeLisle). Kitty, a multi-lingual martial-arts expert cat with an academic spy background, is initially appalled and angered by Dudley's stupidity and his improvised-on-the-fly crime-fighting methods; the ancient enmity between their feline and canine ancestors adds another wrinkle. However, during the evolution of the series, they become more accommodating and friendly, each learning from the other and becoming an effective duo in the process. Kitty, however, is wont to remind Dudley that *she* is the "professional" spy in their relationship, and he is simply an "amateur." Her higher level of intelligence is reinforced, but Hartman's scattershot, pie-in-the-face approach makes her more a stereotype than an empowering character. The "good" guys in the series include the Chief, a.k.a. Herbert Dumbrowski (Daran Norris), a diminutive flea (he has to use a video monitor so his underlings can see him) whose aura of experienced, no-nonsense authority is repeatedly punctured by his use of bizarre non sequiturs in the midst of the action ("I need to carbo load before my ballet class") and other unconventional behaviors; and Keswick (Jeff Bennett), the short, stuttering head of the lab, whose proficiency at creating brilliant inventions is rivaled only by his fear of females (even Kitty) and his intense resentment toward his parents.[29] Other than a few other "agents" who function more as extras than full-fledged characters, nobody else seems to work at T.U.F.F.

Just as in *Get Smart*, the villains are even more incompetent than the heroes. The Diabolical Order of Mayhem (D.O.O.M.), led by the self-absorbed and self-indulgent Verminious Snaptrap (Matthew Taylor, doing what appears to be an impression of Ed Wynn), acts more like an incompetent vaudeville comic than a super-villain. Snaptrap's ineptitude is reinforced by his inability to come up with "original" plans for his crimes (a sad metaphor for the series itself), as well as his capriciousness toward his henchmen. The unfortunate Larry

(Norris), Snaptrap's brother-in-law, is his main victim; it is not uncommon for Larry to be physically assaulted or dropped in a shark tank.

The series' two other major villains are The Chameleon and Bird Brain. The Chameleon (Norris, doing an excellent Peter Lorre imitation), a reptilian character able to transform himself into anything or anybody with the aid of a specially built suit, is hindered by the fact that he is even dumber than Dudley. Bird Brain (Rob Paulsen), an avian mad scientist, hinders himself with his personal flamboyance and lack of preparedness. He is often reduced to playing Abbott and Costello–type word games with his henchmen ("Who?" "What?" "Where?")—which are, oddly enough, one of the funnier elements of the show.

Admittedly, then, the series does have its assets, as reflected by the Emmy and Annie nominations and awards it earned. In technical terms, it is cel animation at its sleekest and most finessed, and a very good argument for continuing the use of this form of animation in the face of the growing prominence of CGI. The background art, particularly the skyline of Petropolis and its individual buildings, as well as the corps of vehicles and weapons used by the competing forces of good and evil, are well thought out and detailed. The individual character designs, as well, give off the impression that Petropolis is a highly sophisticated community of anthropomorphized characters of all species, shapes and sizes. Unfortunately, Hartman only allows us to see this from the outside, not within, which is where the problems with the series begin. The acting is too often overtly hysterical and tinged with lunacy (Trainor and Taylor in particular) for the jokes to be properly "sold" or the action to have true dramatic tension. Likewise, there is a tendency to constantly repeat character and plot points to the audience, as if they were somehow going to be quizzed on them later. Particularly annoying is the habit of having one character from the "good" side say something pertinent to the plot, and then to cut directly to a character from the "bad" side saying *the exact same thing*, or vice versa. The ambience of the series suggests that all the characters, good and bad, are not only aware of the fact that they *are* characters, but also that they believe that the comedy material with which they have been supplied is utterly worthless. Therefore, they feel compelled to constantly shout, roll their eyes, jump up and down, mug at the camera and do other such things to "punch things up." It is surprising that they, particularly Dudley, never double over laughing at themselves in the midst of a "take." The most egregious example of this can be seen at the end of an episode, where the characters, in a way entirely divorced from the last scene they have played, will suddenly plaster beaming grins on their faces and jump up in the air with arms and legs spread, like living exclamation points. Clearly, this project is *not* meant to be taken seriously, but we don't need to be constantly reminded of that.

Still, there are exceptions to the rule, such as an episode in which T.U.F.F. and D.O.O.M. are (implausibly) forced to share office space after blowing up each other's headquarters with tactical missiles (a neat mini-parody of the Cold War). In another above-average episode, T.U.F.F. is profiled on a television reality show about crime-fighters and is made to appear even more inept and incompetent than usual. (A priceless sequence shows Dudley taking several dozen takes to say his own name correctly!) Yet these standouts, unfortunately, are few and far between. While the animation of the series is excellent, Hartman, as executive producer, lacked the discipline and control he had shown in his two prior series in terms of the creative planning, and this filtered down to the writers and voice actors, damaging the overall series. Hartman knew he was making a comedy with *Fairly Oddparents*, and an action series with *Danny Phantom*, and governed himself accordingly in both situations. With *T.U.F.F. Puppy*, he couldn't make up his mind whether the series was to be one or the other, and a good setting and premise are wasted in the process. Not that the viewers seemed to notice or care, as the series soon developed a cult following comparable to those of his prior hits.

As Told by Ginger

This engaging Emmy-nominated Klasky-Csupo series, created by Emily Kapnek and running from 2000 to 2004, deals with the problems of a girl in middle school from the perspective of the title character, Ginger Foutley (Melissa Disney first, Shayna Fox later). Another prime example of the "middle-school angst" sub-genre of television animation (see Chapter 6 and below for other examples), it benefitted from Kapnek and her colleagues drawing on their own childhood years for material, as she later explained to Jerry Beck:

> Everything you see ... [in the series] ... was drawn from someone's personal experience. I myself felt very much like a fish out of water in junior high school. We moved to suburbia, where we were much less privileged than the other families. That feeling of being an outsider became the basis of the show. I drew upon that sense of constantly trying to fit in and still maintain a sense of individuality.[30]

This neo-realist approach is apparent in other aspects of the program as well. The characters regularly wear different types of clothing depending on the context of the episodes, defying the traditional television animation tradition of keeping characters' appearances consistent. It also evolved chronologically, as Ginger and company moved from junior high to high school, another unusual production move that reflect a realistic discourse. What truly gives the series its sense of realism is the starkness of the individual narratives. In one episode, for instance, Ginger's sanity is openly questioned by all around her when she writes what is perceived to be a "troubling" poem. Such subtle yet strong elements made the series a success both with its target audience, among which it retains a cult following.

Invader Zim

This series was the work of California native Jhonen Vasquez, noted for his achievements as a graphic novelist and music-video director. The action centers on the title character, Zim (Richard Horvitz). An alien from the planet Irk, Zim had nearly doomed his home planet with his reckless actions, so his superiors send him off to the "insignificant" planet Earth to be rid of him. Here, Zim and his dimwitted robot sidekick, Gir (Rosearik Simons), enroll in a local elementary "skool" [sic] while making their home base in the suburbs. The only one in the world, it seems, who knows the truth about Zim is a young paranormal expert named Dib (Andy Berman), who lives with his Goth sister, Gaz (Melissa Fahn), and his father, Professor Membrane (Rodger Bumpass). The series proper focuses on the elaborate attempts of the child-like Zim to "rule the world," and the equally elaborate attempts of Dib to stop him. Despite the rather limited format of the series, it ran from 2001 to 2003, when it was canceled due to low ratings and high-budget costs.

ChalkZone

Two long-serving television animation industry veterans—writer Bill Burnett and producer Larry Huber—were responsible for this project, which ran from 2002 to 2005. Much like William Hanna and Joseph Barbera before them, Burnett and Huber's partnership was built on their differences as much as their similarities, though Huber admitted that, ultimately, they shared the status of being "two big guys who never grew up."[31] This series reflects that mentality, as it focuses on an alternate universe, in which "all [of] the things that people [especially children] have drawn over the centuries still live."[32] Therefore, as Burnett notes, the idea of the series itself "is very empowering to kids: when they create a work of art, they're actually bringing something to life."[33]

Burnett and Huber achieved the imaginative aspects of the series by contrasting them with the aptly named "real" community of Plainsville, where the series protagonist, Rudy Tabootie (E.G. Daily), resides. An artist, Rudy happens upon a magical piece of chalk which allows him to enter ChalkZone, where all drawings are gifted with life. He is periodically accompanied there by his confidant, Penny Sanchez (Hynden Walch), and assisted by Snap (Candi Milo), a blue-hooded superhero type. The series' antagonistic characters include the stereotypical bully, Reggie Bullnerd, and his ChalkZone doppelgänger Bullynerd (both Milo), and Rudy's unsympathetic teacher, Mr. Wilter (Robert Cait), who considers Rudy's pursuit of art to be a waste of time.

JIMMY NEUTRON

This project—one of the first to favor CGI over traditional animation techniques—was created and developed by Keith Alcorn, John A. Davis, and Steve Oedekerk in the 1980s. Focusing on a young "boy genius" and his scientifically themed exploits, was revamped in the 1990s via the Lightwave 3-D animation process. The title character, Davis notes, was designed as "my alter ego ... he gets to do all the things I wanted to do when I was a kid but couldn't."[34] After winning a best-of-show prize at a Lightwave competition, Davis met Odekerk, primarily a live-action writer/director, who took a shine to Davis's work. Nickelodeon executives were impressed when they saw the project, so much so that they commissioned an original feature film, *Jimmy Neutron, Boy Genius*. The film was a financial success, as well as being one of the first nominees in the then-nascent Animated Feature Film category at the Academy Awards in 2002. Logically, a series was produced, which ran from 2002 to 2005.

Set in the town of Retroville (which has a 1950s "retro" feel to it, as does the whole series), the focus was on the title character (Debi Derryberry) and his adventures. Other major characters include Carl (Rob Paulsen), Jimmy's asthmatic friend and sidekick; Cindy (Carolyn Lawrence), his intelligent rival-cum-love interest; Sheen Estevez (Jeffrey Garcia), another pal of Jimmy's (who was later featured in a spinoff series, *Planet Sheen*); Nick Dean (Candi Milo), the handsome but accident prone "cool guy"; Libby Folfax (Crystal Scales), Cindy's pal; Jimmy's parents, Judy (Megan Cavanagh) and Hugh (Mark DeCarlo); and Goddard (Frank Welker), Jimmy's robot dog. The major antagonistic characters include Professor Finbar Calamitous (Tim Curry) and his daughter, Beautiful Gorgeous (Wendie Malick); wealthy Eustace Strych (Paulsen), Jimmy's rival for Cindy's affection; and the Twonkies, an alien comet-spawned species reminiscent of *Star Trek*'s Tribbles. The elasticity of the format was most evident by the fact that Jimmy and company, converted to cel form, was able to effectively share the stage with *Fairly Oddparents*' Timmy Turner and co. (see above) in a successful series of specials known, rather fittingly, as *The Jimmy Timmy Power Hour*.

MY LIFE AS A TEENAGE ROBOT

The majority of Nickelodeon's series of the mid-to-late first decade of the 2000s were part of a prominent artistic trend in television animation programming, in which each series

My Life as a Teenage Robot. Shown from left: Tiff, Jenny, Britt (Nickelodeon/Photofest).

had a singular artistic "look" or "feel." *My Life as a Teenage Robot* (*MLAATR*) represented the apotheosis of this trend, and was, by far, the most successful in purely artistic terms. In spite of a voracious cult following, it was a more limited commercial success than some of its peers, lasting for only 40 episodes, which aired between 2003 and 2005. Despite its limited run, *MLAATR* is one of the most cleverly and emotionally staged and written series of recent memory. Particularly noteworthy is its employment of the graphic and literary embellishments of two concurrent "golden ages" in American entertainment: one in theatrical animation; the other in literary science fiction.

◆ ◆ ◆

Series creator Rob Renzetti is an Illinois native, having grown up in Addison, a suburb of Chicago, where he was born in 1967. He attended the University of Illinois at Champaign–Urbana, where he majored in art history. Later, he joined the animation program at Chicago's Columbia College, where he met Genndy Tartakovsky (see Chapter 6 and below). Renzetti and Tartakovsky later became roommates when they studied concurrently at California Institute of the Arts.

As he explained in a 2006 interview with this author:

> I was first hired to do some freelance [work] by a Chicago company called Startoons [sic], working on [*Tiny Toon Adventures;* see Chapter 6] as a clean-up [artist] and [in-betweener]. My first full-time gig was overseas in Madrid, Spain, for a company called Blue Pencil[,] working on *Batman: The Animated Series* [see Chapter 6] as an animator. My first Hollywood gig was for Hanna-Barbera as a storyboard artist.[35]

As a storyboard artist, and, later, a writer and director at Hanna-Barbera between 1992 and 1997 and again from 2000 to 2002, Renzetti was cutting his teeth at a fortuitous period in the history of both the studio and television animation. Chiefly working for his Cal Arts classmates Genndy Tartakovsky and Craig McCracken on *Dexter's Laboratory* (see Chapter 6), *The Powerpuff Girls* (see Chapter 6) and *Samurai Jack* (see below), he also worked briefly as a supervising director on *Whatever Happened to Robot Jones?* (see below). During this time, he produced his first solo project, *Mina and the Count,* for the *What a Cartoon!* anthology series (see Chapter 6). Lured to Nickelodeon in 1997, he made more short projects for the *Oh Yeah* project, including additional *Mina and the Count* films, *Ask Edward*, and the original pilot for *MLAATR*, then titled "My Neighbor Was a Teenage Robot." From the beginning, the project was an artistic partnership between Renzetti and art director Alex Kirwan. Kirwan's graphic sensibilities would become as prominent a part of the final series as would Renzetti's gift for developing the subtle and overt personalities of his characters. Unlike contemporary cases at Nickelodeon and elsewhere, the graphic stylization and character development complemented each other perfectly.

The three-year interval between the original pilot film of 1999 and the series pilot of 2002 allowed Renzetti and Kirwan some time to refine the essential elements of the concept, as well as to define from which artistic and cultural traditions they would draw:

> The style of the pilot is quite different than what the series ended up looking like.... There was a long time where the show remained dormant. I knew there was interest in it as a series, however, and I did work on writing the show "bible" in the years in between. I tried to expand the universe that was only hinted at in the pilot. [This included] coming up with new characters and new facets of the already existing characters and new facets of the existing characters. Some of these characters and concepts were used in the show and some never saw the light of day....
>
> Both Alex and I have a strong affinity for [1930s] design. Rather than solely duplicate the rubber hose style, we tried to marry that style with the flatter "designy" UPA style from the [1950s]. In addition[,] we tried to incorporate a wide array of thirties design beyond what the cartoons of the time looked like. Alex, Joseph Holt, our lead [background] designer, and Seonna Hong, our lead [background] painter, referenced the poster and advertising art of

the time to develop the [background] style of the show. We looked at industrial design for our props. Sci Fi Pulp novels and art were drawn on for the futuristic elements.[36]

This highly unique visual approach—which the creative team came to dub "future deco"[37]—gave the program the visual identity it needed to stand out among the crowd. The art deco design movement, which flourished between the mid–1920s and World War II, was based both on streamlined, geometrically stylized design principles and the influence of the positive attributes of technological change. It was commonplace in architecture, as can be seen in many prominent buildings erected in the 1930s. Too potent a force to be restricted to one medium of artistic expression, it had a powerful influence on graphic media as well. The animated films of the 1930s, particularly those of Max and Dave Fleischer (see Chapter 1), were studded with deco motifs, as were the pioneering science fiction magazines of the same decade, particularly Hugo Gernsback's *Amazing Stories*. The covers of these magazines, executed by such artists as Frank R. Paul and Hans "Wesso" Wessolowski, proved to be as influential in shaping modern science fiction as a genre as were the stories featured within. These were the neglected artistic traditions from which Renzetti, Kirwan and their staff were drawing in creating their universe. Thus, Renzetti was correct in his assessment when he labeled the show "an alternate future—as the future was imagined in the 1930s."[38]

By drawing on past visions of animation and science fiction rather than those of the present, Renzetti had already outlined the unique visual achievement of his series. Yet, as much as it was unique in design terms, it would have fallen flat had it not had compelling stories and characters. Fortunately, Renzetti, unlike most of his Nickelodeon colleagues in this decade, was extremely well equipped in these areas, as the final product clearly showed.

◆ ◆ ◆

Due to Renzetti and Kirwan's affinity for past graphic styles, Tremorton, *MLAATR*'s primary setting has the visual flavor of a science fiction version of Brigadoon, unchanged since the heyday of art deco. It might be expected that the stories and characters would also reflect this retro approach, but this is not entirely the case. They, in fact, reflect the exceptional ease with which Renzetti is able to juggle the retro- and the cutting-edge aspects of his series.

Nothing exemplified this better than the title character herself: Global Response Unit XJ9, better known as Jenny (Janice Kawaye). A well-oiled superheroic machine possessing "the strength of a million and seventy men" and an enormous cache of weaponry besides, Jenny had been programmed to confront and destroy all foreign, domestic and intergalactic enemies. Given her assets, and her highly deceptive physical appearance as a pigtailed, giggly teen, Jenny's job seems fairly easy—sometimes *too* easy. Consequently, she longs to be a normal human teenager and hang out with her "peers." Her creator-cum-"mother," Dr. Nora Wakeman (Candi Milo), eventually allows her to become a student at Tremorton's high school. In Hal Erickson's wonderful turn of phrase, Jenny hoped that maybe she could "go out on a date once in a while without worrying about the future of mankind,"[39] but even this is denied her. The heart and soul of the series, as a result, focuses on the tension existing in Jenny's robot brain and body between the stresses of her "job" and her adopted "alternate identity," and, to the fact that she is more sympathetic (and thus, ironically, "human") than her other Earth-bound associates. This makes her struggle much more compelling than similar crises of consciousness faced by characters in other programs. The variety of ways in which Jenny's various enemies—super-powered and otherwise—scheme to destroy her takes on a deeper level of drama for this reason.

Jenny's multi-faceted character, and her attempts to bridge the obvious divide between her identities, is something Renzetti intended from the start. In a discussion with this author, he clearly outlined the feminist subtext of her character:

> Jenny ... goes through a subtle change through the [evolution of the program]. At first, she is very unsure of herself, her role and her powers. She would give it all away just to fit in and be popular. This may sound trite [,] but I know it is a huge concern to all teenagers. It is something that they all have to struggle with, even those who ultimately shun the acceptance of their peers. Unfortunately for teenage girls, gaining popularity sometimes means fitting yourself into the social [straight jacket] of acceptable feminine behavior. I would argue that there is much less difference between the sexes than we like to think there is. I don't believe in biologically determined "masculine" or "feminine" characteristics.
>
> Jenny has it twice as hard [because, as a robot], she must try to be human as well as "feminine." And this is the one thing that [,] on the biological (or robotic) level, she cannot do. When she tries to fit in, she fails. When she uses the abilities she has, when she is *herself*, she succeeds....
>
> As the show progresses, Jenny gains more confidence in herself and her abilities.... She still has her foibles and weaknesses [,] but also displays confidence and pride in her abilities.... [She] has not only accepted herself but also her unique role as a super-hero....
>
> The message is not meant strictly for the girls in the audience but I hope that it will have a special resonance for them. I think it is important that the media portrays strong female characters without hitting kids over the head with overt lecturing.[40]

Like its contemporary series *Danny Phantom* (see above), *MLAATR* can be read as a picaresque *bildungsroman*, with the heroine's gradual self-discovery at its core. Jenny's growing self-confidence mirrored the confidence of Renzetti, Kirwan and company in presenting her story, and made it a rocket ride of a series in the process.

Like Townsville before it, Tremorton is a community structured on good-and-evil opposites. Consequently, the supporting characters can be firmly separated into two camps: those who are "with" Jenny and those who are "against" her. Most prominent in the "with" camp are those in whom Jenny can most easily confide, and who can console her in turn. The aforementioned Dr. Wakeman is, of course, at the head of this list, even though their relationship crackles with "mother/daughter" tension and can become strained at times.[41] Other friends add different edges. The Carbunkle brothers—tall, red-haired Brad (Chad Doreck) and diminutive, black-haired Tuck (Audrey Wasilewski)—are inadvertently responsible for initiating Jenny into the "outside" world her mother had hidden from her. Both are regularly put in situations from which Jenny must rescue them, reversing the ages-old sexual bias in television animation. The fact that Brad is a vapid idiot and Tuck a young con man add other levels, although the love and respect they have for Jenny is obvious to the viewer even when she doesn't see it. Less prominent, but more fervent in his admiration for Jenny, is Sheldon Lee (Quinton Flynn), a black-haired, pasty-skinned Jewish[42] "geek" whose interest in Jenny is both mechanical and sexual. Though she is initially repelled by him, going so far as to call him a "stalker," Jenny is somewhat won over after he rescues her from peril, returning a favor she had done for him earlier. Gradually, their relationship develops into an affectionate friendship, but, though Sheldon's sexual ardor for Jenny never dims, she is adamant in her refusal to enter this kind of relationship with him, for both she and the audience know it would have disastrous consequences—especially for Sheldon.

As with those of the Powerpuff Girls, Jenny's enemies, the denizens of the show's "against" column, run the gamut from the scarily sublime to the comically ridiculous. There are the fearsome members of the Cluster, a race of largely evil robots, from the planet Cluster Prime, who effectively function as an interplanetary version of the Mafia. Led by the odious Vexus (a brilliantly cast Eartha Kitt), they have made numerous entreaties to Jenny to join them, which she has always heatedly refused. Consequently, Vexus, as well as her various underlings, constantly engage in a variety of physical and mental "hits" on Jenny, some of which nearly destroy her. The climax of this conflict comes in the one-hour special "Escape From Cluster Prime," when Jenny, having temporarily forsaken Tremorton, ends up leading a successful rebellion against Vexus's rule. Jenny has other interplanetary enemies, notably the Space Bikers, an all-girl alien Hell's Angels–type group whose members resemble humanized amphibians. Some of her nastiest enemies, though, are human. The Crust Cousins—British Britt (Moira Quirk) and African American Tiff (Cree Summer)—are the social queens of Tremorton High School, and they view Jenny unfavorably. Thus, they try as often to demolish Jenny mentally as the Cluster does physically, and are quite successful.

It might be said, also, that Jenny is her *own* enemy at times. Though, as Renzetti implies, her self-confidence grows as the show expands its dramatic canvas. In the earliest episodes she is painfully emotionally insecure, and her inability to deal with the demands being made on her and on her friends as a consequence of her actions, carries with it such an emotional punch that the viewer cannot help but empathize. Her efforts to make herself appear more "human," and therefore more "normal," are all the more tragic, considering that, as Renzetti again has suggested, she has had—and will have—more success simply being who she *really* is. Thus, her efforts to renounce her "heritage" and "pass" as a human being are truly poignant. This turmoil makes her decision to reaffirm her robot loyalties at the end all the more satisfying. This program can be read in so many ways, in both sexual and "racial" terms, that it is surprising that it has largely been stashed away in obscurity since its original broadcast run.

MLAATR is a visually and emotionally engaging program, one that has accomplished its creator's aims while also providing a regular stream of comedy and drama. Like its leading character, it is a sleekly designed, effective machine, though not without an occasional malfunction. To viewers, it was enchanting, while, to historians, it is a work of artistic and cultural value.

All Grown Up

The last major collaboration between Nickelodeon and Klasky-Csupo was, fittingly, a sequel to the first one. For a tenth anniversary special for *Rugrats* (see Chapter 6), which was one of the highest-rated programs in the network's history, the studio staff simply presented the now-familiar characters with ten years added to their ages. The result was that some of the characters changed quite a lot, others less so. Despite the relative uniqueness of the concept, there proved to be little that the producers could do with the characters once the format had been established that had not been done, and the initial uniqueness of the idea soon wore off.

Avatar

Created by Bryan Konietzko and Michael Dante DiMartino, and debuting in 2005, this heavily stylized, *anime*-influenced series focused on a young child named Aang (Zack

Eisen), who possesses the ability to "bend" the elements to his will, and therefore becomes the Avatar, a figure responsible for restoring peace to the warring nations of Water, Earth, Fire and Air. He is assisted by Katara (Mae Whitman), who can "bend" water and thus free Aang from an icy prison, and her brother Sokka (Jack DeSena). In spite of impressively mounted graphics, there was little about this series that had not been done in terms of content. In spite of this, it attracted the attention of live-action filmmaker M. Night Shyamalan, who later adapted it into a tepidly received feature film.

CATSCRATCH

This series was created by graphic artist Douglas TenNapel, who had earlier been responsible for developing and creating *Earthworm Jim* and *Project G.E.E.K.E.R.* (see Chapter 6 for both). The project was based on *Gear*, a graphic novel by the artist from 1998, though the network insisted that the concept be cleaned up for television consumption. Even so, there was still a preponderance of toilet humor. The focus of the series, which debuted in 2005, is a trio of fraternal cats—Mr. Bilk (Wayne Knight), Gordon (Rob Paulsen) and Waffle (Kevin McDonald)—who inherit a fortune after their wealthy owner, Mrs. Crandilly, died unexpectedly. They proceed to enjoy the fruits of their new lifestyle, with predictable "cartoonish" results.

THE X'S

Created by Carlos Ramos, this program was notable more for its unique graphic design—dramatic character and art conceptions, with no ink line separations between characters and backgrounds—than its creative elements, which were often leaden and derivative. It foreshadowed Brad Bird's later feature film *The Incredibles*, although the characters here were spies rather than superheroes. The titular family consists of Mr. X (Patrick Warburton), Mrs. X (Wendie Malick), and their two children, teenaged Tuesday (Lynsey Bartilson) and pre-teen Truman (Jansen Panettiere). Working for the Superior agency, they face off against the villainy of SNAFU, led by Glowface (Chris Hardwick), who, like many other cartoon "villains" of this period, come off much more like a simpering, petulant child than a genuine force of evil. Bad, overplayed acting and a lack of interest in developing the characters torpedoed any attempt at artistic development of the series' unique design approach.

KAPPA MIKEY

This project was a genuine case of East meeting West in terms of animation approach and design. Created by Larry Schwarz, and debuting in 2006, the series focused on the title character (Michael Sinterniklaas), an American "cartoon character" who becomes a cast member on a Japanese *anime* series called *LilyMu*. The series proved to be highly effective in satirizing the stereotypical design and character elements of *anime*, particularly the stylized extremes between character "poses," while at the same time providing a "backstage" narrative that made it unique among television animation programs even during this inventive period.

EL TIGRE

Debuting in 2007, this entertaining project, created by Sandra Equihua and Jorge Gutierrez, was a rarity among television animation programs in that it was created and developed by animators with a specific ethnic slant, in this case Mexican/Latino-American, and thus reflected the artistic sensibilities of an underserved demographic among television animation viewers.[43] Drawing on both their personal and ethnic heritages, Equihua and Gutierrez created a compelling narrative dealing with the struggle between good and evil on both personal and metaphysical terms that strongly mirrored the program's idiosyncratic design approach.[44] The title character is the superheroic secret identity of Manny Rivera (Alanna Urbach), the son of a superhero and the grandson of a super-villain based in Miracle City (a thinly disguised Mexico City, where Gutierrez was born and raised). Consequently, he is torn as to whether to use his abilities for good or evil. The struggle is somewhat aggravated by the machinations of his gal pal, Frida Suarez (Grey DeLisle), the black sheep in a family full of police officers and other guardians of the law. Her regular musical performances with the Atomic Sombreros are used as something of a negative mirror image of the climactic musical numbers of *Fat Albert*, in which she tried to persuade Manny of the joys of being bad. She was, nevertheless, entirely supportive of him when he chose to do good. Equihua and Gutierrez clearly enjoyed themselves making this rejoinder to old Latino media stereotypes, and that good feeling extended to their audience as well.

Random! Cartoons

Like *What a Cartoon* and *Oh Yeah* before it (see Chapter 6 for both), this was an omnibus anthology project designed to showcase new visions, creators and ideas in television animation, with the ubiquitous Fred Seibert once again serving as ringmaster. As Seibert himself has noted, the changes that had occurred in the industry dribbled down into this project, particularly in the shift toward more women and more members of racial/ethnic minorities becoming involved in the industry.[45] As with the prior series, a large variety of projects were produced by both newcomers and veterans, though only Eric Robles's *Fanboy and Chum Chum*, an aggressive, slapstick-oriented CGI project, ended up seeing series production after its initial airing.

Wayside

A collaboration with Canada's Nelvana Studios (see chapters 4, 5, 6 and below), this series was based on a series of children's books by Louis Sachar, involving an elementary school constructed on a vertical rather than horizontal structural plan, where the illogical triumphs over the logical. As series director Riccardo Durante has noted, the series "is not about real kids in a real school ... it's about the glory of non-conformity."[46] This was something the characters and plots served to emphasize—a tad too much sometimes. Principal characters include Todd (Michael Cera), the "everyman" and the program's main focus; egotistical Myron (Martin Villafana); Dana (Lisa Ng), the obsessive-compulsive, rule-obsessed class "brain"; Maurecia (Denise Oliver), the helmet-and-rollerblades-wearing "jock girl"[47] who is clearly in love with Todd, but could only display it by punching him (!); and Mrs. Jewls (Kathleen Laskey), the teacher who demonstrates the series' twisted logic (e.g., by throwing a desk out a window to demonstrate gravity).

Back to the Barnyard

Created by Steven Odekerk (see above) and debuting in 2007, this project was based on *Barnyard*, a Nickelodeon-produced CGI feature film, and displayed its source material's lack of inventiveness and inspiration. Based on the exploits of a "male cow" named Otis, the plotlines failed to match the impressive levels of the draftsmanship, and was something of a disappointment.

TAK AND THE POWER OF JUJU

Debuting in 2007, and inspired by a popular video game, this CGI-based project focuses on the coming of age of the title character, a young man living in a stereotypical South Sea island setting, who is in training to become a shaman for his tribe. His adventures take him from his home of Pupununu village to the mythical realm of Juju. As with many CGI-based projects, visual effects took precedence over creative originality, creating singularly uninteresting results.

THE MIGHTY B

One of the more impressive and multi-faceted of the latter generation of Nickelodeon programs, this project, which debuted in 2008, benefitted from skilled work on both sides of the camera. The series was created by animators Cynthia True and Erik Wiese and comedian/actress Amy Poehler, a veteran of *Saturday Night Live* who later starred in the popular live-action sitcom *Parks and Recreation*. True and Weise, Nickelodeon veterans whose credits included *Fairly Oddparents* (see above) and *Spongebob Squarepants* (see Chapter 6), were inspired to develop the lead character after seeing Poehler portray a similar character on the Comedy Central series *Upright Citizens Brigade*. The project thus resembled those the animators had previously worked on, albeit with a far more feminine twist. This was reflected most obviously by the fact that the writing staff was almost exclusively female, an extremely rare occurrence in the often male-dominated world of television animation.[48]

Set in a magical-realist version of San Francisco, California, the focus of the series was on intelligent, resourceful but hyperactive Bessie Higgenbottom (Poehler), a nine-year-old "Honeybee" Scout whose aim in life is to become the all-time most decorated member of her troop. By doing this, she hopes to become The Mighty B, a superhero figure. She lives with her mother, Hillary (Megan Cavanagh), who operates a restaurant; her younger brother, Ben (Andy Richter), who wants to be her sidekick when she becomes Mighty B; and her dog, Happy (Dee Bradley Baker). Bessie also consults one of her fingers, on which she had painted a crude face, when she needs moral support. Fellow Honeybees include Penny (Dannah Feinglass, who doubled as a writer), a portly dimwit obsessed with taffy; Portia (Grey DeLisle), Bessie's bitchy rival; and Gwen (Jessica DiCicco), Portia's Asian best friend.

The feminist nature of the program was evident from the start, but it was presented in an understated way by writers, animators and actors alike, and therefore never assumed the broadly didactic behavior of feminist characters in other series of this time. *The Mighty B* is genuinely funny, engaging and engrossing, and opened up new avenues for presenting the behavior of young female characters in a television animation setting. (An episode in which the Honeybees competed with their Oakland-based rivals, the Dragonflies, in a reality-show setting is particularly revealing, showing the two sides [and a third group, the Black Widows] acting more like members of male street gangs than "female" stereotypes, as well as tapping into the simmering real-life animosities between the two cities by the Bay.) Given the program's excellence, which was rewarded with multiple Annie and Emmy nominations, it was disappointing when it was canceled by Nickelodeon after only two seasons.

❖ ❖ ❖

In its second decade as a television animation provider, Nickelodeon added immeasurably to its legacy by producing a wide variety of series that broadened the cultural vocabulary of television animation. While it was occasionally guilty of trying to further its "brand," and shortened the length of some of its more exceptional products while allowing weaker ones to linger, the company remained committed to taking chances on ideas, viewpoints and concepts that would have been anathema, for a variety of reasons, to the prior generation of television animation backers. For this reason alone, viewers should be grateful to Nickelodeon, and hope that it will continue to provide opportunities for great animators, writers and performers.

Cartoon Network Studios (CNS)

The studio formerly known as Hanna-Barbera had a banner decade during the early 2000s. Retaining the services of many of the animators who had defined its halcyon period, while recruiting veterans and newcomers to its ranks, CNS was able to produce an exceptionally varied group of series, in spite of the fact that it could sometimes, like its rivals Nickelodeon and Disney, arbitrarily terminate these projects for commercially motivated reasons. In spite of a new mandate that required it to exclusively service Cartoon Network (hence the name change), its elastic stretching of the concept of the "cartoon" itself, and crippling financial turmoil in the ranks of its parent company,[49] CNS was generally a reliable repository of creative excellence during this time. The major difference between the Nickelodeon, Disney and CNS was that CNS, due to the fluid nature of its parent network's "brand," was more willing than their competitors to leave their animators to their own devices. This produced mixed results.

◆ ◆ ◆

Before we go on to discuss the network's "greatest hits" during this decade, of which there were many, it is important to get a full understanding of what CNS was producing during this period, as its production mandate was more complex than it would appear on the surface.

Unlike Nickelodeon and Disney, who both supplemented their animated programming with a large portion of live-action material, Cartoon Network was (at least, until recently) committed to providing animation to viewers on an around-the-clock basis. As a consequence, it has been more aggressive and single-minded in its animation production than other studios of the decade, both in terms of its own productions and those commissioned from domestic and foreign animation providers. With the older programs under its control now isolated under a separate channel imprint, Boomerang, Cartoon Network has become more focused on a mandate to produce specific types of original animation. In each case, the audience at which the programming is aimed has determined whether or not the program will be "clean" or "dirty" in comedic content—it can easily go either way. In all cases, a particular, almost rigid, formula is adopted that reflects the channel's mandate. It is called "Cartoon" Network, rather than "Animation" Network, for a specific reason.

CNS product can be subdivided into three categories—comedy, action and adult oriented, though in some cases the categories overlap. The first category is self-explanatory, and it is where the vast majority of the studio's best work has been produced; this will be discussed more fully below. The second category is relatively sparse. There are some interesting projects, however, notably *Ben 10* and its sequel projects, featuring the exploits of a preteen to teenaged superhero, and *The Secret Saturdays*, the saga of a globe-trotting, super-scientific family that reads like an amalgam of *Jonny Quest* (see Chapter 3) and *The Incredibles*. Where the channel's excesses are most evident is, not surprisingly, in the more adult-oriented series, which, with their nudge-nudge-wink-wink sexual humor and obsession with scatology, resemble the incredibly "blue" burlesque shows of the century past. These series include most notoriously *Aqua Teen Hunger Force*, featuring an animated fast food shake and fries and a living meatball as the superheroic protagonists; *Tom Goes to the Mayor*, an exercise in comic angst; and *Assy McGee*, whose protagonist has a posterior for a face! It was fortunate for CNS that these projects aired as late at night as they did. Had they aired earlier, they would not have developed their inexplicably devout cult followings. Most of these were the product of the Atlanta-based Williams Street organization rather than CNS itself.

It is in its comedy-oriented programs, aimed at both children and young adults, that the skill and inventiveness of the CNS animation team is most evident. Balancing the sublime and the ridiculous, while at the same time reflecting the idiosyncrasies of their individual creators, these frequently hilarious programs have created a nearly unbroken streak of mirth and merriment over their broadcast runs, and are very much the equal (and sometimes the superior) of their predecessors and their peers. A close analysis reveals that, while these programs share a mandate and often a structure, each is very much an entity in and of itself, to be judged on its own merits.

Courage the Cowardly Dog

The first of the second generation of Cartoon Network series to emerge was the work of John Dilworth. A New York City native, Dilworth attended the New York School of Visual Art, and then launched his animation career in the short-subject film category in 1985. He produced a number of notable works over the following decade, but the most acclaimed of these was *The Chicken from Outer Space*, which was nominated for an Academy Award in 1995. After this success, Dilworth washed his hands of the medium, claiming that he wanted to do something else. Nevertheless, Cartoon Network was impressed by *Chicken*, and by 1999 they had persuaded Dilworth to begin production of a series based on some of the characters featured in the short; in all, 26 episodes were produced. Since the series' demise, Dilworth has not produced another, preferring to concentrate on his work in the short film format.[50]

His sole series project, *Courage the Cowardly Dog*, naturally preserved the essence of the character he had introduced to viewers of his original short. The title character's (Marty Grabstein) contradictory nature is explained sufficiently by the adverb in the title, although he is periodically able to suppress enough of his generalized fear to act heroically. Courage lives in the appropriately named town of Nowhere, Kansas, with his sympathetic mistress, Muriel Bagge (Thea White), and her crotchety husband Eustace (Lionel Wilson, later Arthur Anderson), who perennially refers to Courage as "stupid." Courage's heroism consists chiefly of rescuing a regularly imperiled Muriel from a variety of bizarrely conceived antagonistic characters, including an evil feline hotel owner named (naturally) Katz. Like Maxwell Atoms's later *Grim Adventures of Billy and Mandy* (see below), the series blended supernatural-based Gothic horror and slapstick comedy in unique and bizarre ways, and soon became an audience favorite. Thus, although Dilworth is himself something of a marginal figure in television animation history, his series, through constant exposure in reruns, is not.

MIKE, LU AND OG

Created by *Rugrats* veteran Chuck Swenson in collaboration with Russians Mikhail Aldashin and Mikhail Shindel, this series, originally airing from 1999 to 2000, is set on the small island of Albonquetine. The title trio are Micheline "Mike" Mavinski (Nika Frost), a Manhattan-raised tomboy who ends up stranded on the island as a foreign-exchange student; Lu (Nancy Cartwright), a haughty princess of the native tribe occupying the island; and Og (Dee Bradley Baker), another native skilled at the art of invention. The series premise was interesting, but the episode content, focusing on what Mike learned from the natives and vice versa, was rather routine. This could not, however, be said for the animation production itself, which was a unique collaboration between three separate animation providers in Russia, America and Korea.[51]

SHEEP IN THE BIG CITY

This series was the creation of Mo Willems, a New Orleans–born writer and artist who is a graduate of the Tisch School of Arts at NYU. He first attracted attention with the cartoon collection *You Can Never Find a Rickshaw When It Monsoons*, based on his European travels. Later, he joined the writing staff of *Sesame Street*, winning six Emmys for his work on the series. He then moved into animation, creating *The Offbeats* for Nickelodeon and then *Sheep* for Cartoon Network. Following the latter program's cancellation, Willems worked for his *Sheep* colleague, Tom "Mr." Warburton, on *Codename: Kids Next Door* (see below). In 2003, he abandoned his animation career to concentrate, like another former animator, Jim Benton (see Chapter 6), on a highly successful career as a children's book writer.

Described by one reviewer as "*The Fugitive* meets *Rocky and Bullwinkle*,"[52] *Sheep in the Big City* (debuting in 2000), the first CNS collaboration with the New York–based Curious Pictures, combined the former's run-or-be-caught formula with the latter's highly irreverent humor. The ovine hero (Kevin Seal), who was drawn in the style of Picasso with both eyes on one side of his head, is an innocent member of the flock of Farmer John (James Godwin) until he is targeted for use as a military weapon by the "insane"[53] General Specific (Seal). Consequently, he was forced to hide out in the Big City. Willems's pun-laden, obvious approach—later a dominant element of his children's books as well—was both an asset and liability to the series. This was evident in the names and behavior of the major characters, among them: Angry Scientist (Willems), the Ranting Swede (Seal), Private Public (Godwin), Lady Richtington (Stephanie D'Abruzzo) and Plot Device—as well as in such devices as a Complimentary Sandwich, which went around praising people. Though the series was well received by critics, it failed to gain sufficient viewership, and was canceled after 26 installments had aired.

GRIM AND EVIL

Launched in 2001, this project, like many Hanna-Barbera projects of the late 1960s, was a two-in-one offering. It was the creation of Maxwell Atoms, the *nom de plume* of Colorado-born animator Adam Burton. He attended the University of the Arts in Philadelphia, and, following his graduation, earned an internship at Film Roman in the mid–1990s. He later worked at Warner Bros. and Wild Brain Studios before joining Hanna-Barbera, working for David Feiss (see Chapter 6) as a writer. As an art student, he developed a personal style that was highly surrealistic, influenced by the television animation and monster science fiction and horror films of the past, and these influences are strongly felt in his own series. The science fiction influence can be seen particularly in the polarized positions of the "good" and "evil" characters, while the reliance on violence and bloodshed of horror films is felt in both the comedy and adventure content. The development and stylization of Atoms's characters is entirely his own, as is the emphasis on nihilism in the plot tones, elements that made this property unique.

The two segments of the program were "The Grim Adventures of Billy and Mandy," which became a separate series in 2003, and "Evil Con Carne." Both had seemingly limited premises, but, in the former series in particular, the writers were able to transcend them. The first project, set in the town of Endsville, features Billy (Richard Horvitz), a cretinous boy, and Mandy (Grey DeLisle), a sadistic blonde-haired girl, whose voice and scowling face rarely show any true empathy or emotion.[54] The series proper began when The Grim Reaper (Greg Eagles), who speaks with a highly improbable West Indian accent (ending many of his sentences with "mon"), arrives to claim Billy's hamster. Through some quick thinking on Mandy's part, the child pair are able to defeat "Grim" in a limbo contest, making him their servant for life. The trio went on to engage in a variety of surrealistic, violent and humorous antics, and defeated a variety of bizarrely crafted supernatural antagonists in the process. This was not quite as simple as it appeared. As Hal Erickson observes, though the series' comedy had a primarily slapstick tone, the tone was far darker than many of its contemporaries: "It was not an unusual sight for Mandy to entomb a tied-up Billy behind a brick wall, simply to teach him a lesson in manners."[55] (Grim, for his part, received even worse treatment at her hands.) Typical nemeses and associates include Eris (Rachel Macfarlane), the Greek goddess of chaos, reincarnated as an impetuous, gap-toothed blonde Valley Girl; Irwin (Vanessa Marshall), an African American schoolmate of Billy's, with an obvious crush on Mandy and a habit of ending his sentences with the word "yo"; Hoss Del Gado (Jim Cummings), an ultra-masculine soldier of fortune reminiscent of Kurt Russell's Snake Plissken characterization in *Escape from New York*; and an elderly African American man (Phil LaMarr) who, believing he is Dracula, dresses the part, and refers to himself in the third person. Savage parodies of Harry Potter and Pokemon—to say nothing of other Cartoon Network shows—added an additional level of humorous menace to the series, one that Atoms and company clearly worked hard to maintain. They were able to take these elements to even greater lengths once the series was extended to a half-hour slot, to the delight, and sometimes the revulsion, of viewers.

The second, and lesser, component, was "Evil Con Carne." The title character of this project is Hector Con Carne (LaMarr), a mad genius type whose body has been destroyed, but whose brain and stomach live on inside a stupid former circus bear named Boskov. With the aid of his two trusted associates, General Skarr (Armin Zimmerman) and Major Doctor Ghastly (DeLisle), Hector attempts to continue his efforts to conquer the world, only to be repeatedly and spectacularly undone in typically slapstick-cartoon fashion. ("These guys should really have considered getting into another line of work," observes Hal Erickson.[56]) General Skarr was later reconstituted in "The Grim Adventures of Billy and Mandy" as the now-retired (and predictably victimized) neighbor of the title characters. An episode in which Con Carne and Ghastly persuade him to come back to the game briefly provided a belated narrative union between the two properties, which simply showed which of the two was the better series.

SAMURAI JACK

After several years of effectively "minding the store" for his friend Craig McCracken on *The Powerpuff Girls* (see Chapter 6), Genndy Tartakovsky was eager to return to the creator's chair. This series allowed him to do so in 2001, with spectacular results.

"I've always loved samurais—I've always been influenced by samurais," Tartakovsky explained to author Allan Neuwirth. "I really wanted to do that."[57] Influenced in particular by iconic Japanese film director Akira Kurosawa's depiction of these proud, noble warriors, Tartakovsky sought to create a similar ambience for his project. However, he ran into the proverbial brick wall in terms of content—samurai narratives typically contain a large amount of stylized violence and bloodshed, and, even in the more liberal-minded context of 21st century television animation, Cartoon Network was not willing to underwrite a series which had this kind of graphic violence as its *raison d'etre*. Other animators might have thrown up their hands and walked away from the project at that moment, but not Tartakovsky. He simply retooled it until it was acceptable to the network and himself.

> "I really can't *cut* anybody," he explained to Neuwirth later:
> ...and there's really no fun in doing samurai action if I can't.... So I thought, "What if they're all robots? ... I can get away with some ... hard-core fighting?" That's where the whole sci-fi element came from. Like, "Then maybe he's thrown into the future, and there's this wizard, and so on." I knew that I didn't want it bound to one world ... so the story started to come together out of the necessities that I needed to make the show [emphasis in original].[58]

After selling the series to studio programming boss Mike Lazzo strictly by comparing it to the 1970s TV action series *Kung Fu*, Tartakovsky was off to the races. "If there was [any animator] we could trust [to deliver on a project at that time], it was Genndy," noted studio executive Linda Simensky.[59]

He didn't let them down, not by any means.

Samurai Jack is a superbly executed series that proves Tartakovsky is one of the living masters of the art of animation. Unlike so many other series of the time, which place a priority on dialogue and sound to carry stories, this series' storytelling is almost exclusively visual in a way not seen since the silent-film era. Influenced by both Japanese *anime* and the stylized Disney feature animation of the 1950s, Tartakovsky highlights the visual elements of his series in a way that is impossible for the viewer to ignore. Even simplistic-seeming material, such as having raindrops fall on a flower, is directed in such a way that its importance to the story is always maximized. Due to the above-noted issues of presentation, Tartakovsky tends to limit the most "violent" aspects of the series to climactic fight sequences, but he builds toward them in such a way that they are the centerpiece of the stories, not simply a cheaply contrived excuse for the characters to drop the gloves with each other, as can happen on other series. Tartakovsky's work on *The Powerpuff Girls* had shown him how to balance action and story, and he applied this philosophy to *Samurai Jack*.

As with other series of this time, the seeming thinness of the series' written concept is belied by the ferocity of its visual imagery. The series proper focuses on the title character (Phil LaMarr), who is, as typical in the action genre, a man of few words who lets his actions do the talking. As a boy, he had witnessed his society conquered and enslaved by Aku (Makoto Iwamatsu), an evil, shape-shifting wizard, and he is determined to get his revenge in any way possible. Hoping to return to his homeland via the proper portal between realms, Jack travels constantly in search of this vessel, all the while pursued by Aku and his robot henchmen.

The fights between Jack and the robots (who "bleed" oil when injured) typically serve as the climax of the stories. In other hands, the storylines might have become dull and pedestrian, but it is a credit to Tartakovsky's skill and imagination as an animator that he does not let this happen.

Since the end of this series in 2004, Tartakovsky has supervised the animation of the *Star Wars* series *Clone Wars* for Cartoon Network, and, after relocating to Sony Pictures Animation, the direction of the animated feature film *Hotel Transylvania*. Reportedly, a *Samurai Jack* feature film is in the works, to be produced by Fred Seibert's Frederator studios under Tartakovsky's direction.

CODENAME: KIDS NEXT DOOR

A second collaboration with Curious Pictures, this series, *Kids Next Door* (*KND*) was an audaciously conceived but well executed project by Tom Warburton, who signed his work simply as "Mr." Warburton. A Pennsylvania native, he is a graduate of Kutztown University of Pennsylvania, where he did his first work in animation. Shuttling between a variety of houses in New York City, he did layout work on *Doug* and character designs for *Pepper Ann* (see Chapter 6) before pitching *KND*, an outgrowth of an earlier pilot called *Kenny and the Chimp*. After the pilot series of films, Warburton was commissioned to develop a series even though he had no prior experience as a "show runner." The series, which made its debut in 2002, was well received, and ultimately ran for six seasons on the network.

Like *The Secret Files of the Spydogs* (see Chapter 6) before it, and *T.U.F.F. Puppy* (see above) after, *KND* attempted to combine typical cartoon "slapstick" comedy with the freewheeling action-oriented approach of espionage films and television programs, but the concept was ultimately undone by ham-fisted overacting, chiefly by the "villains." There was an interesting satirical dimension at work in *KND*, which included suggesting in the credits that the crew also had *its* share of spies. The series was constructed on a literal "generation gap," as the ten-year-old protagonists literally battled their "evil" elders (particularly teenagers and adults who wanted to the restrict the "rights" and mobility of children), and dissenters among their own ranks, particularly the Delightful Children from Down the Lane, who served as a caricature of "proper" child behavior. (The satiric potential in this was not carried as far as could have been, likely because of the intended audience.) The title group themselves were quite diverse. They consisted of "Numbuh" [*sic*] One, a.k.a. Nigel Uno (Ben Diskin), the sunglasses-sporting, British-accented leader; "Numbuh" Two, a.k.a. Hoagie Gilligan (Diskin), the technical specialist; "Numbuh" Three, a.k.a. Kuki Sanban (Lauren Tom), the Asian mistress of diversionary tactics; "Numbuh" Four, a.k.a. Wallabee Beetles (Dee Bradley Baker), master of the art of mortal combat; and "Numbuh" Five, a.k.a. Abby Lincoln (Cree Summer), the African American undercover agent. Despite the variety of their ominous foes, they proved to be highly effective, provided "they weren't slowed down by their basic immaturity and childhood neuroses," notes Hal Erickson.[60] As is often the case with television animation, this could be said of the series itself, considering how childishly most of the adult and teenaged characters behaved, which made the KND seem all the more mature, due to their more nuanced behavior.

It was, in fact, this aspect of the series that Warburton wanted to emphasize, as well as how this contrasted with their "stock" personalities as a team, as he later explained to Joe Murray:

> To be honest, the characters ... have always been your basic, stereotypical "team" personalities at their very core ... the fearless leader, the brainy inventor kid, the airhead, the tough guy, the cool chick.... But ... it's about how you take those basic, boring traits and play upon them. That's what defines who they *really* are and what makes them interesting.... What makes the tough guy weak? What is the fearless leader afraid of? The best way to find out these things is over time. Fortunately, we had six seasons ... in which to really explore the kids and learn more and more about them.[61]

For all the flaws of the series' concept and execution, this element proved to be its saving grace. Like other television animation producers of the time, Warburton understood that you could not produce a series revolving around child characters without portraying them in a manner that reflected inner conflict and confusion its target audience would simply reject it. If Warburton's plots were far-fetched, his characters' weaponry absurd, and his villains one-dimensional silhouettes, his lead characters were not, and, if only for a moment, they managed to make the absurd believable and the nonsensical threatening.

Whatever Happened to Robot Jones?

Oddly enough, the title of this series is something its admirers have been asking since its departure. Of the CNS series of this decade, it was one of the shortest lived, airing only a handful of episodes in 2002 before its abrupt termination. Perhaps the network's decision to initially broadcast it in a late-night timeslot had something to do with it.[62]

Created by Greg Miller, the series focused on the title character (Bobby Block), a semi-human, stereotypically monosyllabic "speaking" robot who attends middle school to learn the "customs" of the human race, which he then reports back to his parental "units" (Grey DeLisle and Maurice La Marche). During his time as a pupil, he befriends two local boys, Socks (Kyle Sullivan) and Cubey (Myles Jeffrey), unintentionally harasses Principal Madman (Jeff Bennett), who bears a strong resemblance to Adolf Hitler; he even develops a crush on Shannon Westaberg (DeLisle), a female nerd with braces and an artificial leg—which somehow convinces Robot Jones that she is a sister robot posing as a human being.

Just as it started getting interesting, it was over. This was a shame, because it was a well-executed series, possessing a superb retro design scheme very much reminiscent of the 1970s episodes of *Schoolhouse Rock*. Nevertheless, it likely convinced series producer Rob Renzetti that he could produce another series about a robot (see *My Life as a Teenage Robot* in the Nickelodeon section above), and for that, at least, we should be glad.

Harvey Birdman, Attorney at Law

This inventive and satirical program, which debuted on the network in 2002, was by far the most artistically successful of the network's adult-oriented programs, simply because its structure and content never allowed it to get too filthy. It was a highly successful televisual example of the literary art of recontextuality—taking characters or entire stories from a previously existing fictional narrative and repurposing them. This has become commonplace in literary and genre fiction circles recently, particularly with public domain materials of the 19th century, but copyright control and enforcement tends to limit the extent to which it can be employed for commercial purposes in the visual media. The creators of this series were fortunate to be able to have nearly the entire classic Hanna-Barbera canon available to them, and they proceeded to milk the opportunity for all it was worth.

The series focused, naturally, on the title character, Harvey Birdman (Gary Cole). Presumably the same Birdman of *Birdman and the Galaxy Trio* (see Chapter 3) fame, he has since retired from the superhero business to adopt a more remunerative career as a lawyer. Some of his old habits remain, however, such as continuing to wear a mask and wings in public. Fittingly, the head of the law firm at which he works is his old superhero boss, Falcon 7 or, rather, Phil Ken Sebben (Stephen Colbert)—who was given a more direct, earthy personality here. This series was a wicked parody of both standard TV legal dramas and the whole Hanna-Barbera studio archive. The two judges Birdman usually argued in front of, for example, were Hiram Mightor (Cole), formerly "The Mighty" of 1960s television animation fame (see Chapter 3), and Mentok the Mind Taker (John Michael Higgins), a supposedly reformed ex-villain who is not above using his abilities to make the jury vote in his favor. Yet what really set the series apart was the recontextualized manner in which the writers utilize the vintage Hanna-Barbera characters. Some examples: Race Bannon and Dr. Benton Quest fighting for custody of Jonny Quest; Secret Squirrel acting as a flasher; Shaggy and Scooby Doo brought in on charges of drug possession; Boo Boo Bear acting as a Unabomber-styled terrorist; and so on. What really took the cake, however, was the decision to recast Fred Flintstone as a Godfather-styled mobster—and to have him "persuade" Birdman to take his case by depositing Quick Draw McGraw's severed head in his bed![63]

Whatever your feelings about the Hanna-Barbera programs, it is hard not to enjoy the program. Though they are usually thought of as carefree and funny, cartoon characters often also have self-centered or pompous qualities like other "actors"; seeing them so severely cast against "type" here is simply hilarious. Hopefully, other studios will think highly enough of *their* characters to be willing to cast them against type.

Atomic Betty

A Canadian import developed by Kevin Gillis (see Chapter 4) which debuted in 2004, this project owed its concept, at least in part, to the literary "space operas" of the 1930s, particularly those of Edmond Hamilton, Jack Williamson and E.E. "Doc" Smith. Not surprisingly, the show itself was partially set in Canada, which gave it a unique position in the overcrowded American market. The title character (Tajja Isen) is a seemingly normal young girl on the surface, but is, in fact, one of the super-powered "Galactic Guardians" who defends the universe from evil. The series managed to mine effective storylines from the contrast between Betty's two "roles" in life, but its attempts at humor were far less successful, due in part to the reticence of the writing.

Foster's Home for Imaginary Friends

Given that he had so radically reshaped viewer expectations for television animation with *The Powerpuff Girls* (see Chapter 6), there was undoubtedly a lot of pressure on Craig McCracken to develop a follow-up project. He ultimately did deliver worthy a project in 2004, after his previous series had ceased production. However, it was entirely characteristic of McCracken to present a follow-up series that heavily deviated from his prior work in both artistic conception and overall moral tone. If *Powerpuff Girls* had showed that McCracken had few peers as an action-oriented animation director, *Foster's*, which also developed a strong cult following, showed that he had even fewer peers as a comedy-oriented director.

McCracken himself made clear the artistic and tonal distinctions between his two projects in an interview with Joe Murray:

> In my mind, *Powerpuff* is much more of a "cartoon," whereas *Foster's* is more like an animated sitcom. *Powerpuff* is shorter, more gag-driven, and the characters are slightly more two-dimensional, while *Foster's* is much more story-driven and the characters are a bit more complex. From a production side, *Powerpuff* utilized more hand-drawn animation produced overseas ... [while] *Foster's* was animated digitally in [the] Flash [system]....
>
> ...I think I'm constantly trying to make the cartoons I wished I had seen when I was young. With *Powerpuff*[,] I wanted to make a show like the Adam West *Batman* series, where a kid could watch it for the action and adventure of it and an adult could watch it for its campy silliness. *Foster's* was just the opposite. I wanted to make a show where kids and adults could enjoy the exact same thing at the exact same time, very much like *The Muppet Show* was for my family and me.[64]

In both instances, he succeeded with flying colors. He had already proved that he could juggle the sublime and the soporific in the comparatively limited format of *Powerpuff*, and the "animated sitcom" format he used for *Foster's* allowed him to successfully mine more adult-oriented approaches to humor and morality that the good-and-evil universe of *Powerpuff* did not permit. Just as *Powerpuff* balanced the serious concerns of the superhero sub-genre with its more mundane aspects, *Foster's* applied these aspects to both the title establishment and the world in which it existed, leavening heavy morality with Mack Sennett–styled slapstick comedy, especially in the climaxes. If McCracken had not already established himself as a unique television animation *auteur* with *Powerpuff*, he most certainly did so with *Foster's*.

◆ ◆ ◆

Foster's is concerned with the by-products of a realistic childhood pursuit: the creation of imaginary friends to either supplement or supplant those in the real world.[65] The major difference is that, rather than being invisible and inaudible to people except the creator, McCracken's "imaginary" friends are not only real, but also sentient, and have lives and feelings fully independent of those who conceived them. Rather than being an asset to their creators, they instead become a burden as they grow older, and, supposedly, must put away "childish" things. Enter Foster's Home for Imaginary Friends (or, simply, "the house"), which exists as something of a halfway house for these individuals who have been shed by their original owners and are awaiting adoption by new owners. This process is not nearly as clear-cut as it seems, for sometimes the needed break between creator and creation is not as thorough as it should be.

A case in point is that of the two protagonists of the series. Mac (Sean Marquette) is a grade-school–aged boy who, though outwardly somewhat "civilized," has a wilder aspect to his personality that has only recently been tamed. The major by-product of this is his highly undisciplined imaginary friend Blooregard Q. Kazoo (Keith Ferguson—simply brilliant), "Bloo" for short, a facetious, anarchic con man who inhabits the body of one of the villains of the *Pac-Man* video game. Forced to abandon Bloo by his mother simply because she can no longer abide the destructiveness he fosters in Mac, Mac reluctantly commits Bloo to Foster's, though he manages to arrange a regular visiting schedule so that they can remain in touch. That is a good thing, considering that, while they are as fractious in their relationship as any estranged married couple, they seem to need each other as Mac reluctantly grows up. Meanwhile, Bloo begins, slowly and defiantly, shaping the place to his own desires, not unlike

Randall McMurphy's reshaping of the asylum in *One Flew Over the Cuckoo's Nest*. He is ultimately punished (multiple times) by both the house management and the series producers for these transgressions, but it never deters him, and the fact that he escapes McMurphy's tragic end only increases the potency of his frequent rebellions. He is willing to listen to Mac, and often *only* Mac, when he considers himself to be in the wrong. To paraphrase Jean-Paul Sartre, Mac realizes that while Bloo literally is *of* him, he is also *not* him.[66] As he becomes more mature, he is better able to criticize Bloo's less-mature behavior, and Bloo is able to recognize this and respect Mac.

This profound relationship is at the heart of the series, but it is by no means the only one that deserves consideration. Even more than in McCracken's previous series, the ability (or lack thereof) of the characters to take personal responsibility for their actions, and the extent to which they feel guilt over them, forms a major dimensional element. This is seen chiefly in the relationship between the house management, functioning as superegos, and their mixed attempts to control the Id impulses of their more destructive patrons, which are also prominently at play.

The dichotomy is amplified by the fact that the two highest levels of "authority" in the house are not in as much control as they should be. Madam Foster (Candi Milo), the house founder, is a dotty old woman who can be as disruptive and troublesome as any of her charges, and, therefore, while she is respected and revered, her actual power is nominal. Her own imaginary friend, Mr. Herriman (Tom Kane), a stubborn, punctual, English-accented and very Victorian/Edwardian humanized rabbit, struts around like he owns the place, in the manner of a British military commander. As most of the imaginary friends (with the notable exception of Bloo) are intimidated by him, he is able to wield at least some power. The true power in the house belongs to Madam Foster's granddaughter, Frankie (Grey DeLisle), whom Herriman patronizingly refers to as "Miss Frances." A tall, college-aged redhead, Frankie has spent her entire life knowing and dealing with imaginary friends, and knows precisely that, because they come in a variety of different forms and outlooks, she must adopt different ways of dealing with them. She can either turn on the charm or apply the lash, depending on what serves her purposes. In Bloo's case, she serves as the Nurse Ratched to his McMurphy, lecturing and cajoling him when he tries to con her or others in the house into doing his bidding, and repeatedly insisting that he "reform" himself. The fact that Mac develops a crush on her that deepens as the series progresses may be a subliminal outgrowth of his respect for her as the only one other than himself who has a chance of restraining Bloo.

Other characters in the series can be separated into those, like Bloo, who are willing to challenge the establishment, and those who are not. The unwilling are Wilt (Phil LaMarr), a basketball player who repeatedly apologizes for actual or imagined violations; Eduardo (Tom Kenny), a Mexican escapee from Maurice Sendak's notebook for *Where the Wild Things Are*, who, despite his outward appearance of fearsomeness, is actually quite docile, given his obsession with potatoes; and Coco (Milo), a bird-like creature capable only of saying her own name, but with the proper inflections to get multiple meanings across. The establishment challengers are made up mostly of outsiders or trespassers to the house. They include Goo (DeLisle), a hyperactive young lady with a runaway train of an imagination; Cheese (Milo), a reckless, disruptive dimwit who makes Bloo look *good* by comparison; and Duchess (DeLisle), a reincarnated pre–Lenin White Russian who cannot seem to do *anything* without the aid of "servants"—like a highly resentful Frankie. The most threatening character, and the one closest to being a true "villain," is Berry (DeLisle), who appears in only two episodes. Though sweet and innocent on the outside, she is, in fact, a rapacious villainess with an enormous secret crush on Bloo. In both of her appearances, she recklessly, and fruitlessly, attempts to connect with Bloo and destroy Mac. She is the closest thing to a truly antagonistic character on the series, since the others recklessly vacillate between "good" and "bad"—a unique marker of McCracken's approach.

Foster's is unique not simply because of the skill of the voice acting (especially DeLisle's) and the cleverness of the scripts, but because of McCracken's overall vision and orchestration of the series. Unlike other producers, he is never content to simply establish a formula for a project and allow it to progress until it wears out. He and his staff experiment constantly with providing innovative ways of telling the stories, with a variety of unique camera setups and—a distinguishing mark of his first series—rapid-fire comic pacing, a myriad of different settings and plots, and, significantly, never allowing us to assume that we truly "know" the characters. The fact that McCracken is a risk taker in terms of narrative progress and character design has allowed him to work in a way that attracts fans and keeps them attracted to a project.

When the series ceased production in 2009, McCracken resigned from Cartoon Network, reportedly angered by the fact that live-action "reality" programming was entering into the lineup. He has developed a new project for Disney called *Wander Over Yonder*, scheduled to debut sometime in 2013. Based on both *Powerpuff* and *Foster's* (for which he won two Emmys), McCracken has carved a formidable niche for himself in the history of American television animation.

CAMP LAZLO!

Like Craig McCracken, Joe Murray faced a challenge in developing a follow-up to a project that had garnered both acclaim and awards, in his case *Rocko's Modern Life* (see Chapter 6) for Nickelodeon. Yet Murray, unlike McCracken, kept his trademark design style intact for his follow-up; the primary change was in character and plot tone. While *Rocko* focused on adult anthropomorphic characters, *Camp Lazlo!* focused instead on characters who could easily be the children of the prior group, and therefore required a less aggressive tone. Murray was able to accomplish this shift easily because he had always prided himself on character development above jokes—the latter emerging from the former—and because he and his staff were once again working hard to make sure that the audience for this series could connect with the characters on an emotional level, regardless of the absurdity of their adventures. Murray was able to work effectively with his second project in a way that his first project, excellent as it was, barely hinted at.

Having taken a sabbatical between production of the two series (*Rocko* ending in the late 1990s, *Lazlo* beginning in 2005), during which he worked as a children's book illustrator, Murray adopted a more simplified background approach than in his prior series, though his characters still had the wide eyes and beaming grins that were his trademark.[67] Besides shifting in orientation to another age demographic, he abandoned the prior series' emphasis on an urban environment in favor of nature and the great outdoors. This was important, considering that the show focused both on an organization (scouting for both boys and girls) and an institution (summer camp) where these values were considered to be paramount.[68] Murray, presented them in the hilariously subversive manner that only television animation can execute successfully, which added considerably to the show's appeal. The effort paid off for Murray as he won the awards denied his earlier project, including Emmys and the international Pulcinella award for achievement in children's television.

Like Disney's later *Phineas and Ferb* (see below), though in a more limited and restrained way, *Lazlo* focuses on the potentials and pitfalls related to the seemingly endless summer and what might be accomplished in the season. Nobody understands this better than the trio who serves as the focus of most of the storylines. Lazlo (Carlos Alazraqui), the title character, is a Brazilian monkey whose personality is a combination of Candide, Frank Merriwell and Natty Bumppo. An eager, almost zealous member of the Bean Scouts, he is immensely resourceful in terms of wilderness survival, and unfailingly polite. He is limited in other aspects of his life, however, making him an easy target for scammers. That he is often shunned by his fellow campers at run-down Camp Kidney does not concern him in the least, as he finds solace in romping with his bunk mates—Raj (Jeff Bennett), an East Indian–accented elephant, and Clam (Alazraqui), an "albino pygmy rhino" [*sic*], who speaks only in clipped, rudimentary grammar. This trio is far less emotionally "mature" than the other masculine inhabitants of Camp Kidney (to say nothing of their female counterparts, the Squirrel Scouts, on the other side of Leakey Lake at Acorn Flats), and Murray often uses their naïveté to make them the butt of jokes. Especially in the case of Lazlo, this proves to be a reasonable shield against the more objectionable aspects of Camp Kidney, as he seems untainted by the moral corruption that comes to engulf most of the other characters in the series.

That corruption is evident in a survey of the characters. Camp Kidney's bullmoose scoutmaster, Algonquin Lumpus (Tom Kenny), is a bespectacled old reprobate who shows very little affection toward his charges, viewing his job instead as merely a corporate stepping stone. This attitude both offends and worries his right-hand man, Slinkman (Kenny), a slug who makes token efforts to "relate" to the boys in ways Lumpus refuses to do. Bereft of the strong authority they need, the Camp Kidney boys have devolved into factions based on actual or perceived friendships, and try to outdo one another in internal contests to prove their mental and physical "manhood." Edward Platypus (Doug "Mr." Lawrence) serves as Camp Kidney's answer to both H.L. Mencken and Sergeant Bilko, ridiculing his mental "inferiors" repeatedly while he cons them shamelessly out of their pride and worldly goods, with only Lazlo and his associates being able to resist him. The other Kidney campers are a sorry lot, headlined by Samson (Steve Little), a hypochondriac guinea pig with a nasal, Truman Capote whine for a voice. In most respects, they are outdone by the Squirrel Scouts, particularly the vivacious, free spirited, and highly athletic Patsy Smiles (Jodi Benson), a mongoose, whose active pursuit of Lazlo as a friend is informed by a sexualized intimacy in her tone to which he seems oblivious. The fact that her father is Commander Hoo Ha (Bennett), the aggressive, bullying Bean Scout boss who frequently and vituperatively harasses Lumpus for his failings, gives us a key to why she stands out in comparison to her milder colleagues, just as Lazlo stands out from his.

As with his prior series, Murray needed only to establish the initial characters and the relationships between them to allow his audience to fill in the blanks, and then took things from there. In "Hello, Dolly," for example, we discovered that the ultra-masculine Edward has a secret fetish for playing with his Veronica (read: Barbie) doll, complete with a variety of accessories. In the course of the episode, when the doll escapes its hiding place, he could not own up to it being his for fear of ridicule, and then is placed in the awkward position of trying to blow it up for the amusement of his colleagues. (Lumpus, when informed of the possible blowup, worries that one of *his* dolls would be the victim!) In the animation accompanying the closing credits of that episode, this subversive comment on masculinity was amplified by showing nearly all of the male characters playing with copies of the Veronica doll! A later episode, "The Book of Slinkman," carries this absurdity even further. By accident, the new guidebooks for the Bean and Squirrel Scouts are sent to the wrong places, so Slinkman ends up guiding the boys through exercises clearly meant for the girls before the mistake is discovered. Thus, we see the boys cheerfully making dresses—and then *wearing them*—without complaint. That Murray is so willing to put his characters in difficult physical and emotional situations like this was offset by the cheerful, accepting manner in which the boys and girls just *did* what their "adult" leaders told them to do—even when this could be dangerous. This heavy-handed lack of true responsibility is represented not only by Lumpus but also by his perennially bewildered female counterpart, Miss Jane Doe (Benson), her rough-and-tumble adjutant, Miss Mucus (Jill Talley), and the spectacularly ugly mayor of the nearby town of Prickly Pines, appropriately dubbed Pothole McPucker.

Unlike some of his counterparts, Murray has never luxuriated in vulgarity, nor "oversold" his jokes and gags to the point of irritation. With *Camp Lazlo!*, he produced a series that was purposely in synch with the placid setting he provided himself: serious when it needed to be serious; funny when it needed to be funny. His measured Tex Avery-meets-Billy Wilder style and the elegant crafting of his characters made it stand out considerably from its contemporaries. Though he has now abandoned television in favor of the Internet, one hopes he will eventually return, for he represents what is best about television animation when its most damaging attributes and aspects are held in check.

THE LIFE AND TIMES OF JUNIPER LEE

The creation of comic-book author Judd Winick, this series, one of a number in this decade to feature an ethnic protagonist in the lead, ran from 2005 to 2007, and was one of the few CNS series of the time to attempt to combine humor and action with relative success. While the Chinese-American title character (Lara Jill Miller) seems normal, she soon discovers that she is, in fact, the new holder of the title of "Te Xuan Ze," the keeper of the balance between the worlds of human creatures and more magical ones, a title previously held by her grandmother (Amy Hill). Her chief assistants are her younger brother, Ray Ray (Kath Soucie) and a magically gifted pug named Monroe (Carlos Alazraqui). Like some other programs in the action/comedy sub-genre, the difficult balancing act between the heroine's normal and supernatural roles occupies the heart of the action, although it is lightened at times.

HI HI PUFFY AMIYUMI

A comedy/music-hybrid series running from 2004 to 2006, this project was based on a popular Japanese music duo. Series creator and producer Sam Register, the then head of CNS, who would later head up Warner Bros. Television Animation (see below), was an admirer of the group and wished to use the series as a vehicle for introducing them to American audiences. Not surprisingly, the show's animation had a large *anime* element to it even though it was produced in America. The series proper focused on animated doppelgängers of group members Ami Onuki (Janice Kawaye) and Yumi Yoshimura (Grey DeLisle) and the scrapes they got into, often at the hands of their less-than-ethical manager Kaz (Keone Young).

MY GYM PARTNER'S A MONKEY

Early episodes of this series betrayed a limited format and premise. However, as it progressed over a lengthy four-season run, it proved to be far more durable and funny than expected, and became host to a unique brand of hilarious satirical comedy that even turned on itself once in a while. *My Gym Partner's a Monkey (MGPAM)* benefitted not only from good writing but also from imaginative direction and acting.

The series was the creation of the husband-and-wife team of Timothy Cahill (who doubled as the primary series director for much of its run) and Julie McNally Cahill, who also served as executive producers. They had worked together, both before and after their marriage, in a variety of capacities for other projects at Warner Bros., culminating in their playing a major role in producing and developing *Detention* (see below). They switched to CNS for *MGPAM*, which immediately became one of the network's, and the studio's, biggest hits. It ultimately ran for 96 episodes between 2005 and 2008, in addition to a special and a feature-length film.

The premise—and its satirical potential—was outlined in the main title sequence. Middle-school student Adam Lyon (Nika Futterman), based on a fairly obvious "clerical error," is transferred from his old institution to Charles Darwin Middle School, and suddenly finds himself to be the token human in an otherwise all-animal universe. Naturally, he experiences culture shock at first, but gradually gets "in touch" with his "inner animal" thanks to his fellow students.[69]

Adam's initiation into the culture of CDMS is partially accomplished by his accommodating—yet quick-to-anger—personality, and the fact that most of the student body is open-minded enough to befriend him in turn. No one exemplified this more than Jake Spider-monkey (Tom Kenny), the Sergeant Bilko in residence, who is just as willing to view Adam as an "easy mark" as he is to becoming Adam's "best friend." Like other animated friendships, theirs is never an entirely placid one, due to the fact that Jake is forever roping in a reluctant Adam as an accessory to his schemes. Their personal connection is underlined by having them trade lines and bits of business like a pair of seasoned vaudevillians, aware of each other's strengths and weaknesses, which becomes more evident in the later, more experimental years of the series. The ease with which Adam engages with Jake is demonstrated in his interactions with his other "peers" as well. These include Windsor Gorilla (Rick Gomez), a highly intelligent primate; Slips Python (Gomez), a snake with an affable "stoner" air; Lupe Toucan (Grey DeLisle), an aggressive Latino avian; and Ingrid Giraffe (DeLisle), whose imposing size, symbolized by an enormously long neck that keeps her head out of camera range much of the time, is belied by her typically apologetic, timorous personality and her passionately voiced but never-realized crush on Adam. At the opposite end of the friendship scale is the fearsome Bull Sharkowski (Phil LaMarr), an avowed bully who harasses Adam as much, if not more, than the other students.

The Cahills and their talented writing staff never placed their audience in the position of knowing everything about CDMS and its inhabitants, which was part of the charm of the program. This applied not only to Adam and his fellow students, but, more significantly, to those who taught and supervised them. This latter group wore their character flaws on their sleeves, making their effectiveness at their jobs rather questionable. Most notable is the principal, Poncherello Pixiefrog (Maurice LaMarche), a pompous, acerbic idiot who, like many of the comic characters in Dickens, is utterly unaware of this. He is a skilled administrator in spite of the fact he can easily be crushed by anyone around him; he avoids this chiefly by puttering around on a motorized scooter. Like Mr. Spacely in *The Jetsons* (see Chapter 3), the comic potential of Pixiefrog is chiefly gained in contrasting him *in extremis* size-wise with other characters, particularly in confrontations in his office, which has a pond for his desk. Other faculty characters are presented in a way that reflect how their personalities and lack of "human" intelligence impairs their effectiveness at their jobs. To cite but a few examples: school secretary Geraldine Warthog (DeLisle) is perpetually exasperated with the demands of her job, although we never actually see her "working" at it; guidance counselor Maurice Mandrill (LaMarche) is an obvious and unashamed hippie whose "New Age" philosophy is undermined by his use of mental and physical violence to get others to agree with him; and school nurse Gazelle (DeLisle) analyzes cases and delivers diagnoses with both placid stupidity and crude sadism.

Given the fact that the American educational system, through financial problems, a lack of oversight and foresight, and an inability to connect with minority students, among other things, was in crisis mode during the 2000s, *MGPAM*, and other depictions of school environments during this decade, can be read as a satire of these issues. Yet the Cahills and their talented writing staff (including Tom Sheppard, Mitch Larson and William Reiss, among others) never limited themselves to this opportunity. In the final two seasons, they openly upended the format of the series to pursue any satirical avenues they wished. This arguably made the project even better, and subtly enhanced the themes of majority/minority conflict that had always been present in the program's subtext. It climaxed in an utterly bizarre installment wherein the local school board capriciously decides to replace the entire CDMS staff—and even some of the students—with badly functioning robots as a cost-cutting measure. But a mere description of any *MGPAM* episode cannot convey the clever lunacy with which it was executed. This is a series that needs to be seen to be believed.[70]

Since the show's demise, the Cahills have remained active in the business by producing a series version of the *Littlest Pet Shop* toy line for Hasbro. However, one hopes that they will eventually return to producing under their own names and concepts, for, with *MGPAM*, they clearly established themselves alongside Jay Ward, Matt Groening, Joe Murray and Seth Macfarlane in the pantheon of television animation's great satiric wits.

Squirrel Boy

That this generally mild project was the creation of Everett Peck, who had earlier been responsible for creating the raunchy *Duckman* (see Chapter 6) for Klasky-Csupo, is probably the most surprising thing about it. Peck was, as executive producer, much more in direct control of this series than his previous one, so this project likely reflects his true style. Be that as it may, it also reflected a formula CNS already seemed to be running into the ground, and, while well animated, it suffered from a lack of innovation in the writing. The focus of the series is mild-mannered Andy Johnson (Pamela Adlon) and his relationship with his hyperactive, scheming pet squirrel, Rodney (Richard Horvitz). Other characters include Andy's parents (Kurtwood Smith and Nancy Sullivan) and Rodney's dimwitted squirrel buddy, Leon (Tom Kenny).

The Marvelous Misadventures of Flapjack

This inventive and surreal project was the creation of artist/animator Mark Van Orman, who typically signs his work with the nickname "Thurop." Born in Norfolk, Virginia, in 1976, Van Orman grew up in Panama City, Florida, and frequently fantasized about living an adventurous life near the ocean. Later, after his family had moved away from the area, he returned, and spent some time as a beachcomber on nearby Shell Island, which helped provide him with the impetus for this series project.

After earning his stripes as an animator and writer on *The Powerpuff Girls* (see Chapter 6), *The Grim Adventures of Billy and Mandy* (see above), and *Camp Lazlo!* (see above), Van Orman pitched the initial version of *Flapjack* to CNS in 2001. Rejected, but given positive feedback, he reformatted the project and resubmitted in 2003. This led to the production of the series itself, which ran from 2007 to 2010.

Flapjack, which combines traditional cel animation (in the main action) with stop-motion effects (chiefly in the imaginative main title sequence), is a genuine television animation version of the popular literary sub-genre known as "steampunk": an imaginative, though not always flattering, restructuring of the culture and technology of the 19th century through contemporary eyes. The main story echoes the principal themes in the juvenile works of Robert Louis Stevenson, while the technology and its cultural use/misuse echoes the science fiction of Jules Verne, H.G. Wells and Sir Arthur Conan Doyle. Van Orman, however, is clearly intent on giving as much as he borrows, and his bizarre and frequent manipulations of characters and setting gives the program a particularly raffish charm rarely seen in television animation.

Set in the rustic oceanside community of Stormalong Harbor, the series focuses on the title character (Van Orman[71]), a high-voiced, blond, wide-eyed boy with a seemingly unquenchable thirst for "adventure" (a word he often says as if it were written entirely in capital letters). His two principal companions and guardians reflect alternate potential paths awaiting him when he reaches manhood. Captain K'nuckles (Brian Doyle-Murray) is, like most of Stormalong's other denizens, an irrepressible reprobate passing himself off as a professional "adventurer." Flapjack adores him unquestionably, even when he is the object of his cons. Bubbie (Roz Ryan), on the other hand, is a matronly whale who has reared Flapjack ever since rescuing the foundling from the sea, and she is determined that he be brought up in a "good" way: i.e., with K'nuckles's influence minimized. The tension between K'nuckles and Bubbie over Flapjack's future—with Bubbie's case undermined by her own deviant behavior—hangs over the series, taking on the Biblical dimension of the fight for immortal souls between God and the Devil. Flapjack never recognizes this conflict, due to his irrepressible boyish innocence and goodwill, which endears him to viewers even when the rest of the series is disturbing. A case in point is the character of Peppermint Larry (Jeff Bennett), who operates a popular candy store (candy taking on the same role that alcohol would in a more adult-oriented story). His addiction is so severe that he has constructed a candy "wife"—and frequently speaks to "her" as if "she" were a sentient being.

Flapjack's primary focus, however, is the title character's progression toward mental and physical manhood, and this Van Orman portrayed in compelling terms, both dramatic and comic. While it is sad to see him gradually shed his faith in the goodness of the world as he matures, he learns that there is no other way to proceed, and that not even K'nuckles and Bubbie can help him. Even though there is a considerable amount of comedic potential in the narrative, Van Orman never surrendered the gravity of the series, adding immeasurably to its impact.

CHOWDER

A far more comic take on the *bildungsroman* theme, this hilarious series seemed to take its cue from the nonsense-driven universes of Lewis Carroll and Edward Lear, with portions of Dr. Seuss thrown in for good measure. *Chowder* was created by Carl Harvey Greenblatt, an Ashkenazi Jew born in Plano, Texas, in 1972; he is typically billed as C.H. Greenblatt.

Another of the veteran artists who worked his way up the television animation ladder, Greenblatt attended the University of Austin as an advertising major, and then broke into animation as a storyboard artist on *Spongebob Squarepants* (see Chapter 6). Later he moved to CNS to work on *The Grim Adventures of Billy and Mandy* (see above) before launching *Chowder*, which ran from 2007 to 2010. The series, like many of its peers, clearly demonstrates the comedic skills of its creator, as well as an understated message not to take the program as seriously as do the characters.

Set in the community of Marzipan City, which consists of both human beings and anthropomorphized animals and has an economy almost exclusively based on food (reflected particularly in the character names), the focus is on the title character (Nicky Jones), a purple rabbit-bear hybrid. A hyperactive youngster with a clear but undiagnosed case of ADHD, Chowder is the apprentice of the veteran, white-haired, egotistical chef Mung Daal (Dwight Schultz), who is prone to exaggerate both his culinary skills and his attractiveness to women. The other employees of Mung Daal Catering are Mung's wife, Truffles (Tara Strong), a "mushroom pixie," and Schnitzel (Kevin Michael Richardson, and later John DiMaggio), a "rock monster" whose entire vocabulary consists of properly modulated variations of the word "Rada." Chowder's closest friend is Gazpacho (Dana Snyder), a wooly mammoth who operates a stand in the city market. The bane of Chowder's existence is Panini (Liliana Mumy), a ten-year-old pink rabbit who clearly views Chowder as her boyfriend—despite his repeated insistence to the contrary.[72] Panini is the apprentice of the pompous, flute-nosed, obese Endive (Mindy Sterling), Mung's principal rival in the cooking trade. Mung and Endive's hatred of each other fueled many of the episodes. Others were driven by the need to make particular Seussian dishes ("Froggy Apple Crumple Thumpkin," "Burple Nurples," "Minced Meach Pie," "Thousand Pound Cake," etc.) to appease hungry clients. Greenblatt and his staff were particularly adept at Carrollian wordplay and anarchic, Mack Sennett–styled slapstick comedy, with the result being that nearly every episode is a comedic gem. As was typical in television animation of this time, the show and its staff themselves were often the subject of the humor, as when Greenblatt was depicted in one live-action episode as a puppet conscience (conspicuously wearing an "I Love the Ladies" T-shirt) to a confused Schnitzel.

A multiple Emmy- and Annie-award nominee, *Chowder* could have run far longer than it did, but Greenblatt (and, more specifically, CNS) were likely right in concluding it before it wore out its welcome. Following its cancellation, Greenblatt and many of his staff members relocated to Disney, where they worked their magic under Greenblatt's former boss Maxwell Atoms on *Fish Hooks* (see below). Greenblatt has since sold a new series to Nickelodeon. Hopefully, when it emerges, it will provide the cleverly executed comedy in the tradition of *Chowder*.

Adventure Time, *The Regular Show*, and *The Amazing World of Gumball*

These most recent CNS shows (the former two debuted in 2010; the latter, in 2011) reflect, in the main, a once-confident studio unsure of what direction to pursue. The latter two programs are utterly juvenile in different ways, while the first is a more sophisticated blend of high and low comedy, reflecting this indecision.

Adventure Time is a collaboration between CNS and Fred Seibert's Frederator studio (see above), who brought the project to CNS after Frederator's primary distributor, Nickelodeon, rejected it. The series was created by Pendleton Ward, who shared executive-producer credit with Seibert. A native of San Antonio, Texas, Ward is a California Institute of the Arts graduate who worked on *The Marvelous Misadventures of Flapjack* (see above). The original pilot for the series aired as a segment of Nickelodeon's *Random! Cartoons* before developing a cult following on the Internet, which encouraged CNS to pick it up for development. From the beginning, the show's unique production development and creative construction were apparent. Having previously worked on a series where the storyboard artists were given considerable creative latitude in episode construction, Ward applied the same methodology to the production of his series, with the result being that no two segments of the series are alike in either content or tone. Often, the artists worked independently of each other to prevent creative *ennui*. Ward also insisted on the actors recording their dialogue together as a group, a practice rarely used in television animation. This is also evident in the series, as the dialogue delivery is far less frantic and rushed than it can be in other series; these performers clearly have to wait their turn to speak rather than vocally riding roughshod over one another.

Drawn from different sources (Ward cited *Dungeons and Dragons* and video games as his main sources, while Seibert compared the animation style to that of Max Fleischer (see Chapter 1), *Adventure Time* manages to draw from these sources while transcending them. Set in the post-apocalyptic Land of Ooo, the protagonists are Finn (Jeremy Shada), an ambitious and eager, if somewhat spacey young man, and Jake (John DiMaggio), his slacker-minded, shape-shifting dog. In the manner of Robert E. Howard's *Conan*, this duo peddles their heroic skills to anyone who wishes to recruit them, and consequently they enter into a variety of adventurous situations, some dramatic, some comic, but many utterly stupid. Friends and foes of the duo include the resourceful Princess Bubblegum (Hynden Walch), the kinky Ice King (Tom Kenny), Marceline, The Vampire Queen (Olivia Olson), the alien Lumpy Space Princess (Ward), BMO (Niki Yang), a sentient video game console, and the anthropomorphic miniature elephant Tree Trunks (Polly Lou Livingston). This variety of characters, and the variety of settings related to them, meant that, more than any other contemporary series, each installment of the project had to stand alone. Thus, while some of the episodes work well, others were simply confusing.

◆ ◆ ◆

The Regular Show follows this same "stoner" methodology, not surprising that its genesis and creation were remarkably similar to that of *Adventure Time*. It is the creation of animator James Garland Quintel—usually billed simply as "J.G.," who was born in Hanford, California, in 1982. He attended the California Institute of the Arts, where his short film *The Naïve Man from Lolliland* won an award at the Nicktoons Film Festival and was singled out for praise by Fred Seibert. After apprentice work as a storyboard artist for *Camp Lazlo!* and *The Marvelous Misadventures of Flapjack* (see above), Quintel pitched *The Regular Show* to CNS, with Craig McCracken and Rob Renzetti, among others, voicing admiration for it. Although Quintel thought it lacked commercial potential, CNS disagreed, and he suddenly found himself "running" his own show.

The show—whose tagline, "It's anything but," contradicts the normality of the title—focuses on a typically mismatched animal pair who are theoretically employed as park groundskeepers, but shirk actual work at every opportunity. Mordecai (Quintel), a tall, acerbic Blue Jay, and Rigby (William Salyers), a pugnacious, troublesome raccoon are the star duo. Other characters on the show, which exude a discomfiting, surrealistic vibe throughout, include Benson (Sam Marin), a humanized gumball machine who is Mordecai and Rigby's boss; Skips (Mark Hamill), a Yeti groundskeeper; Pops Maellard (Marin), the surprisingly naïve, lollypop-headed co-manager of the park; and Mitch "Muscle Man" Sorenstein (Marin), yet another groundskeeper. Though its content could be dull and thin at times, it won an Emmy in the short form animation category in 2012.

◆ ◆ ◆

The Amazing World of Gumball is the maiden voyage of Cartoon Network Development Studios Europe (CNDSE), an England-based CNS subsidiary that was created in 2007. Ben Bocquelet, the series creator, was originally hired by CNDSE to assist animators in pitching projects to the network, but when CNDSE decided to have the animators pitch projects, Bocquelet took several characters from rejected projects and put them together in a traditional school/family setting. The result was a surrealistic but well received project that continues to air.

The series, which features traditional cel animation laid over uber-realistic backgrounds for contrast, focuses on the dysfunctional Watterson family: Gumball (Logan Grove), an overly emotional 12-year-old blue cat; Darwin (Kwesi Boakye), a goldfish who is Gumball's younger brother; Anais (Kyla Kowalewski), Gumball and Darwin's highly intelligent younger sister, a diminutive pink rabbit; Nicole (Teresa Gallagher), their workaholic, martial-arts expert, blue cat mother; and Richard (Dan Russell), their dimwitted, pink rabbit father. Gumball attends Elmore Middle School, where he suffers under the tyranny of his teacher, Miss Simian (Sandra Dickinson first, Hugo Harrison later), and the bullying of the dinosaur Tina Rex (Russell). Meanwhile, Gumball attempts to act on his romantic feelings for classmate Penny Fitzgerald (Jessica McDonald), an antlered peanut. The series was clearly made up of disparate parts, given the vast difference between the character design (including both animation and Muppet-like puppetry) and the realistic designs of the backgrounds, to say nothing of the characters' vacillating behavior. One can only hope that CNDSE will be able to produce better material in the future.

◆ ◆ ◆

The early 2000s were a remarkably fecund period of animation activity at Cartoon Network Studios, with a consistently high level of production. However, the studio has suffered in more recent years from creative indecision and mismanagement, as well as from its decision to admit live programming into what had once been an all-animation environment. Due to these and other decisions, it has lost many of its key animation providers of the 2000s: Atoms, Willems, Murray, Winick, Warburton, McCracken, Tartakovsky, Van Orman, Greenblatt, the Cahills. Whether or not the studio can continue to attract and maintain talent on the level of these one-of-a-kind performers remains to be seen.

Disney in the 2000s

Like Cartoon Network and Nickelodeon, Disney Television Animation[73] (DTA) took as its primary audience the child, "tween" and teen demographics and marketed its products accordingly. However, Disney took a very different approach compared to the other studios. Where its two rivals adapted and amplified the traditional Hanna-Barbera slam-bam formula, Disney seemed much more comfortable emulating the quieter entertainment-plus-education formula pioneered by Lou Scheimer at Filmation during the 1970s and 1980s. In part, this was due to the fact that the studio's product was broadcast chiefly through a network source (Disney-owned ABC) for most of the decade, and therefore had to obey stricter content regulations than the more free-wheeling cable producers. The traditionally conservative production mindset of the Disney studio was also at work here, although it gradually broadened and became less restrictive, especially after longtime studio boss Michael Eisner was forced to resign as a consequence of a corporate revolt in 2006. Disney *did* continue the creator-driven production mode of its rivals, and in consequence, the series should be judged on their own terms rather than as "Disney" productions. The relationship with Disney would be both a blessing and a curse for the animators. The curse was that their work was often ignored by the larger mass media, who maintained biased stereotypes about Disney as a repressive, dystopian corporate oligarchy. The blessing, however, was that they could produce their work under a relatively secure cloud of anonymity absent from the other two studios, and could, therefore, focus more closely on the quality of their work. The result, in many cases, was some superbly crafted and intelligently written television animation that quite clearly ranks among the genre's finest achievements.

Like the other studios, Disney expanded and diversified its cable holdings during this period. The first category was programming aimed at very young children (*Jake and the Never Land Pirates, Handy Manny, Doc McStuffins, Little Einsteins, Stanley*), which aired chiefly on the Disney Junior cable channel. While certainly engaging its target audience, its entertainment value for mature viewers was negligible. The second category includes derivative adaptations of studio-owned properties from other media, including *Tarzan, Lilo and Stitch, Buzz Lightyear of Star Command* (from *Toy Story*), *The Emperor's New School* (based on *The Emperor's New Groove*), *House of Mouse, Mickey Mouseworks*, etc. While all were handsomely animated (Disney never stints on technical quality), these series were very thinly written, chiefly because they all assumed a direct familiarity with the source material that not all viewers would necessarily have.

DTA's best products, as already noted, were based on the creator-driven model, and each was thus a reflection of their creators' vision. This is an important point to consider, especially when these projects are analyzed in depth, which is something the intimidating heritage and hegemony of the Disney studio name has limited in the past.

THE WEEKENDERS

This program is the *ne plus ultra* example of the "middle-school angst" sub-genre of 1990s and 2000s, with full emphasis on the "angst." As it debuted in 2000, it fittingly kicked off a decade of creative excellence coming from the studio. It represents all of the strengths of DTA's creator-driven production model—superb writing with excellent translation into action and smooth animation—while functioning as a cleverly modulated, restrained retort to other studios' frantic production styles. It is a model program that deserves far more attention than it received during its original production run.

The series was created and chiefly written by the talented Doug Langdale, who had earlier collaborated with artist Douglas TenNapel on television animation productions during the 1990s (see Chapter 6). As a California native, it seems that he followed the famed writing axiom, "Write what you know." What makes the series stand out so boldly from its peers was its execution by Langdale and principal director Steven Lyons. It is a highly nuanced, character-driven series with a particular emphasis on exploring all the dimensions of the characters and their relationships with one another and the world around them. They did so in a way that belies most television animation stereotypes, gathering comedy from realism rather than exaggeration—in spite of occasional bursts of ebullience from both writer and director. This is clearly noted in examining the particularly well-handled characterizations of its four 12-year-old leads.

First, there is Tino Tonitini (Jason Marsden), who functions as an interlocutor between the show and the audience (not unlike the Stage Manager in Thornton Wilder's play *Our Town*). Short, blond, and unfailingly eager, he is emotionally insecure despite his obvious intelligence (reflected chiefly by his proficiency at chess) and his sly, ever adept wit (he is one of the very few television animation characters who can be funny only through his words).[74] His perceived failings, though heightened by personal exaggeration, are displayed to the audience chiefly because he is the focus of most of the stories, with his friends good-naturedly mocking his neurotic and "weird" behavior. In most episodes, Tino paints himself into a social or emotional corner that he fears will ultimately overwhelm him (in one memorable instance, he confronted his fear of clowns). He is able to work through the situation with the aid of his three close friends, as well as his sensitive and understanding divorced mother (Lisa Kaplan), whose obsession with vegetarian cooking provided the series with one of its surprisingly large collection of subtly stated, interlocking running gags.

Carver Descartes (Phil LaMarr) provides another wrinkle in the story. The middle child in a family of prosperous buppies,[75] he has an almost obsessional devotion to fashion trends, particularly regarding shoes (his aim in life is to become a shoe designer). This materialistic attitude, coupled with a cocksure ego, puts him in contrast to his more down-to-earth colleagues, and adds a bit of hidden tension to his conflicts with them. (It also belies the intellectual prowess his name might imply.) Like Tino, Carver suffers from the particularly "masculine" delusion that he is always right, something his female friends are delighted to quash.

Lor McQuarrie (Grey DeLisle) is the lone female in the family, so it is not a surprise that she is both a tomboy and a highly proficient athlete—in addition to also being a proud Scot. At first glance, she seems to be merely a target for "dumb jock" jokes. Langdale, however, does not traffic in pure stereotypes, so Lor's personality and emotions are re-shaped continually over the course of the series. Her personal insecurities rival Tino's in many ways, especially regarding her largely inept pursuit of her *inamorata*, Thompson Oberman. But, unlike Tino, she has the inner security and confidence to believe that her way of doing things is the best way—even if it clearly is *not*.

Last, but certainly not least, there is Tish[76] Katsufrakis (Kath Soucie). The fact that her nickname is "The Brain" should tell you a lot about her, though not everything. She is one of the most literate characters in television animation history, given the range and depth of the quotes and references she dispenses, with a particular fondness for Shakespeare. Likewise, she is a skilled actress, a prolific writer, and an aspiring psychologist, with an aim of making one of these professions her full-time career. Nevertheless, she suffers, like the others, from punishing levels of emotional insecurity and self-doubt.[77] While Tish is prone to flaunt her intelligence to the point of aggravation (unless someone, usually Lor, insists she cut it out), we are clearly meant to interpret this as a front for her emotional insecurity. This takes on a deeper level when we discover that she is a second-generation immigrant, with parents from an "Old Country" that, despite being unidentified, seems to be a Soviet bloc state based on the internal evidence.[78] Thus, Tish's mental baggage is cultural and personal, as when she goes through "Momatuche," her culture's equivalent of a Bat Mitzvah.

As the series title implied, the installments are always set during weekends, usually starting on Friday evenings and resolved by the following Sunday (at which point Tino would bid us adieu with a cleverly modulated "Later days!"), with the proper silent movie intertitles used to bridge the episode segments. The overall tone was one that was quite intelligent, as noted by historian Hal Erickson:

> The dialogue exhibited a level of literacy that might startle those who think that all Saturday-morning cartoonery [sic] is brainless; there weren't many other programs in which one would hear a middle-schooler [Tish] congratulate her comrades by proclaiming "Kudos to us!" Nor was there an abundance of animated series wherein a nervous preteen drama queen [again, Tish] was shepherded through her first appearance by the ghost of William Shakespeare. Particularly pleasing was the series' depiction of its adult characters—not as the anal-retentive, rule-imposing tyrants we'd seen in so many other cartoon weeklies, but instead as recognizable human beings with affectionately detailed personality quirks.[79]

This was precisely what was so unique about the program. *The Weekenders* was a conscious, symbolic break with the traditions of television animation aimed at "tweens." It did *not* attempt to portray any of its characters as stereotypes; instead, it celebrated the uniqueness and intelligence of all of its characters, without sacrificing humor in the process. Thanks to the clever writing and directing, and the skilled voice acting behind its four leads (the four performers were never better, particularly Marsden and Soucie), it was an approach that really paid off.

The series has largely been off the radar since its original broadcast run ended in 2003, but this may change with its release on YouTube and DVD by Disney (although in a limited run format). There is every opportunity for Tino, Carver, Lor and Tish to help another generation of middle schoolers confront their concerns and fears in the same colorful, funny way.

CLERKS

Clerks was DTA's sole attempt at a prime-time network project, based on the 1994 Kevin Smith film of the same title. Smith was an executive producer of the series, which first aired in 2000, in addition to reprising his characterization of Silent Bob from the film. The content was similar to other television animation programs aimed at adults, as well as Smith's fan base. Six episodes were made, though only two aired before ABC canceled the series.

TEACHER'S PET

Many DTA projects of the early 2000s benefited from the recruitment of artists and writers to work with the Disney staff. In this case, in a series which ran from 2000 to 2002, a gifted artist *and* a gifted writing team were employed to work on a series idea with great potential that was ultimately, despite the best of intentions, squandered.

The artist was Gary Baseman, the Los Angeles–born child of Ukrainian immigrants and a graduate of UCLA best known for his designs for the board game *Cranium*. The lead character of the series was inspired by his own dog, and the theme based on his interest in dual identity politics.[80] The writing team consisted of Bill and Cheri Steinkellner, a married couple who have written and produced extensively for Broadway and live-action sitcoms (notably *Cheers*). As a consequence, the final project represented a polarization between Baseman's signature drawing style—reminiscent of the "rubber hose" school of theatrical animation of the 1930s—and the Steinkellners' more realistic attempts at developing character and motivation. As Hal Erickson notes, the series design suggested a free-wheeling ambience: "At any moment, Spot might discard his book and staff and begin singing "Smile, Darn Ya, Smile" with Bosko and Honey."[81] This was at odds with the "realistic" attempts at dialogue. Yet when, under the direction of Timothy Bjorklund, it somehow worked, as reflected by the several Emmys the show received.

Despite the unrealistic ambience, there was a token attempt at a serious underlying story. The articulate dog, Spot (Nathan Lane, and later Kevin Schon), had tired of being cooped up at home, so he decided to "pass" as a human being named Scott so that he could attend school with his human master, Leonard Helperman (Shaun Fleming). The latter was not pleased at the idea, considering that he was already struggling with having his mother, Mary Lou (Debra Jo Rupp), as his teacher. In the kind of bizarre twist of fate only possible in television animation, Spot/Scott soon became the most popular and intelligent kid at school, much to Leonard's annoyance. The mental strain of Spot/Scott maintaining "both" identities, and his increasingly frayed relationship with Leonard, provided the program's emotional pivot. Watching and commenting from the sidelines were the other two Helperman pets—Mr. Jolly (David Ogden Stiers), a lethargic cat, and Pretty Boy (Jerry Stiller), an antagonistic parrot.

While the show was moderately entertaining, particularly when Lane was portraying Spot/Scott, it suffered from identity and control concerns, as much off-screen as on. Disney was careful to take note of this, as later programs would not suffer nearly as much from creative control problems.

LLOYD IN SPACE

This series, which ran only for a single season in 2001-02, was produced by Paul Germain and Joe Ansolabehere, the same team responsible for *Recess* (see Chapter 6), though one would never know it by looking at it. Whereas in the previous series innovation was the rule, this time "Paul & Joe" settled for derivation.

To begin with, there was the shopworn "kids in space" idea, which had been overused by this time. Add to that the "middle-school angst" sub-genre (see above), and you basically have what the show was about. The protagonist is Lloyd Nebulon (Courtland Mead), who lives in a floating, talking space station with his mother, Captain Nora Nebulon (April Winchell), and younger sister Francine (Nicolette Little). He attends Luna Vista School, under the tutelage of Miss Bolt (Tress MacNeille), where his closest friends include a living brain named Douglas (Pamela Hayden), cyclopean Kurt (Bill Fagerbakke) and token human Eddie (Justin Shenkarow).

Germain and Ansolabehere kept much of the on-and-off screen team responsible for making *Recess* together, which explains the overlap between the two series' voice credits, but the producers were not able to make lightning strike twice. In some respects, the show was overshadowed by the producers' ultimately successful crusade to have their production company logo receive equal billing time with Disney's (Germain did not wish to have a "dead man" take credit for *his* work).[82]

THE PROUD FAMILY

This is one of the relatively few television animation programs revolving around African Americans; it was produced *by* African Americans as well. *The Proud Family*, originally intended for Nickelodeon before being redirected toward Disney, was widely commended for its generally positive tone and characters. (The show was the recipient of an Image Award from the NAACP in 2003.) That being said, it also had detractors, especially those who were *not* African American, who did not understand or appreciate the fundamentally "inside" nature of the show's humor.

The project was created by animator Bruce W. Smith, a Los Angeles native who had studied at the California Institute of the Arts. After gaining experience working in the industry for Bill Melendez (see Chapter 3) and Baer Animation, he directed *Bebe's Kids*, a 1992 animated feature film based on the stand-up comedy routines of African American comedian/actor Robin Harris. This project earned Smith the attention of veteran African American TV producer Ralph Farquhar, with whom he formed Jambalaya Studios to produce *Proud*. The film's "inside" humor—based on modes of personal presentation and vocal delivery intimately known to African Americans but not necessarily to outsiders—forms the core of what would later be both appealing and appalling about *The Proud Family*.

For the title family, "Proud" is both a surname and a rather fitting adjective. Father Oscar (Tommy Davidson) is a confectioner for whom prosperity always seems to be just around the corner, even when it falls directly out of his grasp. Mother Trudy (Paula Jai Parker), meanwhile, has a more secure career as a veterinarian, and is prone to reminding her husband—with stereotypical brazenness—where the real power in the house lies. Their 14-year-old daughter, Penny (Kyla Pratt), upon whom the majority of the storylines focus, is an emotional mixture of her parents, combining her mother's outspokenness with her father's feckless sense of faith. Completing the family setting are the young toddlers Bebe and Cece (both Tara Strong) and "Sugar Momma" (JoMarie Payton), Penny's grandmother and Oscar's mother, who is as well-equipped to advise her grandchild as she is to openly chastise her son for his supposed shortcomings. Sugar Momma seems more affectionate toward her other son, Bobby (Cedric the Entertainer), a 1970s "funk" music singer.

While the show can be commended for advocating positive racial relations, there remain some troubling aspects. As with the later *Cleveland Show* (see above), there is a tendency to resort to a style of humor that can be traced back to racism from the past,[83] particularly the interactions of the women vis-à-vis the men. Likewise, there is the implicit, though unstated, assumption that lighter-skinned "high yellas" (Trudy and Penny) are intellectually and morally superior to African Americans with darker skin (Oscar).

Certainly, if you are comfortable with the program's raucous, loud and uninhibited African American–comedy style, you will have no problem with *The Proud Family*. If you weren't, then it would be best to avoid it.

FILLMORE

Like *The Weekenders* before it, *Fillmore*, which ran from 2002 to 2004, was remarkable chiefly because of what it was *not* rather than what it was. It boldly rejected traditional storytelling approaches in favor of a practice that more directly and stridently affirmed it as a unique cultural product. Yet where *The Weekenders* subtly recast the sitcom in its own image, *Fillmore* did so with a sub-genre rarely portrayed successfully comically in television animation—the crime/mystery drama. That it managed to do so effectively, without compromising the dignity of its characters, was a significant achievement. That it has never been replicated by another series underlines the significance of that achievement.

The project was the creation of television writer and producer Scott M. Gimple, who hailed from New Jersey and went on to study at USC. Before and after working on *Fillmore*, he served as a writer for various other series (including animated programs for Disney and Nickelodeon), and for comics as well, chiefly for Matt Groening (see Chapter 6) and his Bongo line. Currently, Gimple is a member of the production team of the popular AMC live-action series *The Walking Dead*.

Gimple and director Christian Roman structured the program so that it felt familiar to viewers of prime-time TV police dramas—the committing of a crime and its solution—though this was done in a style that was foreign to the traditional joke-and-gag practices of television animation and direction. The focus of each episode remains exclusively on the characters and story, with almost no attempt to insert blatant bits of comic "business" into the narratives. If humor is present, it seems to be more by accident than design. This meant that the handling of the crimes and their investigations were conducted in appropriately sober tones, not unlike in the adult television models. Given that the program was originally broadcast during a difficult sociopolitical period in American history, in which the definition of youth and adult crime was being pushed by school shootings on one hand and terrorism on the other, the soberness of the approach served as both an attempt to understand the roots of juvenile crime, while satirizing the excesses of adult law enforcement. It succeeded in both aims. As Gimple himself put it, "This show is not about middle school. This *is* middle school [emphasis in original]."[84] Few viewers would disagree with him on that point.

Set chiefly in and around the campus of X Middle School, reputedly in Minnesota,[85] *Fillmore* is the ongoing story of its eponymous lead, Cornelius Fillmore (Orlando Brown). An acerbic, bald African American, Fillmore is a former juvenile delinquent who has become an active member of the school's Safety Patrol as an alternative to punishment. Though occasionally overzealous in executing his duties, he is unfailingly honest and fiercely loyal to his colleagues, and not about to be "bought." His loyalty in particular extends to his partner, Ingrid Third (Tara Strong). Another ex-delinquent, Ingrid is highly intelligent (possessing a photographic memory) and athletic, as is demonstrated in the show's numerous on-foot chase sequences. Her relationship with Fillmore is symbiotic; she is able to keep his more tempestuous emotions under control just as he restricts her intellectual pretensions. They are also highly effective in getting the job done in spite of the personal and social obstacles they must face. Other members of the Safety Patrol crew include the perpetually angry Junior Commissioner Vallejo (Horatio Sanz); forensic expert Tehama (Lauren Tom); and bumbling red-headed dimwit Danny O'Farrell (Kyle Sullivan), who provides what little broad comedy the series allows.

Though there is no shortage of relatively villainous male and female thugs and punks for the Patrol to confront in their investigations, their greatest enemy is, ironically, one they can do nothing to stop. Principal Dawn Folsom (played with genuinely intimidating menace by Wendie Malick) is always willing to put on a smiling face for the school's internal media about what a good job the Patrol is doing, but, in private, she considers them arrogant do-gooders whose services she could easily do without. With that in mind, she does as much as she can to undermine them. Folsom, whom Hal Erickson accurately described as a "pampered, ego-driven political hack,"[86] seems to view herself as a besieged Charles I surrounded by incipient twelve-year-old Oliver Cromwells. She and her largely impersonal vice principal, Raycliffe (future *Survivor* host Jeff Probst), treats all the students, not simply the Patrol, with the contempt she feels they deserve. She seems to have power far beyond the realistic limits of her job, and is blatantly willing to use it to prevent influential suspects from being nabbed by the Patrol, making her a formidable adversary. Nevertheless, justice always wins out in the end.

Gimple, Roman and their colleagues made the show colorful by making the X student community highly diverse, in particular by pockmarking it with a group of clubs, teams and personal alliances that effectively served as subcultures. The possibilities for story ideas seemed endless and inspired, making the abrupt termination of the series after only 26 episodes a pity. Still, many of those episodes were of a unique quality. "The Unseen Reflection" deserves particular praise for realistically exploring the complicated factional disputes (and almost religious devotion) involved in science fiction/fantasy/horror fandom—and, surprisingly, the degree to which some authors hold their own fans in contempt.

Fillmore provided a remarkable window into a world rarely understood or taken seriously, and it is highly commendable for that reason. It provided a model for middle-school students who were intelligent and able to forcefully and fearlessly confront their fears and concerns.

KIM POSSIBLE

This engaging action-comedy series, which debuted in 2002, managed, like many of its peers, to carefully balance its two dominant elements. Consequently, while its lead character and plot structure presented strident feminist overtones in the action element, the comedy component cut any pretensions down to size.

That the series balanced these elements so deftly is a tribute to its veteran writing/producing team, Bob Schooley and Mark McCorkle, who had worked together on previous projects. Schooley and McCorkle had been directed by the Disney brass to develop an animated project aimed directly at nine- to fourteen-year-olds, but which could also attract older viewers. Discussion of the idea led to an epiphany on McCorkle's part; he suggested the show focus on one Kim Possible, who can do "anything," prompting Schooley to suggest that she be paired with Ron Stoppable, who is unable to do what Kim does so with seeming effortlessness. "After that ... the show was practically done," McCorkle observed sagely.[87]

You might assume that the series would have a plethora of puns derived from the two lead characters' names. Yet that would be underestimating the skill of this particular writing team.

The heroine (Christy Carlson Romano) is, on the surface at least, a "typical" high school student, circa 2002. What separates her most from her peers, however, is the fact that she is also a globe-trotting, martial arts–wielding agent of justice, fighting and defeating a variety of foes in a way that she herself would say was "no big." Hal Erickson elaborates: "Sure, Kim evaded bad guys left and right, dodged avalanches, steered clear of brain-transfer machines, even got suspended over a fiery cauldron once in a while, but she always managed to wiggle out of her current predicament with her wits and sense of humor intact—and just in time to finish her homework and get her chores done."[88] Kim was chiefly accompanied by the aforementioned Ron Stoppable (Will Friedle), who, despite being a bumbling goof much of the time, is one of the few confidants "KP" really has outside of her family, and their ultimate development of a romantic relationship was a predictable outcome. Ron is, in turn, accompanied by his pet, Rufus (Nancy Cartwright), a naked mole rat.

The development of stories and plots for the series was logical enough, chiefly involving Kim biting off more than she could chew in one or both of her "roles" and having to pay the price. Yet any potential stagnation in the stories and characterization was countered with comic zest, as well as an understanding that the villains were thinly developed stereotypes. Dr. Draken (John DiMaggio), Kim's principal nemesis, is a typical example: a tall, blue-skinned "mad genius" with dueling scars, he is in love with himself in typical comic-opera fashion. Others were cast in the same mold, with the notable exception of Sheego (Nicole Sullivan), an ex–super heroine who is more than a match for "Kimmy" in combat. Still, there was an overall casual air, with humor managing to take the edge off even the more extreme action sequences. The injection of new plot devices was done similarly without fanfare: the revelation that Ron is Jewish, and the fact that his family later adopts a female Asian baby (whom Ron had to look after) were simply plot devices. This lack of overall seriousness was much appreciated in a sub-genre that, like Dr. Draken, often took itself too seriously for the audience to do likewise.

For some critics, such as David Koening, Disney's development of intelligent and superhuman women characters in the 1990s and 2000s seemed to be a Freudian overcompensation for its portrayal of women as passive and weak in prior decades. *Kim Possible* undoubtedly falls into this category, and provided some inspiration for its female demographic. The fact that she did not take herself entirely seriously, just as the series itself did not, suggests an often neglected but very important criteria for being a good hero—being able to recognize and laugh at your mistakes.

TEAMO SUPREMO

This series, which originally ran in 2002, was a rare and unfortunate case of DTA using someone else's idea rather than coming up with one of its own. Very obviously indebted to *The Powerpuff Girls* (see Chapter 6), though the creators of the series did not acknowledge this, *Teamo Supremo* came off as weak compared to the earlier series. The series focused on a trio of pre-teen superhero types—Captain Crandall (Spencer Breslin), Skate Lad (Alana Ubach), and Rope Girl (Ubach) in confronting rather transparently derivative villainy—most of these "bad" guys clearly had failed their *Powerpuff* auditions. There were some nice touches, including having the trio report to a state governor (Martin Mull), who is far more "hip" than expected, but these were not enough to overcome the shallowly defined characters and premise of the series.

DAVE THE BARBARIAN

This was Doug Langdale's second collaboration with Disney, after *The Weekenders* (see above), which it barely resembled in terms of plot and tone. Given the fact that this series emphasized broad slapstick comedy rather than character-based humor, this was probably a wise choice. Like Langdale's earlier effort, this series was a broad comic satire á la *Rocky and Bullwinkle*, which suggests that there was far more individualism in the studio's television animation productions than its detractors were willing to admit.

Debuting in 2004, *Dave* is a bizarre skewering of the clichés of sword-and-sorcery fantasy. Set in the kingdom of Udrogoth, it focused on the three children of the King and Queen, who were theoretically left in charge while their parents traveled the world, fighting evil. The title character (Danny Cooksey) is charged with protecting the kingdom due to his size, strength and gender, although he is somewhat ill-equipped for the task. His older, "valley girl" sister, Candy (Erica Luttrell), is the official Regent, though she prefers shopping to "ruling." Nevertheless, she has hidden reserves of physical and mental powers that are highly useful in the face of crisis. The family circle is completed by its youngest child, Fang (Tress MacNeille), a somewhat primitive tomboy, and Uncle Oswidge (Kevin Michael Richardson), an incompetent magician. Dave is further "assisted" by his talking, opinionated sword, Lula (Estelle Harris), who frequently interjects wisecracks into the dialogue. The principal villain of the series was the Dark Lord Chuckles the Silly Piggy (Paul Rugg), whose name signifies his highly contradictory personality. The show's humorous ambience was indebted to the work of Jay Ward, most obviously due to the fact that Langdale employed a narrator (Jeff Bennett) to set the scene and occasionally to banter with the characters. An episode in which Chuckles captures the narrator and forces him to the tell the episode from the villain's point of view showed the extent of Ward's influence over Langdale, something that had only been hinted at in *The Weekenders*. Another clear influence on the series was Mark Twain, as revealed in an episode that served as an effective 21st century riff on *A Connecticut Yankee in King Arthur's Court*. Doug Langdale has proven himself to be a notable talent. More is welcome from him in the future.

AMERICAN DRAGON

Like *Kim Possible*, this is an action-comedy hybrid, and like *Juniper Lee* and *El Tigre* (see above), it focused on an "ethnic" hero. This mostly average (but still interesting) series was never able to present something truly original.

Created by Jeff Goode, the series, which debuted in 2005, focused on Jake Long (Dante Basco), a 13-year-old Asian American living in New York. Jake was descended from an ancient race of shape-shifters who were able to transform themselves into dragons for purposes of defense. As the series evolved, Jake developed this ability. His closest friends are Trixie (Miss Kitty) and Spud (Charlie Finn). His confidants and assistants in his magical role include his grandfather, Lao Shi (Keone Young), and the supernaturally gifted Fu Dog (John DiMaggio). In contrast, Jake's enemy was Professor Rotwood (Paul Rugg), a European-accented, supernatural conspiracy theorist who served as his teacher. Jake's love interest is Rose (Mae Whitman), a classmate who is also Huntsgirl, a skilled ninja from a tribe, ironically, sworn from ancient times to kill Jake and his family.

THE BUZZ ON MAGGIE

While Disney was a prolific and flexible producer of the "middle-school angst" subgenre, it had its limits, as this series demonstrated. Originally airing in 2005, it was the creation of Dave Polsky, whose background in live-action became a hindrance to the series; meanwhile, Dave Wasson supervised the show's visual "look." This was the first Disney series to be animated in the Flash digital media system, with the animation work done in Canada and India. Otherwise, it was not an impressive series, relying too much on blatant, ineffective puns and hackneyed storylines.

The focus of the series was Maggie Pesky (Jessica DiCicco), a pre-teen fly, and her adventures in the town of Stickyfeet. Others in the cast include Rayna (Cree Summer), Maggie's best friend; Maggie's siblings Aldrin (David Kaufman), Pupert (Thom Adcox) and Bella (a silent infant "maggot"); her parents, Chauncey (Brian Doyle-Murray) and Frieda (Susan Tolsky); and her enemy, Dawn Swatworthy (Tara Strong).

THE REPLACEMENTS

This uniquely formatted series had a strong and flexible premise at its core, and, at least during its first season, a skilled narrative. Unfortunately, the promise it had shown in its first year was undermined in the second, due to a radical redesign of the characters and setting and a tendency to simply recycle the established ideas of the first year.

The series was the creation of Dan Santat, a children's book illustrator and a graduate of the University of California at San Diego and the Art Center School of Design. It was, fittingly, based on one of his ideas for a children's book, which accounts in some ways for its thin premise. The execution of the series was chiefly in the hands of Nickelodeon veterans who had migrated to Disney: executive producer Jack Thomas, director Heather Martinez and writer Scott Peterson. What resulted was something of an artistic tug-of-war between the house "styles" of Nickelodeon and Disney, with one or the other taking prominence at different times. This was effective for the series at times, but undermined it at others—particularly regarding consistent character behavior.

Like many television animation series, the premise was boldly and directly announced in the main title sequence to attract the viewer's attention. The focus is on the sister-and-brother duo of Riley (Grey DeLisle) and Todd (Nancy Cartwright), who live in an orphanage until they come across the services of the mysterious Fleemco company. Fleemco, headed by the mysterious Conrad Fleem (Jeff Bennett), engages in a variety of businesses, but its main purpose seems to be "replacing" incompetent people with beings who are more capable of doing the job. With Fleemco's assistance, Riley and Todd are able to acquire parents, whom they believe are the ideal—Dick Daring (Daran Norris), an "Evel Knievel"–type stuntman who has clearly been knocked on the noggin too many times, and Agent K (Kath Soucie), an aging but still attractive British spy reminiscent of *The Avengers'* Emma Peel. Brought together, the family is dysfunctional; Riley and Todd have to adjust to their new "normal" lives as middle-school students in Pleasant Hills, while Dick and K have to adjust to the new demands of parenting. Fortunately, when the going gets tough, Todd and Riley can place a call to Fleem and request that someone be "replaced."

The personality quirks of the two central characters, just as with other series of this kind, provide the plot movement, and the differences between them say as much about Riley and Todd as do their familial bonds. Riley is an *uber* feminist, though the comic tone of the program does punish her when she (frequently) overdoes things. A gifted scholar and a skilled athlete (particularly at baseball, bowling and badminton), she aspires to become a journalist/filmmaker. Like many fictional smart girls, she has the capacity to give well-considered tongue lashings, elaborate expressions of personal and social indignity, and somewhat deluded overstatements of her aims. This latter element is most dominant in her romantic pursuit of her baseball teammate Johnny Hitswell (Dee Bradley Baker), with the frenzied zeal and lascivious aims of a stalker. (They eventually do begin dating in the second season, but this ends when Johnny dumps her, justly, for being possessive and overly controlling.) Her "replacements" are done chiefly as an extension of her huffing, puffing and blowing approach to social justice, particularly when it comes to her fellow students. However, they usually do not measure up to her exacting standards, prompting her to call Fleemco to take them back or—in at least one case—to "fire" them herself. While it is true that Riley is a feminist character in a number of respects, she is also a caricature of feminist traits, in particular her loudly stated opinions. She is dangerous when crossed or provoked, but when hurt by life, which happens quite often, she reacts in a way that belies her pretensions and shows the vulnerable little girl within.

Todd, on the other hand, lacks Riley's intelligence and social crusading abilities, though he possesses considerable personal guile. A 21st century Tom Sawyer, he will not lift a finger to do something when it is possible for others to do so, and, even when he *must* take action, he would prefer to have friends take the lumps for him. In this context, his "replacements" are undertaken less to ease the burden on others, as with Riley, than to make life easier for himself. Riley, of course, resents Todd using the "replacement" function as a "get out of jail free" card, and tells him this, loudly and often, but it does not deter him, however reckless and disruptive the final results. What the siblings do share is an ability to admit when they have made mistakes that have become damaging to themselves and the larger community. Riley is, however, able to take her punishments more stoically than Todd.

This seemingly simple framework was overlaid on a number of highly satirical portraits of American society in the first decade of the 21st century, particularly in the previously noted first season. Most of the adults in this depiction (with the exception of the highly resourceful Agent K) are idiots, whose ineptitude Riley and Todd remedy through the "replacement" function and their own skills and resources. The few who are not stupid are played as corrupt and unworthy of respect. The key example of this is Cutler (Bennett), the miserly principal of George Stapler Middle School (which Riley and Todd attend). Of course, not all the students are angels, either. The naïve Riley—who is almost country-bumpkin–like in the earliest episodes—is manipulated by the archetypal "mean girl" Sierra McCool (Tara Strong). But Riley eventually came into her own and was able to fight social bullying on her own terms. The point of the series is clear: life is difficult and there are no easy solutions, regardless of what a "replacement" might offer. The only way to deal with life is to be mature and confront it on one's own terms, something Riley was able to do much more easily than Todd.

Had the series not suffered creatively in its second year, it might have gone down in history as one of the most potent satires in television animation history. At least on the stellar terms of the first year, it was, but it was unable to transcend the clichés and stereotypes it was burdened with in order to maintain this standard.

Ying Yang Yo

This series was another Disney/Nickelodeon hybrid, as it was created and produced by Bob Boyle, who had cut his teeth working on *The Fairly Oddparents* (see above). A co-production of Disney and the George Elliott studio of Canada, it debuted in 2006, as an elaborate anthropomorphic parody of the "kung fu" film genre (see Chapter 4). The title trio includes Ying, a pink female rabbit; Yang, a blue male rabbit; and Yo, their elderly panda *sensei*. Ying and Yang aim was to become Woof Foo Knights so that they could become warriors and thus expel the villain-in-residence, Carl the Evil Cockroach Wizard.

Phineas and Ferb

It is impossible for any work of art to be perfect, especially in the eyes of a mass audience. Viewers—and especially critics—are capable of forming entirely diverging opinions on the same book, film, television series, or audio recording, and what are assets to one viewer or listener are deficits to another. Consequently, it is not perfection that actually matters in art, but the illusion of perfection—the idea that something seems to flow or move effortlessly when, in reality, it involves a considerable amount of unseen work—which is something viewers and critics can appreciate.

Consider, for example, *Phineas and Ferb*. In its on-camera narratives and off-screen construction—particularly regarding its structure and staging—it achieves perfection at times. The ease with which the title characters and their friends accomplish their aims is unrealistic, and their immediate success at endeavors for which others have to work a lifetime, minimize the struggles necessary to achieve the so-called "American dream." However, this satire is deliberately tempered by the matter-of-factness with which the characters go about their business. The writers insist that the characters are not challenging or mocking the world with their endeavors—they are simply finding unique ways to kill time during a long, hot summer, and that is how the creators intended the series to be viewed.

Debuting in 2007, *Phineas and Ferb* was the work of two distinguished television animation veterans: Dan Povenmire and Jeff "Swampy" Marsh. Povenmire, born in 1963 in Mobile, Alabama, worked on *Hey Arnold!*, *Spongebob Squarepants*, *The Simpsons* and *Rocko's Modern Life* (see Chapter 6) before making his mark on *Family Guy* (see Chapter 6) as the director of the same kind of elaborate musical numbers that would dominate *Phineas and Ferb*. Marsh, three years Povenmire's senior, is a native of Santa Monica, California. He spent several years working in animation in America before relocating to England. He returned to America to work with Povenmire, his colleague on *Rocko*, when the latter sold the *Phineas* concept to Disney.

The series, which the creators first developed while working on *Rocko*, borrowed from their childhood experiences. The central theme echoed Povenmire's mother's admonitions to use his summer vacation time wisely, while the structure of the family at the center of the show mirrored Marsh's. Both of these elements were unique, but Povenmire and Marsh added to it by making music as much as action the focus of the series. No other series, save perhaps *Fat Albert and the Cosby Kids* (see Chapter 4), has used music so often—and in so many genres and in such diverse ways—to both explain and advance its plots. Similar innovations exist in the characterizations of the major figures in the story, as well as the use of a show-within-a-show idea—both will be discussed in depth below. In spite of parting ways when *Rocko* ended, the partners were committed to the concept, and Povenmire pitched the series to Cartoon Network and FOX, both of whom turned it down. Disney, however, accepted. An executive there was aware of Povenmire's work on *Family Guy* and encouraged the development of the project as a segmented, 11-minute series, which is how it was presented. Povenmire and Marsh then presented a demo reel that they had storyboarded and voiced, which further convinced the Disney staff that they knew what they were doing, and which allowed the studio to grant them autonomy to pursue the project as they wished. This has continued and the series has become one of Disney's biggest hits, and a marketing bonanza besides.

Debuting in 2007 and running almost continuously since then, the series is set in the seemingly normal community of Danville (modeled in part on Povenmire's hometown), and focuses on the summer exploits of Phineas Flynn (Vincent Martella) and Ferb Fletcher (Thomas Sangster), stepbrothers with a close-knit relationship. Not willing to waste a single opportunity available to them, they often launch ambitious plans typical of the ramblings of their elementary school-aged peer group. Unlike the others, however, they are able to accomplish *exactly* what they want to do. If, for example, they want to build a roller coaster, they build a completely functioning roller coaster and track—no questions asked, no obstacles considered. Likewise, when they create "'Swinter,' a highly improbable combination of summer and winter, by disrupting the elements, the illogic of the idea is never challenged, and it functions successfully. In their actions, Phineas, a P.T. Barnum–styled devisor and showman, and Ferb, a laconic, Liverpudlian-accented engineer and builder, are assisted by plenty of what Joseph Campbell would call "cosmic helpers" to get the job done. The most prominent of these is Isabella Garcia-Shapiro (Allyson Stoner), a "cute," highly intelligent and very resourceful young lady always ready and able to pitch in—in part because she has an enormous crush on Phineas, a fact he does not acknowledge. As the head of her local troop of Fireside Girls, she is able to draft her willing and active colleagues into assisting with Phineas and Ferb's projects, serving as everything from auto racing pit stop crew to flight attendants. Two other prominent assistants are Baljeet (Malik Pancholy), an East Indian intellectual (or "nerd," if you prefer), and Buford (series writer Bobby Gaylor), the local bully, whose intellectual and physical gifts are employed by Phineas and Ferb, mostly without complaint.

The one disruptive force in all of this is Candace Flynn (Ashley Tisdale), Phineas's sister and Ferb's stepsister. "High strung" is too mild an adjective to describe her. Her two aims in life, it seems, are: first, to "bust" Phineas and Ferb by reporting their behavior to her mother before whatever device, object or idea they have constructed that day mysteriously disappears into the ether, as it always seems to do; and second, to make Jeremy Johnson (Mitchell Musso), her boyfriend. She is ultimately successful at that, since Jeremy is a nice, accepting and understanding guy with the patience of Job. The former goal remains frustratingly elusive, however. If it were possible to do so on a Disney show, she would constantly be cursing her bad luck. What compounds this is that often the "proof" she needs to convince her mother of the extent of Phineas and Ferb's transcendence of the limits of "bad" behavior disappears mysteriously at the very last minute, leaving her mother unconvinced and Candace stuttering impotently, a human version of a deflating balloon. Early episodes might lead you to believe that this tall, black-eyed, redheaded victim of the whims of the cosmos was constructed strictly as an antagonist and nothing more, but this is not the case. Of the leading figures, Candace is the only one whose character has evolved, as she has gradually shed many of her fears to become a competent young woman in every aspect—save for nailing that elusive "bust." Like many classic "Aspies," Candace is single-mindedly, almost obsessively, devoted to her two "causes," and almost loses the friendship of her closest chum, Stacy (Kelly Hu), over them. She is able to overcome a fair number of her fears and concerns to act fearlessly and independently; this is important as the show would practically grind to a halt without her perpetual scheming and *kvetching* related to everything and everyone around her. This is not exclusively Phineas and Ferb's fault, either. Suzy (Kari Wahlgren), Jeremy's younger sister, behaves toward Candace in a way that makes her the female doppelgänger of Stewie Griffin, perpetually asserting herself against the older girl. The forces that defeat Candace against Phineas and Ferb also defeat her in her interactions with Suzy, because the younger girl is able to present herself as the innocent toddler she only appears to be, while Candace is unable to convince others of the threat Suzy poses to her. With all this against Candace, it's not surprising that she is often heard screaming loudly and hysterically, and is periodically consoling herself with her teddy bear in her house's panic room. What *is* surprising is that such a fashion-conscious girl would be seen wearing the same red sweater and white skirt every day, but such are the vagaries of television animation.

We next come to the equally fascinating and funny "show within a show," featuring Phineas and Ferb's fedora-clad pet platypus, Perry (Dee Bradley Baker). When not attended to by the boys masters and their family, Perry is a secret agent for the OWCA (Organization Without A Cool Acronym), reporting to the uni-browed spymaster Major Monogram (Marsh). With the exception of Monogram and his "unpaid" intern, Carl (Tyler Mann), this group consists entirely of animals like Perry, though their opponents are all recognizably human. Perry himself is fairly one-dimensional in personality, like his masters (think Buster Keaton portraying James Bond). This cannot, however, be said for his principal enemy,

Heinz Doofenshmirtz (Povenmire). "Doof," as he is called (even by himself), is a frustrated mad scientist, but, unlike others of this type, he is completely without confidence in his own abilities, and prone to loudly burdening others on his failings as a husband, father and man, like a barroom drunk undergoing psychoanalysis. (This is a signature of Povenmire and Marsh's style: inverting common and stubbornly persistent stereotypes.) His inventions, with which he intends to wreak havoc on the world, frequently have names ending in the suffix "-inator." The inventions seem to be related to some arcane childhood trauma he witnessed growing up in the remote community of Gimmelshtoop, in the Ruritanian country of Druselstein, which seems to be the same place as the origin of Tish Katsufrakis (see above) and her parents. It is Doof's failings, not any successes he might have had, that we witness in his encounters with Perry. Not only must Doof endure the platypus escaping the traps he has constructed for him, but Perry also destroys his inventions, when Doofenshmirtz doesn't destroy them himself in the process of chasing Perry. Then there is the matter of being constantly ribbed by his ex-wife, Charlene (Alison Janney), who provides the alimony on which he lives, and his teenaged daughter Vanessa (Olivia Olson), who doesn't think highly of the old man or his line of work, to say nothing of his giant, cheerful but bumbling robot assistant, Norm (John Viener). Not self-sacrificing enough to be truly tragic, nor competent enough to be a purely comic figure, Doofenshmirtz is a truly pathetic figure.

The show proper and the show-within-a-show were artfully connected by Povenmire and Marsh, with an incident from one show directly impacting the events of the other. In this fashion, the possibilities for plots seemed endless as the producers built a fictional world with a large number of supporting characters and settings, not unlike the approach of *The Simpsons* (see Chapter 6). Clearly, the producers intended to get as much traction out of the concept as they could, and they sweetened the pot every time they had a chance. The two, 11-minute-segment-per-show concept is limiting and, periodically, they would have to go beyond this to achieve what they wanted. Thus, several of the later episodes are full 22-minute stories, two-part episodes, one-hour specials or, in one case (*Across the Fourth Dimension*), a full-length movie. In all cases, however, the highly flexible format remained intact, rumbling toward the inevitable conclusion. Povenmire and Marsh more than justified their faith in this series through their surprisingly deep and multi-faceted execution of what appears on the surface to be a limited idea. They managed to provide multiple layers and interpretations in every installment, even if longtime fans believed that they knew how things were going to turn out in the end.

Through all of this, Povenmire and Marsh have never insulted the intelligence of the audience; instead, they focused on what is possible for all of us to achieve during the hot expanse of the warmest season of the year. This is a theme that appeals to both children and adults alike, and has been chiefly responsible for this program's remarkable staying power.

Fish Hooks

As with *The Replacements*, this series was an uncomfortable mash-up—almost a shotgun wedding—between the Disney house style and that of a more liberal outlet, in this case Cartoon Network Studios. While some strong, funny episodes were produced, they were outweighed by the overall tone of the series, which was probably more annoying than the producers intended. The fact that nearly all of the voice actors hammed it up mercilessly, and the writing played to this weakness, hurt the final product.

The project was a collaboration between Noah Z. Jones, a New York–born graphic artist and children's book animator who supervised the program's overall visual tone as art director, and Cartoon Network veteran Maxwell Atoms (see above), who supervised the writing and animation. While Atoms and his crew, including another Cartoon Network veteran, C.H. Greenblatt (see above), managed to keep the more Rabelaisian aspects of the CNS studio style in check (in deference to their new employer's stricter attitude regarding such material), there were elements in the series that reflected their old home base. This series had a full-throttle directness that, while commonplace in CNS products, was utterly foreign to Disney, and therefore Disney's efforts to impose its values were more evident than in their other series. As a result, *Fish Hooks* is a mixed bag, enjoyable at times, but utterly frustrating at others. Yet it has its followers, as represented by its winning of a BAFTA award in England in 2011.

Fish Hooks focuses on the exploits of a group of fish attending a high school in glass bowls in a pet shop. The lead characters in the program are Oscar (Justin Roiland, who doubled as a writer), a catfish with an Afro, and Milo (Kyle Massey), a hyperactive Siamese fighting fish with a prominent fin on his head. These two are said to be "brothers," although the fact that they are different species makes this plot device unlikely. Comedy exists in the contrast between the studious, perpetually nervous Oscar and the annoying "party guy" Milo. However, both are upstaged at regular intervals by the female lead, who has delusions of becoming an "acting superstar." Bea Goldfishberg (Chelsea Staub Kane) is a feminist drama queen who regularly makes herself the center of attention. (Oscar has a crush on her, although, typically, he has difficulty putting his thoughts into words.) Like Riley Daring before her, Bea is, in many ways, a negative caricature of a feminist. Rather than being passive, she charges through life like a deranged lunatic, trilling some of her dialogue in stereotypically "feminine" ways, but bluntly screaming at other characters when they oppose or question her. Her much-vaunted "acting" abilities are continually on display, whether ineptly disguising herself as a delivery "man" with a fake moustache, or painting her face in the school colors to show herself a true "fan" (or, in her case, *fanatic*).

Unfortunately, much of the remainder of the program is based, first, on the epic mood swings of the characters, and, second, on banal plot repetition, awful puns, and an overall smugness in tone. The regular cast of characters and guest-stars, including Richard Simmons, routinely turned in over-the-top performances. The problem was clear—Jones, Atoms and Greenblatt had clearly chosen to base their plotting and characterizations on outdated models, which stood in sharp contrast to the unique inter-media approaches used to create the overall feel of the series.

Jones has gone on to develop another series for Canadian television, this one called *Almost Naked Animals*, and, judging by the fact that it offers the rambling tone and blatant overacting of *Fish Hooks*, he evidently believes that this is what television animation is *supposed* to be.

Gravity Falls

Certainly one of the most accomplished series of the still-young 2010s, this cleverly written and animated series walks a tightrope between narrative logic and illogic with surprising ease. That it is designed this way is clear from the outset, but what sets it apart is the way series creator and principal writer Alex Hirsch and supervising producer Rob Renzetti (see above) orchestrate the often-bizarre goings-on with a clear sense of control and an ambitious satirical style absent in other shows of this kind. Just when you think you can tell how things are going to go, you are repeatedly thrown curveballs, and often you cannot make sense of the story until the end of the program.

Hirsch, a California native who has written and acted for a number of Cartoon Network and Disney series before branching out on his own, was able to clearly articulate what his show was about in the pilot episode. Using a full episode, 22-minute format with "cold" openings and closing "tags," the series resembles *The Replacements* in that it features a brother-and-sister duo. That is where the resemblance ends. This duo is made up of fraternal twins—a rare bird for television animation—and have unique personalities which add a considerable charm to the series.

Dipper (Jason Ritter) and Mabel Pines (Kirsten Schaal) are exiled for the summer by their parents to the (fictional) town of Gravity Falls, Oregon, where their "Grunkel" Stan (Hirsch) operates the Mystery Shack, a 21st-century equivalent of P.T. Barnum's New York–based 19th-century "museum" of "oddities." Most of the material featured is flagrantly false, and Stan himself is a caricature of a carnie and medicine show barker, but, somehow, the incredibly stupid tourists who flock to his door fail to notice this. Stan's two employees—goofy handyman Soos (Hirsch) and seemingly apathetic teenage counter server Wendy (Linda Cardinelli) seem to be aware of this, but they never want to let Stan know. Of the twins, Dipper seems to be the more level-headed and studious, with Mabel much more prone to expressing herself flamboyantly with girlish glee and Gracie Allen–styled fuzzy logic. Both can turn on a dime, though, and, while they are occasionally at odds, they know that their close Gemini relationship ties them together on a permanent basis. As with many twins, their inner "knowledge" of each other is uncanny, giving their relationship a depth absent in other brother-sister pairings of the era.

Being restless "tweens," Dipper and Mabel tire of the routine of the shop, and frequently escape it by delving into the mysterious secrets of the town, in the fashion of the earlier and similar live-action series *Twin Peaks* (which also had a Pacific Northwest setting). Dipper is particularly predisposed to exploration, and this is intensified when, in the environs of the woods, he discovers a mysterious book which seems to be equal parts *Necronomicon*, *Golden Bough* and *Commonwealth of Elves, Fauns and Fairies*. This book is unique, however, in that it includes lore about Gravity Falls. It isn't much of a surprise when things get downright crazy, intense and absurd in the pilot, and in every subsequent episode. Among other plot-lines, they encounter: a race of gnomes who disguise themselves as zombies; a group of animate wax statues; Gideon Gleeful (Thurop Van Orman), a Marjoe Gortner–styled professional "psychic" with an obsessive crush on Mabel; a photocopier able to make sentient human clones; a U.S. president whose existence and exploits are (somewhat justifiably) hidden from the "official" record of U.S. history; Summerween, the only-in-Gravity-Falls summer variation on Halloween; and a nervous time traveler.

These decidedly "weird" elements gave the program color, but the real heart of the show was the coming of age of the twins themselves: Dipper's symbolized by his awkward romantic pursuit of Wendy; Mabel's by her inept attempts to "improve" her personality to gain friends among the locals; and both trying to cope with the physical, mental and emotional changes threatening their closeness. Not that the show isn't funny—it is hilarious—but Hirsch and Renzetti don't allow us to think of any of the characters as walking joke machines. You can always count on Dipper to come to Mabel's defense, and vice versa, and you know exactly why. It is more difficult to explain other elements of the series, but this is not the place to go into deeper psychological speculation to which the show lends itself. *Gravity Falls* is highly enjoyable inspite of its absurdities.

◆ ◆ ◆

Over the past decade, Disney Television Animation has developed into one of the best studios of its kind. It rarely allows its product to be overtly flamboyant in presentation, and, even when it does, there are still likeable elements. While Cartoon Network Studios and Nickelodeon often overwhelm you with their presentation styles, Disney is more restrained, and, in many ways, more likeable, in its approach. While it may never achieve the stature its parent company once held in the field of television animation, the fact that DTA has been such a standard bearer of quality in an often unstable genre and medium—and promises to continue to be so in the future—is a clear indication of its prominence.

Other Voices

The gradual decline of the Saturday-morning network television and syndication markets severely reduced the number of producers who were not affiliated with Fox, CNS, Nickelodeon or Disney. Yet there remained a few outside of this loop who were willing to continue, and, based chiefly on corporate connections rather than quality, they managed to get airtime during the decade. Some of the material was not up to the demanding standards of the new industry power brokers, but some of it was. Had they been executed or distributed more effectively, they would surely have made a bigger impact.

WARNER BROS.

The decline of this studio from its peak achievements of the 1990s was one of the saddest aspects of the story of television animation in the 21st century. Chiefly, it was the result of factors beyond its control. The decline was hastened first by the departure of Jean MacCurdy and Tom Ruegger, who had supervised the studio's excellent 1990s product, and then by its parent company's hasty and ill-conceived merger in 2003 with the Internet service provider America On Line, which led to financial decline and boardroom bloodshed. While its corporate sibling CNS was largely isolated from the mêlée due to the strength of its "brand" and the solid work of its individual producers, Warner Bros. Television Animation was left rudderless and lacking corporate guidance. The fact that its work was primarily distributed on the perennially malnourished, studio-owned WB network (until it folded midway through the first decade of the 2000s) meant that its was now seen by fewer people—which was just as well, considering the diminishing quality of the work.

Warner Bros. seemed no longer to be interested in backing series which had some genuine original creative merit; instead, it simply raided the archives for material and tried to present it in "new" ways. Their inappropriate use of the Looney Tunes and Merrie Melodies canon for new purposes is notable, suggesting that the owners of media properties do not always make good decisions regarding their trust. *Baby Looney Tunes*, to cite one notable example, was a self-explanatory throwback to the offensive 1980s. Other series which repurposed the legendary gang, from *Duck Dodgers* and *Loonatics Unleashed* to *The Looney Tunes Show*, have been just as incomprehensible. Had Friz Freleng, Chuck Jones, Tex Avery and Bob Clampett been able to witness this shameless manipulation of their legendary characters, they most certainly would have cried foul.

Also reflecting poor judgment at the studio was its decision to animate nearly every DC Comics property available to it, hoping to recapture the success of the earlier *Superman* and *Batman* projects. Some of these properties, such as *Krypto the Superdog*, *Legion of Super*

Heroes, and *Teen Titans*, had their origins decades in the past, and little effort was made to update their approach for the new century. Although the programs were all strongly animated and staged (the aforementioned series in particular), the overall tone of this group of shows was that everyone off camera was simply running in place, not using much creativity.

The few properties not already owned by Warner did not vary much from other studio projects. *Baby Blues*, based on the comic strip by Rick Kirkman and Jerry Scott, offered little that was not in its source. *Mucha Lucha*, a spirited exercise in Mexican American goodwill, had some good moments, but also little to distinguish itself from other series of the era. *Detention* was essentially *The Breakfast Club* for middle-school students, though it featured the unique quirk of having one of the students communicate exclusively through his talking yo-yo.

Columbia Tristar/Sony Television

Of the major film studios working in television animation production in the 1990s, Warner and Sony were the only ones to continue production into the 2000s. While Warner had to meet television-network quotas, however, Sony worked on a freelance basis, offering its services wherever a place could be found for it on the dial. The result was evident in the disparity of the quality between Sony's individual productions, from inept to compelling.

There were, of course, adaptations of studio-owned properties, such as *Stuart Little*, and properties borrowed from elsewhere, such as a none-too-faithful version of Ozamu Tezuka's *Astro Boy* and, parallel to that, one of Frank Miller's comic-book robots *Big Guy and Rusty*. Occasionally, the studio aspired to produce more engaging products like its rivals, succeeding in this line with *Generation O!*, the saga of a pre-teen pop-music star appropriately named Molly O. It also hit the dirt with some offerings, as with *D'Myna Leagues*, a hackneyed exercise in anthropomorphism masquerading as the tale of a provincial minor-league baseball team, and *Jackie Chan Adventures*, a shameless vehicle for the martial-arts film star.

The strongest series to emerge from Sony—and one of the strongest of the entire decade—was far above other Sony product in design and execution. *Boondocks*, based on the comic strip by African American artist Aaron McGruder (who also produced the series), made its debut in 2006. This bold, uncensored story of life in a modern African American community, generally eschewed the good-natured conviviality and joviality often present in other media portraits of African Americans, especially in television animation. The Freemans—serious, opinionated "domestic terrorist" Huey (Regina King), would-be thug Riley (King), and their grandfather Robert (John Witherspoon)—serve as the focus of the program. Many of the episodes derive their shock value from McGruder's brutal caricatures, earning him scornful attacks from those he has parodied. McGruder deserves considerable praise for portraying his race in realistic terms, something other producers have rarely done.

Viacom

For a brief period during the summer of 2003, the owner of Nickelodeon presented three adult-oriented television animation series on another of its cable outlets. John Kricfalusi's *Ren and Stimpy Adult Party Cartoon* (see Chapter 6) was one of these. Another was *Gary the Rat*, created by Mark and Robb Cullen. This clever series, indebted to Franz Kafka, focuses on a human lawyer (Kelsey Grammer, whose production company underwrote the project) who turned into an anthropomorphic rat as a form of punishment for his past sins.

How he manages to cope with his new identity, as well as the inept efforts of a Brooklyn-accented exterminator to get rid of him, formed the crux of the show, which was much more entertaining overall than its limited premise would suggest. The third series was *Stripperella*, developed by Stan Lee, which was essentially a soft-core bump-and-grind show masquerading as a superhero narrative: the focus was on a professional stripper (Pamela Anderson), who was the title character. The "adult" aspect of this series was altogether too obvious (the lead character's name is Erotica), and, though it had some good comic moments, this was an obstacle to the series' creative growth that it could not overcome.

Nelvana

Canada's leading television animation studio remained as productive as ever during the early 2000s, even if much of its more recent output has been derivative and hackneyed. These one-dimensional series, such as *Anatole*, *Maggie the Ferocious Beast*, *Marvin the Tap Dancing Horse* and *The Backyardigans*, appealed only to very young viewers. Yet the studio was capable of occasional surprises, such as *Braceface*, a sitcom-style vehicle starring Alicia Silverstone. The most mature and surprising of these ventures was *Clone High*, created by future animation and live-action directors Phil Lord and Christopher Miller. *Clone High* focuses on teenaged clones of famous historical figures interacting within the confines of a high school. Though the behavior of the teens was odd compared to that of the actual figures, this was not the point of the show, which was to parody the over-utilized clichés of live-action series aimed at teens, in particular the focus on "very special" episodes. It was exceptionally effective at this.

DIC

Andy Heyward managed to produce a few final series under the DIC name before folding his company into the Cookie Jar umbrella in the early 2000s. For the most part, they were a continuation of what had gone on before. *Stargate* was a by-the-numbers adaptation of the popular film of a few years earlier (produced with MGM, the distributor of the film), while *Mary Kate and Ashley in Action* provided an old-fashioned, limp vehicle for the now-teenaged former stars of the live-action sitcom *Full House*. The most distinguished of these projects was *Liberty's Kids*, produced for PBS, focusing on the lives of a group of children in Revolutionary War–era America, and featuring legendary newscaster Walter Cronkite as the voice of another legendary American, Benjamin Franklin.

Hit Entertainment

This company was one of the few newer organizations to enter into television animation production during this decade. It was originally Henson International Television, a division of the Jim Henson Company (see Chapter 5). But when Henson entered into negotiations to sell his company to Disney in 1989, the executives of the division, led by Peter Orton, bought it themselves. Originally a distributor only, it entered into series production following the success achieved by its products, particularly *Barney and Friends*. It is currently owned by Mattel and administered through another Mattel subsidiary, Fisher-Price. While it primarily produces live-action series aimed at younger viewers, it has also produced some animated series aimed at the same market through its HOT subsidiary. Notable in this category is an English import, *Bob the Builder*, and *Angelina Ballerina*, the saga of a female mouse with terpsichorean ambitions.

Conclusion

While the early 21st century was not an entirely pleasant period for television animation or its creators, there was an overall feeling of mobility and an adventurous spirit active in the genre that had not be felt since the pre-censorship period of the mid-to-late 1960s. Television animation, once marginalized and ridiculed, was able to show its relevance to a wide variety of viewers, and a chameleon-like ability to adapt to their diverse and unique demands. Whereas a widening cable spectrum, waning network power, and the increasing employment of non–TV sources such as YouTube threatened to make traditional television broadcasting irrelevant, television animation has continued to keep the faith for its genre and medium alike. A belittled artistic format, once accused of being manufactured by "child molesters," looks, at last, to be achieving artistic and commercial respect, and to be showing itself as one of the most potent and diverse bodies of artistic achievement ever devised.

Conclusion: Where Are We Going?

As I write these words (July 2013), the future of television animation is healthy in some respects, and not so in others. Traditional Saturday-morning TV network distribution has effectively come to an end, due to abandonment and neglect on the part of its one-time patrons. As a consequence, the forum by which television animation was most fully able to express its virtues and flaws no longer exists. Cable television providers have, however, stepped into the breach to provide television animation with forums that were more appropriate for its services, as well as treating the programs and their creators with far greater attention and respect than their predecessors were ever accorded during the network era. This has allowed television animation to diversify in a multitude of exciting, creative ways, as noted in Chapters 6 and 7, and it bodes well for its future and evolution in the 21st century. Yet here, too, as we have seen, producers can easily come into conflict with potential backers if they are not able to create product, or "run" their series, in a way that reflects the backer's "brand." Likewise, these backers are prone to use legal means to enforce financial control over the product, and to ration the broadcast of "their" series in such a way that overlooks the intentions of the actual creators and producers—which should always be paramount in assessing the merits of individual television animation programs.

I have hopefully noted throughout this text that television animation must be understood creatively as both individual series and an ongoing, unified narrative process which is continually being added to and, possibly, improved. It is unique among television genres in that its programs are an indication of how a cultural product can change over time and yet remain, for the most part, structurally constant and consistent. *The Flintstones* and *The Simpsons*, for example, both reflect the consistent popularity of the situation comedy as a programming format, but the former program is as much a child of the 1960s as the latter is of the 1990s, and both can only be fully understood in these historical contexts. It is also possible to chart the abrupt cultural change that television animation has documented, particularly in the highly noticeable shifts in the mindset and sociopolitical outlook and feelings of American children and teenagers. This has not been documented to the same full extent in other media, and reflects the significant manner in which television animation has come to serve as a vehicle for empowering the otherwise powerless members of its audience.

◆ ◆ ◆

Because television animation has suffered an inordinate amount of cultural belittling and public shaming during the 20th century, the true, unbiased cultural study of it as a genre has been limited, and remains relatively virgin territory for media scholars and researchers. As noted in the introduction, popular sentiment has always decreed that more visible and popular programming typically gets far greater scholarly attention than less popular series. Yet popularity alone should never be used as a nexus for creative quality. There are many lesser-known series that are arguably superior in creative quality to more "popular" ones, as my text has hopefully demonstrated.

The difficulty of assessing television animation texts on their own terms in the past, caused by the control of them by network and syndication distributors and copyright owners, has been countered firmly in recent years by the advent of means of accessing complete runs of series in their original, unedited forms, specifically through DVD issues and the website YouTube. The latter in particular is an invaluable resource, as it provides access to a wide variety of film and TV texts which had previously only been available in private or institutional film libraries. YouTube is also an excellent litmus test for gauging the popularity of individual programs, as many of the site's many content "posters" have fashioned multimedia presentations as tributes to particular programs that truly reflect their devotion to these series. These are attributes to the site that detractors of it, like those of television animation itself in the 1960s and 1970s, simply do not understand.

Consequently, it will now be possible to construct television animation criticism that has the potential for being truly objective, without being entirely demeaning at one end (as detractors are prone to being) or overly reverential at the other (as too many devoted "fans" of series often are). And I, for one, welcome that.

◆ ◆ ◆

Those who attempt to analyze television animation, either as a whole or through individual programs, must be cautious and, especially, attentive. From the beginning, based on the heritage of vaudeville comedy and superhero action that has always been its lifeblood, television animation has always been paced faster than other television formats. If you are not willing to pay attention to a series as it evolves, and with the same care you would devote to viewing paper-based sources, you should not attempt it. This is due to the fact that the patterns of communication are very different than that of other art forms. Non-verbal body movements communicate as much about internal character composition and development as does dialogue, while even seemingly irrelevant spoken words can provide essential keys to understanding the bare essence of entire characters and series. The level of inheritance from other, prior media sources is key here, and it has always remained a key element of the genre's long-lasting survival. In our modern era of being able to communicate ideas effectively and immediately through social media, television animation's typically hectic pacing is as relevant to understanding our everyday lives as it has ever been.

We must, however, *never* make the mistakes made by prior generations of detractors— painting the entire genre with the same brush. Even when cultural products come from a similar supplier, or are based on a similar cultural background, these projects have always truly reflected the mindsets of the individuals responsible for creating them, as much as the writings of a published author reflect that author's opinions and no one else's. Whether the work was produced as a genuinely creative, artistic expression, or, simply and bluntly, to make money, this must always be the final consideration of television animation's worth, be it from a small, localized organization such as Total Television or an aggressive multi-national corporation such as Disney. It is only through understanding the work via the creators' intentions and its historical context that these works can truly be understood. For this reason, this is the approach that I have used to analyze all of the series in this text.

Television animation in the United States has been fortunate in a number of respects. Most prominent is the fact that it has remained a consistent throughout across the entire history of commercial television broadcasting in America. Very few other genres can make this claim. Appropriately, another is the soap opera, as much a victim of daytime ghettoization as television animation was and, in some cases, continues to be. Other once-popular genres, such as the Western, have utterly faded away from the television landscape, while the longevity of others, such as "reality" programming, has yet to be fully determined. The situation comedy, like the soap opera a holdover from radio, is the major prime-time survivor in this category, although it is less recognizable in format today than it was at the beginning of television's history. Oddly enough, television animation has survived- and thrived- by being able to parody and appropriate all of these programming trends for its own uses, and, in the process, make itself relevant and socially aware to multiple, successive generations of television viewers.

Television animation has also benefited from the consistent presence of producers who, while often seemingly comfortable within cultural restrictions, challenge and confront them by both direct and indirect means. William Hanna and Joseph Barbera, in spite of the seeming sterility of their artistic production methods, were always willing and able to produce work that accommodated accepted social views while subtly mocking them. Similarly, Lou Scheimer was willing to use Filmation as a vehicle for traditional moralizing, but his plots frequently allowed for subtle, restrained moments of social rebellion. At the other end of the spectrum were rebellious comedy producers, such as Jay Ward and Bob Clampett, who always did things "their" way when the networks wanted them done "our" way, and paid a heavy price for doing so. The legacy of these producers lives on in the filmmakers most heavily influenced by them—Groening, Macfarlane, Renzetti, Tartakovsky, McCracken, Murray, et al.—who will, in turn, likely influence the work of a third generation of television animators to come.

For all its seeming emphasis on frivolous comedy and escapist action, television animation's characters and producers are, for the most part, admirable. Both on screen and off, characters and producers both are principled and intelligent people (or other beings) who do not back away from challenges. They say important things when and where it is necessary for them to be said, and, even when they are fairly obviously corporate shills, exude a warm, welcoming atmosphere rarely seen elsewhere in the competitive medium of television. Given that this is the case, it is no wonder that television animation has been with us for so long, and that it will likely remain with us for as long as television itself continues to exist.

◆ ◆ ◆

As the noted jazz musician Jaco Pastorius once observed, it ain't bragging if you can back it up. That is something that television animation's creators and characters alike can always do. While we may not think all of them admirable or genuinely entertaining sometimes, we can still recognize the level of artistic achievement that is always present in the final broadcast product. In this way, television animation, in parts and as a whole, has always mattered to television viewers, and it always will.

Chapter Notes

Introduction

1. Quoted in Hal Erickson, *Television Cartoon Shows: An Illustrated Encyclopedia, 1949–2003*, 2d ed., 2 vols. (Jefferson, NC: McFarland, 2005), 1: 25.
2. Robert Scholes, *Textual Power* (New Haven: Yale University Press, 1985), 2.
3. David Marc and Robert J. Thompson, *Prime Time, Prime Movers* (Syracuse: Syracuse University Press, 1995).
4. John Kenneth Muir, *A History and Critical Analysis of* Blake's 7, *the 1978–1981 British Television Space Adventure* (Jefferson, NC: McFarland, 2001), 31–32.
5. S.T. Joshi, *The Weird Tale* (Holicong, PA: Wildside Press, 1990), 3, 5.
6. Marshall McLuhan, *Essential McLuhan*, ed. Eric McLuhan and Frank Zingrone (Concord, ON: House of Anansi, 1995), 135.

Chapter 1

1. Television animation, for our purposes, refers to animation originally produced for exhibition on television. Theatrical animation refers to animation originally produced for exhibition in motion picture theaters. This is an important, if often unstated, distinction between the two forms which has particularly affected the study and understanding of the former, and one that must be made to understand the two forms on separate ideological and creative terms.
2. The best book-length study of this interactive relationship, with particular emphasis on how it influenced comedy in the early years of film, is Henry Jenkins, *What Made Pistachio Nuts? Early Sound Comedy and the Vaudeville Aesthetic* (New York: Columbia University Press, 1992).
3. For a historical analysis of vaudeville and its influence on later performance forms, see Robert W. Snyder, *The Voice of the City: Vaudeville and Popular Culture in New York* (New York: Oxford University Press, 1989); Anthony Slide, *The Vaudevillians: A Dictionary of Vaudeville Performers* (Westport, CT: Arlington House, 1981); John E. DiMeglio, *Vaudeville U.S.A.* (Bowling Green, OH: Bowling Green University Press, 1973); Douglas Gilbert, *American Vaudeville* (New York: Dover, 1940); and Albert F. McLean, Jr., *American Vaudeville as Ritual* (Lexington: University of Kentucky Press, 1965).
4. Snyder, xiii.
5. Ibid.
6. Susan J. Douglas, *Listening In: Radio and the American Imagination* (New York: Times Books, 1999), 106.
7. Quoted in Snyder, 29.
8. Jenkins, *What Made Pistachio Nuts?*, 63.
9. For a book-length biographical study of Sennett, see Simon Louvish, *Keystone: The Life and Clowns of Mack Sennett* (London: Faber and Faber, 2003).
10. Scott Siegel and Barbara Siegel, *American Film Comedy* (New York: Prentice Hall, 1994), 255.
11. Ibid.
12. Barry Putterman, *On Television and Comedy* (Jefferson, NC: McFarland, 1995), 49.
13. Ibid., 51.
14. For a book-length study of Roach's work, see Richard Lewis Ward, *A History of the Hal Roach Studios* (Carbondale: Southern Illinois University Press, 2005).
15. Putterman, 50–51.
16. An excellent study of Chaplin's impact on the culture of America—including film comedy—is provided by Charles J. Maland in *Chaplin and American Culture: The Evolution of a Star Image* (Princeton: Princeton University Press, 1989).
17. For the full history of theatrical animation in the silent and sound eras, see Leonard Maltin, *Of Mice and Magic: A History of American Animated Cartoons* (New York: Plume, 1987 [1980]); Michael Barrier, *Hollywood Cartoons: American Animation in Its Golden Age* (New York: Oxford University Press, 1999); Stefan Kanfer, *Serious Business: The Art and Commerce of Animation in America from Betty Boop to* Toy Story (New York: Da Capo Press, 1997); and Norman M. Klein, *Seven Minutes: The Life and Death of the American Animated Car-*

toon (New York: Verso, 1993). While, as expected, these texts are laudatory in their treatment of theatrical animation, they share a negative attitude towards television animation as a bastardized, cost-cutting exercise that this book seeks to redress.

18. Maltin, 2.
19. Ibid., 3–6. For a full biographical study of McCay, see John Canemaker, *Winsor McCay: His Life and Art* (New York: Harry N. Abrams, 2005).
20. Ibid., 4–6.
21. Kanfer, 29–31.
22. Winsor McCay, quoted in Maltin, 1.
23. Ibid., 7–10.
24. Ibid., 11.
25. Ibid., 13.
26. Ibid., 17.
27. Ibid., 22.
28. Ibid., 23. For a biographical study of this character, of the silent films he appeared in animated by Messmer and others under Sullivan's name, and his later, less prominent, existences as a television animation character, see John Canemaker, *Felix: The Twisted Tale of the World's Most Famous Cat* (New York: Pantheon, 1991).
29. Ibid., 24.
30. Ibid., 26–27.
31. Two of the most recent and best biographies of the man and his legacy are Neal Gabler, *Walt Disney: The Triumph of the American Imagination* (New York: Knopf, 2006), and Michael Barrier, *The Animated Man: A Life of Walt Disney* (Berkeley: University of California Press, 2007). The latter, understandably, focuses more on his work in animation than does the former.
32. Maltin, 29.
33. Ibid., 30.
34. Ibid.
35. This aspect of Disney's career is covered in great detail in Russell Merritt and J.B. Kaufman, *Walt in Wonderland: The Silent Films of Walt Disney* (Baltimore: Johns Hopkins University Press, 1993). The authors take great pains to explain how Disney's work was initially heavily indebted to the silent film animators discussed earlier, and how he ultimately transcended them.
36. Gilbert Seldes, quoted in Maltin, 35.
37. Klein, 19.
38. Maltin, 38.
39. Ibid., 51–53.
40. Ibid., 72.
41. Ibid.
42. Ibid., 83.
43. Kanfer, 44–45. For a full discussion of the studio's creative legacy, see Leslie Cabarga, *The Fleischer Story* (New York: Da Capo Press, 1988 [1976]). For a personal biography of Max Fleischer, see Richard Fleischer, *Out of the Inkwell: Max Fleischer and the Animation Revolution* (Lexington: University of Kentucky Press, 2005).
44. Maltin, 84.
45. Ibid., 95–98.
46. For an extended analysis of this school of animation, see Barrier, *Hollywood Cartoons*.
47. For histories of these studios, see Maltin, 125–157, 199–208, 189–198, 209–221, respectively. Terrytoons was the only one of this group to last into the television era, producing more specifically for television after its acquisition by CBS in 1955; its television productions will discussed elsewhere in this book.
48. Ibid., 100.
49. Paul Buhle, *From the Lower East Side to Hollywood: Jews in American Popular Culture* (New York: Verso, 2004), 77.
50. Maltin, 102.
51. For a history of this document, see Thomas Doherty, *Hollywood's Censor: Joseph I. Breen and the Production Code Administration* (New York: Columbia University Press, 2007).
52. For a detailed history of this character and his appearances across the media, see Fred Grandinetti, *Popeye: An Illustrated History of E.C. Segar's Character in Print, Radio, Television, and Film Appearances, 1929–1993* (Jefferson, NC: McFarland, 1994). His appearances as a television animation character will be discussed elsewhere in this book.
53. Maltin, 106–107.
54. Ibid., 112.
55. Ibid., 113–114.
56. For the history of this studio, which lasted into the television era with mostly undistinguished product, see Maltin, 311–322. Its contributions to television animation production will be discussed elsewhere in this book.
57. The origins of this character and his early appearances, which strongly influenced the look and feel of these first animated films, are discussed in Gerard Jones, *Men of Tomorrow: Geeks, Gangsters and the Birth of the Comic Book* (New York: Basic Books, 2004). For a full history of Superman's career across the media, see Les Daniels, *Superman in Color: The Complete History* (San Francisco: Chronicle Books, 1998), and Bruce Scivally, *Superman on Film, Television, Radio and Broadway* (Jefferson, NC: McFarland, 2008). The character's later appearances in television animation will be discussed elsewhere in this book.
58. Maltin, 120.
59. Ibid., 121–122.
60. Ibid., 124.
61. Ibid., 159.
62. Ibid., 160. For a full-length biography of Lantz, see Joe Adamson, *The Walter Lantz Story: With Woody Woodpecker and Friends* (New York: G.P. Putnam's Sons, 1985).
63. Maltin, 161–162.
64. Ibid., 165–166.
65. Ibid., 167.
66. Ibid., 171.
67. Ibid., 182. Lantz's censorship troubles, and their enduring impact on other television animation series, will be discussed elsewhere in this book.
68. In addition to being discussed prominently in texts already cited, the studio and its products have also been discussed in several stand-alone books. Among these are Jerry Beck and Will Friedwald, *Warner Broth-*

ers *Animation Art: The Characters—The Creators—The Limited Editions* (New York: Beaux Arts Editions, 1997); Steve Schneider, *That's All Folks! The Art of Warner Brothers Animation* (New York: Henry Holt, 1988); Jerry Beck and Will Friedwald, *Looney Tunes and Merrie Melodies: A Complete Illustrated Guide to the Warner Brothers Cartoons* (New York: Henry Holt, 1989); and Kevin S. Sandler, ed., *Reading the Rabbit: Explorations in Warner Brothers Animation* (New Brunswick: Rutgers University Press, 1998).

69. Maltin, 224.

70. For the contributions of Stalling and other composers to the development of theatrical animation, see Daniel Goldmark, *Tunes for 'Toons: Music and the Hollywood Cartoon* (Berkeley: University of California Press, 2005).

71. For an autobiographical study of this seminal figure, see Mel Blanc and Philip Bashe, *That's Not All Folks* (New York: Warner Books, 1988).

72. Maltin, 256.

73. For a countdown of the results of this poll, see Jerry Beck, ed., *The Fifty Greatest Cartoons* (North Dighton, MA: JG Press, 1994).

74. This studio and its television productions will be addressed elsewhere.

75. Maltin, 274-75.

76. Ibid., 281.

77. Ibid., 282.

78. Ibid.

79. Ibid.

80. The complete story of this duo and their films is chronicled in Patrick Brion, *Tom and Jerry: The Definitive Guide to Their Animated Adventures* (New York: Harmony Books, 1990).

81. See Chapter 3.

82. For a full study of this phase of Avery's career, see John Canemaker, *Tex Avery: The MGM Years 1942-1955* (Atlanta: Turner, 1996).

83. Jones' television animation productions for MGM will be discussed elsewhere in this book.

84. Maltin, 323.

85. Quoted in Maltin., 324.

86. Gilbert Seldes, quoted in Maltin., 330.

87. Gilbert Seldes, quoted in Maltin., 330-31.

88. Ibid., 333.

89. Ibid., 342.

Chapter 2

1. For some essential readings on this time in the context of American history, see Lynn Spigel, *Make Room for TV: Television and the Family Ideal in Postwar America* (Chicago: University of Chicago Press, 1992); Cecilia Tichi, *Electronic Hearth: Creating an American Television Culture* (New York: Oxford University Press, 1991); James L. Baughman, *Same Time, Same Station: Creating American Television 1948-1961* (Baltimore: Johns Hopkins University Press, 2007); J. Fred MacDonald, *One Nation Under Television: The Rise and Decline of Network TV* (Chicago: Nelson-Hall, 1990); and Lynn Spigel, *Welcome to the Dreamhouse: Popular Media and Postwar Suburbs* (Durham: Duke University Press, 2001).

2. Janet M. Davis, *The Circus Age: Culture and Society Under the American Big Top* (Chapel Hill: University of North Carolina Press, 2002), 30-32.

3. Brander Matthews, quoted in Michael Denning, *Mechanic Accents: Dime Novels and Working Class Culture in America*, 2d ed. (London: Verso, 1998), 9. See also J. Randolph Cox, *The Dime Novel Companion: A Source Book* (Westport, CT: Greenwood Press, 2000).

4. For a comprehensive historical study of vaudeville and its influence, see Robert W. Snyder, *The Voice of the City: Vaudeville and Popular Culture in New York* (Chicago: Ivan R. Dee, 2000).

5. Robert Sklar, *Movie Made America: A Cultural History of American Movies* (London: Chappell, 1978 [1975]), 18.

6. Ibid., 134-140.

7. For a history of this document and its most strident enforcer, see Thomas Doherty, *Hollywood's Censor: Joseph I. Breen and the Production Code Administration* (New York: Columbia University Press, 2007).

8. Spigel, *Make Room for TV*, 15.

9. Tom Sito, *Drawing the Line: The Untold Story of the Animation Unions from Bosko to Bart Simpson* (Lexington: University Press of Kentucky, 2006), 213. Sito's book is extremely useful for animation historians, since it deals extensively with labor issues in the industry, something rarely discussed in other texts.

10. Keith Scott, *The Moose That Roared: The Story of Jay Ward, Bill Scott, a Flying Squirrel and a Talking Moose* (New York: Thomas Dunne Books/St. Martin's Griffin, 2000), 4. This is in many ways the definitive study of Ward and his studio.

11. Ibid., 6-7.

12. Alex Anderson, quoted in Jeff Kiseloff, *The Box: An Oral History of Television* (New York: Viking, 1995), 456.

13. Scott, 10.

14. Alex Anderson, quoted in Kiseloff, 456.

15. Scott, 9, 12-13.

16. Ibid., 14-15.

17. Ibid., 15.

18. Hal Erickson, *Television Cartoon Shows: An Illustrated Encyclopedia, 1949-2003*, 2d ed., 2 vols. (Jefferson, NC: McFarland, 2005), 1: 225. This is a historic and seminal text for understanding the evolution of television animation in America, even if one disagrees with the opinions Erickson provides for the individual programs.

19. Scott, 19.

20. Ibid.

21. An exception to this is the issuing of two story cycles, "Crusader Rabbit vs. the State of Texas" and "Crusader Rabbit vs. the Pirates," on Rhino Home Video in 1991. See Erickson, 225. [WHICH VOL?]

22. Ibid.

23. Reproduced in Scott, 22.

24. Ibid., 24-25.

25. Ibid., 26-27.

26. Erickson, 1: 225–226.
27. Erickson, 2: 839.
28. Ibid.
29. For a history of this programming genre, see Tim Hollis, *Hi There, Boys and Girls: America's Local Children's TV Programs* (Jackson: University of Mississippi Press, 2001).
30. Erickson, 1:13.
31. For an understanding of these studios and their work during this period, as well as generous examples of their artwork, see Amid Amidi, *Cartoon Modern: Style and Design in Fifties Animation* (San Francisco: Chronicle Books, 2006).
32. Sito, 189.

Chapter 3

1. The work of Hanna and Barbera has been extensively documented, more than that of their peers, reflecting their exalted status within and outside of the American television animation community. For books on the studio's output, see Ted Sennett, *The Art of Hanna-Barbera* (New York: Viking, 1989); Michael Mallory, *Hanna-Barbera Cartoons* (New York: Hugh Lauter Levin Associates, 1998); and Jerry Beck, *The Hanna-Barbera Treasury* (San Rafael, CA: Insight Editions, 2007). Equally valuable and revelatory are the two men's autobiographies: Joseph Barbera, *My Life in 'Toons* (Atlanta: Turner, 1994), and William Hanna and Tom Ito, *A Cast of Friends* (New York: Da Capo, 2000 [1996]).
2. Barbera, 25–26.
3. For a detailed analysis of the films, see Sennett, 13–45. For a full-length version of same, see Patrick Brion, *Tom and Jerry* (New York: Crown, 1990).
4. Joseph Barbera, quoted in Sennett, 45.
5. Hanna and Ito, 77.
6. In the early 1960s, the company moved to a specially-built facility on Cahuenga Boulevard, where it remained well into the 1990s. The building is currently occupied by its corporate (and, in many ways, ideological) successor, Cartoon Network Studios.
7. Sennett, 49.
8. Barbera, 136.
9. Mallory, 32–36.
10. Ibid., 37–38.
11. For more on Butler's life and career, see Ben Ohmart and Joe Bevilacqua, *Daws Butler: Characters Actor* (Boalsberg, PA: Bear Manor Media, 2005). For background on Messick, see "Don Messick," Wikipedia.org. See also Mallory, 38–39.
12. See the section on Bob Clampett at the end of this chapter.
13. Barbera, 123.
14. Erik Barnouw, *The Sponsor: Notes on a Modern Potentate* (New York: Oxford University Press, 1978).
15. Barbera, 124–126.
16. Quoted in Barbera, 134.
17. Hanna and Ito, 101.
18. Sennett, 52.
19. Ibid.
20. Hal Erickson, *Television Cartoon Shows: An Illustrated Encyclopedia, 1949–2003*, 2d ed., 2 vols. (Jefferson, NC: McFarland, 2005), 1: 420.
21. Hanna and Ito, 102.
22. Daws Butler, quoted in Sennett, 59.
23. Ibid.
24. For an extended study of anthropomorphism in animation and its hidden meanings, see Paul Wells, *The Animated Bestiary: Animals, Cartoons and Culture* (New Brunswick: Rutgers University Press, 2009).
25. Erickson, 2: 932.
26. Ibid.
27. For an extensive history of the Western as a TV genre, see Gary Yoggy, *Riding the Video Range: The Rise and Fall of the Western on Television* (Jefferson, NC: McFarland, 1995).
28. Yogi was replaced during the final season of the *Huckleberry Hound* series by "Hokey Wolf," featuring the title character, a lupine con artist (Daws Butler impersonating Phil Silvers), and his small fox sidekick, Ding-a-Ling (Doug Young). This series essentially followed the same con-artist format as had earlier projects. See Erickson, 1: 420.
29. Erving Goffman, *The Presentation of Self in Everyday Life* (Garden City, NY: Doubleday, 1959).
30. For a complete episode list, see Mallory, 132–141.
31. Alexander Burnham, "Bert Lahr Wins Right to Sue Over Mimicking of His Style," *New York Times*, March 29, 1962.
32. Ohmart and Bevilacqua, 112–113.
33. Erickson, 2: 933.
34. Hanna and Ito, 111.
35. Barbera, 5.
36. For a complete historical overview of this groundbreaking series, see T.R. Adams, *The Flintstones: A Modern Stone Age Phenomenon* (Atlanta: Turner, 1994).
37. Joseph Barbera, quoted in Sennett, 80–81.
38. Joseph Barbera, quoted in Sennett, 81.
39. Joseph Barbera, quoted in Sennett, 83.
40. For a fuller discussion of the political implications of this sub-genre, see Lynn Spigel, "From Domestic Space to Outer Space: The 1960s Fantastic Family Sitcom," in Spigel, *Welcome to the Dreamhouse: Popular Media and Postwar Suburbs* (Durham: Duke University Press, 2007), 107–140.
41. Spigel, "From Domestic Space," 107–140.
42. Jack Gould, "TV: Animated Cartoons—'The Flintstones' in Debut on Channel 7," *New York Times*, October 1, 1960.
43. This division becomes most apparent when comparing the plotlines of the two periods. Early episodes tended to focus more on social concerns in line with the perceived "adult" audience—i.e., joint ownership of property ("The Swimming Pool"), efforts to improve one's economic stature through ownership of a small business ("The Drive-In"), and social conflicts between husbands and wives ("The Flintstone Flyer," series pilot). By 1963, however, with the shift towards a perceived child-dominated audience, fantasy had become

the dominant component, involving such elements as alien invasion ("Ten Little Flintstones"), miniaturization ("Itty Bitty Fred"), mad scientists ("Dr. Sinister"), and restrained elements of Gothic horror and the supernatural ("The Gruesomes"). In both contexts, however, the essential appearance and mindset of the characters did not change. For a listing of episode synopses, see Mallory, 86–129, and Adams, 146–187.

44. For a biographical study of this actor, see Alan Reed and Ben Ohmart, *Yabba Dabba Doo ... or Never a Star: The Alan Reed Story* (Albany, GA: Bear Manor Media, 2009).

45. K.A. Cuordileone, *Manhood and American Popular Culture in the Cold War* (New York: Routledge, 2005), 138.

46. Mallory, 107.

47. M. Keith Booker, *Drawn to Television: Prime Time Animation from* The Flintstones *to* Family Guy (Westport, CT: Praeger, 2006), 5.

48. Erickson, 1: 340.

49. This point was raised both by scholars of the time and contemporary historians to suggest ways that men were limited in the home in ways that they were not in more public settings. For a historical overview, see William H. Whyte, Jr., *The Organization Man* (Garden City, NY: Doubleday, 1957), and David Reisman, Nathan Glazer and Reuel Denny, *The Lonely Crowd* (New Haven: Yale University Press, 1969 [1950]). For historical and contemporary views of manhood and its evolution (or, to some, de-evolution), see Cuordileone, *Manhood and American Political Culture in the Cold War*; R.W. Connell, *Masculinities*, 2d ed. (Berkeley: University of California Press, 2005); Michael S. Kimmel, *Manhood in America: A Cultural History*, 2d ed. (New York: Oxford University Press, 2006); James Gilbert, *Men in the Middle: Searching for Masculinity in the 1950s* (Chicago: University of Chicago Press, 2005); John F. Kasson, *Houdini, Tarzan and the Perfect Man: The White Male Body and the Challenge of Modernity in America* (New York: Hill and Wang, 2001); and Gary Cross, *Men to Boys: The Making of Modern Immaturity* (New York: Columbia University Press, 2008).

50. Most prominently in "The Golf Champion" (1960; here called the Loyal Order of Dinosaurs); "The Beauty Contest" (1962); "The Picnic" (1962); "Here's Snow in Your Eyes" (1962); "The Buffalo Convention" (1962); "Ladies Night at the Lodge" (1964); "Pebbles' Birthday Party" (1964); and "Masquerade Party" (1966). See Mallory, 86–129, and Adams, 146–187.

51. A term that has since entered the North American vocabulary for someone perceived to be a power broker or bigwig.

52. This allowed the program to enter and satirize the social debates on the influence of parenting on child development and the emergence of numerous "experts" on child rearing. See Gilbert, *Men in the Middle*, 20–21.

53. Booker, 5.

54. Brooks Atkinson, "Critic at Large—Cartoon *Flintstones* Possesses Freshness Rarely Found in TV Comedy," *New York Times*, October 4, 1963.

55. Paul Wells, *Animation in America* (New Brunswick: Rutgers University Press, 2002), 93–94.

56. Mallory, 90.

57. Ibid., 114.

58. Barbera, 142.

59. For a production history, see Erickson, 2: 864–866.

60. For information on the Silvers series, see Tim Brooks and Earle Marsh, *The Complete Directory to Prime Time Network and Cable TV Shows*, 8th ed. (New York: Ballantine, 2003), 934.

61. Val Adams. "News of TV and Radio-Cartoons," *New York Times*, September 24, 1961.

62. John Stephenson, quoted in Sennett, 116.

63. Booker, 36–37.

64. Ibid., 36.

65. For a lengthier discussion of these ideas and their implications, see Thomas Sugrue, *The Origins of the Urban Crisis: Race and Inequality in Postwar Detroit* (Princeton: Princeton University Press, 2005 [1996]).

66. For more on this idea, see Whyte, *The Organization Man*; Riesman, Glazer and Denny, *The Lonely Crowd*; and Cuordileone, *Manhood and Popular Culture in the Cold War*.

67. For a listing of episode summaries, see Mallory, 146–153.

68. Erickson, 2: 865.

69. For a production history, see Erickson, 1: 445–449. For an episode guide, see Mallory, 156–164.

70. Lisa Yaszek, *Galactic Suburbia: Recovering Women's Science Fiction* (Columbus: Ohio State University Press, 2008), 3–4.

71. Due to this, George conforms to the attitudes defined by Whyte in *The Organization Man* towards suppressing individual interests in favor of the company's interest. His deference towards Mr. Spacely provides a sharp contrast to his controlling patriarchal interests at home.

72. *The Jetsons: The Complete First Season*, Warner Home Video, Disc 2, Episode 14.

73. Ibid., Disc 4, Episode 22.

74. Ibid., Disc 1, Episode 2.

75. This was a popular cultural stereotype that producers latched on to for "comic" effect. For the evolution of the type, see Grace Palladino, *Teenagers: An American History* (New York: Basic Books, 1996), and Ilana Nash, *American Sweethearts: Teenage Girls in Twentieth Century Popular Culture* (Bloomington: Indiana University Press, 2006).

76. For a study of the early evolution of rock and roll and the opposition which existed to it in its earliest years, see Ed Ward, Geoffrey Stokes and Ken Tucker, *Rock of Ages:* The Rolling Stone History of Rock 'n' Roll (New York: Summit, 1986).

77. For a production history, see Erickson, 1: 452–456. For a list of episodes, see Mallory, 170–177.

78. Christopher Lehman, *American Animated Cartoons of the Vietnam Era: A Study of Social Commentary in Films and Television Programs, 1961–1973* (Jefferson, NC: McFarland, 2006), 47–48. See also J. Fred MacDonald, *Television and the Red Menace: The Video Road*

to Vietnam (New York: Praeger, 1985) for an understanding of the impact of the political atmosphere of the time on television depictions of foreign affairs issues.

79. Booker, 31.
80. Ibid., 32.
81. Sennett, 121.
82. Ibid., 123.
83. Hal Erickson notes that this character was intended as a parody of Chester Goode (Emmy-winner Dennis Weaver), the limping deputy of Marshall Matt Dillon (James Arness), on *Gunsmoke* (CBS 1955–75), right down to Chester's practice of making bad coffee! See Erickson, 2: 523.
84. Sennett, 126.
85. For a biographical study of this controversial figure, see Sally Bedell, *Up the Tube: Prime Time TV and the Silverman Years* (New York: Viking, 1981), which concentrates on the later aspects of his career at the expense of his pioneering work in Saturday morning television and elsewhere. Saturday morning television will be discussed more extensively in the following chapter.
86. Fred Silverman, quoted in Sennett, 137.
87. Ken Spears, quoted in Sennett, 137.
88. Alex Toth, quoted in Sennett, 140.
89. Joseph Barbera, quoted in Sennett, 141.
90. Sennett, 138–139. The "and" in the title of this series, and its later contemporaries, does not imply co-equality among the features, nor that they appeared together. The segment billed first was the lead feature, with two segments per episode; the second was the supporting feature, appearing only once.
91. Sennett, 141.
92. Warner Home Video issued the series on DVD in 2011, for sale exclusively through Amazon.com and the company's website. I do not have access to it at this time.
93. Fred Silverman, quoted in Sennett, 144.
94. Ibid., 148.
95. For the history and evolution of the company, see in particular Les Daniels, *Marvel: Five Fabulous Decades of the World's Greatest Comics* (New York: Harry N. Abrams, 1991); Stan Lee and George Mair, *Excelsior! The Amazing Life of Stan Lee* (New York: Fireside, 2002); Jordan Raphael and Tom Spurgeon, *Stan Lee and the Rise and Fall of the American Comic Book* (Chicago: Chicago Review Press, 2003); and Ronin Ro, *Tales to Astonish: Jack Kirby, Stan Lee and the American Comic Book Revolution* (New York: Bloomsbury, 2004). While, at this time, the company leased its characters to other producers, it would, in the 1980s, develop its own production facilities to animate its own characters and others. This aspect of the company will be discussed elsewhere in this book.
96. Sennett, 150. The issue of the perception of violence in the narratives as opposed to its actual *presence*, and, indeed, what actually constitutes or should constitute "violence" in media narratives will be discussed in Chapter 4.
97. ACT and its impact will be more fully discussed in Chapter 4.
98. Joseph Barbera, quoted in Sennett, 151.

99. Fred Silverman, quoted in Sennett, 151.
100. Sennett, 153.
101. For a biographical study of this pioneering homosexual comedian, film and TV character actor and long-time center square in the original version of *Hollywood Squares*, see Joe Florenski and Steve Wilson, *Center Square: The Paul Lynde Story* (New York: Advocate Books, 2005). Lynde's legacy endures in television animation beyond his death, as Seth MacFarlane's portrayal of Roger the alien on *American Dad* is an evocative re-creation of Lynde's trademark sibilant vocal style.
102. For a biography of this durable animation and live-action performer, see Gary Owens and Jeff Lenburg, *How to Make a Million Dollars with Your Voice (or Lose Your Tonsils Trying)*, (New York: McGraw-Hill, 2004). For his arguably most famous role, see Hal Erickson, *From Beautiful Downtown Burbank: A Critical History of Rowan and Martin's Laugh-In* (Jefferson, NC: McFarland, 2000).
103. Barbera, 120. In the 1980s the company was acquired by the Great American Broadcasting concern, which acquired much of Taft's assets. In 1991, Turner Broadcasting acquired the company and folded it into its cable empire, with the now semi-retired Hanna and Barbera sharing the title of chairman of the board. They also served as members of the board of Cartoon Network when it was created in 1995, and were retained in honorary positions following Time Warner's acquisition of Turner's assets in 1996, which they held until their respective deaths (Hanna in 2001, Barbera in 2006).
104. Sennett, 158–159; Erickson, 2: 721.
105. Fred Silverman, quoted in Sennett, 159.
106. See Timothy Burke and Kevin Burke, *Saturday Morning Fever: Growing Up with Cartoon Culture* (New York: St. Martin's Griffin, 1999), 105–111, for a well done deconstruction of the series.
107. Ibid.
108. For the complete history of the Ward studio, see Keith Scott, *The Moose That Roared: The Story of Jay Ward, Bill Scott, a Flying Squirrel and a Talking Moose* (New York: Thomas Dunne Books/St. Martin's Griffin, 2000). A production history is featured in Erickson, 2: 677–685. Also of potential use and value is Louis Chunovic, *The Rocky and Bullwinkle Book* (New York: Bantam, 1996).
109. Scott, 44–45.
110. Ibid., 32–35.
111. Ibid., 37–41.
112. Ibid., 41–43.
113. Bill Scott, quoted in Scott, 45–46.
114. Scott, 46–47.
115. Ibid., 48.
116. Ibid., 49–51. See also Frees' biography by Ben Ohmart, *Welcome Foolish Mortals: The Life and Voices of Paul Frees* (Albany, GA: Bear Manor Media, 2004), esp. 84–91.
117. Scott, 51–53. See also June Foray, Mark Evanier and Earl Kress, *Did You Grow Up with Me, Too? The Autobiography of June Foray* (Albany, GA: Bear Manor Media, 2009), esp. 93–103.

118. Scott, 56.

119. Ibid., 54–57. See also "William Conrad," Wikipedia.org.

120. Scott, 118.

121. Ibid. For a biographical sketch of Horton, see Anthony Slide, *Eccentrics of Comedy* (Lanham, MD: Scarecrow Press, 1998).

122. Scott, 153.

123. Chunovic, 32.

124. Ephraim Katz, Fred Klein and Ronald Dean Nolan, *The Film Encyclopedia, 3d ed.* (New York: Harper Perennial, 1998), 285.

125. Scott, 127–128. For a full-length biography, see Ben Ohmart and Charles Stumpf, *Walter Tetley: For Corn's Sake* (Albany, GA: Bear Manor Media, 2004).

126. For Butler's work with Ward, see Scott, 119–121.

127. Ibid., 79. This company was also responsible for producing the animation for Total Television Productions (see below in "Other Voices"), which ultimately led to erroneous confusion and conflagration between Ward and Total Television's work that persisted for a number of years. The studio remained in its existence until 1969, when General Mills withdrew its sponsorship. Ward, for his post–*Rocky and Bullwinkle* projects, returned to centralizing his product in the Los Angeles area.

128. Erickson, 2: 681.

129. MacDonald, in *Television and the Red Menace*, provides a lengthy discussion of the creative context in which these characters and others like them existed.

130. *Rocky and Bullwinkle and Friends: The Complete Series 1959–1964*, Season 3, Disc 4, Episodes 28–33.

131. Ibid., Season 4, Disc 1, Episodes 6–9.

132. Ibid., all discs. The series is also discussed on pp. 29–31 of the booklet accompanying the set.

133. Stefan Kanfer, *Serious Business: The Art and Commerce of Animation in America from Betty Boop to Toy Story* (New York: Scribner, 1997), 207.

134. Scott, 125; Erickson, 2: 678.

135. Jay Ward, quoted in Scott, 125.

136. Pierre Berton, *Hollywood's Canada: The Americanization of Our National Image* (Toronto: McClelland and Stewart, 1975).

137. Jay Ward, quoted in Scott, 122.

138. Dwight Newton, quoted in Scott, 154.

139. Scott, 154.

140. For an extended discussion of this conflict, see ibid., 154–157, and Erickson, 2: 683.

141. Chunovic, 56–66, 73.

142. Ibid., 68–69.

143. Ibid., 67–68; Erickson, 2: 684.

144. Erickson, 2: 684.

145. Scott, 214–219.

146. Ibid., 224.

147. Erickson, 1: 415–416.

148. Ibid., 1: 416.

149. For the history of this groundbreaking science fiction/fantasy anthology series, see Marc Scott Zicree, *The Twilight Zone Companion* (New York: Bantam, 1982).

150. Scott, 243–255.

151. Quoted in Erickson, 1: 368.

152. Scott, 262–263.

153. Ibid.

154. Erickson, 1: 369.

155. Ibid., 1: 368.

156. Ibid., 1: 369.

157. Scott, 294–307.

158. Jay Ward, quoted in Scott, 275–276.

159. Scott, 305–306.

160. Ibid., 309–311.

161. Erickson, 1: 478.

162. For the Val-Mar/Gamma connection, see Scott, 255–256. For an overview of the company's history, see Buck Biggers and Chet Stover, *How Underdog Was Born* (Boalsberg, PA: BearManor Media, 2005).

163. Erickson, 1: 478–479.

164. Ibid., 2: 841.

165. Ibid., 2: 883–884.

166. Ibid., 2: 883.

167. Ibid., 1: 124.

168. For the history of the company, see Rick Goldschmidt, *The Enchanted World of Rankin/Bass: A Portfolio* (Issaquah, WA: Tiger Mountain Press, 1997), and Rick Goldschmidt, *Rudolph the Red Nosed Reindeer: The Making of the Rankin/Bass Holiday Classic* (Bridgeview, IL: Miser Brothers Press, 2001). For shorter biographical studies, see Jeff Lenburg, *Who's Who in Animated Cartoons: An International Guide to Film and Television's Award-Winning and Legendary Animators* (New York: Applause Theatre and Cinema Books, 2006), 23–24 and 297–98.

169. Arthur Rankin, Jr., quoted in Lenburg, *Who's Who*, 297.

170. Goldschmidt, *Enchanted World*, 8–9, 11–13, 90–99.

171. For fuller details, see Goldschmidt, *Enchanted World*, 2–23, and Goldschmidt, *Rudolph the Red Nosed Reindeer*.

172. Arthur Rankin, Jr., quoted in Goldschmidt, *Enchanted World*, 3.

173. Lenburg, *Who's Who*, 93–95.

174. Leonard Maltin, *Of Mice and Magic: A History of American Animated Cartoons* (New York: Plume, 1987), 276.

175. Ibid., 345; Erickson, 2: 614–617.

176. See Erickson, 2: 806–807.

177. David DePatie, quoted in Erickson, 2: 807.

178. Ibid., 1: 408–409.

179. Maltin, 319.

180. Erickson, 2: 635.

181. For analysis of the individual segments based on studio origin, see Erickson, 2: 632–637, and Fred Grandinetti, *Popeye: An Illustrated History of E.C. Segar's Character in Print, Radio, Television and Film Appearances, 1929–1993* (Jefferson, NC: McFarland, 1994), 62–68.

182. Erickson, 2: 476–477.

183. Ibid., 1: 127–128. See also Mitch Axelrod, *Beatletoons: The Real Story Behind the Cartoon Beatles* (New York: Wynn, 1991).

184. Ibid., 1: 213.
185. Maltin, 338; Erickson, 1: 370–371.
186. Maltin, 338.
187. Ibid., 342.
188. Erickson, 2: 556.
189. Ibid., 1: 245.
190. Maltin, 147.
191. Paul Terry, quoted in Maltin, 147.
192. Maltin, 147–148.
193. Alex McNeil, *Total Television, 4th ed.* (New York: Penguin, 1996), 129.
194. Erickson, 2: 546–547.
195. Maltin, 151.
196. Erickson, 1: 65.
197. Maltin, 153–154; Erickson, 1: 241–242.
198. Maltin, 153; Erickson, 1: 401–402.
199. Erickson, 1: 99.
200. Jon Gibson and Chris McDonnell, *Unfiltered: The Complete Ralph Bakshi* (New York: Universe, 2008).
201. Maltin, 155.
202. For the history and development of their two most famous specials, see Lee Mendelson with Bill Melendez, *"A Charlie Brown Christmas": The Making of a Tradition*, ed. Antonia Felix (New York: Harper, 2005), and Lee Mendelson and Bill Melendez, *"It's the Great Pumpkin, Charlie Brown": The Making of a Television Classic* (New York: Harper, 2006).
203. David Michaelis, *Schulz and Peanuts: A Biography* (New York: HarperCollins, 2007), 346.
204. Lenburg. *Who's Who*, 235–237.
205. Ibid., 237.
206. Michaelis, 347.
207. Ibid., 347–349, 357–358.
208. Lee Mendelson, quoted in Lenburg, *Who's Who*, 237.
209. Chuck Jones, quoted in Maltin, 307.
210. Ibid., 308.
211. For an essential Seuss biography, which significantly discusses his work in animation, see Judith and Neil Morgan, *Dr. Seuss and Mr. Geisel* (New York: Random House, 1995).
212. Chuck Jones, *Chuck Amuck: The Life and Times of an Animated Cartoonist* (New York: Farrar, Straus and Giroux, 1999 [1989]), 274.
213. Jeff Lenburg, *The Encyclopedia of Animated Cartoons, 3d ed.* (New York: Checkmark, 1999), 291–292; Jones, 274.
214. Lenburg, *Encyclopedia*, 359.
215. Chuck Jones, quoted in Maltin, 308.
216. For biographical information on Clampett, see Lenburg, *Who's Who*, 45–48, and Jeff Lenburg, *The Great Cartoon Directors* (New York: Da Capo, 1993 [1983]), 93–122.
217. Erickson, 1: 126.
218. Ibid.
219. Lenburg, *Who's Who*, 49–50.
220. Art Clokey, quoted in Lenburg, *Who's Who*, 50.
221. Erickson, 1: 387.
222. Lenburg, *Who's Who*, 50–51.
223. Erickson, 1: 388.
224. Art Clokey, quoted in Lenburg, *Who's Who*, 50.
225. Erickson, 1: 236; Lenburg, *Who's Who*, 50–51.
226. Lenburg, *Who's Who*, 51.
227. For further biographical information about Oriolo see Lenburg, *Who's Who*, 270–271, and John Canemaker, *Felix: The Twisted Tale of the World's Most Famous Cat* (New York: Pantheon, 1991), 147–152.
228. For the media history of this character, see Lenburg, *Who's Who*, 270; Maltin, 313–316; and Erickson, 1: 188–190.
229. Erickson, 1: 325.
230. Canemaker, 150.
231. Erickson, 1: 326.
232. Ibid., 1: 450–451; 2: 543.
233. Ibid., 2: 528–530.
234. For Culhane's version of his relationship with Krantz, see Shamus Culhane, *Talking Animals and Other People* (New York: St. Martin's Press, 1986). See also Maltin, 321–322.
235. Erickson, 2: 529.
236. Ibid., 2:777–780. For a slightly more detailed study of the series, see Edward Gross, *Spider-Man Confidential: From Comic Icon to Hollywood Hero* (New York: Hyperion, 2002), 108–120.
237. Erickson, 2: 675.
238. Karen Mazurkewich, *Cartoon Capers: The Adventures of Canadian Animators* (Toronto: McArthur, 1999), 96, 132.
239. Erickson, 2: 534.
240. Ibid., 1: 352.
241. Ibid., 1: 686.
242. Ibid., 1: 416–417.
243. Ibid., 2: 751.
244. Lenburg, *Who's Who*, 78–79.
245. Fred Bronson, *The Billboard Book of Number One Hits* (New York: Billboard Books, 1992), 36, 47.
246. Erickson, 1: 514.
247. "Hal Seeger," Wikipedia.org.
248. Erickson, 2: 598–599.
249. Ibid., 2: 551–553.
250. Ibid., 1: 113–114.
251. Ibid., 1: 65.
252. Ibid., 161.
253. Ibid., 1: 217–218.
254. Ibid., 1: 748.
255. "Larry Harmon," Wikipedia.org.
256. Erickson, 1: 154.
257. Ibid., 1: 488–489.
258. Ibid., 1: 497–498.
259. Ibid., 1: 172–173.
260. For a thorough study of the radio and television programs, see Melvin Patrick Ely, *The Adventures of Amos 'n' Andy: A Social History of an American Phenomenon* (New York: Free Press, 1991).

Chapter 4

1. An excellent overview of life and politics in the late 1960s and 1970s is found in Rick Perlstein, *Nixonland: The Rise of a President and the Fracturing of America* (New York: Scribner, 2008).

2. ACT's identification of itself as a "grassroots" organization of concerned parents gave it considerable leverage in this debate. Because they were parents themselves, they were concerned deeply with their children's exposure to the more damaging aspects of television, in particular violence and the commerical nature of Saturday morning television. Such concerns were also at the heart of the formation of the Children's Television Workshop (CTW) during this period. CTW's entrance into television production, first on the publicly-funded National Educational Television (NET), and then on its successor, the Public Broadcasting Service (PBS)—particularly with its most famous program, *Sesame Street*—tipped the scales considerably in the argument for educational elements within programming directly aimed at children. This would have severe consequences for the future of television animation. For a study of ACT's activities and network television's reaction to them, see Heather Hendershot, *Saturday Morning Censors: Television Regulation Before the V Chip* (Durham: Duke University Press, 1998). A recent and excellent study of the CTW through the lens of its most famous program is Michael Davis, *Street Gang: The Complete History of Sesame Street* (New York: Viking, 2008).

3. Hendershot, 21.

4. For a discussion of the debate over violence in the media, see Harold Schechter, *Savage Pastimes: A Cultural History of Violent Entertainment* (New York: St. Martin's Press, 2005).

5. Janet M. Davis, *The Circus Age: Culture and Society Under the American Big Top* (Chapel Hill: University of North Carolina Press, 2002), 30–32.

6. Brander Matthews, quoted in Michael Denning, *Mechanic Accents: Dime Novels and Working Class Culture in America*, 2d ed. (London: Verso, 1998), 9. For a full historical view of the form, see J. Randolph Cox, *The Dime Novel Companion: A Source Book* (Westport, CT: Greenwood Books, 2000).

7. For a comprehensive historical study of vaudeville and its influence, see Robert W. Snyder, *The Voice of the City: Vaudeville and Popular Culture in New York* (Chicago: Ivan R. Dee, 2000).

8. Robert Sklar, *Movie Made America: A Cultural History of American Movies* (London: Chappell, 1978 [1975]), 18.

9. Ibid., 134–140.

10. For a history of this document and its most strident enforcer, see Thomas Doherty, *Hollywood's Censor: Joseph I. Breen and the Production Code Administration* (New York: Columbia University Press, 2007).

11. Lynn Spigel, "Seducing the Innocent: Television and Childhood in Postwar America," in *Welcome to the Dreamhouse: Popular Media and Postwar Suburbs* (Durham: Duke University Press, 2007), 186.

12. Ibid.

13. Ibid., 186–193.

14. Reproduced in ibid., 194.

15. For a full history of this ongoing debate, and its impact on both American children and the media, see Stephen Mintz, *Huck's Raft: A History of American Childhood* (Cambridge: Belknap/Harvard University Press, 2004), Mintz's central metaphor—using Huckleberry Finn's Mississippi river raft as a symbol for the turbulence and instability of childhood—is perfectly suited to studying both the debates over American television animation and the personalities of many of its younger characters.

16. For an overview of child-rearing ideas in this period, such as the influential ones of Dr. Benjamin Spock, see Paula S. Fass, "Bringing It Home: Children, Family and Technology in the Postwar World," in Mark C. Carnes, ed., *The Columbia History of Post–World War II America* (New York: Columbia University Press, 2007), 79–105.

17. Lawrence Undang, ed., *The Random House Dictionary of the English Language: College Edition* (New York: Random House, 1968), 1469.

18. Les Brown, "TV Enlists Educators to Aid in Children's Shows," *New York Times*, April 4, 1974.

19. Jack Gould, "Of Scapegoats and Headlines," *New York Times*, July 13, 1969.

20. Critics argued that, out of misguided animation for animated characters, children might conceivably act out their performances and injure or kill themselves as a result. The "imitation" argument was given considerable force in 1993, when a five-year-old Ohio boy burned his house down with a cigarette lighter, supposedly under the influence of the television animation program *Beavis and Butthead*. See Stefan Kanfer, *Serious Business: The Art and Commerce of Animation in America from Betty Boop to* Toy Story (New York: Scribner, 1997), 206–208, 226.

21. Timothy Burke and Kevin Burke, *Saturday Morning Fever: Growing Up with Cartoon Culture* (New York: St. Martin's Griffin, 1999), 2.

22. Walter Lantz, quoted in Danny Peary, "Reminiscing with Walter Lantz," in Danny Peary and Gerald Peary, ed., *The American Animated Cartoon: A Critical Anthology* (New York: E.P. Dutton, 1980), 199.

23. See Hanna and Barbera quotes in Ted Sennett, *The Art of Hanna-Barbera* (New York: Viking, 1988), 42.

24. As recently as 2001, the surgeon general was reporting that "the label 'violence' is [or should be] reserved for the most extreme end of the physical aggression spectrum," which calls into question earlier, broader-based definitions of the term used to attack television animation in the 1960s and 1970s. See Rose M. Kundanis, *Children, Teens, Families and Mass Media: The Millennial Generation* (Mahwah, NJ: Lawrence Erlbaum Associates, 2003), 72.

25. Jason Mittell, "The Great Saturday Morning Exile: Scheduling Cartoons on Television's Periphery in the 1960s," in Carol A. Stabile and Mark Harrison, ed., *Prime Time Animation: Television Animation and American Culture* (New York: Routledge, 2003), 51.

26. Terry Ramsaye, quoted in Leonard Maltin, *Of Mice and Magic: A History of American Animated Cartoons* (New York: Plume, 1987), 37.

27. Kanfer, 182.

28. Newton Minow, quoted in Kanfer, 191.

29. Walter Lantz, quoted in Maltin, 182.

30. However, later reissues of these films for home viewing, first on VHS and later on DVD, have done much to rectify this problem by presenting the original theatrical release prints.

31. The history and evolution of the field is told in Gerard Jones, *Men of Tomorrow: Geeks, Gangsters and the Birth of the Comic Book* (New York: Basic Books, 2004).

32. Spigel, "Seducing the Innocent," 191–192.

33. For a monograph-length study of Wertham's life and career, and his negative impact on the evolution of American comics and television, see Bart Beaty, *Frederic Wertham and the Critique of Mass Culture* (Jackson: University Press of Mississippi, 2005).

34. David Hajdu, *The Ten Cent Plague: The Great Comic Book Scare and How It Changed America* (New York: Farrar, Straus and Giroux, 2008), 97–103, 229–244.

35. Ibid., 107.

36. Ibid., 116–117.

37. Ibid., 278–282.

38. Amy Kiste Nyberg discussed the history and evolution of the Code in *Seal of Approval: The History of the Comics Code* (Jackson: University of Mississippi Press, 1998).

39. Joseph Barbera, quoted in Sennett, 151.

40. The nadir of this was perhaps most notably FCC Chairman Nicholas Johnson, in the 1970s, referring to television animation producers as "evil men" and "child molesters" for what he misinterpreted as their intentions for manipulating their audience. See Hal Erickson, *Television Cartoon Shows: An Illustrated Encyclopedia*, 2d ed., 2 vols. (Jefferson, NC: McFarland, 2005), 1: 25.

41. Philip H. Dougherty, "Advertising: How to Be First on the Block," *New York Times*, January 8, 1967.

42. See, for examples, Carol Rinzler, "Trying to Like Those Saturday TV Kid Shows," *New York Times*, January 25, 1976; John F. McDermott, "The Violent Bugs Bunny et al.," *New York Times*, September 28, 1969; John J. O'Connor, "Laugh It Up, Kiddies—It's Bad for You," *New York Times*, June 18, 1972; Beatrice Berg, "Goodbye Bang Burn Stab Shoot," *New York Times*, November 9, 1969; John Leonard, "Since the Kiddies Are Hooked…Why Not Use TV for a Head Start Program?" *New York Times*, July 14, 1968; Sam Blum, "De-Escalating the Violence on TV," *New York Times*, December 8, 1968; Jane Brody, "TV Violence Cited as Bad Influence," *New York Times*, December 17, 1975; and Jack Gould, "Of Scapegoats and Headlines," *New York Times*, July 13, 1969.

43. Mrs. Irvin Hendryson, quoted in Robert Windeler, "Violence in TV Cartoons Being Toned Down," *New York Times*, July 20, 1968.

44. Joseph Barbera, quoted in Windeler, "Violence…"

45. Dr. Murray Korengold, quoted in Windeler, "Violence…"

46. Dr. Murray Korengold, quoted in Windeler, "Violence…"

47. Dr. Murray Korengold, quoted in Windeler, "Violence…"

48. Chuck Jones, quoted in Digby Diehl, "On Saturdays, Super-Heroes and Talking Animals," *New York Times*, March 5, 1967.

49. David DePatie, quoted in Diehl, "On Saturdays…"

50. See Carmen Luke, *Constructing the Child Viewer: A History of the American Discourse on Television and Children 1950–1980* (Westport, CT: Praeger, 1999), for an overview of many of these studies.

51. Hendershot, 32.

52. Ibid., 209–210, 213–214.

53. Gary Grossman, *Saturday Morning TV* (New York: Dell, 1981), 356.

54. Ibid.

55. Hendershot, 67; Joseph Turow, *Entertainment, Education and the Hard Sell: Three Decades of Network Children's Television* (New York: Praeger, 1981), 84–88.

56. Grossman, 357; Erik Barnouw, *The Sponsor: Notes on a Modern Potentate* (New York: Oxford University Press, 1978), 91–95.

57. Grossman, 356.

58. Hendershot, 81–90.

59. Erickson, 1: 23.

60. Kanfer, 205.

61. Joseph Barbera, quoted in Grossman, 358.

62. Erickson, 1: 26.

63. Quoted in Kanfer, 207.

64. Erickson, 1: 27.

65. Karen Hill-Scott and Horst Stipp, "Saturday Morning Children's Programs on NBC, 1975–2006: A Case Study of Self-Regulation," in Michelle Hilmes, ed., *NBC: America's Network* (Berkeley: University of California Press, 2007), 240–241.

66. Ibid., 241.

67. Ibid., 242–244.

68. Ibid., 251. In recent years, the network has experimented with bringing animation back to its Saturday morning schedule, but these programs are chiefly imports from network-owned cable channels and are not directly commissioned by the network itself, as was the case in the heyday of Saturday morning.

69. Ibid., 249–251.

70. Joseph Barbera, quoted in Hendershot, 210.

71. Erickson, 2: 934.

72. Ibid., 2: 802–804.

73. Ibid., 2: 802.

74. Ibid., 2: 804.

75. Ibid., 2: 802.

76. Timothy Burke and Kevin Burke, *Saturday Morning Fever: Growing Up with Cartoon Culture* (New York: St. Martin's Griffin, 1999), 215.

77. Ibid., 27.

78. See below for further examples of Hanna-Barbera programming during this period.

79. Erickson, 2: 716.

80. Aimee Dorr, quoted in Erickson, 2: 717.

81. Lou Scheimer telephone interviews with author, 2006, 2009. All references to Lou Scheimer and Filmation in this book's text are based on this source unless otherwise cited.

82. Lou Scheimer, quoted in Edward Palmer, *Children in the Cradle of Television* (Lexington, MA: D.C. Heath, 1987), 101.

83. Erickson, 2: 685.
84. Ibid.
85. Ibid., 2: 811.
86. Christopher Lehman, *American Animated Cartoons of the Vietnam Era: A Study of Social Commentary in Films and Television Programs 1961–1973* (Jefferson, NC: McFarland, 2006), 68.
87. Ibid., 79; Erickson, 2: 811.
88. Lehman, 78–79.
89. Erickson, 2: 811.
90. Bruce Scivally, *Superman on Film, Television, Radio and Broadway* (Jefferson, NC: McFarland, 2008), 72.
91. Erickson, 1: 91.
92. Ibid., 1: 92–93. See also Fred Bronson, *The Billboard Book of Number One Hits*, 3d ed. (New York: Billboard Books, 1992), 258, for the history of the production of the record and others like it, and Kim Cooper and David Smay, eds., *Bubblegum Music Is the Naked Truth: The Dark History of Prepubescent Pop, from the Banana Splits to Britney Spears* (Los Angeles: Ferral House, 2001), for a historical overview of the "bubblegum" pop music subgenre of which they were a part.
93. Norm Prescott, quoted in Erickson, 1:93.
94. Erickson, 1: 99.
95. Louis Calta, "Bill Cosby to Star in Children's Show Saturdays on CBS," *New York Times*, April 26, 1972.
96. For biographical studies of Cosby's life and career, see Ronald L. Smith, *The Cosby Book* (New York: S.P.I. Books, 1993), and Bill Adler, *The Cosby Wit: His Life and Humor* (New York: Carroll and Graf, 1986). See also Gerald Nachman, *Seriously Funny: The Rebel Comedians of the 1950s and 1960s* (New York: Pantheon, 2003), 562–590.
97. Quoted in Adler, 105.
98. Ibid., 26.
99. Nachman, 580.
100. Adler, 89.
101. Hendershot, 201; Smith, 126.
102. Smith, 128; Adler, 89–90.
103. Erickson, 1: 323.
104. For the history of the treatment of African Americans on television specifically, see J. Fred MacDonald, *Blacks and White TV: African Americans in Television Since 1948*, 2d ed. (Chicago: Nelson-Hall, 1992), and Donald Bogle, *Prime Time Blues: African Americans on Network Television* (New York: Farrar, Straus and Giroux, 2001). *Fat Albert*, likely due to its "marginal" status as a television animation program, is not discussed significantly in either text.
105. Hendershot, 196.
106. Lehman, 163–164.
107. Historian Thomas Sugrue analyses many of the issues and concerns related to African American and urban origins, which *Fat Albert* frequently drew upon, in his detailed study *The Origins of the Urban Crisis: Race and Inequality in Postwar Detroit* (New Brunswick: Princeton University Press, 2005 [1996]).
108. Lehman, 164, 181.
109. The history of this staple of African-American patois has recently been chronicled by music historian Elijah Wald in *The Dozens: A History of Rap's Mama* (New York: Oxford University Press, 2012).
110. Hendershot, 215.
111. Ibid., 200.
112. This was, of course, a rather simplistic way of dealing with a complex situation for real-life African American urban communities. The drug culture, as shown particularly in the "blaxploitation" film *Superfly* (Gordon Parks, Jr., 1972), was a major problem for urban African American at this time, and a key source of the social, economic and political divisions that continue today. As with many of the issues related to urban African American populations, it was a consequence of the isolation of African Americans in urban ghettoes, which were and are "areas with densely packed tenements and visible poverty, plagued with disease and crime" (Sugrue, *The Origins of the Urban Crisis*, 37). However, as an animated program aimed at children, *Fat Albert* was limited as to how to how it could approach this topic for its audience. Given this limitation, "Dope Is for Dopes" manages to discuss this issue in a constructive and effective manner, making the gravity of the situation apparent to its audience.
113. Hendershot, 199–200.
114. Ibid., 200.
115. Erickson, 1: 324.
116. Hendershot, 208–215.
117. Erickson, 1: 324.
118. Ibid.
119. Hendershot, 206–208. For a concise study of an earlier and more heavily criticized television series with a similar format, see Melvin Patrick Ely, *The Adventures of Amos 'n' Andy: A Social History of an American Phenomenon* (New York: Free Press, 1991).
120. Erickson, 1: 386–387.
121. Historian David J. Skal has examined the evolution and decline of these figures extensively in his work. See in particular *The Monster Show: A Cultural History of Horror* (New York: Norton, 1993), *Screams of Reason: Mad Science and Modern Culture* (New York: Norton, 1998), and *Hollywood Gothic: The Tangled Web of Dracula from Page to Stage to Screen* (New York: Faber and Faber, 2004).
122. Erickson, 2: 553.
123. Quoted in Erickson.
124. Ibid., 1: 24.
125. Ibid., 2: 790.
126. It was also, significantly, the only Best Series Emmy won so far by the cumulative Star Trek franchise, although it has been nominated for and won in many more slightly minor Emmy categories over the years.
127. 2: 791. "Highbrow" in this sense refers to a traditionally-defined bias towards entertainment geared at intelligent consumers, as opposed to "lowbrow," referring to material downplaying this bias in favor of more guttural and visceral content aimed at less discriminating consumers. More recently, a middle ground, called "nobrow," has emerged, balancing elements of both. For lengthier analysis of the terms, see Lawrence Levine, *Highbrow/Lowbrow: The Emergence of Cultural*

Hierarchy in America (Cambridge: Harvard University Press, 1988), and Peter Swirski, *From Lowbrow to Nobrow* (Montreal: McGill-Queen's University Press, 2005).

128. The creation of animation footage by tracing images based on previously filmed live-action footage.

129. Erickson, 2: 942–943.

130. Ibid., 2: 943.

131. Ibid., 2: 881.

132. Ibid., 2: 882.

133. Ibid., 2: 488.

134. Ibid., 2: 730.

135. William Hanna and Tom Ito, *A Cast of Friends* (New York: Da Capo, 2000 [1996]), 193–194.

136. Tom Sito, *Drawing the Line: The Untold Story of Animation Unions from Bosko to Bart Simpson* (Lexington: University Press of Kentucky, 2006), 258.

137. Quoted in Sito, 259.

138. Sito, 260.

139. Quoted in Sito, 260–261.

140. Sito, 261.

141. Lou Scheimer, quoted in Sito, 267.

142. Joseph Barbera, *My Life in Toons* (Atlanta: Turner, 1994), 121.

143. Ibid., 196.

144. Hanna and Ito, 148–149.

145. The most notable signing in this regard was Irish-born singer Danny Hutton, later co-founder of the 1970s rock powerhouse Three Dog Night. See Bronson, 291.

146. Barbera, 176.

147. Tim Brooks and Earle Marsh, *The Complete Directory to Prime Time Network and Cable TV Shows, 8th ed.* (New York: Ballantine, 2003), 502.

148. Barbera, 197–199.

149. By name, *Hey There, It's Yogi Bear*, released in 1964, and *The Man Called Flintstone*, released in 1966. Both were distributed theatrically by Columbia Pictures, the parent company of the studio's then-TV distributor, Screen Gems. (The latter film, in fact, opens with Wilma Flintstone impersonating Columbia's torch-holding female logo.)

150. Barbera, 196–197.

151. Ibid., 225–230.

152. Sennett, 192–201.

153. Ibid., 202–209.

154. This FCC mandated legislation forced the three television networks to make available an evening time slot- which was eventually agreed to be 7:30 p.m. Eastern Standard Time- available to their affiliated stations so this latter group could provide local programming aside from their ubiquitous newscasts in the slot. However, most stations simply could not afford to do this anymore, so they chose instead to fill the slot with programming from syndicators, either new (like *Father*), or old sitcoms, game shows (*Wheel of Fortune* and *Jeopardy*!), or Hollywood-themed "information" programs (*Entertainment Tonight*), the latter groups gaining prominence in the 1980s. See Erickson, 2: 893, for more information.

155. Ibid.

156. Ibid.

157. Ibid., 2: 894.

158. Ibid., 2: 687.

159. This author's candidate for the most improbable and unlikely fictional character name ever devised.

160. As Barbera himself has noted, this was the result of a standoff between producer and network similar to that between CBS and Filmation over *Fat Albert*: the studio wanted to produce new episodes of the series, while the network, citing issues of additional costs, did not. Barbera, 179–181.

161. "Henry Corden," Wikipedia.org. Like Alan Reed, Mel Blanc and Jean Vander Pyl would play their *Flintstones* roles until their own deaths (1989 and 1999, respectively), while the role of Betty simply became a revolving door part.

162. "The first minority heroine in animated cartoons...," according to studio historian Ted Sennett (164).

163. Burke and Burke, 121.

164. Erickson, 1: 384.

165. Sennett, 169.

166. Ibid., 170.

167. For further, deeper analysis of the genre, see Lehman, *American Animated Cartoons of the Vietnam Era*; Donald Bogle, *Toms, Coons, Mulattoes, Mammies and Bucks* (New York: Continuum, 2001 [1973]); and Nelson George, *Blackface* (New York: HarperCollins, 1994).

168. Sennett, 175.

169. Ibid., 176.

170. When Barbera approached Stephenson about the role, Stephenson asked him why he had not simply approached Flynn himself for the part. Barbera responded, significantly, that they had indeed tested Flynn's voice, but that "he didn't sound right" (Sennett, 264).

171. Ibid., 178.

172. A second, more authentic version of the series would be animated by the studio in the 1990s. See Chapter 6.

173. Sennett, 180.

174. For the media history of the character, see Yunte Huang, *Charlie Chan: The Untold Story of the Honorable Detective and his Rendezvous with American History* (New York: W.W. Norton, 2010).

175. Erickson, 1: 396. The Globetrotters themselves did not play themselves in the series (thus setting a precedent for most series featuring real-life athletes in the future), leaving the vocal chores to veteran African American actors, such as Scatman Crothers and Eddie "Rochester" Anderson. For a revealing portrait of the real-life Globetrotter organization, see Ben Green, *Spinning the Globe: The Rise, Fall and Return to Greatness of the Harlem Globetrotters* (New York: Amistad, 2005).

176. Sennett, 183.

177. Ibid.

178. Ibid., 185.

179. Ibid., 187–191. Unfortunately, as Barbera was later to write, things were far less harmonious off-screen on the project than on. The live-action footage Kelly

filmed for the project was not entirely in line with the studio's complementary animation, causing the studio to make a number of necessary cuts and revisions. Kelly was furious when he saw the results, claiming Hanna and Barbera had "really screwed" him with a "terrible job." As a consequence, he blackballed the animators, making NBC threaten them with not airing the project (a decision which was ultimately reversed), and crediting himself as the producer alone when it aired. As a result, Kelly alone accepted the Emmy for the project when it was awarded, even though it was Barbera who suggested the project idea to Kelly in the first place (Barbera, 162–165).

180. For the complete history of the studio, see Rick Goldschmidt, *The Enchanted World of Rankin/Bass: A Portfolio* (Issaquah, WA: Tiger Mountain Press, 1997).

181. Arthur Rankin, Jr., quoted in Goldschmidt, 103.

182. Erickson, 1: 112.

183. Ibid.

184. Ibid., 1: 119–120.

185. For an outline of the Freleng/Seuss relationship, see Judith and Neil Morgan, *Dr. Seuss and Mr. Geisel* (New York: Random House, 1995).

186. "Clerow" was Wilson's real given name, as well as the name of his production company.

187. Friz Freleng, quoted in Jeff Lenburg, *The Encyclopedia of Animated Cartoons*, 3d ed. (New York: Checkmark Books, 2009), 12.

188. Jeff Lenburg. *Who's Who in Animated Cartoons* (New York: Applause Theatre and Cinema Books, 2006), 95.

189. Erickson, 1: 304–305.

190. Ibid., 1: 424.

191. Ibid., 1: 565–566.

192. Daniel Stoffman, *The Nelvana Story: Thirty Animated Years* (Toronto: Nelvana, 2002), 9.

193. For a book-length study of this process, see J. Fred MacDonald, *Television and the Red Menace: The Video Road to Vietnam* (New York: Praeger, 1985).

194. Erickson, 1: 582.

195. Erickson, 2: 914–915.

Chapter 5

1. James L. Baughman, *The Republic of Mass Culture: Journalism, Filmmaking and Broadcasting in America Since 1941*, 3d ed. (Baltimore: Johns Hopkins University Press, 2006 [1992]), 211–212.

2. Quoted in Hal Erickson, *Television Cartoon Shows: An Illustrated Encyclopedia 1949–2003*, 2d ed., 2 vols. (Jefferson, NC: McFarland, 2005), 1: 28.

3. Tom Englehardt, "The Shortcake Strategy," in Todd Gitlin, ed., *Watching Television* (New York: Pantheon, 1986), 88–89.

4. Stan Lee and George Mair. *Excelsior! The Amazing Life of Stan Lee* (New York: Fireside, 2002), 207–208.

5. For the history and establishment of the process of syndication in television, see Hal Erickson, *Syndicated Television: The First Forty Years 1947–1987* (Jefferson, NC: McFarland, 2001).

6. Timothy and Kevin Burke, *Saturday Morning Fever: Growing Up with Cartoon Culture* (New York: St. Martin's Griffin, 1999), 64.

7. Ted Sennett, *The Art of Hanna-Barbera* (New York: Viking, 1988), 215.

8. Fred Silverman, quoted in Sennett, 226.

9. Ibid.

10. Erickson, 2: 753–754.

11. Joseph Barbera, *My Life in 'Toons* (Atlanta: Turner, 1994), 184–185.

12. Gordon Clark, quoted in Erickson, 1: 755.

13. Barbera, 185–186.

14. Sennett, 226.

15. His voice and mannerisms mark him as one of the first, and few, openly "gay" characters in television animation.

16. Quoted in Sennett, 226.

17. The first character of her kind in television animation.

18. Burke and Burke, 162–163.

19. Erickson, 1: 485.

20. Joseph Barbera, quoted in Sennett, 217.

21. Sennett, 218.

22. Erickson, 1: 486.

23. Sennett, 218.

24. Erickson, 2: 738.

25. Ibid., 1: 145.

26. Ibid., 1: 346.

27. Ibid., 2: 638.

28. Ibid., 2: 639.

29. Fred Grandinetti, *Popeye: An Illustrated History of E.C. Segar's Character in Print, Radio, Television and Film Appearances, 1929–1993* (Jefferson, NC: McFarland, 1994), 68–75. Grandinetti also reproduces a script from *The All-New Popeye Hour* on pp. 251–256, which goes to show chiefly how poorly written it was in comparison to the classic Fleischer cartoons.

30. William Hanna and Tom Ito, *A Cast of Friends* (New York: Da Capo, 2000 [1996]), 205.

31. Sennett, 236.

32. Erickson, 1: 757.

33. Ibid.

34. Barbera, 241–242.

35. Erickson, 1: 342.

36. Burke and Burke, 109.

37. Erickson, 1: 210.

38. Barbera, 211.

39. Ibid., 212.

40. Barbera, 213.

41. Sennett, 239.

42. Hanna and Ito, 210–211.

43. Ironically, their old nemesis, ACT founder Peggy Charren, received a similar prize that same year from the Los Angeles-based Academy's sibling organization, the New York-based National Academy of Television Arts and Sciences, at their annual Daytime Emmy ceremonies.

44. Erickson, 2: 861.

45. Ibid., 1: 145.

46. Ibid., 2: 786.
47. For a concise, if sensationalized, history of the company, see Jerry Oppenheimer, *Toy Monster: The Big, Bad World of Mattel* (Hoboken, NJ: John Wiley and Sons, 2009).
48. For the rise and fall of the toy line, see Oppenheimer, 121–133.
49. Erickson, 1: 405.
50. Ibid.
51. Although, as Timothy and Kevin Burke have suggested, "anyone [watching the show] who couldn't figure out the secret was in need of emergency brain surgery" (Burke and Burke, 160).
52. See Charren and Lautenberg quotes in Oppenheimer, 126.
53. Burke and Burke, 160–161.
54. Erickson, 2: 735.
55. Quoted in ibid.
56. Kathleen McDonnell, *Kid Culture: Kids and Adults and Popular Culture* (Toronto: Second Story Press, 1994), 132.
57. Denise Lowe, *Women and American Television: An Encyclopedia* (Santa Barbara: ABC-CLIO, 1999), 15, 25; Gary Cross, *Kids' Stuff: Toys and the Changing World of American Childhood* (Cambridge: Harvard University Press, 1997), 214; Susan Faludi, *Backlash: The Undeclared War Against American Women* (New York: Anchor Books, 1991), 63–64.
58. Burke and Burke, 160.
59. Erickson, 1: 373.
60. Hal Erickson (*Television Cartoon Shows*, 1: 158–159) seems to believe that this was done so subtly that Filmation underplayed it in its publicity for the series because the studio itself seemed to be unaware of it all. I disagree; subtle progressive moves such as this were common under Lou Scheimer's watch, and for him not to have been aware of the lead character's race during the production of the series seems to me to be inconceivable.
61. Tom Sito, *Drawing the Line: The Untold Story of the Animation Unions from Bosko to Bart Simpson* (Lexington: University Press of Kentucky, 2006), 279.
62. Ibid., 279–280.
63. As of this writing, a now-retired Lou Scheimer continues to reside in Los Angeles. The final product of the Filmation studio was the feature film *Happily Ever After*, released in 1990 to limited fanfare. See Jeff Lenburg, *Who's Who in Animated Cartoons* (New York: Applause Theatre and Cinema Books, 2006), 311–313, for a fuller biographical portrait.
64. Sito, 278–279.
65. Walt Disney, quoted in Neal Gabler, *Walt Disney: The Triumph of the American Imagination* (New York: Alfred A. Knopf, 2006), 519–520.
66. Walt Disney, quoted in Gabler, xix.
67. Michael Eisner and Tony Schwartz, *Work in Progress* (New York: Random House, 1998), 19. See also James B. Stewart, *Disney War* (New York: Simon & Schuster, 2005), 22, 24–29.
68. In classic Machiavellian fashion, Eisner later betrayed Roy Edward Disney to secure his hold on the company, prompting the latter to lead a grass-roots campaign against him in the 2000s which played a major role in ending Eisner's tenure at the company. This, however, is irrelevant to the story at hand, and I will not discuss it here. For the full story of these corporate Disney issues, see Stewart book listed above.
69. Stewart, 208–209, 244.
70. Ibid., 2; Eisner and Schwartz, 152.
71. Erickson, 1: 922.
72. For a more detailed episode guide, see Bill Cotter, *The Wonderful World of Disney Television: A Complete History* (New York: Hyperion, 1997), 236–237. This is a remarkably detailed, well-researched book that covers a wide variety of Disney television productions in detail. Unfortunately, there is no information for any programs after 1997; an updated edition, given the great volume of product produced after this date, is very much in order.
73. The majority of the Disney company's television animation productions have placed "Disney's" ahead of the title in official billing (although the possessive apostrophes have been removed in more recent years). Some chroniclers of TV animation history, such as Hal Erickson and Jeff Lenburg, have gone along with this in listing the series in their alphabetical chronologies, but I will not here. The imposition of the company's name in the title implies a suggested level of strict control that distorts the actual production and decision making processes involved with the series, as well as the intent of the actual creators of the work, so I will identify the series in this text by name without referring to the studio in doing so.
74. Erickson, 1: 254–256; Cotter, 237–243.
75. Cotter, 243.
76. Gary Krisel, quoted in Erickson, 1: 293.
77. Ibid., 1: 295.
78. Ibid., 1: 293–294. For a full-length study of Barks and his work, see Thomas Andrae, *Carl Barks and the Disney Comic Book: Unmasking the Myth of Modernity* (Jackson: University of Mississippi Press, 2006).
79. Cotter, 243–248.
80. For an outline of these films and their production, see Christopher Finch, *Disney's Winnie the Pooh: A Celebration of the Silly Old Bear* (New York: Disney Editions, 2000).
81. Ibid., 1: 587.
82. The extent and versatility of Cummings' skill will become apparent to the reader by the number of times his name appears in the voice credits of other series discussed in this book.
83. Erickson, 1: 201.
84. Quoted in ibid.
85. Ibid., 1: 624.
86. Ibid., 1:399.
87. Ibid., 2: 846.
88. Ibid., 2: 601.
89. Ibid., 1: 202.
90. Ibid.
91. Norris would have better luck with TV in the 1990s, when he starred in the hit CBS series *Walker, Texas Ranger*.

92. Erickson, 1: 490.
93. Erickson, 2: 631.
94. The series has been issued on DVD as *Ruby-Spears Superman* to distinguish it from the later Warner series.
95. Erickson, 2: 813.
96. Literally, "Broadcasting, Information and Communication."
97. Erickson, 1:29.
98. Sito, 276.
99. Andy Heyward, quoted in Erickson, 1: 430.
100. Ibid., 1: 186.
101. Burke and Burke, 164.
102. Erickson, 1: 127.
103. DIC only produced the animation for the first season of this series; Saban Entertainment took over for the balance of the run.
104. Haim Saban, quoted in G. Wayne Miller, *Toy Wars* (New York: Random House/Times Books, 1998), 139.
105. Ibid., 145–47, 155–56.
106. Ibid., 138–39.
107. Lenburg, 305–307.
108. Erickson, 1: 359.
109. Lorenzo Music, quoted in Erickson, 1: 359.
110. Erickson, 1: 359.
111. Ibid., 1: 360.
112. Ibid., 1: 360.
113. Mark Evanier, quoted in Erickson, 1: 360.
114. Miller, 140.
115. Erickson, 1: 298.
116. Ibid., 2: 571.
117. Margaret Loesch, quoted in Erickson, 2: 573.
118. Miller, 11–23.
119. Margaret Loesch, quoted in Miller, 140.
120. See Burke and Burke, 170–173, for an effective deconstruction of the project.
121. In the early 2010s, Hasbro revived the project under the title *My Little Pony: Friendship Is Magic*. While the ultra-feminine Ponyland setting and characters were retained, the writing and characterization brought a shade more vinegar into the sweetness, in the fashion of later productions such as *The Powerpuff Girls*. This was no accident when you consider than this *Pony* had as its executive producer Lauren Faust, a veteran *Powerpuff Girls* writer (and the wife of *Powerpuff* creator Craig McCracken, to boot).
122. For the history of the company, see Daniel Stoffman, *The Nelvana Story: Thirty Animated Years* (Toronto: Nelvana, 2002).
123. Erickson, 1: 133.
124. Lenburg, *Who's Who*, 253
125. Erickson. *Television Cartoon Shows*. 2: 835.
126. Jon Gibson and Chris McDonnell. *Unfiltered: The Complete Ralph Bakshi* (New York: Universe, 2008), 211.
127. Erickson, 1: 549, is the source of the quote. The film sequence featuring the act is broken down in Gibson and McDonnell, 214, and shows the true content of the misunderstood segment.
128. Donald Wildmon and Randall Nutton, *Don Wildmon: The Man the Networks Love to Hate* (Wilmore, KY: Bristol Books, 1989), 179–180.
129. Ralph Bakshi, quoted in Gibson and McDonnell, 217.
130. Peter Kenter and Martin Levin, *TV North* (Vancouver: Whitecap Books, 2001), 143.
131. For the history of the company, see Rick Goldschmidt, *The Enchanted World of Rankin-Bass* (Issaquah, WA: Tiger Mountain Press, 1997).
132. Don Duga, quoted in Goldschmidt, 81.
133. Goldschmidt, 83.
134. Peter Bakalian, quoted in Goldschmidt, 119.
135. Arthur Rankin, Jr., quoted in Goldschmidt, 120.
136. Lenburg, *Who's Who*, 298.
137. Jeff Lenburg, *The Encyclopedia of Animated Cartoons* (New York: Checkmark Books, 2009).

Chapter 6

1. The full history of the network's creation and growth is told in Daniel M. Kimmel, *The Fourth Network: How FOX Broke the Rules and Reinvented Television* (Chicago: Ivan R. Dee, 2004).
2. For television's involvement in this practice, see J. Fred MacDonald, *Television and the Red Menace: The Video Road to Vietnam* (New York: Praeger, 1985).
3. Among these are John Ortved, *The Simpsons: An Uncensored, Unauthorized History* (Vancouver: Greystone Books, 2009); Chris Turner, *Planet Simpson: How a Cartoon Masterpiece Documented an Era and Defined a Generation* (Toronto: Random House, 2004); Steven Kezlowitz, *The World According to the Simpsons* (Napierville, IL: Sourcebooks, 2006); and Nancy Cartwright, *My Life as a Ten-Year-Old Boy* (New York: Hyperion, 2000). Other texts, listed in the bibliography, have analyzed the show in philosophical and psychological terms, and thoroughly listed the episodes chronologically. Similar sources exist online; space prevents me from addressing all of them and the myriad ways they look at the program episodes as the canonical texts they truly are.
4. Ortved, 12.
5. David Marc and Robert J. Thompson, *Prime Time, Prime Movers* (Syracuse: Syracuse University Press, 1995 [1992]), 62.
6. Turner, 15.
7. For many people, this has become the default term to describe the Simpsons and other fictional animated families that have come in their wake. However, it serves more to demonstrate the prejudices of the critics of these programs than it does their actual content—especially when one considers that there really is no such thing as a properly "functional" family to compare them to.
8. Turner, 15–16.
9. Ortved, 54.
10. Hal Erickson. *Television Cartoon Shows: An Illustrated Encyclopedia, 1949–2003, 2d ed.*, 2 vols. (Jefferson, NC: McFarland, 2005), 2: 743.

11. Industry jargon for the individual, usually the single "executive producer" or one of many, who directly oversees the day-to-day production of a television series.

12. Ortved, 57.

13. Gerard Jones, *Honey, I'm Home: Sitcoms Selling the American Dream* (New York: St. Martin's Griffin, 1992), 267.

14. Ortved, 53.

15. M. Keith Booker, *Drawn to Television: Prime Time Animation from* The Flintstones *to* Family Guy (Westport, CT: Praeger, 2006), 50.

16. Ralph Waldo Emerson, "The Transcendentalist," in Stephen E. Whicher, ed., *Selections from Ralph Waldo Emerson* (Boston: Houghton Mifflin, 1957), 195.

17. Turner, 195.

18. Ibid., 221.

19. Mike Judge, quoted in Jeff Lenburg, *Who's Who in Animated Cartoons* (New York: Applause Theatre and Cinema Books, 2006), 167.

20. Jeff Lenburg, *The Encyclopedia of Animated Cartoons, 3d ed.* (New York: Checkmark Books, 2009), 542.

21. An American term referring to small towns whose names are identifiable by the fact that they are written in bold letters on the side of the water towers that dominate their landscape. Other examples of this type of community will follow in later identified programs in the following two chapters.

22. Erickson, 1: 480.

23. Ibid.

24. Ortved, 184.

25. Ibid., 185.

26. Lenburg, *Who's Who*, 221–222.

27. Erickson, 1: 315.

28. Booker, 83.

29. Erickson, 1: 315.

30. One can only hope that the real man is not nearly as clinically insane as Macfarlane's fictional doppelganger clearly is.

31. Tim Brooks and Earle Marsh, *The Complete Directory to Prime Time Network and Cable TV Shows 1946–Present, 8th ed.* (New York: Ballantine, 2003), 856.

32. Lenburg, *Who's Who*, 186–187.

33. John Kricfalusi, quoted in Jerry Beck, ed., *Not Just Toons: Nicktoons* (New York: Melcher Media, 2007), 12. This excellent, heavily illustrated book is the definitive study of Nickelodeon's animated productions, mainly because the series creators are the ones telling the stories of the series, rather than having editor Beck do it for them.

34. Erickson, 2: 661.

35. Thelma Scumm, quoted in Erickson, 2: 661.

36. Jim Jinkins, quoted in Beck, *Not Just Toons*, 26.

37. Peggy Charren, quoted in Erickson, 1: 281.

38. Erickson, 1: 281.

39. Lenburg, *Who's Who*, 54–55, 181–182.

40. Erickson, 2: 693; Paul Germain, Arlene Klasky and Gabor Csupo, quoted in Beck, *Not Just Toons*, 32.

41. Erickson, 2: 694.

42. Paul Germain, quoted in Beck, *Not Just Toons*, 32.

43. Joe Murray, *Creating Animated Cartoons with Character* (New York: Watson-Guptill, 2010), 14. This book—part memoir but mostly how-to—is enormously useful for anyone wanting to understand the current state of the art and business models of television animation, not only due to its depiction of Murray's own life and career but due to the extensive interview segments he conducts with colleagues and contemporaries as well.

44. Erickson, 2: 675–676.

45. Joe Murray, quoted in Beck, *Not Just Toons*, 42.

46. Murray, 85.

47. Chuck Swenson, quoted in Beck, *Not Just Toons*, 49.

48. Craig Bartlett, quoted in Beck, *Not Just Toons*, 55.

49. Craig Bartlett, quoted in Beck, *Not Just Toons*, 56.

50. Erickson, 1: 410.

51. Mitch Schauer, quoted in Brooks and Marsh, 58.

52. Fred Seibert, telephone interview with author, 2003.

53. Fred Seibert, quoted in Beck, *Not Just Toons*, 90.

54. Eryk Casemiro, quoted in Beck, *Not Just Toons*, 96.

55. Lenburg, *Who's Who*, 140.

56. Allan Neuwirth, *Makin' Toons* (New York: Allworth Press, 2003), 48–55; Lenburg, *Who's Who*, 140–141; Eric Coleman, Kevin Kay, Margie Cohn and Steven Hillenburg, quoted in Beck, *Not Just Toons*, 109.

57. Lewis was, in fact, Hillenburg's model for the character (Steven Hillenburg, quoted in Beck, *Not Just Toons*, 109), and, fittingly, is just one of the show's many ardent celebrity fans (Lenburg, *Who's Who*, 141)—a unique factor in the show's ongoing existence and popularity.

58. Steven Hillenburg, quoted in Beck, *Not Just Toons*, 109.

59. Erickson, 2: 785–786.

60. Eryk Casemiro, quoted in Beck, *Not Just Toons*, 123.

61. Eryk Casemiro, quoted in Beck, *Not Just Toons*, 123.

62. Ted Turner and Bill Burke, *Call Me Ted* (New York: Grand Central, 2008), 261.

63. Ibid., 239.

64. Ibid., 290–292.

65. Ibid., 292–294.

66. Fred Seibert, telephone interview with author, 2003.

67. Erickson, 2: 622.

68. Erickson, 1: 61.

69. Michael Mallory, *Hanna-Barbera Cartoons* (New York: Hugh Lauter Levin Associates, 1998), 194.

70. Ibid., 196.

71. Ibid., 196–197.

72. Lenburg, *Who's Who*, 331–332.

73. Genndy Tartakovsky, quoted in Mallory, 198–199.

74. Lenburg, *Who's Who*, 332; Mallory, 199.

75. Erickson, 1: 243.

76. Genndy Tartakovsky, quoted in Mallory, 200.

77. The characters also were featured in a theatrical short film that preceded *The Powerpuff Girls Movie* in 2002—fitting considering Tartakovsky's role in the latter program's initial success.

78. Lenburg, *Who's Who*, 332.

79. Ibid., 80.

80. David Feiss, quoted in Lenburg, *Who's Who*, 80.

81. Erickson, 1: 218.

82. Mallory, 203.

83. Ibid., 204.

84. Ibid.

85. Lenburg, *Who's Who*, 230.

86. Craig McCracken, quoted in Murray, 106–107.

87. Neuwirth, 73.

88. Ibid., 77. The quotes are from McCracken.

89. Brooks and Marsh, 950.

90. Charlotte Baum, quoted in David Zurawik, *The Jews of Prime Time* (Hanover: Brandeis University Press, 2003), 178.

91. Erickson, 2: 821.

92. Jim Cummings, quoted in Erickson, 1: 234.

93. Erickson, 1: 385.

94. Bill Cotter, *The Wonderful World of Disney Television: A Complete History* (New York: Hyperion, 1997), 267.

95. Erickson, 1: 266.

96. Ibid., 1: 269.

97. Ibid., 1: 267.

98. Ibid.

99. Ibid., 1: 268.

100. For more detailed studies of Spielberg, see Joseph McBride, *Steven Spielberg: A Biography* (New York: Simon & Schuster, 1997); John Baxter, *Steven Spielberg: The Unauthorized Biography* (London: Harper Collins, 1997); and more recently, Nicole Laporte, *The Men Who Would Be King* (Boston: Houghton Mifflin Harcourt, 2010). The major flaw with these texts is that they almost completely gloss over Spielberg's extensive contributions to both theatrical and television animation as an innovative producer in both fields. A comprehensive study of this work is in order and would likely be welcomed by animation scholars like myself.

101. Erickson, 2: 853.

102. Ibid., 2: 856.

103. This is a television industry term for a general reference used for setting establishment and character construction and development, to prevent any creative inconsistencies from emerging in the final product.

104. Jerry Beck and Will Friedwald, *Warner Bros. Animation Art* (New York: Warner Brothers/Beaux Arts Editions, 1997), 156–157.

105. Beck and Friedwald, 157; Lenburg, *Encyclopedia*, 638.

106. Tom Ruegger, quoted in Beck and Friedwald, 157.

107. For a detailed study of this aspect of the show's following, see Bill Mikulak, "Fans Versus Time Warner: Who Owns Looney Tunes?" in Kevin S. Sandler, ed., *Reading the Rabbit: Explorations in Warner Brothers Animation* (New Brunswick: Rutgers University Press, 1998), 195–208.

108. Erickson, 2: 854.

109. Kathleen McDonnell, *Kid Culture: Kids and Adults and Popular Culture* (Toronto: Second Story Press, 1994), 146.

110. Ibid., 148.

111. Tom Ruegger, quoted in Beck and Friedwald, 159.

112. Beck and Friedwald, 160.

113. Erickson, 1: 86.

114. Beck and Friedwald, 160.

115. Erickson, 1: 350.

116. Paul Rugg, quoted in Erickson, 1: 350.

117. Beck and Friedwald, 168.

118. Jean MacCurdy, quoted in Erickson, 1: 119.

119. Paul Dini, quoted in Erickson, 1: 119.

120. Bruce Timm, quoted in Paul Dini and Chip Kidd, *Batman Animated* (New York: Harper Entertainment, 1998), xii-xiiii. This lavish, fully illustrated tome is highly informative about the conception and production of the series, and is one of the best books ever written about an individual television animation program or series of such for that reason.

121. Beck and Friedwald, 170.

122. Paul Dini, quoted in Beck and Friedwald, 170.

123. Erickson, 1: 301.

124. Erickson, 1: 302.

125. Erickson, 2: 728–729; Jim Benton, e-mail interview with author, 2004.

126. Erickson, 1: 199.

127. For the history of the company, see Daniel Stoffman, *The Nelvana Story: Thirty Animated Years* (Toronto: Nelvana, 2002).

128. For the full history of the company, see William Urseth, *Death Spiral* (Toronto: ECW Press, 2008).

129. For these corporate concerns, see Sean Howe, *Marvel Comics: The Untold Story* (New York: Harper, 2012).

130. A later attempt to revive the series in live-action form on the FOX network was, however, a failure in all respects, as it was unable to convey the graphic lunacy of the animated or comic book versions.

131. Quoted in Erickson, 1: 160.

132. Erickson, 1: 275.

133. Lenburg, *Who's Who*, 275–76, 326–28.

134. For a lengthier study of the series, see Toni Johnson-Woods, *Blame Canada!* South Park *and Popular Culture* (New York: Continuum, 2007).

Chapter 7

1. Jeff Lenburg, *Who's Who in Animated Cartoons* (New York: Applause Theater and Cinema Books, 2006), 222.

2. Seth Macfarlane, quoted in Lenburg, *Who's Who*, 222.

3. Lenburg, *Who's Who*, 222.

4. M. Keith Booker, *Drawn to Television: Prime*

Time Animation from The Flintstones *to* Family Guy (Westport, CT: Praeger, 2006), 97.

5. Tim Brooks and Earle Marsh, *The Complete Directory to Prime Time and Cable TV Shows, 1946–Present* (New York: Ballantine, 2003), 116.

6. Brooks and Marsh, 565. For a fuller analysis of this programming trend, see J. Fred MacDonald, *Television and the Red Menace: The Video Road to Vietnam* (New York: Praeger, 1985).

7. Booker, 97–98.

8. Quoted in Booker, 98.

9. Booker, 98.

10. Ibid., 99. Booker's book, for all its merits in discussing other, earlier programs, was published in 2006, and therefore deals only with the earliest episodes of this series, when Roger's character had yet to fully develop. As a regular viewer who has seen the show and the character change and develop over the years, I can assure you that Roger—whatever he is—is truly gay—one of the gayest in television animation history, in fact.

11. Ibid., 100.

12. This and many other similar jokes mark this program as the true "dirty old man" series of Macfarlane's oeuvre.

13. For a more elaborate overview of the historical stereotyping of African Americans in the mass media, particularly television, see Donald Bogle, *Toms, Coons, Mulattoes, Mammies and Bucks* (New York: Continuum, 2001 [1973]); J. Fred MacDonald, *Blacks and White TV* (Chicago: Nelson-Hall, 1992); Melvin Patrick Ely, *The Adventures of Amos 'n' Andy* (New York: Free Press, 1991); Kristal Brent Zook, *Color by FOX* (New York: Oxford University Press, 1999); and Donald Bogle, *Prime Time Blues* (New York: Farrar, Straus and Giroux, 2001). For two slightly more "realistic" depictions of African Americans during this time period, see my discussion of *The Proud Family* and *Boondocks* below.

14. Butch Hartman, quoted in Jerry Beck, ed., *Not Just Cartoons: Nicktoons* (New York: Melcher Media, 2007), 134.

15. Fred Seibert, quoted in Beck, *Not Just Cartoons*, 134.

16. Butch Hartman, quoted in Beck, *Not Just Cartoons*, 134.

17. Hal Erickson, *Television Cartoon Shows: An Illustrated Encyclopedia, 1949–2003, 2d ed.*, 2 vols. (Jefferson, NC: McFarland, 2005), 1: 311.

18. Quoted in Erickson, 1: 311.

19. This interesting casting choice recalls the theatrical tradition of having the same actor playing Captain Hook and Mr. Darling in stage productions of *Peter Pan*, and may likely serve the same purpose of comparing and contrasting the reasoning and behavior behind both halves of the dual role. In the case of *Fairly OddParents*, however, it serves mainly to reinforce the fact that Timmy's "surrogate" parents have more true affection and interest in him than his "real" ones do- a rather disturbing subtext, if you take the show more seriously than was likely intended.

20. For a recent history of that "profession," see Miriam Forman-Brunell, *Babysitter: An American History* (New York: New York University Press, 2009).

21. For examples, see Beck, *Not Just Cartoons*, 136–137.

22. Butch Hartman, quoted in Beck, *Not Just Cartoons*, 187.

23. Butch Hartman, quoted in Beck, *Not Just Cartoons*, 187.

24. Butch Hartman, quoted in Beck, *Not Just Cartoons*, 187.

25. The sexual tension between Danny and Sam was something of an elephant-in-the-room device for most of the series' run, but, at the end of it, they were able to openly acknowledge their love for each other.

26. In this obvious sense, Lancer is an exception to the rule of the decade for adult male non-villainous characters, who are typically portrayed as incredibly stupid idiots. His air of learning and erudition is repeatedly reinforced in a very unusual way by Hartman, notably by having him use works of literature ("Paradise Lost!," "Great Gatsby!," etc.), as exclamations. However, in other ways, he is denied full humanity in the series narrative, notably by being denied a first name, which tends to reinforce the fact that he was clearly designed simply as a comic foil.

27. For examples, see Beck, *Not Just Cartoons*, 190–191.

28. This naturally occasions a comparison between this series and those of Joe Murray (see Chapter 6 and below), whose works operate under a similar format. Murray, however, tends to focus on developing his characters from within before making them the subject or target of jokes, and therefore allows the audience to sympathize with them in this way. Hartman does just the opposite here; by allowing his animators to prioritize the jokes and gags over and above the characters and their development, the latter suffer immensely, and the audience is never allowed to view them in the multi-dimensional fashion allowed to their counterparts in Murray's series.

29. This was a major comic subplot of the series, for some odd reason. Dudley lived with his mother (and was often verbally bullied by her), while Kitty bore resentment towards hers. This was not restricted to the "good" guys, as Snaptrap also lived with *his* mother.

30. Emily Kapnek, quoted in Beck, *Not Just Cartoons*, 129.

31. Larry Huber, quoted in Beck, *Not Just Cartoons*, 152.

32. Bill Burnett, quoted in Beck, *Not Just Cartoons*, 152.

33. Bill Burnett, quoted in Beck, *Not Just Cartoons*, 152.

34. John Davis, quoted in Beck, *Not Just Cartoons*, 159.

35. Rob Renzetti, e-mail interview with author, May and December 2006.

36. Rob Renzetti, e-mail interview with author, May and December 2006. For a full display of this program's highly unique design style, see Rob Renzetti, Alex Kirwan and Eric Homan, eds., *The MLAATR Sketchbook* (New York: Frederator Books, 2004).

37. Rob Renzetti, quoted in Beck, *Not Just Cartoons*, 170.
38. Rob Renzetti, e-mail interview with author, May and December 2006.
39. Erickson, 2: 574.
40. Rob Renzetti, e-mail interview with author, May and December 2006.
41. Dr. Wakeman is portrayed with a strong *mittel Europa* accent, and therefore "tagged" as a possible U.S. immigrant, although this is not mentioned in the text. Jenny's attempts at entering into the human world resemble the assimilationist patterns of some second-generation immigrants, and Dr. Wakeman's opposition to this resembles that of their first-generation immigrant parents. This is most strongly coded by Wakeman always referring to her creation by her "given" name, XJ9, and not her assumed "human" one. Actress Milo adds another layer by drawling out the "9" in "XJ9" so that it resembles the German word *nein*, which, significantly, means "no."
42. This is strictly my reading of his character, though some internal evidence suggests this is the case.
43. In this respect, it reflected a growing trend among television animation producers (other examples will be provided below), to recognize the growing cultural and economic importance of the Latino demographic in America, though *El Tigre* was more blatant in embracing this heritage, and thus more effective.
44. See Gutierrez and Equihua quotes in Beck, *Not Just Cartoons*, 229.
45. Fred Seibert, quoted in Beck, *Not Just Cartoons*, 236.
46. Riccardo Durante, quoted in Beck, *Not Just Cartoons*, 244.
47. Jillian Ruby, quoted in Beck, *Not Just Cartoons*, 244.
48. Cynthia True and Erik Weise, quoted in Beck, *Not Just Cartoons*, 270.
49. These will be more fully addressed in the section on Warner Brothers Television Animation below, as this studio was more adversely effected by them than was CNS.
50. Lenburg, *Who's Who*, 64–65.
51. Jeff Lenburg, *The Encyclopedia of Animated Cartoons* (New York: Checkmark Books, 2009), 564.
52. Quoted in Erickson, 2: 732.
53. Erickson, 2: 732.
54. For these reasons, she is the scariest non-villain television animation character in the genre's history, in my opinion.
55. Erickson, 1: 386.
56. Erickson, 1: 386.
57. Genndy Tartakovsky, quoted in Allan Neuwirth, *Makin' Toons* (New York: Allworth Books, 2003), 78.
58. Genndy Tartakovsky, quoted in Neuwirth, 78.
59. Linda Simensky, quoted in Neuwirth, 78.
60. Erickson, 1: 208.
61. Tom Warburton, quoted in Joe Murray, *Creating Animated Cartoons with Character* (New York: Watson-Guptill, 2010), 91.
62. Erickson, 2: 901.
63. Ibid., 1: 144.
64. Craig McCracken, quoted in Murray, 107, 109.
65. For an outline of the realistic discourse on this topic, see Marjorie Taylor, *Imaginary Companions and the Children Who Create Them* (New York: Oxford University Press, 1999).
66. For Sartre's concept of imagination and creation, see his book *The Imagination* (New York: Routledge, 2012).
67. Murray discusses the evolution and development of the series in *Creating Animated Cartoons with Character*.
68. For a detailed study of the latter institution and its relation with the former, see Leslie Paris, *Children's Nature: The Rise of the American Summer Camp* (New York: New York University Press, 2010).
69. Whether the Cahills intended this or not, the choices of names for their protagonist and the institution he attends become highly and satirically symbolic over the course of the program's run, particularly regarding the division between organized, traditional religion (Adam), and more progressive schools of scientific thought (Charles Darwin). Adam's gradual embrace of his inner animal also, subliminally, reflects the sentiments of a traditional phrase from pre–United States Puritan primers: "In Adam's fall, we sinned, all."
70. Thankfully, it can be. Cartoon Network has issued two DVDs of the project, although an issue of the complete series is still in order. It can also, like a surprisingly large number of the series in this book, be viewed on YouTube.
71. Wikipedia reports that Paul Reubens had originally been cast in the role, but Van Orman assumed the part himself when Reubens failed to attend the initial recording session.
72. Oddly enough, the last episode of the series actually shows the two of them married with children!
73. "Walt" was officially dropped from the entire corporate masthead of the company in the early 2010s, so I will use this term to refer to the studio, even though most bore the full Walt Disney Television Animation name.
74. Tino's vacillation between high intelligence and emotional insecurity, which drive a number of plots in the series, has led me to privately conclude that he is challenged with Asperger's Syndrome, where this is common. There is no direct evidence of this in the program plots or dialogue, however.
75. Black Urban Professionals—the African American equivalent of "yuppies."
76. Short for "petratishkovna," which apparently means "girl with one nose."
77. In this context, Tish can be seen as being challenged, like Tino, with Asperger's Syndrome; their friendship in this context is highly apt.
78. Her parents' accents and behavior tend to reinforce this view, as does the traditional stereotyping of these people. Her university professor father (Jeff Bennett), speaks in a manner reminiscent of the Mad Russian (Bert Gordon), a recurring character on Eddie Cantor's radio program during the 1930s, while her mother

(Kerri Kenney), is reminiscent of Molly Goldberg, the matriarch of the fictional Jewish family of radio and television fame.

79. Erickson, 1: 271.
80. Ibid., 1: 270.
81. Ibid., 1: 271.
82. Paul Germain, quoted in Erickson, 1: 263. In retrospect, this may explain the decision to drop "Walt" from the company name noted earlier, so that future TV animation producers would understand that they were dealing with a functioning company and not simply the trustees of the legacy of a "dead" man.
83. See the texts cited in note 13 for fuller explanation.
84. Scott M. Gimple, quoted in Erickson, 1: 259.
85. Jeff Lenburg (*Encyclopedia*, 481), makes this assertion, but my viewing of the series does not confirm this.
86. Erickson, 1: 259.
87. Liner to *Punk Jazz: The Jaco Pastorius Anthology* (Rhino/Atlantic 2003).
88. Erickson 1: 474.

Bibliography

Primary Sources

PERSONAL INTERVIEWS

Adler, Charlie. Telephone, 2008.
Benton, Jim. E-mail, 2004.
Huber, Larry. Telephone, 2006.
Renzetti, Rob. E-mail, May and December 2006.
Rogers, Amy Keating. E-mail, December 2006.
Scheimer, Lou. Telephone, 2003 and 2006.
Seibert, Fred. Telephone, 2006.

NEWSPAPER ARTICLES

Adams, Val. "For Super-Heroes, New Frontiers." *New York Times,* Mar. 20, 1966. 131.
_____. "News of TV and Radio-Cartoons." *New York Times,* Sept. 24, 1961. X23.
_____. "News of TV and Radio-Loggia's Triple Role." *New York Times,* Apr. 3, 1960. X15.
Atkinson, Brooks. "Critic at Large: Cartoon Flintstones Possess Freshness Rarely Found in Acted TV Comedy." *New York Times,* Oct. 4, 1963. 55.
Bart, Peter. "Studios to Revive Animated Shorts." *New York Times,* Jan. 15, 1965. 20.
Berg, Beatrice. "Goodbye Bang, Burn, Stab, Shoot." *New York Times,* Nov. 9, 1969.
Blum, Sam. "De-Escalating the Violence on TV." *New York Times,* Dec. 8, 1968. 401.
Brody, Jane. "TV Violence Cited as Bad Influence." *New York Times,* Dec. 17, 1975. 74.
Brown, Les. "Children in CBS Study Largely Indifferent to Race." *New York Times,* June 12, 1975. 75.
_____. "TV Enlists Educators to Aid in Children's Shows." *New York Times,* Apr. 4, 1974. 83.
Burnham, Alexander. "Bert Lahr Wins Right to Sue Over Mimicking of His Style." *New York Times,* May 29, 1962. 29.
Calta, Louis. "Bill Cosby to Star in Children's Show Saturdays on CBS." *New York Times,* Apr. 26, 1972. 91.
Culhane, John. "The Men Behind Dastardly and Muttley." *New York Times,* Nov. 23, 1969.
Curry, Kay. Letter to the Editor. *New York Times,* Nov. 23, 1969. SM21.
D.A.K. "In Search of Jay Ward." *New York Times,* May 7, 1989. H31.
Diehl, Digby. "On Saturdays, Super-Heroes and Talking Animals." *New York Times,* Mar. 5, 1967. 125.
Dougherty, Philip H. "Advertising: How to be First on the Block." *New York Times,* Jan. 8, 1967. 142.
Everitt, David. "Cute Animals with a Cutting Edge." *New York Times,* Dec. 8, 1996. H36.
"Excerpts from National Panel's Statement on Violence in TV Entertainment." *New York Times,* Sept. 25, 1969. 38.
Gent, George. "NBC and CBS Announce Changes in Children's TV." *New York Times,* Mar. 22, 1968. 95.
_____. "Networks Say They Eliminated Most Violent Children's Shows." *New York Times,* Jan. 13, 1972.
Gould, Jack. "ABC's 'Jonny Quest' a Series for the Young." *New York Times,* Sept. 19, 1964. 54.
_____. "Gosden and Correll, Long 'Amos 'n' Andy,' Lend Voices to Cartoon Series." *New York Times,* Oct. 4, 1961. 91.
_____. "Of Scapegoats and Headlines." *New York Times,* July 13, 1969. D19.
_____. "TV: Animated Cartoon—'The Flintstones' in Debut on Channel 7..." *New York Times,* Oct. 1, 1960. 39.
_____. "TV Review: Fewer Pows and Sockos of a Saturday Morn." *New York Times,* Sept. 8, 1969. 83.
_____. "TV: Violence as a Program Staple Prompts Concern." *New York Times,* June 10, 1968. 91.
_____. "TV Violence Held Unharmful to Youth." *New York Times,* Jan. 11, 1972.
Kaplan, David A. "Rocky and Bullwinkle Brave the Comeback Trail." *New York Times,* May 7, 1989. H31.
Leonard, John. "Since the Kiddies Are Hooked—Why Not Use TV for a Head Start Program?" *New York Times,* July 14, 1968. SM5.
McDermott, John F. "The Violent Bugs Bunny, et al." *New York Times,* Sept. 18, 1969. SM95.
"Mel Blanc Is Hurt in Coast Car Crash." *New York Times,* Jan. 26, 1961. 19.

O'Connor, John J. "Lap It Up, Kiddies—It's Bad for You." *New York Times*, June 18, 1972. D17.
_____. "Of Moose, Mounties and Their Mentors." *New York Times*, Mar. 13, 1991. C13.
_____. "TV: ABC Presents Its New Fare for Children." *New York Times*, Oct. 13, 1972. 78.
_____. "TV: Effecting Changes in Children's Programming." *New York Times*, Sept. 27, 1972. 94.
Rinzler, Carol. "Trying to Like Those Saturday TV Kids Shows." *New York Times*, Jan. 25, 1976. 71.
Rosenthal, Jack. "Panel Links Violence to That on TV." *New York Times*, Sept. 18, 1969. 1; 94.
Schumach, Murray. "Animated, Yes—Frantic, No." *New York Times*, Aug. 28, 1960. X11.
Shepard, Richard F. "Lincoln Center Signs a TV Firm." *New York Times*, Dec. 30, 1959. 45.
"Taft Broadcasting Eyes Colorful Deal." *New York Times*, Nov. 13, 1965. 35.
Thompson, Howard. "'Hey There, It's Yogi Bear,' New Color Cartoon, Opens Here." *New York Times*, July 30, 1964. 16.
Weaver, Warren, Jr. "Violence Found Uncurbed on TV." *New York Times*, July 6, 1969. 35.
Windeler, Robert. "NBC Is Dropping Violent Cartoons." *New York Times*, Nov. 25, 1968. 94.
_____. "Violence in TV Cartoons Being Toned Down." *New York Times*, July 20, 1968. 53.
Yarrow, Andrew L. "Jay Ward, 69, the TV Cartoonist Who Created Bullwinkle, Is Dead." *New York Times*, Oct. 14, 1989. 32.

Secondary Sources

Abate, Michelle Ann. *Tomboys: A Literary and Cultural History*. Philadelphia: Temple University Press, 2008.
Abramson, Albert. *The History of Television, 1942 to 2000*. Jefferson, NC: McFarland, 2003.
Adams, T.R. *The Flintstones: A Modern Stone Age Phenomenon*. Atlanta: Turner, 1994.
Adamson, Joe. *Tex Avery: King of Cartoons*. New York: Popular Library, 1975.
_____. *The Walter Lantz Story*. New York: G.P. Putnam's Sons, 1985.
Adler, Bill. *The Cosby Wit: His Life and Humor*. New York: Carroll and Graf, 1986.
Alberti, John, ed. *Leaving Springfield:* The Simpsons *and the Possibility of Oppositional Culture*. Detroit: Wayne State University Press, 2004.
Amidi, Amid. *Cartoon Modern: Style and Design in Fifties Animation*. San Francisco: Chronicle Books, 2006.
Anderson, Christopher. *Hollywood TV: The Studio System in the Fifties*. Austin: University of Texas Press, 1994.
Andrae, Thomas. *Carl Barks and the Disney Comic Book: Unmasking the Myth of Modernity*. Jackson: University Press of Mississippi, 2006.
Annam, David. *Robot: The Mechanical Monster*. New York: Bounty Books, 1976.
Aries, Phillippe. *Centuries of Childhood: A Social History of Family Life*. New York: Vintage, 1962.

Ashby, Leroy. *With Amusement for All: A History of American Popular Culture Since 1830*. Lexington: University Press of Kentucky, 2006.
Asimov, Isaac, and Karen Frankel. *Robots: Machines in Man's Image*. New York: Harmony Books, 1985.
Auletta, Ken. *Three Blind Mice*. New York: Random House, 1991.
Austin, Joe, and Michael Nevin Willard, eds. *Generations of Youth: Youth Cultures and History in Twentieth-Century America*. New York: New York University Press, 1998.
Axelrod, Mitch. *Beatletoons*. New York: Wynn, 1991.
Ayres, Brenda, ed. *The Emperor's Old Groove: Decolonizing Disney's Magic Kingdom*. New York: Peter Lang, 2003.
Balio, Tino, ed. *Hollywood in the Age of Television*. Boston: Unwin Hyman, 1990.
Banet-Weiser, Sarah. *Kids Rule! Nickelodeon and Consumer Culture*. Durham: Duke University Press, 2007.
Barbera, Joseph. *My Life in 'Toons*. Atlanta: Turner, 1994.
Barcus, F. Earle. *Images of Life on Children's Television—Sex Roles, Minorities and Families*. New York: Praeger, 1983.
_____, and Rachel Wolkins. *Children's Television: An Analysis of Programming and Advertising*. New York: Praeger, 1977.
Barnouw, Erik. *The Sponsor: Notes on a Modern Potentate*. New York: Oxford University Press, 1978.
_____. *Tube of Plenty*. New York: Oxford University Press, 1975.
Barrier, Michael. *The Animated Man: A Life of Walt Disney*. Berkeley: University of California Press, 2007.
_____. *Hollywood Cartoons: American Animation in its Golden Age*. New York: Oxford University Press, 1999.
Basinger, Jeanine. *A Woman's View: How Hollywood Spoke to Women 1930–1960*. Hanover: Wesleyan University Press, 1993.
Baughman, James L. *The Republic of Mass Culture*. Baltimore: Johns Hopkins University Press, 2006.
_____. *Same Time, Same Station: Creating American Television 1948–1961*. Baltimore: Johns Hopkins University Press, 2007.
_____. *Television's Guardians: The FCC and the Politics of Programming*. Knoxville: University of Tennessee Press, 1985.
Baxter, John. *Steven Spielberg: The Unauthorized Biography*. London: HarperCollins, 1997.
Beaty, Bart. *Frederic Wertham and the Critique of Mass Culture*. Jackson: University Press of Mississippi, 2005.
Beck, Jerry. *The Animated Movie Guide*. Chicago: Chicago Review Press, 2005.
_____. *The 50 Greatest Cartoons*. North Dighton, MA: JG Press, 1994.
_____. *The Hanna-Barbera Treasury*. San Rafael, CA: Insight Editions, 2007.
_____. *Not Just Toons: Nicktoons*. New York: Melcher Media, 2007.
_____. *Warner Brothers Animation Art*. New York: Warner Brothers/Beaux Arts Editions, 1997.

_____, ed. *Animation Art*. London: Flame Tree, 2004.

_____, and Shalom Auslander. *I Tawt I Taw a Puddy Tat: Fifty Years of Sylvester and Tweety*. New York: Henry Holt, 1991.

_____, and Will Friedwald. *Looney Tunes and Merrie Melodies*. New York: Henry Holt, 1989.

Bedell, Sally. *Up the Tube: Prime Time TV and the Silverman Years*. New York: Viking, 1981.

Bendazzi, Giannalberto. *Cartoons: 100 Years of Cinema Animation*. Bloomington: Indiana University Press, 1994.

Benjamin, Walter. *The Work of Art in the Age of Its Technological Reproducibility and Other Writings on Media*. Cambridge: Belknap/Harvard University Press, 2008.

Berger, Arthur Asa. *The TV Guided American*. New York: Walker, 1976.

Bergreen, Lawrence. *Look Now, Pay Later*. Garden City, NY: Doubleday, 1980.

Berton, Pierre. *Hollywood's Canada: The Americanization of Our National Image*. Toronto: McClelland and Stewart, 1975.

Bettelheim, Bruno. *The Uses of Enchantment*. New York: Alfred A. Knopf, 1977.

Bianculli, David. *Teleliteracy*. New York: Continuum, 1992.

Biggers, Buck, and Chet Stover. *How Underdog Was Born*. Boalsberg, PA: Bear Manor Media, 2005.

Biskind, Peter. *Seeing Is Believing: How Hollywood Taught Us to Stop Worrying and Love the Fifties*. New York: Pantheon, 1983.

Blanc, Mel, and Philip Bashe. *That's Not All Folks*. New York: Warner Books, 1988.

Bly, Robert. *The Sibling Society*. Reading, MA: Addison-Wesley, 1996.

Bodgroghkozy, Aniko. *Groove Tube*. Durham: Duke University Press, 2001.

Bogle, Donald. *Prime Time Blues: African Americans on Network Television*. New York: Farrar, Straus and Giroux, 2001.

_____. *Toms, Coons, Mulattoes, Mammies and Bucks*. New York: Continuum, 2001.

Bogart, Leo. *The Age of Television*. New York: Frederick Ungar, 1972.

Booker, M. Keith. *Drawn to Television: Prime Time Animation from* The Flintstones *to* Family Guy. Westport, CT: Praeger, 2006.

_____. *Strange TV: Innovative Television Series from* The Twilight Zone *to* The X Files. Westport, CT: Greenwood Press, 2002.

Boorstin, Daniel J. *The Image: A Guide to Pseudo-Events in America*. New York: Vintage, 1987.

Boyd, Todd. *Am I Black Enough for You?* Bloomington: Indiana University Press, 1997.

Brion, Patrick. *Tom and Jerry*. New York: Harmony, 1990.

Britton, Wesley. *The Encyclopedia of TV Spies*. Albany, GA: Bear Manor Media, 2009.

Bronson, Fred. *The Billboard Book of Number One Hits*. New York: Billboard Books, 1992.

Brooks, Ann. *Postfeminisms*. London: Routledge, 1997.

Brooks, Tim, and Earle Marsh. *The Complete Directory to Prime Time Network and Cable TV Shows*, 8th ed. New York: Ballantine Books, 2003.

Broughton, Irv, ed. *Producers on Producing*. Jefferson, NC: McFarland, 1986.

Brown, Les. *Television: The Business Behind the Box*. New York: Harcourt Brace Jovanovich, 1971.

Brown, Lyn Mikel. *Raising Their Voices*. Cambridge: Harvard University Press, 1998.

Brunvand, Jan Harold. *The Study of American Folklore: An Introduction*. New York: W.W. Norton, 1968.

Buckingham, David, ed. *Small Screens: Television for Children*. London: Leicester University Press, 2002.

Buhle, Paul. *From the Lower East Side to Hollywood*. London: Verso, 2004.

Burke, Timothy, and Kevin Burke. *Saturday Morning Fever: Growing Up with Cartoon Culture*. New York: St. Martin's Griffin, 1999.

Butler, Judith. *Gender Trouble*. New York: Routledge, 1990.

Cabarga, Leslie. *The Fleischer Story*. New York: Nostalgia Press, 1976.

Caldwell, John Thornton. *Televisuality*. New Brunswick: Rutgers University Press, 1995.

Callaghan, Steve, ed. *Family Guy: The Official Episode Guide, Seasons 1–3*. New York: Harper, 2005.

Canemaker, John. *Felix: The Twisted Tale of the World's Most Famous Cat*. New York: Pantheon, 1991.

_____. *Tex Avery: The MGM Years, 1942–1955*. Atlanta: Turner, 1996.

_____. *Winsor McCay: His Life and Art*. New York: Harry N. Abrams, 2005.

Cantor, Joanne. *Mommy, I'm Scared*. New York: Harcourt Brace, 1998.

Cantor, Muriel. *The Hollywood TV Producer: His Work and His Audience*. New York: Basic Books, 1971.

Capsuto, Stephen. *Alternate Channels: The Uncensored Story of Gay and Lesbian Images on Radio and Television*. New York: Ballantine, 2000.

Carlyle, Thomas. *On Heroes, Hero Worship and the Heroic in History*. Lincoln: University of Nebraska Press, 1966.

Carnes, Mark C., ed. *The Columbia History of Post–World War II America*. New York: Columbia University Press, 2007.

Cartwright, Nancy. *My Life as a Ten-Year-Old Boy*. New York: Hyperion, 2000.

Casey, Bernadette, et al. *Television Studies: The Key Concepts*. London: Routledge, 2002.

Castleman, Harry, and Walter Podrazik. *Watching TV*. New York: McGraw-Hill, 1982.

Cater, Douglass, and Stephen Strickland. *TV Violence and the Child: The Evolution and Fate of the Surgeon General's Report*. New York: Russell Sage Foundation, 1979.

Cawley, John, and Jim Korkis. *The Encyclopedia of Cartoon Superstars*. Las Vegas: Pioneer Books, 1998.

Charren, Peggy, and Martin W. Sandler. *Changing Channels: Living (Sensibly) with Television*. Reading, MA: Addison-Wesley, 1983.

Chunovic, Louis. *One Foot on the Floor*. New York: TV Books, 2000.

_____. *The Rocky and Bullwinkle Book.* New York: Bantam, 1996.
Clark, Beverly Lyon, and Margaret Hignonett, eds. *Girls, Boys, Books, Toys.* Baltimore: Johns Hopkins University Press, 1999.
Clute, John, and John Grant, eds. *The Encyclopedia of Fantasy.* New York: St. Martin's Press, 1997.
_____, and Peter Nicholls, eds. *The Encyclopedia of Science Fiction.* New York: St. Martin's Press, 1993.
Cohen, Karl. *Forbidden Animation.* Jefferson, NC: McFarland, 1997.
Cole, Barry, and Mal Oettinger. *Reluctant Regulators.* Reading, MA: Addison-Wesley, 1978.
Coloroso, Barbara. *The Bully, The Bullied, and The Bystander.* Toronto: HarperCollins, 2002.
Condry, John. *The Psychology of Television.* Hillsdale, NJ: Lawrence Erlbaum Associates, 1989.
Connell, R.W. *Masculinities.* Chicago: University of Chicago Press, 2005.
Considine, David. *The Cinema of Adolescence.* Jefferson, NC: McFarland, 1985.
Coogan, Peter. *Superhero: The Secret Origins of a Genre.* Austin: MonkeyBrain Books, 2006.
Cotter, Bill. *The Wonderful World of Disney Television: A Complete History.* New York: Hyperion, 1997.
Crafton, Donald. *Before Mickey.* Cambridge: MIT Press, 1982.
Cross, Gary. *The Cute and the Cool: Wondrous Innocence and Modern American Children's Culture.* New York: Oxford University Press, 2004.
_____. *Kids' Stuff: Toys and The Changing World of American Childhood.* Cambridge: Harvard University Press, 1997.
_____. *Men to Boys: The Making of Modern Immaturity.* New York: Columbia University Press, 2008.
Cohen, Lizabeth. *A Consumers' Republic: The Politics of Mass Consumption in Postwar America.* New York: Vintage, 2003.
Cooper, Kim, and Davin Smay, eds. *Bubblegum Music Is the Naked Truth.* Los Angeles: Feral House, 2001.
Cowan, Geoffrey. *See No Evil.* New York: Simon & Schuster, 1978.
Cox, J. Randolph. *The Dime Novel Companion: A Source Book.* Westport, CT: Greenwood Press, 2000.
Culhane, Shamus. *Talking Animals and Other People.* New York: St. Martin's Press, 1986.
Cuordileone, K.A. *Manhood and American Political Culture in the Cold War.* New York: Routledge, 2005.
Czitrom, Daniel. *Media and the American Mind from Morse to McLuhan.* Chapel Hill: University of North Carolina Press, 1982.
Daniels, Les. *Marvel: Five Fabulous Decades of the World's Greatest Comics.* New York: Harry N. Abrams, 1991.
_____. *Superman in Color.* San Francisco: Chronicle Books, 2009.
Davis, Janet M. *The Circus Age: Culture and Society Under the American Big Top.* Chapel Hill: University of North Carolina Press, 2002.
Davis, Jeffery. *Children's Television 1947–1990.* Jefferson, NC: McFarland, 1995.
Davis, Michael. *Street Gang: The Complete History of Sesame Street.* New York: Viking, 2008.
De Lauretis, Teresa. *Alice Doesn't.* Bloomington: Indiana University Press, 1984.
Denning, Michael. *The Cultural Front.* London: Verso, 1996.
_____. *Mechanic Accents: Dime Novels and Working-Class Culture in America.* London: Verso, 1998.
Diamant, Lincoln. *Television's Classic Commercials: The Golden Years 1948–1958.* New York: Hastings House, 1971.
Dijkstra, Bram. *Evil Sisters.* New York: Alfred A. Knopf, 1986.
DiMeglio, John. *Vaudeville U.S.A.* Bowling Green, OH: Bowling Green University Popular Press, 1973.
Dini, Paul, and Chip Kidd. *Batman Animated.* New York: HarperEntertainment, 1998.
Dobson, Nichola. *Historical Dictionary of Animation and Cartoons.* Lanham, MD: Scarecrow Press, 2009.
Doherty, Thomas. *Hollywood's Censor: Joseph I. Breen and the Production Code Administration.* New York: Columbia University Press, 2007.
_____. *Teenagers and Teenpics.* Boston: Unwin Hyman, 1988.
Douglas, Susan. *Listening In: Radio and the American Imagination.* New York: Times Books, 1999.
_____. *Where the Girls Are: Growing Up Female with the Mass Media.* New York: Times Books, 1994.
Dow, Bonnie. *Prime Time Feminism.* Philadelphia: University of Pennsylvania Press, 1996.
Early, Frances, and Kathleen Kennedy, eds. *Athena's Daughters.* New York: Syracuse University Press, 2003.
Edgerton, Gary. *The Columbia History of American Television.* New York: Columbia University Press, 2007.
Eisner, Michael, and Tony Schwartz. *Work in Progress.* New York: Random House, 1998.
Ellison, Harlan. *The Glass Teat.* New York: Ace, 1983.
Ely, Melvin Patrick. *The Adventures of Amos 'n' Andy: A Social History of an American Phenomenon.* New York: Free Press, 1991.
Emerson, Ralph Waldo. *Selections from Ralph Waldo Emerson.* Ed. Stephen Whicher. Boston: Houghton Mifflin, 1957.
Engelhardt, Tom. *The End of Victory Culture: Cold War America and the Disillusioning of a Nation.* New York: Basic Books, 1995.
Erickson, Hal. *From Beautiful Downtown Burbank.* Jefferson, NC: McFarland, 2000.
_____. *Syndicated Television: The First Forty Years, 1947–1987.* Jefferson, NC: McFarland, 1989.
_____. *Television Cartoon Shows: An Illustrated Encyclopedia 1949–2003*, 2 vols. Jefferson, NC: McFarland, 2005.
Erikson, Erik. *Identity: Youth and Crisis.* New York: W.W. Norton, 1968.
Esslin, Martin. *The Age of Television.* San Francisco: W.H. Freeman, 1982.
Everitt, David. *King of the Half Hour: Nat Hiken and the Golden Age of TV Comedy.* Syracuse: Syracuse University Press, 2001.

_____. *A Shadow of Red: Communism and the Blacklist in Radio and Television*. Chicago: Ivan R. Dee, 2007.
Faludi, Susan. *Backlash*. New York: Anchor Books, 1991.
Finch, Christopher. *Disney's Winnie the Pooh*. New York: Disney Editions, 2000.
Fingeroth, Danny. *Superman on the Couch*. New York: Continuum, 2004.
Fischer, Stuart. *The Hanna-Barbera Story*. Baltimore: PublishAmerica, 2011.
_____. *Kids TV: The First Twenty Five Years*. New York: Facts on File, 1983.
Fishwick, Marshall. *Seven Pillars of Popular Culture*. Westport, CT: Greenwood Press, 1985.
Fiske, John. *Television Culture*. London: Routledge, 1987.
_____. *Understanding Popular Culture*. Boston: Unwin Hyman, 1989.
_____, and John Hartley. *Reading Television*. London: Methuen, 1978.
Florenski, Joe, and Steve Wilson. *Center Square: The Paul Lynde Story*. New York: Advocate Books, 2005.
Foray, June, Mark Evanier and Earl Kress. *Did You Grow Up with Me, Too?: The Autobiography of June Foray*. Albany, GA: Bear Manor Media, 2009.
Forman-Brunell, Miriam. *Babysitter: An American History*. New York: New York University Press, 2009.
_____. *Made to Play House: Dolls and the Commercialization of American Girlhood*. Baltimore: Johns Hopkins University Press, 1993.
Fowles, Jib. *The Case for Television Violence*. Thousand Oaks, CA: Sage, 1999.
Friedman, Lester. *Hollywood's Image of the Jew*. New York: Frederick Ungar, 1982.
_____, ed. *Cultural Studies: Medicine and Media*. Durham: Duke University Press, 2004.
Fleischer, Richard. *Out of the Inkwell*. Lexington: University of Kentucky Press, 2005.
Frye, Northrop. *Anatomy of Criticism: Four Essays*. Princeton: Princeton University Press, 1990.
Gabler, Neal. *An Empire of Their Own*. New York: Doubleday, 1988.
_____. *Life, the Movie: How Entertainment Conquered Reality*. New York: Alfred A. Knopf, 1998.
_____. *Walt Disney: The Triumph of the American Imagination*. New York: Alfred A. Knopf, 2006.
Gans, Herbert. *Popular Culture and High Culture: An Analysis and Evaluation of Taste*. New York: Basic Books, 1974.
Geissman, Grant. *Foul Play: The Art and Artists of the Notorious 1950s E.C. Comics*. New York: HarperCollins, 2005.
George, Nelson. *Blackface*. New York: HarperCollins, 1994.
Gerani, Gary, and Paul Schulman. *Fantastic Television*. New York: Harmony Books, 1977.
Geraghty, Lincoln, and Mark Jancovich, eds. *The Shifting Definitions of Genre: Essays on Labeling Films, Television Shows and Media*. Jefferson, NC: McFarland, 2008.
Gibson, Jon, and Christopher McDonnell. *Unfiltered: The Complete Ralph Bakshi*. New York: Universe, 2008.
Gilbert, Douglas. *American Vaudeville*. New York: Dover, 1940.
Gilbert, James. *A Cycle of Outrage: America's Reaction to the Juvenile Delinquent in the 1950s*. New York: Oxford University Press, 1986.
_____. *Men in the Middle: Searching for Masculinity in the 1950s*. Chicago: University of Chicago Press, 2005.
Gilligan, Carol. *In a Different Voice*. Cambridge: Harvard University Press, 1982.
Gimple, Scott M., ed. *The Simpsons Forever*. New York: HarperPerennial, 1999.
Gitlin, Todd. *The Whole World Is Watching: Mass Media in the Making and Unmaking of the New Left*. Berkeley: University of California Press, 2003.
_____, ed. *Watching Television*. New York: Pantheon, 1986.
Glick, Ira, and Sidney Levy. *Living with Television*. Chicago: Aldine, 1962.
Goffman, Erving. *The Preservation of Self in Everyday Life*. Garden City, NY: Doubleday, 1958.
Goldmark, Daniel. *Tunes for 'Toons: Music and the Hollywood Cartoon*. Berkeley: University of California Press, 2005.
_____, and Charlie Kell, ed. *Funny Pictures*. Berkeley: University of California Press, 2011.
Goldschmidt, Rick. *The Enchanted World of Rankin/Bass*. Issaquah, WA: Tiger Mountain Press, 1997.
_____. *Rudolph the Red Nosed Reindeer*. Bridgeview, IL: Miser Brothers Press, 2001.
Graff, Harvey J., ed. *Growing Up in America: Historical Experiences*. Detroit: Wayne State University Press, 1987.
Grandinetti, Fred. *Popeye: An Illustrated History*. Jefferson, NC: McFarland, 1994.
Gray, Herman. *Watching Race: Television and the Struggle for Blackness*. Minneapolis: University of Minnesota Press, 2004.
Green, Ben. *Spinning the Globe: The Rise, Fall and Return to Greatness of the Harlem Globetrotters*. New York: Amistad, 2005.
Greenfield, Patricia Marks. *Mind and Media*. Cambridge: Harvard University Press, 1984.
Gross, Edward. *Spider Man Confidential*. New York: Hyperion, 2002.
Grossman, Dave, and Gloria DeGaetano. *Stop Teaching Our Kids to Kill*. New York: Crown, 1999.
Grossman, Gary. *Saturday Morning TV*. New York: Dell, 1981.
Hajdu, David. *The Ten Cent Plague: The Great Comic Book Scare and How It Changed America*. New York: Farrar, Straus and Giroux, 2008.
Hamamoto, Darrell Y. *Nervous Laughter: Television Situation Comedy and Liberal Democratic Ideology*. New York: Praeger, 1991.
Hanna, William, and Tom Ito. *A Cast of Friends*. New York: Da Capo, 2000.
Harries, Dan. *Film Parody*. London: BFI, 2000.
Haskell, Molly. *From Reverence to Rape*. Chicago: University of Chicago Press, 1987.

Hawes, Joseph, and N. Ray Hiner, eds. *American Childhood*. Westport, CT: Greenwood Press, 1985.

Hazard, Patrick D., ed. *TV as Art*. Champaign, IL: National Council of Teachers of English, 1966.

Heinecken, Dawn. *The Warrior Women of Television*. New York: Peter Lang, 2003.

Heins, Marjorie. *Not in Front of the Children*. New York: Hill & Wang, 2001.

Herman, Edward, and Noam Chomsky. *Manufacturing Consent: The Political Economy of the Mass Media*. New York: Pantheon, 2002.

Hendershot, Heather. *Saturday Morning Censors: Television Regulation Before the V Chip*. Durham: Duke University Press, 1998.

Henry, Charles P. *Culture and African American Politics*. Bloomington: Indiana University Press, 1990.

Hersch, Patricia. *A Tribe Apart*. New York: Fawcett Columbine, 1998.

Herz, J.C. *Joystick Nation*. Boston: Little, Brown, 1997.

Hilmes, Michelle. *Hollywood and Broadcasting: From Radio to Cable*. Urbana: University of Illinois Press, 1990.

_____, ed. *NBC: America's Network*. Berkeley: University of California Press, 2007.

Himmelstein, Hal. *On the Small Screen*. New York: Praeger, 1981.

_____. *Television Myth and the American Mind*. New York: Praeger, 1984.

Hodge, Robert, and David Tripp. *Children and Television*. Cambridge: Polity Press, 1986.

Hollis, Tim. *Hi There, Boys and Girls!* Jackson: University Press of Mississippi, 2001.

Holtzman, Linda. *Media Messages: What Film, Television and Popular Music Teach Us About Race, Class, Gender and Sexual Orientation*. Armonk, NY: M.E. Sharpe, 2000.

hooks, bell. *Communion: The Female Search for Love*. New York: William Morrow, 2002.

_____. *Feminism Is for Everybody: Passionate Politics*. Cambridge: South End Press, 2000.

_____. *Feminist Theory: From Margin to Center*. Cambridge: South End Press, 2000.

_____. *Outlaw Culture: Resisting Representations*. New York: Routledge, 1994.

Horowitz, Susan. *Queens of Comedy*. London: Gordon and Breach, 1997.

Houseman, Jerry Paul. *A Study of Selected Walt Disney Screenplays and Films and the Stereotyping of the Role of the Female*. Ann Arbor: University Microfilms, 1974.

Howe, Michael J.A. *Television and Children*. Hamden, CT: Linnet Books, 1977.

Illick, Joseph. *American Childhoods*. Philadelphia: University of Pennsylvania Press, 2002.

Inglis, Ruth. *The Window in the Corner*. London: Peter Owen, 2003.

Inness, Sheri. *Tough Girls: Women Warriors and Wonder Women in Popular Culture*. Philadelphia: University of Pennsylvania Press, 1999.

Innis, Harold. *The Bias of Communication*. Toronto: University of Toronto Press, 2006.

_____. *Empire and Communications*. Toronto: Dundurn Press, 2007.

Isaacs, Susan. *Brave Dames and Wimpettes*. New York: Ballantine, 1991.

Jacobs, Will, and Gerard Jones. *The Comic Book Heroes*. New York: Crown, 1985.

Jenkins, Henry. *Textual Poachers: Television Fans and Participatory Culture*. New York: Routledge, 1992.

_____. *What Made Pistachio Nuts? Early Sound Comedy and the Vaudeville Aesthetic*. New York: Columbia University Press, 1992.

_____, ed. *The Children's Culture Reader*. New York: New York University Press, 1998.

Johnson-Woods, Toni. *Blame Canada! South Park and Contemporary Culture*. New York: Continuum, 2007.

Johnston, Ollie, and Frank Thomas. *The Disney Villain*. New York: Hyperion, 1993.

Jones, Chuck. *Chuck Amuck: The Life and Times of an Animated Cartoonist*. New York: Farrar, Straus and Giroux, 1989.

Jones, Dudley, and Tony Watkins, ed. *A Necessary Fantasy?* New York: Garland, 2000.

Jones, Gerard. *Honey, I'm Home: Sitcoms Selling the American Dream*. New York: St. Martin's Press, 1992.

_____. *Killing Monsters: Why Children Need Fantasy, Super Heroics and Make Believe Violence*. New York: Basic Books, 2002.

_____. *Men of Tomorrow: Geeks, Gangsters and the Birth of the Comic Book*. New York: Basic Books, 2004.

Joshi, S.T. *The Weird Tale*. Holicong, PA: Wildside Press, 2003.

Kackman, Michael. *Citizen Spy*. Minneapolis: University of Minnesota Press, 2005.

Kaminsky, Stuart and Jeffrey Mahan. *American Television Genres*. Chicago: Nelson-Hall, 1985.

Kammen, Michael. *American Culture, American Tastes: Social Change and the Twentieth Century*. New York: Alfred A. Knopf, 1999.

Kanfer, Stefan. *Serious Business: The Art and Commerce of Animation in America from Betty Boop to "Toy Story."* New York: Scribner, 1997.

Kaplan, E. Ann, ed. *Psychoanalysis and Cinema*. New York: Routledge, 1990.

Kasson, John. *Houdini, Tarzan and the Perfect Man: The White Male Body and the Challenge of Modernity in America*. New York: Hill & Wang, 2001.

Katz, Ephraim, et al. *The Film Encyclopedia*. New York: HarperPerennial, 1998.

Kaveney, Roz. *Superheroes! Capes and Crusaders In Comics and Films*. London: I.B. Tauris, 2008.

Kaye, Evelyn. *The Family Guide to Children's Television*. New York: Pantheon, 1974.

Kelley, Michael. *A Parents' Guide to Television*. New York: John Wiley and Sons, 1983.

Kenner, Hugh. *Chuck Jones: A Flurry of Drawings*. Berkeley: University of California Press, 1994.

Keslowitz, Steven. *The Simpsons and Society*. Tucson: Hats Off Books, 2004.

_____. *The World According to The Simpsons*. Napierville, IL: Sourcebooks, 2006.

Kett, Joseph. *Rites of Passage*. New York: Basic Books, 1977.
Kimmel, Daniel. *The Fourth Network*. Chicago: Ivan R. Dee, 2004.
Kimmel, Michael. *Manhood in America*. New York: Oxford University Press, 2006.
Kinder, Marsha. *Playing with Power in Movies, Television and Video Games*. Berkeley: University of California Press, 1993.
_____, ed. *Kids' Media Culture*. Durham: Duke University Press, 1999.
Kisseloff, Jeff. *The Box: An Oral History of Television*. New York: Viking, 1995.
Klein, Norman M. *Seven Minutes*. New York: Verso, 1993.
Kline, Stephen. *Out of the Garden: Toys and Children's Culture in the Age of Marketing*. Toronto: Garamond Press, 1993.
Koening, David. *Mouse Under Glass*. Irvine, CA: Bonaventure Press, 2001.
Kundanis, Rose. *Children, Teens, Families and Mass Media: The Millenial Generation*. Mahwah, NJ: Lawrence Erlbuam Associates, 2003.
Laporte, Nicole. *The Men Who Would Be King*. New York: Houghton Mifflin Harcourt, 2010.
Lawson, Tim, and Alisa Persons. The *Magic Behind the Voices: A Who's Who of Cartoon Voice Actors*. Jackson: University Press of Mississippi, 2004.
Leacock, Stephen, ed. *The Greatest Pages of American Humor*. New York: Sun Dial Press, 1936.
Lebeau, Vicky. *Lost Angels*. London: Routledge, 1995.
Lee, Stan, and George Mair. *Excelsior: The Amazing Life of Stan Lee*. New York: Fireside, 2002.
Leff, Leonard, and Jerrold Simmons. *The Dame in the Kimono*. New York: Grove Weidenfeld, 1990.
Lehman, Christopher. *American Animated Cartoons of the Vietnam Era: A Study of Social Commentary in Films and Television Programs 1961–1973*. Jefferson, NC: McFarland, 2006.
Leibert, Robert, John Neale, and Emily Davidson. *The Early Window: Effects of Television on Children and Youth*. New York: Pergammon Press, 1973.
Lenburg, Jeff. *The Encyclopedia of Animated Cartoons*. New York: Checkmark Books, 2009.
_____. *The Great Cartoon Directors*. New York: Da Capo, 1993.
_____. *Who's Who in Animated Cartoons*. New York: Applause Theatre and Cinema Books, 2006.
Lesser, Gerald. *Children and Television: Lessons from "Sesame Street."* New York: Vintage, 1974.
Levine, Lawrence. *Highbrow/Lowbrow: The Emergence of Cultural Hierarchy in America*. Cambridge: Harvard University Press, 1988.
Lewis, Justin. *The Ideological Octopus*. New York: Routledge, 1991.
Lewis, Robert M., ed. *From Travelling Show to Vaudeville: Theatrical Spectacle in America, 1830–1910*. Baltimore: Johns Hopkins University Press, 2003.
Lichter, S. Robert, Linda S. Lichter, and Stanley Rothman. *Watching America*. New York: Prentice-Hall, 1991.
Lipsitz, George. *Time Passages: Collective Memory and American Popular Culture*. Minneapolis: University of Minnesota Press, 1990.
Louvish, Simon. *Keystone: The Life and Clowns of Mack Sennett*. London: Faber and Faber, 2003.
Lowe, Carl, ed. *Television and American Culture*. New York: H.W. Wilson, 1981.
Lowe, Denise. *Women and American Television: An Encyclopedia*. Santa Barbara: ABC-CLIO, 1999.
Lucanio, Patrick. *Them or Us*. Bloomington: Indiana University Press, 1987.
_____, and Gary Coville. *American Science Fiction Television Series of the 1950s*. Jefferson, NC: McFarland, 1998.
Luke, Carmen. *Constructing the Child Viewer: A History of the American Discourse on Television and Children 1950–1980*. New York: Praeger, 1990.
Lukin, Josh, ed. *Invisible Suburbs: Recovering 1950s Protest Fiction*. Jackson: University Press of Mississippi, 2008.
MacDonald, J. Fred. *Blacks and White TV: African Americans in Television Since 1948*, 2d ed. Chicago: Nelson-Hall, 1992.
_____. *One Nation Under Television*. Chicago: Nelson-Hall, 1990.
_____. *Television and the Red Menace: The Video Road to Vietnam*. New York: Praeger, 1985.
Maland, Charles. *Chaplin and American Culture*. Princeton: Princeton University Press, 1989.
Mallory, Michael. *Hanna-Barbera Cartoons*. New York: Hugh Lauter Levin Associates, 1998.
Maltin, Leonard. *Of Mice and Magic*. New York: Plume, 1987.
_____, ed. *Leonard Maltin's Movie Encyclopedia*. New York: Dutton, 1994.
Marc, David. *Comic Visions: Television Comedy and American Culture*. Malden, MA: Blackwell, 1997.
_____. *Demographic Vistas: Television in American Culture*. Philadelphia: University of Pennsylvania Press, 1997.
_____, and Robert J. Thompson. *Prime Time, Prime Movers*. Syracuse: Syracuse University Press, 1995.
Martin, William. *With God on Our Side*. New York: Broadway Books, 1996.
Martyn, Warren, and Adrian Wood. *I Can't Believe It's a Bigger and Better Updated Unofficial* Simpsons *Guide*. London: Virgin, 2000.
Mast, Gerald. *The Comic Mind*. Chicago: University of Chicago Press, 1979.
Maurer, David. *The Big Con: The Story of the Confidence Man*. New York: Anchor Books, 1999.
May, Elaine Tyler. *Homeward Bound*. New York: Basic Books, 1988.
Mazurkewich, Karen. *Cartoon Capers*. Toronto: McArthur, 1999.
McBride, Joseph. *Steven Spielberg: A Biography*. New York: Simon & Schuster, 1997.
McCann, Jesse L., ed. The Simpsons *Beyond Forever*. New York: HarperPerennial, 2002.
_____. The Simpsons *One Step Beyond Forever*. New York: HarperPerennial, 2005.

McDonnell, Kathleen. *Honey, We Lost the Kids: Re-Thinking Childhood in the Multimedia Age.* Toronto: Second Story Press, 2005.

_____. *Kid Culture: Kids and Adults and Popular Culture.* Toronto: Second Story Press, 1994.

McGirr, Lisa. *Suburban Warriors: The Origins of the New American Right.* Princeton: Princeton University Press, 2001.

McLean, Albert F., Jr. *American Vaudeville as Ritual.* Lexington: University of Kentucky Press, 1965.

McLuhan, Marshall. *Essential McLuhan.* Ed. Eric McLuhan and Frank Zingrone. Toronto: House of Anansi Press, 1995.

_____. *Understanding Media: The Extensions of Man.* Ed. W. Terrence Gordon. Corte Madea, CA: Gingko Press, 2003.

_____, and Eric McLuhan. *Laws of Media: The New Science.* Toronto: University of Toronto Press, 1988.

McNeal, James. *Children as Consumers.* Lexington, MA: D.C. Heath, 1987.

McNeil, Alex. *Total Television.* New York: Penguin, 1996.

Medved, Michael. *Hollywood vs. America.* New York: HarperPerennial, 1992.

Meehan, Diana. *Ladies of the Evening.* Metuchen, NJ: Scarecrow Press, 1983.

Melody, William. *Children's Television: The Economics of Exploitation.* New Haven: Yale University Press, 1973.

Mendelson, Lee, and Bill Melendez. *A Charlie Brown Christmas: The Making of a Tradition.* Ed. Antonia Felix. New York: HarperResource, 2000.

_____, and _____. *It's The Great Pumpkin, Charlie Brown.* New York: Harper, 2001.

Merritt, Russell, and J.B. Kaufman. *Walt in Wonderland: The Silent Films of Walt Disney.* Baltimore: Johns Hopkins University Press, 1993.

Meyrowitz, Joshua. *No Sense of Place: The Impact of Electronic Media on Social Behavior.* New York: Oxford University Press, 1985.

Metz, Robert. *CBS: Reflections in a Bloodshot Eye.* Chicago: Playboy Press, 1975.

Michaelis, David. *Schultz and Peanuts.* New York: Harper, 2007.

Miller, G. Wayne. *Toy Wars.* New York: Random House, 1998.

Miller, Toby. *Spyscreen.* Oxford: Oxford University Press, 2003.

Minow, Newton, and Craig LaMay. *Abandoned in the Wasteland: Children, Television and the First Amendment.* New York: Hill & Wang, 1995.

Mintz, Stephen. *Huck's Raft: A History of American Childhood.* Cambridge: Belknap/Harvard University Press, 2004.

Misiroglu, Gina, ed. *The Superhero Book.* 1st ed., Detroit: Visible Ink Press, 2004; 2d ed., 2009.

_____, and Michael Eury, ed. *The Supervillain Book.* Detroit: Visible Ink Press, 2006.

Mitchell, Glenn. *The Marx Brothers Encyclopedia.* London: B.T. Batsford, 1996.

Modell, John. *Into One's Own.* Berkeley: University of California Press, 1989.

Modleski, Tania. *Feminism Without Women.* New York: Routledge, 1991.

Montgomery, Kathryn. *Target: Prime Time.* New York: Oxford University Press, 1989.

Moody, Kate. *Growing Up on Television: The TV Effect.* New York: Times Books, 1980.

Morgan, Judith, and Neil Morgan. *Dr. Seuss and Mr. Geisel.* New York: Random House, 1995.

Muir, John Kenneth. *The Encyclopedia of Superheroes on Film and Television.* Jefferson, NC: McFarland, 2004.

_____. *A History and Critical Analysis of Blake's 7, the 1978–1981 British Television Space Adventure.* Jefferson, NC: McFarland, 2001.

Mullan, Bob. *Consuming Television.* Oxford: Blackwell, 1997.

Murray, Janet. *Hamlet on the Holodeck.* New York: Free Press, 1997.

Murray, Joe. *Creating Animated Cartoons with Character.* New York: Watson-Guptill, 2010.

Nachman, Gerald. *Seriously Funny: The Rebel Comedians of the 1950s and 1960s.* New York: Pantheon, 2003.

Naha, Ed. *The Science Fictionary.* New York: Seaview, 1980.

Nash, Ilana. *American Sweethearts: Teenage Girls in Twentieth Century Popular Culture.* Bloomington: Indiana University Press, 2006.

Nathanson, Paul, and Katherine Young. *Spreading Misandry.* Montreal: McGill-Queen's University Press, 2001.

Newcomb, Horace. *TV: The Most Popular Art.* Garden City, NY: Anchor Press, 1974.

_____, ed. *Television: The Critical View*, 6th ed. New York: Oxford University Press, 2000.

_____, and Robert S. Alley. *The Producers' Medium.* New York: Oxford University Press, 1983.

Neuwirth, Allan. *Makin' Toons: Inside the Most Popular Animated TV Shows and Movies.* New York: Allworth Press, 2003.

Nodelman, Perry. *The Pleasures of Children's Literature.* New York: Longman, 1992.

Novick, Peter. *That Noble Dream: The "Objectivity Question" and the American Historical Profession.* Cambridge: Cambridge University Press, 1998.

Nyberg, Amy Kiste. *Seal of Approval: The History of the Comics Code.* Jackson: University Press of Mississippi, 1998.

O'Connor, John E., ed. *American History/American Television: Interpreting the Visual Past.* New York: Frederick Ungar, 1983.

O'Donnell, Victoria. *Television Criticism.* Los Angeles: Sage, 2007.

Ohmart, Ben. *Welcome Foolish Mortals: The Life and Voices of Paul Frees.* Boalsberg, PA: Bear Manor Media, 2004.

_____, and Joe Bevilacqua. *Daws Butler, Characters Actor.* Boalsberg, PA: Bear Manor Media, 2005.

_____, and Charles Stumpf. *Walter Tetley: For Corn's Sake.* Boalsberg, PA: Bear Manor Media, 2005.

O'Neill, William. *American High: The Years of Confidence 1945–1960.* New York: Free Press, 1986.

Oppenheimer, Jerry. *Toy Monster: The Big, Bad World of Mattel*. New York: John Wiley and Sons, 2009.
Orenstein, Peggy. *Schoolgirls*. New York: Anchor Books, 1994.
Ortved, John. *The Simpsons: An Uncensored, Unauthorized History*. Vancouver, BC: Greystone Books, 2009.
Osgerby, Bill, and Anna Gough-Yates, eds. *Action TV*. London: Routledge, 2001.
Owen, David. *The Man Who Invented Saturday Morning and Other Adventures in American Enterprise*. New York: Villard, 1988.
Owens, Gary, and Jeff Lenburg. *How to Make a Million Dollars with Your Voice (Or Lose Your Tonsils Trying)*. New York: McGraw-Hill, 2004.
Ozersky, Josh. *Archie Bunker's America*. Carbondale: South Illinois University Press, 2003.
Palladino, Grace. *Teenagers: An American History*. New York: Basic Books, 1996.
Palmer, Edward. *Children in the Cradle of Television*. Lexington, MA: D.C. Heath, 1987.
Paris, Leslie. *Children's Nature: The Rise of the American Summer Camp*. New York: New York University Press, 2010.
Parish, James Robert, and Michael R. Pitts. *The Great Science Fiction Pictures*. Metuchen, NJ: Scarecrow Press, 1977.
Pawlewski, Cheryl. *Glued to the Tube: The Threat of Television Addiction to Today's Family*. Napierville, IL: Sourcebooks, 2000.
Pearl, David, Lorraine Bouthliet, and Joyce Lazar, eds. *Television and Behavior—Volume 2*. Washington, D.C.: U.S. Dept. of Health and Human Services, 1982.
Peary, Danny, and Gerald Peary, eds. *The American Animated Cartoon: A Critical Anthology*. New York: Dutton, 1980.
Pearson, Patricia. *When She Was Bad*. New York: Viking, 1997.
Pecora, Norma Odom. *The Business of Children's Entertainment*. New York: Guildford Press, 1998.
Perlstein, Rick. *Nixonland: The Rise of a President and the Fracturing of America*. New York: Scribner, 2008.
Perry, Jeb. *Universal Television*. Metuchen, NJ: Scarecrow Press, 1983.
Piling, Jayne, ed. *A Reader in Animation Studies*. London: John Libbey, 1997.
Pohl-Weary, Emily, ed. *Girls Who Bite Back*. Toronto: Sumach Press, 2004.
Postman, Neil. *Amusing Ourselves to Death*. New York: Penguin, 1985.
_____. *The Disappearance of Childhood*. New York: Laurel, 1984.
Powers, Ron. *The Beast, the Eunuch, and the Glass-Eyed Child*. New York: Harcourt Brace Jovanovich, 1990.
Pratkanis, Anthony, and Elliot Aronson. *Age of Propaganda*. New York: W.H. Freeman, 2001.
Press, Andrea. *Women Watching Television*. Philadelphia: University of Pennsylvania Press, 1991.
Pungente, John, SJ, and Martin O'Malley. *More Than Meets the Eye*. Toronto: McClelland and Stewart, 1999.
Pustz, Matthew J. *Comic Book Culture: Fanboys and True Believers*. Jackson: University Press of Mississippi, 1999.
Putterman, Barry. *On Television and Comedy*. Jefferson, NC: McFarland, 1995.
Raphael, Jordan and Tom Spurgeon. *Stan Lee and the Rise and Fall of the American Comic Book*. Chicago: Chicago Review Press, 2003.
Reed, Alan, and Ben Ohmart. *Yabba Dabba Doo, Or Never a Star: The Alan Reed Story*. Albany, GA: Bear Manor Media, 2009.
Reisman, David, Nathan Glazer, and Reuel Denny. *The Lonely Crowd*. New Haven: Yale University Press, 1969.
Renzetti, Rob, Alex Kirwan, and Eric Homan, eds. *The MLAATR Sketchbook*. New York: Frederator Books, 2004.
Reynolds, Richard. *Super Heroes: A Modern Mythology*. Jackson: University of Mississippi Press, 1992.
Richmond, Ray. *TV Moms: An Illustrated Guide*. New York: TV Books, 2000.
_____, ed. *The Simpsons: A Complete Guide to Our Favorite Family*. New York: HarperPerennial, 1997.
Riley, Denise. *"Am I That Name?"* Minneapolis: University of Minnesota Press, 1998.
Ro, Ronin. *Tales to Astonish: Jack Kirby, Stan Lee and the American Comic Book Revolution*. New York: Bloomsbury, 2004.
Ross, Steven. *Working Class Hollywood: Silent Film and the Shaping of Class in America*. Princeton: Princeton University Press, 1998.
Rovin, Jeff. *Aliens, Robots and Spaceships*. New York: Facts on File, 1995.
_____. *The Illustrated Encyclopedia of Cartoon Animals*. New York: Prentice Hall, 1991.
Rutstein, Nat. *"Go Watch TV!"* New York: Sheed and Ward, 1974.
Ryfle, Steve. *Japan's Biggest Mon-Star: The Unauthorized Biography of "The Big G."* Toronto: ECW Press, 1998.
Sandler, Kevin, ed. *Reading the Rabbit: Explorations in Warner Brothers Animation*. New Brunswick: Rutgers University Press, 1998.
Sartre, Jean-Paul. *The Imagination*. London: Routledge, 2012.
Sarris, Andrew. *The American Cinema: Directors and Directions, 1929–1968*. New York: E.P. Dutton, 1968.
Schechter, Harold. *Savage Pastimes: A Cultural History of Violent Entertainment*. New York: St. Martin's Press, 2005.
Scheimer, Lou, and Andy Mangels. *Lou Scheimer: Creating the Filmation Generation*. Raleigh: TwoMorrows, 2012.
Scheiner, Georgeanne. *Signifying Female Adolescence*. Westport, CT: Praeger, 2000.
Schelde, Per. *Androids, Humanoids and Other Science Fiction Monsters*. New York: New York University Press, 1993.
Schneider, Cy. *Children's Television: The Art, the Business and How It Works*. Chicago: NTC Business Books, 1987.

Schneider, Steve. *That's All Folks: The Art of Warner Brothers Animation*. New York: Henry Holt, 1988.

Scholes, Robert. *Textual Power*. New Haven: Yale University Press, 1985.

Schramm, Wilbur, Jack Lyle, and Edwin B. Parker. *Television in the Lives of Our Children*. Stanford: Stanford University Press, 1961.

Scivally, Bruce. *Superman on Film, Radio, Television and Broadway*. Jefferson, NC: McFarland, 2008.

Scott, Keith. *The Moose That Roared*. New York: Thomas Dunne Books/St. Martin's Griffin, 2000.

Seger, Linda. *When Women Call the Shots*. New York: Henry Holt, 1996.

Segrave, Kerry. *American Television Abroad: Hollywood's Attempt to Dominate World Television*. Jefferson, NC: McFarland, 1998.

Seiter, Ellen. *Sold Separately: Parents and Children in Consumer Culture*. New Brunswick: Rutgers University Press, 1995.

Seldes, Gilbert. *The Public Arts*. New York: Simon & Schuster, 1956.

_____. *The Seven Lively Arts*. Mineola, NY: Dover, 2001.

Sennett, Ted. *The Art of Hanna-Barbera*. New York: Viking, 1989.

Shaheen, Jack. *The TV Arab*. Bowling Green, OH: Bowling Green State University Popular Press, 1984.

Sheras, Peter, and Sherrill Tippins. *Your Child—Bully or Victim?* New York: Fireside, 2002.

Siegel, Scott, and Barbara Siegel. *American Film Comedy*. New York: Prentice-Hall, 1994.

Sito, Tom. *Drawing the Line: The Untold Story of the Animation Unions from Bosko to Bart Simpson*. Lexington: University Press of Kentucky, 2006.

Skal, David J. *Hollywood Gothic: The Tangled Web of Dracula from Page to Stage to Screen*. New York: Faber and Faber, 2004.

_____. *The Monster Show: A Cultural History of Horror*. New York: Norton, 1993.

_____. *Screams of Reason: Mad Science and Modern Culture*. New York: Norton, 1998.

Sklar, Robert. *Movie Made America: A Cultural History of American Movies*. London: Chappell, 1978.

_____. *Prime Time America*. New York: Oxford University Press, 1980.

Skornia, Harry. *Television and Society*. New York: McGraw-Hill, 1965.

Slater, Robert. *This Is CBS*. Englewood Cliffs, NJ: Prentice-Hall, 1988.

Slide, Anthony. *Eccentrics of Comedy*. Metuchen, NJ: Scarecrow Press, 1998.

_____. *The Television Industry: A Historical Dictionary*. Westport, CT: Greenwood Press, 1991.

_____. *The Vaudevillians*. Westport, CT: Arlington House, 1981.

Smith, Ronald. *The Cosby Book*. New York: S.P.I. Books, 1993.

Smoodin, Eric. *Animating Culture: Hollywood Cartoons from the Sound Era*. New Brunswick: Rutgers University Press, 1993.

Snyder, Robert W. *The Voice of the City: Vaudeville and Popular Culture in New York*. Chicago: Ivan R. Dee, 2000.

Sobchack, Vivian. *Screening Space*. New York: Ungar, 1987.

Solomon, Charles, ed. *The Art of the Animated Image*. Los Angeles: American Film Institute, 1987.

Spigel, Lynn. *Make Room for TV: Television and the Family Ideal in Postwar America*. Chicago: University of Chicago Press, 1992.

_____. *Welcome to the Dreamhouse: Popular Media and Postwar Suburbs*. Durham: Duke University Press, 2001.

_____ and Michael Curtin (eds.) *The Revolution Wasn't Televised*. New York: Routledge, 1997.

Stabile, Carol, and Mark Harrison (eds.) *Prime Time Animation: Television Animation and American Culture*. New York: Routledge, 2003.

Stark, Steven. *Glued to the Set*. New York: The Free Press, 1997.

Starker, Steven. *Evil Influences: Crusades Against the Mass Media*. New Brunswick: Transaction, 1988.

Steiner, Gary. *The People Look at Television*. New York: Alfred A. Knopf, 1963.

Stewart, James B. *Disney War*. New York: Simon & Schuster, 2005.

Sterling, Christopher, and Mark Kittross. *Stay Tuned*. Belmont, CA: Wadsworth, 1978.

Stoffman, Daniel. *The Nelvana Story: Thirty Animated Years*. Toronto: Nelvana, 2002.

Sugrue, Thomas. *The Origins of the Urban Crisis: Race and Inequality in Postwar Detroit*. Princeton: Princeton University Press, 2005.

Swirski, Peter. *From Lowbrow to Nobrow*. Montreal: McGill-Queen's University Press, 2005.

Tasker, Yvonne. *Spectacular Bodies*. London: Routledge, 1993.

Taylor, Marjorie. *Imaginary Companions and the Children Who Create Them*. New York: Oxford University Press, 1999.

Telotte, J.P. *Replications*. Urbana: University of Illinois Press, 1995.

_____. *Science Fiction Film*. New York: Cambridge University Press, 2001.

Thompson, Robert J. *Adventures on Prime Time: The Television Programs of Stephen J. Cannell*. New York: Praeger, 1990.

Thoreau, Henry David. *Walden and Civil Disobedience*. New York: Airmont, 1965.

Tichi, Cecilia. *Electronic Hearth: Creating an American Television Culture*. New York: Oxford University Press, 1991.

Trites, Roberta Seelinger. *Disturbing the Peace*. Iowa City: University of Iowa Press, 2000.

Tuchman, Gaye, ed. *The TV Establishment*. Englewood Cliffs, NJ: Prentice-Hall, 1974.

_____, Arlene Kaplan Daniels, and James Benet, eds. *Hearth and Home*. New York: Oxford University Press, 1978.

Turner, Chris. *Planet Simpson: How a Cartoon Masterpiece Dominated an Era and Defined a Generation*. Toronto: Random House, 2004.

Turow, Joseph. *Entertainment, Education and the Hard Sell*. New York: Praeger, 1981.

———. *Playing Doctor*. New York: Oxford University Press, 1989.

Urdang, Lawrence, ed. *The Random House Dictionary of the English Language: College Edition*. New York: Random House, 1968.

Wadlington, Warwick. *The Confidence Game in American Literature*. Princeton: Princeton University Press, 1975.

Wald, Elijah. *The Dozens: A History of Rap's Mama*. New York: Oxford University Press, 2012.

Walkerdine, Valerie. *Daddy's Girl: Young Girls and Popular Culture*. Cambridge: Harvard University Press, 1997.

Walters, Suzanne Danuta. *All the Rage*. Chicago: University of Chicago Press, 2001.

Ward, Ed, Geoffrey Stokes, and Ken Tucker. *Rock of Ages: The Rolling Stone History of Rock and Roll*. New York: Summit, 1986.

Ward, Richard L. *A History of the Hal Roach Studios*. Carbondale: Southern Illinois University Press, 1994.

Wasko, Janet. *Understanding Disney*. Cambridge: Polity, 2001.

Watkins, Mel. *On the Real Side*. New York: Simon & Schuster, 1994.

Watson, Mary Ann. *The Expanding Vista*. New York: Oxford University Press, 1990.

Watts, Stephen. *The Magic Kingdom: Walt Disney and the American Way of Life*. Boston: Houghton Mifflin, 1997.

Weibel, Kathryn. *Mirror, Mirror*. Garden City, NY: Anchor Books, 1977.

Wertham, Frederic. *Seduction of the Innocent*. New York: Rinehart, 1954.

Wells, Paul. *The Animated Bestiary: Animals, Cartoons and Culture*. New Brunswick: Rutgers University Press, 2009.

———. *Animation and America*. New Brunswick: Rutgers University Press, 2002.

———. *Animation: Genre and Authorship*. London: Wallflower, 2002.

———. *Understanding Animation*. London: Routledge, 1998.

West, Mark I. *Children, Culture and Controversy*. Hamden, CT: Archon, 1988.

Westfahl, Gary. *Science Fiction, Children's Literature and Popular Culture: Coming of Age in Fantasyland*. Westport, CT: Greenwood Press, 2000.

Whelehan, Imelda. *Modern Feminist Thought*. New York: New York University Press, 1995.

Whitfield, Stephen. *The Culture of the Cold War*. Baltimore: Johns Hopkins University Press, 1995.

Whyte, William, Jr. *The Organization Man*. Garden City, NY: Doubleday, 1957.

Wild, David. *The Showrunners*. New York: HarperCollins, 1999.

Wildmon, Donald, and Randall Nutton. *Don Wildmon: The Man the Networks Love to Hate*. Wilmore, KY: Bristol Books, 1989.

Wilentz, Sean. *The Age of Reagan: A History 1974–2008*. New York: HarperCollins, 2008.

Willeford, William. *The Fool and His Scepter*. Chicago: Northwestern University Press, 1969.

Williams, Raymond. *Television*. New York: Routledge, 2003.

Wilson, Edmund. *Axel's Castle: A Study in the Imaginative Literature of 1870–1930*. New York: Collier Books, 1991.

Winn, Marie. *The Plug In Drug*. New York: Penguin, 1985.

Wolf, Naomi. *Fire with Fire*. Toronto: Random House, 1993.

Wong, Eugene. *On Visual Media Racism*. New York: Arno Press, 1978.

Woods, Harold, and Geraldine Woods. *Bill Cosby: Making America Laugh and Learn*. Minneapolis: Dillon Press, 1989.

Woolery, George. *Children's Television: The First Thirty-Five Years. Part 1: Animated Cartoon Series*. Metuchen, NJ: Scarecrow Press, 1983.

Wright, Bradford. *Comic Book Nation: The Transformation of Youth Culture in America*. Baltimore: Johns Hopkins University Press, 2001.

Yoggy, Gary. *Riding the Video Range*. Jefferson, NC: McFarland, 1995.

Zicree, Marc Scott. *The Twilight Zone Companion*. New York: Bantam, 1982.

Zipes, Jack. *Happily Ever After: Fairy Tales, Children and the Culture Industry*. New York: Routledge, 1997.

———. *When Dreams Came True: Classical Fairy Tales and Their Tradition*. New York: Routledge, 1999.

Zook, Kristal Brent. *Color by FOX*. New York: Oxford University Press, 1999.

Zurawik, David. *The Jews of Prime Time*. Hanover: Brandeis University Press, 2003.

Index

A.K.A. Cartoons 301
A Squared 208
Aames, Willie 150
ABC 27, 53, 54, 58, 60, 63, 65, 66, 70, 71, 73, 75, 78, 79, 80, 86, 88, 92, 93, 95, 102, 106, 108, 110, 111, 112, 128, 129, 140, 142, 143, 144, 151, 152, 153, 154, 155, 157, 158, 159, 160, 161, 162, 163, 165, 172, 173, 179, 181, 183, 184, 189, 196, 197, 198, 199, 202, 203, 204, 208, 209, 210, 211, 220, 221, 226, 227, 230, 231, 233, 238, 242, 250, 262, 273, 274, 276, 277, 278, 280, 291, 292, 348, 350
ABC Afternoon Special 158
Academy of Television Arts and Sciences 186, 228
Ace Ventura 244, 298
Action for Children's Television 71, 115, 123, 125, 126, 127, 137, 140, 144, 170, 190
Adams, Don 91, 151, 154, 208, 280
Adcox, Thom 356
Adler, Charlie 183, 254, 266, 283
Adlon, Pamela 343
Adventure Time 345, 346
Adventures of the Gummi Bears 198
advertising 6, 30, 32, 37, 38, 39, 45, 47, 83, 86, 87, 92, 93, 99, 106, 111, 119, 120, 121, 123, 126, 129, 130, 189, 211, 250, 260, 261, 322, 345
Aeon Flux 302
"Aesop and Son" 79, 82
Al Brodax 95, 106
Al Guest Studios 107
Aladdin 275

Aladdin and His Wonderful Lamp 21, 24
Alaskey, Joe 283
Alazraqui, Carlos 340, 341
Albee, E.F. 11
Alcorn, Keith 320
Aldashin, Mikhail 331
Alexander, Adrienne 180
Alexander, Joan 131
Alf 210, 300
Alf Tales 210
Alice in Wonderland 158
All Dogs Go to Heaven 295
All Grown Up 325
The All-New Popeye Hour 180
Allen, Chris 68, 88
Allen, Dayton 98
Allen, John 99
Allen Gregory 310
Almost Naked Animals 362
Alvin and the Chipmunks 203, 204
Amazing Spider Man and the Incredible Hulk 219
Amazing Stories 238
Amblimation 281
Amblin Entertainment 281
American Dad 306, 307, 308
American Dragon 356
American Family Association 224
American-International Pictures 149
American Pop 223
An American Tail 281, 312
Amsterdam, Morey 161
Anamorphism 108
Anatole 366
Anderson, Alex 36, 77, 296
Anderson, Arthur 330
Anderson, Pamela 366
Andes, Keith 70
Andrusco, Gene 163
Angelina Ballerina 366

Animagic 92, 93, 160, 161, 162, 226, 227
Animaniacs 284, 285, 286
anime 270, 291, 301, 325, 326, 333, 341
Ansara, Michael 205
Ansolabehere, Joe 278, 351
"The Ant and the Aardvark" 94
Antonucci, Danny 301
Appel, Richard 309
Aqua Teen Hunger Force 330
Arbuckle, Roscoe "Fatty" 12
Archie's TV Funnies 132
Arthur 299
As Told by Ginger 319
Ask Edward 322
ASK 292
Asner, Edward 149, 238, 300
Associated Artists Productions 102
Assy McGee 330
Astaire, Fred 160, 161
Astro Boy 365
Astronut Show 98
Atomic Betty 225, 336
Atoms, Maxwell 330, 331, 345, 362
Attack of the Killer Tomatoes 300
Avatar 325
The Avengers 300, 357
Avery, James 222
Avery, "Tex" 24, 102, 121, 178, 182, 253, 291, 311, 341, 364
Azaria, Hank 234

Babar 221
Baby Blues 365
Baby Looney Tunes 364
Back to the Barnyard 327
Back to the Future 286
Backus, Jim 29, 96
Baer Animation 352

403

Bagdasarian, Ross 108, 203
Bagdasarian, Ross, Jr. 109, 203, 204
Baggy Pants and the Nitwits 163
Bailey's Comets 163
Bakalian, Peter 228
Baker, Dee Bradley 308, 328 331, 334, 357, 360
Baker, Joe 202
Bakshi, Ralph 98, 106, 107, 211, 214, 223, 224, 249
Baldwin, Gerald 176
Baldwin, William 316
Banas, Carl 107
Bannister, Frank 166
Barbera, Jayne 147
Barbera, Joseph 28, 29, 40, 41, 42, 43, 44, 45, 46, 47, 49, 52, 53, 67, 68, 71, 73, 74, 119, 123, 124, 127, 128, 130, 145, 146, 147, 148, 149, 156, 157, 165, 172, 173, 174, 175, 178, 183, 184, 185, 186, 187, 201, 204, 207, 226, 238, 245, 261, 264, 267, 296, 314, 319, 370, 371
Barge, Gene 43
Barker, Mike 306
The Barkleys 163
Barks, Carl 199
Barney and Friends 366
Barnyard Commandos 301
Barre, Raoul 15
Barron, Phil 210
Bartilson, Lynsey 326
Basco, Dante 356
Baseman, Gary 350
Bass, Jules 92, 226, 227, 371
Batchelor, Joy 162
Batfink 110
Batman 95, 108, 110, 111, 129, 142, 145, 152, 247, 288, 289, 294, 322, 337, 364
Beals, Dick 68, 179
Bean, Orson 161, 226
Beany and Cecil 46, 102, 103, 211, 249
Beany and Cecil Meet Billy the Squid 102
Beasley, Allyce 279
Beavis and Butthead 239, 302
Bebe's Kids 352
Beck, Jackson 91, 131
Beck, Jerry 284, 289, 319
"The Bedrock Cops" 182
Beethoven 297
"Beetle Bailey" 95
Beetlejuice 221
Bell, Michael 142, 176, 178, 182, 202, 204
Bellflower, Nellie 203
Ben 10 330

Benaderet, Bea 55
Benedict, Ed 45, 249, 267
Benedict, Tony 45
Benjamin, H. Jon 311
Bennett, Jeffrey 267, 277, 287, 297, 317, 335, 340, 344, 356, 357
Benny, Jack 72, 157, 160, 253, 258
Benson, Jodi 340
Benton, Jim 294, 331
Berger, Gregg 215, 254
Berger, Holly 208
Bergman, Mary Kay 294, 313
Berman, Andy 319
Berry, Dr. Gordon 134
Besser, Joe 163
Better off Dead 293
Beverly Hills Teens 210
Bianchi, Bruno 207
Bickenbach, Richard "Bick" 43, 45
Bigfoot and the Muscle Machine 219
Big Guy and Rusty 365
Biggers, Buck 91
Bikel, Theodore 226
Biker Mice from Mars 300
Billingsley, Barbara 218
Billionfold 314, 315
Bird, Brad 238, 326
Birdman and the Galaxy Trio 70, 336
Birdz 298
The Biskitts 179
Bjorklund, Timothy 351
Black Beauty 158
Blackstar 187
Blackton, J. Stuart 14
Blakeslee, Susan 313
Blanc, Mel 26, 46, 55, 61, 64, 65, 66, 72, 150, 154, 157, 183, 202, 266
Blaster's Universe 298
blaxploitation 136, 155
Blazing Dragons 298
Bliss, Lucille 36, 68, 176
Block, Bobby 335
Blu, Susan 183, 202
Bluhdorn, Charles 196
Bluth, Don 205, 207, 261, 295
Boakye, Kwesi 347
Bob the Builder 366
Bobby's World 293
Bob's Burgers 310
Bochco, Steven 238
Bocquelet, Ben 347
Boen, Earl 275
Bolke, Bradley 91
Bonsall, Shull 37
Booker, M. Keith 56, 59, 237, 246, 306

Boomerang 329
Boondocks 365
Boone, Richard 161
Booth, Shirley 161
Bosley, Tom 150, 162
Bosustow, Stephen 29, 30, 96
Bouchard, Loren 310
Bowers, Charles 15
Boyle, Bob 358
Braceface 366
Bracken, Eddie 227
Braverman, Bart 202
Bravestarr 192, 193
Bravo, Danny 63
Bray, John Randolph 14
Breslin, Spencer 355
Brillstein, Bernie 210
Britt, Melendy 191, 202
Brodax, Al 95, 106
Brooks, Avery 276
Brooks, James L. 233, 292
Brothers Grunt 301, 302
Brown, Joe E. 64, 65
Brown, Orlando 353
Browne, Roscoe Lee 300
Bruno the Kid 292
Bucky and Pepito 111
Bucky O'Hare and the Toad Wars 300
Buena Vista 195
Buhle, Paul 21
Bulifant, Joyce 188
"Bullwinkle's Corner" 83
Bumpass, Rodger 258, 313, 319
Buono, Victor 227
Burke, Kevin 153, 177, 183, 190, 192, 209
Burke, Timothy 153, 177, 183, 190, 192, 209
Burness, Pete 30, 79
Burnett, Alan 288
Burnett, Bill 319
Burnett, Leo 47
Burns, George 160
Burns, Jack 150
Burton, Adam 331
Burton, Corey 198, 200
Burton, LeVar 276
Burton, Tim 221, 238
Butch Cassidy and the Sundance Kids 153
Butler, Daws 46, 47, 48, 49, 50, 51, 61, 62, 64, 65, 69, 71, 78, 79, 82, 151, 153, 157, 163
Buzz Lightyear of Star Command 348
Buzzi, Ruth 164, 180

C Bear and Jamal 292
Caesar, Sid 168
Cahill, Julie McNally 342

Cahill, Timothy 342
Cait, Robert 320
Calico 222, 301
Callaway, Bill 157, 173
Callier, Frances 309
Calvin and the Colonel 112, 214
Camp, Hamilton 176
Camp Candy 211
Camp Lazlo! 339, 341, 344, 346
Campanella, Joseph 300
Campbell, David 277
Canemaker, John 105
Cannon, Robert "Bobe" 30, 96
Capital Cities Communications 208, 273
Capitol Critters 238, 262
"Captain Caveman" 182
"Captain Caveman and Son" 183
Captain Caveman and the Teen Angels 154, 182
Captain Kangaroo 97, 98, 110, 166
Captain N: The Game Master 211
Captain Planet and the Planeteers 290
Cardinelli, Linda 363
Carlson, Len 225
Carlton Your Doorman 215
Carney, Art 226
Carroll, Pat 179, 180
Carson, John 68
Cartoon All-Stars to the Rescue 228
Cartoon Network 7, 73, 90, 108, 231, 244, 248, 256, 260, 261, 262, 263, 264, 265, 266, 269, 270, 272, 273, 277, 278, 287, 301, 305, 306, 311, 329, 330, 331, 332, 333, 334, 347, 359, 362, 363, 364
Cartoon Network Development Studios Europe 347
Cartwright, Nancy 179, 180, 182, 234, 252, 274, 285, 331, 354, 357
Casper 105, 286
Cassidy, Ted 68, 70, 157, 158, 164
Castalleneta, Dan 234, 255, 276, 297
Cathy 214, 215
Catscratch 326
Caudell, Toran 255, 279
Cavadini, Cathy 271
Cavanagh, Megan 320, 328
CBS 46, 53, 54, 58, 66, 67, 68, 69, 70, 71, 73, 87, 91, 92, 93, 96, 97, 98, 99, 100, 108, 109, 111, 123, 127, 128, 131, 132, 137, 138, 139, 142, 144, 145, 150, 151, 152, 153, 157, 158, 160, 163, 164, 165, 166, 173, 178, 179, 180, 181, 183, 187, 188, 197, 203, 204, 206, 209, 215, 217, 218, 219, 220, 222, 223, 224, 227, 230, 233, 238, 251, 260, 274, 275, 292, 297, 306, 317
CBS Cartoon Theater 97
Cedric the Entertainer 352
censorship 6, 7, 11, 20, 24, 40, 41, 86, 87, 89, 113, 114, 115, 118, 120, 121, 122, 123, 125, 127, 128, 130, 139, 142, 143, 145, 147, 150, 156, 159, 168, 169, 178, 186, 215, 216, 284, 293, 303, 367
The Centurions 205
Cera, Michael 327
CGI 296, 298, 318, 320, 327, 328
Chalkzone 319
Challenge of the Gobots 181
Chalopin, Jean 207, 212
Channel Umptee-Three 296
Chaplin, Charlie 11, 12, 13, 15, 44, 47, 164
Charest, Micheline 299
Charles, Larry 296
A Charlie Brown Christmas 99
A Charlie Brown Thanksgiving 100
Charlotte's Web 149
Charren, Peggy 71, 126, 190, 250, 284
Children's Television Workshop 292
Children's Television Act 194, 231, 300
Chip 'n' Dale's Rescue Rangers 200
Chipmunk Punk 203
Chipmunks Go to the Movies 203
C.H.O.M.P.S. 149, 157
Chowder 344, 345
Chuck Jones Enterprises 101
Chuck Norris' Karate Kommandos 205
Chung, Peter 302
CINAR 299
Clampett, Bob 26, 46, 76, 102, 107, 245, 248, 364, 370
Clarke, Cam 222
Claymation 222
Clerks 350
Clerow Wilson and the Miracle of P.S. 14 165
Clerow Wilson's Great Escape 165
Clokey, Art 103
Clone High 366
Clone Wars 334
Clue Club 153
Coal Black and De Sebben Dwarfs 102
Coca, Imogene 160
Codename: Kids Next Door 331, 334
Cohl, Emile 14
Cohn, Harry 44
Colbert, Stephen 336
Cole, Gary 336
Cole, Jack 202
Coleman, Dabney 279
Coleman, Townsend 222, 301
Collins, Judy 227
Collins, Rickey D'Shon 279, 315
Collyer, Bud 131
Columbia Pictures 20, 42, 44, 192, 210, 296
Columbia Tristar/Sony Television 296, 365
Colvig, Vance 51
Comedy Central 243, 300, 302, 328
Comics Code Authority (CCA) 122
Conn, Didi 173
Connelly, Joe 112
Conreid, Hans 85, 87, 88, 161, 173
Conroy, Kevin 289
Coogan, Jackie 157
Cook, Donovan 269, 280
Cookie Jar Entertainment 208, 366
Cooksey, Danny 184, 284, 355
Cool McCool 95
Cool World 224
Coonskin 223
C.O.P.S. 211
COPS 295
Corden, Henry 66, 152, 163, 183, 203
Corey, Jeff 300
Correll, Charles 112
Cosby, Bill 132, 133, 134, 135, 136, 137, 138, 139, 190, 193, 211, 359
A Cosmic Christmas 167
Cotter, Bill 198, 275
Courage the Cowardly Dog 330
Courageous Cat and Minute Mouse 111
Court, Alyson 221
Covington, Treadwell 91
Cowan, Bernard 106
Cox, Wally 91
Craig, Tony 277
Crawford, Jan 135
"Crazy Claws" 178
Creston Studios 112
Cro 292
Cronkite, Walter 366
Crothers, Scatman 155
"Crusader Rabbit" 5, 35, 36, 37, 38, 46, 64, 74, 76, 77

Cryer, Jon 316
Culhane, Shamus 24, 76, 77, 106, 107, 110, 169
Cullen, Mark 365
Cullen, Peter 178, 179, 192, 200, 204
Cullen, Robb 365
Culliford, Pierre 174, *See* Peyo
Cummings, Brian 182, 197
Cummings, Jim 198, 200, 256, 272, 274, 275, 287, 297, 298
Curious Pictures 331, 334
Curry, Tim 238, 257, 320
Curtin, Hoyt 45, 72
Curtin, Jane 226
Cyrano de Bergerac 96, 158

D'Abruzzo, Stephanie 331
Daily, E.G. 252, 271, 320
Daly, Tim 289
Dan 108, 226, 255, 267, 276, 297
Danny Phantom 311, 314, 315, 316, 324
Daria 302
Darkwing Duck 274
Darling, Jennifer 179, 181
Darnoc, J. *see* William Conrad
Darrow, Henry 143
Dauterive, Jim 311
Dave the Barbarian 355
Davey and Goliath 104
Davey Crockett on the Mississippi 158
David, Jeff 158
David, Keith 276
Davidson, Tommy 352
Davis, Jason 279
Davis, Jim 214, 215, 216, 292
Davis, John A. 320
Davis, Sammy, Jr. 149
Davis, Tom 226
Dawber, Pam 203
Day, Dennis 161
DC Comics 70, 128, 131, 188, 189, 206, 258, 280, 287, 289, 290, 364
Dear Dumb Diary 295
Dearie, Blossom 129
De Brunhoff, Jean 221
De Brunhoff, Laurent 221
DeCarlo, Mark 320
Dees, Julie 177
Defenders of the Earth 220
Delany, Dana 289
DeLisle, Grey 313, 315, 317, 327, 328, 332, 335, 338, 339, 341, 342, 343, 349, 357
Delmar, Kenny 91, 92
DeLuise, Dom 151
De Lyon, Leo 58
Denison, Bob 142

Denver, the Last Dinosaur 223
DePatie-Freleng 94, 147, 162, 164, 165, 214, 217
DePatie, David 94, 125, 162, 172
Deputy Dawg 98
Dermer, Bob 225
Derryberry, Debi 320
DeSena, Jack 326
Detention 342, 365
The Devil and Daniel Mouse 167
Devlin 158, 209, 296
Dexter, Jerry 69, 153, 173, 202
Diamond, Bobby 69
DIC 172, 191, 198, 202, 207, 208, 209, 210, 211, 212, 213, 221, 231, 249, 265, 290, 291, 366
DiCenzo, George 187
DiCicco, Jessica 328, 356
Dickinson, Sandra 347
Dilbert 296
Diller, Barry 196
Diller, Phyllis 151
Dilworth, John 264, 330
DiMaggio, John 242, 345, 346, 354, 356
DiMartino, Michael Dante 325
Dingbat and the Creeps 202
Dini, Paul 189, 282, 289
Dink, the Little Dinosaur 206
"Dino and the Cavemouse" 182
Dino Riders 220
Dinobabies 301
"Dino's Dilemmas" 183
Dinosaucers 210
Diskin, Ben 255, 334
Disney 17, 18, 19, 20, 21, 22, 23, 24, 25, 26, 27, 28, 29, 30, 38, 43, 51, 82, 90, 106, 146, 148, 161, 162, 168, 172, 194, 195, 196, 197, 198, 199, 200, 201, 205, 208, 209, 213, 214, 217, 219, 225, 231, 244, 250, 260, 272, 273, 274, 275, 276, 277, 278, 279, 280, 282, 290, 294, 295, 297, 305, 311, 329, 333, 339, 340, 345, 347, 348, 350, 351, 353, 354, 355, 356, 357, 358, 359, 360, 361, 362, 363, 364, 366, 370
Disney, Melissa 319
Disney, Roy 195, 196, 216
Disney, Roy Edward 196
Disney, Walt 13, 16, 19, 24, 43, 45, 72, 82, 86, 99, 103, 120, 135, 143, 145, 172, 186, 189, 194, 195, 196, 197, 214, 223, 226, 273
Disney Channel 196, 275, 280
DiTillio, Larry 189
Ditko, Steve 106
DiVono, Sharman 216

Dixon, Peg 106
D'Myna Leagues 365
Doc McStuffins 348
Dr. Katz, Professional Therapist 302
Dr. Seuss 30, 100, 164, 165, 214, 344
Dr. Seuss on the Loose 165
Dog City 300
Dohrn, Walt 280
Dolenz, Micky 153, 157, 294, 301
Donkey Kong Country 298
Doreck, Chad 324
Dorfman, Leo 131
Dorn, Michael 266, 276
Dorough, Bob 129
Dorr, Aimee 129
Doug 50, 65, 67, 209, 250, 251, 254, 258, 278
Douglas, Susan 10
Doyle-Murray, Brian 344, 356
Dragon Tales 296
Dragon's Lair 204
Drak Pack 173, 297
Drake, Alfred 227
Duck Dodgers 364
Duckman 251, 343
Ducktales 198, 200, 274
"Dudley Do-Right of the Mounties" 36, 85
Duga, Don 226
The Dukes 181
Dumb and Dumber 298
Dumb Bunnies 298
Dunford, Gary 224
Dungeons and Dragons 217, 346
Dunn, Nora 287
Durante, Jimmy 50, 93, 202
Durante, Riccardo 327
Dwyer, Mickey 174
Dynomutt 152, 157

Eagles, Greg 332
Earthworm Jim 297, 326
Easter Fever 168
Eastman, Kevin 222
Eccles, Teddy 69
Ed, Edd 'n' Eddy 301
Ed Graham Productions 111
Education/Information (E/I) criteria 231, 279
Edwards, Vince 205
Eek! The Cat 276, 293, 295, 298
Efron, Marshall 178, 179, 181
Eiffeth, Glenn 302
Eiler, Virginia 70
Einstein, Bob 291
Eisen, Zack 45, 272, 326
Eisenberg, Jerry 45, 65, 71, 217
Eisner, Michael 162, 172, 194, 196, 260, 273, 284, 348

Ellison, Casey 205
Embassy 160
Emergency + 4 166
Emmerich, Roland 296
Enberg, Dick 150
Engel, Julius "Jules" 108
Equihua, Sandra 326
Erhard, Bernard 181
Erickson, Hal 1, 36, 37, 48, 51, 60, 91, 95, 103, 105, 106, 127, 128, 140, 151, 163, 164, 166, 168, 178, 187, 191, 197, 200, 205, 206, 209, 214, 221, 222, 234, 246, 253, 273, 278, 279, 293, 313, 323, 332, 334, 350, 353, 354
Erwin, John 189
Esser, Carl 163
Evanier, Mark 216, 296
"Evil Con Carne" 332
Exo-Squad 297

Fagerbakke, Bill 258, 351
Fahn, Melissa 319
Fairly Oddparents 257, 301, 311, 312, 313, 314, 315, 318, 320, 328, 358
Family Dog 238
Family Guy 98, 244, 246, 247, 248, 305, 306, 308, 309, 311, 312, 359
Famous Studios 22, 105
Fanboy and Chum Chum 327
Fangface 202
The Fantastic Four 300
Fantastic Voyages 301
Farmer, Bill 274
Farquhar, Ralph 352
Fat Albert and the Cosby Kids 132, 133, 134, 135, 136, 137, 138, 139, 141, 190, 192, 193, 211, 255, 327, 359
FCC 3, 87, 108, 112, 121, 126, 287
"Fearless Fly" 110
Feinglass, Dannah 328
Feiss, David 264, 265, 332
Ferdin, Pamelyn 151
Ferguson, Keith 337
Ferrer, Jose 227
Fiedler, John 200
Fillmore 280, 352, 353, 354
Film Roman 172, 213 214, 235, 291, 292, 293, 298, 331
Film Roman Presents Animated Classic Showcase 292
Filmation 111, 112, 115, 127, 129, 130, 131, 132, 133, 134, 135, 137, 138, 139, 140, 141, 142, 143, 144, 145, 146, 147, 152, 159, 162, 163, 169, 172, 187, 188, 189, 190, 191, 192, 193, 194, 201, 206, 210, 231, 249, 282, 287, 347, 370
Films by Jove 292
Filmways 201
Finn, Charlie 356
Fish Hooks 345, 361, 362
Fish Police 238, 262
Fisher, Bud 15
Five Weeks in a Balloon 158
Flaherty, Joe 184
Flapjack 344, 346
Flash digital media system 356
Fleischer, Dave 20, 21, 22, 23, 323
Fleischer, Max 15, 19, 20, 21, 43, 104, 109, 110, 131, 346
Fleming, Shaun 351
The Flintstone Family Adventures 182
"Flintstone Funnies" 183
The Flintstone Kids 183
The Flintstone Kids "Just Say No" Special 183
The Flintstones Comedy Show 182
Flowers and Trees 18
Flynn, Herbert 108
Flynn, Quinton 324
Fontana, D.C. 140
Fonz and the *Happy Days Gang* 173
Foofur 179, 181
Foray, June 78, 86, 88, 89, 198, 199
Ford, Paul 65
Format Films 108
Forte, Will 309
Foster, Alan Dean 141
Foster, Ame 180
Foster, Ami 205
Foster's Home for Imaginary Friends 336, 337, 338, 339
Fox, Shayna 259, 319
FOX network 198, 212, 216, 230, 234, 239, 260, 285, 291, 294, 299
Fox Worldwide Cable 213
"Fractured Fairy Tales" 82
Fractured Flickers 79, 87
Fraggle Rock 220
Fraidy Cat 144
Frakes, Jonathan 276
Fraley, Patrick 192, 193, 222
Francks, Cree Summer 208
Franken, Al 226
Frankenstein Jr. and the Impossibles 68
"The Frankenstones" 182
Fraquin, Andre 174, 275
Freakazoid! 286
Freberg, Stan 46, 78, 161, 197
Fred Calvert Productions 166
Fred Wolf Studios 301
Frederator 256, 262, 311, 312, 334, 345
Free Willy 298
"Freedom Force" 142
Frees, Paul 66, 68, 70, 78, 85, 88, 89, 95, 112, 160, 161
Freleng, Isadore "Friz" 26, 27, 28, 94, 162, 163, 164, 165, 166, 179, 295, 364
Frewer, Matt 295
Friedle, Will 354
Fritz the Cat 223
Frost, Nika 331
"The Frostbite Falls Review" 37, 77, 296
Frosty the Snowman 93
Frosty's Winter Wonderland 161
Frye, Solelil Moon 205
The Funtastic World of Hanna-Barbera 184
Fusco, Paul 210, 300
Futterman, Nika 342

G.I. Joe 181, 209, 219, 290
Gallagher, Teresa 347
Galtar and the Golden Lance 181
Gannaway, Roberts 277
Garbage Pail Kids 218
Garcia, Jeffrey 320
Garfield and Friends 214, 215, 216, 292, 296
Gargoyles 276, 277
Garrett, Brad 297
Garrett, Patsy 69
Garson, Greer 161
Gary, Linda 142, 190
The Gary Coleman Show 180
Gary the Rat 365
Gately, George 202, 209
Gator, Wally 64
Gautier, Dick 179
Gaylor, Bobby 360
Gaynes, George 205
Geffen, David 221, 286
Gene Deitch Studios 95, 97
Generation O! 365
George Elliott Studio 358
George of the Jungle 88
George Shrinks 298
Gerald McBoing Boing 30, 77, 96
Gerber, Joan 150, 163
Gerbner, George 140
Germain, Paul 251, 278, 351
Getzler, Buddy 108
Ghostbusters 74, 192, 210
Ghostley, Alice 296
Gibson, Henry 149, 179, 197
Gilbert, Ed 193
Gilbert, Edmund 273
Gilliam, Stu 163

Gilligan's Planet 188
Gillis, Kevin 224, 336
Gillis-Wiseman 224
Gilpin, Peri 316
Gilvezan, Dan 180
Gimple, Scott M. 280, 352
Ginott, Haim 129
Glover, John 289
"Go Go Gophers" 92
Gobel, George 160
Godwin, James 331
Godzilla 158, 296
Goffman, Erving 51
Goldberg, Whoopi 185, 218
Goldhar, Marvin 225
Goldie Gold and Action Jack 203
Goldman, Danny 176
Goldman, Les 100
Goldschmidt, Rick 92, 226
Gomez, Reagan 309
Gomez, Rick 342
Goober and the Ghost Chasers 153
Goode, Jeff 356
Goof Troop 274
Gordon, Barry 154, 182, 222
Gori, Kathi 154, 155
Gorshin, Frank 161
Gosden, Freeman 112
Gosfield, Maurice 58
Gottfried, Gilbert 276
Gough, Michael 200
Gould, Chester 96, 272
Gould, Jack 54
Goyette, Desiree 215
Grabstein, Marty 330
Gracie Films 234, 292
Grammer, Kelsey 365
Gramps 312
Grantray-Lawrence 106
Grape Ape 156
Gravity Falls 362
Great American Broadcasting 186, 260
Greatest Adventure: Stories from the Bible 185
Greenblatt, C.H. 344, 362
Greene, Lorne 149
Grey, Joel 160
Griffith, Andy 161
Grim Adventures of Billy and Mandy 330, 332, 344, 345
Grim and Evil 331
Grimm's Fairy Tales 213
Grimmy 292
Groening, Matt 233, 234, 237, 239, 242, 243, 310, 311, 343, 353, 370
Gross, Milt 28
Grossman, Gary 127
Grove, Logan 347
Guaraldi, Vince 99

Guillaume, Robert 238
Guisewite, Cathy 214
Gulf and Western 196
Gulliver's Travels 23, 71, 158, 294
Gumbasia 104
Gutierrez, Jorge 326

Hackett, Buddy 162, 238
Hajdu, David 122
Hal Seeger Productions 109
Halas, John 95, 162
Hale, Jennifer 272
Haley, Jackie 150
Hall, Monty 151
Halloween Is Grinch Night 165
Hamill, Mark 289, 347
Hamilton, Kim 142
Hammerman 290
Handy Manny 348
Haney, Bob 131
Hanna, William 5, 6, 26, 28, 29, 40, 41, 42, 43, 44, 45, 46, 47, 48, 49, 50, 51, 52, 53, 54, 56, 58, 59, 60, 61, 62, 63, 64, 65, 66, 67, 68, 70, 71, 72, 73, 74, 76, 77, 79, 80, 81, 84, 90, 108, 110, 111, 113, 115, 118, 119, 127, 128, 129, 130, 132, 139, 142, 144, 145, 146, 147, 148, 149, 150, 151, 152, 153, 154, 155, 156, 157, 158, 159, 162, 163, 164, 166, 169, 170, 173, 174, 175, 176, 177, 178, 179, 181, 183, 184, 185, 186, 187, 193, 194, 198, 201, 202, 203, 204, 207, 209, 212, 216, 217, 220, 225, 226, 231, 238, 244, 245, 248, 249, 256, 260, 261, 262, 263, 264, 265, 267, 269, 272, 277, 280, 282, 287, 288, 290, 293, 295, 296, 297, 298, 312, 314, 319, 322, 329, 331, 335, 336, 347, 370
Hanna-Barbera 5, 6, 26, 28, 29, 40, 41, 43, 44, 45, 46, 47, 48, 49, 50, 51, 52, 53, 54, 56, 58, 59, 60, 62, 63, 64, 65, 66, 67, 68, 70, 71, 72, 73, 74, 76, 77, 79, 80, 81, 84, 90, 108, 110, 111, 113, 115, 118, 127, 128, 129, 130, 132, 139, 142, 144, 145, 146, 147, 149, 150, 151, 152, 153, 154, 155, 156, 157, 158, 159, 162, 163, 164, 166, 169, 170, 173, 174, 175, 176, 177, 178, 179, 181, 183, 184, 185, 186, 187, 193, 194, 198, 201, 202, 203, 204, 207, 209, 212, 217, 220, 225, 231, 238, 244, 248, 249, 256, 260, 261, 262, 263, 264, 265, 267, 269, 272, 277, 280, 282, 287, 288, 290, 293, 295, 297, 298, 312, 322, 329, 331, 335, 336, 347
Hanna-Barbera's Superstars 184
Hannah, Jack 24
Harding, Noelle 205
Hardwick, Chris 326
Hardy, Oliver 13, 111
Harman, Hugh 25, 27, 28
Harman-Ising Studios 102
Harmon, Larry 95, 111, 131
Harnell, Jess 285, 309
Harrington, Joe 91
Harrington, Pat, Jr. 151
Harris, Estelle 356
Harris, Jo Ann 153
Harris, Jonathan 296
Harris, Robin 352
Harrison, Hugo 347
Hartman, Butch 311
Harvey Birdman, Attorney at Law 335
Hastings, Bob 154
Hathcock, Bob 199
Hayden, Pamela 351
He-Man 181, 189, 190, 191, 192, 227
Hearst, William Randolph 15
Heathcliff 202, 203, 209
Heavy Traffic 223
Hecht, Albie 315
Heidi's Song 149
Help! It's the Hair Bear Bunch! 157
Helppie, Kathleen 179
Helppie, Kathy 197
Hendershot, Heather 137
Hendryson, Mrs. Irvin 124, 140
Henry, Mike 309
Henson, Jim 217, 218, 220, 300, 366
Here Comes Garfield 215
Here Comes Peter Cottontail 160
Here Comes the Grump 94
Hero High 187
Herriman, George 15
Hershfield, Harry 28
He's Bonkers 275
Heyward, Andy 207, 212, 290, 291, 366
Hi-Hi Puffy Amiyumi 341
Hibbert, Edward 298
Hickman, Darryl 179
Higgins, John Michael 336
Hilberman, David 29, 38
Hill, Amy 341
Hill, Dana 274
Hill, Jonah 310
Hirsch, Alex 362
Hirsh, Michael 167
Histeria! 287
Hit Entertainment 366

Holland, Savage Steve 276, 293
Holland, Tina 150, 153
Holloway, Sterling 200
Holt, Bob 156, 179
Hong Kong Phooey 155, 156
"Hoot Kloot" 94
Hoppity Goes to Town see *Mr. Bug Goes to Town*
Hoppity Hooper 79, 88
Horton Hears a Who! 100
Horvitz, Richard 256, 319, 332, 343
Hot Wheels 108
Hotel Transylvania 160, 334
The Houndcats 163
House of Mouse 348
How I Got into College 293
How the Grinch Stole Christmas 100
Howard, Ron 173
Howdy Doody 104
Hu, Kelly 360
Huber, Larry 319
Hubley, John 30, 77
Huffington, Arianna 309
Huge, Thom 215
Hughes, Howard 195
Humanitas Prize 211
"The Hunter" 91
Hurd, Earl 14
Hurtz, Bill 30, 76, 79
Hurwitz, Mitchell 310
Huston, John 161, 226

I Am the Greatest: The Adventures of Muhammad Ali 166
Inch High, Private Eye 154
The Incredible Hulk 300
Ingels, Marty 156, 181
Inhumanoids 220
"The Inspector" 94
Inspector Gadget 207, 208, 209, 212, 221, 274
Intergalactic Thanksgiving 168
Invader Zim 319
Irene, Georgi 181
Irving, George S. 161, 226
Isen, Tajja 336
Ising, Rudolf 25, 27, 28
ITC 217, 227
It's Punky Brewster 205
It's the Great Pumpkin, Charlie Brown 100
Ives, Burl 93, 161
Iwamatsu, Makoto 333

Jabberjaw 154
Jack and the Beanstalk 158
Jack Frost 161, 162
Jack Kinney Studios 95
Jackie Chan Adventures 365

Jackson, Roger 272
Jackson Five Show 162
Jacobs, Christian 198
Jacobs, Renae 222
Jacoby, Billy 204
Jacquemin, Bob 198
Jake and the Never Land Pirates 348
Jambalaya Studios 352
James Bond Jr. 295
Janis, Conrad 203
Janney, Alison 361
Jason of Star Command 142
Jay, Tony 274
Jayce and the Wheeled Warriors 209
Jean, Al 235, 292
Jeffrey, Myles 335
Jeffries, Herb 150
JEM 220
Jenkins, Allen 59
Jenkins, Henry 11
Jessel, George 160
The Jetsons Meet the Flintstones 184
Jim Henson Company 300
Jim Henson's Muppets, Babies and Monsters 218
Jimmy Neutron, Boy Genius 320
Jinkins, Jim 250, 273, 277
John Sutherland Productions 99
"Johnny and Mr. Do-Right" 37
Johnny Cypher in Dimension Zero 105
Johnson, Arte 163, 164
Johnson, Ashley 279
Johnson, Brett 198
Johnson, Cherie 205
Johnson, Gerry 55
Joliffe, David 154
Jones, Chuck 26, 29, 100, 101, 124, 164, 166, 203, 214, 364, 364
Jones, James Earl 227
Jones, Nicky 345
Jones, Noah Z. 361
Jonny Quest 63, 64, 65, 67, 286, 314, 330, 336
Joseph, Jackie 153
Josie and the Pussycats 153
Judge, Mike 239, 242, 243, 302, 310
Jumanji 296
Jungle Cubs 244, 277
Juster, Norton 100

Kane, Bob 95, 111, 288
Kane, Chelsea Staub 362
Kane, Tom 272, 338
Kanfer, Stefan 121, 127
Kaplan, Lisa 349

Kaplan, Marvin 58
Kapnek, Emily 319
Kappa Mikey 326
"Karate Kat" 227
Karloff, Boris 100
Karman, Janice 203
Kasem, Casey 73, 153
Kassir, John 259, 283
Katayama, Tetsuo 207
Katz, Jonathan 302
Katzenberg, Jeffrey 196, 284, 286
Kaufman, David 286, 315, 356
Kavner, Julie 234
Kawaye, Janice 323, 341
Kay, Kevin 315
Kaye, Danny 160
Kayro Productions 112
Keane, Margaret 270
Keaton, Buster 13, 360
Keefe, Peter 222, 301
Keith-Albee-Orpheum 11, 33
Keller, Lew 30, 79
Kelly, Walt 101, 280
Kenny, Tom 272, 338, 340, 342, 343, 346
Keystone Studios 12
"Kid Champion" 38
Kid 'n' Play 294
Kid Power 162
The Kid Super Power Hour with Shazam 187
Kidd Video 209
Kideo TV 209
Kim Possible 193, 354, 354, 355, 356
King, Alan 226
King, Kip 179
King, Regina 365
King Features 21, 95
"The King Features Trilogy" 95
King Leonardo and His Short Subjects 91
King of the Hill 150, 239, 241, 246, 291, 302, 311
Kinney, Jack 95, 274
Kirby, Jack 70, 164, 203, 205
Kirschner, David 261, 262, 263
Kirshner, Don 132
Kirwan, Alex 322
Kissyfur 210
Kitaen, Tawny 293
Kitt, Eartha 325
Klasky-Csupo 234, 235, 251, 252, 254, 257, 259, 278, 299, 311, 319, 325, 343
Klein, Dennis 238
Kligman, Paul 106
"Klondike Kat" 92
Klutter 293
Knight, Wayne 326
Knotts, Don 151, 152

Koensgen, John 210
Konietzko, Bryan 325
Koonce, Ken 199
Kopp, Bill 276, 287, 293
Korengold, Dr. Murray 124, 140
Korman, Harvey 58
Kowalewski, Kyla 347
Krantz, Steve 106, 107, 169, 212, 223
Krazy Kat 15, 95
Kricfalusi, John 211, 223, 248, 253, 259, 261, 265, 277
Krisel, Gary 198
Krypto the Superdog 364
The Kwicky Koala Show 178

Lacewood Productions 225
Lady Lovelylocks and the Pixietails 211
Laemmle, Carl 23
Laird, Peter 222
La Marche, Maurice 168, 208, 243, 285, 335, 342, 343
LaMarr, Phil 332, 333, 338, 342, 349
Landau, Martin 300
Lane, Nathan 351
Langdale, Doug 259, 297, 348, 355, 356
Lange, Christina 179
Lansbury, Angela 161
Lantz, Walter 23, 24, 25, 119, 121
Larry Harmon Productions 95, 111, 131
Larson, Mitch 343
Laskey, Kathleen 327
Lassie's Rescue Rangers 144
Last of the Curlews 159
Last of the Mohicans 158
Lathan, Sanaa 309
Laugh-O-Grams 17
Laurel, Stan 13, 111
Laverne and Shirley 173, 174, 180
Laverne and Shirley in the Army 173
Laverne and Shirley with the Fonz 173
Lawrence, Andrew 279
Lawrence, Carolyn 320
Lawrence, Doug, "Mr." 254, 258, 340
Lawrence, Robert 106
Laws, Maury 160, 227
Lazer Tag Academy 205
Lazzo, Mike 265, 333
Lear, Norman 150, 296
Lee, Stan 70, 106, 164, 171, 216, 294, 300, 366
Legion of Super Heroes 364
Lehman, Christopher 63, 135
Leigh, Katie 198

Leonard, Sheldon 112
The Leprechaun's Christmas Gold 226
Lesser, Elana 203
Lewis, Steve 163
Liberty's Kids 366
The Life and Adventures of Santa Claus 227
Life in Hell 233
Lightwave 320
Lilo and Stitch 348
limited animation 40, 44, 77, 95
Linus the Lionhearted 111
Liquid Television 302
Little, Nicolette 351
Little, Rich 151
Little, Steve 340
Little Clowns of Happytown 220
Little Drummer Boy, Book II 161
Little Einsteins 348
Little Lulu 299
The Little Mermaid 274, 294
Little Nemo in Slumberland 14
The Little Rascals 181
Little Rosey 298
Little Shop 300
Littlest Pet Shop 343
Livingston, Polly Lou 346
Livingston, Stanley 151
Lloyd, Harold 13, 47
Lloyd in Space 351
Loc, Tone 292
Loesch, Margaret 212, 216, 218, 299
London, Robby 207
Long, Nia 309
Loonatics Unleashed 364
Looney Tunes 25, 138, 253, 280, 281, 283, 284, 286, 364
The Lorax 165
Lord, Phil 366
Lorimar-Telepictures 227
Loubert, Patrick 167
Lovitz, Jon 292
Luke, Keye 158
Lundy, Dick 24
Luttell, Bob 154
Luttrell, Erica 355
Lynch, David 309
Lynde, Paul 72, 149, 150, 308
Lyons, Steven 348

Macchio, Ralph 212
MacCurdy, Jean 282, 288, 290, 364
Macfarlane, Rachel 307, 332
Macfarlane, Seth 90, 243, 244, 245, 246, 247, 248, 255, 267, 305, 306, 310, 311, 312, 343
MacGeorge, Jim 153, 178
Mackall, Steve 275

MacNeille, Tress 198, 200, 243, 255, 283, 285, 287, 351, 355
Macron 1 213
Mad, Mad, Mad Monsters 160
Mad Monster Party 160
Madeline 291
Magee, Michael 225
Maggie and the Ferocious Beast 366
Magnon, Jymn 198
Maliani, Michael 207
Malick, Wendie 320, 326, 353
Malinger, Ross 279
Maltese, Michael 27, 45, 72
Maltin, Leonard 1, 14, 15, 17, 19, 20, 22, 23, 24, 94, 95, 96, 97, 98
Mandel, Howie 293
Mann, Tyler 360
"Manta and Moray" 142
Mantooth, Randolph 166
Maple Town 213
Marc, David 4
Marcus, Sid 24
Marin, Sam 346
Mark VII 166
Marquette, Sean 337
Mars, Kenneth 179, 182
Marsden, Jason 277, 349
Marsh, Jeff "Swampy" 359
Marshall, Lewis 45
Marshall, Mona 208
Marshall, Penny 173
Marshall, Ron 161
Marshall, Vanessa 332
Marsupilami 275
Martella, Vincent 359
Martin, Andrea 184, 297
Martin, Ross 158
Martinez, Heather 357
The Marvel Action Universe 220
Marvel Comics 70, 164, 171, 188, 219, 294
Marvel Entertainment 216
Marvel Superheroes 106, 219
Marx Brothers 160, 285
Mary Kate and Ashley in Action 366
M.A.S.K. 209
Mask 298
Maslansky, Paul 206
Mason, Eric 143
Massey, Kyle 362
Matheson, Tim 63, 68
Mattel 102, 107, 108, 112, 170, 181, 185, 189, 218, 366
Matthews, Gerry 112
Matthieson, Tim 70
Matty's Funnies with Beany and Cecil 102
Max, the 2000-Year-Old Mouse 107

McCall, David 129
McCann, Chuck 173
McCay, Winsor 14, 30
McCorkle, Mark 354
McCracken, Craig 90, 264, 265, 268, 269, 311, 314, 316, 322, 333, 336, 339, 346
McDonald, Jessica 347
McDonald, Kevin 326
McDowall, Roddy 226, 227
McFadden, Bob 112
McGiver, John 160
McGovern, Terry 199, 274
McGregor, Christina 205
McGruder, Aaron 365
McKeon, Nancy 204
McKimson, Robert 26
McLuhan, Marshall 7
McMillan, Norma 69, 92
McWhirter, Julie 154, 163, 173
Mead, Courtland 279, 280, 351
Medina, Julio 143
"Meet the Inventor" 96
Melendez, Bill 98, 99, 100, 214, 215, 255, 352
Melendez, Sonny 203
Melvin, Allan 64, 65, 145
Men in Black 296
Mendelson, Lee 98, 99, 100, 214, 215
Menken, Shepard 109
Mercer, Jack 110
Merrie Melodies 25, 26
Messick, Don 46, 48, 61, 63, 64, 65, 66, 68, 69, 70, 71, 72, 73, 153, 156, 158, 161, 173, 176, 202, 283
Messmer, Otto 15, 105
Meugniot, Will 294
MGM 26, 27, 28, 29, 42, 43, 44, 45, 100, 101, 142, 158, 164, 178, 187, 201, 214, 260, 261, 262, 280, 295, 296, 314, 366
Michaels, Lorne 226
Mickey Mouseworks 348
"Microwoman and Super Stretch" 142
Mighty Max 292
"Mighty Man and Yukk" 202
Mighty Morphin Power Rangers 212, 294
Mighty Mouse Playhouse 97
Mighty Thor 106
Mike, Lu and Og 331
Miller, Christopher 366
Miller, Greg 335
Miller, Lara Jill 341
Miller, Ron 195
Miller, Sidney 181
Milne, A.A. 199
Milo, Candi 265, 320, 323, 338

Mina and the Count 322
Mini Monsters 227
Minow, Newton 87, 121
Mintz, Charles 20
Mintz, Dan 311
Mirkin, David 235
Mirman, Eugene 311
Mish, Michael 204
Mission: Magic 140
Mr. Bogus 301
Mr. Bug Goes to Town 23
"Mr. Know It All" 83
Mr. Magoo's Christmas Carol 96
Mister T 204
Mitchell, John 44, 47, 52, 53
Mitchell, Shirley 151
Mittell, Jason 119
Moby Dick and the Mighty Mightor 69
Mohr, Gerald 70
Monchichis 181
Monnickendam, Freddy 181
Monster Force 297
Moore, Alan 290
Morgan, Harry 227
Morita, Pat 212
Mork and Mindy 203, 205
Morley, Robert 100
Morris, Garrett 168
Morris, Howard 64, 65, 66, 145, 216
Morse, Robert 161, 162, 180
Mortal Kombat 292
Mosher, Bob 112
Moss, Gene 108
Most, Donny 173
The Most Important Person 166
Mostel, Zero 161
Mother Goose and Grimm 292
Motion Picture Screen Cartoonists 147
Mouse on the Mayflower 93
MTV 215, 239, 248, 261, 301, 302
MTV Downtown 302
MTV Oddities 302
Mucha Lucha 365
Muir, John Kenneth 4
Mulgrew, Kate 276
Mull, Martin 316, 355
Muller, Romeo 227
Mummies Alive! 291
Mumy, Liliana 345
Muppet Babies 183, 217, 218, 220
Murakami, Jimmy 222
Murakami-Wolf-Swenson 197, 222
Murdoch, Rupert 230
Murray, Bill 215
Murray, Joe 253, 255, 258, 269, 334, 337, 339, 343

Muse, Ken 43
M.U.S.H. 144
Mushi Studios 162
Music, Lorenzo 198, 215
Musso, Mitchell 360
Mutt and Jeff 15
My Gym Partner's a Monkey 341, 342
My Life as a Teenage Robot 31, 193, 257, 315, 320, 321, 335
My Little Pony and Friends 219
My Mom's Having a Baby 165
My Pet Monster 221

The Naïve Man from Lolliland 346
Napoleon Dynamite 310
Naranjo, Ivan 143
Nash, Clarence 51
National Association for Better Broadcasting 94, 140, 144
NBC 36, 37, 46, 53, 66, 68, 70, 71, 73, 80, 86, 87, 91, 93, 94, 95, 96, 98, 101, 104, 128, 132, 141, 145, 148, 151, 152, 153, 154, 157, 158, 161, 162, 163, 164, 165, 166, 173, 174, 175, 176, 178, 179, 180, 181, 182, 184, 187, 188, 198, 203, 204, 205, 209, 210, 211, 216, 217, 219, 220, 226, 230, 231, 290, 294, 300, 317
Nelson, Frank 163, 182
Nelvana 167, 168, 169, 172, 209, 220, 221, 225, 244, 298, 327, 366
Nelvanamation 167, 220
Nestor, the Long Eared Christmas Donkey 162
The New Adventures of Gilligan 188
The New Fantastic Four 164
The New Scooby-Doo Mysteries 184
Newman, Laraine 226, 287
Ng, Lisa 327
Nichols, Charles, "Nick" 45, 149
Nichols, Nichelle 141, 276
Nickelodeon 7, 90, 213, 218, 224, 231, 248, 249, 250, 251, 252, 253, 254, 255, 256, 258, 259, 260, 261, 264, 273, 277, 278, 305, 311, 312, 313, 315, 320, 321, 322, 323, 325, 327, 328, 329, 331, 335, 339, 345, 346, 347, 351, 353, 357, 358, 364, 365
Nightmare Ned 280
Nolan, William 24
Noozles 213
Norris, Daran 313, 317, 357
North, Noelle 198
Norton, Cliff 150

Oakley, Bill 235
O'Connor, Carroll 163
The Oddball Couple 163
Oedekerk, Steve 320, 327
Of Mice and Magic 1
Ogle, Robert Allen 178, 179
Oh Yeah Cartoons! 312, 322, 327
O'Hanlon, George 61
O'Hara, Catherine 168, 184
Oliver, Denise 327
Oliver Twist 294
Olson, Olivia 346, 361
Olym-Pinks 165
One Crazy Summer 293
1001 Arabian Nights 30
Oppenheimer, Alan 173, 176, 181, 189, 193, 197, 205
Oriolo, Don 292
Oriolo, Joe 104, 105
Orion Pictures 201, 295
Orton, Peter 366
O'Shaughnessey, Colleen 316
Osmond family 162
Oswald the Lucky Rabbit 24
Ouimette, Stephen 221
Out of the Inkwell 20, 109
Owens, Gary 68, 72, 108, 157
Pac-Man 181
Page, Laurel 154
Palace Theatre *see* vaudeville
Pallilo, Ron 204
Palmer, Edward 130
Pancholy, Malik 360
Pandamonium 217
Panettiere, Jansen 326
Paramount 5, 20, 22, 23, 34, 95, 106, 141, 149, 196, 203, 223, 233, 261, 311
Pariot, Barbara 153
Parker, Paula Jai 352
Parker, Randolph "Trey" 303
Parmelee, Ted 30, 79
Parris, Pat 154, 179
Patchett, Tom 210
Patterson, Don 24
Patterson, Ray 45, 106
Paulsen, Rob 198, 220, 222, 263, 274, 285, 287, 292, 296, 301, 316, 318, 320, 326
Paymer, David 296
Payne, Julie 216
Payne Fund 33, 117
Payton, JoMarie 352
PB&J Otter 250, 280
PBS 134, 217, 299, 366
"Peabody's Improbable History" 83, 107
Peanuts 98, 99, 214, 215, 255
Peary, Hal 161
Pebbles and Bamm-Bamm 152

Pebbles, Dino and Bamm-Bamm 182
Peck, Everett 251, 343
Pepper Ann 279, 280, 334
Percival, Lance 95
Perlman, Ron 316
Pershing, Diane 142, 205
Peter Potamus Show 65
Peters, Bernadette 285
Peters, Brock 181
Peters, Mike 287, 292
Peterson, Scott 357
Petty, Lori 289
Peyo *see* Culliford, Pierre
Pfish and Chips 312
Phil Roman Entertainment 214
Phillips, Barney 69
Phineas and Ferb 340, 358, 359, 360
Pink Panther 94, 163, 165, 166, 179, 295
The Pink Panther and Sons 179
Pinky and the Brain 285
Pinocchio 93, 226, 294
Pinocchio's Christmas 226
Pintoff, Ernest 96
Pippi Longstocking 298
Planet Sheen 320
Playhouse 38, 99
Please Don't Eat the Planet 168
Poe, Edgar Allan 30
Poehler, Amy 328
Pogo 101, 280
Pole Position 209
Police Academy 206
Polsky, Dave 356
Pontoffel Pock, Where Are You? 165
"Popeye" 95, 102, 111
The Popeye and Olive Comedy Show 180
Popeye and Son 180
Popeye Meets Ali Baba and His Forty Thieves 21
Popeye the Sailor Meets Sinbad the Sailor 21
Porky in Wackyland 102
Pound Puppies 179
Povenmire, Dan 359
Pratt, Hawley 165
Pratt, Kyla 352
Premavision Studios 104
Preminger, Otto 161
Prescott, Norman 131
Price, Judy 223
Price, Vincent 160, 184
Prime Time Access Rule 150
Problem Child 297
Probst, Jeff 353
Production Code 21, 33, 117, 121, 122, 195

Project G.E.E.K.E.R. 296, 326
pro-social education 128, 130, 133, 134, 136, 137, 145, 171, 177, 193, 194, 204, 205, 207, 215, 220, 228, 231, 252, 259
Prostars 290
PTA 124
A Pup Named Scooby Doo 184
The Puppy Who Wanted a Boy 204
The Puppy's Further Adventures 204
The Puppy's Great Adventures 204
Puss Gets the Boot 28, 43

Quack Pack 277
Quimby, Fred 28, 29, 43
Quintel, James Garland 346
Quirk, Moira 325

The Raccoons 225
Radomski, Eric 288
Rainbow Brite 210
Rambo 205
Ramos, Carlos 326
Random Cartoons 327
Rankin, Arthur, Jr. 92, 226
Rankin-Bass 92, 159, 226
Raw Toonage 275
Ray, Aldo 163
Reaves, J. Michael 189
Recess 278, 351
Red Seal Pictures 20
Reed, Alan 55, 64, 150, 152
Reilly, Charles Nelson 144, 182, 227, 300
Reiner, Carl 112
Reiss, Mike 292
Reiss, William 343
Reitherman, Wolfgang, "Woolie" 200
Reitman, Ivan 210, 297
Rembrandt Films 95
Ren and Stimpy 211, 250, 253, 256, 258, 259, 265, 365
Ren and Stimpy Adult Party Cartoon 365
Renaday, Pete 209, 222
Renzetti, Rob 269, 316, 322, 335, 346, 362
The Return of the King 226
Return to Oz 93
Return to the Planet of the Apes 163
Reynolds, Debbie 149
Rhoda 215
Richards, Billie Mae 93, 161
Richards, Lou 181
Richardson, Kevin Michael 308, 309, 316, 345

Richardson, Salli 276
Richie Rich 183, 293
The Richie Rich / Scooby Doo Hour 183
Richter, Andy 328
"Rickety Rocket" 202
Ridgely, Robert 142, 181, 203
Ritchard, Cyril 160, 161
Ritter, Jason 363
Ritter, John 218, 227, 238
RKO 43, 92, 142, 195
Roach, Hal 12, 181
Road, Mike 27, 63, 68, 69, 247
Roberts, John 311
Robinson, Bumper 183
Robinson, Craig 309
Robles, Eric 327
Robocop 220, 295
Robotix 219
Rock and Rule 221
Rocket Robin Hood 107
Rockin' with Judy Jetson 184
Rocko's Modern Life 253, 258, 339, 359
Rocky and Bullwinkle 30, 31, 46, 78, 79, 80, 81, 83, 84, 85, 86, 87, 88, 90, 156, 331, 355
Rod Rocket 131
Roddenberry, Gene 140, 141
Roger Ramjet 107
Roiland, Justin 362
"Roland and Ratfink" 94
Rolie Polie Olie 298
Roman Holidays 151
Roman, Phil 213, 214, 216, 291, 293
Roman, Susan 225
Romano, Christy Carlson 354
Romie-O and Julie-8 168
Rooney, Mickey 160, 161
Rose, Sue 279
Ross, Joe E. 155, 157
Ross, Neil 205, 296
Ross, Steve 287
Rotoscope 19, 20
RS Holdings 202
Rubik the Amazing Cube 204
Ruby, Cliff 203
Ruby, Joe 45, 67, 157, 201, 207
Ruby-Spears Enterprises 172, 201, 202, 203, 206, 209, 289, 312
Rude Dog and the Dweebs 220
Rudolph the Red Nosed Reindeer 93, 161
Rudolph's Shiny New Year 161
Ruegger, Tom 180, 189, 282, 286, 289, 364
Ruff and Reddy 46, 47
Rugg, Paul 286, 356
Rugrats 251, 252, 255, 257, 278, 325, 331

"runaway" animation 146, 147
Rupp, Debra Jo 351
Russell, Dan 347
Ryan, Michael 294
Ryan, Roz 344
Rye, Michael 198

Saban 172, 213, 222
Saban, Haim 212, 213, 294
Saban Entertainment 207, 212, 294
Sabella, Paul 295
Saber Rider and the Star Sheriffs 223
Sabrina 291
Sagal, Jeff 297
Sailor Moon 291
St. Patrick, Matthew 316
Salyers, William 346
Sam Singer Productions 110
Samson and Goliath 70
Samurai Jack 322, 333, 334
Sangster, Thomas 359
Sansom, Ken 200
Santa Claus Is Comin' to Town 160, 227
Santat, Dan 357
Sanz, Horatio 353
Saperstein, Henry 30, 96
Sarlatte, Bob 204
Scales, Crystal 320
Schaal, Kirsten 311, 363
Schaal, Wendy 307
Schatzberg, Steve 179
Scheffler, Marilyn 154, 180, 183
Scheimer, Erika 140
Scheimer, Lane 131, 182, 188
Scheimer, Lou 111, 115, 116, 130, 131, 134, 135, 138, 139, 141, 142, 145, 147, 172, 187, 188, 189, 190, 192, 193, 194, 347, 370
Schell, Ronnie 153, 179
Schlesinger, Leon 25, 26, 27
Schmock, Jonathan 179
Scholes, Robert 4
Schon, Kevin 351
School's Out 279, 313
Schooley, Bob 354
Schoolhouse Rock 129, 335
Schultz, Dwight 345
Schulz, Charles 98, 214
Schwarz, Larry 326
Scooby Doo 69, 73, 74, 151, 152, 153, 157, 159, 182, 183, 184, 204, 262, 336
Scooby Doo and the Ghoul School 159, 184
Scooby Doo and the Reluctant Werewolf 184
Scooby Doo Meets the Boo Brothers 184

Scooby's All-Star Laff-A-Lympics 152
Scott, Bill 30, 40, 76, 78, 82, 83, 85, 86, 88, 89, 96, 197, 198
Scott, Bryan 164, 209
Scott, Raymond 110
Screen Actors Guild 38
Screen Gems 29, 44, 47, 53, 110, 296
Scully, Mike 235
Seal, Kevin 331
Sealab 2020 158
Seduction of the Innocent 124
Segall, Pamela 240, 279
Segar, E.C. 21, 180
Seibert, Fred 256, 261, 263, 311, 312, 327, 334, 345, 346
Seldes, Gilbert 18, 30
Sennett, Mack 12, 23, 119, 258, 337, 345
Sennett, Ted 43, 44, 47, 67, 68, 70, 71, 154, 173, 176
Seven Arts 105
Seville, David *see* Bagdasarian, Ross
Shada, Jeremy 346
Shannon, Dave 278
Shawn, Dick 161
Shazzan 69
She-Ra: Princess of Power 191
Shearer, Harry 234
Sheep in the Big City 331
Sheldon, Jack 129
Shenkarow, Justin 255, 351
Sheppard, Tom 343
Sherlock Holmes in the 22nd Century 291
Shindel, Mikhail 331
Short, Martin 184, 211
Shows, Charles 45, 77
Shuster, Joe 22
Siegel, Barbara 12
Siegel, Jerry 22
Siegel, Scott 12
Silly Symphonies 18
Silo, Susan 179
Silverhawks 227
Silverman, Fred 66, 67, 68, 69, 71, 73, 98, 109, 123, 131, 132, 153, 173, 174, 176, 217
Silvers, Phil 48, 58, 65, 82, 168
Silverstone, Alicia 366
Simensky, Linda 270, 333
Simmons, Grant 106
Simmons, Richard 362
Simon, Sam 234
Simons, Rosearik 319
Sinbad Jr. 111
Singer, Sam 110, 111
Singleton, Penny 61
Sinterniklaas, Michael 326

Sit Down, Shut Up 310
Sito, Tom 146
Skelton, Red 86, 161
Sklar, Robert 33, 116
Sky Commanders 181
Sky Hawks 108
"slash" system 15
Smith, Bruce W. 352
Smith, Clive 167
Smith, Hal 151, 200
Smith, Kevin 350
Smith, Kurtwood 343
Smith, Yeardley 234
Smokey Bear Show 93
Smothers Brothers 160
The Smurfs 174, 175, 176, 177, 178, 179, 209, 275
The Snorks 181
Snow White and the Seven Dwarfs 19, 29
"Snuffy Smith" 21, 95
Snyder, Dana 345
Snyder, Kenneth 107, 108, 112, 166
Snyder, Robert 10
Snyder, Tom 302
Soles, Paul 106
Sony Pictures Animation 334
Sorkin, Arleen 289
Soucie, Kath 198, 252, 274, 278, 297, 316, 341, 349, 357
South Park 245, 303
Soyuzmultifulm 292
"Space Barton" 38
Space Ghost and Dino Boy 68
Space Kidettes 68, 202
Spacecats 300
Sparktaus and the Sun Beneath Sea 213
Spears, Ken 45, 67, 157, 201, 207
Spears, Steve 181
Speed Buggy 157
Speed Racer 105, 301
Spence, Irv 43
Spicy City 224
Spider-Man 106, 107, 219, 220, 300
Spider Man and His Amazing Friends 219
Spider Woman 164
Spielberg, Steven 207, 238, 261, 275, 281, 286, 297
Spigel, Lynn 34, 54, 117
Spike and Mike's Twisted Festival of Animation 269
Spiner, Brent 276
Sporn, Michael 211
Sport Billy 188

Springfield, Rick 140
Squirrel Boy 343
Stalling, Carl 26, 110
Stang, Arnold 58
Stanley 151, 163, 348
The Star Com: U.S. Space Force 211
Star Trek 70, 140, 141, 145, 276, 320
Star Wars 190, 245, 291, 334
Starcom 210
Stargate 366
Steamboat Willie 17
Stein, Ben 314
Steinkellner, Bill 350
Steinkellner, Cheri 350
Stephenson, John 56, 58, 63, 65, 66, 68, 69, 71, 154, 157, 161, 178
Sterling, Mindy 345
Stern, Joe 142
Stickin' Around 298
Stiers, David Ogden 351
Stiller, Jerry 351
Stitch, Patricia 154
Stone, Doug 209
Stone, Matthew, "Matt" 303
Stoner, Allyson 360
Stoner, Sherri 285
Stones, Tad 198
Stop the Smoggies 299
Storch, Larry 91, 227
The Stories from the Bible 185
Stover, Chet 91
Strangis, Judy 151, 157
Strawberry Shortcake 221
Street Frogs 227
Stripperella 366
Strong, Tara 271, 313, 316, 345, 352, 353, 356, 358
Struthers, Sally 273
Stuart Little 365
Styne, Jule 96
Sudeikis, Jason 309
Sullivan, Kyle 335, 353
Sullivan, Nancy 343
Sullivan, Nicole 355
Sullivan, Pat 15
Summer, Cree 208, 284, 287, 297, 325, 334, 356
Super Bwoing 94
"Super Chicken" 89
Super Dave 291
Super Friends 128, 129, 138, 142, 206
Super President and Spy Shadow 94
Super Six 94
Super Sunday 219

Superman 22, 129, 131, 206, 288, 289, 364
Suter, Eric 135
Sutherland, Hal 111, 130
Sutherland Learning Associates 166
Swamp Thing 290
Swenson, Charles 222
Swenson, Chuck 331
Swift, Allen 91
syndication 6, 7, 37, 64, 87, 88, 92, 95, 96, 97, 98, 102, 104, 105, 106, 107, 111, 112, 132, 145, 150, 162, 167, 169, 172, 178, 184, 188, 189, 190, 191, 198, 199, 200, 201, 203, 204, 206, 207, 208, 210, 211, 215, 217, 218, 222, 223, 228, 231, 262, 273, 274, 276, 277, 282, 284, 290, 292, 295, 300, 301, 306, 364, 369

Taft Broadcasting 73, 139, 169, 173, 185, 186, 201
Tak and the Power of JuJu 328
Takamoto, Iwao 45, 71, 149
Take Me Up to the Ballgame 168
Talboy, Tara 154
Tale Spin 273
Tales of the Wizard of Oz 93
Talkartoons 20
Talley, Jill 341
Tartakovsky, Genndy 264, 269, 316, 322, 333
Tarzan 88, 142, 145, 187, 348
Tarzan and the Super Seven 142, 187
Tashlin, Frank 26
Tate, Grady 129
Tattertown 224
El Tigre 326
"Tom Terrific" 97
"Tooter Turtle" 91
Treyz, Oliver 53
T.U.F.F. Puppy 311, 317, 318, 334
Twas the Night Before Christmas 160
Twentieth Century–Fox 36, 103, 163, 204, 233, 251, 265
20,000 Leagues Under the Sea 158

A Unicorn in the Garden 30

Valdez, Socorro 143

"Web Woman" 142
"The World of Commander McBragg" 91